Indiana-Michigan Series in Russian and East European Studies

Alexander Rabinowitch and William G. Rosenberg,
general editors

Russian
Folk
Art

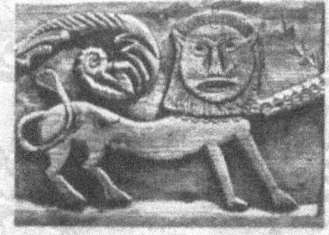

Alison Hilton

Indiana University Press

Bloomington and Indianapolis

Research for this book was supported in part by a grant from
the International Research and Exchanges Board (IREX),
with funds provided by the National Endowment for the
Humanities, the United States Information Agency, and
the U.S. Department of State, which administers the Soviet
and East European Training Act of 1983 (Title VIII).

This book is a publication of

Indiana University Press
601 North Morton Street
Bloomington, Indiana 47404-3797 USA

www.iupress.indiana.edu

Telephone orders   800-842-6796
Fax orders   812-855-7931
Orders by e-mail   iuporder@indiana.edu

♾ The paper used in this publication meets the minimum requirements
of the American National Standard for Information Sciences—
Permanence of Paper for Printed Library Materials, ANSI Z39.48–1992.

Manufactured in the United States of America

The Library of Congress has catalogued the hardcover edition as follows:

Hilton, Alison.
    Russian folk art / Alison Hilton.
        p. cm.   (Indiana Michigan series in
    Russian and East European studies)
    Includes bibliographical references (p. —) and index.
        ISBN 978-0-253-32753-6 (cl. : alk. paper)
        1. Folk art—Russia (Federation). 2. Decorative
    arts—Russia (Federation) I. Title. II. Series.
    NK975.H55 1995
    745′.0941—dc20   94-30901

ISBN 978-0-253-22335-7 (pbk.)

1   2   3   4   5   16   15   14   13   12   11

Contents

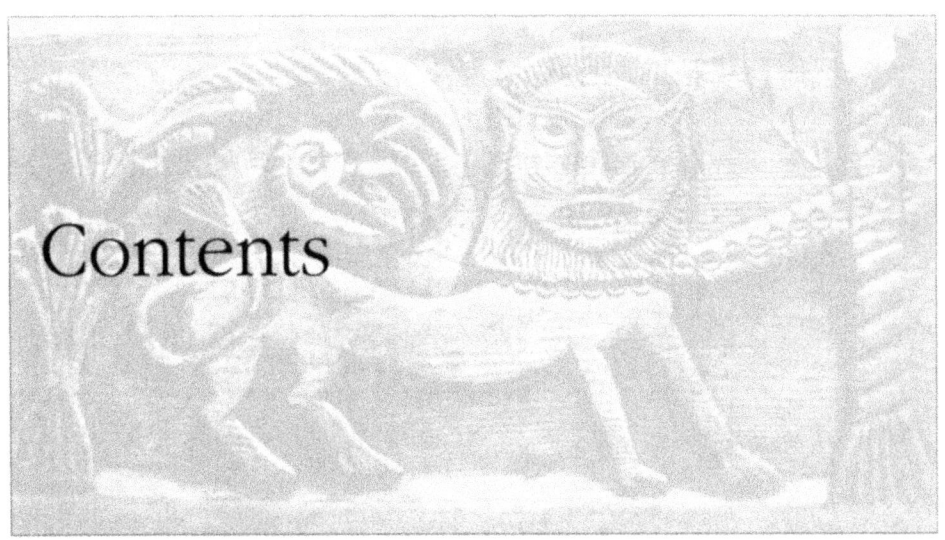

PART I

THE ARTS IN PEASANT LIFE

PART II

MATERIALS AND FORMS

List of Illustrations

List of Illustrations

List of Illustrations

List of Illustrations

Preface to the Paperback Edition

A century ago, the Russian artist Ivan Bilibin traveled to Arkhangel'sk and Vologda provinces to study the folk art of the Russian north. Authentic folk art was dying out, he feared, and he urged that remnants of folk arts be preserved and allowed to develop naturally. Collecting specimens for museums was less productive than teaching young artists the skills that could enable them to adapt to changing conditions. Bilibin's report, published in 1904 in the journal *World of Art (Mir iskusstva)*, inspired efforts made throughout the late Imperial and Soviet eras to invigorate national artistic traditions. Scholars and artists realized that forms and motifs from the past could provide aesthetic fulfillment for modern communities and individuals. Though their original meanings had been lost, familiar forms could help make even radically new political messages understood. Folk art proved vital to Soviet culture in ways that earlier generations of artists never imagined.

The adaptability of folk art is equally important in the post-Soviet era. Thanks to the expanding tourist market, particularly tours of the Golden Ring and Russian north, contemporary folk artists have new opportunities to practice their art and exhibit and sell their work. Many participate in art fairs abroad. But the local resonance of folk arts is even more significant, as the number and variety of exhibitions and publications in the fifteen years since the publication of *Russian Folk Art* demonstrate. In 2007, curators of the Russian Museum in St. Petersburg reinstalled the permanent exhibition of folk arts and published a lavishly illustrated guidebook. The museum's Department of Folk Art also organized temporary exhibitions and scholarly conferences focusing on the arts of distinct regions, such as Kargopol. Other museums with major folk art collections have improved their facilities, published new catalogs, organized conferences, developed educational programs, and created engaging websites. The interaction of scholars and contemporary folk artists, a key component of Soviet arts policy discussed in the book's concluding chapter, has not diminished despite cutbacks in state support. In the past five years, museums and universities in Moscow, St. Petersburg, and many regional centers such as Vologda, Kirov, Arzamas, Orel, and Arkhangel'sk sponsored conferences on contemporary practice.

Preface to the Paperback Edition

xiv

Museums and schools throughout the country use folk arts along with stories and songs in educational programs for children, ensuring familiarity with Russian traditions for the next generation. One such project was based on this book. In 1997, my colleague Mary Ann Allin and I collaborated with curators from six Russian museums to organize an exhibition of Russian folk art for American audiences. The Trust for Mutual Understanding and the Cultural Foundation SWASH supported a curatorial conference and a subsequent reconfiguration of the project to create a virtual exhibition in the form of a website, "The World of Russian Folk Art" (www.rusfolkart .ru). Over the next decade, the foundation's director, Evgenia Zimnukhova, developed a program called "Journey to the World of Russian Folk Art" for children's homes and rehabilitation centers in small towns in the Leningrad region, with activities such as weaving, making wooden toys, and performing traditional music. Museums, ethnographic specialists, and folk music ensembles contribute to the project, as do contemporary folk artists, whose work is featured on the website. Although initially designed for American audiences, the ongoing virtual exhibition has turned out to be of greater interest and applicability for Russians seeking a way to understand their national heritage.

Bilibin's prophetic insights about the nature of folk art were an inspiration to me as I worked on this book. I would like to reiterate the appreciation I expressed in the original preface to the institutions, folk art specialists, and colleagues in Russia and in this country who offered me their expertise, and moral support. Other friends and colleagues, including the Porudominskii family, the Kolodzei family, Irina Karasik, Rosalind Blakely, Abbott Gleason, Anne Odom, Scott Ruby, Priscilla Roosevelt, and Blair Ruble, have enriched my understanding of Russian culture. The Trust for Mutual Understanding, the Cultural Foundation SWASH, the Wright Family Foundation, Hillwood Museum and Gardens, and Georgetown University provided practical support in many ways. I continually thank the museum curators and others involved in the exhibition and website projects: Alexander Grekov, the late Olga Arzumanova, Elena Mokhova, Lidia Iovleva, Natalia Sosnina, Svetlana Zhizhina, Valentina Zhiguleva, and especially Evgenia Zimnukhova and Mary Ann Allin for nourishing my fascination with Russian folk art. Finally, I wish to thank students and many readers who have sent me questions and comments about Russian folk art over the years.

Washington, D.C., 2011

Preface

Folk art embodies both the creative experience of individual artists and the traditions and values held by their communities. In Russian peasant culture, music, drama, and visual art formed components of vital social rituals of remarkable longevity and geographical range. Studies of Russian folk art have demonstrated that some visual images and patterns were based on traditions and beliefs from the distant past, while other designs reflected local historical experiences or individual responses to the surrounding world. Objects made and used by peasants such as serving bowls and other domestic utensils and garments for daily wear and ceremonial occasions physically linked tradition and daily life.

"Folk art" is sometimes mistakenly equated with "primitive," "naive," or "amateur" art and valued as a communal, unconscious expression of a "popular" spirit. But the folk art of any culture is complex, reflecting many interwoven layers of social and economic life, religious belief, and artistic ability and sensitivity. Some early studies of folk art emphasized a human instinct for making useful objects as beautiful as possible and held that folk art originated and flourished in an era in which the makers and consumers of crafted objects shared the beliefs and practices of a common culture.[1] Such cultural ties began to weaken, it was believed, with the Renaissance and Enlightenment; the industrial revolution and the rise of capitalism widened the gap between urban and rural life, between literary and oral cultures, between elite and popular or folk arts.

In Russia, divisions existed between Scandinavian overlords and local Slavic populations of Kievan Rus', between Muscovite princes and the rural peasantry, and between the educated landed gentry and the serfs in the eighteenth and nineteenth centuries. The social and economic gaps were more extreme in largely rural and undeveloped Russia than in the West. And yet, in retrospect, some observers in the postemancipation period felt that a shared culture, with its Slavic and Byzantine religiosity, its strong oral traditions, and its emphasis on ritual and symbol, continued to mold the identities of Russians of all classes. Folk art objects were seen as authentic manifestations of a shared cultural identity, and the study of folk art took on exceptional importance during the late nineteenth century, a period of transition and stress for the nation. The intensity of feeling about Russian folk art was reflected in the overlapping concepts of "national," "folk," and "popular" in the term *narodnoe iskusstvo,* "folk art." The word *narod,* "people," is closer to the German *Volk* than to English approximations of this idea. It connotes a sense of nationhood and national traditions. Some early studies of Russian folk art were inspired by the belief that living folk art preserved the deeply rooted historical identity of the Russian nation.

The study of folk and popular arts in any culture involves study of the makers and users of the objects as well as the pieces themselves. Problems arise when subjective qualities associated with a given culture are too insistently ascribed to folk art. For example, early commentary on American folk art was filled with praise for Yankee ingenuity and such phrases as "an honest and straightforward expression of the spirit of a people," "independence of school or tradition," "enterprise and courage," and "in harmony with democratic social institutions."[2] During the Soviet period, writing on Russian folk art was similarly riddled with political and philosophical statements, on the one hand denigrating it as dependent on the conditions of serfdom, and on the other elevating it as a pure expression of the genuine spirit of the people. More than one essay on Russian folk art began with Lenin's declaration that "art belongs to the people."[3] In many ways, the values ascribed to folk art by outside observers reflected the perceived needs of the larger society.

Russian folk art, like the art of many cultures in which the written word is not the primary means of communication, is often unsigned, but it is by no means impersonal. Carved house facades, painted furnishings, and smaller articles made by peasants or by masters of specialized crafts are often inscribed with names, dates, proverbs, or other messages. Many works can be ascribed to one of several hundred Russian folk artists known by name and reputation; many more pieces can be identified on the basis of style with specific districts or villages. Primarily the product of peasant artists working in their own villages and for local markets, Russian folk art had the capacity to absorb and adapt forms and ideas acquired from the larger environment. Folk art also had remarkable esthetic appeal beyond the original purposes of its makers or users; its influence on modern art, for instance, could not have been anticipated by its creators.

The organization of this book corresponds to my own process of examining the various components of folk art. As an outside observer, I am aware of my personal esthetic responses to forms and materials; at the same time I have tried to see as fully as possible what qualities were important to the makers and users of folk art. I begin by approaching the settings within which folk artists worked: the village, household, and market; then I move to the specific materials and techniques of the major types of art. After establishing the concrete aspects of folk art production, distribution, and use (mainly in the nineteenth and twentieth centuries), I turn to a broader context of historical evolution. Finally, I reflect on processes of survival and revival of folk art forms to the present day.

The functions of folk art within the village and the roles of individual masters, craft artels, and regional markets are shown in Part I, "The Arts in Peasant Life." The concept of cumulative originality, as distinct from individual invention on the one hand or communal production on the other, helps to explain the character of Russian folk art. Study of the style, imagery, and social contexts of folk art reveals its capacity to preserve ancient forms while absorbing and adapting new images that reflect historical changes as perceived by the peasants. Peasant culture, although predictably conservative and slow to change, was not static, and folk art evolved along with the culture. In addition, material conditions of peasant life varied from one area to another. The differences between the central agricultural regions, where serfdom prevailed and peasants were bound to the land, and the less fertile north, where trapping, forestry, and a variety of crafts provided a living for free peasants, were crucial in determining the kinds of arts practiced and the range of their distribution through markets. In all periods and regions, the ability to maintain the significant core of a local tradition while responding to new stimuli was essential to the success of the folk artist and to the validity of his or her work for the peasant community.

Identifying the concrete components of an art tradition brings into focus the balance between individual creativity and the outlook of a community. In Part II, "Materials and Forms," the relationships between styles and the physical characteristics of folk art are illustrated. The principal media include the woodworking and textile arts fundamental to every peasant community and specialized arts, such as birch-bark and bone carving, metalwork, and ceramics, characteristic of particular regions and towns. This section will clarify the meanings of folk art (*narodnoe tvorchestvo*), applied art (*prikladnoe iskusstvo*), handcraft production or cottage industry (*kustarnaia promyshlennost'*), and craft or trade (*remeslo*) and will show how these categories overlapped in Russia. A composite picture will emerge of the various artistic traditions that coexisted in northern and central Russia and that employed similar repertoires of images and patterns.

The question of what specific forms meant and why certain designs survived for centuries is raised in Part III, "Designs and Their Meanings." The answer depends upon an understanding of peasant communities, the tenor of daily life, and the special features of seasonal events and stage-of-life ceremonies as practiced in villages in various parts of the country. It requires an appreciation of the dual aspect of folk religiosity, known as *dvoeverie* ("dual faith") in Russian. Part III describes manifestations of *dvoeverie* in nineteenth- and twentieth-century village rituals, suggests how pervasive motifs in folk art may have been derived from ancient Slavic sources, and shows how certain formal patterns evolved over the centuries, absorbed elements from Byzantine and western European art, and reflected historical events and daily life in Russia. This section questions the common conception of the separation between court and people in historical times and emphasizes the importance of periodic interaction between the spheres of folk and urban or court art.

Part IV, "Preservation and Revival of Russian Folk Art," considers the historical role of folk art in the formation of a concept of Russian "national" identity from the eighteenth to the twentieth century. Here, the theme of interaction between folk art and high culture takes on new dimensions. The section begins with a discussion of the ambiguous situation of serf artists, peasants trained in professional skills and Western styles. It considers the radical changes in peasant life in the mid-nineteenth century, examines the nature and degree of the often cited decline in folk art, and evaluates the efforts by intellectuals and professional artists to revive the peasant arts. The following chapter identifies the quite different emphasis in modernist reinterpretations of folk art in the early twentieth century, when many professional artists explored the "primitive" styles of Russian folk arts as alternatives to overused European conventions in art. After the 1917 Revolution, artists and art administrators sought to enliven and validate new forms of "mass culture" with adaptations of folk designs and motifs. The final chapter examines the cultural significance of Russian folk art for the former Soviet state. The differences in the positions of folk artists and of Russian artists trained in modernist, international artistic idioms are obvious. Yet even artists and writers who approached folk art from outside, and who used specific motifs or interpreted folk traditions according to their own goals, demonstrated the elasticity of folk art in new and vital ways.

The fundamental question of the integrity or validity of folk art is addressed throughout the book. Can traditional visual forms remain effective once the traditional structures of folk society have disappeared? Traditional peasant piety, with its core of pagan and Christian beliefs, weakened after the emancipation of the serfs in 1861 and practically disappeared after the 1917 Revolution. Did folk art decline when its imagery no longer instilled belief? If folk art is defined narrowly as consisting of objects made by peasants for their own use, should handcrafts made for the market or for upper-class patrons be considered folk art? Is today's thriving Russian folk art industry merely commercial souvenir production, or does it preserve identifiable esthetic traditions? The question of validity is closely tied to the evolution of forms, examined in Part III, and to the changes in rural life and folk art revivals discussed in Part IV. The book as a whole argues that folk art is not isolated from the realities of history, commerce, and social change; in all its variety of media, styles, and functions, folk art is a crucial link connecting the esthetic, social, and spiritual values of Russian culture.

Finally, this book is concerned both with esthetic aspects of folk art that might be called universal, such as the formal harmony between decoration and underlying structure emphasized in studies of every national folk art tradition, and with the formal and thematic elements specific to Russia. Aside from a few comparative notes, it concentrates on northern and central European Russia, regions with great wealth and variety of folk art and extensive documentary material on peasant life and regional history.

These regions are best represented in the major national collections of folk art, partly because they have been the focus of important expeditions by ethnographers and art historians to record and collect objects and to talk with local artists about their working methods, their positions in the villages, and their attitudes about their art. Moreover, the large quantity of material in all media has encouraged many scholars to develop methods of structural and semiotic analysis, relating abstract forms to social roles, kinship patterns, and folklore theory.[4]

I have relied a great deal on the results of expeditions—the objects now in museums and publications—as I could not take part in fieldwork. In the Soviet period, many areas (northern Vologda Province and the villages on the Volga River near Nizhnii Novgorod) were out of bounds to foreigners, and as an outsider I would not have been privy to the social relationships and family traditions of the village artists. Even more helpful than the publications of these scholars were discussions with Ol'ga Kruglova, Serafima Zhegalova, and other researchers who had taken part in early expeditions in the 1950s and 1960s, which had identified the main centers of painting along the Northern Dvina River. Curators from the State Historical Museum in Moscow, the State Russian Museum and the Hermitage in St. Petersburg, and other institutions sponsoring these expeditions returned regularly and stayed in contact with some of the artists; their long-term familiarity with the regions and the physical and cultural contexts for the art was invaluable. In the course of their research, directed to particular regions and their specialized arts, these scholars assembled the widest possible range of pieces, studied and classified them according to material and styles, and used this concrete evidence to build up a census of artists and artist families, and to form a picture of artistic production, distribution, use, and esthetic evaluation of folk art in each region. Their approach sought to focus as closely as possible on the meaning of the artworks for their makers and users.

Other scholars whom I consulted not only studied local folk arts but also participated in government-sponsored efforts to support local and regional arts by establishing market outlets, assisting in obtaining materials, and even improving physical conditions in rural villages.[5] This kind of activism, with its precedent in prerevolutionary Russia, differs from "pure" scholarly study in that it ultimately changes the relationship of both makers and users to the traditional crafts.

Preface

No amount of documentation, theoretical study, or applied research conveys the sensory richness of the art itself. Very few examples of Russian folk art can be found outside of the national and regional museums in the former Soviet Union. The major collections in these museums are organized according to the prevailing methods of study and classification of art objects. Curatorial departments are identified by material: for folk art the main categories are wood, textile, metal, and ceramics, though some types of folk art, such as toys, are made of several materials. In addition to the basic media designations, collections are kept and exhibited according to historical contexts (particularly in the State Historical Museum in Moscow, and in the Department of Russian Culture of the Hermitage in St. Petersburg). Several regional museums and the Museum of Ethnography in St. Petersburg contain some displays of environments—such as a corner of a peasant's house, a bench in a carving workshop, or costumed mannequins holding threshing tools—but a sense of context is generally lacking in Russian art museums.

The media-based organization of museum collections naturally affects research and publication. The overwhelming proportion of articles and monographs on folk art are studies of the specialized techniques and materials described in Part II of this book. I have drawn upon these studies in addition to the museum collections, appreciating the concreteness and detail of the many works cited in the notes and bibliography. However, my goal was different. Rather than examining objects as illustrations of certain categories of art, I wanted to see how various kinds of art functioned together in the peasant household, in the village, or in the larger sphere of commerce. In addition to understanding the meaning of folk art for its actual makers and users, I wanted to see what the art might convey to other audiences: to scholars, about peasant life in particular times and places; to artists, about formal possibilities not encountered in academic art; to other viewers moved by the beauty and animation inherent in all kinds of folk art. The book presents an interpretation of Russian folk art rather than a catalogue of objects or an encyclopedic survey of styles and motifs. While representing the varieties of folk art as broadly as possible, it focuses on the historical developments and types of work that best reveal the interactive relationship of art and life essential to folk art.

This study grew out of my interest, shared by many art historians, in the values that nineteenth- and twentieth-century artists invested in folk and popular art. In the late 1960s, I first became aware of the bold colors and designs of Russian peasant costume and painting through the works of Natal'ia Goncharova, Vasilii Kandinskii, and other early twentieth-century artists. A conference at the University of Minnesota, held in connection with the exhibition "Russian Art 1800–1850" in 1978, gave me the chance to examine stylistic connections between folk art and "high" art in this earlier period, but at the time I knew only scattered published examples of Russian folk art. I began a more methodical study of Russian folk art with encouragement from many friends and colleagues, and financial support from scholarly institutions, for which I am deeply grateful. In 1982 the Kennan Institute for Advanced Russian Studies awarded me a short-term research grant, and a Senior Research Scholar Fellowship from the International Research and Exchanges Board allowed me to carry out research in the Soviet Union during the autumn and winter. A Georgetown University faculty summer grant helped me to make a start on the long process of reading, assembling material, and writing. I would like to thank the staffs of these institutions, of the Library of Congress, and of the American Embassy in Moscow for assistance of many kinds.

For information and inspiration I am indebted to the late Viktor M. Vasilenko, Professor of Art History at Moscow State University. One of the pioneers of Soviet folk art scholarship, he generously aided my research, introduced me to scholars in museums and institutes, many of them his former students, and shared with me his boundless love and understanding of Russian culture. My working base in Moscow was the State Historical Museum, and I thank the Director, K. G. Levykin, and the Secretary for Academic Affairs, Vera P. Zykova, for access to collections that soon after my stay went into long-term storage pending renovation of the museum. Curators in the departments of ceramics, metals, textiles, and wood, all authors of major studies of these media, were generous with their time and expertise; I would particularly like to thank Galina Dul'kina for help with ceramics, Luisa Efimova for showing me textiles and costumes, and Zoia Popova, Serafima Zhegalova, and Svetlana Zhizhina for introducing me to every form of carved and painted wood in their department and at the museum's branches at the Novodevichii Convent and elsewhere in the city. Elena V. Kamenetskaia assisted me at the Museum of Folk and Applied Art in Moscow. At the Tretiakov Gallery, Deputy Director Lidiia Iovleva and other curators arranged access to relevant paintings and helped me in numerous other ways.

At the Sergiev-Posad Museum-Preserve, I would like to thank Deputy Director Vera M. Zhiguleva for help with material on folk costume and on the history of the museum. I am especially grateful for opportunities to examine distaffs and other objects from the Northern Dvina River area with the late Ol'ga V. Kruglova, the scholar who identified the distinctive styles of painting and carving in the region in the 1950s. Galina Dain, at the Toy Museum in Sergiev-Posad, kindly showed me the impressive collection in her charge. I received practical help and the benefit of many discussions with curators and researchers at other museums: the Abramtsevo Estate Museum near Moscow; the Smolensk Museum Reserve, its affiliate, the Talashkino Estate Museum, and the Linen exhibition in Smolensk; and the Vologda Regional Museum of Local Studies and its branch at the Spasso-Priliutskii Monastery. Other collections, including those of the Iaroslavl' Kremlin Historical-Architectural Museum-Preserve, the Nizhnii Novgorod Regional History Museum, the Ipat'ev

Monastery Museum in Kostroma, the Murom Art Museum, and the wooden architecture museum-reserves in Novgorod, Suzdal', and Kizhi, added to my knowledge of regional folk arts.

In Leningrad (St. Petersburg), Lidiia Molotova, director of the Museum of Ethnography of the Peoples of the USSR, was especially helpful with material on costume and women's headwear. At the State Russian Museum, I would like to thank Evgeniia Petrova and Nikandr Mal'tsev for ready assistance with access to materials, Mal'tsev, Irina Boguslavskaia, and Natal'ia Taranovskaia in folk art, and Kira Mikhailova in early nineteenth-century painting. At the State Hermitage Museum, Galina Komelova and Irina Ukhanova showed me materials in the vast Department of Russian Culture.

Long after this first research trip, when I was finishing the text, I returned to Moscow in 1990 for a conference on "Folk Art and Contemporary Culture" sponsored by the Academy of Arts and the Ministry of Culture of the USSR. I am grateful to Mariia Nekrasova for organizing the exhibition and conference, for inviting me to give a paper, and for introducing me to folk art scholars and practitioners from all parts of the Soviet Union and adjacent countries—a concentrated experience of the enormous range of folk art studies in the former Soviet Union. The visit gave me the chance to meet again with scholars who had helped me earlier and enabled me to see my own research in a new perspective.

The people I have mentioned, and many others, went far beyond the requirements of duty or professional courtesy in a period of very difficult relations between our two countries. Vasilenko, in particular, also helped me to understand some of the politically determined conventions in scholarly publications of the 1930s through the 1970s, and to appreciate both positive values and severe restrictions signaled by ideological vocabulary about "the people," "the masses," "capitalism," "nationality," and "democracy." Besides sharing their expertise, all communicated to me a sense of devotion to scholarship in the face of daunting obstacles. My impressions were confirmed by subsequent contacts, and I will always be grateful for what I learned from these colleagues.

Finally, I would like to thank friends and colleagues in this country, who read all or parts of my text at various stages, alerted me to problems, suggested improvements, and brought material from their own fields to my attention. I am indebted to Marjorie Balzer and Ben Eklof for insights from anthropology and peasant studies, and to the publisher's outside readers for many helpful criticisms and suggestions. Peg Weiss, Janet Kennedy, Richard Stites, and Elizabeth Lipsmeyer gave me valuable advice, and Wendy Salmond, William Brumfield, and John Bowlt discussed aspects of their own work related to my interests. Three people were most important in helping me to visualize the scope and purpose of the book, and in seeing it through every stage. Janet Rabinowitch, as sponsoring editor, represented a fine standard of scholarship and writing; having encouraged me to take on the subject of Russian folk art, she maintained a wonderful balance of eagerness and patience over the years. Elizabeth Lipsmeyer asked the difficult questions, waited for comprehensible answers, and gave me constant moral support. My mother, Hildegard Hilton, read the text, made careful corrections, and contributed in more subjective ways as well. For this project, and for my other work, she was the model I emulated.

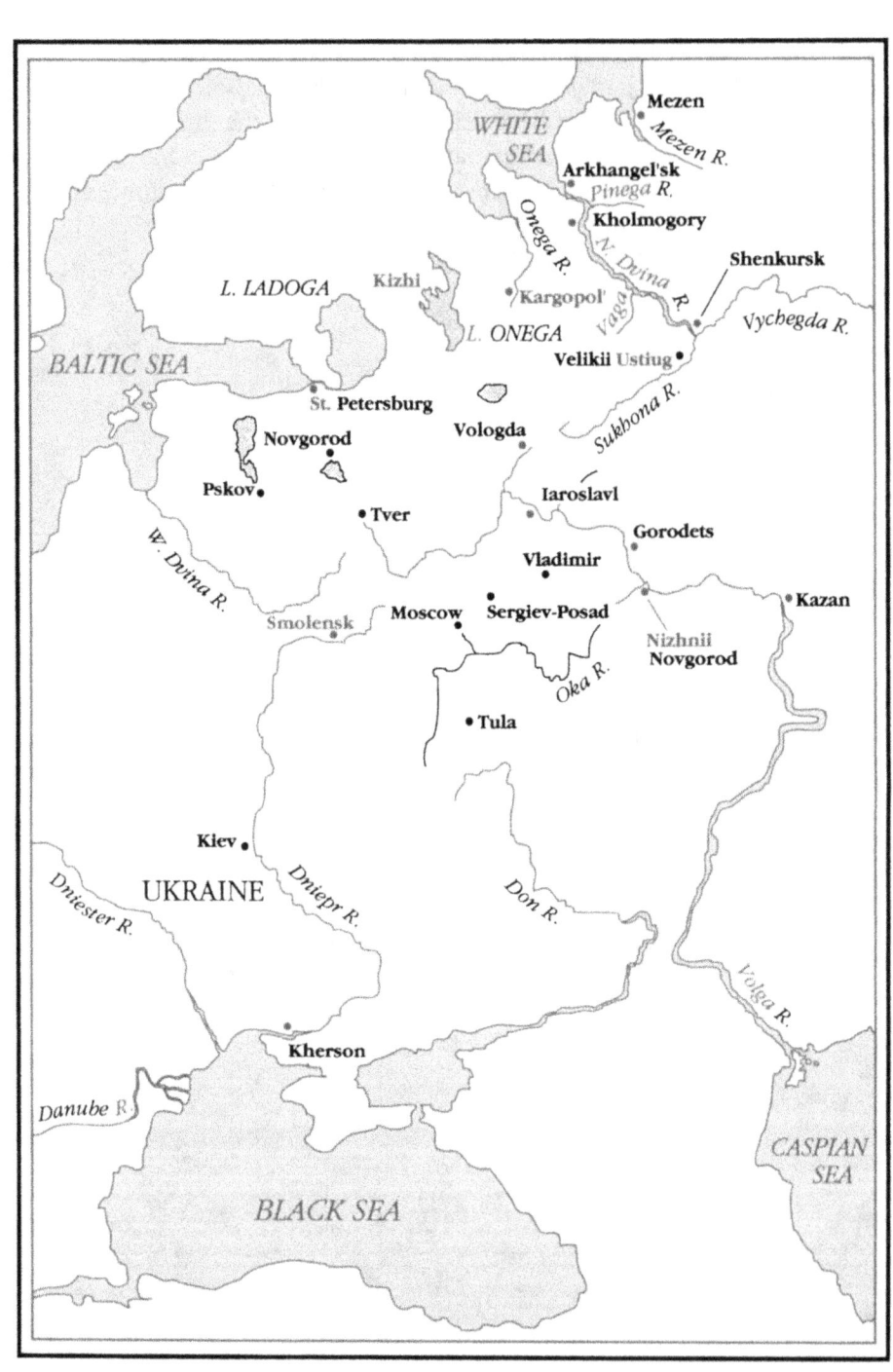

Note on Transliteration

Russian proper names and common terms in the text are given in a modified form of the Library of Congress system of transliteration that approximates their written appearance in Russian. Pronunciation follows a few basic rules. Consonants are pronounced much as they are in English; the "soft sign" (shown as ') indicates that the preceding letter, such as *r'*, *l'*, *t'*, is "softened," or slightly aspirated. The vowel spelled as *e* is pronounced as "ye" (e.g., *endova* is pronounced "yendova") or sometimes "yo" (e.g., *matreshka* is pronounced "matryoshka"). The vowels *a, i,* and *u* are pronounced as in other European languages; the *-yi* or *-ii* endings of adjectives and proper names are lengthened *i* sounds. Personal names are usually transliterated as, e.g., Aleksandr, Petr, Mariia, except in the case of tsars, i.e., Peter I, Catherine II.

Several Russian words related to folk arts, used frequently in the text, are defined in a glossary at the end of the book.

Abbreviations

The following abbreviations have been used in the photo captions:

Abramtsevo	Abramtsevo Estate Museum, Moscow region
GE	State Hermitage, St. Petersburg
GIM	State History Museum, Moscow
GRM	State Russian Museum, St. Petersburg
GTG	State Tretiakov Gallery, Moscow
Kolomenskoe	Museum-Preserve of the 16th–19th Centuries, Kolomenskoe
ME	Museum of Ethnography, St. Petersburg
MNI	Museum of Folk Art, Moscow
Sergiev-Posad	Sergiev-Posad State History and Art Museum-Preserve
Sergiev-Posad Toy Museum	Museum of Toys, Academy of Pedagogical Sciences, Sergiev-Posad
Smolensk	Smolensk Museum of Art History and Architecture
Vologda	Regional Museum of Local Studies, Vologda

Russian Folk Art

PART I

The Arts in Peasant Life

Tradition and Discovery

I worked the way my father worked; my father worked the way my
grandfather worked. And so that thread . . . of tradition has stretched and
stretched down to us.

— Antip Ershov, 1958[1]

I can remember vividly stopping on the threshold of this amazing
spectacle. The table, the benches, the stove . . . the closets,
the sideboards — everything had been painted with multi-colored
and bold ornaments.

— Vasilii Kandinskii, 1913[2]

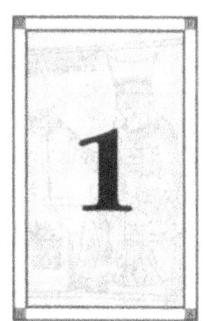

The strength of folk art traditions, sometimes submerged but flexible enough to survive and develop from one generation to the next, is linked to the conservatism of peasant life. Folk art belongs to communities rather than to individuals, and to many generations rather than to one period. Its basis is the repetition and preservation of special traits, ways of handling materials, treatment of form and volume, line and ornament, color and texture, and choice of certain subjects or decorative forms (fig. 1.1).

Folk art reflects community ideas about what is beautiful or appropriate for a given object or function. Even when an artist tries a new design, or copies a motif from a book or an object reflecting urban fashions, the underlying local tradition remains apparent. Several folk masters interviewed by Aleksandr

Saltykov in the late 1950s gave thoughtful responses to his questions about the nature of *narodnost'* ("folk"-ness), the differences between folk painting and "easel" painting, the traits of local styles, and the role of tradition. Arkhip Ermilovich Ershov, a maker of distaffs decorated with paint and wood inlay from the village of Semenovo, near Nizhnii Novgorod on the Volga, defined the quality of folk tradition by example.[3] He mentioned one local artist who did beautiful work but began drawing his lines very finely, instead of boldly like the other Volga-area painters, until he "lost the local character." In contrast, another artist came to the area from Moscow, lived in Semenovo for a year or two, and "tried to make pieces just like ours—but it didn't come out right—and why? Because he did not work the way we did." Ershov explained: "I worked the way my father worked; my father worked the way my grandfather worked. And so that thread, the thread of tradition, stretched and stretched down to us. But that man never held that thread—he worked in his own way."[4]

The esthetic preferences of a particular group were reinforced through a process of teaching by example. This instruction was not a matter of drill or mechanical repetition, however; there was room for personal choice. Thinking again about learning, practicing, and becoming a master, Ershov added: "[Artists] sometimes think that once a tradition exists, it will live forever, without change. No, I work the way my father worked, but not quite the same way. And my father also worked like my grandfather, but not entirely like him. We each have something of our own, but we still hold on to that thread."[5]

The concept of cumulative originality, as distinct from individual invention or communal activity, helps to clarify the nature of folk art.[6] The notion that folk art was a spontaneous or unconscious expression of a communal spirit was largely a product of early nineteenth-century romantic social theories. In reality, most objects we consider folk art were made for specific purposes by individual peasants or town artisans who were known for their abilities in particular art forms. Many articles were inscribed with names, dates, verses, and proverbs (fig. 1.2), and the names and specializations of several hundred Russian folk artists are known.[7] Nevertheless, the common household arts, the making of textiles and garments and the fashioning of utensils and tools of wood, were practiced by most Russian peasants until the late nineteenth century. Even untrained peasants, exposed only to a few examples of decorative art forms at regional fairs, had the skills to make simple objects attractive, to add something festive to their ordinary routines and sometimes dreary surroundings. Beauty was not an abstract concept, and art was not a self-sufficient element in peasant life. Ornament was always integral to an object that had either a utilitarian or a ceremonial function.[8] Russian scholars often use the term *tselostnost'*, "completeness" or "integrity," to explain this quality.[9]

Since the objects made by Russian peasants were used daily over long periods of time, surviving examples are sometimes so worn that only traces of their original decoration can be seen. But enough remains to show that the purpose for which a piece was made determined the type of decoration. Representational and abstract forms had meanings tied to the function of the object, to the people who used it, or to a special occasion, such as a wedding or the first day of harvest. The relation between form and function seems direct and self-evident. However, surveying a wide range of folk art in many media and from various parts of Russia reveals intriguing geographical and historical patterns in this relationship, along with apparent exceptions to those patterns. One approach to analyzing the decoration of folk art objects, enunciated by Viktor M. Vasilenko, poses a series of questions. What is depicted on the object? What did these forms mean to the peasants who used them? How did these forms attract attention? How and why did so many of these forms survive, with hardly any change, from generation to generation?[10] Vasilenko and other scholars theorized that the most persistent designs were symbols of "good magic," possessing special powers. They speculated that some forms originated as stylized animals, plants, or hybrid creatures found in pre-Christian cultures of the southern steppes. In historic times, according to

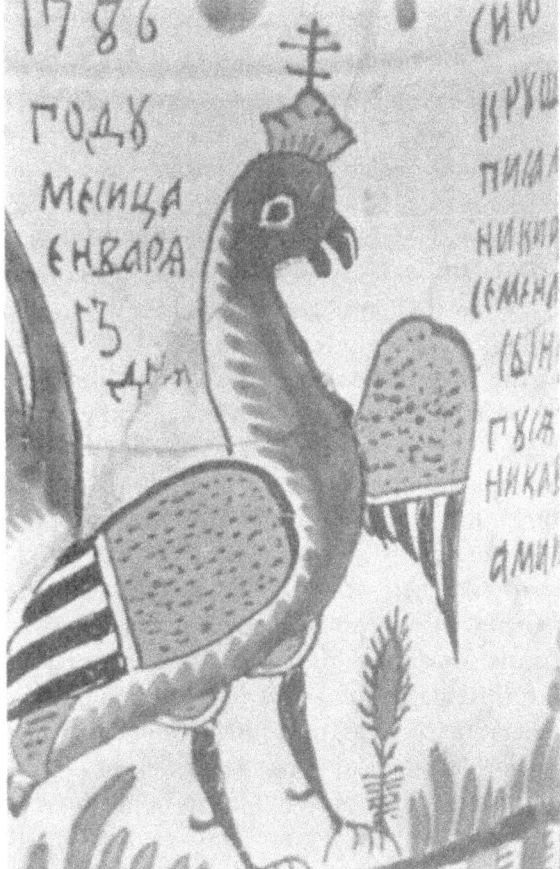

this view, distinctive styles that developed in Kiev, Novgorod, Vladimir, and Suzdal' before the Mongol invasions in the thirteenth century and in Moscow from the fifteenth to the seventeenth centuries, were gradually transmitted to outlying areas through the circulation of manuscript miniatures and portable church furnishings, and by itinerant artisans. These new styles modi-

FIG. 1.2   Plate. Majolica. Detail of inscription. Gzhel', 1786. GIM.

fied, but did not erase, the underlying patterns, just as Christianity did not entirely replace pagan beliefs.

Although the premise that folk art reflected ancient Russian culture was hypothetical and left open possibilities for misinterpreting later images and practices, it provided a useful framework for observation. Students of Russian folk culture in the nineteenth and early twentieth centuries recorded customs still alive in rural villages, ranging from rituals surrounding the chief events of life or marking the agricultural seasons and saints' days, to the prosaic details of daily tasks. Observation of local practices was supplemented by travelers' accounts and official documents concerning the resources, manufacturing, and trade of a region. Researchers worked back and forth in time, using physical evidence from earlier or related cultures to fill gaps, attempting to establish, if not the source of a particular form or practice, at least a sense of the distant roots of a tradition.

In Russia, the vast expanses and the hardships of travel seem to have helped rather than hindered the study of folklore and folk art. Protected by great forests from interference or exploitation, the villages northeast of Vologda, settled in the sixteenth and seventeenth centuries by exiles from Novgorod, appeared virtually unchanged in the nineteenth century.[11] Traces of the more distant past, forms resembling objects dating from pre-Mongol Novgorod found in the major excavations of the city after World War II, have been examined by Vasilenko, B. A. Rybakov, S. K. Prosvirkina, and others.[12] Surveying the common stock of images found in all forms of peasant art, Vasilii Voronov concluded that except for a few topical motifs related to such events as Peter the Great's capture of a Swedish fortress on the Neva and Napoleon's invasion of Russia, nearly all the images could be traced to origins in pagan Russia.[13] For example, the female figure with arms raised in an orant position (fig. 1.3), prominent in all types of woodwork and textiles, is visually close to icons of the Virgin of the Sign (*Bogomater' znameniia*), but probably reflects more ancient forms of the female divinities Mokosh or Mother Moist Earth (*Mat' syra zemlia*). Other motifs that often accompany this figure in folk art, including flowers, branches, and the Tree of Life, horsemen or hunters, horses, deer, ducks and other birds, fish, and various mythical creatures, may have originated with the female nature cults. Semiotic studies of folk art emphasize certain decorative patterns and their iconographic development over the centuries as manifestations of several interrelated layers of meaning.[14]

Russian peasants were not alone in decorating dwellings, garments, and objects used in daily life with forms that symbolized or evoked aspects of nature through resemblance, association of ideas, or a conventional identification; formal and functional parallels existed in other national traditions.[15] Similarities between Russian decorative and symbolic forms and those of neighboring peoples point to contacts in the remote past, especially with Scandinavians (the Varangians who founded the Kievan dynasty) and North-

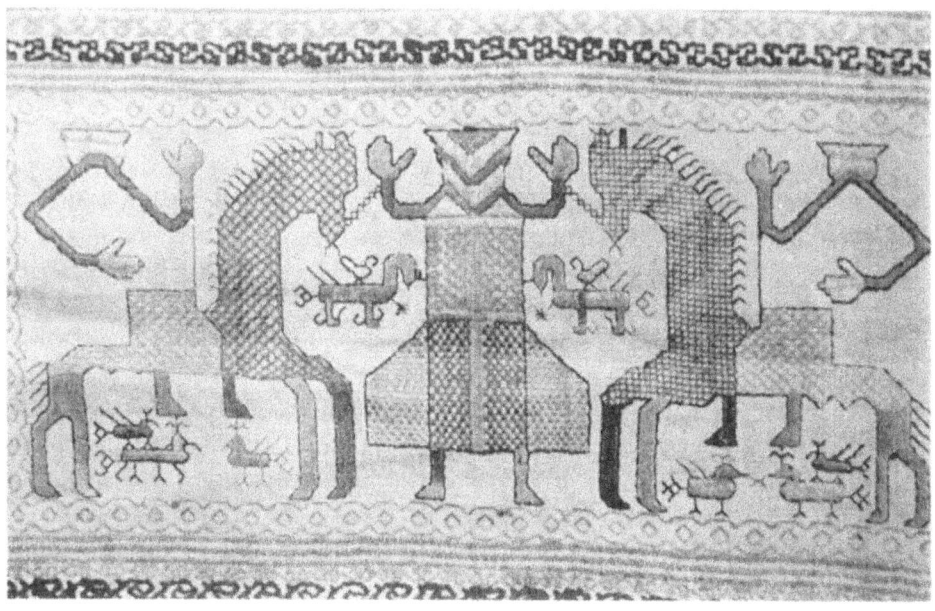

FIG. 1.3 Border of headdress. Embroidery on linen. Female figure with raised hands, flanked by riders. Kargopol', 19th century. MNI.

ern Slavs, who settled in the Western Baltic region while the Eastern Slavs moved into central Russia, around the eighth century. Historically, trade and war generated important artistic contacts.[16] Comparative studies of European folk art by Helmuth Bossert, Bernward Deneke, and Reinhard Peesch offer several ways of analyzing and interpreting formal and iconographical relationships.[17] Museum collections and books on national folk arts also reveal formal and functional parallels; for example, distaffs from Finnish Karelia and from Bosnia, looms, scutchers, mangels, and other tools for working linen from Schleswig-Holstein and Pomerania, spoons from Romania, and gingerbread molds from several regions of Germany are strikingly similar to their Russian counterparts. Beyond the practical fact that certain shapes are suited to particular tasks, the decorative forms suggest artistic kinship. The folk arts of northern and eastern Europe, Ukraine, the Caucasus, Central Asia, Siberia, and other regions with which the inhabitants of central and northern Russia had contact are not covered in this book.[18] However, neighboring art traditions evidently influenced some folk artists, as did periodic encounters with artists and works from Moscow, Nizhnii Novgorod, and other urban centers.

THE ARTS IN PEASANT LIFE

The producers of Russian folk art were not isolated sociologically. Peasants who made objects for their own use rubbed shoulders with artisans and tradesmen in market towns. In the winter months many families engaged in *kustar'* art, piecework for sale, traveling to markets once or twice a week, or selling their wares through middlemen.[19] Statistical records of provincial markets and travelers' accounts seldom drew distinctions among products such as honeycombs or candle-wax and artifacts such as carved birch-bark containers, bast shoes, braided trim, and other items crafted by peasants. Peasant artists also found employment in the workshops of monasteries and in artels and factories producing textiles, ceramics, metalware, and other goods, sometimes for middle-class urban buyers. When peasant artisans produced specialized art objects, such as silver boxes with niello designs, for well-to-do townspeople, they often employed the same motifs and techniques that they used for birch-bark or carved woodenware. Conversely, peasant artists readily adapted urban art forms to their own familiar materials. The interaction of peasant art and church or court art was important in all historical periods. But the nature of this interaction changed in the eighteenth century, affected by Peter I's westernizing policies, the rise of serfdom, and the separation of gentry and peasantry. In turn, the geographic and ethnographic studies promoted by Catherine II and the copious studies of Russian history and culture inspired by Slavophilism in the nineteenth century contributed to an identification of peasant and folk culture with Russian national qualities.

Contemporary study of folk art and folklife must consider, above all, the relationship of artistic traditions both to communities, defined broadly or locally, and to individual artists. Unfortunately, brief references to folk art in books on Russian art or studies of peasant life tend to point out "typical" forms and images and to emphasize communal or regional characteristics; uncommon styles or subjects that cannot be readily categorized are disregarded. However, some more specialized studies of peasant woodcarving, painting, textiles, ceramics, and other arts show that such objects often reflected personal responses to current events or stimuli from other art forms, and that they embodied individual esthetic preferences. Each regional repertoire of designs appropriate to certain types of objects had room for variations. The relationship of the individual folk artist to local tradition, what I have called "cumulative originality," is a recurrent theme of this book. The major public collections of Russian folk art, field research, and oral histories recorded by Soviet scholars provide sufficient material to present accurate and vivid pictures of individual artists' styles, methods of working, and ways of life.[20]

A broad definition of Russian folk art includes the overlapping categories of peasant art, urban crafts, and *kustar'* art (small-scale home industry). In the late nineteenth century, professional artists worked with peasants to "improve" the quality of traditional crafts. With different motives, artists in early twentieth-century vanguard groups studied folk art to understand its principles of decoration, apply them to their own work, and teach them to others. Today, in almost every region and sphere of activity, professional and folk artists interact: contact rather than isolation is the rule. How will this blurring of boundaries affect the preservation of folk art traditions in Russia?

It is likely that folk and professional artists will continue to approach their work differently.[21] A folk artist brings his or her skills and perceptions to a traditional task, while a professional artist expresses individual perceptions or feelings, even if this means departing from a traditional form or canon. The professional artist might strive for originality for its own sake or for the sake of creating something universal. The folk artist, in contrast, works within a local, familiar, and natural discipline and preserves the integrity of the object and the generative core of folk art tradition.

While the folk artists and the main users of folk art expected objects to be made in ways customary to their villages, the special visual qualities of the houses, furnishings, clothing, and tools made by peasants seemed remarkable to those unfamiliar with local traditions. The spectacle of color and ornament in peasant houses of Vologda Province, which amazed Vasilii Kandinskii in 1899 and had a profound and lasting effect on his art, was part of the daily experience of local peasants. The village artist might pay attention to small variations in a design or technique, but visitors would see the most striking features: finely carved facades, colorful garments, the sounds and motions of village festivities. In many cases, visitors saw what they expected to find. But thanks to the sometimes naive but detailed observations of outsiders, a great deal of information about Russian peasant life and art in different regions has been preserved.

Prompted by Catherine the Great's empire-building policies in the eighteenth century, the Russian Academy of Sciences and geographical and economic commissions sponsored expeditions throughout the territories of Russia and Siberia. The first work to offer a comprehensive picture of the peoples of Russia was the four-volume *Description of All Peoples Inhabiting the Russian Empire, Their Customs and Rituals, Beliefs, Dwellings, Clothing and Other Notations*, published in St. Petersburg in 1776–77.[22] The author, German ethnographer Johann Gottlieb Georgi, supplemented his own observations with those of other travelers, Russian and foreign. Over 100 colored engravings, mostly of figures in native costumes, inspired a series of porcelain figurines of the peoples of Russia made at the Imperial Porcelain Factory in the 1780s.

In 1791, Petr I. Chelishchev, traveling through northern Russia, compiled extensive reports on the economy of the trade centers on the White Sea and the Northern Dvina River. He made special note of the well-established guilds of ivory carvers, silversmiths, icon painters, fabric printers, and others in the trading center of Arkhangel'sk, and distinguished between these specialized arts and carpentry, "all done by peasants from neighboring villages."[23]

In the early nineteenth century, Evdokii Ziablovskii's six-volume *Geographic Description of the Russian Empire* included information on craft guilds in all the major towns and noted the importance of "various kinds of handwork" made by peasants for sale at regional markets.[24]

Influenced by the Enlightenment and the revolutions in America and France, Aleksandr Radishchev wrote and published *Journey from Petersburg to Moscow* in 1790. Radishchev's purpose was not ethnography but protest. Denouncing the system of serfdom and the condition of the peasantry, he portrayed peasant life in negative terms, as in this description of a peasant's hut: "Four walls, half covered, as was the whole of the ceiling, with soot; the floor full of cracks and at least two inches in accumulated dirt. . . . A wooden bowl and some vessels called plates; a table, hewn with an axe . . . ."[25] Nothing here, or in his comments on clothing, daily activities, and customs, suggests comfort, let alone esthetic pleasure. Radishchev's treatment of peasant life in this work set the tone for much of the writing about rural Russia in the nineteenth century.

Early nineteenth-century Russian literature portrayed some worthy peasant characters, including intelligent and sensitive serfs, and in the 1840s and 1850s several writers introduced long descriptions of village settings along with narratives in "peasant" dialect.[26] Slavophile convictions probably inspired studies of folk life in this period, as they influenced research on folk music;[27] such works paid little attention to visual arts, however. Research on the peasant economy published after the emancipation of the serfs in 1861 noted the decline of peasant *kustar'* art production in the face of manufactured goods, but rarely included any specific description of the art. However, one author, V. P. Bezobrazov, noted the Russian peasant's fondness for decoration, commenting that next to singing, popular prints and decorated tableware "constitute the major esthetic enjoyment of our people."[28]

Chiefly concerned with exposing the terrible living conditions of the peasantry, some writers nevertheless commented on their ingenuity in the face of adversity. Sergei Kravchinskii, a populist activist who wrote under the name Stepniak, characterized the creativity of peasants in 1888:

> They make all kinds of goods which do not require expensive machinery for their manufacture: earthen, steel, iron, leathern wares; woollen, cotton and linen stuffs; carts and harness; hats, furniture, mats, carpets, lithographs and ikons, ropes, musical instruments, candles, soap, glass, beads, bronze and silver finger and earrings; they bring up singing-birds, they knit laces, they hew grindstones. They do everything which a ready mind, coupled with a hungry stomach, can suggest.[29]

Foreign travelers who immersed themselves, even briefly, in the atmosphere of Russian rural life were sometimes struck by details that would have been taken for granted by Russians. Their writings offer vivid glimpses of peasant life and of the roles of physical objects in daily routines and seasonal rituals. The earliest description of Russian woodcarving, in one of few documents dating before the Mongol invasion, was the Arab traveler Ahmed Ibn Fadlan's account of his journey up the Volga in A.D. 922. Each time his ship stopped at a pier, every merchant on board took bread, meat, onions, and milk to place before a tall wooden pillar, carved with the face of a man and surrounded by smaller wooden forms and a row of poles.[30]

Much later, in the sixteenth and seventeenth centuries, European travelers admired Russian wooden architecture with its large-scale relief carving done by peasants using only a hand-axe. The English explorer Richard Chancellor, who traveled from Arkhangel'sk to Moscow in the late sixteenth century, praised the weathertight construction of peasant houses. Other foreigners visiting trading towns along the Volga noted that Russian merchants, instead of renting shops and warehouses, had local carpenters at each port build temporary wooden structures to house their goods.[31] More striking displays of woodworking skill, the great wooden churches of the north and the unique wooden palace at Kolomenskoe built for Tsar Aleksei Mikhailovich in the 1660s, aroused enthusiastic responses. The German traveler Jacob Rietenfels saw the just-completed palace and wrote that it was "so marvelously adorned with carving and gilt that one could take it for a toy newly out of its box."[32] Many considered the palace one of the great wonders of the world.

More revealing than admiring comments about remarkable sights are foreigners' observations about the appearance and atmosphere of ordinary towns and villages. Theophile Gauthier, who visited Russia in the 1830s, was fascinated by icons, their presence in every house and their aura of veneration as much as their appearance. His descriptions of peasants' garments, sleds, houses, and baths, and of inns, monasteries, and markets, are rich in visual detail. He noticed everything, from the lanterns and spires of the St. Sergius Monastery to the souvenirs for sale at its gates: felt shoes, fur mittens, dishes from Tula, medallions of St. Sergius, and rolls from the convent bakery with scenes from the Old and New Testament stamped on their smooth brown crusts.[33] Gauthier was interested in Russia partly because of romantic associations dating from the time of Napoleon's invasion. Some travelers displayed political and philosophical biases in their accounts of life in Russia. The Marquis Astolphe de Custine, who spent several weeks in 1839 visiting Petersburg, Moscow, Sergiev-Posad, Iaroslavl', and Nizhnii Novgorod, took note of the landscape and architecture but did not recognize anything he would call art among the people. He found the country alien and was chiefly interested in demonstrating the connection between the "brutalization, sly obstinacy and anarchic" nature of the serfs and Nicholas I's autocracy.[34]

By the mid-nineteenth century there were European business communities in most of Russia's commercial centers, as well as a surprising number of tourists, who, as one long-time English resident put it, "being desirous of change, take the voyage to Russia as one promising more novelty than . . . France or Switzerland."[35] One Englishman motivated by curiosity was Charles Lutwidge Dodgson, who toured Russia in 1867. Knowing some Russian, and with friends to show him around, he visited cities, palaces, cathedrals, monasteries, markets, and even a "genuine" Russian inn or *traktir*. Like any tourist en route through the countryside, he thought of "applying at a peasant's cottage for bread & milk, as a pretext for seeing the interior and their mode of life."[36]

The most detailed accounts were by people who spent more than a few weeks in the country and who were more or less trained in sociological observation. The German agrarian expert Baron August von Haxthausen's lengthy record of the year he spent studying "the condition of the country and . . . its national life" is deservedly the most famous.[37] Haxthausen emphasized the patriarchal character of the country and the importance of the village commune as the basis of all social relationships: a microcosm of the nation. He related many of his observations of family life, social classes, crafts, manufacture, wage earning, trade, agriculture, education, and entertainment to this idea. In almost every region, Haxthausen had opportunities to witness village meetings and inspect farms and peasant houses. In a village not far from Iaroslavl', he recorded the domestic arrangements:

> We ascended a staircase, to the dwelling-room (*izba*), which had no other furniture than a bench running round it. Opposite the door in the corner stood the image of the saint, with a lamp burning under it; and on the walls were some shelves, upon which were placed all kinds of vessels and utensils. Spinning-wheels and hand-looms testified to the widely disseminated linen manufacture in this district. An enormous stove, built up with bricks, filled one third of the room; this in winter is a sleeping-place; beside it a small staircase led down to the lower part of the house (*patpolye*), which serves as a store, and where the smaller animals, fowls and swine, take up their abode in the night . . . . On the other side of the staircase were some closets, [with] boxes, one for each member of the family, containing clothes . . . .[38]

The author was surprised by the cleanliness of the room and the freshness and purity of the air, thanks to the constantly burning fire and open windows. His description stands in sharp contrast to Radishchev's comments on the dirty interiors, with layers of soot serving as insulation. Haxthausen declared: "The taste for ornament is very prevalent among the Great Russians, and indicates a high capacity for civilization."[39]

Depending on the time of year in which he visited a particular region, Haxthausen gave accounts of local festivals or recurring events such as the week for collecting the tax (*obrok*) in mid-May, the autumn day set for releasing or giving up farmland (known as the second St. George's Day), and seasonal bazaars at which linen and local produce were sold.[40] In the larger towns, Iaroslavl', Torzhok, and Tver', he noted the chief manufactured articles, such as boots, gold embroidery, and woven linen, and described the artisans' guilds and their methods of distributing work and income. Haxthausen obtained statistics and other details on the economies of the various regions from local governors and from official reports, such as the *Journal of the Ministry of the Interior*, sources still indispensable for study of folk culture.

An Illustrated Description of the Russian Empire, written in 1855 by Robert Sears, contained a methodical, region-by-region description of the country, with lists of the main towns and district centers, their inhabitants, occupations, and major products. More than a straightforward presentation of facts, the book revealed subtle social and economic relationships. Reporting on Iaroslavl' and Rostov, Sears stated that linen, cotton, and woolen stuffs, leather, silk, hardware, and tobacco were the principal manufactures, but "independently of these, the peasants are almost everywhere partially occupied with weaving stockings and other fabrics, and making gloves, hats, harness, wooden shoes and various rural implements."[41] Sears discussed the various categories of peasants and serfs and their occupations, and included an engraving of peasant carpenters building a cottage. In an account of seasonal markets and the goods sold by peasants, he noted: "The Russians have a peculiar talent for making figures and toys out of the most worthless materials in the world: straw, shavings, ice, dough, they turn all to account."[42]

An English gentlewoman who lived in Russia for ten years before publishing her description of the country in 1855 made particularly precise and insightful comments on folk culture. She described several months' stay in Arkhangel'sk Province, visits to Samoyed camps and to Russian villages along the Northern Dvina River, journeys through Vologda Province to the remote settlements of the Old Believers, visits to monasteries and provincial towns, and longer stays in major cities such as St. Petersburg, Iaroslavl', Kostroma, and Moscow. Although warned by members of her own class that the peasants were "nothing but brutes," this Englishwoman weighed positive and negative aspects in her observations.

> A Russian village is generally composed of a long row of wooden houses on each side of the post-road, with usually a line of birch-trees in front. Some of the well-to-do peasants, or those amongst them who are the most ingenious, have the eaves of their cottages ornamented in a very pretty manner with a kind of border of so light and elegant a description that it may be compared to wooden lace; the windows, where there are any, are decorated in the same manner.[43]

Her enjoyment of peasant creativity was counterbalanced by her remark that "at the entrance of the villages we generally saw painted on the same board the number of men and cows contained in each; the fair sex were not thought *worth the trouble* of being enumerated."[44] Although less methodical than official provincial records, this narrative conveys the features of peasant culture that were most striking to an outside observer.

In addition to written accounts, photographs and prints of Russian popular life, including entire series of colored engravings illustrating folk dances, weddings, and other customs, or "popular types," peasants, coachmen, peddlers, and artisans (fig. 1.4), appeared in both Russian and foreign publications. Valuable for their details of townscapes as well as costumes, most of these works conform to the romantic idealization of the peasantry that can be seen in the decorations of porcelain and other luxury goods of the same period.[45]

After the emancipation of the serfs, the depiction of peasants changed in all media, in decorative arts, painting, and creative writing as well as in travel accounts and ethnological studies. Some works, such as those of Sergei Kravchinskii and other members of the Russian populist movement, were political in intent. Providing ample, even exhaustive, detail about the long working hours, meager pay, and hard daily lives of the peasants involved in cottage industry, Kravchinskii gave little information about the artistic aspects of peasant crafts.

Many astute foreign observers in Russia from the 1870s to the end of the century were interested not only in the general "condition" of the peasantry, but also in particular regional conditions, social traditions, and beliefs, which determined the patterns of peasants' lives. The noted British traveler Sir Donald Mackenzie Wallace devoted a good deal of space to the custom of the *beseda*, the evening conversation and singing that accompanied routine work such as spinning or making bast shoes. He identified such predictable community activity as a kind of touchstone against which variations in behavior might be measured. While confirming the importance of the *besedy*, he did not pay any attention to the forms of the spinning implements or the methods of plaiting *lapti* (bast shoes).[46]

One of the most specific and visual of all the travel accounts is the American Isabel Hapgood's narrative of an excursion up the Volga in 1895. Her descriptions of peasants' houses are even more detailed than those of Haxthausen, with greater attention to the materials and ornamentation of various utensils, furnishings, and garments, as well as the exact procedures for placating the house sprite or *domovoi*.[47]

Standing apart from the travelers' accounts and studies of the peasantry, a few works on Russian art included folk art. Eugene Viollet-le-Duc's *Russian Art: Its Origins, Constituent Elements, Its Apogee and Its Future*, published in French in 1877 and in Russian in 1879, included the author's engravings of exteriors and interiors of peasant houses and other decorative forms.[48] Declaring that "over the centuries, the house of the Russian peasant has not changed," the author showed both the practicality and visual richness of Russian folk art and architecture. This book was among the first to suggest stylistic affinities

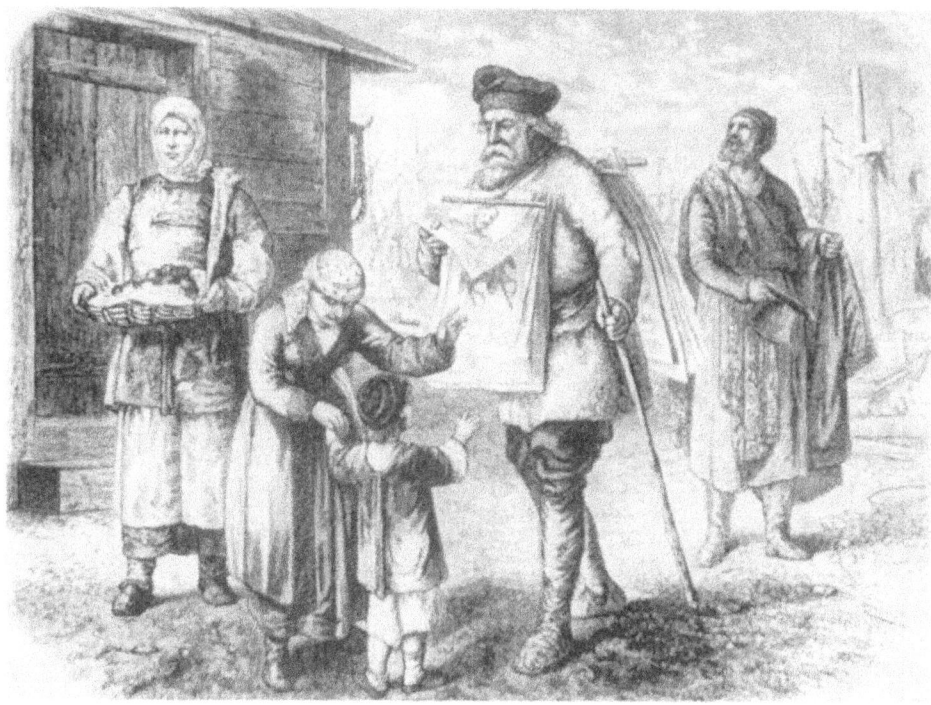

FIG. 1.4 "Russian Folk Types": fruit seller, *lubok* peddler, rag seller. From Herbert Roskoschny, *Russland: Land und Leute* (1882).

between Russian folk art and decorative traditions of Byzantium and Asia. The most detailed, and significant, study of the ornamentation of Russian folk art was by Vladimir V. Stasov, the eminent publicist and critic who championed national art represented by the "Mighty Handful" composers and the "Wanderers" association of artists. Stasov's *Russian Folk Ornament*, published in 1872, included beautifully printed color plates illustrating samples of historical and contemporary embroidery and lace (fig. 1.5), and extensive historical commentary.[49]

Folk art figured prominently in the work of creative writers and artists. Nikolai Leskov's 1873 story "The Sealed Angel," about a group of Old Believers, treats with great sensitivity the virtually miraculous art of an itinerant icon painter.[50] The realist painter Il'ia Repin, recalling his childhood in Ukraine, credited an itinerant painter, Trofim Chaplygin, and his lifelike and mouthwatering rendering of a watermelon slice with first awakening Repin's own

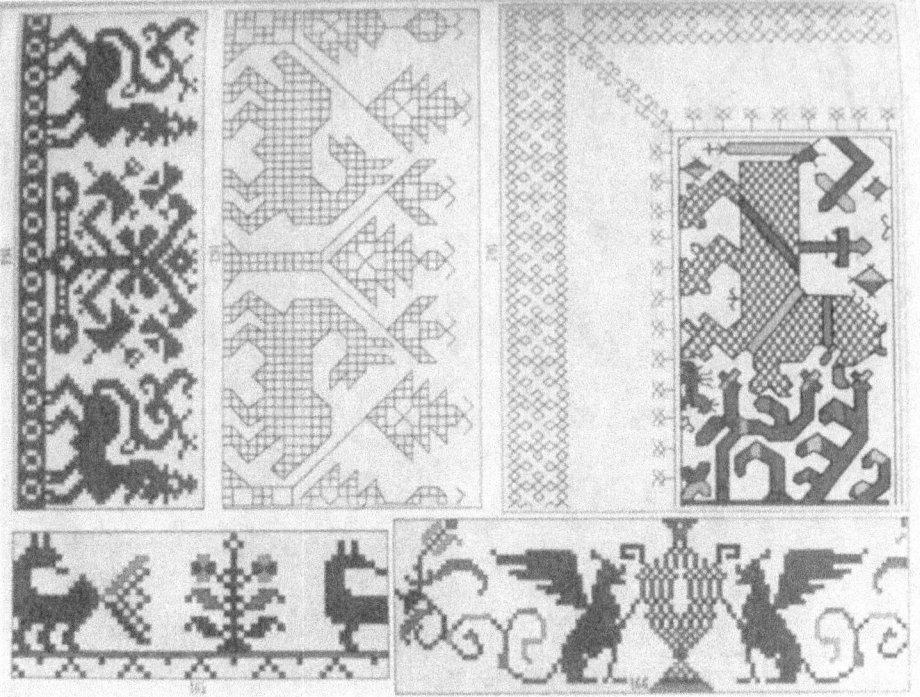

FIG. 1.5   Towel borders. Plate from
Vladimir Stasov, *Russkii narodnyi ornament*
(1872).

interest in art.[51] The artist recalled the strong visual impressions of his childhood home, its walls decorated with humorous popular prints (*lubki*), and especially the enormous stove of white chalk clay, "painted by hand with
wonderful boldness by the women and girls." The young Repin watched as
"their bast brushes of various forms and sizes, embellished with many colors,
made miracles of unique art."[52] A generation later, Vasilii Kandinskii experienced the "miracle" of folk painting in the remote north, and Kazimir
Malevich had a powerful formative experience watching an ordinary housepainter at work.[53] Leskov, Repin, Kandinskii, and Malevich expressed an im-
pulsive, perhaps instinctive awareness of the strengths of peasant art. Many
professional artists at the turn of the century were engaged in a more deliberate revival of folk art forms and development of the cottage crafts (*kustar'*)
industry. We will return to the activity of the Abramtsevo colony and other
art circles in the 1880s and 1890s and the very different approaches to folk art
by artists of the neoprimitivist movement in chapters 16 and 17. In the fol-

lowing chapters, we will begin to look at the environment of folk art from a broad perspective, that of the peasant village. We will then focus on the household, its furnishings, and the activities of daily life. Finally we will turn to more specialized skills and tasks, markets for folk art, and the experiences of individual artists working in this traditional setting.

Village and *Izba*

The taste of the Russian peasant for pictorial decoration manifests itself
incessantly. . . . In the *izba*, one . . . encounters painted
images everywhere.

— E. E. Viollet-le-Duc (1877)[1]

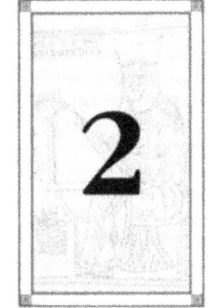

The physical layout of Rus- sian villages in the nineteenth
and early twentieth centuries varied only slightly from
region to region. A row of wooden houses lining a river
bank or a dirt road, spaced far enough apart to avoid the spread of fire; a
church and a bathhouse, windmills, storage sheds, and other outbuildings
were the main features. Early maps show four basic types of peasant settlement: the *pogost*, originally a country church together with related buildings;
the *svoboda* or *sloboda*, a village exempted from the work obligation to the
state; the *selo*, a market town or large village; and the *derevnia*, a small village or
hamlet, usually without its own church, supply store, or other amenities.[2]

Locations of hills, woodlands, and rivers and the directions of sunlight
and prevailing winds affected the layout of the village. The linear arrangement, the most ancient type and still most common in the nineteenth century,
had buildings set in lines along the bank of a lake or river, or along the sides
of a road. A typical farmstead included the dwelling, the *izba*, close to the
street, a barn, a hayshed, and a kitchen garden; the outbuildings were usually
arranged to form a yard (*dvor*), enclosed by a low fence of sticks or woven
twigs. Outbuildings were usually connected to the main structure in the
north, and placed apart in the more temperate south. Sometimes bathhouses
were built in a cluster near a river or lake, and storage sheds and workshops

for crafts were grouped at the edge of the village. The farmland, beyond the village, was divided into narrow strips; each household was assigned several strips, which lay in diverse parts of the village holdings. The lots were rotated among the households according to an established system (usually based on the number of taxable persons in each family). The practice allowed fair apportionment of the arable land, though it hindered efficient farming.[3] It also meant that, while farming activity took place at some distance from the home, domestic tasks and the crafts that occupied peasants during the winter months could often be done communally.

The grouping of ten to twenty dwellings formed a visual unit. Constructed of logs and fairly uniform in design, peasant houses boasted special areas which could be embellished according to the taste and skill of the individual carpenter, sometimes with an effect described by travelers as "wooden lace."[4] The ridgepole of the roof, the gable ends, the horizontal board that separated the triangular pediment from the square base of the house, the uprights at each corner, and especially the framing of the windows and doors could be carved to accentuate their structural functions or, in many cases, to underline their importance in symbolic ways (fig. 2.1). Decorative plant and animal forms, mythic and magical creatures, or initials and dates also identified the dwelling with its owners.

Well-built and prosperous villages were not the rule everywhere. One former peasant wrote about his birthplace near Voronezh: "An experi-

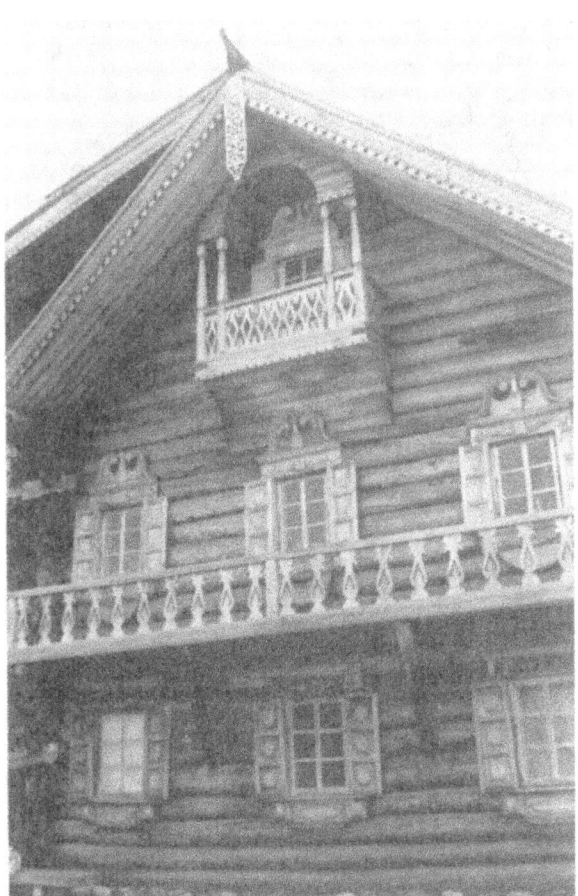

FIG. 2.1   Oshevnev house. Lake Onega region, 1876. Kizhi Museum-Preserve.

enced person coming to the village of Karachun for the first time can see at once from the buildings that it is not rich and that the inhabitants live poorly. He is not mistaken. . . . Only the *izby* are made of logs; the yards are fenced with wattle, full of gaps—a sure sign that the owners have no pigs or sheep. . . . Not all have the wooden gates whose decoration is the pride of the Russian peasant."[5]

Wood was the most readily available building material throughout European Russia, and there is evidence that it was used and that woodworking skills were valued from earliest times. Tenth-century chronicles from the Pecherskii Monastery in Kiev use the term *rubit'*, "to cut with an axe," to record that Sviatopolk ordered a city to be built and that Vladimir had a church built.[6] All parts of a building—the foundations, frame, walls, doors, and shingles—could be cut and joined tightly with a hand-axe. Saws were rarely used even in the nineteenth century. Before the seventeenth century, not only monasteries and military outposts but even large towns such as Novgorod, Iaroslavl', and Moscow were made of wood. Illustrations in manuscripts and details on icons showing monastic foundations offer valuable evidence on the appearance and building techniques of early Russia.[7] Major excavations in Novgorod, in the aftermath of the devastating bombing of the city during World War II, confirmed the textual and pictorial evidence of the ubiquitous use of wood. As early as the eleventh century, Novgorod had streets paved with oak beams and oak drains and gutters. Surviving buildings from the seventeenth century in Pskov, Moscow, and Suzdal' probably followed wooden models; although stone and brick replaced some wooden parts, massive oak beams and door frames remained. The substantial houses of the boyars, the landowning nobility of early Russia, and the modest peasant *izby* clearly shared the same prototypes.[8]

The word *izba* seems to have been derived from the tenth-century Kievan *istopka*, bathhouse.[9] Later *istopsa* and *ist'ba* referred to a house with a reception area, or to a building in general. *Klet'*, another early term for a building with four walls, later designated the very simplest wood structure, whereas *izba* was a house heated with a clay or tile oven. Variations on the *izba* plan had to do with size and the number of walls. A *piatstenok*, or five-walled type, was comparatively large, and had a wall dividing living and storage space. A separate storeroom, sometimes called a *klet'*, was below or to the side of the main room; other structures might be attatched to the main building, as often in the north. Regardless of size, the main room, the *izba* itself, was defined by the large stove and was the only heated room in the dwelling. It sometimes accommodated ten to twenty people.

Regional variations reflected climate and local economies. Three major types of *izba* developed in the north, in central Russia along the Volga River, and in the south and Ukraine.[10] In the heavily forested north (Arkhangel'sk, Olonets, Vologda, and Novgorod provinces), where the winters were long and severe, living areas were raised off the ground, over a cellar (*podklet'*), or over stables to take advantage of rising heat from animals' bodies. Northern peasant houses built in the nineteenth century, such as those in the Kizhi Museum-Preserve on Lake Onega, were as large as twenty-one meters across the front facade and about eight meters high at the roof peak. Arranged in an L or U shape around a courtyard, each housed an extended family, live-stock, storage areas for hay and grain, a bathhouse, and a well. In central Russia (between the Volga and Smolensk), houses were smaller, with at-tached or separate sheds for storage and livestock arranged on a variety of plans. In the temperate south (Kaluga, Orel, Kursk, Voronezh, and Tam-bov), houses usually lacked basements and had adjacent sheds and enclosed yards for stock. The Ukrainian peasant house, called a *khata*, was built of wood or of stone or clay, usually covered with plaster and whitewash, with an earthen floor and a thatched roof. The exterior and interior walls were often painted with brightly colored designs, like those Il'ia Repin recalled from his childhood.

The most distinctive exterior decoration appeared in the north and in the Volga area. The complex arrangement of wings and outbuildings in northern *izby* provided interesting fields for decoration, especially on covered stairs or passages from one part to another.[11] Carving was limited to narrow bands of openwork tracery setting off the eaves, the window frames, and the balcony extending across the facade at the upper story; painting was sometimes added under the wide eaves and balconies, where it was sheltered from the weather. A striking feature of northern houses was the *okhlupen'* (fig. 2.2), a large figure carved from the root end of a larch tree used as the ridgepole, placed so that it protruded over the facade of the house. Carved in the shape of a horse, duck, or deer, the *okhlupen'*, also called *konek* (from *kon'*, "horse"), probably preserved a form of ancient Slavic or Scandinavian origin. In an-cient times, the figure may have represented a nature deity or protective spirit, and even after the original meaning was lost, it was still carved as a necessary part of a house.

Along the Volga, houses were simpler in structure; the facade facing the street was broader, and the entrance was usually at the front rather than the side. Built of pine logs about two feet thick, the body of the simplest *izba* was visually dominated by the rough, curved horizontals and by the complex pat-terns of their notching at the corners. In the region around Gorodets and Nizhnii Novgorod, elaborate carving was used to set off the main architec-tural elements.[12]

The evolution of architectural carving in this region may be connected with the expansion of boatbuilding under Peter I, although it is difficult to draw exact parallels. In its early stages (roughly the seventeenth and eighteenth centuries), external decor consisted of a few flat, planed boards that contrasted with the rough texture of the logs and accentuated the main demarcations of the house front: the pediment, the eaves, and the windows. Boards called "wings," *kryl'ia* (fig. 2.3), covering the butt ends of the roof beams and extending down at the sides, were often carved in openwork patterns like those on the embroidered towels draped around the insides of windows.

The frontal board, *lobnaia doska* (from *lob*, "forehead"), also called *krasnaia doska* or *ochele*, was the most important detail; it separated the pediment from the lower part of the facade (fig. 2.4). Window surrounds, *nalichniki* (fig. 2.5), and shutters were initially carved modestly, but later the largest (*krasnoe*, "beautiful") window received more elaborate carving, in deep relief rather than openwork. Other parts of the facade were embellished with ever richer carving during the nineteenth century. The single frontal board was replaced by two or three parallel frontal boards (fig. 2.4), and above them an arrangement of stepped-back carved panels emphasized the triangular form of the pediment. The frame of the upper window was enlarged and sometimes decorated in the form of an arch with columns. The carved designs on the headpiece (*ochele*) of the window repeated some of the forms carved on the frontal board.

The second stage in the development of exterior carving resulted from a new type of roofing, which allowed a shallower slope and a still broader facade. The framing of the pediment became even more emphatic, giving the effect of a complete triangle above a series of horizontal friezes. The friezes might be continued onto the sides of the house, and

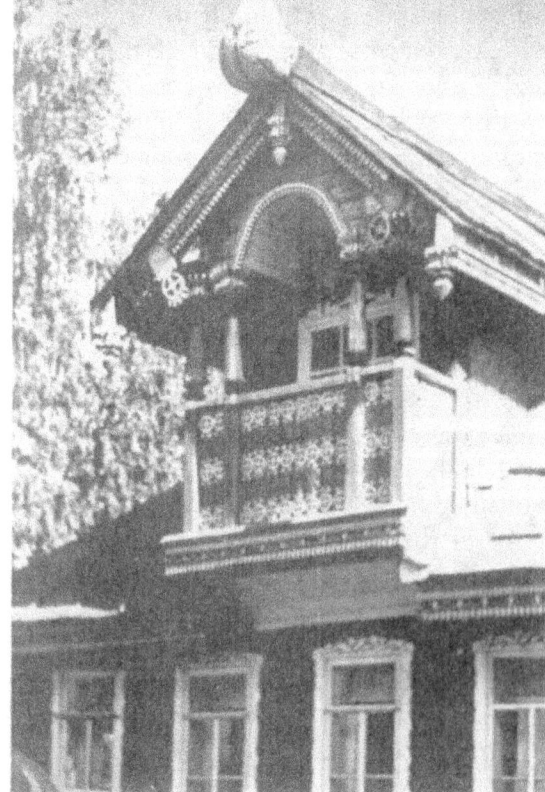

FIG. 2.2 *Okhlupen'*, ridgepole on house. Volga region, 19th century. From Makovetskii, *Arkhitektura russkogo narodnogo zhilishcha.*

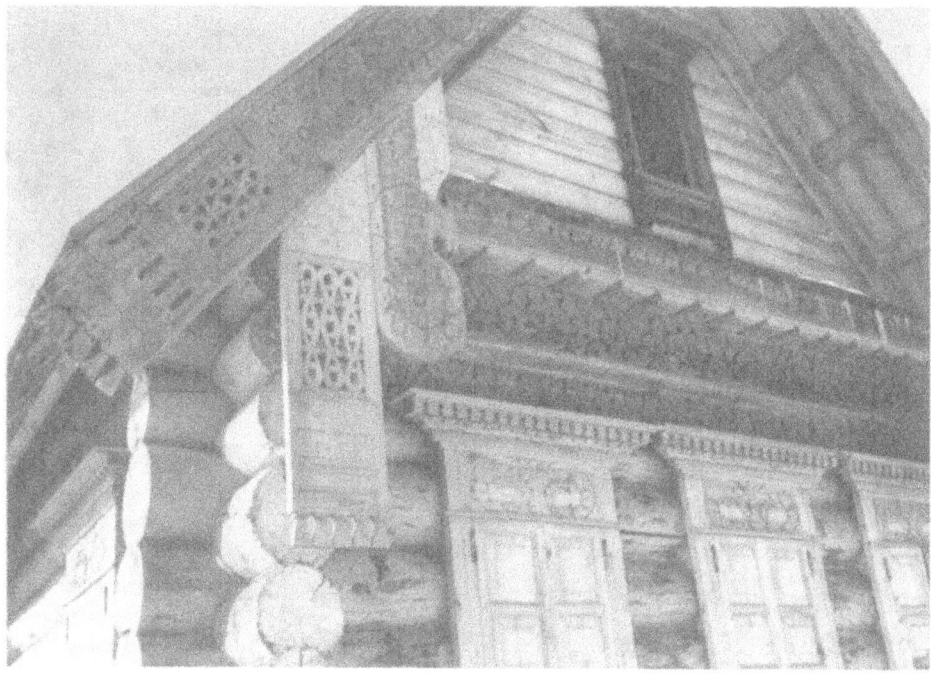

FIG. 2.3 House from central Russia, detail of eaves and *kryl'ia*. 19th century. Suzdal' Preserve.

would also be richly carved, especially if the house was on a corner and the side was visible from the road. At this stage (by the 1840s and 1850s through the 1880s), the carvers had large areas in which to work. They devised elaborate compositions, mingling purely decorative motifs with figures and inscriptions, and extending the *lobnaia doska* outward to suggest a mezzanine or balcony of a city house. They filled the pediment completely with carving in a sequence of triangular frames, one inside another, stepped back to give an illusion of depth. Many houses of this period are marked with carved dates and names or initials of the owners or master carvers (fig. 4.4). This was the apogee of architectural carving. In the last decades of the century, carving tended to be flatter and schematic; areas previously emphasized, including the frontal boards and *nalichniki*, were sometimes left plain. In some regions sawn ornamentation replaced deep relief carving.

Surface decoration included geometrical patterns, often reminiscent of the classical egg-and-dart motif; meanders and denticulation; deeply carved leaf and flower swags set off by bunches of fruit; and highly animated birds,

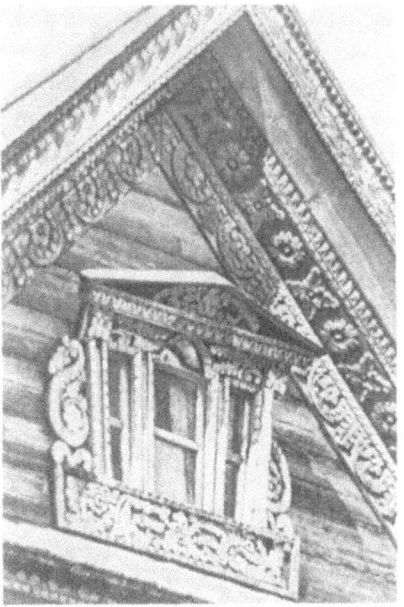

FIG. 2.4   Pediment of house in Volga
region. 19th century. From Makovetskii,
Arkhitektura russkogo narodnogo zhilishcha.

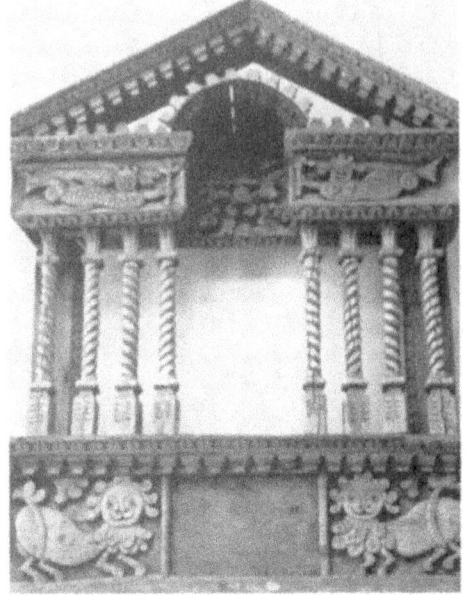

FIG. 2.5   Window surround (*nalichnik*).
Nizhnii Novgorod region, second half
of the 19th century. Sergiev-Posad.

animals (fig. 2.6), and mythical beings described in chapters 10 and 12, the
beregina (protective spirit) (fig. 2.7), *vodianoi* (water sprite), or *sirin* (paradise
bird) (fig. 2.8). The types of ornament, styles of carving, and special motifs
varied with location, the wishes of the householder, and the skill of the
master carver. But in all cases, practices of architectural decoration developed in peasant villages over long periods, and forms evolved in tandem
with other aspects of peasant art, particularly those related to the interior
arrangement and furnishings of the *izba*, and to the tasks and activities carried out in this setting.

The dominant feature inside any *izba* was the large clay oven, or *pech'*,
occupying one corner to the left or right of the main door (fig. 2.9).[13] The
adjacent area, the *chulan*, was the women's side of the house; it contained the
water barrel, a table for preparing food, and storage cupboards for dishes and
cooking supplies. Raised sleeping platforms, *polaty*, fit next to the oven, sometimes extending over the entrance area; low benches, *lavki*, built along the
other walls, were used for seating, for sleeping, or sometimes to support free-
standing cupboards. The large loom usually stood in the center of the room.
Wrought-iron lighting fixtures held wooden splints to provide light for eve-

ning and winter tasks.[14] The simple, functional arrangement of the *izba* was a remarkably efficient one for the varied requirements of a peasant family.

The spiritual focus of the home was the icon corner, located diagonally opposite the oven. Called the *krasnyi ugol* ("red" or "beautiful corner"), it had at least one icon, sometimes an icon case (*bozhnitsa* or *kiot*), and usually a small table holding candles and family mementos beneath. Anyone entering the *izba* would bow to the icons before greeting the hosts or speaking. Guests of honor were seated in the icon corner, and matchmaking rituals and parts of the marriage rites were conducted there. When a member of the family died, the body would be laid out so that the head lay closest to the icon corner, and the feet near the door.[15]

In most areas, the interior walls were at least partly finished, planed and smoothed to the height of a man. In prosperous houses, the most important features were set off by carving or painting. Carving was seldom as elaborate as that on the exteriors. Painting, however, confined to sheltered parts of the exterior, could be much more lavish inside. Carved panels around the oven, *pripechnye doski*, painted to stand out from the whitewashed clay surfaces, were found in houses on the Volga.[16] In the north, in Karelia, Arkhangel'sk, and Vologda provinces, east to the Urals, a long tradition of painting interiors, going back to twelfth-century churches and sixteenth-century boyar houses, may have influenced the styles of painting in peasant houses of the nineteenth century.[17] Many of these mural paintings were done by the same skilled artists who decorated the bowls, distaffs, and other household objects. By the nineteenth century, entire towns became known as centers of decorative painting. Viatka in the northern Urals and Tiumen' to the east of the mountains were especially famed, judging by documents referring to *tiumenskie krasil'shchiki* ("Tiumen' painters"). As many as three to five hundred master painters traveled each year along the major routes through the region, stopping at regular points, where they could be met and engaged by customers.[18]

Styles of decorative painting included geometrical accenting of structural parts; freehand renderings of plants, animals, and genre scenes; and mottled or rippled patterns imitating the costly woodwork and marble of fashionable city dwellings. Most artists favored oil-based paint of an ocher tone or red for contrast. In parts of Vologda Province, paint served mainly to enhance carved geometrical patterns of rhomboids, circles, or squares within the framework of the wall panels. A more complicated type of painting replaced geometrical shapes with flowering branches, berries, birds, or bouquets in baskets. The surface of a wall was divided into ten or twelve rectangular panels, and the decorative motifs were painted freehand and with small variations from one panel to another. Doors of the larder or cupboards bore similar floral motifs, contrasting checkerboard designs, brightly clothed male and female figures bearing bottles or other symbols of hospitality, and dramatic images such as roaring lions (Fig. 2.10).[19] The entire room was treated as an ensemble, with a

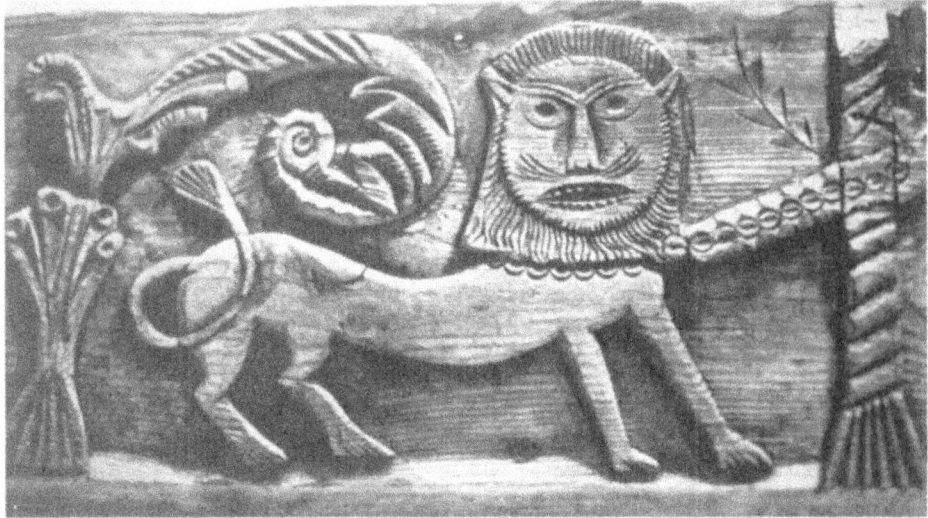

FIG. 2.6 Frontal board with lion.
Volga region, 19th century. From
Makovetskii, *Arkhitektura russkogo
narodnogo zhilishcha.*

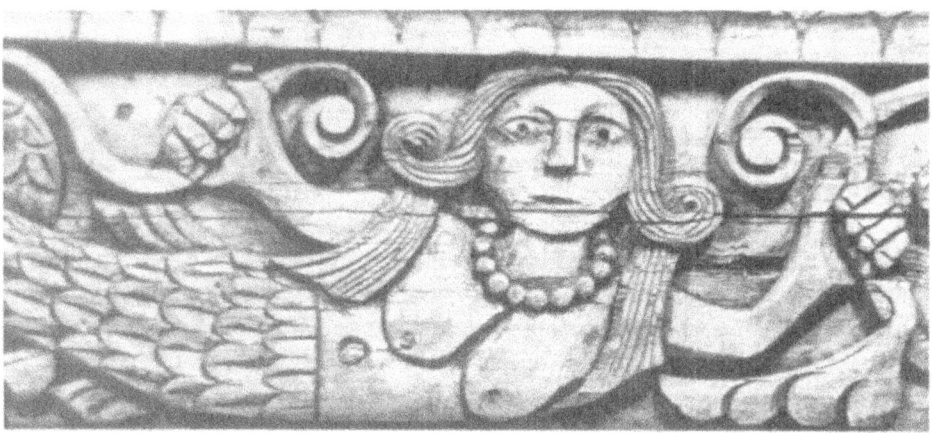

FIG. 2.7 Frontal board with *beregina.*
Volga region, 19th century.
Kolomenskoe.

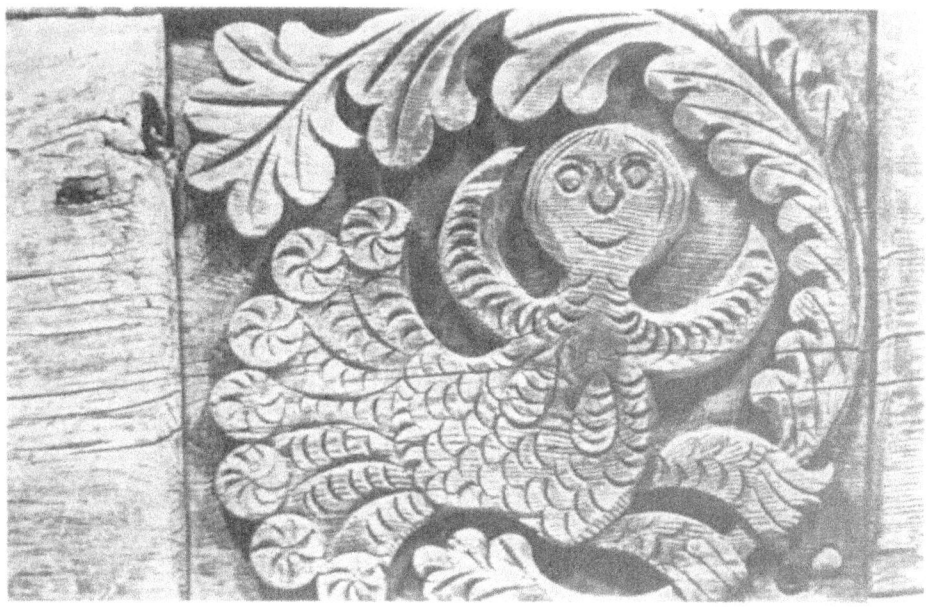

FIG. 2.8   *Sirin* carved on frontal board.
Nizhnii Novgorod region, 1870s.
Sergiev-Posad.

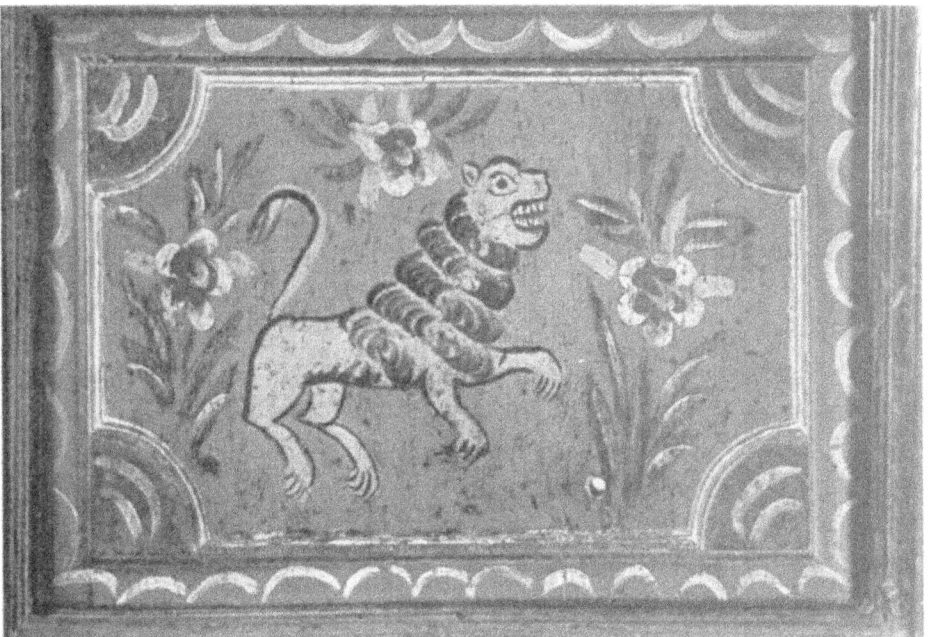

FIG. 2.10   Lion, detail of painted
cupboard door. Vologda Province, late
19th century. Sergiev-Posad.

striking sense of decorative unity. The separate panels were drawn together by the red or ocher background, by repetition of the main shapes, and usually by some kind of continuous border. For instance, a frame of plain red surrounding each panel would lead into a band of the same color extending across the width of each wall, and around the frames of windows and doors.

The combined effect of brightly painted walls and cupboards, the utensils stored on beams or open shelves, the textiles, and the candlelit icon corner could be stunningly beautiful. Visiting peasant houses in remote villages of northern Vologda Province, Vasilii Kandinskii said that he felt as if he were stepping into a living painting, saturated with color and symbol.[20] The lively harmony of shapes, patterns, and colors inside the *izba* embodied the unity of form, function, and meaning in traditional village life.

Domestic Tasks
and Tools

Husband plaits the *lapti* / Wife spins the thread.
Both want to get rich. / They never get to bed.
—Rhyme from an eighteenth-century *lubok*[1]

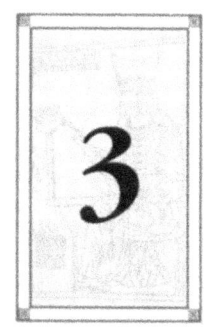

The most essential and time-consuming activities in the village were connected with raising grain, vegetables, and livestock; preparing food; and making and caring for clothing (figs. 3.1, 3.2). Tools for these tasks, intended for rugged use, were crafted with great care and decorated in ways that showed their central importance in peasant life.

Most farming tools were made by the peasants themselves or by the village blacksmith. A light, wheelless plow (*sokha*) with an iron share was used in the northern forested areas; heavier, wheeled plows, which had to be pulled by teams of horses or oxen, were used for fallow fields and virgin soil, especially in the south. The main hand tools were the scythe (*kosa*), the sickle (*serp*), and the flail (*tsep*); these, like winnowing baskets, troughs, and barrels, were rarely decorated. One farming implement that received special attention was the yoke, *duga*, for harnessing horses to wagons or sleighs. Tall and bow-shaped, curved to fit a single horse or a pair, it was painted with stripes, lozenges, hearts, or bright floral patterns, sometimes carved, or hung with small metal bells. Representations of decorated yokes appear in the scenes of sleigh rides painted on distaffs and other household utensils (fig. 3.3). A festive or ceremonial occasion or an important seasonal event such as the first day of plowing called for decoration; an ordinary yoke would not merit such work.

The storage, preparation, and serving of food required several types of utensils and containers. Utilitarian and practical as they were, many utensils recalled the forms of ancient ceremonial vessels. Even modest households possessed some richly decorated and obviously cherished articles. The oldest forms of utensils were used for serving and drinking beverages on important ceremonial occasions.[2] Large vessels, *kovshy*, for serving mead, beer, and kvass; dippers, *nalevki*, used for ladling the drinks into individual cups; and dipper-shaped cups for drinking were made from the earliest times (one found in a peat bog in the Urals may date from the second millennium B.C.) and were probably widespread by the sixteenth century. Because communities were isolated, each area had its own shapes and decorative styles: forms typical of Tver', Vologda, Kozmodemiansk, and other regions were known by this time. One of the most distinctive types of *kovsh*, also called *skobkar'*, was shaped like a swimming bird with the head and tail forming handles (fig. 3.4). The form probably originated in the north, in Vologda and Arkhangel'sk provinces.[3] Sometimes the head and tail of a horse replaced the bird forms. The carver followed the natural grain of the wood, often using the tree root, and created the features with only the most economical strokes of his adze.

A deeper, more massive form of *skobkar'* was made in Iaroslavl'. Mos-

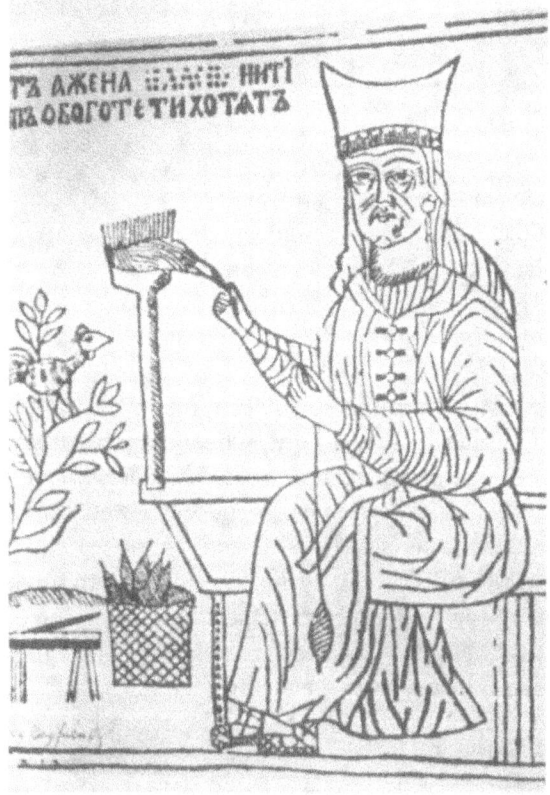

FIG. 3.2 "Husband plaits the *lapti*, wife spins the thread." *Lubok*. Wood engraving, detail, spinning. 1770s. Public Library, St. Petersburg.

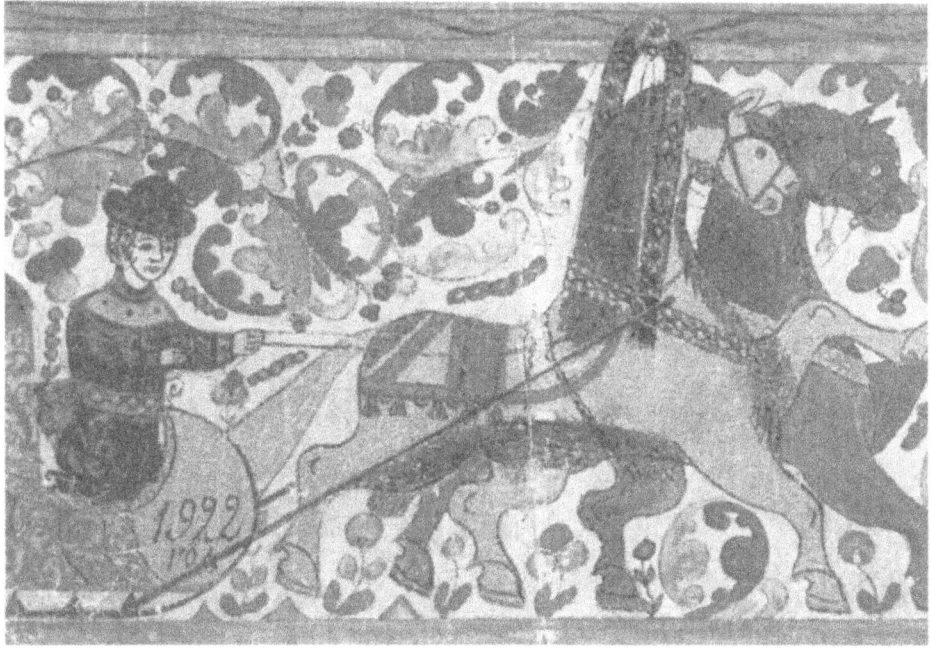

FIG. 3.3 Vasilii Amosov, distaff.
Detail showing sleigh and decorated
horse yoke. Borok, Arkhangel'sk
Province, 1922. Sergiev-Posad.

cow dippers, broader, with shorter handles, were called *sudy*, "boats," in
seventeenth-century documents. Smaller dippers followed these regional variations. The long handles of ladling dippers were often treated more elaborately than those of the *skobkar'* type. Dippers from Kozmodemiansk (fig. 1.1)
had architectural forms, with towers and archways surmounted by horses and
birds. Some dippers from Kostroma were brightly painted rather than carved.
A type from Tver', called the *koniukh* or "horse" dipper, had two or three horse
heads extending upward from steeply sloping sides. Surface ornament on the
dippers included abstract rosettes and wavy lines, stylized symbols of the sun,
wind, and water.

Other early forms of vessels were the *bratina* and *endova*. The name *bratina*
derived from *bratchina* or *bratovshchina*, a feast of brothers; the large, spherical
vessels generally had lengthy inscriptions referring to the reunions of relatives. *Endovy*, deep, spouted vessels (fig. 3.6), appeared later than the other
types, but were widespread by the sixteenth century. Made of fine woods,

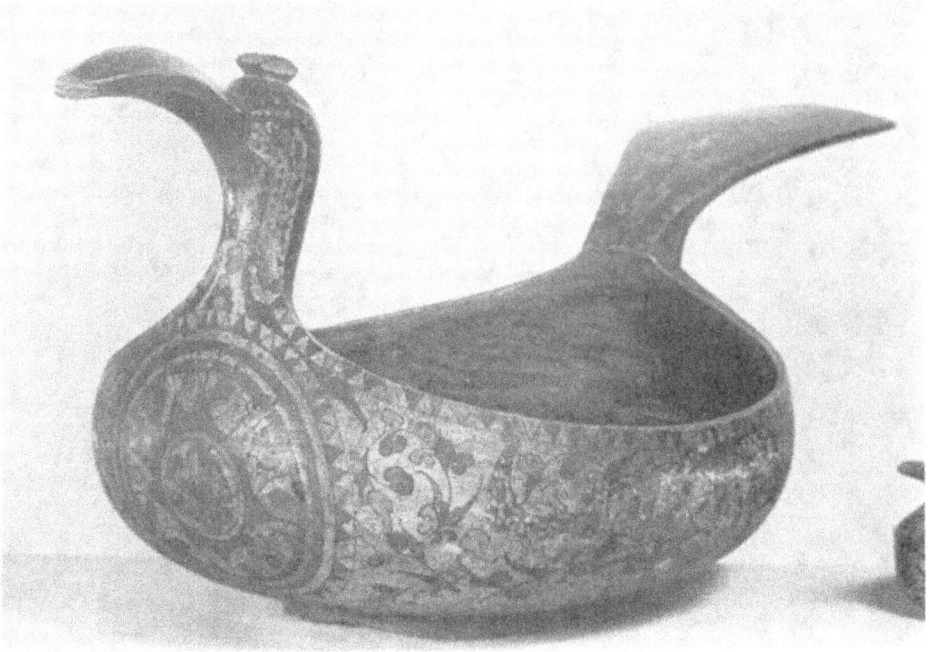

FIG. 3.4 *Kovsh-skobkar'*. Permogore,
Arkhangel'sk Province, early 19th
century. Sergiev-Posad.

they were ornamented with elegant carving in the Tver' region, or with painting in the Northern Dvina region.

Serving and storage vessels used regularly in peasant households were
simpler in shape and decoration. The main serving dishes were large bowls,
up to fifty centimeters in diameter, from which a whole family ate. Bowls for
individual servings, called *stavi*, had lids that could be used simultaneously as
dishes; they were ingeniously designed so that smaller lidded cups, *stavtsi* and
stavchiki, could fit inside the larger *stavi* for storage.[4]

In the nineteenth century, shallow wooden plates and platters were
sometimes decorated to imitate dishes of porcelain or metal. The well-known
Khokhloma ware from the Nizhnii Novgorod district was painted with cin-
nabar and metallic powder and covered with varnish which gave an effect of
gilt. Elsewhere, especially along the upper Volga and Northern Dvina, plates
and drinking cups featured brightly painted figures, animals and plants, buildings, and scenes of tea drinking or other social activities. Among the most
varied and intricately decorated utensils were ladles and spoons: the natural

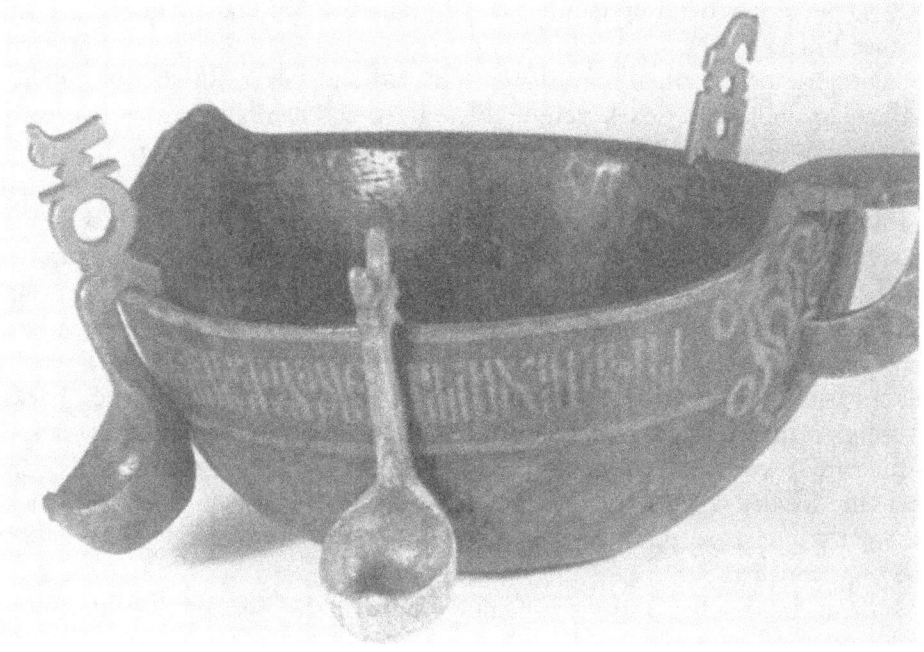

FIG. 3.5 *Kovsh* for festive table. Volga region, 18th century. Sergiev-Posad.

shapes of the bowls and handles gave rise to imaginative renditions of vegetable and animal forms as well as abstract designs. Among the favorite motifs were horses, birds, and architectural forms carved in the round (those from Kozmodemiansk were similar to carvings on dippers from that region); realistic fish with widely gaping mouths, as if biting at the handles (probably from Kostroma); and religious scenes, such as St. George and the dragon or St. Sergei of Radonezh with a bear, on spoons made for monastic use or as souvenirs for pilgrims.[5] Inscriptions in ink on the handles or bowls include initials, dates, place names, and sometimes blessings.[6]

Wooden storage containers were lathe-turned or coopered; a special type, called *buraki* (fig. 3.7), were canisters made of birch bark, double-layered so that they could hold liquids. Those made in villages along the Northern Dvina were brightly painted, with flat bands of color or floral designs, while those from Velikii Ustiug were decorated with openwork ornament known as birch-bark lace, sometimes backed with colored tinfoil or mica inserts. Another technique was plaiting or weaving narrow strips of birch bark to form a watertight surface. These forms, unique to the north of

THE ARTS IN PEASANT LIFE

Russia, were practiced by families and communities of craftsmen and are still in use today.

Because of the ritual importance of bread and salt in Russian hospitality, saltcellars and bread boxes were highly valued and carefully made. Two types of salt containers, the chair and the swimming bird, originated in the distant past. The chair form, shaped like a princely throne, was most common in central Russia. Its rectangular or polygonal base, which contained the salt, was covered by a flap lid and attached to an upright back. All surfaces were filled with painted, intaglio, or openwork designs, which were almost always abstract and symmetrical. Duck-shaped saltcellars, recalling the northern *skobkar'* dippers, were ingeniously constructed, with a sliding lid in the form of a duck's back and wings (fig. 3.8). Some pieces carried ducklings on their backs; others were modeled on geese or swans, or horses or rams instead of waterbirds. A sense of their beauty and personal value was expressed by one peasant woman visited by museum curators. She refused to sell her duck-shaped saltcellar to the museum, explaining, "Without her, the house would be impoverished."[7]

Bread boxes (fig. 3.9) were made of bast or thin wood, the side pieces

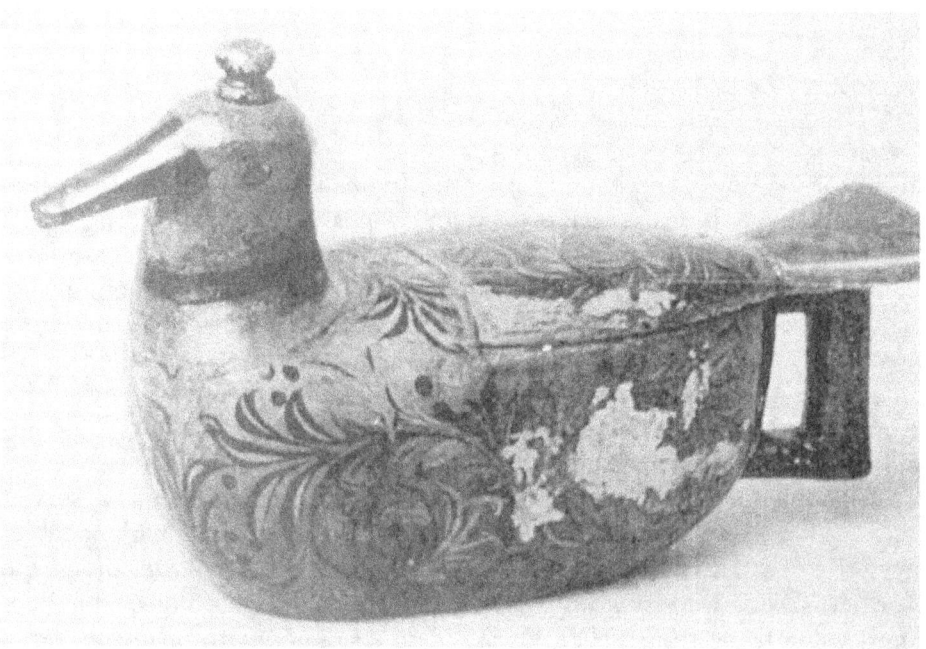

FIG. 3.8 Duck-shaped saltcellar.
Carved and painted wood. Khokhloma,
Volga region. ME.

steamed into long curves, the sides and tops banded by narrow strips of bast, and made to fit tightly. Although the uniform oval shape did not lend itself to sculptural variation, the large, flat surfaces were ideal for painted designs. Some designs, such as a large fish surrounded by smaller figures eating and drinking, were humorously appropriate. Many bread boxes from the Northern Dvina region were painted by the same artists who painted other utensils, cupboards, cradles, and distaffs in the northern villages. The imagery of these decorations provides a wealth of information about daily life, and also about the development and intermingling of various layers of symbolism and representation in the iconography of folk art.

Among the implements of daily life, those designed for the textile arts brought together the requirements of different crafts. Distaffs, looms, scutchers, and other tools were made to fulfill the specific functions of spinning, weaving, sewing, or laundering cloth. Often these objects bore the imprint of an individual personality. As the constant companions of women's main activities, they had to suit an individual's hand and style of work, and distaffs were frequently decorated with a particular woman in mind. They were meant to

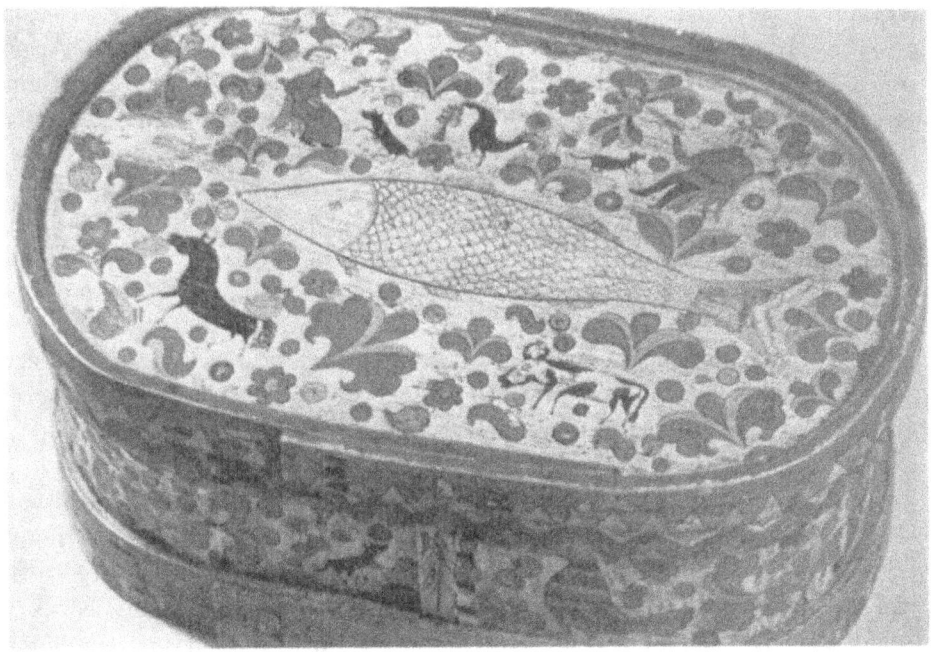

FIG. 3.9 Bread box with lid. Bast, painted on white ground. Permogore, early 19th century. Sergiev-Posad.

be used, shown off at social gatherings, and treasured. Finally, just as some textiles had ritual importance, for instance embroidered towels used in greeting ceremonies or to embellish the icon corner and garments worn for the first day of harvest, the tools for making these textiles were also invested with special meaning.

The massive loom, *tkatskii stan*, virtually an architectural feature, dominated the women's side of the *izba*.[8] Its main structural parts were decorated like the beams of houses, though the carving was shallower and more sparing. Well-preserved remains of thirteenth-century looms found in Novgorod indicate that the design changed little.[9] Small parts of looms, such as the shuttles (*chelnoki*), pulleys (*bloki*) for lifting the thread, *prituzhalniki* for stressing the warp, and *nabilki* for fixing the thread, were often carved in the form of ducks, geese, horses, or horses' heads. Archeologists have related the horse forms to ornaments found in women's graves and have suggested an ancient origin and perhaps a symbolic, protective function for these motifs.[10]

Most tools for working with textiles, such as the scutcher (*trepalo*) for beating and breaking down the tough flax fibers before spinning, the battledore (*valek*) for beating linen cloth against stones during laundering (fig. 3.10), and the rocker (*rubel'*) for rolling and smoothing out the linen cloth after washing, received such hard use that few survived in good condition. But remaining examples confirm both regional variation in their ornamentation and a pervasive preference for certain patterns and symbolic motifs such as horses and birds. The blade-shaped scutchers, lightweight because they had to be lifted and brought down with repeated chopping motions of the wrist, were decorated simply with openwork carving or painting, while their sturdy, curved handles were often shaped like horses. The *shveika*, a sewing implement that stood upright on a bench to hold an end of cloth in a clamplike jaw or with the aid of pins, was also frequently carved with a horse shape at the top (fig. 3.11). The *rubel'*, grooved on the convex bottom surface to aid in flattening the cloth, might seem to rock over the material with a galloping motion; its handle, carved like a running horse, would enhance this fantasy (fig. 3.12). Other wooden implements for the textile arts include pins for making lace (*kokliushki*), very small and simply ornamented, and carved boards for use in printing cloth (*nabivnie doski*), which were quite varied and will be discussed in detail in chapter 6.

Distaffs (*prialki*) (fig. 3.13) were the only implements preserved well enough and in sufficient quantity to allow thorough study of their forms, styles of decoration, and geographical variations. Made of a single piece or two joined pieces of wood, the distaff consisted of an upright blade (*lopastka*), usually topped by a comb to hold the flax fibers, and a base (*dontse*), on which the spinner sat to hold it steady while she worked. Spinning wheels, called "self-spinners" because the thread was controlled mechanically, were known but not widely used in the nineteenth century. Probably introduced from the

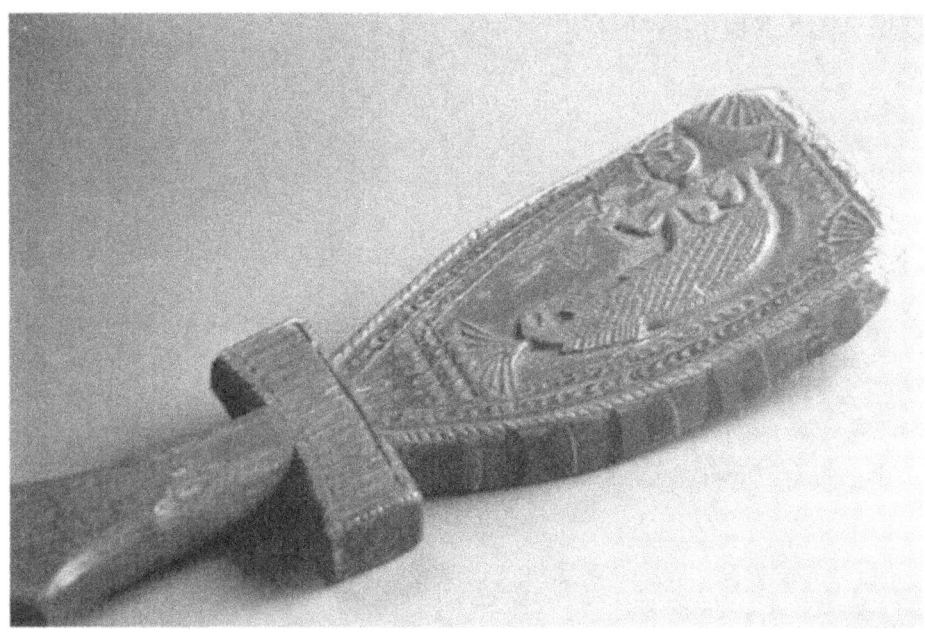

FIG. 3.10 *Valek* (battledore), carved with *beregina*. Carved and painted wood. Nizhnii Novgorod region, late 18th or early 19th century. MNI.

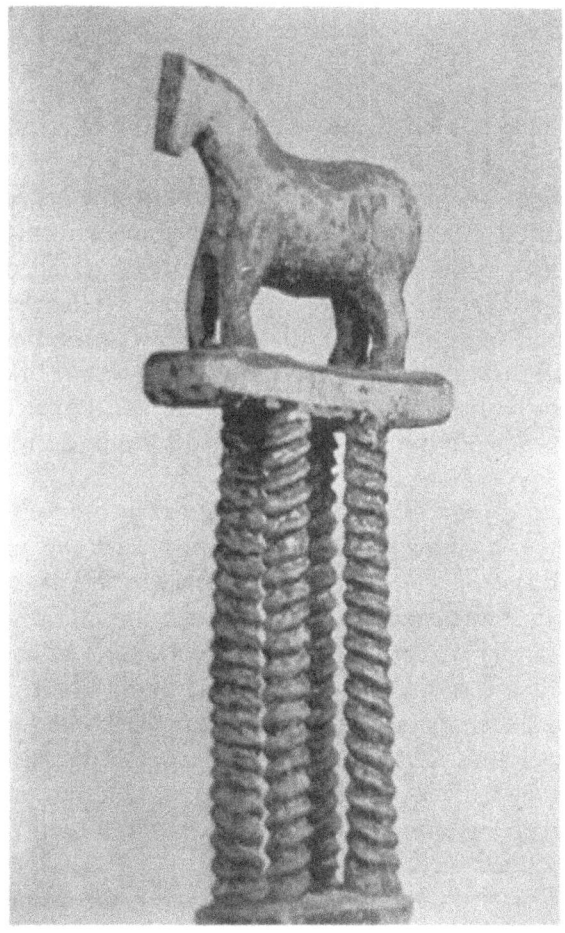

FIG. 3.11 *Shveika*, sewing implement. Carved and painted wood. Arkhangel'sk region, late 19th century. Sergiev-Posad.

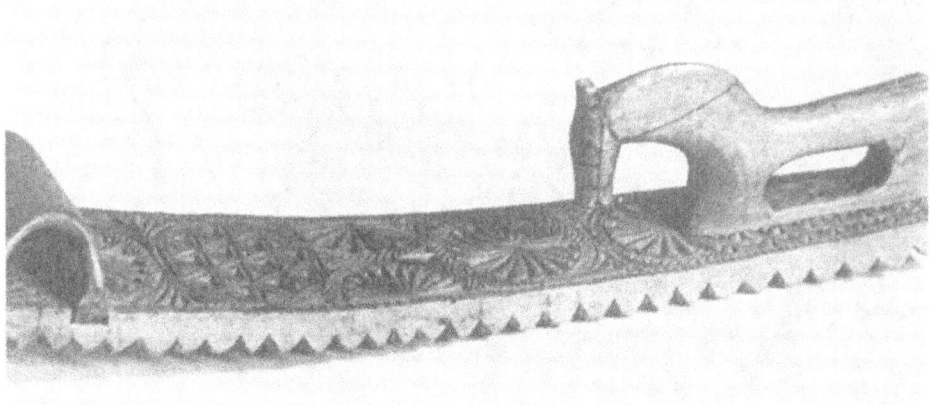

FIG. 3.12 *Rubel'*, rocker for smoothing linen. Carved wood. Volga region, 19th century. Sergiev-Posad.

West, they were common only in areas such as the Seredskaia region of Iaroslavl' Province, which had ties with the Baltic.[11]

Spinning was a constant task for women of all ages. Thanks to the easily portable distaff, it could be carried out in company—one reason why the large spinning wheels never replaced the distaffs. Evening gatherings called *besedy* or *posidelki*, at which groups of women sat together to spin while they talked or sang, sometimes accompanied by men with accordions and other instruments, were often depicted on the painted blades of distaffs (fig. 3.14). Other social scenes, such as tea parties and sleigh rides, were also popular motifs, perhaps because images of lively occasions helped to relieve the tedium of spinning.

Distaffs with scenes of wedding processions were among the most splendidly painted; it was customary for a young woman's fiance or her parents to give her a specially decorated distaff to celebrate her betrothal or marriage. One such wedding gift, from the northern village of Borok, was inscribed "This distaff [belongs to] Aleksandra Mikhailovna Klestova. 1890. [Painted by] V. Amosov." Painted with brilliant colors and a good deal of gold leaf and with carefully drawn details, it included a portrait of the artist himself with his betrothed, dressed in their best clothes, setting out in a carriage on the customary three-day wedding journey.[12] Even in regions where floral motifs or abstract patterns were preferred to figurative painting, distaffs often carried inscriptions or forms that symbolized such a life ritual.

The basic structure of the distaff was simple, but there was a surprising range of variation in design. Nearly forty distinct regional types of distaffs

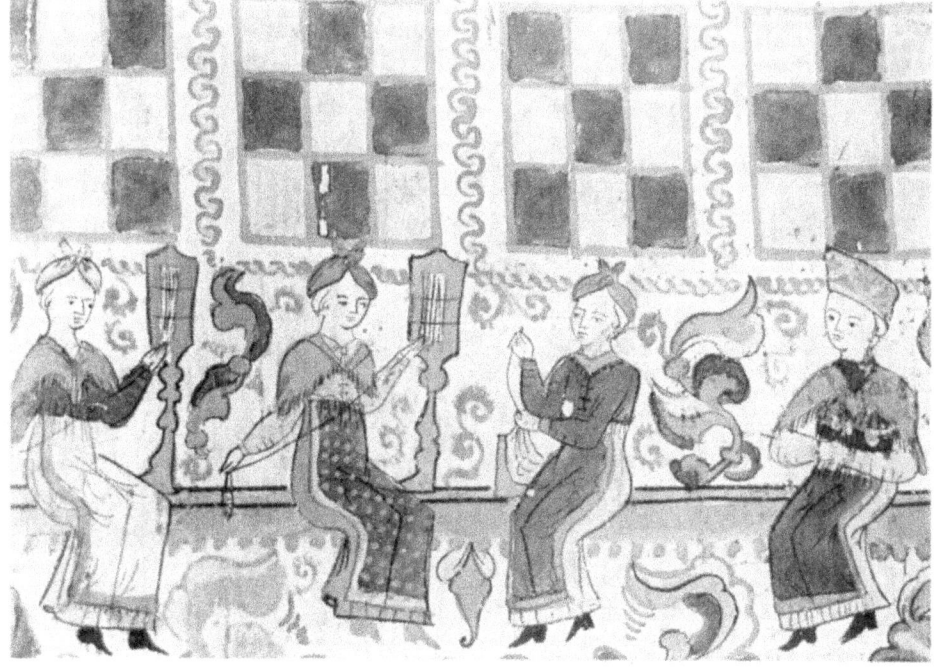

FIG. 3.14 Distaff. Painted wood.
Detail showing women sewing and
spinning with one-piece distaffs.
Permogore, early 19th century.
Sergiev-Posad.

have been classified by Voronov, Kruglova, and others.[13] According to their
construction, distaffs fell into two types: one-piece distaffs made from the
lower part of a tree trunk with a root projecting at a right angle (fig. 3.14),
and two-part distaffs consisting of a base with a socket for attaching the upright blade and comb (fig. 3.15). The one-piece distaffs were made in the
heavily forested northern regions, the detachable ones in the Volga region,
near Nizhnii Novgorod and Gorodets. The main variations in form were
determined by the proportions of the blade, whether it was flat or columnar,
whether the decoration was openwork or three-faceted or contour carving,
and whether painting was applied over the carving or used alone to decorate
the blade.

One of the most ancient forms, found in the Iaroslavl' region, was the
columnar distaff, with a small comb on a tall stem, carved so that the interior
was hollowed out and the faceted surface was pierced (fig. 3.13). An icon of
the Annunciation in the Trinity Monastery at Sergiev-Posad showed a colum-

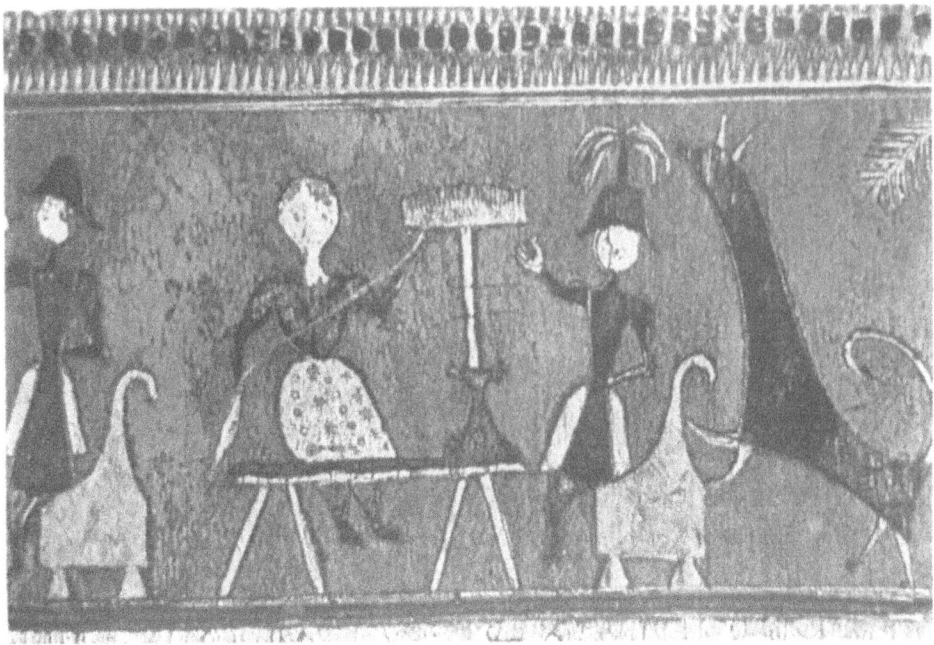

FIG. 3.15   Lazar Mel'nikov, distaff.
Carved and painted wood. Detail
showing use of two-part distaff.
Gorodets, 1866. GIM.

nar distaff in use.[14] Another early form was the tower-shaped or *terem* type,
also found in Iaroslavl' and the neighboring districts of Griazovets and Bui.
The stem, a wide board, nipped in gently near the top and surmounted by an
elaborate stepped comb, was shaped like a palace or *terem*. The three-faceted
carving of the body also suggested architectural forms, while contour carving
on the upper part might depict scenes of tea drinking, dancing, or wedding
rites (fig. 5.2).

In addition to their distinctive shapes, distaffs of each region were identified by certain combinations of carved and painted decoration. Both freely
painted floral designs, similar to those on interior walls and cupboards, and
more geometric patches of color painted over faceted carving were characteristic of certain districts of the Vologda and Arkhangel'sk regions. In some
areas, only painting was used: most strikingly in the Mezen' River area of the
Arkhangel'sk region, where parallel friezes of running horses or deer, painted
schematically, with long galloping legs and flowing manes or branching
antlers, were combined with patterns of triangles and linear hatching on a

vivid gold-orange ground (fig. 6.4). Villages on the Northern Dvina River were noted for vivid, colorful paintings of peasant life with considerable specific detail of costume, furnishings, and even facial expressions. These distaffs, along with other household furnishings such as bread boxes and wooden dishes made by some of the same artists, convey a lively sense of the special occasions which they sometimes commemorated, as well as the daily life in the region.

Most activities of the peasant household, including making tools for domestic tasks, were seasonal, determined by the agricultural cycle. Festivities connected with the first day of taking the herds to pasture, St George's Day (April 23), and the beginning of the first grain harvest, around St. Peter's Day (June 29), required specially decorated garments and tools, as well as ceremonial bowls for the feasts.[15] The harvesting of flax in late summer and the soaking and beating of the fibers were followed in the autumn and winter by the long processes of spinning and weaving cloth, sewing garments for everyday wear, and embroidering shirts and towels for dowry chests.

Winter was also the time for engaging in handcraft work that did not fill immediate requirements of the family. It was a trying, wearisome time, according to the peasant writer Ivan Stoliarov.[16] Isolated for days, in a smoky room without enough light, with children sprawled in every corner, peasants could not have found it easy to produce work of high quality. Nonetheless, even peasants in remote, landlocked villages made use of the time and local resources, as Kravchinskii noted in the 1880s, to make goods for local barter or sale at markets, sometimes on a piecework basis. This seasonal activity was most important in villages along the major trade arteries, such as Khokhloma, on the Volga, famed for its "wooden gold" painted bowls and spoons; Borok on the Northern Dvina, known for painted distaffs; and the villages of Khlebiankha, Koskovo, Kurtsevo, Repino, and Serkhovo along the Ugola River, known for their production of carved domestic utensils in the mid-nineteenth century.[17] Making objects for daily use, for special rituals, or for trade was part of the routine of peasant life.

Specialization
and Originality:
Some Peasant Artists

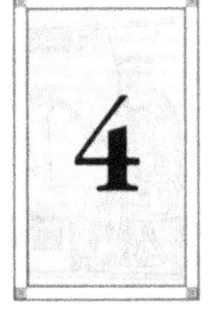

Most peasants had the carpen-
izba, keep it in repair, and
but more specialized tasks be-
try skills needed to build an
make furnishings and tools,
came the province of experts.
In many villages, two or three artels of carpenters or painters were engaged in
carving house fronts, painting interiors, and making household utensils for
their neighbors and for peasants in other villages in the same district. Names
of some of these artists and artist families are known. Even though few works
were signed, villagers could often recall which artist had painted a particular
house or decorated the distaff that had become an heirloom. Not surprisingly,
the same names turned up in connection with work in a variety of media.[1]
Certain towns were identified with particular forms of production. For example, Khokhloma, near Nizhnii Novgorod, was noted for painted wooden
spoons and bowls; Sergiev-Posad, near the Trinity-Sergiev Monastery, was
a center for the manufacture of toys.[2] In some areas, villages cooperated in
production, so that wooden articles were carved by one group and painted
by another.

   A relatively centralized and specialized system of producing and marketing peasant arts coexisted with the more localized village craft economy. This
interaction contributed to the distribution of characteristic forms, decorative

motifs, and stylistic developments in general; it was crucial to the relationship between the manufacture of crafts and other aspects of peasant life.

Topographical and statistical accounts of the Russian provinces attested to the importance of peasant-made goods in regional markets in the eighteenth and nineteenth centuries. Evdokii Ziablovskii's *Geographic Description of the Russian Empire* gave details of the products and markets of each province, statistics on guilds, and information about independent craftworkers, including peasants. The author stated that "the population of Iaroslavl' is much attracted to craftwork and to trade, sending goods great distances. There is scarcely a city in central Russia where products from Iaroslavl' are not to be found."[3] Writing about the Sergiev market, he specifically mentioned "various kinds of handwork" done at home, as piecework: "In some villages not far from the town they make handcrafts out of a white clay that is found locally."[4] In the Nizhnii Novgorod region, he saw that "the wealth of wood" gave rise to "notable crafts," including lacquered bowls of every kind, cups, serving dishes and plates, many tools, and even barges. Ziablovskii listed many other regional specializations: wooden dishes in Orel, textile work in Kaluga, tile and metalwork in Tula, and blacksmith work, turned woodwork, and other crafts in Riazan', emphasizing that the merchants there actively traded not only in imported goods but in "the products of the peasants' hands."[5]

In the far north of Russia, the interaction of peasant and town economy was especially important in the major trade centers on the White Sea, the Northern Dvina, and other rivers. Chelishchev's report on the region in 1791 noted goods made by and for well-to-do peasants. The shops and open markets of Arkhangel'sk displayed women's handwork, such as fabric and belts decorated with gold, silver, and river pearls, along with leather, fur, and other goods brought in from the region and even products from Greenland and the New World. Among the craftsmasters enrolled in the town guilds were ivory carvers, silver- and metalsmiths, woodworkers, barrelmakers, shoemakers, painters, printers of cloth, ropemakers, tailors, and textile workers. Even in Chelishchev's time, young peasant women were coming to the city to work in textile factories.[6] Arkhangel'sk, as the major northern port, attracted skilled workers as well as merchants at a very early stage. A smaller town in the region, Kholmogory, offered less variety in trade, but already supported a well-developed art of carving in walrus ivory and bone.

Of all the northern cities, Velikii Ustiug, at the confluence of the Northern Dvina and the Sukhona rivers, the main distribution point for goods from the region around the White Sea to both central Russia and Siberia, was most varied in its products and maintained the highest level of quality in specialized crafts. Silverwork, especially niello (a technique of engraving on silver, described in chapter 8), was "famous everywhere," Chelishchev wrote, counting sixty-three practitioners of this art at the time of his visit.[7] This art form was to have considerable stylistic influence on one of the most distinctive types of folk art from this area, birch-bark boxes decorated with engraved scenes and cut and stamped patterns. Icon painting, for the church and for the market, was an important occupation in Velikii Ustiug. Chelishchev knew of thirty-five icon painters; he thought that most were justly praised for the high quality of their work, and that some "could be called genuine artists."[8]

Velikii Ustiug boasted five big market squares and a huge mercantile hall (*gostinyi dvor*) with five trading rows, 240 kiosks, and many storage huts. The annual trade fair, the *Prokop'evskaia iarmarka* (from the German *Jahrmarkt*, "yearly market"), was held for three days at the beginning of June, around the feast of St. Procopius. Merchants came from all over, Chelishchev observed, "not bringing wares to sell, but to buy the handwork and produce of the peasants."[9] Velikii Ustiug reached its commercial height in the seventeenth century; it began to decline with the rise of St. Petersburg, but was still a major center for the northeast of Russia in Chelishchev's time and in the nineteenth century.

Specialization in the production of handcrafts led to active commercial relationships and even cooperative manufacturing practices among major towns, villages, and monastic communities in the north. Records from Velikii Ustiug show that thousands of wooden articles were made and marketed in these centers in the seventeenth century. According to an inventory of 1677, several hundred dippers and duck-shaped saltcellars were brought to the market in Velikii Ustiug during the few days of the summer fair. Large quantities came from the Kirill-Belozersk Monastery north of the city of Vologda, a journey of several days on the Sukhona River. Many families in the villages around the monastery were employed in carving the duck-shaped dippers. Some dippers, still plain, were sent to the monastery, where they were decorated with carved borders or painted designs by a team of artists before being sent to the market. Batches of plain wood dippers were also sent to the Velikii Ustiug market and shipped from there farther north, to villages along the Northern Dvina River, where local artists painted designs on them.[10] In this way, utensils of a common type might have decorations reflecting two or more local painting styles.

A special role in the commerce in handcrafts was filled by nearly six thousand annual and seasonal markets that grew up around major monasteries, such as the Trinity-Sergiev Monastery in the Moscow region, the Makarevskii Monastery near Nizhnii Novgorod, and the Kirill-Belozersk Monastery on the White Lake in Vologda Province. All were important pilgrimage centers; the annual fairs had originally catered to pilgrims and were scheduled to coincide with saints' days or church feasts, such as the Assumption, the Ascension, or the Presentation of the Virgin.[11] It was a profitable system: at the largest fair, the *Makarevskaia iarmarka* in Nizhnii Novgorod, the daily attendance reached about 250,000 in 1870.[12] In his 1882 study of rural economy, Bezobrazov emphasized the importance of peasant manufactures at this fair.

His list of products in greatest demand ranged from simple household goods and cheap religious prints bought by peasants to exotic "asiatic" products, silk and gold cloth, porcelain, silver, and other luxury goods.[13] The location and timing of the fairs were important both for full-time and itinerant artisans and for peasants who engaged in handwork as a supplement to farming. The annual fairs not only were fixtures of the religious calendar, but also were firmly tied to the agricultural cycle of the rural year.

Because many forms of peasant art were interrelated, as components in a regional economy, similarities in objects from different regions can point to economic or other cultural ties between one region and another. Research in the Northern Dvina and the Volga areas has been most productive in identifying typological parallels that show historical relationships. For example, the distinctive painting styles on distaffs made around the village of Borok on the Northern Dvina (fig. 4.1) can be traced to sources in Novgorodian icon painting and manuscripts (fig. 4.2), thus providing evidence of the continued presence of families exiled to that area after Ivan IV's sack of Novgorod in the sixteenth century.[14] Similar geographical connections are shown through the forms of ceremonial vessels. The type of *skobkar'* characteristic of Iaroslavl' may be derived from wooden versions of metal vessels from the older city of Novgorod. Moscow "boat"-shaped dippers were probably the models for vessels found in Kozmodemiansk, founded in the seventeenth century as a frontier outpost occupied by the *strel'tsy*, border guards from Moscow. Inscriptions around the rims of the dippers support this hypothesis. One example reads: "This dipper belongs to the *strelets* Yakov son of Nefed of Kozmodemiansk. May good folk drink to the bottom for their own good, for the good is at the bottom, and he who does not drink to the bottom will never see the good."[15]

Folk art of the Volga River area also reflects ties with older cultural centers. Stylistic similarities between Gorodets woodcarving and designs on early icon frames from Vladimir and Suzdal' can be traced to contacts between these regions as early as the twelfth century, under Prince Iurii Dolgorukii, and later, in the seventeenth century, when some of the Old Believers fled to the lands beyond the Volga.[16] There is evidence that the carving on house facades, distaffs, and other household objects, for which craftsmen of Gorodets were famed, probably developed along with the art of boatbuilding along the Volga. Gorodets, Nizhnii Novgorod, Balakhna, Katunki, and other villages were known for carved decorations of riverboats, and Peter I's efforts to increase navigation and trade encouraged this art.[17]

Just as Novgorod, Moscow, and other great cultural centers of pre-Petrine Russia disseminated ideas and styles throughout the more recently settled territories, the trading centers on the Northern Dvina, the Volga, and other major rivers became hubs of artistic influence and exchange. For example, *prianiki*, large spicecakes decorated with stamped patterns (fig. 4.3) made in Gorodets on the Volga, were known in the seventeenth century, and were

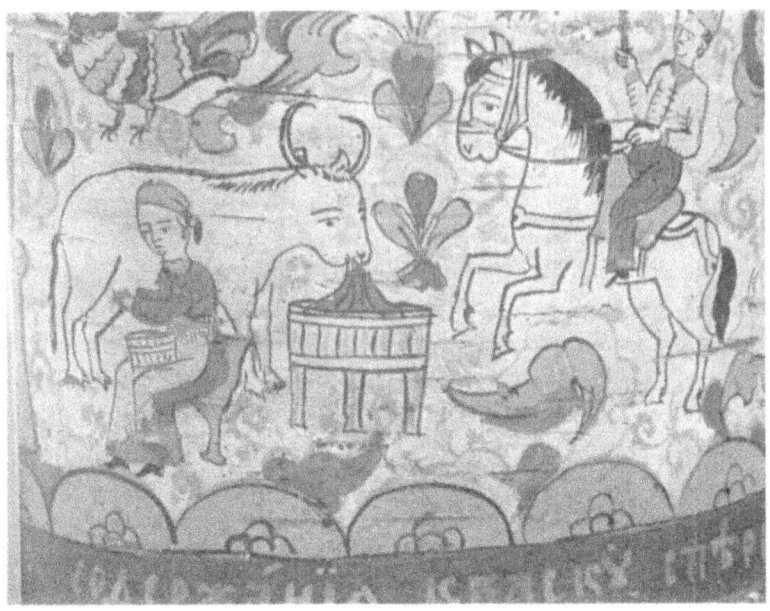

FIG. 4.1 *Burak.* Painted birch bark.
Detail of genre scene and inscription.
Permogore, mid-19th century.
Sergiev-Posad.

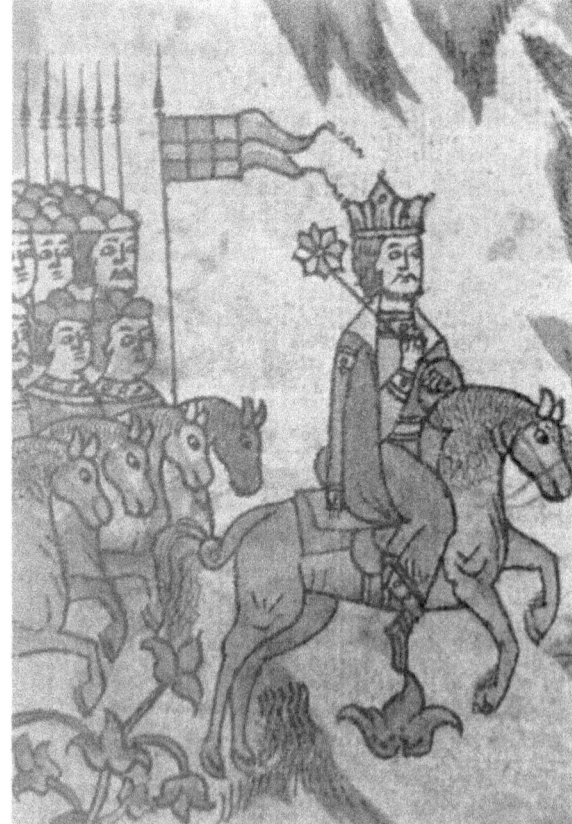

FIG. 4.2 "Prince Dmitrii and
His Army," miniature from *The
Tale of Mamaev's Battle.*
Novgorod, 17th century.
GIM.

often mentioned in later guidebooks and travelers' accounts.[18] The molds, *prianichnye doski* (figs. 5.4, 5.5), were boards carved with designs of animals, human figures, architectural forms, heraldic motifs, or genre subjects, into which the thick dough was pressed. The boards were made by woodcarvers, but the cakes themselves were baked by specialists, called *prianishniki*. Ingredients for the cakes, chiefly honey from a particular variety of wild bees, became the bases for other peasant industries that flourished throughout the period.[19] The finished spicecakes and the *doski* were sold both in Gorodets and at the great Nizhnii Novgorod trade fair. In this way, the characteristic forms of local woodworking crafts, and all the associated products, enjoyed wide distribution. Location on a great trade route meant that a town's handcrafted goods, especially easily portable objects, might be imitated or adapted in other regions, and the demand for the original products and for specialists in the required crafts would also increase.

Master was the term used in towns and villages to designate a recognized specialist in any of the crafts. In areas where several master painters or master carvers worked within the territory of a few neighboring villages, local informants expressed opinions about the strengths and weaknesses of various masters, indicating that one painter was better at distaffs, while another's style might be more pleasing for walls or cupboards.[20] Evidence that individual skills were recognized as early as the seventeenth century can be seen in ideographic signs, resembling brands or heraldic forms, carved on the logs of houses and other buildings.[21]

Information about individual masters and dynasties of artists is most abundant for the northern parts of Vologda Province and the upper Volga area. These areas were settled chiefly by the Old Believers exiled from Novgorod and Moscow in the sixteenth and seventeenth centuries. Old Believer communities maintained a high level of literacy, and many inscriptions on carved and painted objects, along with written records of contracts, support oral information about the artists. In other areas, too, the conservative character of folklife and the tendency to keep specializations within a family meant that many of the artists still working in the 1920s and 1930s were the descendants of earlier masters and heirs to their stylistic traditions.

Whether or not their names are known, dates and other inscriptions on objects give insights into the artists' purpose or attitude toward pieces. For example, a mold for a spicecake has the date 1792 and the name Emel'ian Ivanov on the back; guild records show that this was the name of a master *prianishnik*, so the mold was in all likelihood ordered by him for his business. In contrast, a *valek* carved with the name Sonia, the date July 20, 1786, and the name Maksim Shapozhnikov, was clearly a gift made by the artist for his bride. Decorated with a trumpeting triton, a double-headed eagle with a scepter, the portraits of two tsars, and in the center a man and woman in wedding dress holding hands, it celebrated the artist's pride in his marriage.[22] Other inscriptions identified objects made or commissioned as gifts for special occasions: the phrase "I present this gift to commemorate" followed by a date and names or initials frequently appeared on the borders of spicecakes (fig. 4.3). The wish that life would be as "sweet as honey" was expressed on a spicecake presented to a newly married couple; an inscription carved on a large spicecake mold, "This cake of honey I give to the one I love," allowed for a variety of occasions and recipients. Variations on the generic formula "To Dmitrii Ivanovich and Natal'ia Efimovna as a sign of respect" were also frequent. Some inscriptions identified an object with a historical event. For instance, the date April 10, 1881, and the words "Battle of Adrianople" carved on the bottom of a distaff base made by Master Gavriil Lavrent'ev Poliakov explain the figures of soldiers that decorate the distaff. Finally, phrases or verses were added to praise the quality of the object itself, such as the large capacity or good contents of a water beaker or a kvass mug.[23]

In any locality, there might be ten to twenty master painters or master carvers in each generation whose names are recorded. Some artists stand out for the high quality of their work, the obvious success of their careers, because pieces they made survived in good condition, or even because they introduced some new form or esthetic idea into the tradition within which they worked. Field research in the area around Nizhnii Novgorod has produced a census of masters' names and, more important, recognition of several individual approaches to the task of decorating window frames and frontal boards. An outstanding master active in the 1880s, Mikhail Malishev, was so well known in the Kstovsky district of the Nizhnii Novgorod region that inhabitants always recog-

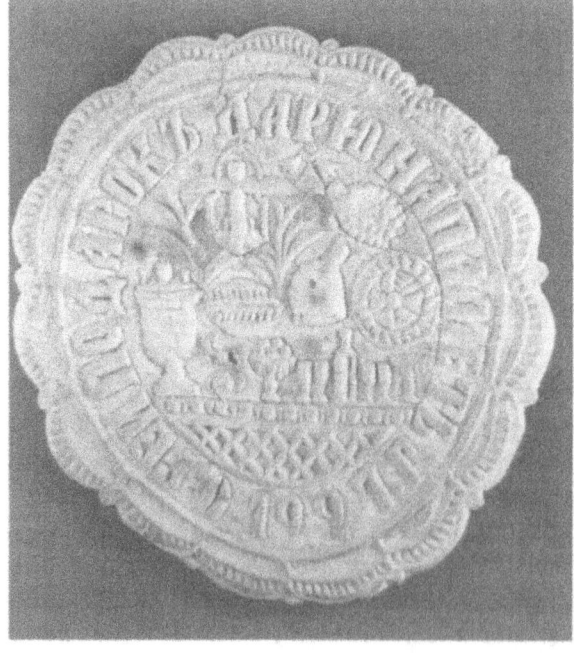

FIG. 4.3 *Prianik,* spicecake with inscription. Baked dough with stamped design. Tula region, 19th century. ME.

nized his initials carved on a frontal board: MMM signified Master Mikhail Malishev (fig. 4.4).[24] Some twenty other masters active in the late nineteenth and early twentieth centuries identified their works by means of carved initials or abbreviated names which local inhabitants could still recognize in the 1950s.[25] One facade distinguished by especially rich floral ornament bore the inscription "Fedar Kon," short for Fedor Konkin, villagers explained; another house, dated 1875 with the initials MRA, could be identified with Master Aleksandr Rodionov. A deeply cut inscription extending the breadth of the frontal board included "1889" and "year" bracketing the information "this house [belongs to] the brothers Fediantsev" and was carved by "Master A. Molodtsov." The names of owners were frequently carved on houses, and local memory preserved these names as well as those of the master carvers.

Interior decoration, including the painting on wood paneling, cupboard doors, and floors and the carving and painting on furnishings and utensils, sometimes bore the names of the artists, particularly if they had some reputation at the time the work was commissioned. Records of names also give information about the careers of artists. In the Northern Dvina region, family names of the house painters who used flat, geometrical designs tended to be localized, indicating a limited geographical range of activity. In contrast, the names of painters who used more varied styles were also found in localities outside their native villages, indicating that by traveling about the region in search of commissions, these artists acquired new stylistic ideas.[26]

The most prolific painters often had family histories in the craft. Timofei Makarov, from Toima on the Pineg River, began working as a child in the 1860s with his father, a painter of distaffs, horse yokes, chests, and church furnishings. Mariia and Avdotiia Chistiakova, sisters from the village of Puchuga in the same area, learned painting from their father, a self-taught itinerant artist. An overlapping of traditions can be seen in the Petrovskii family, a father and two sons active from the 1840s to the end of the century in Churkovskaia village, who decorated their own house in an original fashion. Painted lions and unicorns flanked the windows on the facade; blue leaves and branches covered the logs, and inside, a gallery of Petrovskii family portraits was painted directly on the walls in imitation of framed portraits in city houses.[27]

While there was certainly room for individual taste, most interiors were painted in ways that emphasized the structural elements, uprights, beams, the framework around the oven and cellar, the benches around the walls, and the cupboard doors. This was done either with flat colors following the forms of geometrically carved panels, usually rhomboids or circles within squares, as was common in the Sol'vychegodsk area in Vologda Province, or with more complex arrangements of floral or animal decorations, described earlier. A local painter named Misharin specialized in combinations of floral and geometrical motifs,[28] and other accomplished artists unified their decorations by means of the background color, framing devices, or repeated patterns. Many peasant houses in the Sol'vychegodsk district were well preserved, and members of an expedition during the 1960s were especially struck by their visual harmony.[29] To the east, in Tagil in the Urals, an area with trade connections in Vologda Province, interior painting included similar designs, but was more loosely organized. In houses from the villages of Popovo and Komel'skaia, floral motifs were spread out over entire walls and even onto the ceiling, instead of being arranged within framed panels. An artist named Varlam Riabkov even introduced a tethered camel and a steaming railroad train into one sitting room (fig. 4.5).[30]

The effect of visual unity along with variety of forms and bright, saturated color can be seen in paintings depicting domestic scenes on distaffs (fig. 3.14), bread boxes, and the lids of storage chests. In some paintings, figures are surrounded by floral forms filling almost all the space between them, or are framed by bands of red and yellow rhomboids, or large checkerboard patterns of yellow and black with red borders.[31] This likeness is not surprising, since many artists worked in both spheres of painting, on walls as well as small objects. Others may simply have adapted the mural motifs to the space available on distaffs or containers, adjusting the proportions and colors to fit the given composition. These small portable objects were vehicles by which forms of interior decoration in one region could be conveyed

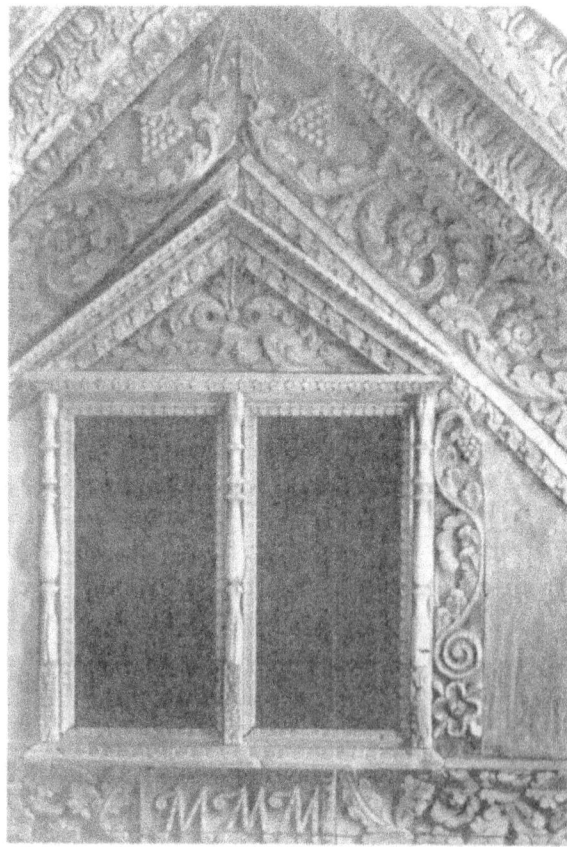

FIG. 4.4 Mikhail Malyshev, pediment of house from Vishenki village, Nizhnii Novgorod region, 1882. Carved wood. Detail showing initials MMM on frontal board. Sergiev-Posad.

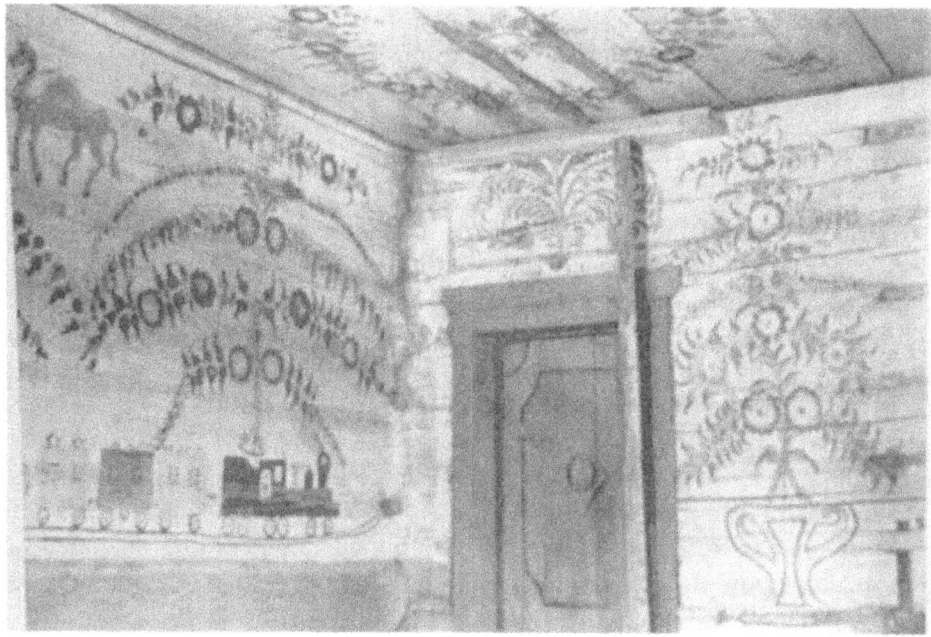

FIG. 4.5 Varlam Riabkov, painted
interior of house, Komel'skaia village,
Sverdlovsk region, Urals, 1897. Detail
of garlands, train, and camel. Alapaevsk
Society for Protection of Monuments.

to another area. The continued activity of traveling artists, added to the wide
distribution of folk art objects, meant that a variety of formal models were
available to artists over a fairly wide territory. This availability makes the preservation of distinctive regional styles and the identification of styles with individual artists and artels all the more significant.

The most detailed information about peasant artists comes from parish
records and from oral accounts gathered by folk art scholars and curators on
visits with practicing artists and with their neighbors and relatives. In the late
1950s, expeditions up the Northern Dvina River found three distinct painting
styles within the region. A group of villages known as Mokraia Edoma, a short
distance from the Permogore landing stage, was the center of the style called
Permogore painting. Farther north, the village of Ul'ianovskaia, located where
the Rakulka River flows into the Northern Dvina, was the home of Rakulka
painting; and farther still, in the villages of Puchuga and Skobeli near the

Borok landing stage, where the river Nizhniaia Toima enters the Northern Dvina, lived the masters of Borok painting.[32]

At Permogore wharf, after climbing the steep bank to the nearest settlement, expedition members entered brilliantly colored houses and were shown distaffs, bowls, and other furnishings by elderly villagers who could still remember the artists who had made them. One woman readily gave the names of several painter families: Khvostov, Khripunov, and Iarygin; the artists she knew personally were the children and grandchildren of Iakov Iarygin, Aleksandr Misharin, and others active in the first half of the nineteenth century.[33] Parish records allowed the researchers to trace these families and find that Iarygin came from a large family, had a wife and children who also painted, and was still working in his seventies. Iarygin painted sleds, cradles, distaffs, serving bowls, and containers with scenes of activities in the home, farm, and woodlands; one early piece showed the artist himself at work painting a horse yoke, with his tools and pigments arranged neatly around him (fig. 4.6). Many artists of the following generations emulated his elegant handling of floral ornament and his exact drawing of figures and domestic detail. The Permogore style blended observation with the stateliness and refinement of the icon- and manuscript-painting traditions preserved in this region.[34]

In the swampy woodlands around Borok, villagers in the 1950s still used objects made by masters of a generation earlier. Ivan Osipovich Burmagin painted icons for churches and "for peasants, painted everything, whatever they brought to him and, for himself, on his own front gate, he painted an angel," according to one elderly man.[35] One master carver, Nikitin, made all the distaffs and other tools needed by Borok peasants, who then took them for decoration to one of several master painters. Pelageia Amosova, who lived in a tiny forest settlement called Pal'niki ("burnt-over place"), belonged to a large family whose members all specialized in painting wooden objects on commission from other peasants. In her nineties when she talked with museum curators in 1959, she explained how she had learned her craft as a child, and how she went about her work.

The Amosov family, like many in the district, were Old Believers, pious and literate. Pelageia's father, Matvei, a painter, taught all his children, using miniatures in religious manuscripts as models, a practice which strengthened their love of linear ornament. The brothers Stepan, Vasilii, Nikifor, Matvei, and Kuz'ma married and moved to nearby villages, but Pelageia remained to work with her father. When he died, he left her all his tools: a wooden ruler, a wooden compass with a goose quill, a brush made of rabbit hair, and a booklet of gold leaf from Suzdal'.[36]

Explaining her technique of painting distaffs (fig. 6.3), Amosova made it clear that the preparation of the surface, the laying out of the design, and all the subsequent steps (described in the next chapter) were as painstaking as those in the making of icons. The various parts of the composition had traditional names and contained specific motifs. Amosova, her brothers, and other Borok artists, such as Fedor Kuznetsov, Vasilii Tret'iakov, and Dmitrii Khripunov, used the same colors (mainly red, green, and yellow with fine black outlines) and chose similar subjects: *posidelki*, tea parties, and sleigh or carriage rides, accompanied by birds, flowering trees, and other ornamental motifs. They used gold leaf to accent important features. The amount of gold determined the selling price of the distaff, and some artists, including Vasilii Amosov, tended to use a great deal (fig. 13.5). An overall similarity of form was to be expected; the shared traits were part of a long-lasting pictorial tradition in this region. But subtle variations in the depiction of figures or horses and in the ornamentation of sleighs, costumes, or interiors were almost as distinctive as signatures. Amosova said that she used stencils left by her father for the more

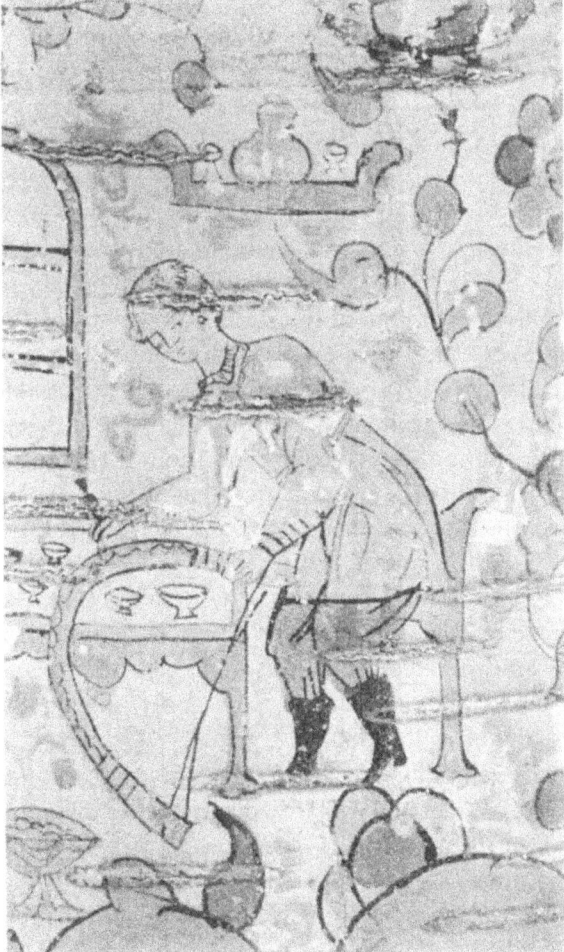

complex subjects, such as the horse and carriage, indicating one way traditions of representation were preserved. But she also drew many forms freehand.

Like other peasant artists, Amosova painted only in the fall and winter when she was free of gardening chores, from the feast of the Intercession of the Virgin until the end of March. Most winters she could make fifty distaffs, and she had no

FIG. 4.6 Iakov Iarygin, *burak*. Painted birch bark. Detail showing the artist painting a horse yoke. Permogore, 1811. GIM.

trouble selling them. "Our work was praised far and wide," Amosova said, adding that some women walked fifty versts (over thirty miles) to buy a distaff from her or her brothers.

In contrast to the local success of the Amosovs and other artists of the Northern Dvina villages, the much wider reputation of the Veprev family, makers of finely ornamented boxes of birch bark, depended partly on the stimuli and the commercial resources of Velikii Ustiug. Birch wood and bark were used throughout the north, and most peasants knew the techniques of plaiting narrow strips of bark and combining two layers of bark to make containers for liquids. But the Veprevs' work went beyond the utilitarian: their trays, snuffboxes, caskets, and other containers of birch were covered with thin layers of birch bark finely cut to create lacelike patterns of vegetation, abstract forms, or figural scenes. The special art of "birch-bark lace," described in more detail in chapter 8, employed several techniques: contour cutting to delineate the major forms, incising the soft birch with thin parallel lines for a hatching effect, or stamping the surface with patterns carved in hardwood. The art was unique to a few villages about twelve kilometers from Velikii Ustiug. Kurovo-Navolok, Pavshino, Klimlevo, and smaller settlements on the river Shemoksa, a tributary of the Northern Dvina, belong to the Shemogodskii region, and the terms *shemogodskaia rez'ba* ("Shemogodskii carving") and *shemogodskaia beresta* ("Shemogodskii birch") are used to describe this type of work.[37]

The extraordinary elegance of the art can certainly be related to the high cultural level of Velikii Ustiug, and to the high technical and artistic quality of its metalwork. Another factor in the development of crafts in the area was the presence of the Monastery of Michael the Archangel, which counted Kurovo-Navolok and the neighboring villages, with their peasant inhabitants, as part of its property in the seventeenth and eighteenth centuries. Until the lands were secularized by Catherine II, the monastery employed the most talented peasant artisans in its workshops. Since the foundation had originated in Novgorod, continuing ties with that city may well have influenced the art of the Shemogodskii villages. Chelishchev mentioned birch articles with stamped or cut-out designs for sale at the Prokop'ev market in Velikii Ustiug.[38] Descriptions of similar articles appeared in customs records and inventories from Velikii Ustiug in the mid-nineteenth century. The first mention of such pieces in a source from outside the area was in the Report on the All-Russian Exhibition at Nizhnii Novgorod in 1882.[39]

It was here that the name of Ivan Afanas'evich Veprev first appeared, as the winner of a bronze medal "for overall high quality, distinguished by careful execution and beautiful carving of baskets, canisters, and caskets of birch inlaid with foil."[40] This distinction was not achieved in a vacuum. Veprev came from a family of skilled birch-bark carvers. Foma Anisimovich Veprev, born in 1808, was the first known carver, and the names of at least nine other

Veprev masters from four generations have been identified. In addition, there were some seventy other masters active in the district by the late nineteenth century, many of them good enough to send works to the city of Vologda for exhibition and sale.[41]

Ivan Veprev, born in 1855, learned the skills of birch carving as a child, and went to work at an artel in Krasavino. A visitor from Moscow happened to see his work, commissioned him to make a decorative box, and later gave him many other orders. The artist's wife later said, "There were other carvers in the village, both older and younger, but they did not get commissions and they were not so well known as Ivan Afanas'evich."[42] Veprev's growing reputation led to the opportunity to exhibit his work at the Nizhnii Novgorod fair in 1882. After his successful debut, Veprev began to mark all his work with a stamp: "Ivan Afanas'evich Veprev. Kres. Shemogsk. vol. der. Kur. Navolok" (Peasant of Shemogodskii Volost', Village of Kurovo-Navolok).[43]

Veprev's work was displayed in the Russian Pavilion at the Paris Universal Exposition of 1900, along with examples of embroidery, woodcarving, and other peasant arts and the *kustar'* products of the Abramtsevo, Solomenko, and other folk art revival workshops.[44] It attracted attention for its sophistication and elegance of form, in contrast to the general expectation of simplicity and naiveté in folk art.

Although they worked with the simplest and most readily available materials, the Veprevs and the other specialists in carving "birch-bark lace" were more akin to urban craftsmen than to those artists from more remote areas who made objects primarily for local peasant use. The ornamentation of Veprev's boxes suggests the fluid linear contours and delicate foliage motifs found in ivory carving and in fine inlay work on furniture. Other artists modeled their designs for birch-bark boxes on the genre scenes and topographical views typical of silver and niello snuffboxes made in Velikii Ustiug. Alternatively, they adapted motifs from illustrations in printed books—another indication of their literate, urban orientation.[45]

During the early part of the twentieth century, the art of birch-bark carving continued to flourish in the villages around Kurovo-Navolok. Veprev taught his children how to carve birch bark, and in 1908 he helped to found a local craft school in Pogorelovo. Beginning with fifteen pupils, the school had forty-six by 1918.[46] One of Veprev's grandsons, Nikolai Vasil'evich Veprev, spoke with folk-art scholars Voronov and Vasilenko in the 1960s, and described his own early training with his father and brother, and subsequent apprenticeship with Ivan Afanas'evich.[47] By the time Nikolai became a master, around 1920, the craft was becoming organized under government sponsorship, much like other regional crafts discussed in chapter 18. The fourteen villages occupied with birch-bark carving established artels to maintain craft standards, to arrange for participation in trade fairs and craft exhibitions, and to select works to send to foreign markets and exhibitions. Nikolai Veprev won a prize at the 1936 Paris Exposition, and he in turn taught a younger generation of artists.

The Veprevs' work had close affinities with urban arts, and their success in receiving commissions and winning recognition beyond the boundaries of their village owed much to the growing interest in the *kustar'* crafts. However, by virtue of their training and their practice within a local tradition, these artists still belonged firmly within the sphere of peasant art. The artists in the Amosov and Veprev families, regardless of their differing spheres of activity, all represent the continual process of give and take between local customs and external influences. They exemplify the roles of individual artists who work within a tradition and simultaneously enrich and change it. Similar patterns existed in other peasant arts such as weaving and needlework, bonecarving, ceramics, and metalwork. In each case, the artists' esthetic choices were based partly on local materials, practices, and the requirements of a local clientele, and partly on contact with styles from outside the area, and awareness of the possibilities of urban or regional markets.

There were certainly a few exceptions. One artist whose work deserves special note stood somewhat apart from the usual situation of peasant artists, although there is no question that his work was genuine folk art and filled a specific role in village life. Vasilii Timofeevich Savinov lived in Timirevo in the Egor'evskii district in Riazan' Province south of Moscow.[48] Like other peasants, he farmed his land; like many he traveled to Moscow to earn money during the winter. He began carving wooden figures as a hobby during his free time. Villagers came to watch, and soon asked him to carve things for them. He made all the usual tools and furnishings, but since he was self-taught, he fashioned them in his own way, without recourse to traditional models.

Among Savinov's earliest known works are two wood figures dated 1870. Just over one meter high, they represent a man holding a long-stemmed pipe and a woman with a bucket (fig. 4.7). The man has a full beard and wears a hat and a double-breasted jacket; the woman wears a headscarf, a jacket, an apron with zigzag lines scratched along its border, a skirt, and boots—ordinary working clothes rather than festive peasant costume. Both figures are hollow; the man's widely gaping mouth and a hole under the woman's chin once served as entrances to these nesting boxes for starlings (*skvorechniki*). Old nests of the last inhabitants remain inside both figures. These insect-eating birds were always welcomed by peasants, and in Timirevo the villagers began to compete over starling boxes. Everyone wanted the expressive and amusing figures Savinov made (fig. 4.8). Savinov placed a painted couple on the roof of his own house. The man smokes a pipe and the woman, dressed in a variety of wildly spotted garments, holds a large box labled "snuff." Starlings flew in and out from beneath their long, pointed noses. Beehives, with holes bored in the eyes and mouths, were also popular. Not content to carve only useful ob-

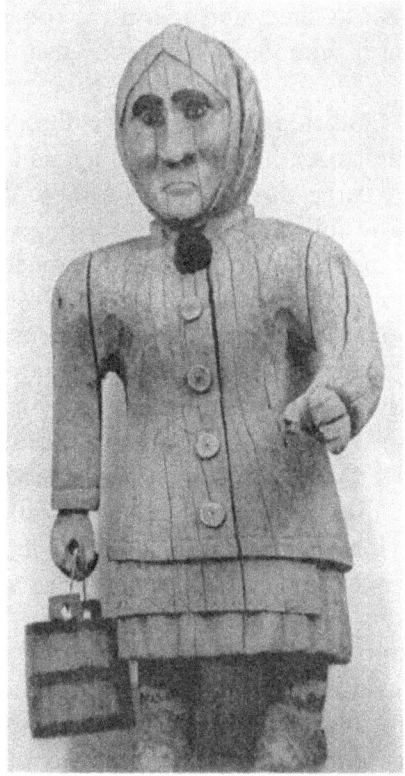

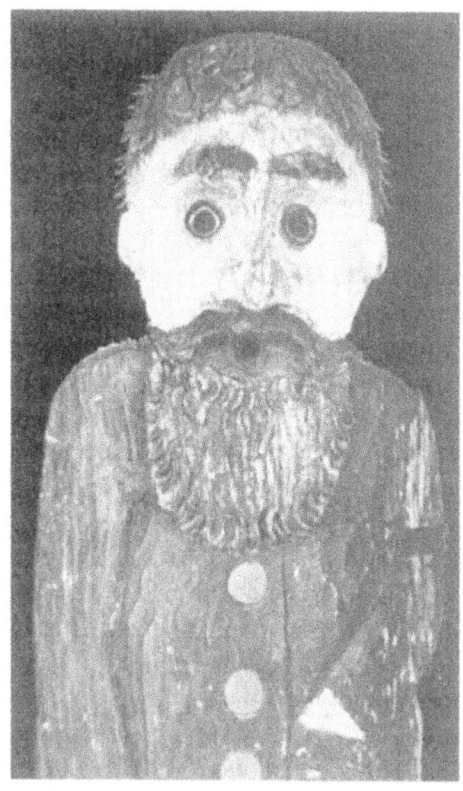

FIG. 4.7 Vasilii Savinov, starling-box figure. Carved wood. Timirevo, Riazan' Province, 1870s. Sergiev-Posad.

FIG. 4.8 Vasilii Savinov, starling-box figure. Carved and painted wood. Timirevo, Riazan' Province, 1880s. GIM.

jects, Savinov fashioned two life-sized figures for his yard, a woman hospitably offering a bottle and glass and a man raising a heavy stick as if to threaten intruders.

Surprisingly, the identity of this highly individualistic artist was unknown until a few years ago. Two of his figures had been acquired by the State Historical Museum in 1895, and were attributed to a certain "Master Timofei Vasil'ev, from the village of Kimerovo in Moscow Province." In the 1920s folk art scholar Aleksandr Nekrasov found the name V. T. Savinov in some records and believed that he had identified the artist, but he had no proof, and so the pieces remained "without passports" for years. One day, two elderly men appeared at the museum and asked to see the curator. They had heard a radio program about starling boxes and beehives carved like men and women, and they remembered such pieces from childhood. Ivan Vasil'evich Savinov and his neighbor Mikhail Gusev recognized them at once and identified other works in the museum storage area as by Vasilii Timofeevich Savinov, Ivan's father.[49]

The demarcation between tradition and innovation is especially vivid on a distaff base carved by Savinov in a stylized human form. At one end, a deeply carved, nearly three-dimensional face with a large open mouth serves as a socket for the detatchable upright blade. The long, flat body is carved in shallow relief with forms sometimes found in other folk art, but here arranged in an unusual way. The Russian imperial double-headed eagle with a crown is carved on the chest, above crossed arms; beneath the arms are three genre scenes and an inscription. First is a hunting scene of two men with gun and spear, a dog, and a raging bear; just below is a horse and sleigh carrying a man, woman, and small child; in the lowest register is an interior scene of a man carving and a woman spinning with a distaff; finally, an eagle with outspread wings marks the edge. A carved inscription reads: "This [distaff] base [belongs to] Salomon[ida] Antipova Savinova 1879."[50] Evidently the figures at work and those in the sleigh represent Savinov himself, his wife, Salomona, and their small son, the future Ivan Vasil'evich.

The juxtaposition of such motifs as a hunting scene, a sleigh ride, and a scene of domestic activity, combined with heraldic eagles and an inscription, falls within a traditional repertoire of designs found on distaffs. However, as the following chapters show, such compositions were usually painted on distaff blades from the north, whereas the Gorodets type with detachable bases featured paired horsemen above decorative bands, with a sleigh ride or domestic scene below. Detachable distaffs were decorated with paint or two-toned inlay work; relief carving was used for geometrical patterns, not figurative scenes. On most distaffs, divisions between motifs were clearly marked. Savinov seems to have taken ideas from various sources, with little concern for the expectations of any one regional tradition. What may be even more unusual is his apparent neglect of symmetry and clearly framed registers in favor of natural poses, movement, and even some attempt at perspective.

Another piece showing Savinov's insistent individuality is a large saltcellar that he made in 1890 (fig. 4.9). Roughly square with rounded corners, it has a lid but not a typical "chair" back; its carved decoration includes a lively assortment of forms. Perched on the lid are three large, realistically detailed chickens, perhaps a nod to the traditional "bird" form of saltcellar. Four grotesquely grinning heads serve as feet on which the cellar rests. Scenes from village life are carved in high relief on all four sides. They include men plowing and sowing seed, a woman cooking *bliny* (yeast pancakes) at her oven, and the same woman taking a plate full of them to a table where three sit waiting to begin the pre-Lenten Maslenitsa feast. In the largest area on the back, four men are seated and two are standing around a table adorned with inlay ornament. An inscription, *"volostnoi sud,"* identifies this as the district council or court, and it could refer to a current issue or debate.[51] All the scenes have precise details of furnishings, clothing, gestures, and facial expressions, and they were probably drawn from Savinov's own life and observations.

Savinov was one of very few folk artists to make life-sized figures, and perhaps the only one to do a life-sized sculpted portrait. A merchant named Bardygin came to the village on a holiday, noticed the starling boxes on Savinov's roof, and sought out the artist. Bardygin bought and commissioned several pieces, including his portrait. Without Savinov's usual humor, the figure, in a civil service uniform with medals, is rather stiff; it is a copy from life, rather than an original conception. Bardygin, like many of his peers, was interested in peasant art and collected it eagerly; he built a small museum and displayed many of Savinov's things there.[52] It was probably this museum that gave Nekrasov a hint of Savinov's existence, but because of the haphazard manner of labeling objects, most of the data on Savinov and his *oeuvre* might have been lost but for a stroke of luck.

Savinov was a natural artist who happened to be a peasant. His position in life certainly helped determine the kinds of objects he made. Clearly familiar with the decorative forms and arrangements traditionally used in architecture and domestic utensils, Savinov was unlike most peasant artists because he did not answer to a tradition. He did not follow proven techniques or work within a recognized local style. An exception to

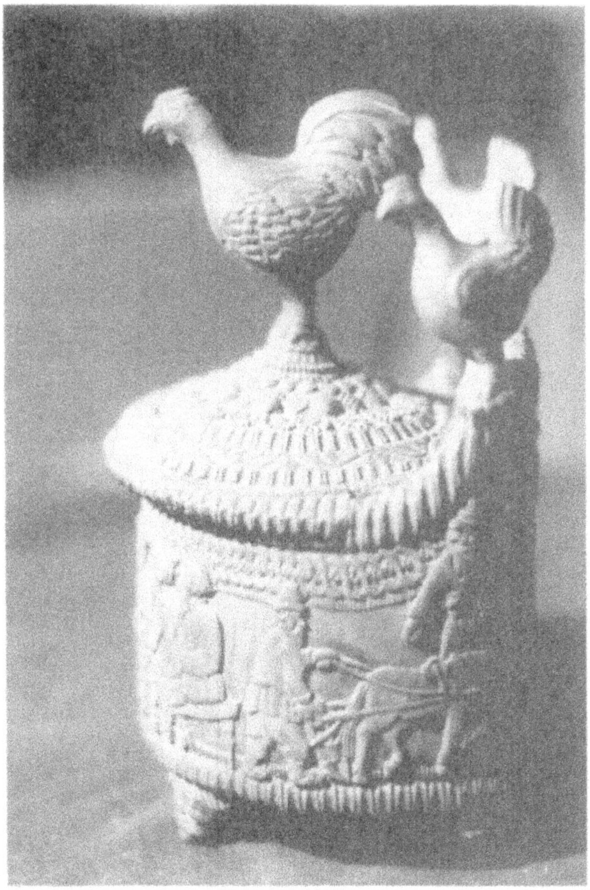

FIG. 4.9 Vasilii Savinov, saltcellar. Carved wood. Timirevo, Riazan' Province, 1890. GIM.

the general picture of the peasant artist in many ways, Savinov nevertheless worked at his special craft as part of a larger cycle of seasonal tasks, and he filled a well-defined position in his community.

There were undoubtedly other artists whose personalities and artistic inclinations were akin to Savinov's. Interviews with folk artists published in the past decade reveal a wide range not only in styles but in artists' attitudes toward marketing their work, their involvement with teaching their skills, and their roles within their communities.[53] Changes in the outlook of peasant artists were consequences of the tremendous social changes that began in the second half of the nineteenth century and have continued into our own time. Today there are still painters, carvers of birch bark, weavers, and toymakers who follow local craft traditions, who do not copy earlier models but produce pieces in much the same spirit. As in the past, artists do not carry out their work in isolation, but in relation to the requirements of local villages, state-supported workshops, and regional or urban markets.

A flexible definition of folk art as being based on traditions and customs shared by the producers and consumers of the work still seems useful for distinguishing authentic folk art from tourist merchandise. But it is even more important to understand that folk artists do not only follow tradition, they contribute to it. Even conservative artists, whose specializations have technical requirements that tend to preserve established forms and methods, need some room for invention, for cumulative originality. In the words of Antip Ershov, the folk artist quoted at the beginning of the book, the artist seeks scope for "adding something of our own" to the "thread of tradition."[54]

PART II

Materials
and
Forms

Wood and Carved Ornament

The wealth of wood gave rise to notable crafts.
— Evdokii Ziablovskii, 1810[1]

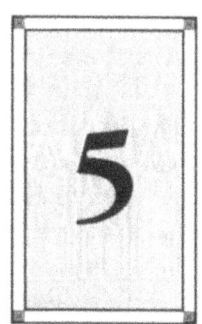

Woodworking skills were basic to life in the forested zones of Russia, and tools and techniques changed very little over the centuries. Although folk artists felt free to add individual touches to their compositions, the characteristics of their work were defined largely by the specific qualities of the materials they used. We have seen how characteristics of folk art were connected with the requirements of the peasant household and village, and in Part III we will see how certain forms and images reflected various layers of tradition. In Part II, by relating formal elements to physical materials and working methods, we will uncover the structural and ornamental foundations of each art form. These foundations serve as reference points for recognizing variations within a given type of art and for understanding the reasons for formal similarities in works in different media or different places of origin.

Decoration applied to crafted objects consists, in the most basic sense, of patterns that contrast with a surface or ground.[2] In the case of wood, the pattern is created by openwork carving, by three-faceted chip carving, inlay, or low or high relief, by painting combined with carving, or by paint alone. In textiles, patterns may be woven, embroidered, printed, or created by a combination of techniques. For other media, such as bonecarving, ceramics, and metalwork, ornamentation also relies on color or textural contrast between figure or pattern and ground. Beyond this elementary principle of contrast, other characteristics of decoration are found in all forms of folk art. Stylistic distinctions are based on several traits, including the degree of symmetry or asymmetry within a design; the presence of an allover pattern or a figural or abstract motif at the center of a decorated area; and the relationship between a central figure and the smaller repeated forms that make up a border. Both central figures and borders are composed to fit the overall shape of the object and to suit the material from which it is made.

These generalizations about style hold true not only for handcrafted objects made by Russian peasants but also for types of folk art requiring complex techniques and collaborative methods of production. The first category includes work in wood and the textile arts; the second includes metalwork, printmaking, lacquerwork, and ceramics. Distinctions between handcrafts and more complex methods are not firm, since metalwork and ceramics were practiced from ancient times and under the most primitive conditions. Moreover, by the late eighteenth century there were workshops and factories producing almost every type of article, whether traditionally made in the peasant home or imported from abroad.[3] However, the physical similarities and differences between the primary peasant arts and the specialized folk arts or urban crafts are important for an understanding of folk art in its broad context.

Woodworking skills were fundamental in building, and the *izba* embodied the principles of design and ornamentation in Russian folk art: clear articulation of structure and integration of the various components of the surface, border ornament, and focal figurative or symbolic motifs. The exterior decoration emphasized features that were structurally or symbolically important. The *okhlupen'* at the end of the ridgepole, the gable ends, the *lobnaia doska* that set off the pediment, and the *nalichniki* framing the windows and doors were decorated with openwork tracery or with carving in high relief. The types of ornament, styles of carving, and special motifs, based on plants, animals, and mythic and magical creatures, varied with location, the wishes of the householder, and the skills of the carver. In all regions, practices of architectural decoration developed in tandem with other types of peasant art, including interior furnishings and the tools and utensils used for domestic tasks. The distinctive environment provided by the decoration and furnishing of the *izba* was made up of many components; each dish, cupboard, or piece of textile was complete in itself, and it was also a "microcosm" of peasant art.[4]

Before looking at specific techniques and individual pieces, we can make a few generalizations about peasant artists' approach to carving. First, in fashioning bowls, distaffs, and three-dimensional architectural features such as the *okhlupen'*, the artist paid attention to the natural grain of the wood, which was often taken from a tree bole or root, using an axe to define the main features of the image. In applying smaller-scale ornamentation to an object, the carver or painter maintained a harmony with the natural form by using appropriate ornament to emphasize the roundness of a bowl, the angle of a bird's neck, or the upright strength of a distaff blade. The decorative use of natural motifs, such as water weeds or ripple-like lines on the body of a duck-shaped *skobkar'* or saltcellar, was one way of maintaining this harmony with nature.

The abundance of wood, the universal building material in Russia, may have generated the characteristic massiveness and rich ornamentation of Russian wooden structures. All varieties of wood and all parts of the tree were used: peasants extracted pine resin, burned charcoal, made matting and shoes of bast, and made toys out of pinecones, needles, and lichen. Some trees were especially valued: the fir, with its straight grain, was most widely used for roofs, for the runners of sleds, and for objects to be decorated such as distaff bases.[5]

The earliest surviving large-scale carvings, found in Staraia Ladoga and Novgorod, in excavation levels of the ninth to twelfth centuries, were tree trunks or roots carved with faces: these recall Ibn Fadlan's descriptions of the carved pillars where Slavic merchants placed offerings. They may have represented the *domovoi* of folklore, a house spirit or goblin believed to protect and serve a home and its inhabitants if properly treated.[6] Three-dimensional sculpture was rare until the eighteenth century, except in work done for the church. Icons carved in relief were widespread in the north. One early seventeenth-century icon from Arkhangel'sk depicts St. George, his horse, and the dragon in high relief, with a fantastically ornamented city tower in shallow relief against a painted background showing the dragon's lair among stylized hills.[7] The warrior saints George and Michael the Archangel were among the most popular carved images, along with the more contemplative saints Nicholas and Paraskeva-Piatnitsa. In some churches, carved, polychrome figures of the evangelists and the annunciation scene appeared on the royal doors of the iconostases in place of the more usual painted icons. Free-standing figures of the mourning Mother of God and John the Evangelist were sometimes placed on either side of a crucifixion. Christ as a Man of Sorrows, a life-size, half-nude figure seated with bent head, was an important image in the churches of Vologda, and a standing figure of King David with a dulcimer was made in the mid-eighteenth century, possibly for a church in Smolensk.[8] The surviving pieces are of high quality. But there was evidently enough inferior work to arouse a church synod of 1722 to prohibit sculptures of saints on account of the "insufficiency of artistic mastery" which turned the holy faces into monstrous images upon which it was "painful and harmful to gaze."[9] Near cities and monastic centers, Vologda and the nearby Spasso-Priliutskii Monastery or Velikii Ustiug and the Monastery of Michael the Archangel, local craftsmen were employed side by side with masters from Novgorod and Moscow. This direct contact gradually introduced new forms, based largely on baroque art of the West, much as shipbuilding in the towns near Gorodets on the Volga affected the styles and techniques of local craftsmen.

The oldest household objects of wood were decorated with carving alone, without the addition of paints. Carving required only the simplest tools, axe and knife, and skills that every peasant practiced almost daily. In contrast, painting demanded more specialized skills, and the pigments had to be made or purchased in towns.[10] The main carving techniques used on all kinds of wood objects, from architectural ornament to spicecake boards, dishes, and domestic implements, were variations on three basic approaches: relief, incision into the surface, and openwork, or cutting through the entire thickness of a board. Each method resulted in particular kinds of ornament and pattern, and certain methods were appropriate for particular types of objects. For example, most architectural features were carved in relief, though openwork was used for balconies and shutters in the north; spicecake molds were carved in relief or reverse relief for different effects. Distaffs were ornamented with all kinds of carving, sometimes with several techniques used together on one piece.[11]

The thin boards and flat surfaces of distaff blades were ideal for carved patterns. The basic techniques were openwork, three-faceted (or V-shaped) incisions, contour carving, incrustation or inlay, and low and high relief. Openwork, which involved cutting all the way through the thin blades, leaving silhouettes of quartered circles, crescents, and intricate interlocking patterns, was used most frequently in Griaznovets, in Vologda Province. In many areas, the comb at the top of the blade was embellished with toothlike indentations cut with a fretsaw, and sometimes rounded at the edges or amplified with additional carved and painted designs.

The most versatile and widely used techniques for geometrical ornament involved three-faceted pyramidal or longer wedge-shaped incisions (commonly called a three-faceted groove, a fingernail groove, or a fine-outline groove), which could be arranged to form a variety of patterns. With only three to six cuts of a knife or chisel, a carver could fashion several distinctive shapes: a triangle; an indented triangle (called a "tooth" shape); an "eye" made up of a series of curved cuts; a "lantern" made by combining an "eye" and a triangle; a four-sided indented pyramid; a "honeycomb"; a straight-sided or curved wedge; and a rhomboid or diamond. These indented shapes could be combined with engraved parallel lines or curves to make additional forms such as a "pinecone," "fish scale," "fir tree," "snake," "spiral," or "lattice."[12] A rosette or sunflower pattern was made by carving long wedges out from a center point, and widening them toward the circumference of an inscribed circle. Rosettes and half-circular fan shapes could be arranged in rows across a surface, or could be overlapped to make patterns that would shift from one center point to another.

An exceptionally fine distaff blade by Master Stepan Ogloblin of Vologda Province[13] features a pinwheel-like rosette, composed of grooves that curve slightly clockwise, combined with an outer band made of overlapping half-rosettes or fan shapes (fig. 5.1). This central form is enclosed by another ring of inward-facing half-rosettes, and the whole circular form is set into the shape of the blade through a combination of half-circle and wedge patterns filling out the corners of the rectangle. This complex composition occupies the upper half of the distaff blade. Beneath it is a lattice-like pattern of six rows of eight squares, each made up of four pyramidal three-faceted cuts, creating an x shape from one corner of each square to the opposite one. The overall grid or lattice pattern can be read as an arrangement of either square or diamond (rhomboid) shapes. This ornamentation, topped by linked cartouches bearing the name of the peasant woman for whom it was made, covers the entire outer side of the distaff blade, the side seen by company. The inner side is plainer, ornamented by an arched pattern containing several rosettes and half-rosettes near the base, and a band containing the artist's name and the date.

Few distaffs are so completely and harmoniously embellished. But similar combinations of three-faceted and longer, grooved incisions are often used to make dense patterns, which contrast with a surface left unadorned or filled with very shallow engraved lines. This effect of contrast is especially notable on the long stems of dis-

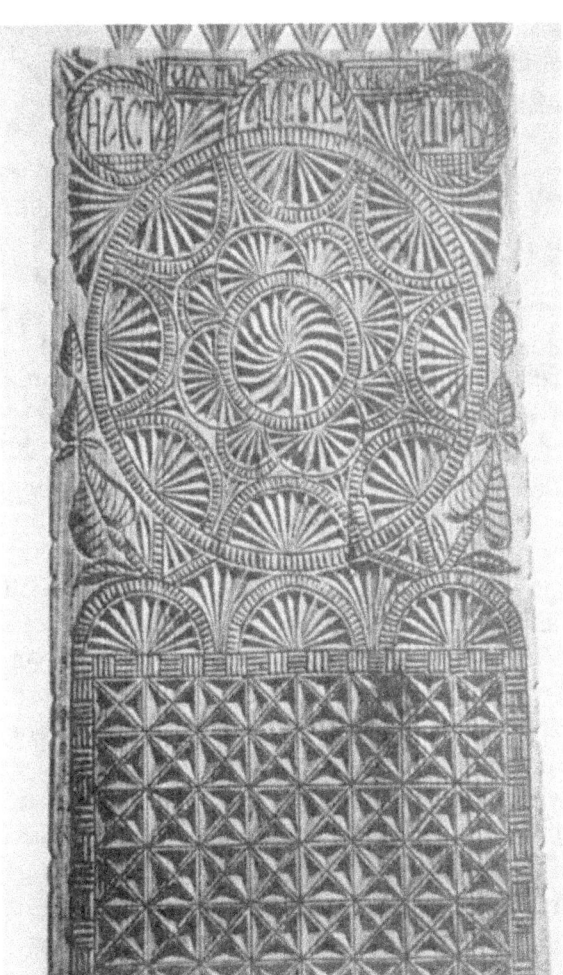

FIG. 5.1 Master Stepan Oglobin, distaff. Wood, three-faceted chip carving. Vologda, 1890. Sergiev-Posad.

MATERIALS AND FORMS

taffs from the Vologda region, and on the hollowed stems of the columnar Iaroslavl' distaffs.

Contour carving was the main technique used in the Iaroslavl' district for distaffs of the *terem* type (fig. 5.2). The nipped-in, hourglass-shaped blades were often decorated at the top with a heraldic figure such as an eagle, while the larger portion below was divided into bands by three-faceted borders, in which two or three figural scenes were displayed.

Distaffs from the Volga River area had different decorative styles from those of the north, because they were made of two pieces, with the blade fitting into a socket at one end of the base, the *dontse*. This two-part form probably appeared in the seventeenth century, when shipbuilding demanded so much timber that distaffs had to be made as economically as possible. However, the decoration was still lavish, especially on the base, which, when not in use, was hung from a peg on the wall. The basic three-faceted, grooved incisions were used for geometric patterns, sometimes in combination with shallower outline grooves almost as fine as engraved lines.

The most important carving technique, unique to Gorodets and the Nizhnii Novgorod Region, was known in Russia as *inkrustatsiia* (incrustation) (fig. 5.3). Comparable to intarsia or inlay work, the method involved scraping or planing a depression in the surface of the wood, into which shapes cut out of thin veneers of water-treated oak were set. The rare veneers came from trees that once grew in the swampy ground around the Uzol River, a small tributary of the Volga. When the river flooded, many trees weakened and fell into the swamp, remaining in the mineral-rich mud until the stream changed its course and the darkened logs surfaced. Gorodets craftsmen valued the wood for its dense grain and dark color, which contrasted with the natural golden oak from which distaff bases were carved.[14]

The cut-out shapes, rarely abstract, except for small diamonds or dots used in borders, were surprisingly lifelike silhouettes of birds, horses, riders, carriages, and figures dancing or promenading. Some of the compositions were highly formal and hieratic, but much of the imagery evidently reflected the bustling life of Gorodets and other Volga port towns. The distaffs were in great demand in these trade centers.

The Mel'nikov family from the village of Okhlebiaka were among the first documented makers of distaffs with incrustation, but peasants in neighboring river villages, including Koskovo, Kurtsevo, Mokrovo, and Ometovo, soon began to specialize in the technique.[15] The process of curing and cutting the wood, matching the grain, and adding the countour-cut details was exacting and time-consuming. Eventually, some artists began to streamline production by using dark paints to imitate the tone of the dark oak used for veneers, and the pure technique of "incrustation" was rarely practiced after the middle of the nineteenth century. However, the vivid silhouettes characteristic of Gorodets decoration continued to influence local styles of carving and painting. The painted distaffs and decorative panels popular later in the century and the distinctive carved toys, known as Gorodets horses and troikas, all emphasized angular and expressive silhouettes.

Like distaffs, sewing implements, loom parts, and tools for washing and smoothing linen were decorated with the same carving techniques. In addition, relief carving, only rarely used on distaff bases, often transformed the handle of a *valek* or *rubel'* into a bird or a horse. Some utilitarian items may not have been decorated at all, but were simply discarded or used for firewood when they wore out. The pieces that survive were obviously cherished as heirlooms because of their beauty and personal value.

Two other kinds of objects were carved but not painted: boards for molding spicecakes, *prianichnie doski*, and boards for printing textiles, *nabivnie doski*. In both cases, the utilitarian functions required specific carving techniques. Spicecakes or honeycakes were made not only in famous centers such as Gorodets but throughout the country, and they were used in festivities and rituals of both the church and the agricultural community. Spicecakes were given to loved ones for birthdays, wedding anniversaries, and funerals; they were presented as tokens of esteem at coronations and other state ceremonies. Each occasion required a special form and design. For instance, on St. George's Day, April 23, when herds were led out to pasture after the winter, the peasants baked round, flat

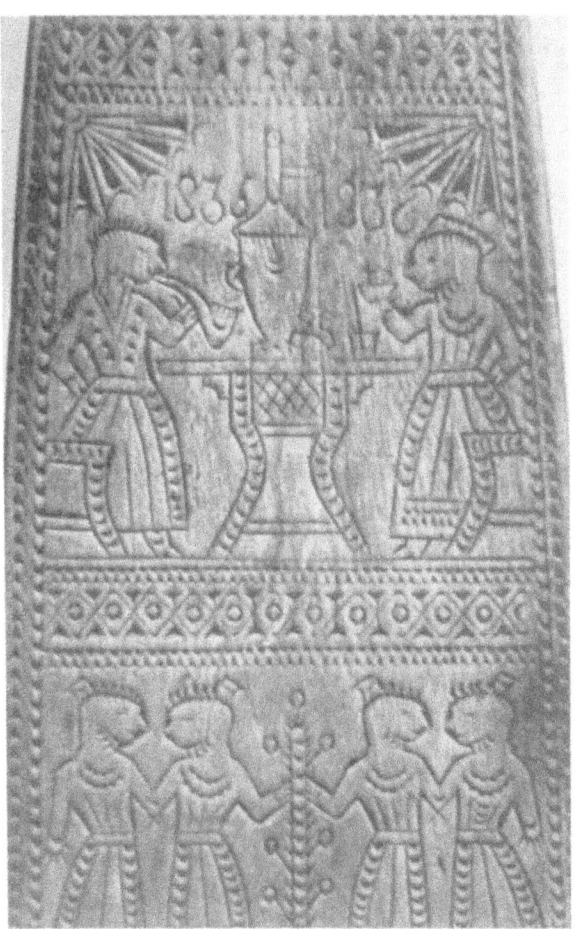

FIG. 5.2 Distaff, *terem* type. Wood with contour carving. Iaroslavl', 19th century. GIM.

rye cakes in the shapes of birds, cattle, sheep, and deer with branching antlers. They gave the cakes to children, hung them in windows, and fed them to the animals so that the herds would return home during the summer.[16] During major market weeks, special games and contests were centered around spicecakes: round cakes about twenty centimeters in diameter were used, and whoever could throw a cake the farthest without breaking it won the contest.[17] The most elaborate and largest cakes, weighing up to 150 pounds, were made for weddings and state festivals.

In the seventeenth century, spicecakes were made in workshops attached to the courts, in the Armory Palace in Moscow and the Admiralty in St. Petersburg, and also in major trade centers, where the workshops were sometimes called factories rather than bakeries. However, there were always independent *prianishniki,* or spicecake makers, who spent the winter and early spring months carving boards to be used during the next market seasons. One board inscribed on the reverse "1778 year this board was made in the month of October the 9th day for this factory of Semen Andreev[ich] Prianishnikov," indicates that the professional designation was already being adopted as a family name.[18]

There were two methods of decorating a spicecake. It could be molded in a raised pattern by pressing the dough into a concave form cut into the surface of the wood (reverse relief), or stamped by means of a raised or relief carving, leaving a concave impression. Both relief and impressed forms were widespread. The earliest spicecake boards, dating from the twelfth and thirteenth centuries in Novgorod, were decorated with sim-

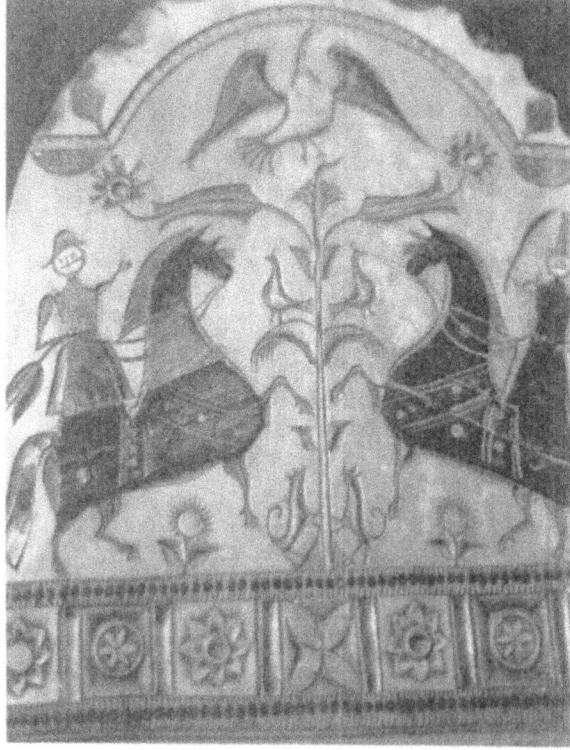

FIG. 5.3 Lazar Mel'nikov, distaff. Wood with "incrustation." Gorodets, 1866. GIM.

ple geometric and floral ornaments. In the seventeenth century, the molds were circular or rectangular, with central decorative motifs, such as a flowering branch or a city gate and tower, surrounded by an ornamental border or by an inscription similar to those on festive bowls of the same period. The imperial double-headed eagle appeared on numerous inscribed boards, usually indicating an honorary presentation for a specific occasion (figs. 5.4, 5.5).

More modest molds, without borders, were decorated with single animals such as lions, horses, or birds. In the nineteenth century some boards were divided into several smaller compartments, each containing a single figure, such as a rooster, fish, sheep, flower, or human being, to obtain multiple cakes with one impression. In the same period, figures of "hussars" or "cavaliers and ladies" became popular, probably adapted from similar images in *lubki*, popular broadsheet prints.[19]

The most distinctive spicecake forms were those with city motifs such as gates flanked by towers with domes, spires, and banners. Though somewhat schematized, most were inscribed with a town's name, since they were sold as souvenirs of the type Isabel Hapgood sought out in Gorodets during her excursion along the Volga in 1895.[20] One enterprising Gorodets baker had a two-part mold made, showing the city gates on one board and a paddle-wheel boat steaming up the Volga on the other.

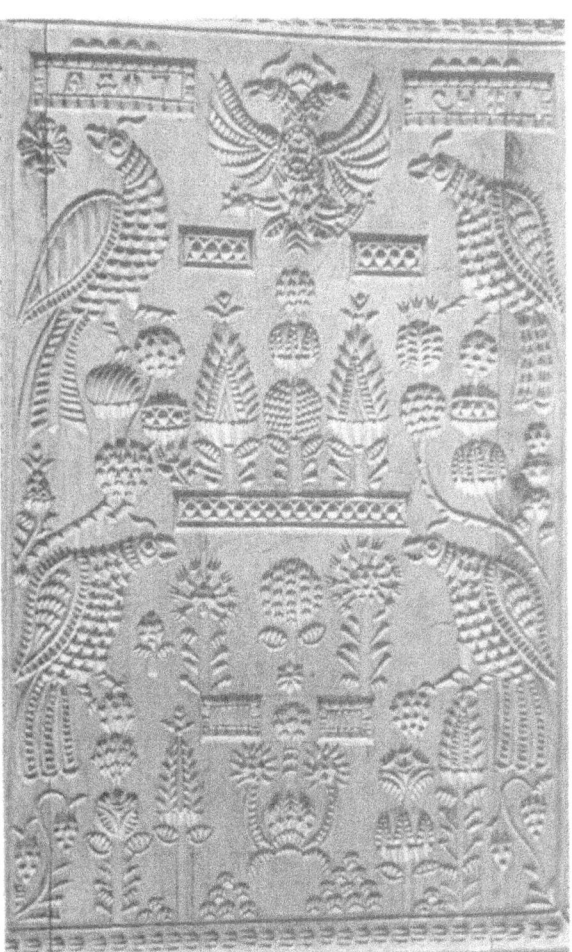

FIG. **5.4** Spicecake mold. Carved wood. 1849. Smolensk.

MATERIALS AND FORMS

Hinged in the middle, the diptych mold could be folded for easy transportation, and it could print two large cakes at once.[21]

Boards for printing cloth (figs. 5.6, 5.7) were known as *manery* ("matrices") or *nabivnye doski* (from *naboika,* "printed cloth"). Made of hardwoods — maple, pear, nut, or birch — to withstand the repeated pressure of printing, the earliest blocks, from the seventeenth and early eighteenth centuries, were large, about fifty centimeters square, and were carved on both sides. In the nineteenth century they were somewhat smaller, carved on one side, and the smaller details of the design were sometimes made of bands of metal.[22] Printing was used to decorate many kinds of textiles: linen and cotton cloth used for peasants' garments and kerchiefs; silk and velvet used in cities; drapes and hangings used in churches. Certain kinds of designs were appropriate for each function. The most widespread design consisted of small repeated forms printed on natural or indigo dyed linen. The boards were generally carved with a basic vertical and horizontal orientation, with stripes, evenly spaced floral motifs, or abstract geometrical designs. In the process of printing, each impression would be aligned with adjoining impressions until the whole cloth was covered. A length of cloth could also be printed with both an allover pattern and a contrasting border

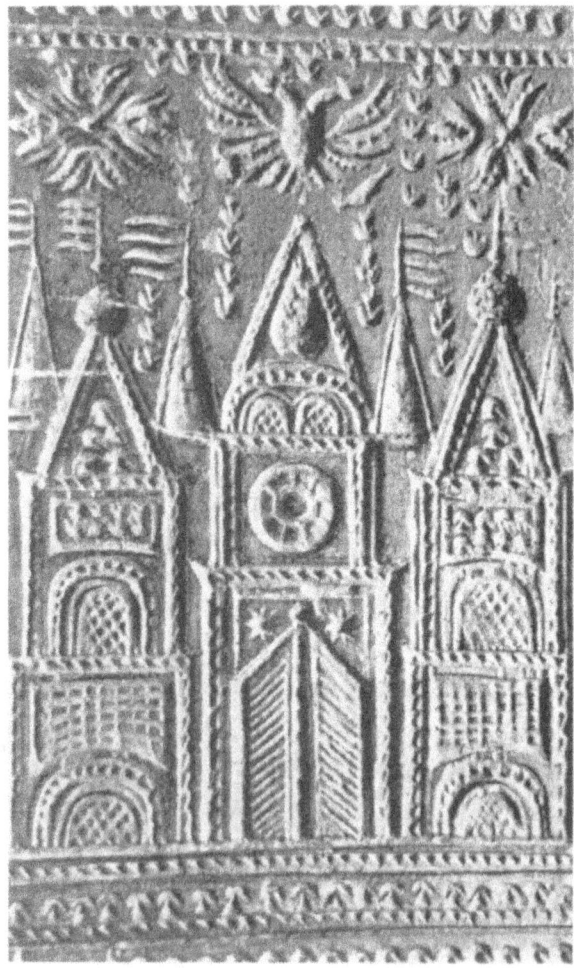

FIG. 5.5 Ceremonial spicecake mold. Carved wood. Late 18th century. From Voronov, *Krest'ianskoe iskusstvo.*

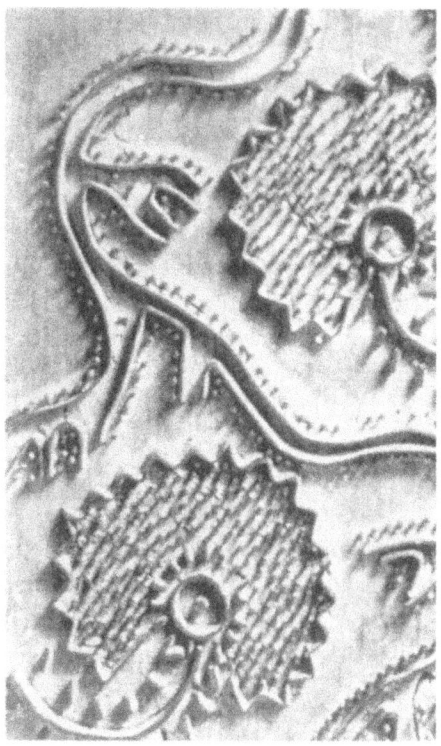

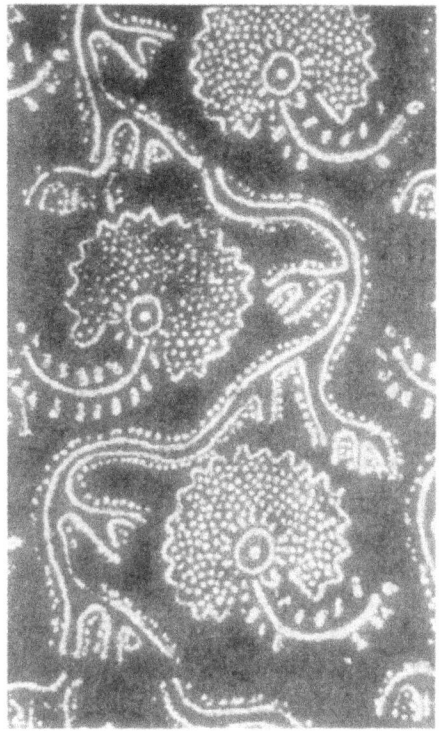

FIG. 5.6   Printingboard. Wood, iron.
19th century. Sergiev-Posad.

FIG. 5.7   Printed cloth sample, linen.
19th century. Sergiev-Posad.

of larger-scale bird or animal motifs, for which separate *manery* would be
used.

A few thousand examples of printing boards are preserved in museums,
along with fragments of printed textiles, representing many periods and regions. The designs on the oldest examples resemble those on carved woodenware, with geometrical forms, triangles, checkerboard patterns, and rosettes
predominating. The common technique of three-faceted incised carving was
the basic method for forming the allover designs to be printed on cloth.
Curved linear incisions, called contour carving, like that found on Iaroslavl'
distaffs, were used for the exuberant floral ornament printed in several colors
on white linen. Decorative printed cloth, for scarves, tablecloths, and hangings (as opposed to plain lengths for clothing), also featured horsemen,
women with upraised hands, and birds, motifs familiar from carved facades

and other household furnishings and, significantly, from embroidery. Some designs were highly inventive. One *doska*, carved with a very convincing still life of a knife, fork, spoon, and fish arranged on a plate, was used to print the complete place setting at intervals around a tablecloth.[23]

The techniques of carving the wooden blocks and those required for dyeing and printing the fabric relate this art form both to the woodworking and textile arts of the peasant household and to the more specialized urban crafts, such as the printing of *lubki* and books. In the nineteenth century, peasant women often took their cloth to professional dyers and printers, or waited for itinerant printers to come to their village with swatches of cloth to show the range of designs possible from the available *manery*. In the north, in Vologda, Arkhangel'sk, and Olonets provinces, and in central Russia, in Iaroslavl', Tver', Kostroma, and Nizhnii Novgorod provinces, entire villages became known as centers for textile printing. Textile boards and spicecake molds are examples of types of folk art that involve characteristics of more than one artistic medium, and more than one group of makers and users. Depending only on the most abundant of materials and the simplest carving techniques, these boards had the capacity to broaden the base of folk art by helping to disperse images and decorative styles and bring new elements into the repertoire of forms used by peasant and town artists alike.

Painting on Wood

Paint enlivened carved forms on frontal boards, the geowalls, and the horses, ducks, domestic implements. Practices varied. Most northern painters had a linear or graphic approach, following methods derived from icon painting, first applying a ground, then outlining the main figures, and finally adding color and linear ornament. Others worked freehand, applying colors directly to the wood; still others used a combination of linear and freehand techniques. The basic tools and pigments were similar in all regions, and both oil-based paints and egg tempera were used. According to Lazar Mel'nikov, a Gorodets distaff maker, the main colors were chrome yellow, vermilion, emerald green, ultramarine, soot black, and white.[1] For interiors of houses, red and ocher grounds predominated, though there were local preferences for other colors. The same lions, *bereginy*, and other creatures from the frontal boards were often painted on cupboard doors, large storage chests, and even the floors.

Similarities between domestic decoration and church decoration in the north suggest interaction between artists engaged in both kinds of work, although the subject has not been studied in detail. Statues and three-dimensional icons were painted; and icons were placed in small shrinelike cases or mounted on wooden iconostases, intricately detailed with carving, gilt, and painting. The same designs, usually in red, yellow, and black with silver or gilt highlights, were used on other church furnishings such as pulpits, candlesticks, and cases for the gospels.

In Vologda and Arkhangel'sk provinces, the so-called provincial schools of icon painting maintained the austere forms and strict methods of the fifteenth and sixteenth centuries, while the Moscow school, following Simon Ushakov, introduced Western-style shading and proportion in the seventeenth century. By the eighteenth century many workshops produced icons on a commercial basis; distributors, called *ofeni*, contracted with peasant painters or with workshops and shipped icons to buyers throughout the country. Some icon workshops used an assembly-line system, with different workers preparing panels, laying and burnishing the gold backgrounds, outlining figures and settings, and painting the faces. Only a few painting centers, notably a group of small villages, Palekh, Mstera, and Kholui, in Vladimir Province, maintained the older icon-painting traditions in a modest way: in the twentieth century these traditions became the source of the new local art of painting miniatures on lacquered papier-mache boxes.[2] In most of the country, however, the availability of cheap, printed icons led to a drastic decline in the quality of icon painting. Icon painters, whether attached to factories or itinerant, were regarded as little more than pieceworkers.

In the Old Believer communities of the north, painting was still regarded with a kind of mystique, as a divinely given art.[3] The founders of painting dynasties, such as the Iarygins and the Misharins from the Northern Dvina area, were Old Believer icon painters.[4] In these areas there was much overlapping of religious and secular life, and it is not surprising that the painted decoration on objects used every day—dishes, distaffs, storage boxes, and furniture—helped to perpetuate styles and images from earlier religious art. Specific techniques of icon painting, such as applying paint and ink over a gold background, were adapted by peasant artists to decorate many household objects. Examples of different kinds of adaptation are the "golden" wood dishes made in Khokhloma on the Volga River, and the distaffs from Permogore and Borok on the Northern Dvina.

Painted and lacquered woodenware from Khokhloma (fig. 6.1) was famous as early as the seventeenth century. Khokhloma-Ukhozheia, literally a clearing in the woods, was one of several properties deeded to the Trinity-Sergiev Monastery in the seventeenth century. This connection with the wealthy church foundation gave the village both an outlet for its wooden products and the technique that made Khokhloma ware distinctive.[5] A special method of varnishing the dishes made them far more durable than plain or painted wood. More important, it made an ideal surface on which to paint calligraphic designs, and it produced a mellow, golden tone, which seemed to transform the wooden dishes into finely chased metalware.

The process of making spoons and bowls was time-consuming. The wood, usually linden, birch, or more rarely fir, had to be seasoned, then carved into the proper shape. Axes and knives were used initially; lathes powered by foot or by water from the many streams running into the Volga were later added in the large workshops. The carved dish was covered with a layer of clay in

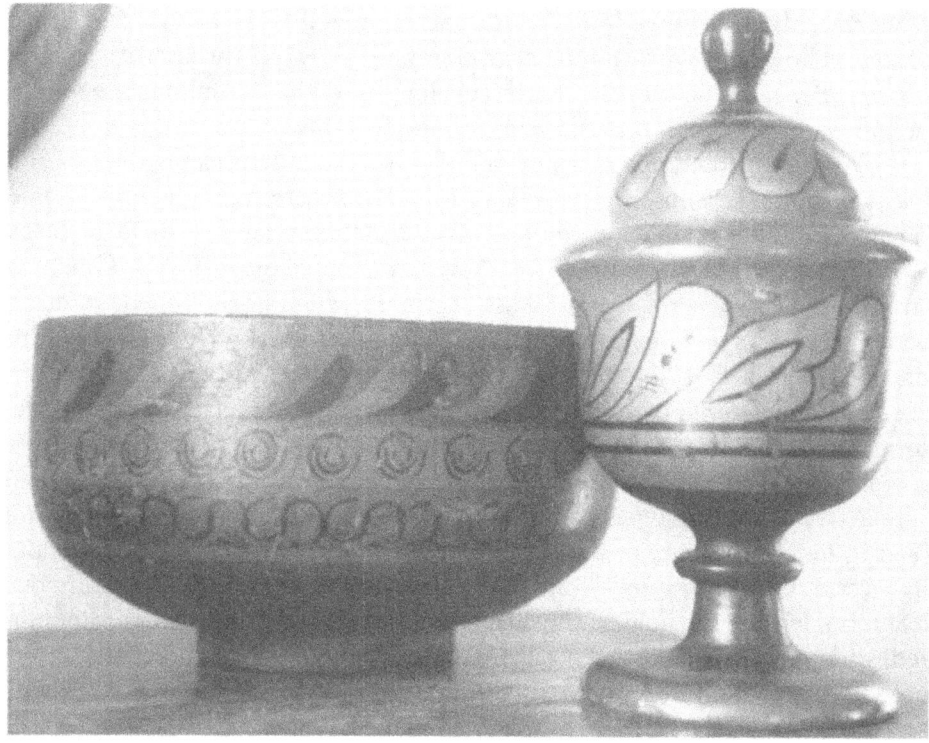

FIG. 6.1 Bowl and goblet. Wood, paint, metallic powder, ink, varnish. Khokhloma, Nizhnii Novgorod region, late 19th or early 20th century. Private collection.

order to seal all the pores of the wood. Several coats of boiled linseed oil were applied, and the dish was dried in an oven. After this process of curing, a dish was ready to paint.

The technique of first preparing a metallic-looking surface with coats of oil, rather than painting with opaque colors directly onto a ground, may have come from icon workshops. In order to economize in the use of gold leaf, some workshops developed the practice of covering the backgrounds with silver chloride and, after painting, coating the entire surface with varnish made of linseed oil and gums, which turned golden when heated in an oven. Peasant artists replaced silver with powdered tin in a process comparable to tinning or tinplating.[6] On this metallic background, the master drew outlines of the main forms in ink. The colors were painted in, and the piece was covered with clear linseed-oil varnish and tempered in an oven. The varnish turned yellow, and with the metal background showing through it appeared golden. Beneath the varnish, the black lines and the vermilion, green, and yellow paint also took on a unified, burnished tone.

The early painted designs were akin to those found on iconostases, on the backs of portable icons, and on metalwork. They were highly graphic, sometimes resembling interlacing ribbons of gold or red against a band of black. Khokhloma ornament was based on a variety of special brushstrokes. One basic stroke was known as the *travka* ("grass") form, in which finely tipped, gradually widening strokes were made parallel to one another or fanning out from a thin line to create a frondlike effect. These strokes could easily conform to and accentuate any curve or scroll in a dish or decorative panel. A more complex form, probably developed at the beginning of the nineteenth century, was sometimes called the "leaf" pattern. The strokes were varied to suggest the silhouettes of specific types of foliage, and were often accented with very fine lines to indicate veining or a curl at the leaf's edge. This pattern could be done in reverse, by painting in a solid black background around the contours of a leaf form, leaving the gold to shine through. Berries and flowers were painted in red, with yellow or gold accents. To represent various species of berries, artists used a combination of techniques: a round or oblong berry was painted with one stroke of a heavily loaded brush, curved and tapering off as the circular form was completed. When the paint dried, fine details, such as the stem and highlights to indicate roundness, were added with a fine brush or pen.

These designs or the methods of painting them were not unique to Khokhloma. They were probably inherited and adapted from the icon painters of the neighboring Semenovo district, as Vasilenko suggested.[7] But the Khokhloma painters took what were primarily border ornaments of icons and transferred them to the bodies of three-dimensional objects. In the process, they gradually departed from the original motifs, adding images and forms from other types of folk art and from nature.

The influence of icon-painting techniques in works produced in the villages around Permogore and Borok on the Northern Dvina River illustrates another way in which folk art adapted older decorative traditions. Storage trunks dating from the seventeenth and eighteenth centuries (fig. 6.2), decorated with figures representing the owners or guardsmen, with heraldic beasts and foliage ornament, reflect the styles and techniques of Novgorod icons and manuscripts.[8] The legacy of Novgorod is particularly strong in the painting styles of Iakov Iarygin, Aleksandr Misharin, and their followers. Clearly arranged compositions with each figure firmly outlined, the egg-based tempera applied smoothly over a white ground, and the calligraphic foliage ornament relate their styles to miniature painting.

Most of the wooden dishes, storage boxes, cradles, and distaffs made in Permogore were embellished with scenes of common activities such as hunting, berry picking, milking, riding in carriages, spinning and weaving, reading and writing, and drinking tea. A box for gathering berries and a distaff depict similar scenes of students reading lessons and miniature painters at work on manuscripts, scenes clearly reflecting the area's religious and literate tradition. Another distaff portrays the figures of a merchant being driven by a coachman, a uniformed envoy on horseback, and a couple drinking tea in a boyar's house. Such images do not record daily life but may rather recall tales of the past. All the details are accompanied by identifying words and phrases, often repetitive and sometimes meaningless, as if the artist believed that a long inscription added value to the piece.[9] The manner of representing faces, costumes and headgear, yoked horses pulling carriages, and views inside buildings on this distaff and those of later periods, seems to follow conventions of Novgorodian manuscript miniatures.[10]

The villages around Borok also maintained the traditional outlined or graphic approach to painting on wood.[11] However, the methods described by the folk artist Pelageia Amosova in the 1950s and the generally larger size of Borok distaffs suggest greater affinity to icon painting than to manuscripts (fig. 6.3).[12] Amosova emphasized the importance of preparing the surface of the distaff blade, as icon painters prepared their boards, with several layers of a ground, a mixture of glue and honey, so that the paint would not soak into the wood.

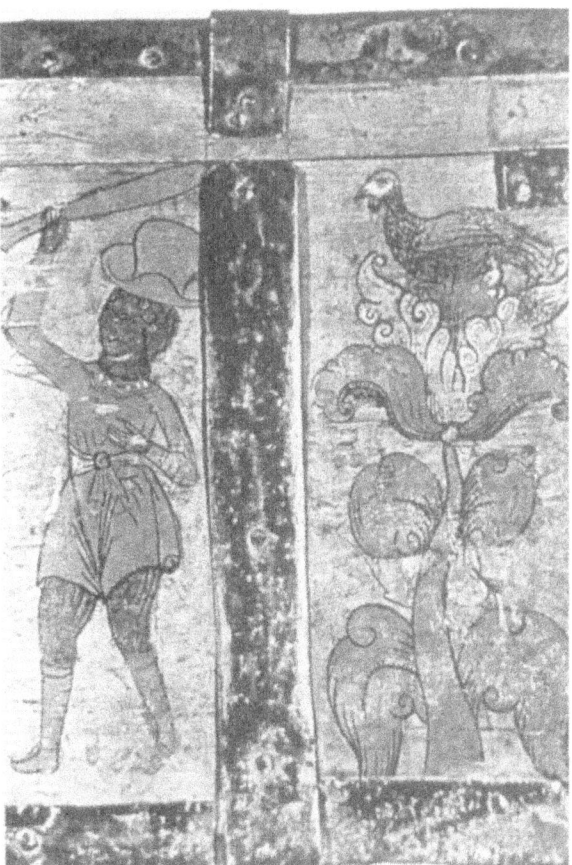

FIG. 6.2 Storage chest. Painted wood, iron. Detail of guard, tree, and peacock. Northern Dvina, first half of 18th century. GIM.

After drying, she smoothed the ground with a pumice stone. Then she applied two coats of whitewash, the first thin and the second thicker, more opaque. When the surface was again dry, the artist used her ruler and a sharp quill pen to draw guidelines across the whole distaff blade, separating the area horizontally into the traditional three bands. Following her father's teaching, she identified these bands as the row "with windows" at the top, the row "with the bird" or the "center row," and the row "with the horse" below. She used the compass to inscribe circles to accent the knobs or "buttons" carved across the top and at the two lower corners of the blade, and the circular bulges along the stem of the distaff. Only after the framework of the composition was outlined came the careful placing and gluing of sheets of gold leaf in the proper areas of the composition, where the bird or flowering branch would be placed in the center section, or to frame the horse in the lower area. The gold was dried and then burnished.

Amosova began the actual painting with a fine brush, first outlining the floral background motifs, then turning to the main figures. She used stencils left by her father for the complex subjects, such as the horse and carriage, but drew many figures freehand. She always paid careful attention to the relationship between contours of the main figures and the subsidiary decorative flourishes. This part of the process might take two days.

The distaffs painted by Amosova, her brothers, and neighbors share a number of characteristics in the choice of red, yellow, and green colors, the frequent use of gold accents, the fine black outlines, and the division of the surface into three parts. The rectangular shape made it easier for artists to adhere to a clear-cut composition on distaffs than on any other type of utensil. Hundreds of Northern Dvina distaffs display the same pattern, with the topmost section symmetrical and generally architectural, the center often containing a bird, a flowering tree, or some other heraldic image, and the bottom portion filled with a lively, asymmetrical scene of a sleigh or carriage ride (fig. 13.5). The sources of these motifs and the reasons for their prevalence will be discussed in chapters 12 and 13. One reason for the traditional aspect and the careful craftsmanship of these compositions is that they were meant to be admired at *posidelki*, gatherings at which women did their spinning together. The most elegant compositions were on the face or outer side of the distaff.

The inner side of most distaff blades was divided into two parts, the upper containing floral ornamentation, the lower a genre scene, most often a *posidelka* or another social scene such as a tea party. In some examples, the vertical pattern of figures seated on a long bench and the upright blades of their distaffs is set against a contrasting effect of curving foliage ornament. Scenes of tea parties sometimes introduce details of decor or costume borrowed from popular illustrations or from glimpses of upper-class provincial life. But at the same time they give an impression of formality and social ritual, with the figures arranged around a large, centrally placed samovar. The back of the distaff was sometimes inscribed with a personal message, especially if it was a gift; alternatively, it might be left with an unpainted area in the center of the blade so that a small mirror could be attached there.

Rakulka painting, named for the Rakulka River, and centered in the village of Ul'ianovskaia between Permogore and Borok, is the third major style of the area. Less linear and more painterly than the neighboring styles, it is characterized by rich, deep colors, green and reddish brown, on a golden ocher background. Without using outlines to determine the main forms of a composition, the Rakulka artist applied the paint freehand (or "free-brush" in Russian) to the untreated wood surface, then added a few fine contour strokes to accent the forms. A few Rakulka berry baskets and other small articles survive, but most artists preferred to paint distaffs.[13] The front of a distaff blade was divided into three parts. The stem, much broader than those of Borok and Permogore distaffs, was decorated with a branch with three spreading leaves. The center of the blade contained a square frame enclosing a bird, depicted with only a few dark strokes. The uppermost section, the largest and most boldly painted, was filled with an S-shaped branch bearing large leaves and twining tendrils. The inner side of the distaff was usually painted in the same way.

Freehand painting was not confined to any one region or group of artists; its distribution throughout the region, from Arkhangel'sk, Olonets, and Kargopol', through Vologda Province, and farther northeast toward the Urals along the rivers Vaga, Uftiuga, and Sukhona, may reflect increasing trade throughout these territories.[14] This kind of painting was particularly well suited to mural scale decoration, and the large, bold brushstrokes evident on some walls and cupboard doors suggest affinities to fresco painting.[15]

In freehand painting, whether geometrical or floral, the artists worked quickly, using wide brushes and sometimes bits of cloth or their fingers to spread the paint. Despite the rapid, relatively spontaneous handling of the paint, most compositions were balanced, if not perfectly symmetrical. Among the favorite motifs were flowering branches or baskets of flowers, usually placed in the center of a wall panel, on a cupboard door, or along the vertical axis of a distaff blade. These motifs contained virtually no suggestion of depth, but the edges of leaves or petals might be touched with a lighter green or rose tint, giving a slight effect of volume. On some pieces, especially on birch bark ornamented with small-scale designs, the artist used a fine black line to add a graphic contour or accent on top of the painted form. There were local variations within this approach. On distaffs from a village on the Vychegda River in Arkhangel'sk Province, flowers were arranged in a wreath around a brightly painted rosette; on those from another village, not far away on the river Vaga, blossoms were invariably arranged one above the other.[16]

Two distinct distaff types employed characteristics of both graphic and free-brush painting: the Mezen' type, from the Mezen' River basin in the north of Arkhangel'sk Province (fig. 6.4), and the Gorodets distaffs from the Volga area. Mezen' distaffs, painted in the village of Palashchel'e, were once widely distributed in the north, along the Mezen', Pinega, Pechora, and Northern Dvina rivers. In contrast to the three-part or centrally oriented compositions of most other northern distaffs, the Mezen' distaffs were divided horizontally into eight or more narrow rows made up of repeated abstract patterns or friezes of running horses or reindeer. The inner side of the blade was usually more casually arranged, with motifs such as riverboats, hunters with guns and dogs, or promenading ladies and cavaliers.

The geometrical patterns and the animals' bodies were painted freehand in a brownish-red or orange ocher against a golden or light orange background. Fine lines of black (soot mixed with oil) were drawn in to indicate the legs, manes, reins, or antlers of the horses or deer, or the zigzag, wave-like, or spiral lines which made up the bands of ornament. The quick, calligraphic lines produced a strong feeling of motion from left to right.

Gorodets artists also worked in both freehand and linear styles. A few distaffs and many storage containers were decorated with foliage designs painted freehand (much like those on Rakulka pieces) or with figures painted in thick black lines, accented with touches of

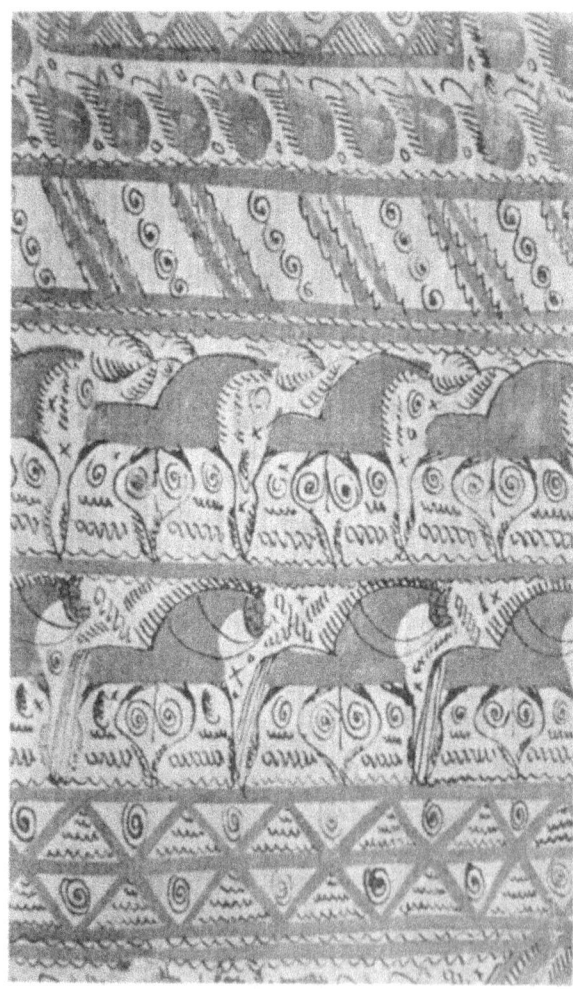

FIG. 6.4 Distaff. Wood, paint, soot-based ink. Mezen', Arkhangel'sk Province, early 20th century. Sergiev-Posad.

color. This type of painting was most common on bast boxes (*lukoshki*), on boxes for spindles (*mochesniki*), and on looms, sewing implements, and toys.[17] Some spindle boxes had designs reminiscent of Khokhloma dishes, produced in a neighboring district and sold in the same markets (mainly the *Makarevskaia iarmarka* in Nizhnii Novgorod). Others had more in common with Gorodets distaffs, with clearly defined human figures, horses, birds, and sometimes hints of landscape.

Gorodets distaffs with incrustation, made in the early and mid-nineteenth century, were hieratical in composition, but still conveyed a sense of liveliness and motion through the combination of schematized silhouette inlay for the bodies of horses or soldiers, and lightly engraved lines for arms, legs, sabers, or the branches of flowering trees. But when Gorodets artists used paint to replace the intricate and time-consuming techniques of inlay, they also had to find ways of creating both the silhouette effect and the flexibility of line. Lazar Mel'nikov was one of those who worked in both techniques: incrustation with painted accents and paint alone. By the end of the nineteenth century, several other artists developed styles combining firm, emphatic silhouettes and linear accents. The motifs of riders, flowering trees, and perching birds remained much the same as those on earlier distaff bases, and even the color scheme tended to preserve the strong contrast of light and dark, with the main figures painted black or ultramarine, accents of red, yellow, or green, and sometimes fine white lines over the dark shapes to indicate details of harness or costume.

Combining the techniques of geometrical carving, incrustation, and painting on a distaff base dated 1866, Mel'nikov arranged the composition as a series of horizontal bands containing different types of motifs (fig. 6.5). The traditional symmetrically balanced horsemen, tree, and perching bird filled the upper half of the base. A carved ornamental band separated this composition from a band of small painted figures on a bright red background—including two fashionable ladies with parasols, a man with a pipe, a woman spinning with a distaff, a cavalier, and a large dog—components of familiar genre scenes. Finally, at the lower border, a wider band contained a rearing horse, two dogs, three men, a bird, and two rosettes. This transitional piece, combining formulaic and descriptive approaches, indicates the essentially graphic and countour-oriented bases of Gorodets painting.

In slightly later pieces decorated with paint alone, the tight contours and extremely symmetrical compositions yielded to much more pliant lines and freer placement of figures within the frame. A distaff base by Vasilii Lebedev depicts a pair of riders, a "cavalier" and a fashionably dressed woman, in place of the traditional horsemen flanking a tree in the upper section. The figures look out of the picture, and the horses' noses and tails actually break out of the painted frame of the composition. On other distaffs, the portion formerly reserved for the horsemen, tree, and bird was occupied by a scene of a festive meal, so exact in its details that neighbors would recognize the participants. Painters Ignatii Lebedev, Petr Sundukov, and Ignatii Mazin all did many scenes of this sort in the early twentieth century. A distaff Mazin made for his fiancee (fig. 6.6) includes arched windows, artfully draped curtains, carved pillars, and even a parquet floor drawn in perspective: the trappings of city fashion as well as sophisticated representational devices. Mazin once told a scholar that he thought such elegant scenes more attractive to peasants than more traditional images.[18]

Many Gorodets masters replaced the traditional three-tier compositions with more spacious, and therefore more flexible, two-part paintings; the upper section increased in size and importance until it became almost an independent picture, while the more traditional symmetrical and heraldic motifs became part of a decorative border. Mazin painted not only distaffs but chair seats, storage boxes, and toys; he also began to produce paintings that were not part of the decoration of any object. He painted horizontal panels with scenes from peasant life, including a series of vignettes showing the preparation of flax, spinning and weaving, and the construction and decoration of a distaff. In style and technique, these scenes were outgrowths of his distaff paintings. But when distaffs became less than essential tools in the 1920s and 1930s, artists

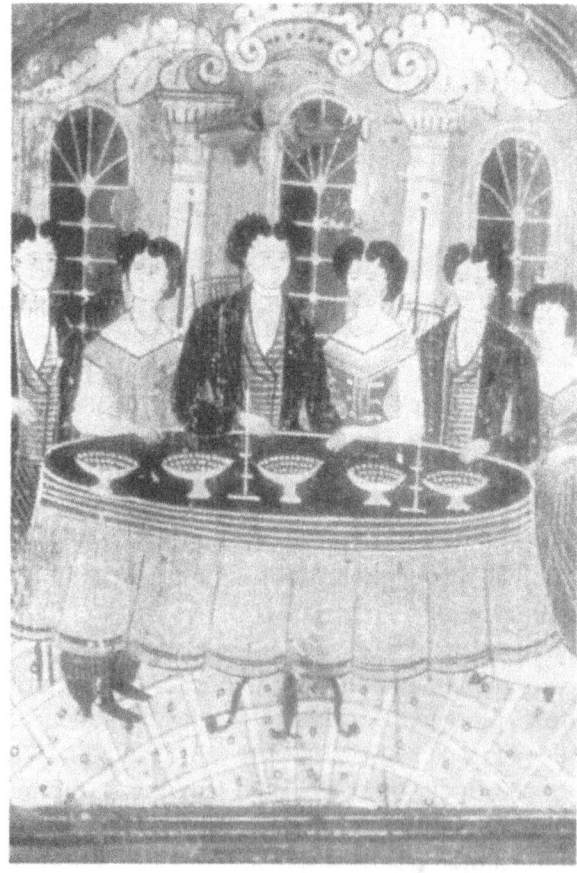

FIG. 6.6 Ignatii Mazin, distaff. Painted wood. Detail, interior scene. Gorodets, early 20th century. GIM.

such as Mazin had to find other areas in which to practice. These panels might be regarded as expansions of the small genre bands on traditional distaffs, but they were really closer in intention and function to the easel paintings that embellished town dwellings.

Textile Arts and Costume

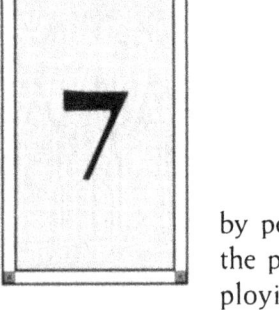

The festive garments worn compared with the decor of of many elements, each em- by peasant women might be the peasant house.[1] Made up ploying special techniques, with variations depending on occasion, region, age, status, and taste of the wearer, the peasant costume, like the house, was a complete ensemble. The costumes worn in Arkhangel'sk, Vologda, Novgorod, and Tver' provinces in the north, and in Riazan', Orel, and Voronezh in the south, illustrate the major components of peasant dress and the main forms of decoration.[2]

The basic garment of both men and women was the *rubakha*, a long shirt or shift (calf-length on women) made of homespun linen or commercial fabric, and usually embroidered. Young, unmarried women sometimes wore the *rubakha* alone in the summer, but married women always wore an overgarment, a *sarafan* in the north or a *poneva* (pronounced "ponyova") in the south. The *sarafan* was a full-length, sleeveless dress similar to a jumper. The most elegant *sarafany*, worn only on festive occasions by well-to-do peasants and townswomen in the north, were made of fine linen or silk, cut on a bias so that the four or six gores flared out from the narrow shoulders toward the ground. The shoulders and front were reinforced with a stiff lining and decorated with gold or silver thread, broad ribbons, and metal buttons. *Sarafany* for daily wear were of plain, checkered, or printed cloth, cut on the bias or from six straight widths of cloth, which were gathered at the yoke. *Sarafany* were usually belted at the waist with a sash (*poias*), braided or woven with geometrical designs and trimmed with bells or beads. The *perednik*, a full-length apron worn in most districts, was often the most conspicuous and elaborately decorated part of the costume.

Some occasions called for special costumes. For the first day of hay mowing in June, young women wore a special belted shirt called a "mowing" shirt, *pokosnitsa*, with a bright red or blue skirt (fig. 7.1). One traveler watching a grain harvest on a country estate admired the colorful effect of the peasants ranged across the landscape, "forming a brilliant picture in contrast with the yellow grain, in their blue and scarlet raiment."[3] For visits and holidays, women wore a short circular cape (*epanechka*) or a padded jacket (*dushegreia*) of brocade or velvet with heavy embroidery. Some women had fabric or leather shoes or low boots for holidays, but wore bast shoes (*lapti*) or went barefoot in summer, and wore felt boots in winter.

In the south, the basic costume consisted of a *rubakha* with an embroidered panel at the neck and shoulders and a *poneva*, a wraparound skirt made of three straight lengths of woolen or linen cloth, attached to a belt but not seamed together. They were often double-woven, of wool outside and cotton inside. In the nineteenth century, a true skirt sometimes replaced the *poneva*. The *poneva* was usually woven in a checkered or "windowpane" pattern and ornamented with embroidery and ribbons. A long, richly decorated *perednik* and, for holidays, a long, tunic-like *navershnik* were worn over the shirt and *poneva*.

In all regions, special garments and headdresses were required at particular stages of life, especially at the time of marriage and during the childbearing years. Several recent studies relate the designs and decoration of headdresses to embroidery motifs on other parts of costume, bed linens, and towels used in women's stage-of-life rituals.[4] Headdresses were among the most varied items of costume, ranging from a simple kerchief, *platok*, to elaborate *kokoshniki* worn for weddings. The significance of the head covering may be related to ancient beliefs shared by many cultures about the magic powers of hair. Peasant girls and unmarried women wore their hair in a single, long braid, sometimes entwined with ribbons. As part of the wedding ritual, the bride's plait was unbraided and then rebraided in the married woman's manner, two braids wrapped around the head and covered by a scarf or other headdress. The basic type of women's headdress in the north, the *kokoshnik* (fig. 7.2), varied greatly in shape: half-moon-shaped tiaras, tall miter-like structures, bonnets, pillbox-shaped hats, and caps bordered with netting strung with pearls all appear in eighteenth- and nineteenth-century paintings and in museum collections.[5] All types were covered with brocade, damask, silk, or velvet and embroidered with metallic threads, river pearls, sequins, and real or glass jewels. The *kichka* or *kika* of Riazan' and Tambov in the south had hornlike points at either side, sometimes with feathers or ribbons hanging from them.

Depending on the region, men wore the *rubakha* belted, hanging loosely like a smock or (in Ukraine) tucked into their trousers. The trousers, of plain or striped homespun, were bound into the rag leg wrappings most peasants wore with their plaited bast shoes (*lapti*), or tucked into high boots of felt (*valenki*) or leather (*sapogi*). The *kaftan*, the all-purpose outer garment, was a long, loose-fitting robe of heavy cloth, overlapped across the front to fasten at the left side. The most common hat, seen in mid-nineteenth-century photographs, was of felt, cylindrical and sometimes with a narrow brim. A sheepskin coat, *tulup* if long or *polushubka* if short, and a fur or sheepskin hat, often with earflaps, were worn in winter.

Flax, plentiful throughout most of Russia, was the major material for textiles.[6] Harvesting flax, soaking the sheaves to soften the stalks, drying and beating them to release the separate fibers, carding, spinning, and finally weaving the threads into cloth occupied women for many months of the year. Sometimes hemp, cotton, or wool was blended with flax to make cloth of particular weights or textures. In some regions garments were made of naturally bleached linen; in others, the fabric was dyed or printed, either at home or by itinerant craftsmen. Indigo and red were the most popular colors for

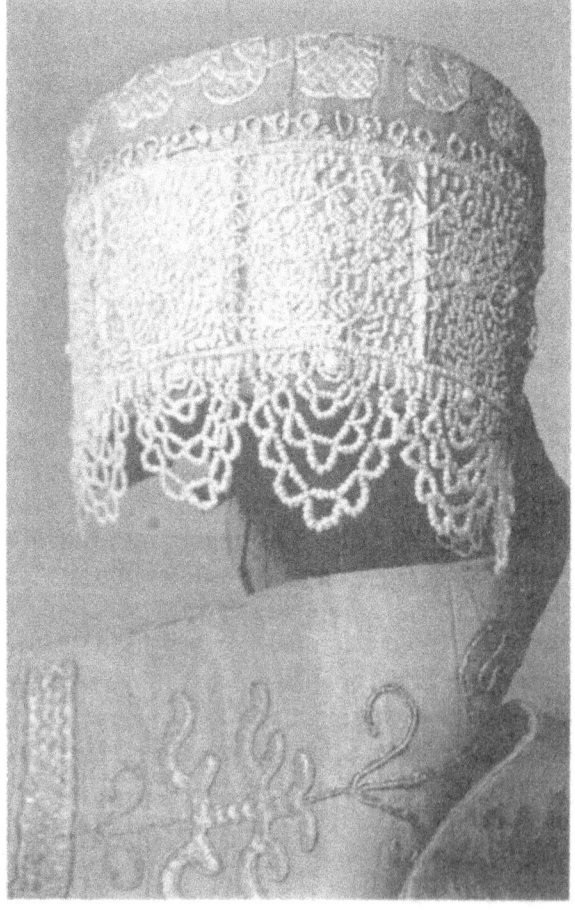

FIG. 7.2 *Kokoshnik* "Maiden's fillet." Embroidery, river pearls. Nizhnii Novgorod region, early 19th century. GRM.

fabric, while red, yellow, green, and black were the main colors in embroidered decorations. Garments, headwear, towels, sheets, bed valances, and table runners were richly embroidered with varicolored threads of flax, cotton, or silk and sometimes trimmed with lace, gold or silver thread, and river pearls.

The decoration of women's costumes and men's shirts and jackets was concentrated on the parts of the garment that were most readily visible and most important in a symbolic sense, such as the neck and shoulder of a shirt (fig. 7.3). On a young woman's *rubakha*, the embroidered design on a yoke or shoulder area was sometimes extended down the length of the sleeve, either on an applied strip of embroidery or in small motifs stitched directly onto the sleeve fabric.[7] Gussets and gores in shirts were usually embroidered or made of a contrasting fabric. *Sarafany* were decorated sparingly, along the edge of the bodice, the shoulder straps, the center of the back, or in a border slightly above the hem. Woven or braided sashes often displayed intricate patterns, and characteristics such as their length, color, and type of weaving identified the wearer's village and her kinship relationships, both important in arranging marriages.[8] Headdresses, always significant indicators of women's status, were the most lavishly decorated components of Russian costume.

Besides articles of clothing, other textiles found in the peasant household such as towel borders, bed valances,

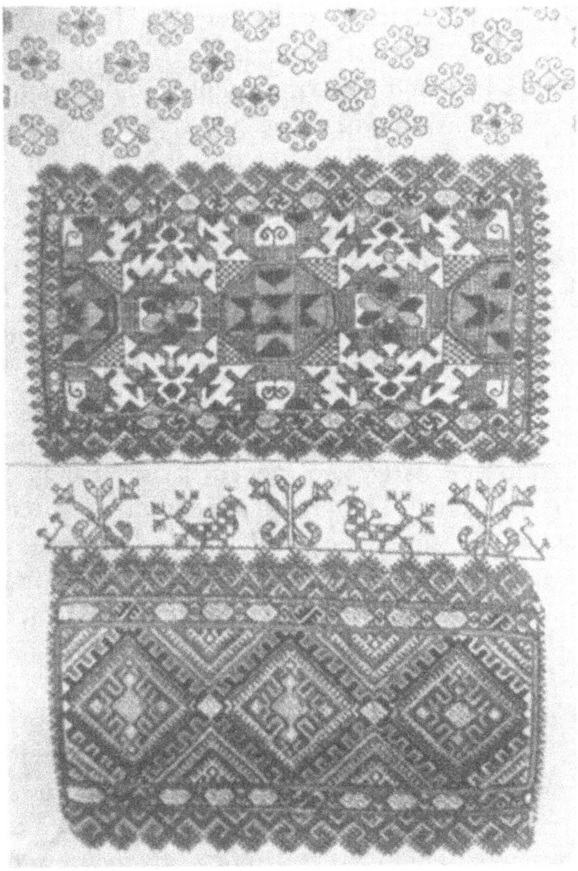

FIG. 7.3 Sleeve of *rubakha*. Embroidery on linen. North Russia, late 19th century. From Bilibin, in *Mir iskusstva* (1904).

sheets, and table runners had both ceremonial and esthetic value. Towels were especially important, as they were draped around windows and icons; dozens were used at various stages in the wedding ceremony; they were held out to receive a newborn child; and they were placed over a grave at the end of a funeral service. Many decorative and ceremonial textiles were made for the same occasions at which decorated serving utensils or distaffs presented as gifts might be used.

Historically, textiles were important in both church and secular settings. In tenth-century Kiev, court women embroidered in their chambers; in twelfth-century Novgorod and fourteenth- and fifteenth-century Moscow, women of royal families and nuns embroidered church vestments and covers for altars, palls, and icons. They used silk and metallic thread, made by wrapping a linen or silk core with strips of gold or silver leaf, a technique used in antiquity and perhaps introduced to Russia from Byzantium. Workshops established in the seventeenth century by the Godunovs in Sergiev-Posad and by the Stroganovs in Sol'vychegodsk made vestments and secular articles of expensive materials, including pearls, silk ribbons, precious stones, and mother-of-pearl plaques, often in designs shared with traditional folk ornament: heraldic lions, unicorns, birds, mythical creatures, and the many-branched tree of life.[9]

Methods of decorating textiles included pattern weaving, usually featuring checkered or "windowpane" designs, for the *poneva* and *perednik*; printing by means of carved wooden matrices; embroidery on strips of plain linen to be sewn to the garment or fit into printed or woven patterns; and crocheted or bobbin lace. In pattern weaving or "embroidered weaving," *branoe tkachestvo*, colored threads were woven through the cloth to make geometrical designs or stylized figural patterns. Some of the woven patterns, including rhomboids, meanders, and swastikas woven with white threads into colored fabric, were given the designations "scythe," "comb," and "rake,"[10] suggesting vivid associations with field work. In the north, where unbleached linen was preferred, weavers drew three or four pairs of warp threads together to create texture and pattern, or added narrow bands of red-on-white patterns into the borders.[11] The art of multicolored pattern weaving was highly developed in the south, especially for making *ponevy*. Variations in color and pattern denoted regional differences, kinship ties, and the age of the wearer. For instance, in one district in Riazan' Province, the *poneva* of a young woman had mainly red threads on a blue or black ground in the checked pattern, called a "red-eye" weave, and that of an elderly woman was woven in the "white-eye" style, with white threads predominating.[12] Several regions exhibited distinct color preferences in weaving: red thread on white in most areas of the north; in the south, patterns of light or red threads against dark backgrounds, or sometimes black on white. The woven patterns would always be seen in combination with the designs and colors of embroidery: in Tambov, bold black geometric designs, some-times with gold and silver threads; in Riazan', red, white, and black; in Tula, white, red, and blue; in Voronezh, black or red on white, or red, yellow, green, blue, and black on red backgrounds; in Smolensk, red, yellow, or-ange, blue, and black. *Ponevy* were also decorated with ribbon or strips of printed fabric along the hem and up the side where the overskirt was fast-ened, and on the inner side of the overlapping section.

Special techniques of weaving were used to make the kerchiefs and shawls worn by all married women. The earliest form of scarf was called *shirinka* (from "width"): made from an entire width of fabric, and embroidered in satin stitch with silk and metallic threads, it was held in the hands at church, during visits, and at wedding ceremonies. Simple scarves were woven by peasant women at home, but by the seventeenth century textile factories in Moscow Province and in the north were producing linen, silk, and brocade scarves, bought by merchant-class women and well-to-do peasants. A distinctive double-weaving technique that created identical patterns on both sides of the fabric was invented at the beginning of the nineteenth century by Nadezhda Merlina. She was not a peasant but a carpet manufacturer of the merchant class, who established a factory in the village of Skorodumovka, part of her estate in Nizhnii Novgorod Province. Merlina's factory employed sixty village women who worked in pairs for six months to weave each shawl; it produced only sixteen shawls and five scarves in a year.[13] Merlina's shawls, made of the finest cashmere from Tibet, could be bought only by wealthy women, but they provided models for less expensive shawls and kerchiefs made in quan-tity on Jacquard looms by the middle of the century. In the 1860s, the town of Pavlovsk in the Moscow district became the center of a thriving shawl-weaving industry, producing wool and cotton scarves marketed throughout the country in the nineteenth century, and still popular today.

Embroidery developed in distinct styles in every region, but achieved the most varied and sumptuous forms in the north of Russia, especially in Arkhangel'sk, Vologda, Olonets, and Tver' provinces (fig. 7.4). The wide range of stitches—satin stitch, cross-stitch and half-cross-stitch, a slanted darning stitch, brick stitch, chain stitch, hooked stitch, and many types of drawn-thread work—allowed a great deal of flexibility in creating designs.[14] Several standard motifs were made up of combinations of the basic stitches, and in turn were put together to make repeated patterns or more complex, figurative designs. Many simple patterns found in borders were based on the rhomboid form with various internal or external elaborations: some of these were commonly called the "frog," "rabbit," "hook," "finger," "comb," "horse," "sheep," and "windmill."[15]

More complex designs, embroidered in metallic threads on *kokoshniki* (fig. 7.5), at the hems of garments, and on the borders of towels and valances, featured the same archaic subjects, stylized figures, animals, trees, and mythological beings found in carved and painted woodwork and other media.[16] In some early nineteenth-century embroideries from Tver′ Province, large single motifs—a tree, bird, or standing woman with upraised arms—dominate the composition, while much smaller figures surround it, filling in the areas left by angles or protrusions.[17] In contrast, many later designs are characterized by balanced two- or three-part compositions, in which each of the main figures is approximately the same size. Sometimes narrower rows of rhythmically repeating or alternating figures were placed above or below the main composition. The border figures were highly stylized, the limbs of a tree conflated with the tail feathers of a peacock, the double heads of a heraldic eagle, or the upraised arms of a female figure. The patterns of the stitchery gave rise to geometric elaboration of branches, feathers, or sunrays, almost to the point of abstraction. The distinction between stylization and abstraction was not always clear or important. As in other media, the most pervasive forms, lozenges or rhomboids, sometimes with internal spirals, swastikas, rays, or crosses—symbols of the sun and its life-giving power—were incorporated into the bodies of heraldic animals and into geometrical border designs. Embroidery stitches, especially variations on the cross-stitch, were well suited to these forms.

The area available for decoration on an apron or shirt was fairly large. An apron or a sleeve might be covered with small repeated abstract forms, but compositions with figures were usually

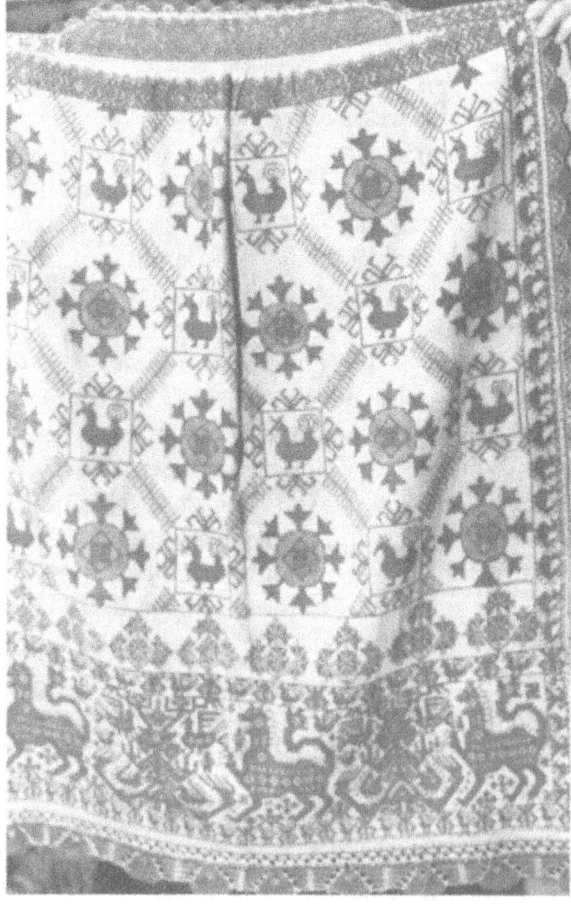

FIG. 7.4 *Perednik* (apron). Embroidery on linen. Vologda Province, 19th century. GIM.

arranged in horizontal bands at the shoulders or hem. Similarly, on towels the main ornamentation was concentrated at the ends, which were meant to hang down around windows or icons, or from a tray held out in ceremonial welcome. Often as much as fifty centimeters in depth, the embroidered towel borders were treated as a series of bands, some wide and displaying figural or heraldic motifs, some quite narrow with repeated patterns, and sometimes with inset bands of weaving, printed fabric, or lace (figs. 12.12–12.14). The borders of wedding towels often included kinship or clan-related patterns, like other textiles for dowry chests and marriage ceremonies. The principle of symmetry was more consistent in textiles than in decorated woodwork. The only exceptions were single figures (peacocks, horses, or horses with riders) in profile, but these figures were paired visually with counterparts at the opposite end of the towel or the other sleeve of a shirt.

Lace (*kruzhevo*), made separately and sewn on to the edges of garments and towels, often complemented the patterns of openwork weaving or embroidery. Though technically more limited than embroidery in the range of designs, lace borders contained the same motifs, such as rhomboids, trees and branches, double-headed eagles, peacocks, and horses (fig. 7.6). Early descriptions of textiles used the term *kruzhevo* for many kinds of trim, including netting strung with river pearls and openwork with embroidery, but in the eighteenth and nineteenth centuries the word meant a band made of threads worked by braiding or crocheting. Metallic threads were often used for lace trim on ecclesiastical textiles and ceremonial costume, but most peasant women worked with undyed thread. The usual method, called "pricked" lace, used a pricked design on a pattern attached to a small rectangular pillow, as a guide for locating pins and forming the loops; another method, without a pattern, required counting the interlacing threads. Small wooden pegs (*kokliushki*) were used to hold the separate threads (fig. 14.4). Crochet hooks were also used to make either a chainlike pattern, *stsepnoe* ("coupled" or "linked") lace, or to work designs into a background of woven net or tulle, a method called *parnoe* ("paired" or "straight") lace. There were many refinements, and several techniques were often used together on a single piece.[18] In the nineteenth century there were twelve important centers of lacemaking, as distinctive stylistically as the embroidery of different regions: Vologda lace, probably the best-known and most widely distributed type, is still prized today.

Printed fabric, *naboika*, was used for *sarafany*, *kaftany*, and other garments, for tablecloths and curtains, and for ecclesiastical vestments and hangings. Sometimes the printed linen or cotton was of such fine quality that it was used in combination with expensive brocade and trim. Early printing blocks and fragments of fabric show the same repeated motifs found in other arts, such as rhomboids, crosses, flowers, foliage, and small birds.[19] Some prints intended as hangings rather than for dress featured large focal figures, such as the Christian saints, legendary characters, and mythical beings found in wood-

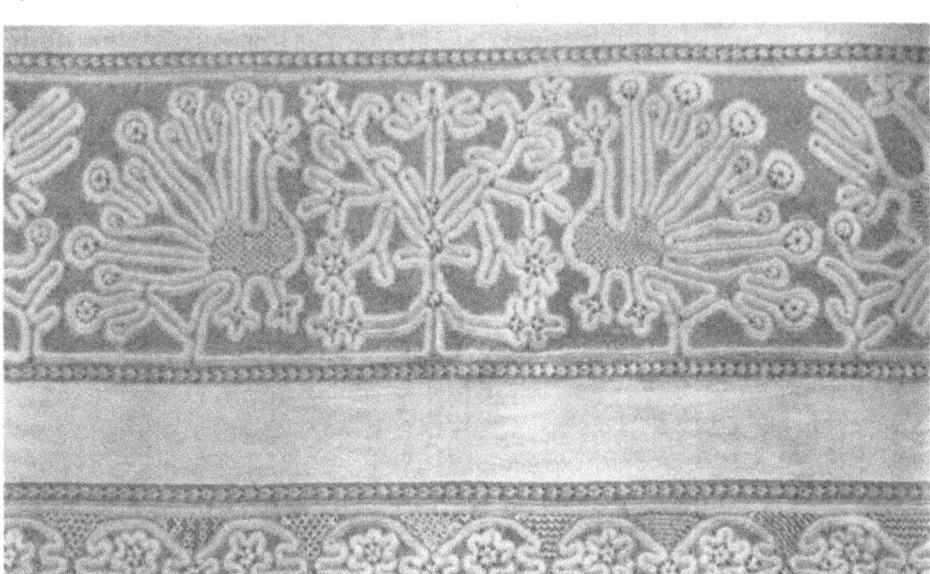

FIG. 7.6　Bed valance. Lace. Nizhnii
Novgorod region, early 19th century.
GIM.

work, tiles, and printed broadsheets (*lubki*). The figures were printed in black
or reddish brown on unbleached linen, sometimes with details of the design
added by hand.

Two techniques were used for printing cloth. In one method, the board
was covered with oil-based paint, placed against a wet piece of linen, and
pressed with a wooden roller; in the other, the printer held the board
against the cloth and struck it with a cloth-covered mallet. By the seventeenth century, additional colors were printed by superimposing two or
three blocks.

In addition to "white-ground" or unbleached fabric, indigo-dyed cloth
became popular, especially among peasants. For dark cloth, a different technique, called "reserved" printing, similar to resist dyeing, was used. The board
was covered with a mixture of clay, vitriol, and glue, called *vapa*, and pressed
onto the white cloth, in effect printing it with this substance. The cloth was
then submerged in a vat filled with the blue dye until it was deeply colored,
except where the reserved designs remained white. This technique was common throughout Russia by the nineteenth century. A wide variety of patterns
could be created through the juxtaposition of different *manery* and the addi-

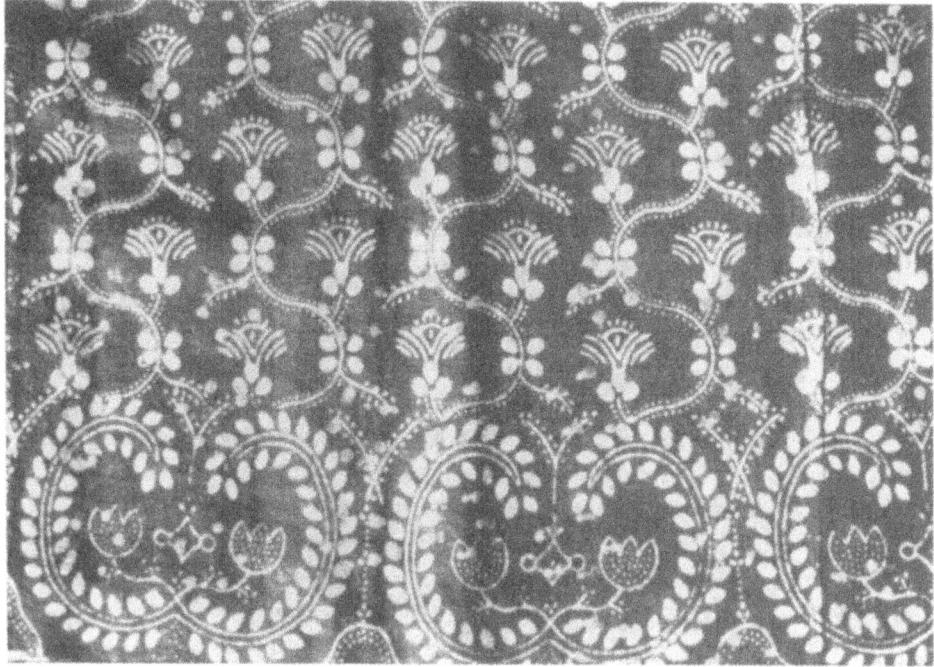

FIG. 7.7 *Naboika.* Repeated pattern and border, on indigo-dyed linen with saffron highlights. Late 19th century. GIM.

tion of stenciled highlights. Indigo prints with foliage motifs were often touched up by hand with "peas" of saffron dye (fig. 7.7).

Printing cloth was not difficult to do at home. Many peasant women owned one or two boards and printed their own borders for curtains, kerchiefs, and pillows, although they took larger orders to specialists in the craft. At certain times of year, traveling printers visited the villages, bringing sample lengths of cloth printed with the various designs in stock. Both the *manery* and the printed cloth could also be purchased at fairs.

In common with wooden objects, textiles sometimes bore names, dates, or other messages. Inscriptions were embroidered, worked in drawn-thread techniques or in crocheted lace, especially on towels made as wedding gifts. Textiles also shared the most important abstract and figural designs found in woodwork; the archaic, symbolic motifs could be rendered in all the textile techniques. Similarities of motif and design could be striking within a given region, but there were also noticeable differences in the ways common forms were applied. For instance, architectural motifs, with their angular forms, were well suited to textiles. But they were usually made into repeated border patterns, in contrast to the specific local references on spicecake boards or birchbark and niello boxes. Figurative decoration in embroidery or lace was usually symmetrical or in repeated patterns. Images reflecting changes in rural life were relatively rare, in contrast to the frequency of genre scenes of tea drinking, promenades, and carriage rides on distaffs and other wooden tools used in the textile arts.

Formal similarities between wood and textile work are most striking in the repeated patterns filling relatively large areas and more concentrated designs in the borders that separate the main sections of a composition. Three-faceted carving or chip carving on distaffs from Vologda Province sometimes covered the entire distaff blade, while variations in the form of the cut created distinctive patterns, such as checks, spirals, and rosettes that would interact with one another and articulate the surface. In a similar way, the basic embroidery stitches could be varied to enliven a large background area or the body of a horse or bird, and simultaneously echo and accentuate patterns in the border areas. In contrast, the painted designs of northern distaffs, featuring spreading floral ornaments and figural scenes, had their closest formal parallel in tambour-style embroidery, with its continuous ribbonlike, rather than squared-off, contours. In both distaffs and embroidery, the demarcations between sections of a composition were established by contrasting geometrical border motifs. In the case of *naboika*, formal similarities were even closer, because the carved printing blocks were made by means of the same techniques used for spicecake molds, stovetile molds, and blocks for printing *lubki*. However, the repeated patterns on printed cloth were always intended to be seen in juxtaposition with embroidered, crocheted, or woven designs which embellished parts of the peasant costume.

Peasant clothing was both conservative and adaptable. The reforms of Peter the Great, requiring all subjects except priests and peasants to wear Western-style clothing, did not change peasant dress. However, just as peasant carvers, painters, and makers of *lubki* and toys picked up ideas from current urban fashions, peasant women willingly used factory-made cloth and trim, often in addition to homemade goods. Cotton embroidery yarn and chemical dyes made from coal-tar products became widely available at the turn of the twentieth century, and they were frequently used in tambour-style embroidery. The bright yellow, purple, green, and orange shapes outlined in white chain stitch were especially striking on red calico cloth. Early twentieth-century towel borders, valances, and hems of *rubakhi* from Olonets in the north exhibit this type of embroidery in combination with strips of ribbon or lace; costumes from Kharkov and Voronezh provinces in the south combined pattern weaving with aniline dyes and strips of purchased trim.[20]

The introduction of machines for weaving, printing, and even embroidery brought further changes. By the 1830s, mechanical printing presses had been introduced in many regions. Although dyers still traveled to small villages, the more efficient printing artels in towns and market centers took over most of the business. Factory-printed calico replaced *naboika* for shirts and *sarafany*. Calico kerchiefs from numerous factories in Vladimir and Moscow provinces, often printed with folklike floral designs on red, easily outsold woven shawls. Gradually, the dyeing and printing of cloth changed from being a peasant art to a town industry.

Weaving also became the province of handicraft artels and regional centers, rather than peasant households. High-quality linen was still woven by hand in the late nineteenth and early twentieth centuries, and peasant weavers could sell fabrics through local outlets and obtain further orders or credit for supplies through such distribution centers. Increasingly, however, competition from factory-made woolen and cotton goods led to the disappearance of linen from the large markets. It was largely thanks to the rescue efforts by artists and others concerned about preserving the traditional crafts that linen weaving, embroidery, and *naboika* enjoyed a revival and some commercial success at the turn of the century.[21] Machine embroidery was common by the early twentieth century, especially for geometrical borders and tambour-style designs. However, like small-scale decorative painting and carving, embroidery and crocheted lace, essentially handwork, were less directly affected than weaving and printing either by changes in technology or by requirements of specialized markets.

What did affect these art forms, however, were changes in village life after the turn of the century. In most regions, traditional peasant costumes were gradually replaced by manufactured town garments, except for occasions such as the first day of harvest or weddings. One American traveler who attended a village wedding in 1895 wrote, prophetically, that the sight of peasants in their colorful shirts and *sarafany* was "becoming a precious rarity."[22] Pelageia Amosova and many of her fellow painters stopped making distaffs at the end of the 1920s because, as she explained, women bought their cloth instead of spinning and weaving it.[23] *Posidelki* no longer had their traditional role, and many of the motifs traditionally depicted on distaffs lost their meaning. Although textile arts adapted to many changes, the disruptions of social structures in the twentieth century brought an end to the evolution of costume as a genre.

Beyond the Village: Specialized Crafts and Urban Folk Art

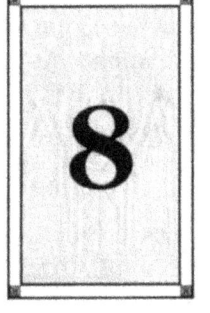

The overlapping of local markets and urban settings of all forms of Russian folk traditions and stimuli from influenced the development art. Even the woodworking and textile arts, most directly connected with peasant life, absorbed motifs and technical innovations from other spheres. This chapter focuses on several types of folk art whose development involved the borrowing and sharing of materials and techniques not available to all peasants, and sometimes relied on urban or distant markets. Some art forms in this category, such as carving in birch bark and bone, were regional specializations influenced by techniques of woodcarving. Crafts requiring special materials, equipment, and skills, such as metalsmithing and pottery, were practiced in most villages, but in urban settings they developed far beyond the level of village technology.

As folk art genres traveled beyond the boundaries of their original villages or regions, they acquired new uses and monetary value as applied or decorative arts. Yet even highly specialized and costly works, such as silver and niello boxes, retained traces of the traditional techniques and images of their sources. The differences between folk art and applied or decorative art had more to do with the attitudes of the artist and the consumer, with intention and audience, than with materials, although the dividing line was not always clear. Increasingly, as folk art reached the great markets of Nizhnii Novgorod, Moscow, and foreign cities, the makers and users of the objects belonged to different cultural environments. On the other hand, the *kustar'* (cottage) industries of the late nineteenth century and many types of decorative and applied arts took forms or motifs from folk arts, or deliberately quoted "primitive" or "folk" styles. The growing contact between folk and professional artists and the mingling of local and cosmopolitan styles and practices may have diluted the purity of folk art, as some nineteenth-century observers feared. However, folk art did not exist in a museumlike vacuum, and it could not have developed in isolation from real life, as the artist Ivan Bilibin pointed out at the turn of the century.[1] The forms, media, and practices described in this chapter were the province of both folk artists and urban artists with professional training. Both groups contributed to the repertoire of images and refinements in techniques. These specialized art forms illustrate, even more clearly than woodworking and textile arts, the complex relationships that determined the development of Russian folk arts.

Carved Lace of Birch Bark and Bone

A special technique of delicate, openwork carving known as "northern lace" was used to decorate small boxes and caskets made in northern Russia of carved birch bark and of animal bone or tusk. Although birch bark was pliable and soft, while bone was dense and sometimes brittle, both substances responded well to techniques for small-scale ornamentation by means of cutting, drilling, engraving, and stamping patterns, and rubbing incised lines with color.

The art of carving birch bark was centered in several small villages on the river Shemoksa, near Velikii Ustiug (fig. 8.1), where masters such as the Veprev family worked from the early nineteenth century.[2] The birch tree, sacred in Russian folklore, was used for every conceivable purpose: the wood for tools and furniture; twigs for the bath; tar for soap and medicine; and thin strips from the layer under the bark for paper.[3] Among the earliest examples of writing found in Russia were letters and signs scratched onto strips of birch bark.

To decorate a birch-bark surface, an artist inscribed lines with a stylus, punched patterns with an awl, or stamped designs by holding a hardwood or metal form against the soft bark and striking it with a small hammer. A writer visiting Velikii Ustiug in the eighteenth century described these techniques, adding that some artists used extremely sharp blades to cut through the birch bark and make a silhouette design.[4] Chelishchev's report on the Prokop'ev

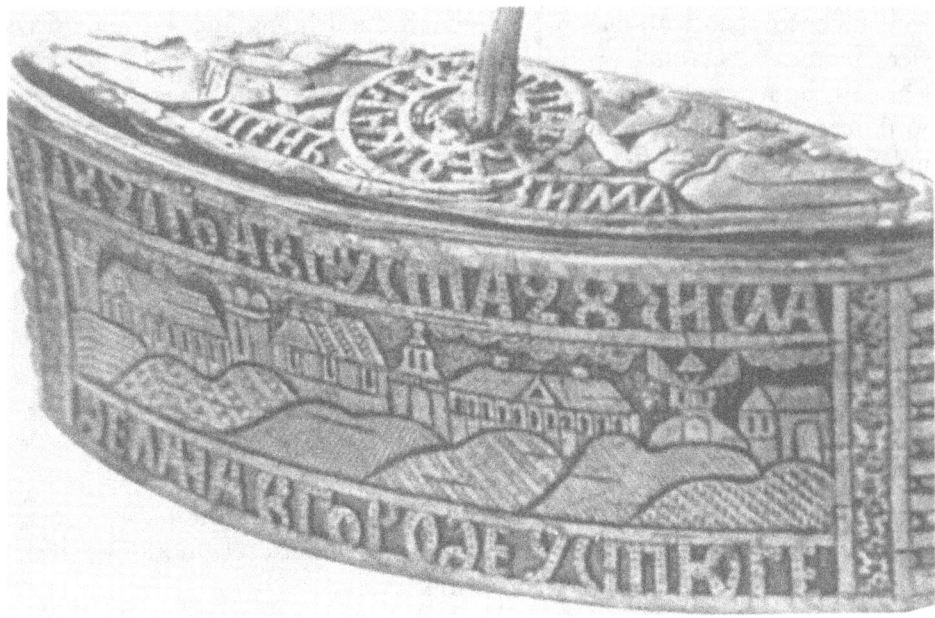

FIG. 8.1 Stepan Bochkarev, snuffbox.
Birch bark, openwork, line engraving.
Detail, Velikii Ustiug vista. Kad'iakov
village, near Velikii Ustiug, Vologda
Province, early 19th century. GIM.

Market at Velikii Ustiug also mentioned birch-bark boxes with stamped and
cut-out designs.[5] By the 1880s, 168 masters from 110 households were engaged in the craft.[6] Some of them advertised their wares. An inscription on
one decorated birch box announces: "In Velikii Ustiug the very best boxes of
first quality—Master boxmaker Grigorii Semenov[ich] Sobonovskii worked
1865, 18th day of March."[7]

The process of making birch containers began in the spring, when villagers from Kurovo-Navolok went into the woods to select several well-grown
birch trees. They cut sections from the upper layers of bark, always leaving a
strip of bark wide enough to keep the trees healthy. When enough bark was
gathered for a year's work, it was conditioned in water, dried, smoothed, and
polished. Then two layers of birch bark were placed one inside the other so
that the grain of one layer ran perpendicularly to that of the other. This lami-
nating made the bark strong and watertight. To make a cylindrical container,
the artist fastened the edges of the birch strips with an ingenious "lock," somewhat like a zipper, made by cutting slits into one edge of the bark and forcing

projections of the other end into them. The cylinder was attached to a base of birch wood. Some containers were stamped or painted with geometrical designs or with flower, leaf, or bird motifs like those on many wooden vessels; others were carved shallowly in patterns much like the rosettes and fans found on chip-carved wooden objects.

For more elegant effects, artists decorated the outer layer of birch bark with openwork carving before attatching it to the inner layer. They sometimes chose a darker-toned wood for the inner layer to create a visual contrast, or inserted thin strips of colored foil or paper behind the openings cut into the outer layer. This technique created an effect comparable to parcel-gilt metalwork, which was one of the arts practiced in Velikii Ustiug. It is likely that the first decorated birch bark was meant to resemble the engraved patterns on metal: in the seventeenth century, large trunks made of wood with ornamental wrought-iron bands were sometimes decorated with panels of birch bark, cut in patterns echoing those of the ironwork. Later, the art of birch-bark carving was devoted mainly to decorating smaller boxes for keeping cards, gloves, tallies for board games, or tobacco.

The varied shapes of the boxes gave rise to interesting compositions and framing devices. Some artists used engraved parallel lines and cross-hatching to give textural variety to the design; others invented intricate patterns of floral, geometrical, and lacelike designs, often including inscriptions done in openwork. The sides, ends, and top of a box, and even the inside of the lid, displayed city vistas; genre scenes much like the tea-drinking or card-playing scenes found on niello work; traditional heraldic and mythical creatures of folklore, such as lions, gryphons, and *bereginy*; and scenes adapted from book illustrations or *lubki*.

The decoration on the lid of a box made by Stepan Bochkarev in 1817 (fig. 8.2) resembles a niello engraving: a picture set within a shadow-box frame made up of five progressively smaller lacelike borders. With realistic scale and perspective, it shows a fox peering into a stone well as a goat pokes its head out—the setting and characters of an Aesop fable. Bochkarev evidently used an illustrated Russian translation of the fables published in St. Petersburg in 1792.[8] He adapted the print without copying it exactly. The expanded background with a house, two kinds of trees and flowers, and the dog and rooster watching the clever fox and unfortunate goat were additions that made the scene more specific and lifelike.

It is not surprising that artists who were literate and in close contact with a large city took advantage of styles and fashions associated with other art forms. Although birch-bark containers originally had a practical function, and decorating them required only simple tools and materials, and although a carver as successful as Ivan Veprev identified himself as a peasant, this art gradually took on the character of an urban specialization rather than a craft based on the requirements of peasant life.

MATERIALS AND FORMS

Carving in bone and walrus tusks went through a comparable evolution from an art tied closely to life in the northern coastal regions, where there was little wood, to a luxury art associated first with the Moscow court and later with international trade. The use of bone dated from prehistoric times, in Russia as elsewhere, and there is evidence that bone embellished with decorative carving was common before the Mongol invasions of Russia in the thirteenth century. Combs and other small items of bone were found in excavations at Pskov and Novgorod. The development of bonecarving as an art form may have been influenced by the Byzantine carvings of elephant ivory brought to Kiev in the tenth and eleventh centuries, but there were independent sources of technique and design in the north.[9] Mammoth bone and tusks were once abundant in Siberia and were carved into miniature animal forms by the Yakuts and other Siberian natives.

Walrus ivory was a major resource in the area bordering the White Sea. Kholmogory, the administrative capital of the northern region, on a tributary of the Northern Dvina River near the White Sea, was a center for deep-sea fishing and for bone and ivory carving. When Arkhangel'sk was founded in 1584 as Russia's northern port, Kholmogory shared the convenience of a trade route between Europe and the interior of Russia. In the sixteenth century, "fishes' teeth" (walrus tusks) were sold in Moscow and abroad; and in 1649 Tsar Aleksei Mikhailovich published an *ukaz* making trade in northern ivory a state monopoly.[10] Northern carvers brought to Moscow to work in the Armory Palace produced extremely fine carved bone icons, decorative panels for furniture, combs, and small luxury items. Some master carvers went to Velikii Ustiug, Sol'vychegodsk, and other northern cities, and artists traveled to Moscow from many parts of Russia, Poland, and Germany in order to work with the Kholmogory bonecarvers and learn their skills. By the late seventeenth century, ivory carving was no longer exclusively a folk art. It was modified by court patronage, by contact with artists trained in European styles, and by access to nontraditional models.

Information about the early ivory carvers in Moscow and Kholmogory exists in records of payments and commissions; master carvers began to gain recognition after Peter the Great took up bonecarving as a hobby during a summer visit to Arkhangel'sk in 1693. In the eighteenth century, bonecarving shared the status and many aspects of style and imagery of other decorative arts at the courts of Empresses Elizabeth and Catherine II,[11] again blurring the distinction between folk and applied art.

The carving techniques, openwork and engraving, required firm control on the hard, smooth surfaces of plaques cut from bone or tusk. Seldom more than an inch or two wide and up to four or five inches long, the plaques had to be cut even smaller to fit curved or indented forms. In openwork carving, an artist took a smoothed plate, drew a design on it, perforated the surface with a drill, and cut outward from the hole with a knife. Special scraping and

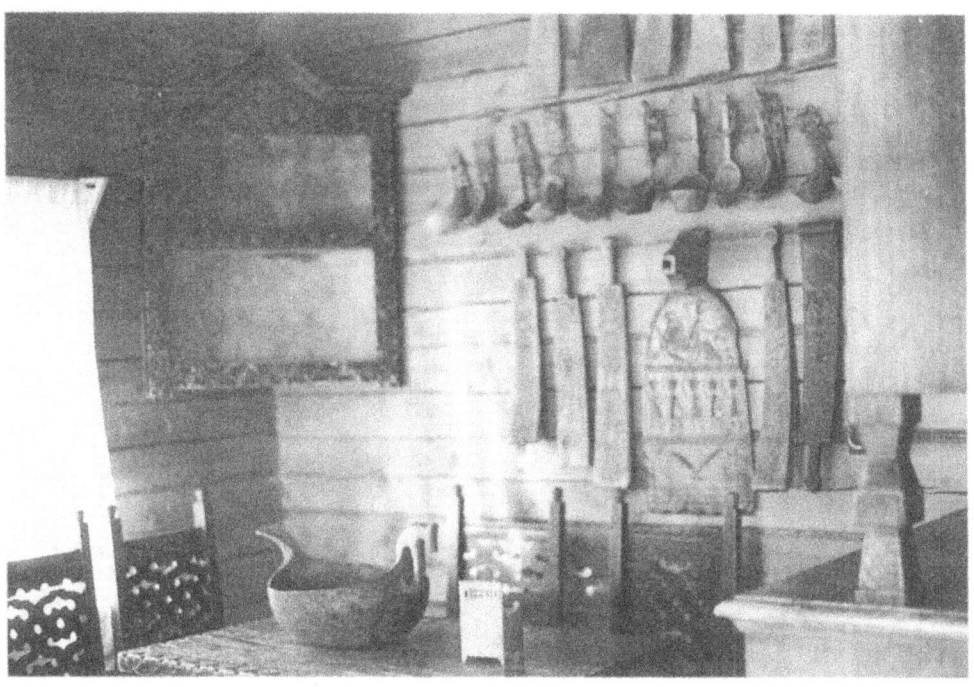

1.1 Folk utensils in the Abramtsevo collection.

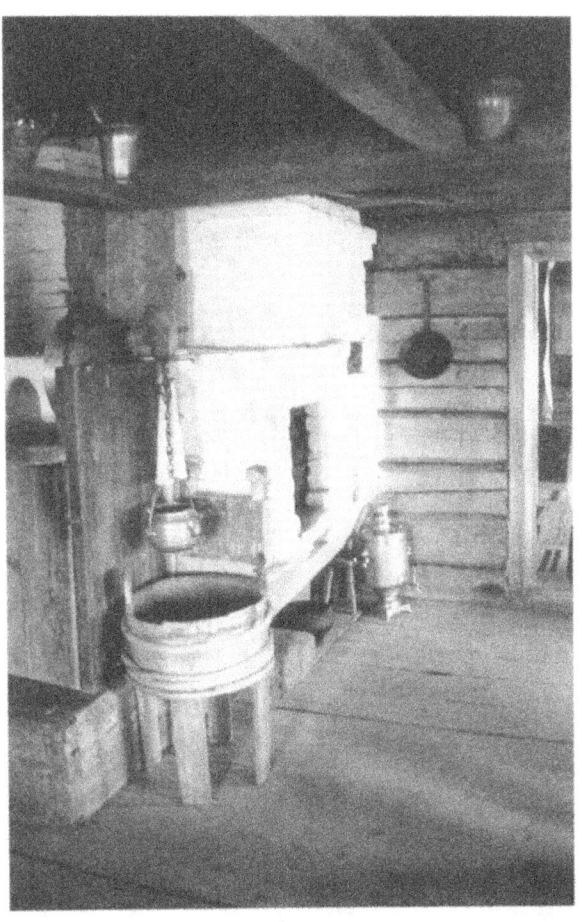

2.9 Iakovlev house, interior of main room. Kleshcheila village, Karelia, 1880–90.

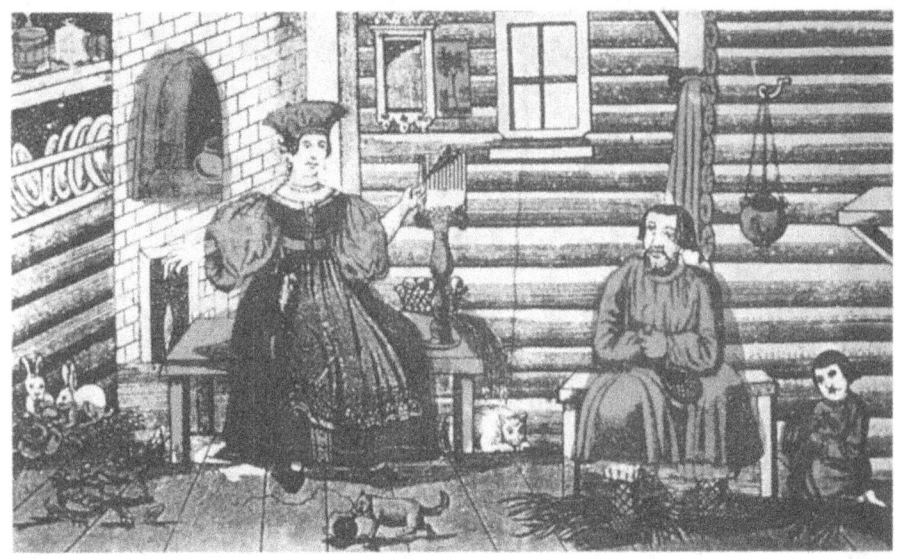

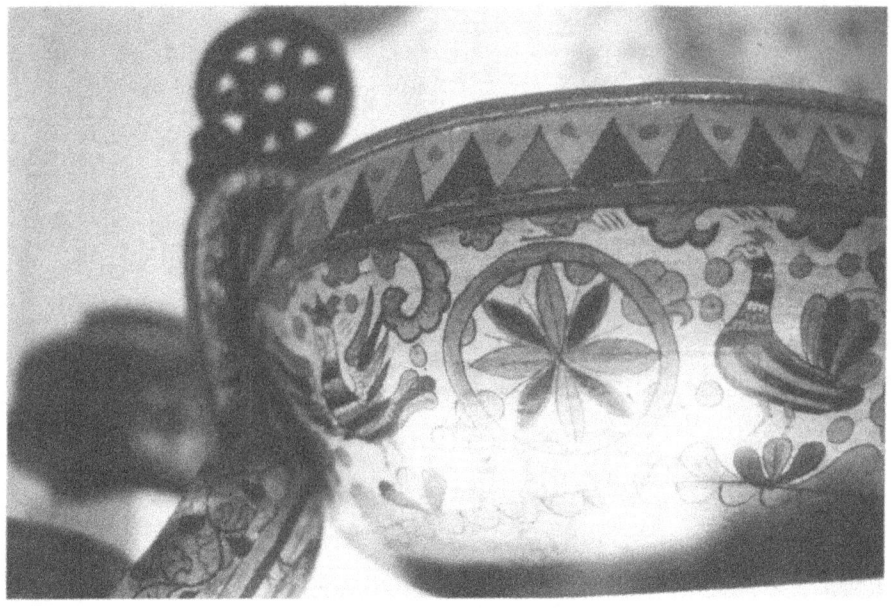

3.1 "Spin away my spinner, don't be lazy." *Lubok.*
Moscow, 1859.

3.6 *Miska* (dinner bowl) with ladle. Northern Dvina,
late 19th century.

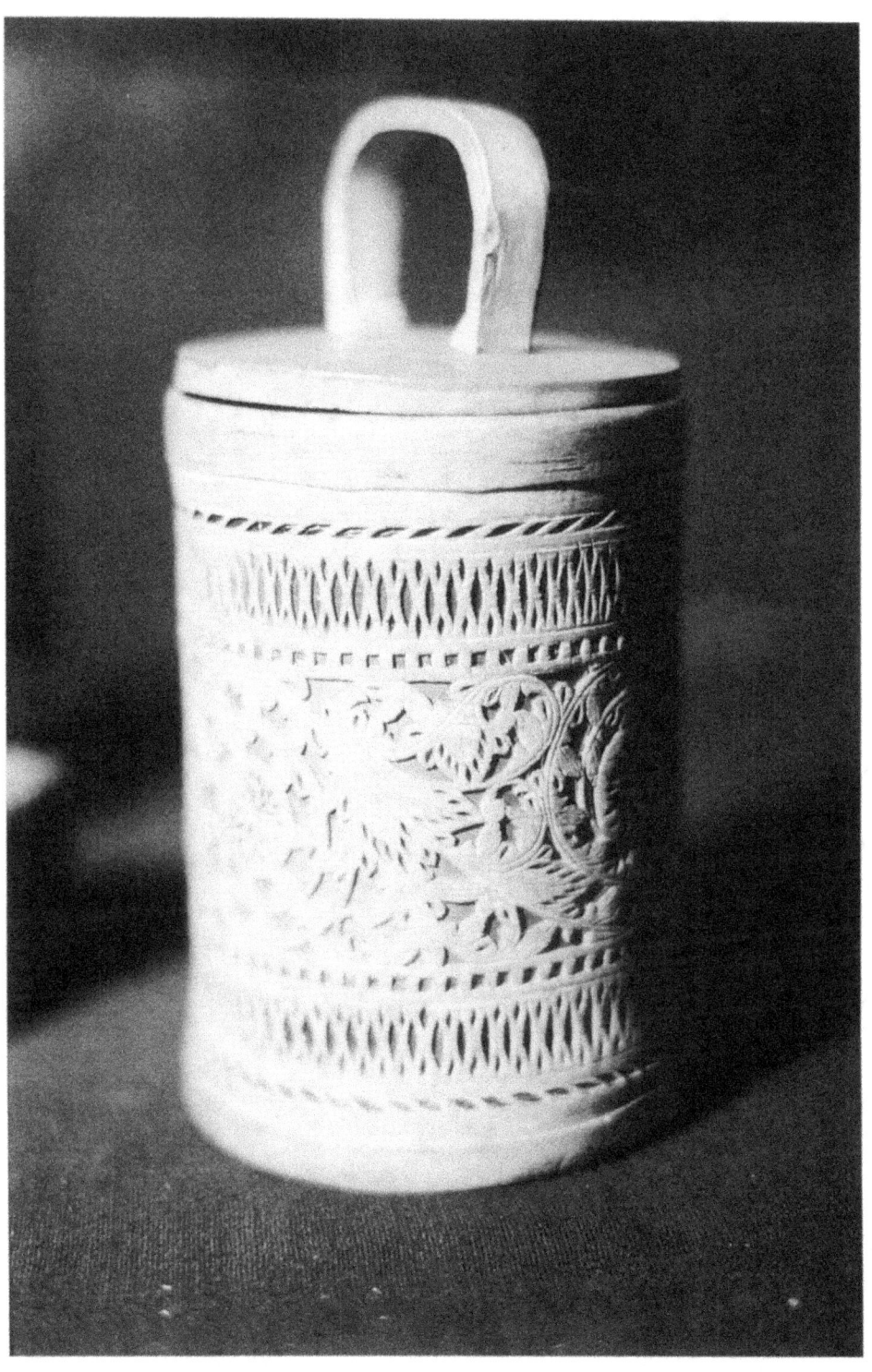

3.7 *Burak* canister. Shemogodsk region, Vologda
Province, early 20th century.

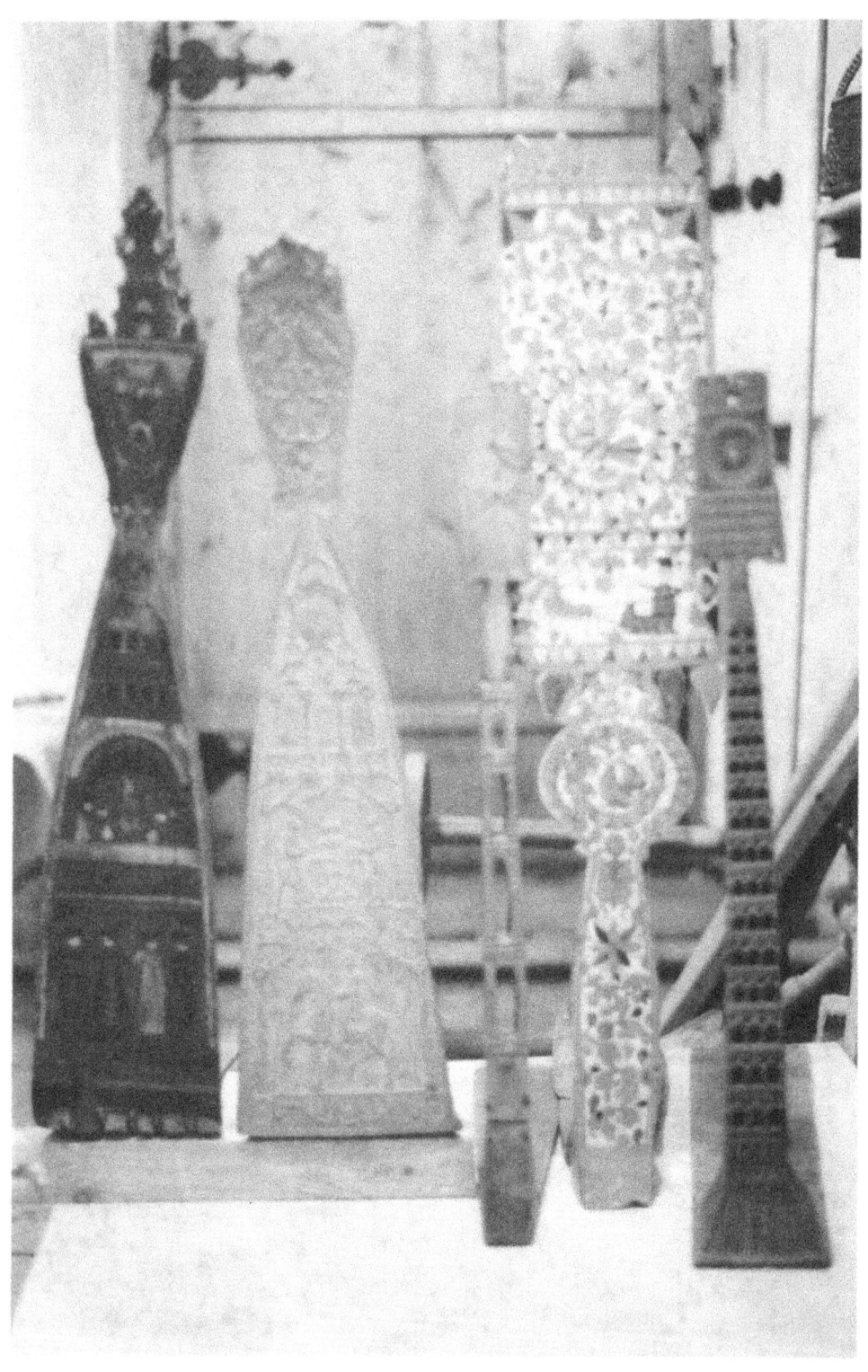

3.13 Group of distaffs. Iaroslavl', Kostroma, and Arkhangel'sk provinces, late 19th and early 20th centuries.

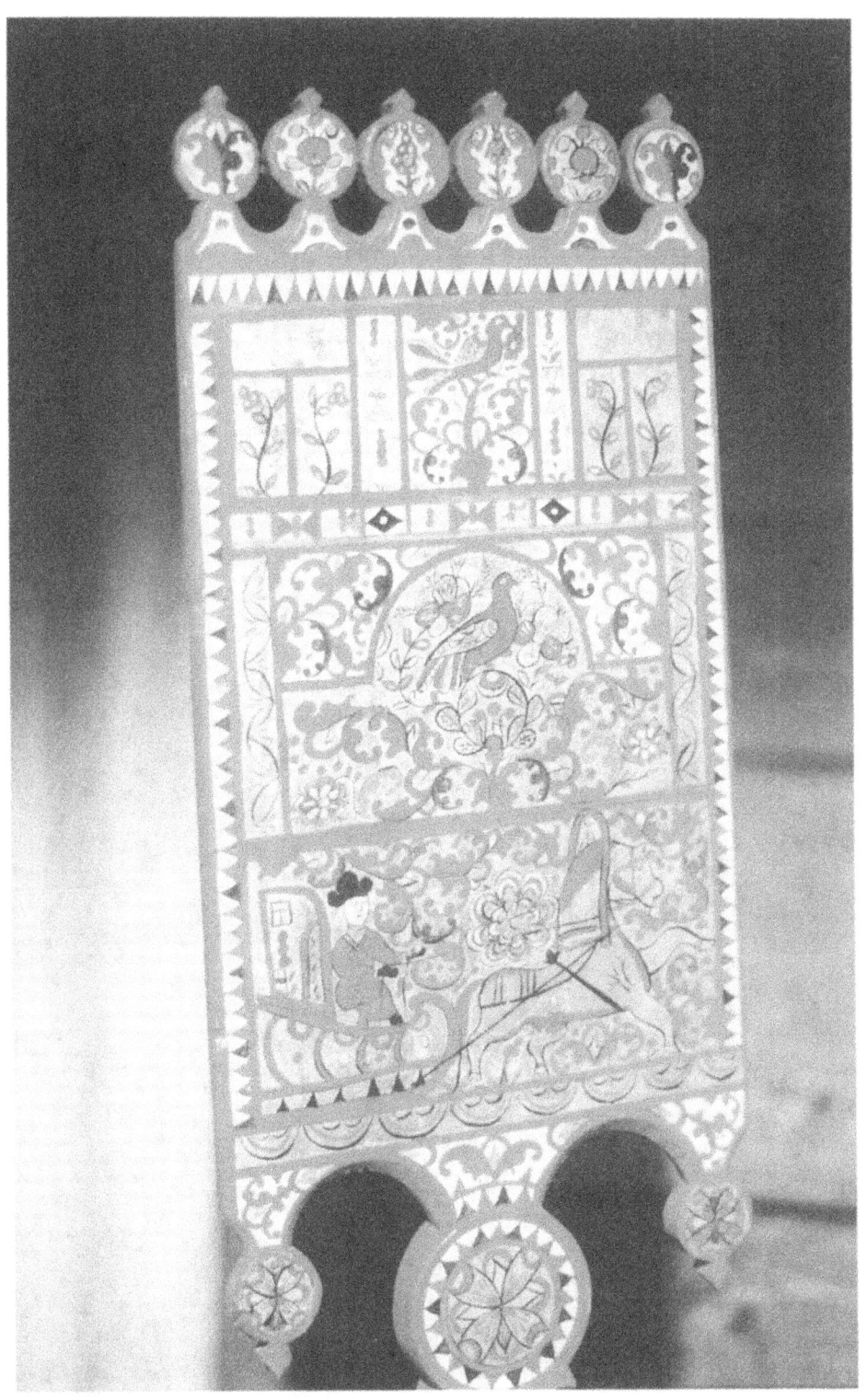

6.3 Pelageia Amosova, distaff blade. Borok, early 20th century.

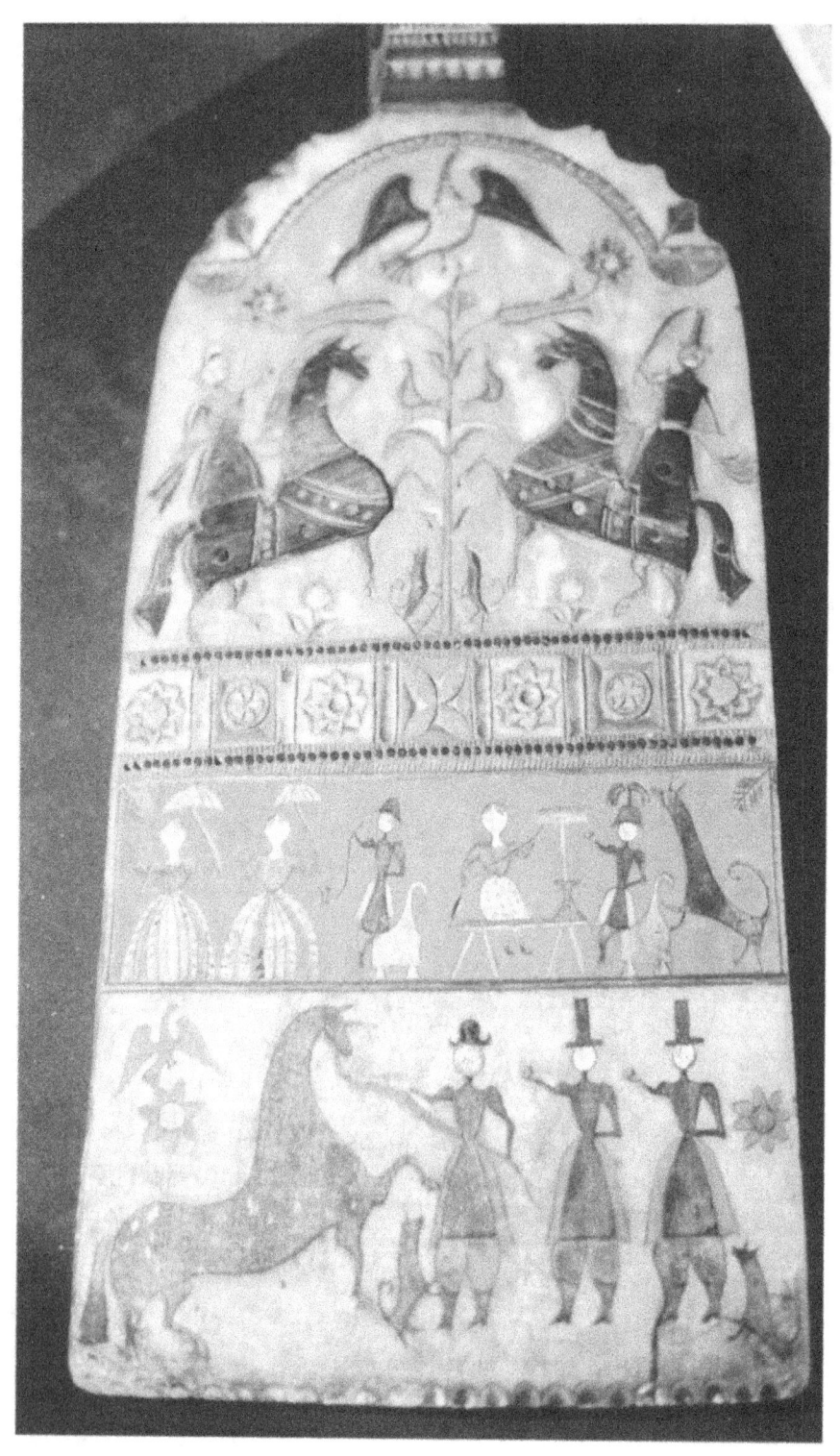

6.5 Lazar Mel'nikov, distaff base. Gorodets, 1866.

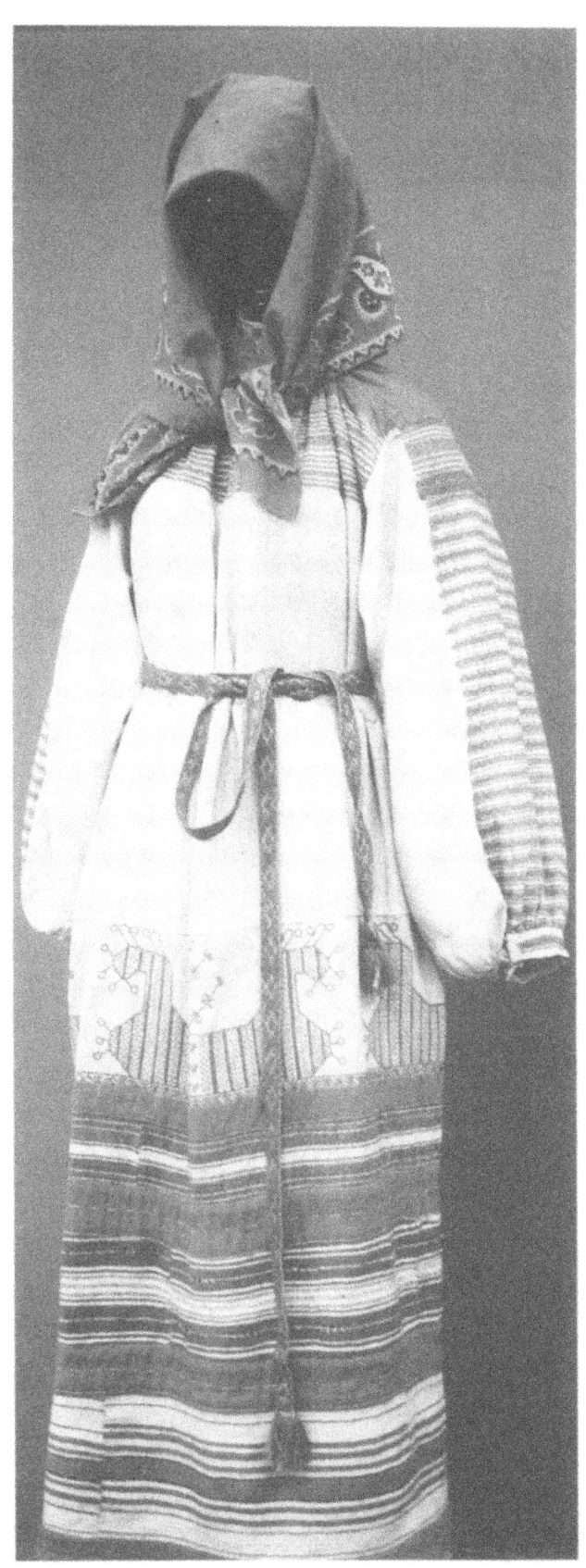

7.1 Dress for haymaking.
Vologda Province, 19th
century.

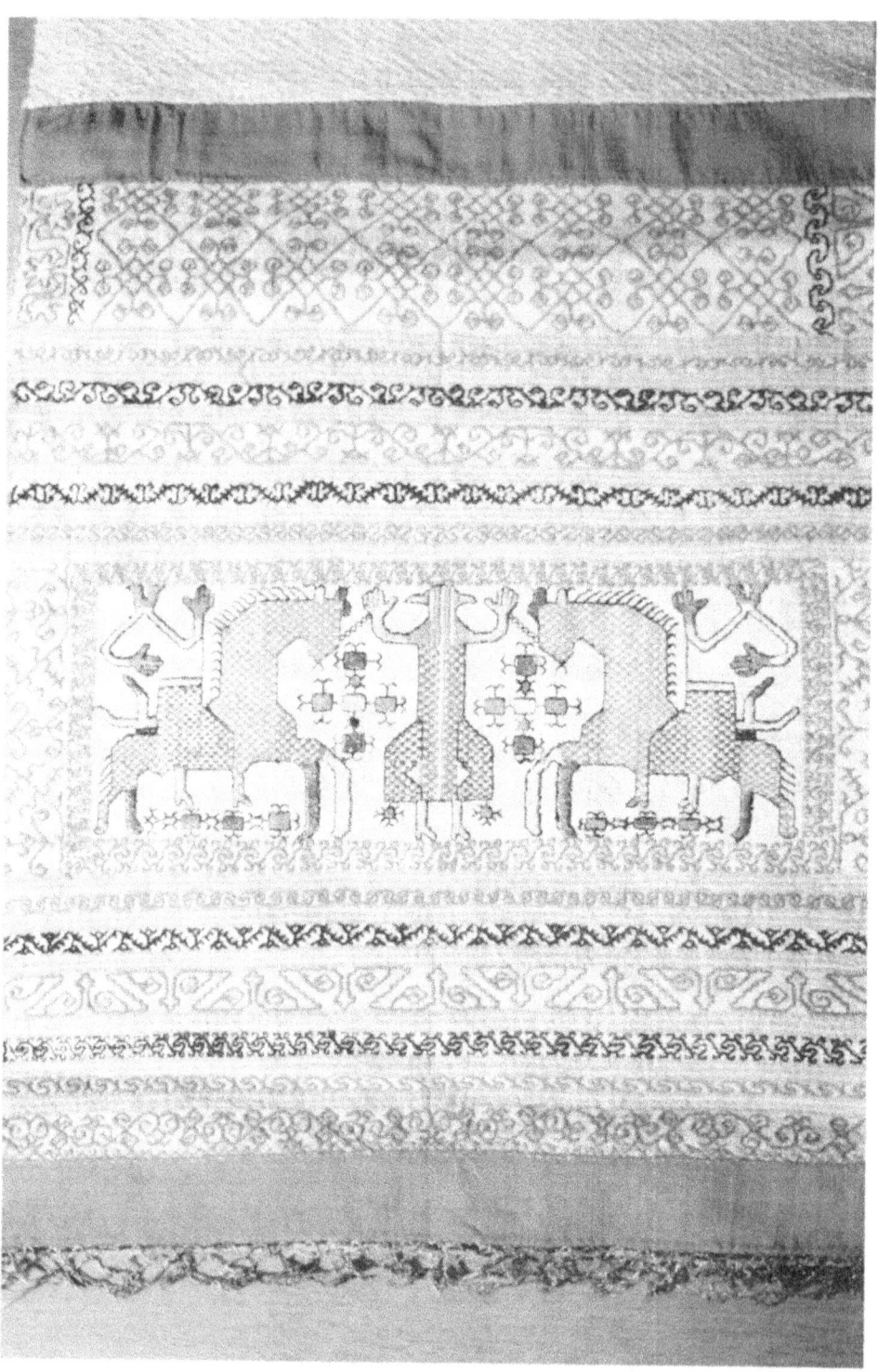

7.5 Border of headdress. Kargopol', 19th century.

8.2 Stepan Bochkarev, lid of box for game pieces.
Velikii Ustiug, 1817.

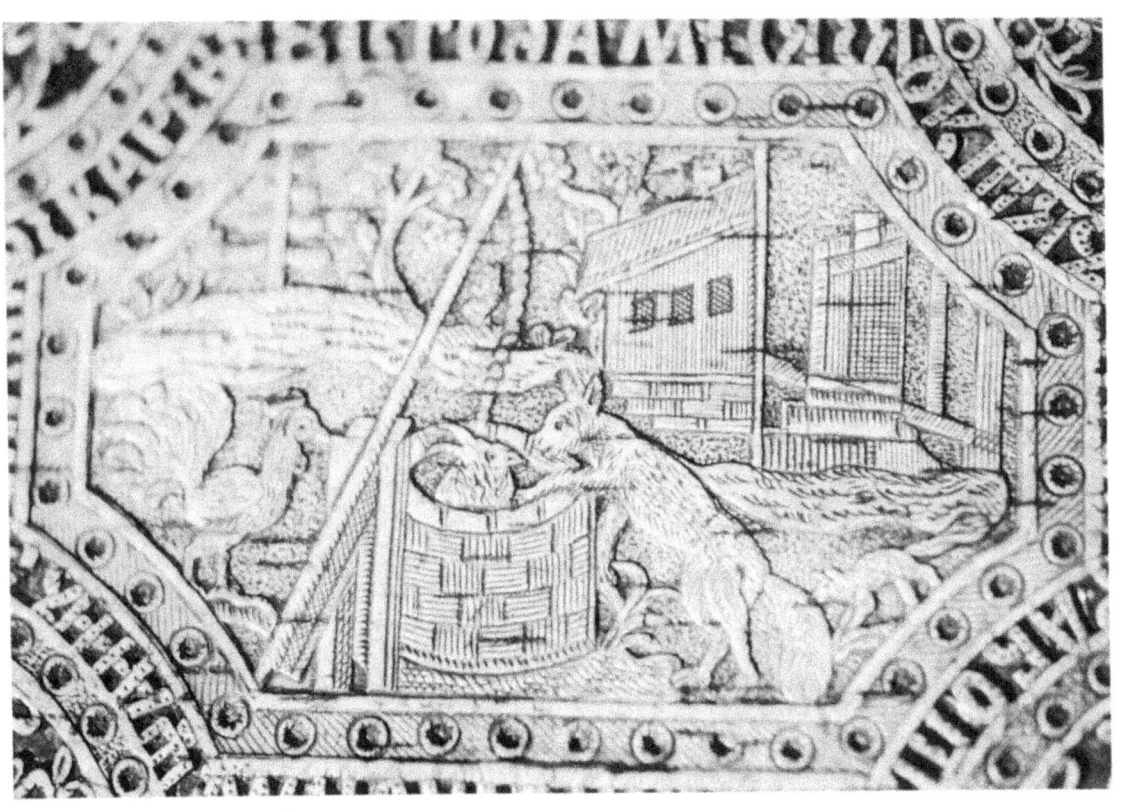

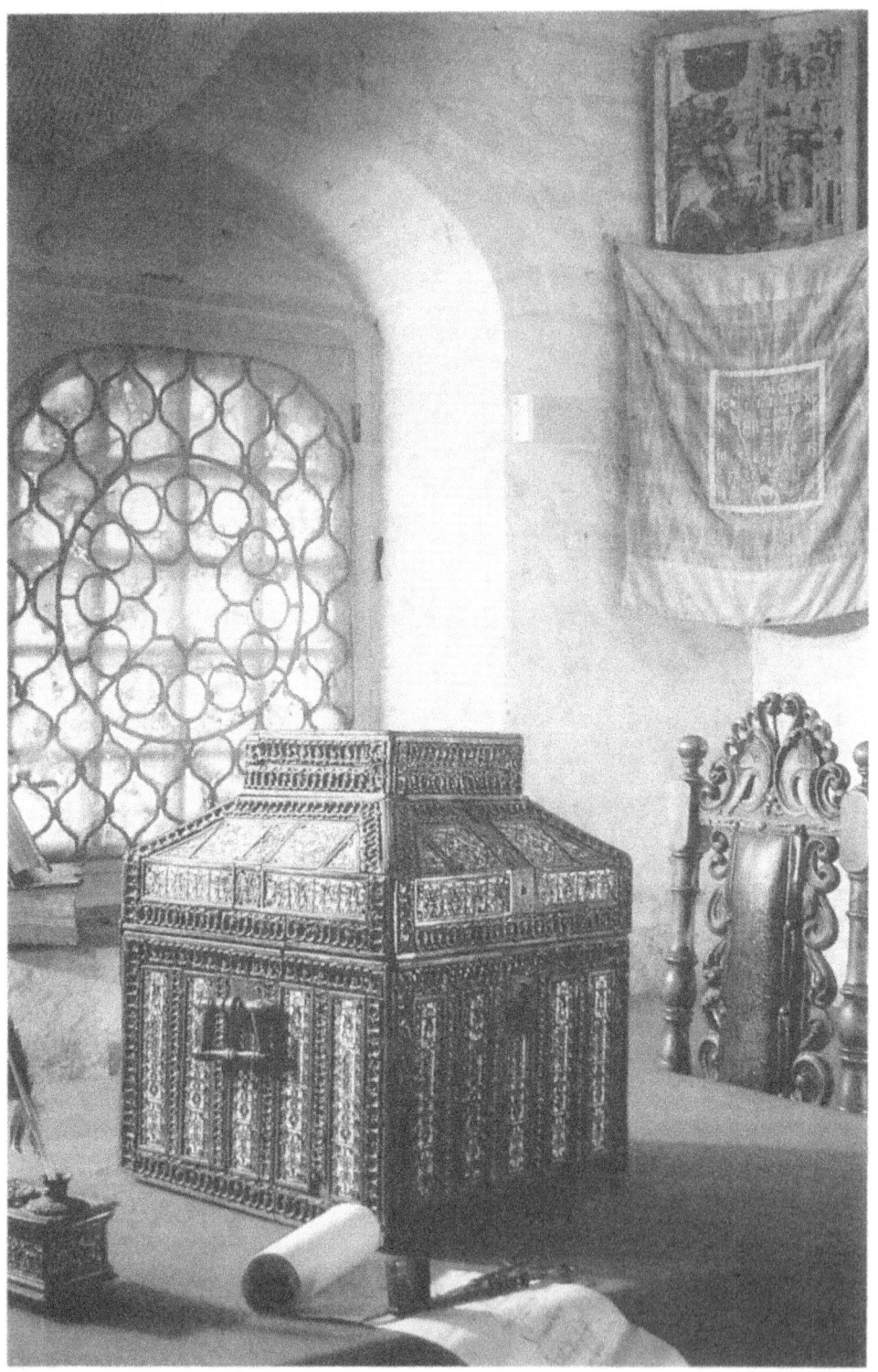

8.4 Casket. North Russia, 17th century.

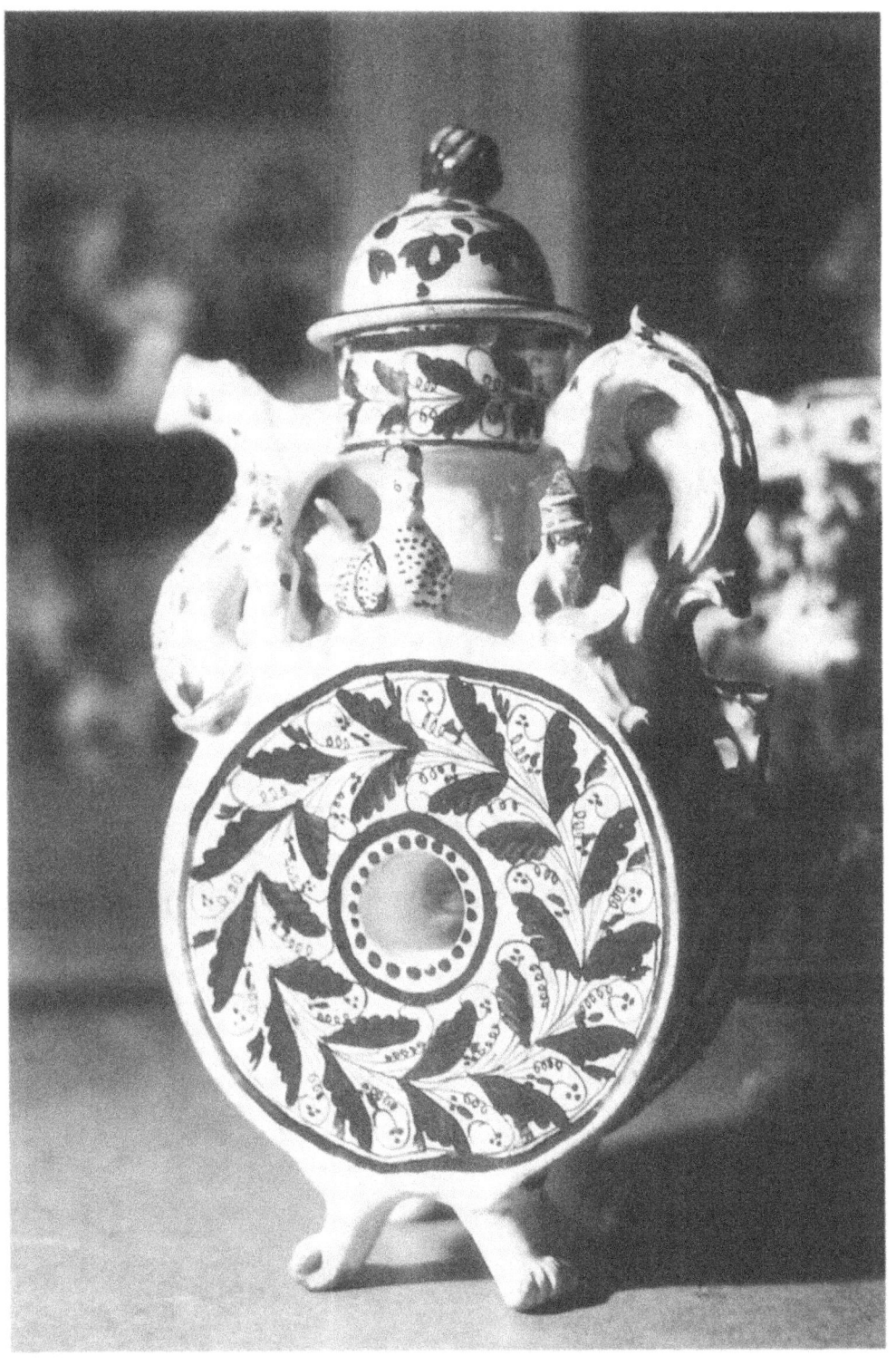

8.13 Kvass pitcher. Gzhel', second quarter
of the 19th century.

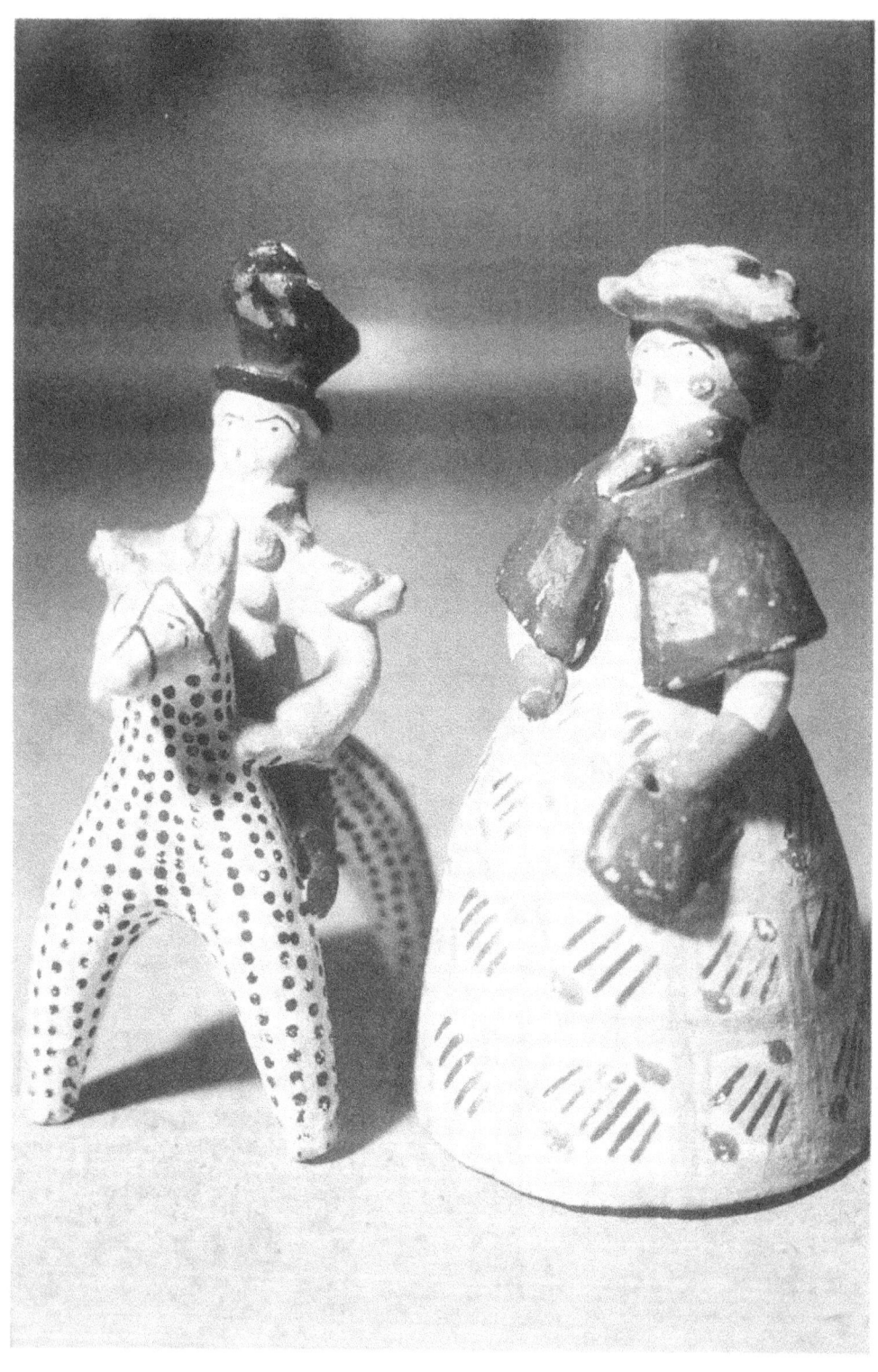

9.5 "Rider and Lady." Dymkovo, late 19th or early 20th century.

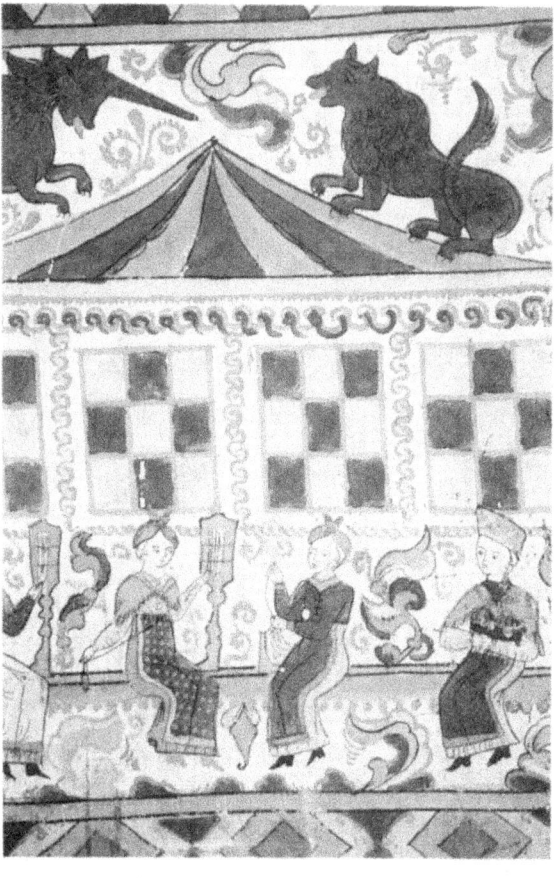

12.8 Iakov Iarygin, distaff blade with lion and unicorn. Permogore, early 19th century.

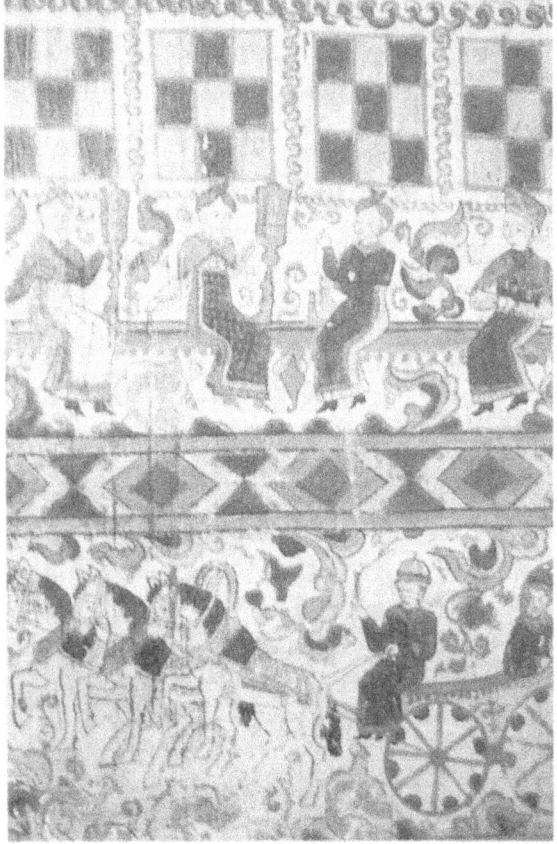

13.3 Iakov Iarygin, distaff blade with spinning scene and journey. Borok, Arkhangel'sk Province, early 19th century.

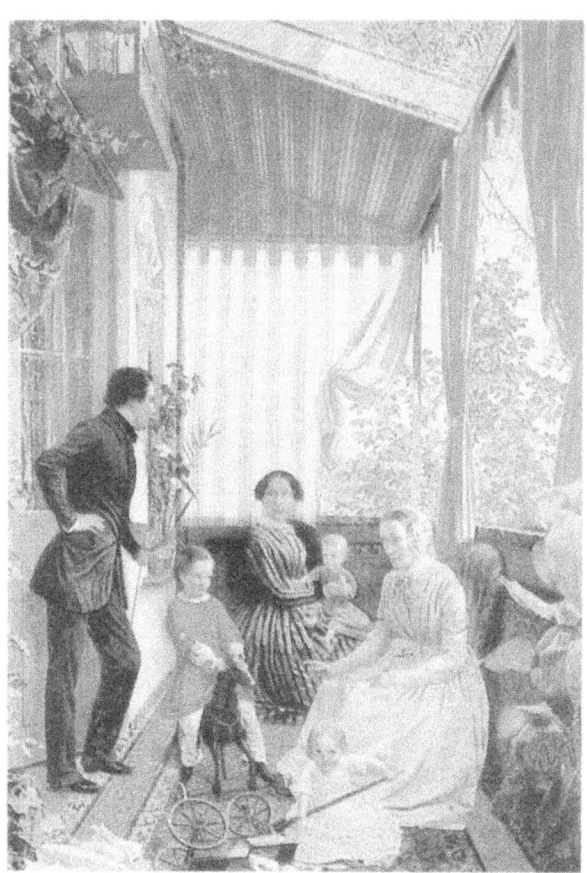

14.7 Fedor Slavianskii, *On the Balcony (Family Portrait)*. 1851.

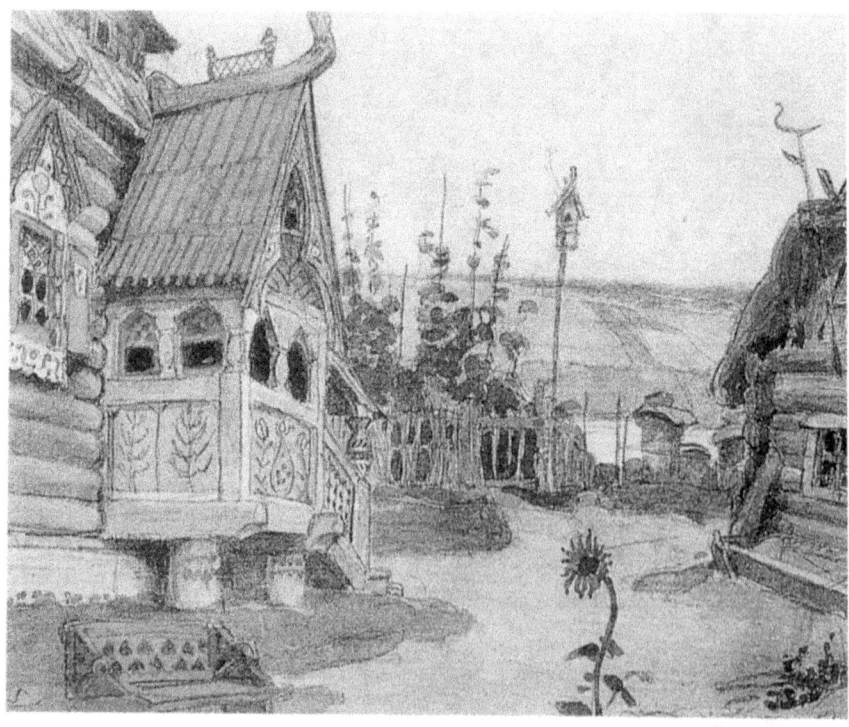

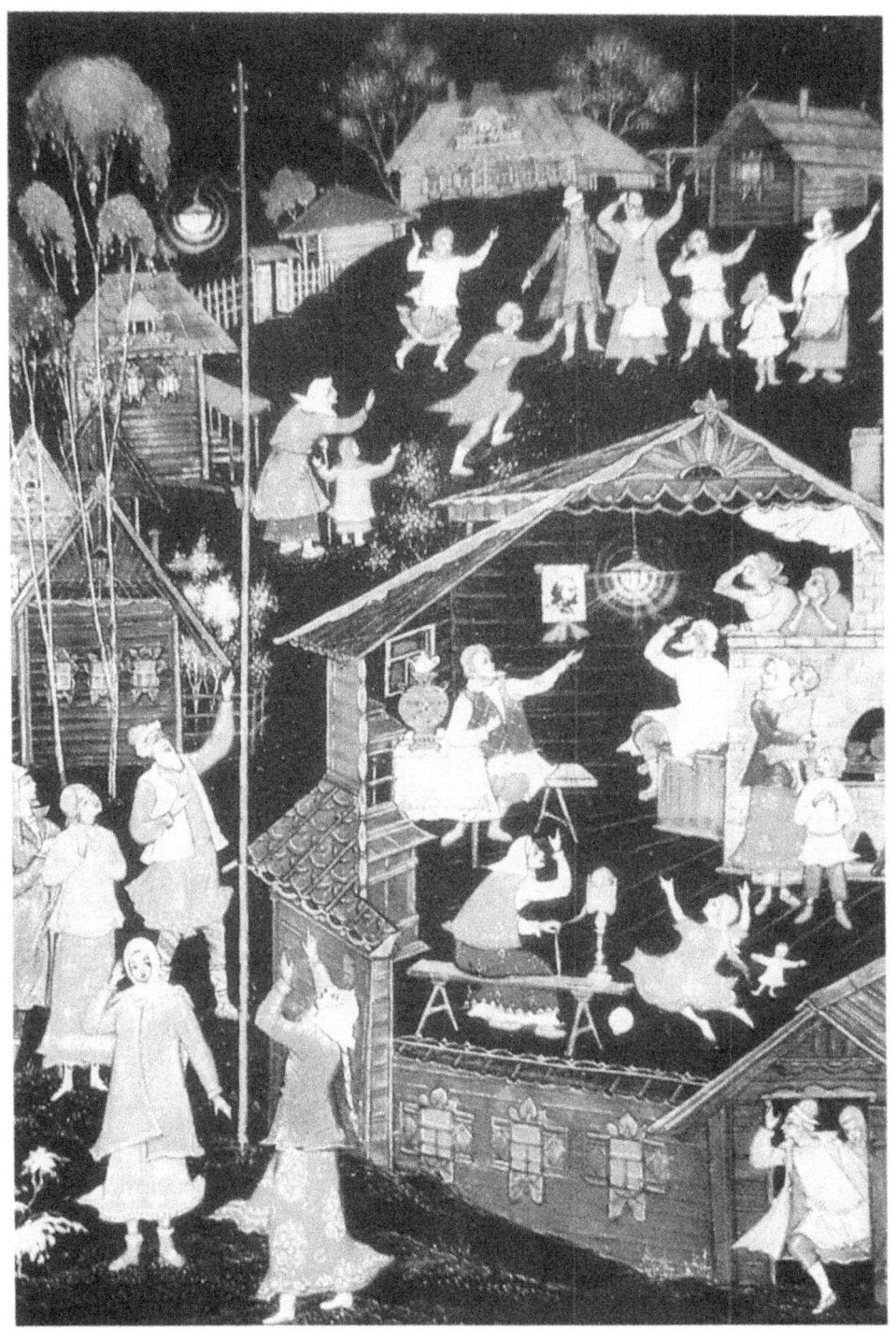

18.6 K. Mel'nikov, *The Lamp of Lenin*. Palekh, 1969.

16.2 Viktor Vasnetsov, set design for
Snegurochka. 1885.

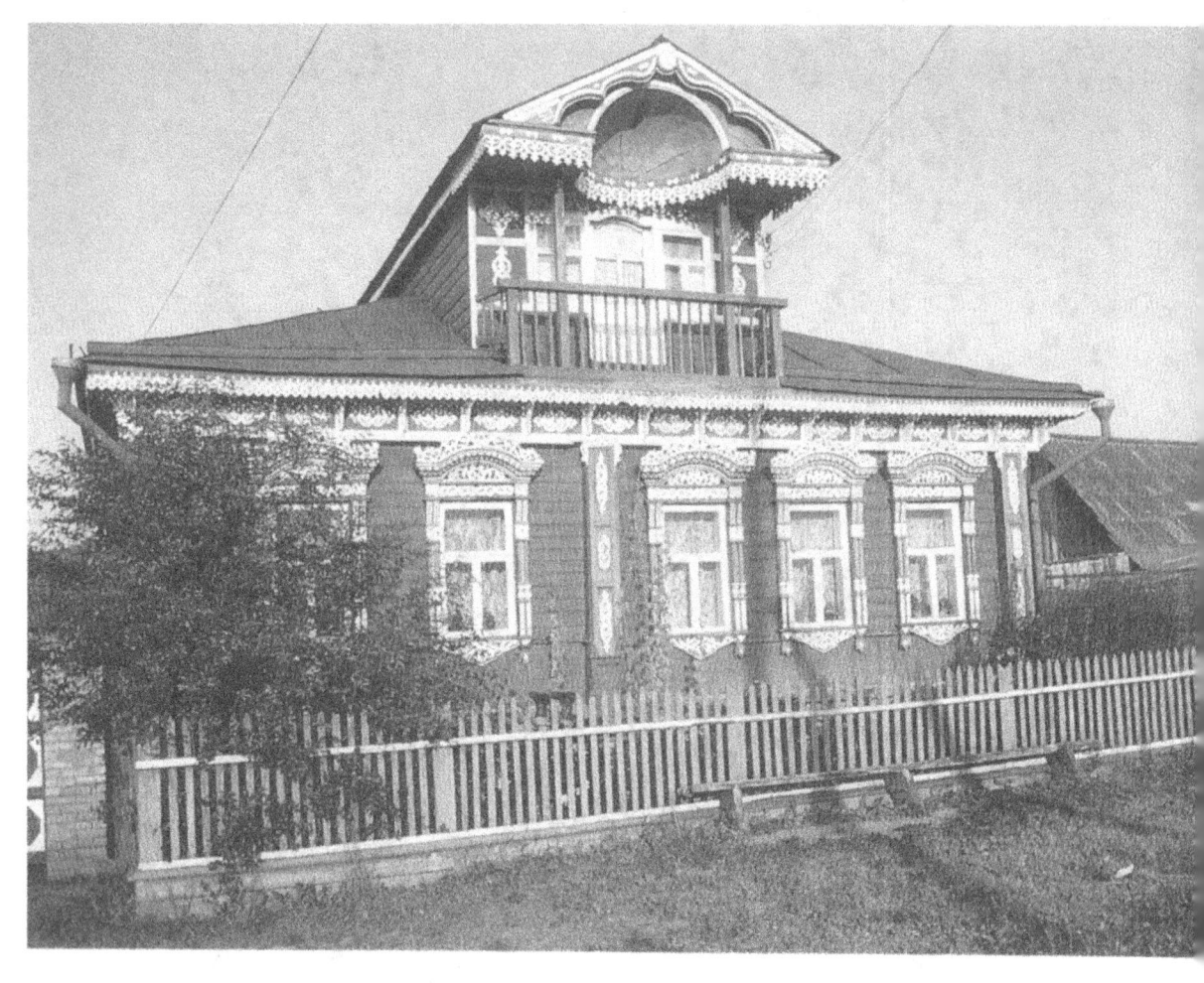

18.17 *Izba* in Suzdal', 20th century.

rubbing instruments were used to remove excess bone. When the outline was cut out, the edges of the cut were rounded with a file to create a soft effect. The work was very slow; bone could chip and splinter, and not every prepared plate could be used for openwork carving.

A coffer or casket with a stepped or sloped lid, called a *teremok* because its shape recalled a palace *terem*, was the most characteristic form for bonework decoration (fig. 8.3).[12] It was made of wood and covered with ivory or bone plates, attached by tiny metal pins. The sides were covered mainly with engraved plaques, with the openwork or low-relief panels arranged rhythmically across the front and lid. Colored foil of an orange-bronze or silvery tint was often placed behind the openwork plaques; sometimes the foil was covered with a thin sheet of mica to create a jewel-like glow behind the delicate contour of the cut-out ornament.

Walrus ivory varies in color: new tusk has a white, opaque outer layer, which gradually turns yellow; fossil tusks turn brownish and violet, while the core is somewhat translucent. Kholmogory artists took advantage of all of these natural tones. Plates engraved with very fine lines were rubbed with green or brown pigment to give them depth and color. The subtle green, violet, tan, or yellow tones contrasted with adjacent white opaque plates with engraved designs into which green or red pigments were worked. Placed next to openwork carving, the tints made the delicate work seem even more lace-like.

The repertoire of motifs was as extensive as that of any other decorative art. Engraved designs were usually flowering branches, birds and animals, or abstract forms. Relief and openwork panels included flowers, birds, mythical creatures, or biblical scenes such as the popular Judgment of Solomon, based on the Bible published in Russia by Johann Piscator in 1631. Other motifs, such as classical putti and personifications of virtues, were derived from Western baroque art via Kop'evskii's symbol and emblem book published under Peter I's auspices in 1705.[13] Genre scenes were probably adapted from those on prints, tiles, and metalwork or based on observation.

The ornamentation of bone combs, brooches, and very small boxes, for which one panel served, was similar to that in birch-bark lace. In both, the delicately cut-out contours of the main figures were set off by a unifying background of finely incised tendrils or cross-hatched lines. But on a *teremok* coffer, made up of several parts, each side requiring ten or more plaques, the principle of decoration was different. Each plaque had its own character and balance, but each panel had to be carefully related to adjacent ones so that the entire arrangement was harmonious. Although the individual elements were minuscule, the composition of a work on this scale was akin to architectural design.

As the bonecarving art of Kholmogory, Arkhangel'sk, Tobol'sk, and other northern centers, based on skills and interests of local peasants, became an

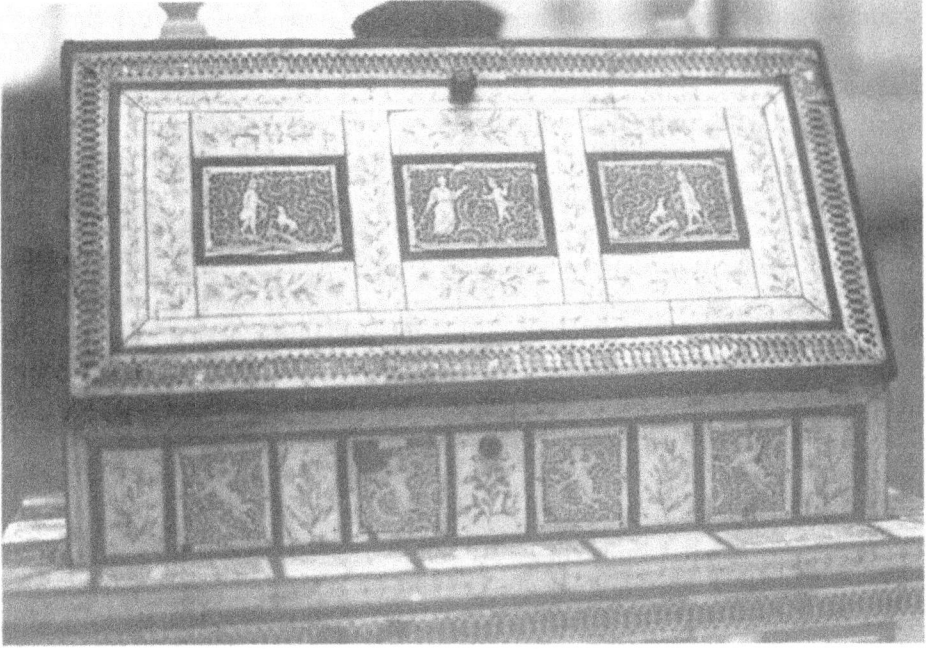

FIG. 8.3 *Larets-teremok* (small lidded chest). Walrus ivory, engraving, stain, foil. Kholmogory, 18th century. GRM.

embellishment of courts, the vocabulary of images and the principles of composition developed along urban, cosmopolitan lines. Nevertheless, the underlying esthetic qualities—the clear relationship between border ornament and figurative elements, the use of repetition and pattern, and the harmony between decoration and structure—remained essentially those of traditional folk art.

Metalwork

Unlike wood, metal was not always available to peasants; houses and entire villages were customarily built without the aid of nails. However, axes, knives, horseshoes, plowshares, sled runners, and other utilitarian items made of iron were always in demand. From the sixteenth century, almost every village had its own blacksmith, a peasant who did this work part-time in exchange for produce and field work from other villagers; some blacksmiths worked regularly and even employed assistants. Smithies were located at the edge of a village or town, on the main road and near a lake or stream, both to guard against the danger of fire and to have a supply of water for tempering. In towns and cities, where a variety of wrought-iron goods were needed, entire quarters were identified with the craft: the important thoroughfare Kuznetskii Most in Moscow was literally "Smith's Bridge."

Blacksmiths' work included chimney fittings and other architectural elements and ornamented furnishings and utensils. From the sixteenth through the nineteenth centuries, blacksmiths made trunks bound with iron bands (fig. 8.4), often decorated with line engravings of plants, animals, and mythical beings; lanterns with mica glazing; lighting stands with clips to hold tapers, often ornamented with spirals or leaf forms; brackets and corbels shaped like flowering branches; hinges, locks, strike plates, and keys of intricate design; and kitchen knives and cabbage-choppers, richly decorated with points and spirals. Architectural ornament of iron or copper was used in the sixteenth and seventeenth centuries, most often with brick or glazed tile facades. In the nineteenth century, a peasant named Sergei Malinnikov made metal weathervanes in the village of Vorsma near Nizhnii Novgorod; he also made decorations for the eaves and ridgepoles from strips of iron cut out into silhouettes of leopards, birds, *bereginy*, and human figures much like those in genre scenes on Gorodets distaffs.[14]

Wrought-iron work was most highly developed in Moscow and in the major manufacturing and trading cities of Nizhnii Novgorod, Iaroslavl', Velikii Ustiug, and Tula. These centers were best known for more refined forms of metalwork. Specialties of Velikii Ustiug and Sol'vychegodsk in the seventeenth century included pitchers, goblets, and desk sets, covered in white or blue enamel with silver floral ornaments, and bowls with delicate miniature paintings of flowers, animals, and other motifs resembling those in prints and tiles. Velikii Ustiug was known for production of articles of etched tin (sometimes called "northern frost") and metal boxes, plates, goblets, and trays decorated in niello on silver.[15] Painting on metal trays was a specialty of Nizhnii Tagil in the Urals. Tula was among the most important centers of metalwork, with its armaments industry and its extraordinary furniture of iron and cut steel.

Tula also became the most important center of samovar production. The samovar (literally "self-boiler"), a metal urn in which water was boiled and kept hot for tea, came into general use in the mid-eighteenth century, and eventually almost every household had one. By the 1830s or 1840s, there were hundreds of workshops and factories making samovars in a variety of shapes and styles. By the end of the century, forty samovar shops in Tula alone were producing 630,000 samovars each year.[16] The components of a samovar were a vertical chimney through the center, in which charcoal or wood was burned; a large cylindrical, oval, or vase-shaped body to contain the water; a base raised on feet, for air circulation; a flared ring at the top of the chimney to hold a teapot; and a spigot to release the hot water. The construction was simple, a matter of shaping and welding cylinders cut from sheets of copper. Any peasant could do this with minimal equipment, even at home, and many factories employed peasants on a piecework basis. The final shaping, welding, forging, and chasing of the samovars was done in the shop by skilled artisans.

The mineral resources of the Ural Mountains made the towns of Ekaterinburg, Nizhnii Tagil, Suksun, and Irginskii major centers of metalwork. By the 1730s, copper deposits were being mined by the government and by major industrialists, the Stroganovs, Osokins, Demidovs, and other families. Their workshops and factories employed local peasant artists, who adapted to metal the familiar wooden forms of tableware and storage containers, *endovy*, *bratiny*, goblets, and caskets (fig. 8.4). They also invented novel types of kettles, hanging washing stands (made like modern soap dispensers with rods and valves at the bottom to release streams of water), and elaborate settings for magnets, important products of the region. Engraved or chased plant tendrils and birds were the preferred ornaments. Hunting birds with outstretched wings decorated drinking cups and flasks from the Demidov and Iugovskii factories (fig. 8.5), and other devices identified work from other firms.[17] Other common motifs were the lion and the unicorn, heraldic images found in Russian art as early as the late fifteenth century,[18] and genre scenes featuring sleigh rides or smartly dressed figures with goblets and bottles.

Work in precious metals, including jewelry,

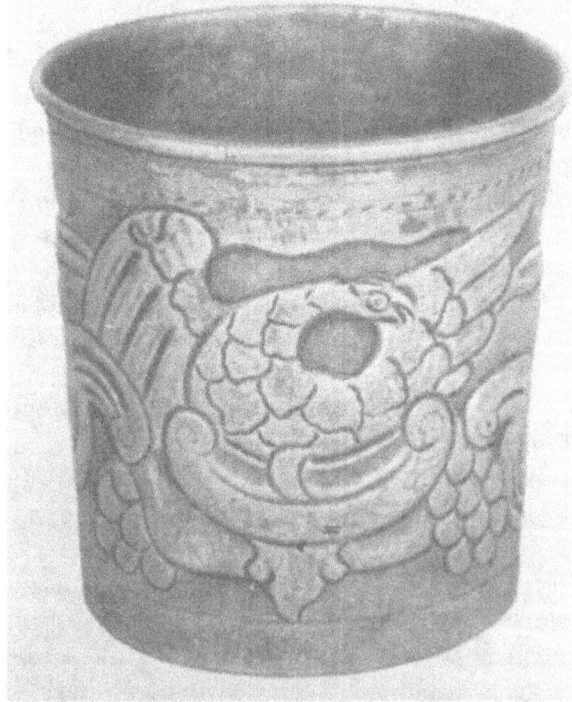

FIG. 8.5 Wine cup. Copper, hammered design. Demidov factory, Urals, second half of 18th century. GIM.

falls outside the sphere of folk art, although some peasant women made earrings and other ornaments of metal wire, beads, and river pearls, and they bought metal buttons for their festival garments.[19] Ecclesiastical metalwork, including bronze icons, crosses, chalices, and gospel covers in silver, gold, filigree work, and enamel, with cut or cabuchon gems, was an important art form and a major sign of wealth and status for monasteries throughout Russia. Peasants were employed in this work, as they were in carving and painting iconostases, but the techniques, forms, and iconography remained distant from the peasants' normal frame of reference.

The area of metalwork most relevant to folk art is the Velikii Ustiug art of *chern'* or niello engraving on silver, which provided models for the makers of birch-bark "lace" and carvers of spicecake molds. The techniques and imagery of niello work were also closely related to popular engraved prints. The method of engraving with niello was adapted from western European models. A metal plate was engraved with a design, and the furrows were filled with a black substance, nigellum, formed by a mixture of copper, silver, lead, and sulphur powders, which fused when heated, leaving a clear black line when cooled and burnished.[20] Russian niello workers used various "secret" mixtures of copper, silver, and lead,[21] which they mixed into a paste, worked over the surface of the plate, fired, burnished, and sometimes gilded. Niello was used to decorate icons and chalices for churches and such secular accessories as flasks and snuffboxes. City vistas and maps of provinces were among the most common designs on such items. Hunting scenes (fig. 8.6), card playing or tea drinking, and other social subjects were also popular. Many artists borrowed subjects from books or popular prints, embellishing them with fanciful baroque border ornament.

These niello pieces might be compared with the birch-bark containers made by artists working within a few miles of Velikii Ustiug. They shared a graphic approach to decoration, and a comparable range of subjects. However, the craft tradition from which birch-bark cutting derived was still essentially a rural, peasant one: although the objects were made for urban markets, they retained an identifiable folk esthetic. Niello work increasingly reflected an urban and cosmopolitan tradition, even when its decorative motifs were based on popular images.

Lubki

Printing on paper from engraved wood blocks or metal plates was similar to printing cloth; the techniques of making the blocks or plates were those of wood- and metalworking. In many ways, the *lubok* (plural *lubki*) fits into the framework of folk art. However, as in the case of English and American

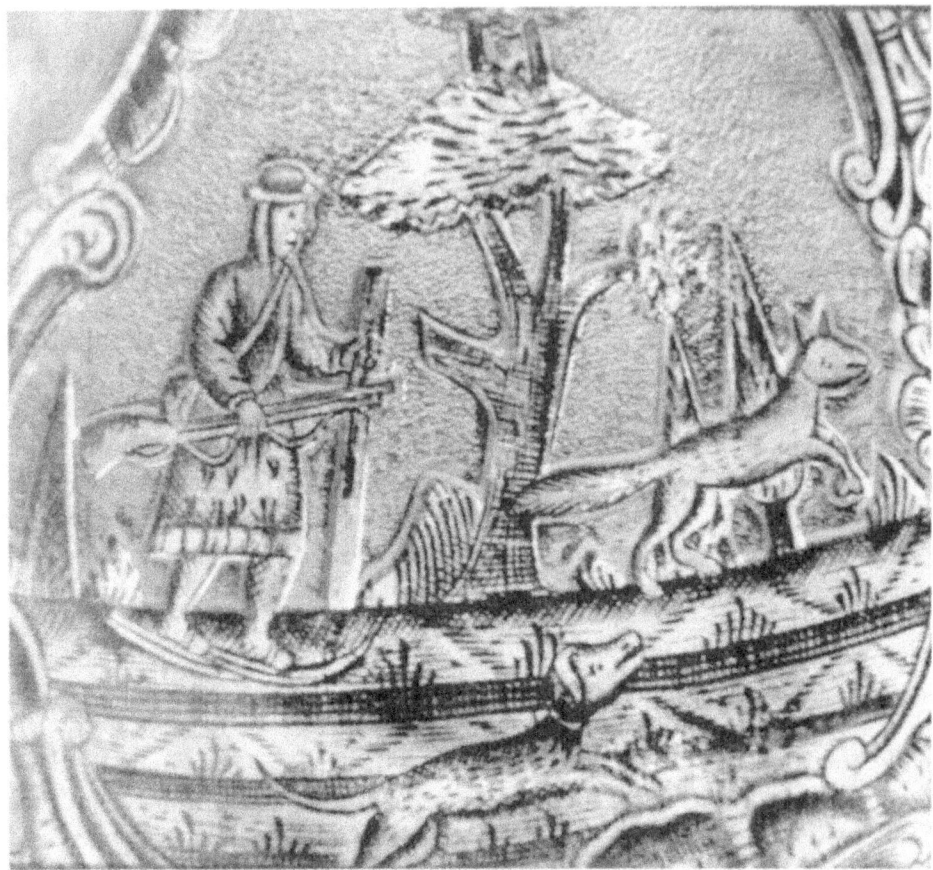

FIG. 8.6 Milk jug. Niello and gilt on silver. Detail of hunting scene. Tobol'sk, 1776.

broadside prints, or French *imagerie populaire d'Epinal, lubki* were often made by professional artists for both urban and rural audiences; moreover, their function was usually to inform, persuade, or entertain people rather than to decorate objects.

The first known wood engraving printed in Russia was an image of the evangelist Luke for the *Apostol* printed for the tsar in Moscow in 1564; it was followed by other printed illustrations in gospel books published in Lithuania and Ukraine.[22] Separate engraved pictures, probably introduced from the West in the seventeenth century, were called *lubochnye kartinki* or *lubki* in Russian.

The term *lubok* was once thought to have derived from *lub*, an archaic word for the *lipa* or lime tree, which yielded excellent wood for carving. A more convincing derivation is from another meaning of *lub*, bast, the soft layer of wood taken from trees in the spring, which was pressed and dried to form soft, thin, elastic, and water-resistant boards widely used for baskets and bread containers.[23] In medieval Kiev and probably in Novgorod, thin strips of bast were also used in place of expensive parchment, since its smooth surface and light weight made it ideal for documents. The writing on these documents was partially ideographic: symbols and pictures conveyed specific meanings, and also probably served as identifying marks in place of signatures. These ideograms or schematic drawings may have been the original *lubochnye kartinki*, or "bast-paper pictures." The use of bast for documents and other purposes was eventually so common that great quantities of the product were sold in markets all over northern and central Russia. The name of Lubianka Square in Moscow originated from the bast market held there.

In addition to the connection of bast with writing, the painted decorations on bread boxes, clothing chests, and other articles commonly made of bast were probably the stylistic forerunners of *lubki*. Strong, quickly painted outlines of figures, round faces with schematic features, background elements, or foliage-like ornament that filled and sometimes even broke through the compositional frame, and bright, flatly applied colors were characteristic of this painting. Moreover, plain sheets of bast, not attached to any utilitarian article, were decorated with amusing pictures and sold in Moscow in the seventeenth century.[24] The styles and subjects of these early funny papers seem to have been carried over to printed broadsheets.

But the earliest *lubki* were quite different in style and purpose. The first printing house was established in Moscow in 1564, and within the next few decades engraved icons and prints copied from illuminated manuscripts and frescoes were being sold in Moscow and at the major monasteries. Religious prints and "picture Bibles" made in Ukraine in the early seventeenth century were modeled on Dutch and German sources, including Piscator's *Theatrum Biblicum*, the popular German *Biblia pauperum*, and engravings by Dürer and other masters, with a few alterations to conform to Orthodox iconography. Engraving on copper was introduced in the mid-seventeenth century, and was encouraged by the court and church. Well-known icon painters, including the influential Simon Ushakov,[25] worked along with engravers to make religious prints. These served as substitutes for the far more costly icons, and were sometimes mounted on wood and framed in the traditional manner with metal facings.

The method of printing was fairly simple. The board or metal plate was covered with a linseed-oil-based ink, which filled the engraved grooves, and the surface was wiped clean; then a sheet of damp paper was laid on the plate and smoothed by hand or pressed. The prints were colored by hand. Large quantities of *lubki* were produced and sold outside the Spasskii Gate of the Moscow Kremlin, and at the vegetable market, where *prianiki* and printing boards were also sold (fig. 8.7).[26]

By the eighteenth century, there was a well-established printers' quarter in Moscow with numerous independent printing shops. The range of subjects increased, stimulated by Peter the Great's employment of printmakers to publicize his achievements and reforms. A popular type depicted a legendary hero such as Alexander the Great or one of the Russian *bogatyri* battling an enemy in such a way that the hero resembled Peter I (usually with a large mustache) and the enemy could be recognized as King Charles XII of Sweden or some other foe (fig. 8.8). Naturally, broadsides opposing Peter's policies or satirizing his appearance and character soon appeared. One of the best-known, entitled *How the Mice Buried the Cat,* shows a large dead cat, with Peter's whiskers, being pulled to his tomb by a procession of mice identified as some of the territories he had conquered.

Dmitrii Rovinskii, the pioneer collector and publisher of a nine-volume study of *lubki* that remains the definitive work in the field, classified them according to several types. His major categories were icons and gospel illustrations; the virtues and evils of women; teaching, alphabets, and numbers; calendars and almanacs; light reading, novels, folktales, and hero legends; stories of the Passion of Christ, the Last Judgment, sufferings of the martyrs; popular recreation including Maslenitsa festivities, puppet comedies, and drunkenness; music, dancing, and theatricals; jokes and satires related to Ivan the Terrible and Peter I; satires adapted from foreign sources; folk prayers; and government-sponsored pictorial information sheets, including proclamations and news items.[27]

Some of these subjects are shared with other folk arts. A few images are found in almost identical form in *lubki*, painted distaffs and bast boxes, carved birch-bark containers, carved bone plaques, niello engravings, ceramic tiles, and toys. For example, illustrations of popular recreation during Maslenitsa and Semik (the seventh Thursday after Easter, Ascension Thursday, considered the beginning of spring in Russia) most often show sleigh and carriage rides popular on those occasions (fig. 10.8). The stylized forms of prancing horses and well-dressed ladies and cavaliers are much like those on Gorodets and Borok distaffs.[28] Images of *bogatyri*, legendary Russian heroes such as Solovei Razboinik ("Nightingale the Robber"), Bova fighting the Centaur Polkan (fig. 8.8), and their ancient prototype Alexander of Macedon, were also popular in other media, especially *prianiki* and glazed tiles; pictures from calendars, emblem books, and topographical views also appeared on tiles and niello ware. Some artists found another way of borrowing, by cutting details from books or *lubki* and placing them under thin sheets of mica to decorate birch and metal trunks or boxes.[29]

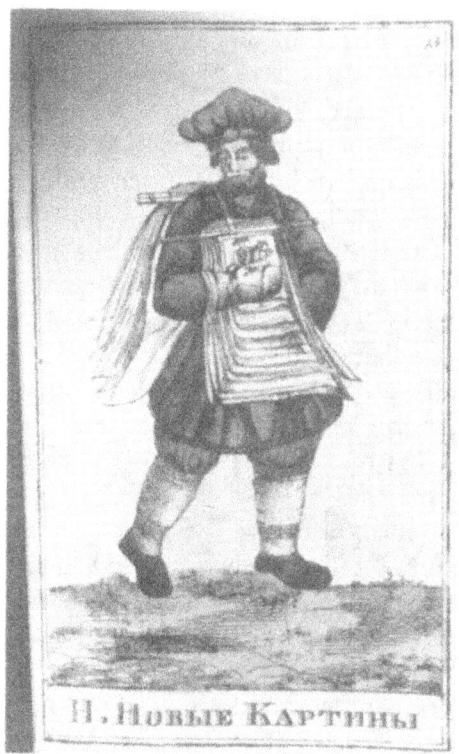

FIG. 8.7 *Lubok* seller, page from alphabet. Hand-colored engraving. Moscow, second half of the 19th century.

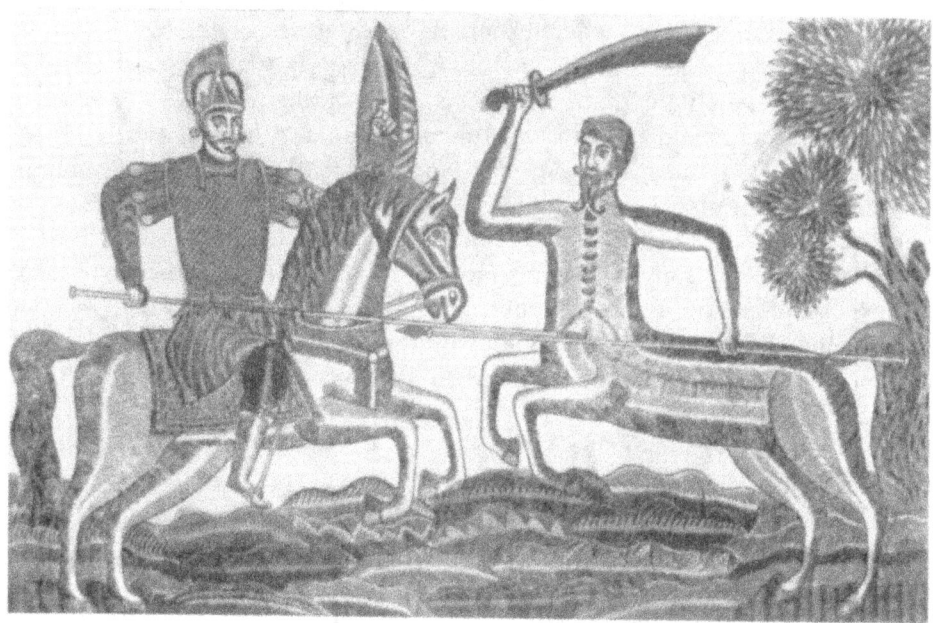

FIG. 8.8 "Prince Bova and Polkan the Centaur." *Lubok.* Hand-colored engraving. 19th century.

There are many other examples of borrowing and sharing motifs. But the sharing was not indiscriminate. Fewer *lubok* pictures were reproduced in other art forms than might be expected, given their wide distribution. Specifically, the function of disseminating information and propaganda was unique to *lubki*. Following the example of Peter I, Catherine the Great made use of *lubki* to publicize the new smallpox vaccine in 1768, and to record Russian victories in the war against Turkey in the 1770s; during the same period a number of private printers inaugurated wall newspapers to announce and illustrate current events and phenomena. The satirical character of many eighteenth- and early nineteenth-century *lubki* was also comparatively rare in other types of folk art. The subject of Napoleon's invasion of Russia gave rise to many *lubki* satirizing French behavior, often very crudely, but appeared only tangentially in other media, in images of soldiers on distaffs, on stovetiles, and in toys.

The audience for these popular prints was "popular" in the broadest sense, including not only peasants but city dwellers and members of the middle class. The artists were largely townspeople accustomed to an abundance of visual stimuli and rapidly changing fashions. At the same time, in isolated communities of Old Believers, religious *lubki* were printed and colored by hand. Hand-colored prints of favorite saints and moralizing illustrations of the Seven Deadly Sins, Life in Hell, and the Fall of Adam and Eve cost only about one kopek, cheap enough for peasants.[30] Sales were especially brisk during Lent, when itinerant peddlers festooned with samples visited village markets, and dozens of small book and *lubok* kiosks were set up near the vegetable markets in Moscow and other towns. Other types of *lubki*, illustrating ribald Russian versions of Punch and Judy shows, with the stock characters Farnos, Foma, Erema, and Paramoshka, or offering humorous advice about marriage and domestic habits, were aimed at both peasants and townsfolk.

There were certainly persistent traces of folklore, popular piety, and peasant experience in the thematic repertoire of *lubki*, just as there were in town life in general.[31] However, the style of presentation in most of these images, combining words and pictures, often with multiple scenes making up a narrative, also points to affinities with theatrical spectacles, fireworks, and other forms of city entertainment, and with the development of popular literature in the nineteenth century.[32]

As *lubki* became readily available to people of all classes, distinctions between peasant and urban subject categories lessened. Scenes of distant cities and records of natural phenomena, such as a comet or the first Persian elephant brought to Russia, and half-understood mythological subjects undoubtedly stimulated peasant artists and found their way, sometimes in altered forms, into the repertoire of folk art. The *lubok* was an art form that originated in the city, under the high auspices of church and tsars, developed largely in tandem with popular culture, interacted directly with other urban art forms such as ceramics and metalwork, and tangentially influenced peasant art.

Lacquer

Lacquerware was another decorative art form introduced to Russia from abroad, promoted by the court, and gradually taken over by private manufacturers and, in the Soviet period, by cooperative artels. However, the art also preserved ties to folk traditions. Lacquer objects of wood or metal coated with a resinous varnish were brought to Europe from China and Persia in the sixteenth century; by the eighteenth century, lacquerware was produced in France, Scotland, and Germany. Peter the Great's Monplaisir Palace in Peterhof, built around 1720, had a room decorated with ninety-four lacquer panels painted in a "Chinese" style by Russian icon painters. This was the first use of lacquer in Russia.

During the second half of the eighteenth century, Russian artists made many small lacquered objects, such as snuffboxes and medallions, decorated chiefly with images of Peter I or Catherine II. A Moscow merchant, Pavel Korobov, began manufacturing lacquer products in 1795.[33] He owned a factory producing lacquered cap visors for the Russian army and thought that he could adapt his equipment and techniques to make snuffboxes on a large scale. Korobov visited the Stobwasser Lacquer Factory in Braunschweig, and invited German craftsworkers to help organize his factory and train local artisans. Many of the original workers were serf artists, purchased by Korobov along with the village of Danilkovo. The neighboring village, Fedoskino, became the main center of lacquer painting in the nineteenth century.

The process of making the lacquer boxes required about seventy days. First strips of cardboard or paper were glued together, wound around a wooden block, and placed inside a wooden frame which could be pressed inward, to compress the cardboard and form the sides of the future box. The pressed sheets were dried, attached to a bottom and a lid, then boiled in linseed oil and oven-dried again. The resulting material was as strong as hard wood, and absolutely uniform in texture.

After sawing off the lid and smoothing the edges, workers covered the blank with a mixture of clay and soot combined with a drying oil. They polished the form with pumice and coated it with several layers of lacquer, black on the outside and vermilion inside, drying it in an oven after each coat. At this stage, an artist painted a design or picture on the lid, and ornamental vine tendrils or dots and lines around the sides. Some boxes, instead of being painted, were decorated with paper engravings glued onto the lids. The articles were given several coats of clear lacquer, dried, and hand-buffed.[34]

Though the process was laborious, it was made as efficient as possible by an assembly-line system, with teams of workers assigned to separate stages. The Fedoskino factory was soon producing over 10,000 pieces in a year; within a generation the production reached nearly 50,000. Petr Lukutin, Korobov's son-in-law, inherited the factory, expanded it, and supervised innovations in technique and style. From the 1820s to the 1850s, lacquerware was known as Lukutin lacquer and, by imperial decree, it carried the tsar's seal. The chief articles were snuffboxes, cigarette cases, matchboxes, trays, tea caddies, desk sets, and decorative plaques. The quality was generally very high. Lukutin established an art school at the factory to train workers not only in traditional methods of icon painting, but also in Western painting methods. The subjects of miniatures ranged from portraits and scenes of famous battles to views of the Kremlin, country landscapes, and genre scenes of haymaking, sleighing, and tea drinking, reminiscent of folk art motifs. The Lukutin factory was most successful, but a few competitors appeared, including the Vishniakov factory established by former serfs of Count Sheremetev. Some of their boxes were painted green to look like malachite inlay. Their miniatures were simple country scenes or adaptations of well-known paintings of peasant life, such as Il'ia Repin's *Seeing Off the Recruit*, unusual for its lack of idealization.[35] The Austen Factory in Moscow produced miniatures with "Chinese" motifs and idealized peasant scenes (fig. 8.9). Nazhevshchikov's small workshop combined mother-of-pearl and metal wire with lacquer, and an unknown artist in St. Petersburg developed a way of making lids with low-relief floral designs.

Most of the pieceworkers and artists in lacquerware factories were originally peasants or serfs, but their boxes and snuffboxes were intended for an urban and wealthy clientele, just as niello ware was. But despite its status as a luxury art, lacquerwork retained some elements of a native artistic tradition. This became obvious in the twentieth century, after the revolution, when efforts were being made to revive the craft. Ivan Golikov, an icon painter from Palekh, saw examples of lacquerwork during a visit to Moscow in 1924, and thought that he and his fellow painters might be able to make similar miniatures (fig. 18.7).[36] They founded the "Artel of Old Painting," with a distinctive style based on icon traditions, imagery from folk stories, and adaptations from popular illustrations of folksongs and from *lubki*.[37] They also introduced modern, Soviet subjects, such as Red Army soldiers and rural electrification, rendered in the same icon-painting style. The nearby villages of Kholui and Mstera developed their own miniature painting schools, using the elegant stylization of icons but emphasizing detailed landscape backgrounds. Fedoskino lacquer also enjoyed a revival, and continued its more realistic painting traditions.

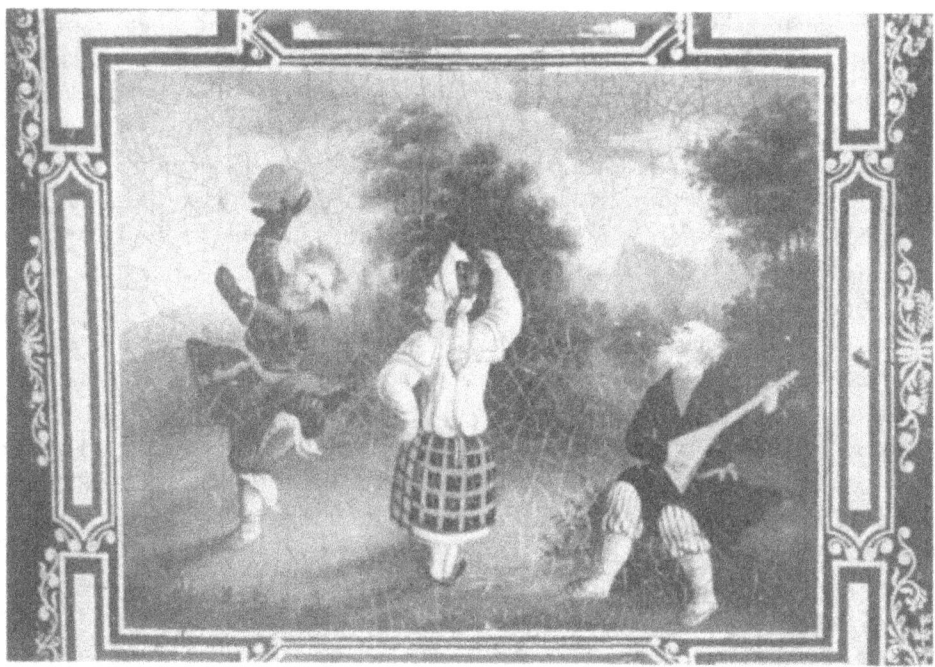

FIG. 8.9 "Peasant Dance" tea caddy. Papier-mâché, oil paint, metallic powder, lacquer. Austen factory, Fedoskino, Moscow Province, mid-19th century. GIM.

Ceramics

Pottery was made by the early inhabitants of South Russia, and was widely used in Kievan Rus'. Wheel-turned and hand-built dishes decorated with undulating incisions, and glazed building tiles were found in excavations of eleventh- and twelfth-century sites. There is no sign of large-scale manufacture and distribution until the fifteenth century, when building programs in Moscow and other formerly wooden cities stimulated production of brick and tile.

Tile, *izrazets*, used in architecture and for facing stoves, was one of the most important ceramic forms. The earliest tiles were small, of unglazed terracotta. Stamped, green-glazed tiles were made in the sixteenth century, colored enameled tiles in the seventeenth century. Smooth blue and white tiles and stamped white tiles, influenced by Dutch and English models, appeared in the eighteenth and nineteenth centuries. Ceramic utensils for domestic use were made in quantity in the early sixteenth century, reaching a peak with the invention of new techniques for making majolica, faience, and porcelain in the late seventeenth and eighteenth centuries. Clay toys, dolls, and whistles were made in many parts of Russia from early times, and remained popular items for cottage production and trade. All three types of ceramics, architectural tiles, domestic utensils, and toys, were produced by both simple and technically complex procedures, and all reflected both folk traditions and urban fashions.

Potteries were located near clay deposits, whenever possible near large towns or monasteries, where the products were in demand. Architectural tiles began to replace expensive stone facing in the fifteenth century. Used in combination with brick, bands of unglazed terra-cotta tile stamped with floral patterns and swags were whitewashed to emulate the effect of carved white stone on the earlier churches of Novgorod and Suzdal'.[38] Tiles were formed by pressing kneaded clay into wooden molds, then drying and baking them; glazing involved coating the tile with glaze, sometimes also enamel paints, and a second firing. Fragments of unglazed stovetiles made in the sixteenth century show pressed floral and geometrical patterns and images of mythical creatures and heroes such as Alexander of Macedon and the Russian *bogatyri.* Green-glazed relief tiles were made in Pskov in the late fifteenth century, and in Rostov, Kostroma, Moscow, and other cities in the mid-sixteenth century. The number of figurative motifs increased, and a variety of geometrical border patterns appeared.

Tilemaking was greatly stimulated by Patriarch Nikon's plan to build his monastery of New Jerusalem at Istra, west of Moscow, in 1654. Nikon summoned the best tilemakers, among them Stepan Polubes, Samoshka Grigor'ev, and Ignat Maksimov from Poland, to decorate the new church with multicolored tiles. The roofline, arches, and portals of the New Jerusalem cathedral were embellished with enameled tiles, the seven iconostases with blue, green, yellow, and brown glazed relief tiles, including tiles formed as the heads of angels at the top story. A decade later, after exiling Nikon, Tsar Aleksei Mikhailovich called the master tilemakers to the Kremlin Armory, and their work made Moscow the center of tile production.

The technique of tile enameling, *tsenina,* a term of unknown origin, also influenced the decoration of other ceramic wares. Many tiles were molded in very high relief, and some figurative reliefs, for instance of the evangelists or of seraphim, extended over several tiles. Such compositions decorated the facades of many brick churches and public buildings in Moscow.[39] They marked the height of architectural tilemaking.

In the eighteenth century, tiles were used chiefly to decorate the large heating stoves of city and town dwellings (fig. 8.10). While the ovens in peasant houses were made of brick or unglazed tiles and simply whitewashed, those in town houses, like those of Germany, Holland, and Scandinavia, were lined with two layers of tiles, the outer layer being decorative. Peter the Great admired Dutch tiles, and he recruited two Swedish prisoners of war to start production of flat, white tiles painted "with blue plants in the Dutch fashion."[40] However, most Russians preferred multicolored tiles, with figures and scenes. Green glaze combined with black outlines was favored, sometimes with contrasting touches of a bright, clear yellow. Five-color compositions, recalling the earlier raised enamel tiles, were even more popular. Russian artists introduced new motifs, from a variety of sources—large floral motifs like those in freehand painting on wood in the backgrounds; framing devices from early manuscripts; scenes from folktales and peasant life—into the range of images adapted from European, classical, and even Oriental sources. Inscriptions, occasionally related to the images but often quite arbitrary, were added in cartouches beneath the scenes.[41] Tile painters sometimes used cartoons which were pinpricked for making guidelines on the unglazed tiles, but for simple or familiar images, many painters worked freehand and quickly. Since the unfired tiles immediately absorbed the water-based paint, this required considerable practice and skill.

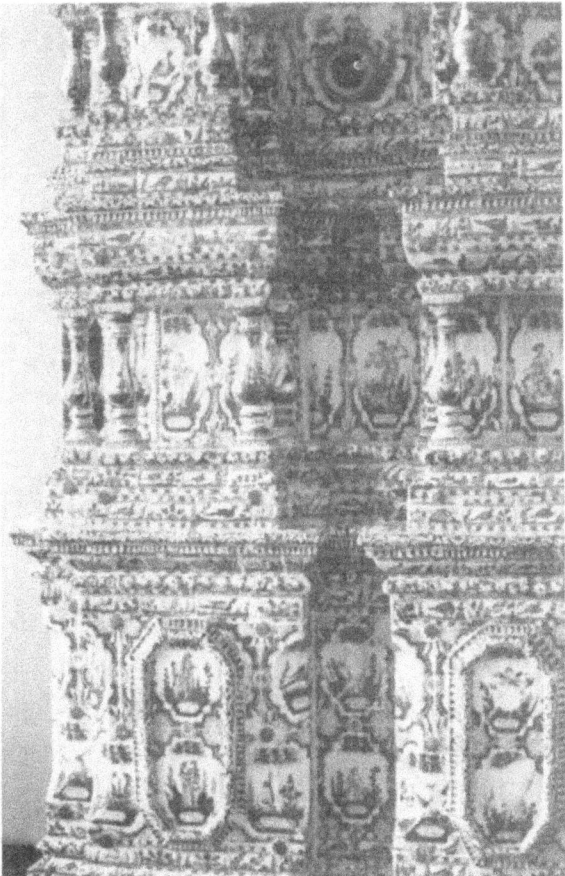

At the end of the eighteenth century, the neoclassical taste in architecture and decorative arts reduced the decorative richness of stovetiles. Plain white tiles with slightly raised borders or low vaselike motifs became fashionable in Moscow. But factories in Kaluga, Sol'vychegodsk, Velikii Ustiug, Totma,

FIG. 8.10 Tile stove. Glazed tile (*izrazets*), central section. 18th century. Suzdal' Archepiscopal Palace Museum.

and other provincial cities continued to make tiles in the earlier styles. Cheaply made tiles illustrated scenes of the 1812 war and genre motifs similar to those on distaffs (fig. 8.11). Finally, in the late nineteenth century, the small ceramics factory at Abramtsevo, where efforts to revive Russian folk and decorative arts were concentrated, produced a number of decorative tile panels, friezes, and fireplaces based on early patterns and featuring motifs from Russian folklore.

The development of domestic ceramics paralleled that of tiles, though technical innovation and design changes occurred for different reasons. Early pottery dishes, either smoke-cured or glazed with a white slip, followed the shapes of wooden or metal *kovshy* and *bratiny*. A few special forms, including a *kumgan* or tall pitcher and a *rukomoi*, a pitcher with a large mouth for washing hands, and flasks of various shapes were made in glazed terra-cotta. They were decorated with fairly simple motifs of trees, birds, stripes, and zigzags in brightly colored enamels on a white ground. Called *tsenina*, like enameled tiles, the thick earthenware of red-tinted clay was thrown on a wheel, and was decorated in bright blue, yellow, green, and brown enamels on white backgrounds in designs reminiscent of those in northern peasant painting.

Majolica was first made in the 1720s, at a pottery owned by the merchant Grebenshchikov, who employed several workers from a group of villages southwest of Moscow, known collectively as Gzhel'.[42] These peasant potters returned home and started their

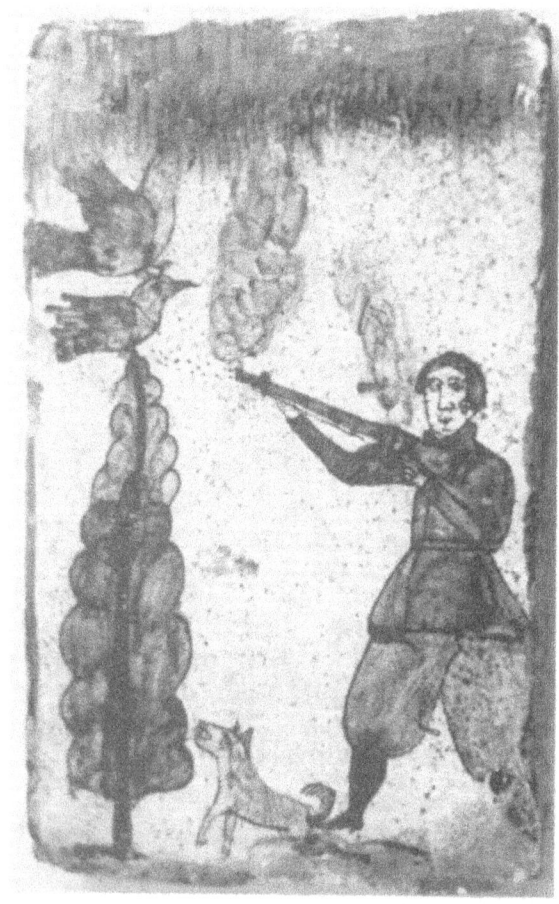

FIG. 8.11 "Hunter" tile. Moscow region (?), 1830s. Kolomenskoe.

own potteries, using the techniques they had learned in Moscow. They were so successful that their majolica ware soon competed with Grebenshchikov's. The merchant tried unsuccessfully to stop his peasant rivals by enserfing them; he finally abandoned his factory in 1774, and Gzhel' became the center of majolica production.

Gzhel' majolica was practical, but many pieces, like their wooden counterparts, were highly inventive in design and decoration. The large pitchers (fig. 8.12), *kumgany* and *kvasniki* (made to serve kvass, a fermented drink), with their distinctive wheel-shaped bodies, high necks, and boldly curved spouts and handles, were decorated in ways that emphasized these features, sometimes treating the spout like a bird's neck or a beak. Pitchers, bowls, and platters were painted with birds, trees, human figures, and buildings with pointed roofs and weather vanes, or with luxuriant floral and geometric patterns, sometimes incorporating dates and verbal inscriptions like those on *lubki*. In the 1780s, Gzhel' potters decorated pitchers with small figures of soldiers or peasants, dogs, and goats, modeled in the round and attached around the handles and rims. They also made figurines or toys representing peasants in typical activities such as carrying water, pulling a child on a sled, or happily fighting, scenes clearly adapted from *lubki*.

Another refinement in Gzhel' ceramics came around 1800, with the discovery of a nearly white clay suitable for semifaience that did not require coating with a

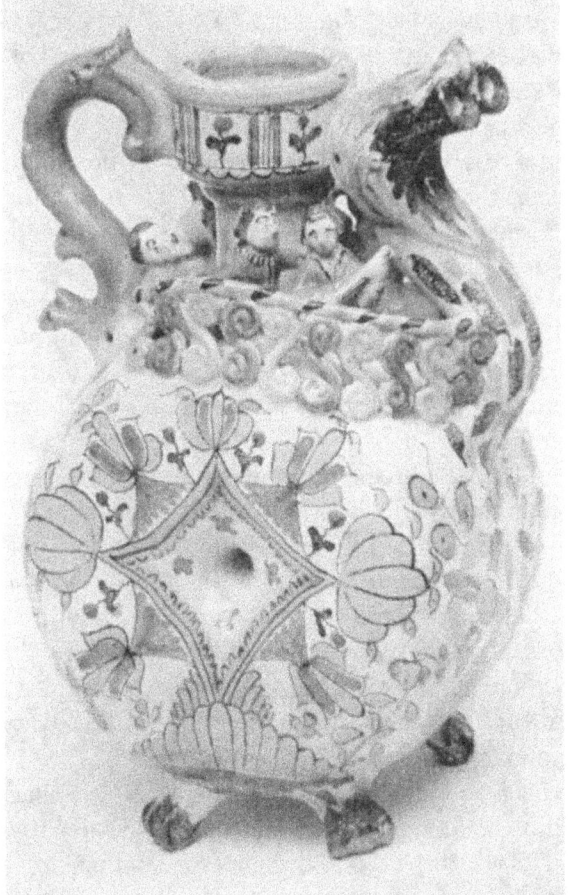

FIG. 8.12 Kvass pitcher. Majolica, polychrome glazes. Gzhel', 18th century. GIM.

white enamel shell before colored designs were added. The new method saved labor and allowed more variety in the brushwork and detailing of designs. Pieces of this type (fig. 8.13) were decorated in semitransparent dark blue or, more rarely, brown glaze, with patterns of leaves, vines, or hatching strokes accenting the roundness of the body of the pitcher, and often a date painted in large numerals around the neck. Small molded figures, like those on majolica pieces, were also perched on the tops of pitchers and inkwells.

Creamy white earthenware, pure faience, was introduced about thirty years later by a peasant, Afanasii Kiselev, and his partners the Terekhov brothers. Kiselev developed a nearly white clay and a variety of devices for decorating the glazed surface, by painting, transfer printing, and combining colored glazes with metallic oxides to produce iridescent, luster effects. The tsar decorated the partners "for improving the manufacture of faience ware and stimulating other appanage peasant potters of the Gzhel' district to manufacture such faience ware of an improved sort."[43] Soon thirty or more potteries were making great quantities of faience tableware, popularly called "Russian Staffordshire." Like stovetiles of the same period, these pieces looked more European than Russian.

The final development in ceramics was the long-awaited mastery of porcelainmaking techniques. Introduced in the mid-eighteenth century from Germany, porcelain manufacture was confined to the Imperial Porcelain Factory outside Petersburg and the Gardner factory near Dmitrov. Rival firms, including Gzhel' potteries, tried to discover the secret formula for porcelain. According to legend, a peasant potter named Pavel Kulikov learned the formula while he was working at a small, German-owned china factory outside Moscow. Kulikov opened his own factory in the village of Volodino and sold chinaware locally and in Moscow. It was not long before two other peasants, Khrapunov and Gusiatnikov, broke into the factory, stole samples of his paste and glaze, and sketched the design of his furnace. Within a generation, factories throughout the Gzhel' area were producing porcelain of high quality, though not at the level of the Imperial Porcelain Factory. Intended for a broad market, the Gzhel' porcelain was decorated in a variety of styles, some resembling contemporary European chinaware, but most deliberately more Russian in character, with landscapes, scenes of battles during the French invasion of 1812 or the Crimean war in the 1850s, familiar monuments of Moscow and St. Petersburg, and scenes of folklife. Small porcelain figurines of peasants and "popular types" enjoyed popularity in the 1840s and 1850s. Based on lubki and popular books, they reflected an idealized, nostalgic image of peasant life that could also be found in other luxury arts and in academic painting and literature of the period.

Outside of Gzhel', several villages in clay-rich districts began to manufacture pottery, sometimes cooperating to set up factories. Skopin, in Riazan' Province, produced sturdy blue and black dishes, but became best known for a distinctive type of kvass jar modeled in the form of an osprey, the skopa, from which the town of Skopin took its name (fig. 8.14). Other vessels were shaped like centaurs and other fantastic creatures from Slavic or Greek mythology, perhaps modeled on *lubki*. Skopin potters followed traditional methods of finding and working their clay, building the forms by hand, stamping or cutting designs into the partly hardened clay, and firing the vessels. They made their own glazes, which they poured over the objects to create many variations of one tone and driplike effects.[44] Many potters displayed their wares on benches or poles in front of their houses, or took them to local fairs. These sculptural dishes and other Skopin ceramics were made more for country and provincial buyers than for middle-class Muscovite tastes.

The potteries of Gzhel' and Skopin achieved the highest level of ceramic manufacture that could still be identified with peasant production and style, as opposed to upper-class applied art. But peasants in other villages near clay deposits made cruder pottery for local markets. Ivan Stoliarov, a peasant who grew up in such a village, described the work as "heavy, dirty, and bad for the health of the potter's entire family."[45] The hardest part was digging clay from deep pits, which were buttressed but sometimes collapsed, like coal pits. The job was done in winter, when the ground was frozen; the clay was stored in sheds and brought into the *izba* for working. Most potters used simple, hand-turned wooden wheels and made

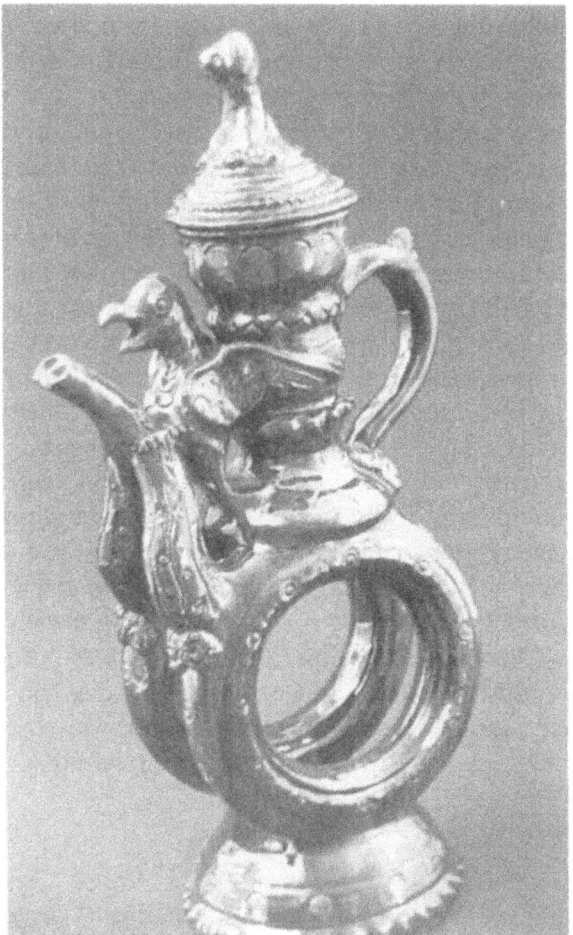

FIG. 8.14 Kvass jug. Terracotta, brown glaze. Skopin, Riazan' Province, 1978. Union of Artists, Moscow.

thick-sided bowls or jugs. These were dried and fired in a large oven, which was difficult to regulate; many batches were lost.

Some pieces were sold unglazed, very cheaply; others were treated before firing with a "glaze" made of tar mixed with sand and a lead powder, which the potters prepared by heating a lead mixture in a large cauldron, stirring it vigorously so that the air would make it oxidize into powder. The entire family helped in the task, the women and children smearing the tar mixture onto the bowls, and the men sprinkling the lead powder. This took from dawn until late at night, and the air was always full of lead dust: "it got into the nose, mouth, throat, and lungs, and even spit had an unpleasant, cloying taste."[46] A family with two adept potters could produce a finished batch of bowls in about two weeks. The next task was to sell them, and this was not easy in a village full of potters. There was a large market in Voronezh, with an area reserved for potters, who paid a small fee and built light shelters where they stayed all summer. Peasants also came from outlying areas once or twice a week to sell glazed or unglazed pots and jugs; sometimes they could sell everything in a day or two, but often they had to try other markets and travel up to a hundred versts, more than sixty miles, in search of buyers.[47] The enormous outlay of effort to make and sell the pots for very little money was more typical than the situation of peasants working in factories or cooperative workshops. But this picture of ordinary peasant ceramics manufacture makes the quality of Gzhel' and Skopin pottery all the more remarkable.

The most varied and intriguing ceramic works are small clay figures of people, animals, and hybrid creatures made in Skopin, Gzhel', and other pottery centers. Modeled by hand, baked in ordinary ovens, and painted rather than glazed, most of these figures were made by peasant women and children for holiday gifts and for sale at local markets. Figures from such widely separated regions as Kargopol' in the far north, Viatka at the northwestern edge of the Urals, and Filimonovo in Tula Province had much in common stylistically, particularly their geometrical ornamentation and bright colors. These figures were the result of acute observation and lively imagination. Kargopol' toys, for all their strange coloration and schematic features, showed the artist's careful attention to how a man blew a horn, how a cat played with string, or how a bear might try to play an accordion. Viatka figures revealed fascination with social interactions and urban fashions introduced by exiled intellectuals in the 1840s, and a purely esthetic joy in the complexities of bows, flounces, bonnets, and brilliant stripes, checks, and flowerlike patterns. In common with other kinds of toys, these ceramic figures were really pieces of nonutilitarian folk sculpture.

Toys in All Media

The Russians have a peculiar talent for making figures and toys out of
the most worthless materials in the world: straw, shavings, ice,
dough, they turn all to account.

— Robert Sears, 1855[1]

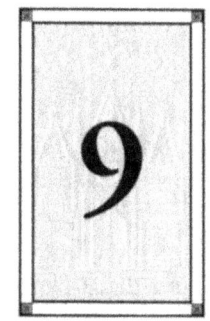

Visitors to Russian markets marveled at the ingenuity and variety of the toys on display. All the materials used by peasant and town artisans for other purposes were also available for fashioning toys. The skills and workshop practices used for the production of carved and painted wooden utensils, ceramic dishes, fabrics, and ornamental items were readily adapted to the making of wood, clay, tin, papier-mâché, and cloth toys. No single technique predominated; all the materials and methods and even most of the images described in this section were represented in toys. Intimately related to peasant life, as children's playthings and as the products of home industries, toys also differed from most crafted objects because of their wide range of media and styles and their flexible relationship to tradition.[2]

The scale of toymaking varied. A parent could take a few spare moments to make a doll out of a piece of firewood and a rag, or an animal out of a twisted branch. But toymaking was also a widespread cottage industry: during the winter each family member worked on some stage of the manufacture, and the total output was sold to middlemen. Large artels and factories employed both peasants and townsfolk in many areas. Sergiev-Posad, the settlement that grew up around the Trinity-Sergiev Monastery near Moscow, was one of the most successful toy-producing centers. An exhaustive statistical study of the light industries of Sergiev made by D. I. Vvedenskii in 1927 showed that a large percentage of local families were occupied by some form of toymaking. The number had grown from 333 households in 1879 to 471 in 1900, 531 in 1912, and over 600 by 1926; at the turn of the century most of the toymaking families were registered as townspeople rather than peasants.[3] Vvedenskii's work covered such questions as the degree of specialization, the size of working units, the cost of materials for various types of manufacture, the outlets for selling, and expected income. It included statistics on several distinct categories of toys: clay toys, lathe-turned toys, toys of mixed materials, painted or poker-burned toys, dolls with clothing, joined wood toys, musical instruments, balls, and various soft toys. These charts and statistics indicate official consciousness of the diversity of the craft and the importance of this type of home industry for the economy of the region.

Long before toys were made for trade, they were certainly present in most households. Toys in all cultures sometimes served as substitutes for real things. In early Russia, some pagan amulets in the form of wood and clay figures may have been kept as both heirlooms and toys after the conversion to Christianity, and in that way preserved from destruction. The chunky wooden doll called a *panka* and the toy horse made from a stump or a branching root, crudely carved with neither features nor limbs, may be close in form and significance to *domovye* found in Novgorod excavations. The same could be true of the small clay figures from Skopin, Kargopol', and other areas, which closely resemble findings from early Kievan and Novgorod sites. Many of these were hollow and pierced to be used as whistles (fig. 9.1). They were probably more than mere playthings and noisemakers. The village of Viatka celebrated the coming of spring, a rite connected with the pagan sun god Iarilo, with a weeklong holiday called the "Whistling Dance," *svistopliaska* (also a colloquial term for pandemonium), during which these whistling figures were played. There was also a peasant superstition that whistling could chase evil spirits out of a bad child.[4]

Thanks to careful records of the Romanov tsars' household expenses, we know that the children of Tsar Mikhail Fedorovich were given "amusing dolls" painted in various colors in 1628.[5] Peter the Great's wife recorded an order of several toys to be sent from Moscow to Petersburg in 1721: three cows, two horses, two deer, four sheep, two pairs of swans, two roosters, one duck, a model town with soldiers, and three balls.[6] Evidently they were the products of Sergiev-Posad.

Even when there was no money to buy toys, it was easy enough to make them of kindling wood, straw, and scraps of fabric. Among the most individualistic and fascinating were figures made of pinecones, lichens, twigs, and moss. Called *lesovniki* or *mokhovniki* (forest or moss people), they embodied the spirits of the deep forest.

Besides such simple toys, which were made almost everywhere, there were regional specializations, just as there were in other folk arts. Wooden horses and horses with carriages or sleighs came from the Gorodets area. Some were of plain wood with a few dark spots and lines for accent, much like the distaffs carved with incrustation. Carved and painted horses and other toys were made by Ignatii Mazin and fellow artists from the nearby village of Kurtsevo. Artists from Bogorodskoe, about twenty kilometers from Sergiev-Posad, specialized in carved toys that they left unpainted, "in white."[7]

Many toys were topical: multifigure scenes of Russian peasants driving out the French during the 1812 war; Russian soldiers beating the Turks in the 1870s; famous generals such as Aleksandr Suvorin on horseback. In the Soviet period, miniature battalions of Red Army soldiers were arranged on a hinged base so that they could be made to move in formation. Toys illustrated typical activities of peasant life: plowing and sowing grain, spinning thread and plaiting *lapti* (fig. 9.2), dancing and playing fiddles and accordions. Several Bogorodskoe toys were based on popular prints of city tradesmen and peddlers, fashionable ladies and cavaliers (fig. 9.3), or "Stages of Human Life." Some quoted works by well-known artists, such as Aleksandr Orlovskii's *Dandy in a Drozbki*, a lithograph popular in the 1820s.[8] Among the favorite subjects were the rural clergy. The figure of a monk carrying a bulging sheaf of grain that almost conceals a seductive young peasant woman among the stalks was a

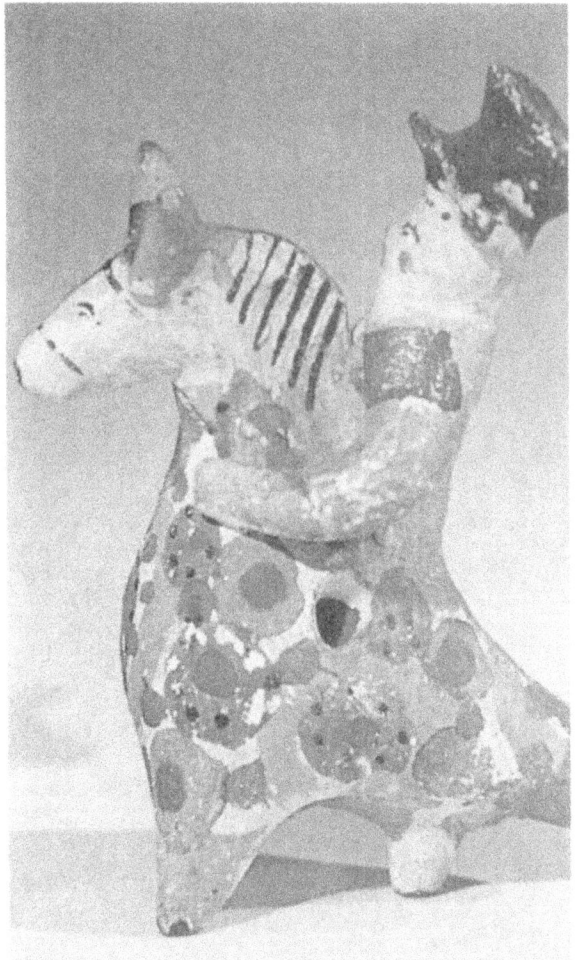

FIG. 9.1 Rider-whistle. Red clay, tempera. Dymkovo, late 19th or early 20th century. Sergiev-Posad Toy Museum.

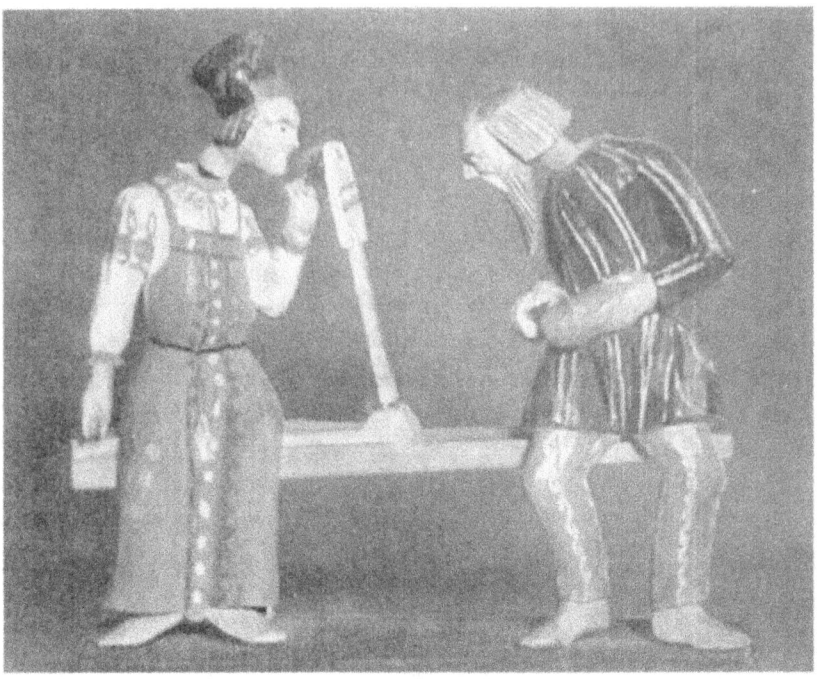

FIG. 9.2 "Spinning and Plaiting *Lapti.*"
Carved and painted wood.
Bogorodskoe, late 19th century. MNI.

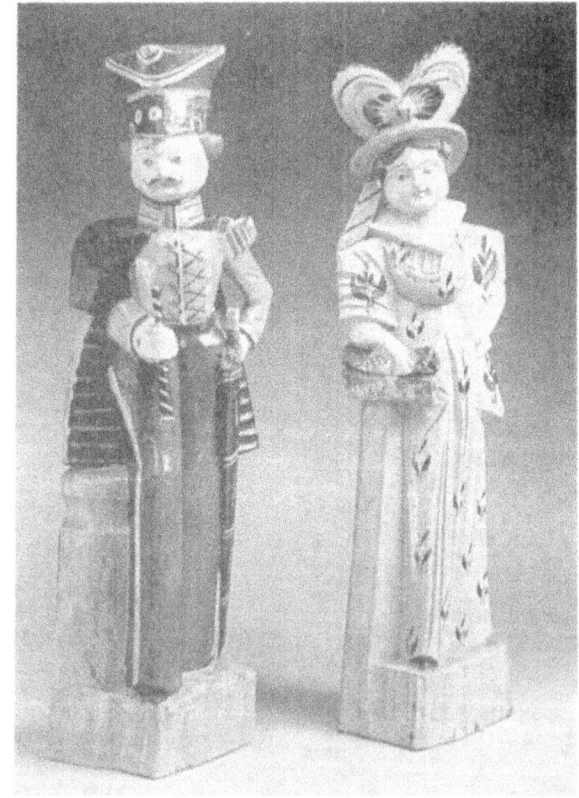

FIG. 9.3 "Lady and Hussar."
Carved and painted wood.
Bogorodskoe, mid-19th
century. Sergiev-Posad Toy
Museum.

familiar image in wood, clay, and even porcelain. A carver named Ryshev from Sergiev-Posad made clever mechanical toys featuring monks whose dark habits dropped down when a knob was twisted, leaving them pink and naked. He sold them for fifty kopeks, until the police caught him and threatened dire punishment unless he swore never to make such toys again. Ryzhev's humor appealed to Nikolai Bartram, a pioneer in the early twentieth-century revival of Sergiev toys; he interviewed the artist and asked whether he had kept his promise. Ryzhev admitted that he continued to make monk toys, but sold them for three rubles.[9] Such irreverence toward the clergy and religious authority was common.[10] More orthodox religious subjects—Jonah and the Whale, the Sacrifice of Abraham, and the Judgment of Solomon—were handled ingeniously in toys with moving parts. Sergiev artists were also known for splendid miniature monasteries, including Rostov the Great and the Trinity-Sergiev Monastery itself, carved and painted to scale, with all the churches, refectories, and bell towers richly detailed and with doors that opened to reveal *trompe-l'oeil* interiors painted on paper.[11]

Toys that could be manipulated and altered were among the best-known products of Bogorodskoe. Musical and dancing animals, pecking birds, and industrious bears chopping wood or washing each other in Russian baths were worked with a push-rod or a ball on strings. Figures with jointed arms and legs held together by elastic bands bowed and danced when their circular stands were pushed. Entire animated groups, regiments of soldiers or herds of farm animals, stood on scissorlike trellises whose action made them move back and forth in rows.

The most famous type of wooden toy was the *matreshka* (commonly rendered in English as "matrioshka"), usually shaped as a peasant woman in a *sarafan*, hollow inside to hold a whole series of smaller nesting dolls. Legends about the origin of the form related it to an ancient mother goddess of Siberian peoples. Travelers told of a mysterious golden statue, hollow and containing many layers or shells of gold. Regardless of any ancient source, the wooden *matreshka*, comfortably rounded and containing a multitude of offspring, was a familiar symbol of fertility and security. The idea of nesting figures may actually have come from Japanese toys. The first documented Russian *matreshka* was designed in the 1890s by Sergei Maliutin, a professional artist and member of the Talashkino folk art revival group; it was shaped on a lathe and carved by the carpenter Zvezdochkin. This was an eight-piece doll, the figure of a woman in a modest *sarafan* and kerchief, inside her a boy, then a girl, and so on, the smallest piece a baby in swaddling clothes. Variants soon appeared: nesting caricatures of artists' friends (such a group was done of the Abramtsevo circle) and characters from Gogol's stories, similar to figures made in porcelain. An eight-piece set depicted General Kutuzov and Napoleon with members of their armies. A particularly ambitious piece began with an outer figure of God the Father holding a dove, enclosing the Roman pope, the

Russian patriarch, a monk, a kulak, a nun, and a sexton in descending order, down to the "dark masses" represented by a blindfolded woman.

Clay toys ranged from the archaic animal and human figures from Filimonovo and the awkwardly humorous creatures from Kargopol', to dolls that showed keen observation of life and fashion in large towns. Among the most sophisticated were clay figures made in Tula, depicting well-dressed women holding parasols, painted in subtle colors, and with natural, individual expressions (fig. 9.4). These figures are similar to wooden ones made in Sergiev-Posad depicting fashionable ladies and cavaliers or hussars, painted to show exact details of uniform or dress, and they reflect the same subjects that appealed to many distaff makers.

The most lively and most varied clay figures were from Viatka, sometimes called Dymkovo toys for the village across the river where most of the makers lived (fig. 9.5). The settlement had been founded in the fifteenth century, when Tsar Ivan III exiled a group of recalcitrant inhabitants of Velikii Ustiug to this remote place at the edge of the Urals. Many of the settlers were arti-

sans, and they pursued a variety of crafts. Toymaking was most successful. By the middle of the nineteenth century, fifty households were making clay toys at the rate of 100,000 figures a year.[12]

Dymkovo figures were made by women and children working together in family units, dividing the labor according to the skill required

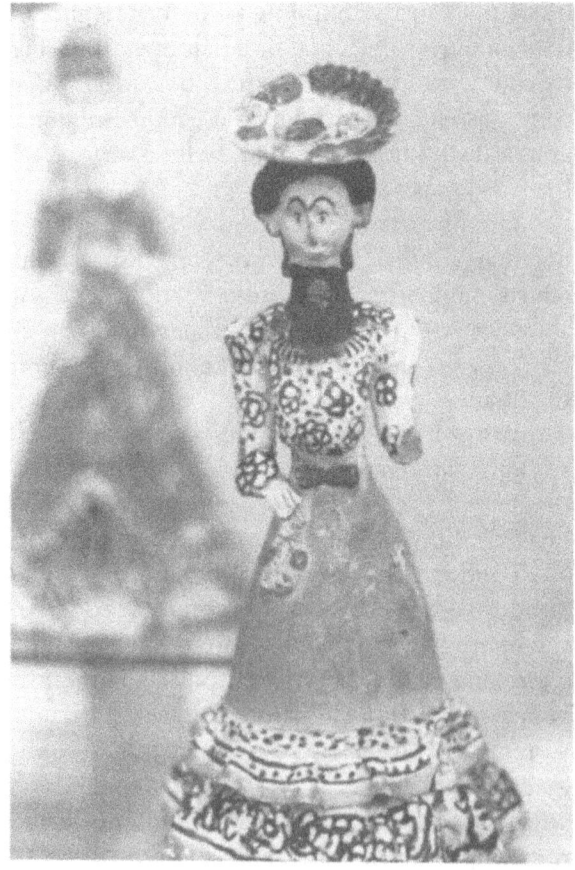

FIG. 9.4 "Ladies with Parasols." White clay, paint. Bol'shie Gonchary, near Tula, 1880s–1890s. Sergiev-Posad Toy Museum.

for each step. The clay was prepared in the fall, mixed with clean sand from brooks, and kneaded, to be ready as soon as the late summer field work was finished. Each person specialized in a particular part of the body: the bell-shaped skirt, trunk, arms, head and bonnet, and other accessories such as parasols, yoke and pails, or a swaddled baby. The limbs were joined to the body, and the seams rubbed with a damp rag or a wet finger, and then the batch of figures was set aside to dry for several days while the family began a new batch.

After drying, the figures were baked over an open fire of eight birch logs. After firing they were placed in a solution of fresh milk and crushed chalk, which made an even, white ground for the paint. The paints, made from dry pigments mixed with egg yolk and either kvass or vinegar, were in six colors: blue, yellow, green, orange, crimson, and black, and sometimes tints and mixtures including light blue, rose, and brown. Small squares of gold leaf could be glued onto the dress or bonnet. The eyes were painted first, with a fine brush saturated with black pigment. The painters used homemade brushes bound with rags to lay in the flat, even paint on the blouse and for most of the stripes and dots that made up the plaid and floral patterns on the skirt; they often used their fingers and left fingerprints. The dolls were finished with coats of egg white.

Most of the figures of women, men, children, and animals reflected village life. They were often grouped as if involved in some activity: feeding animals, milking cows, fetching water, playing guitars or accordions, and dancing. These pieces show how villagers in an area that was once quite remote responded to the influx of exiled Polish and Russian intellectuals in the 1840s, and to the arrival of military garrisons and an urban population in the following decades. The figures were humorous without being satirical, fairly predictable in overall form, but with fanciful touches that made them appealing.

Obviously all these toys filled more than one role. They were playthings first, and later became amusing collectors' items. For the peasants who made them, they offered the possibility of some extra income. However, payment was notoriously low; jobbers bought and shipped toys by the pound—for example, records show 21,328 pounds of toys sent from Sergiev-Posad to Moscow in 1879—so bulk was more important than quality.[13] But toymaking may have given some satisfaction to the artisans who engaged in this activity instead of making fabric, rope, shoes, cakes, or other items to sell at markets. Local resources, traditions, and the reputation of a village for a specialized product partly determined the choice of craft; most peasants involved in toymaking or other handicrafts learned the techniques in early childhood. Carving wood or fashioning figures from clay was a part of family life from fall to early spring, as many nineteenth- and early twentieth-century photographs of peasant families doing such piecework show. One of the senior masters of toymaking in Kargopol', Ul'iana Babkina, who was born in 1888

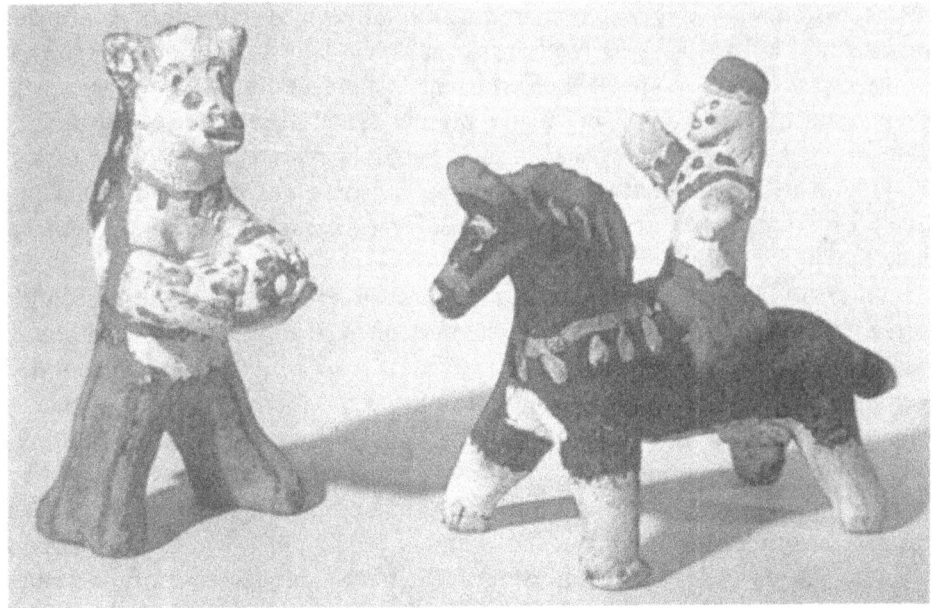

FIG. 9.6 Ul'iana Babkina, "Rider and
Bear." Red clay, tempera. Grinevo
village, Kargopol' District, Arkhangel'sk
Province, 1970s. Sergiev-Posad Toy
Museum.

and lived to age ninety-nine, said that she could not imagine herself *not* making her small clay figures (fig. 9.6); they had always been part of her life from childhood. For Babkina, modeling the clay was like singing.[14] Without glossing over the obvious material difficulties documented by Vvedenskii and others, it is still apparent from the remarkable quality of Russian toys that families who made them took pride in their work.

Several scholars who studied folk toys, including Bartram, Tseretelli, Voronov, Nekrasov, and Bakushinskii, pointed out that toys of all media came closest of all forms of folk art to expressing the central relationships between art and other facets of peasant life. Through their ties to ancient forms of worship, their use as gifts for festivals, their function in amusing and educating the young, toys represented conservation of important, though sometimes subconscious, community traditions. In the techniques of production based on methodical routine but allowing for inventive variations, especially in ornamentation, toymaking represented the fundamental approaches to design and ornament found in all the folk arts. Finally, like games, puppets, popular theater, and folksongs, toys embodied the spirit of play combined with an underlying seriousness of content that brought them close to the original role of art in folklife.

Russians made toys of every conceivable material, and in many ways this category of folk art encompasses the range of materials, styles, methods of production, and means of distribution described in the five chapters in this section. By examining physical materials and working methods in relation to forms and designs in several examples of each genre of folk art, we can appreciate both the pervasive authority and the versatility of traditions. We become aware of standards of quality—harmony, appropriateness, sensory appeal, and even true-to-life humor—that are quite different from those of professional and academic art, but are equally valid. In the following section, we will look at some traditional images and designs from a different perspective, to suggest how certain forms may have developed over time, not only because they were customary in a given region or appropriate to a particular material, but because they had some significance within the historical and social framework of the Russian peasant community.

PART III

Designs
and
Their
Meanings

Amulet, Ornament,
and Ritual

This curiously designed [spicecake] figure is not the fruit of fantasy of
some common baker. . . . It has significance, indeed great
significance, because it is one of the surviving examples of an ancient
Russian pagan mythology.

—Vladimir Stasov, 1872[1]

The focal point of a Russian house, the icon corner with its array of sacred images draped with embroidered towels, gave visual presence to a folk religiosity with roots in both Christian and Slavic cultures. Towels and other household objects surrounded the peasant with forms and images expressing the two levels of belief, *dvoeverie*, that pervaded Russian folk culture from the tenth to the twentieth centuries. The theory that folk art—toy horses, dolls, spicecakes, and the figures embroidered on towels, carved on frontal boards, or painted on domestic implements—had common ancestry in ancient Slavic idols was based on the practice of relating objects found in archeological excavations to motifs found in folklore and contemporary folk arts. Researchers sought to identify forms shared by all types of Russian folk art. Vasilii Voronov wrote in the 1920s:

> If we exclude the widely distributed motifs of the seventeenth century, like the heraldic lion and unicorn, the double-headed eagle, and the sirin-bird; if we separate the many-faceted genre characteristic of the eighteenth century, carriages,

costumes, furnishings, clocks, and so forth; then we are left with the horse, snow leopard, goddesses, the sacred tree, the sacrificial altar, and other graphically vigorous symbols of bygone folk culture.[2]

Voronov's hypothesis was that not only figures but also abstract motifs had significance beyond decoration, that circles, rhomboids, rosettes, swastikas, crescents, stars, zigzags, and wavy lines were based on natural forms and therefore evoked natural powers. This interpretation of Slavic symbolism and cultural identity is too general to be really informative about the specific sources and meanings of folk art motifs. But certainly the varied forms of ornament were means of enhancing the value or significance of an object, making it both personal and powerful. In the preceding chapters, we saw how certain design principles were related to materials, craft traditions, and uses of various objects in peasant households and in the wider sphere of commerce. In this section, we will focus on other kinds of relationships between the formal properties of certain folk art motifs and the changing historical and social contexts in which they evolved. Using some of the same archeological and historical material as did Stasov, Voronov, and other Russian scholars, but without the goal of matching folk art and ritual with archaic prototypes, we can appreciate a complex and irregular evolution of forms through the interaction of several artistic traditions.

The original functions of prehistoric art forms and their development in subsequent cultures cannot be fully traced, despite nineteenth-century speculations, because concrete evidence is meager. However, there is evidence that the evolution of forms in folk art paralleled the transformation of ancient rituals into popular games, songs, and folk theater. Physical manifestations of pagan divinities were absorbed into the images of Christian saints, much as pagan rituals were incorporated into Christian feasts. The development of visual folk culture was akin to that of vernacular language and literature, through the interaction of oral folk epos and written accounts of the lives of saints and secular events.[3]

The human, animal, and abstract forms of Russian folk art may have originated in the lands north of the Black Sea and along the Dniepr River. Slavs or proto-Slavs inhabited this region during the first millennium B.C.; archeological evidence shows some contact with Scythian tribes in the south Russian steppes in the late Bronze Age and early Iron Age (about 1200–750 B.C. and 750–500 B.C.).[4] The Scythians honored their noble dead with burial mounds, furnished with quantities of grave goods, pottery, horse trappings, armor, and gold and silver jewelry. The decoration on these objects reflected a mythology of sun, sky, and earth gods, related to those of Greece, the eastern Mediterranean, and Iran. Many Greco-Scythian motifs were later used by the Slavs: the swimming duck, the horned stag, the female figure with upraised arms, and patterns based on triangles, interlocked circles, and rhomboids.[5]

Between the second and fourth centuries A.D., Goths and other Germanic tribes invaded the northern Black Sea lands, pushing remnants of Scythian and then Slavic cultures into eastern and northern Europe. The Slavs, divided into separate western and eastern groups, moved into the Danube basin, the Balkans, the Baltic, and northeast up the Dniepr River. Scythian-inspired art forms became significant in Russia during the eighth to the tenth centuries, when Slavs moving north encountered Finno-Ugrian, Lithuanian, and Slavic groups from the Baltic region, and when the Varangians from Scandinavia began colonizing the Oka, Volga, and Dniepr River area from the north down to Kiev. The territory that later became Russia, from the Black Sea to the Baltic and east to the Urals, was occupied by several Slavic groups: the Viatichi, Radimichi, Severiani, and others were settled in farming and herding communities before the rise of Kiev, and were listed in the Russian Primary Chronicle. The Byzantine historian Procopius of Caesarea wrote in the sixth century that the eastern Slavs venerated rivers and nymphs and that they offered animal sacrifices to "one god, the creator of lightning, who is lord of all." The tenth-century Arab traveler Ibn Fadlan wrote that they placed offerings before wooden idols. Deities varied from one region or tribe to another; only Perun, god of thunder and lightning, appeared in all the groups.[6]

The closest thing to a Slavic pantheon appeared at a very late stage, when Prince Vladimir of Kiev marked the beginning of his reign in 980 by erecting a group of idols on a hill next to the palace: "a wooden Perun with a silver head and golden mustache and Khors and Dazhbog and Stribog and Simargl and Mokosh."[7] Other divinities were named in later writings: Volos, Svarog, Sviatovit, Rod and Rozhanitsa, Kupalo and Iarilo. Some of these were major gods, others local cult figures. Their traits and functions varied widely, and some Slavic gods may have taken on aspects of related deities of neighboring cultures.[8] Perun, like Zeus, was a god of thunder and lightning; by Vladimir's time, he was probably identified with the Scandinavian Thor as patron of the Varangian warriors who ruled Kiev. Khors and Dazhbog were sun gods; Dazhbog was the son of Svarog, another sun god and master of fire. Stribog, possibly a father god and a deity of the wind, and Simargl, a winged dog which sang and spread its wings to make wind come and distribute seeds, were related to ancient Iranian nature cults. The female deity Mokosh, mentioned in many early sources, was not clearly defined, but may have been an aspect of the ubiquitous Mother Moist Earth, *Mat' syra zemlia,* connected with the earth, fertility, fate, oathtaking, and the occult. Some of the roles and mutations of these gods will be described shortly, as they retained great power in folk belief.

The physical remains of the early Slavic tribes were mainly grave goods (fig. 10.1): small metal ornaments shaped like ducks, roosters, falcons, horses, deer, and some imaginary creatures with two heads or body parts of more than one species.[9] Images of horses, the motifs most pervasive in later folk art, were prevalent in the areas where the Slavs came into contact with the Finno-Ugrians and Balts, the wide, fertile belt of mixed forests and grasslands in the basins of the Dniepr, Oka, Volga, and Kliazma rivers.[10] The Viatichi, Radimichi, Krivichi, Severiani, and Il'men' Slavs made ornaments of bronze, copper, or low-grade silver. They cast most shapes in stone molds, which allowed simple detailing by means of grooves incised within the hollowed-out forms. They employed the lost-wax technique for more complex ornamentation. A linen or woolen thread was soaked in wax and twisted or braided into the required shape. It was covered with soft clay, dried, and fired so that the wax melted and the thread burned away. Molten metal was then poured into the clay mold. The resulting amulets and pendants had intricate contours and graphic patterns of twisted threads resembling filigree work.[11]

Objects found in mound burials included plaques to sew on garments, ornaments for horse trappings, and circular headbands with small ornaments hanging from them. The designs of the headbands and their pendant ornaments were specific to each tribe. The Severian type was a circle with heavy hanging spirals like coiled snakes; the Il'men' or Novgorodian type was a circle with pendant rhomboids decorated with incised rosettes. The Radimichian bands held crescent shapes with hanging triangles, and the Viatichian bands displayed crescent forms with rows of teeth, rays, or petals along their inner edges. The Viatichian pieces, from the fertile Oka River basin and the area around Moscow, showed the fullest development of an arsenal of symbolic forms shared by the other Slavic tribes.[12] The forces of nature, personified by Perun, Khors, Svarog, Mokosh, and other gods worshipped

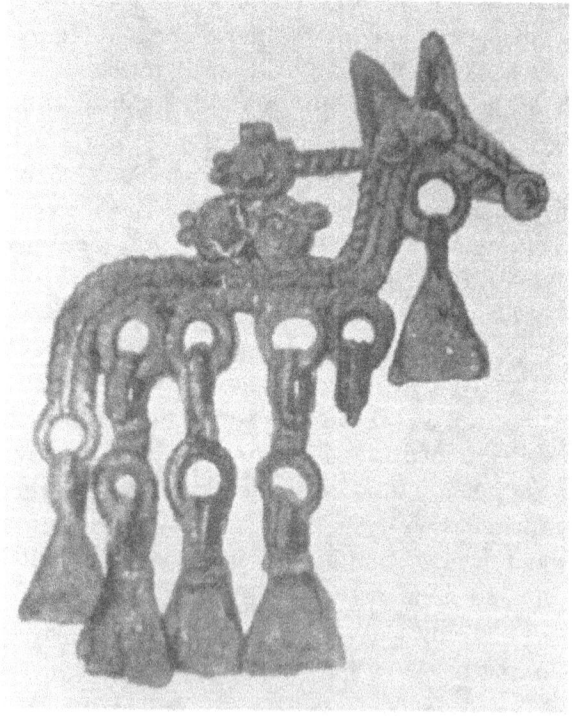

FIG. 10.1 Pendant. Bronze. Viatichian Slavs, 10th to 12th centuries. Vologda Museum.

over a wide territory for many centuries, were perhaps embodied in these ornaments.

The Viatichian ornaments contained both abstract designs and forms based on nature; the ornaments symbolized natural forms by resemblance, association, or convention.[13] The small pendants hanging from the headbands differed from one period to another. The earliest, before the twelfth century, were crescents from which extended seven rays, with soft, slightly rounded contours, almost like the petals of a flower.[14] In later ornaments, the crescents' rays extended in the shape of small axes, sometimes engraved with lightning-like zigzags and solar disks. In the thirteenth century, the ends of the rays were tipped with miniature horses, birds, trees, or abstract rhomboids, disks, or swastikas. All these motifs might be related to the functions of the gods, to the sun and moon, to flowers or the earth's fertility, to thunder and lightning bolts. The axe, an attribute of Perun (or Thor), could also symbolize protection against enemies. The design was widespread in Slavic ornament, appearing on fibulae, headbands, and other jewelry found in *kurgan* burials from the Kiev region north to Riazan', Uglich, and Vladimir.[15]

The bronze headbands with their hanging charms were too heavy to be worn for simple cosmetic reasons. The rituals of making, wearing, and being buried with symbolic amulets were more likely forms of protective magic. The hypothesis that animals and abstract forms symbolized powers of the deities is useful, but there is insufficient material evidence to connect each form with a specific function or meaning. Moreover, there was no consistent roster of Slavic gods. What can be deduced from physical evidence is that the makers of ornamented objects may have sought to evoke more than one divinity by combining different forms on a single object. For instance, on one amulet, a duck was molded so that its very large tail turned into an axe blade. Animals such as the hare, dog, horse, deer, cock, and falcon appeared singly or in pairs (on a bone comb with horse heads at either end), in combination with other animals (a horse shape with a duck in place of the head), and with symbolic forms (a tiny hare with long ears shaped like crescent moons decorating the head of a pin). The amplification suggests a wish to increase the efficacy of a form by doubling or multiplying it, or to cover all needs by conflating the symbols of natural forces or divinities.[16]

Metal ornaments probably replicated designs on objects of wood, bone, textile, and clay, of which few have survived.[17] In addition to personal amulets, the ancient Slavs may have made larger totem-like or apotropaic columns, similar to those described by Ibn Fadlan. Those "idols" and the carved logs found in Novgorod may have given rise to the horse or bird forms of the *okhlupen'* on northern houses and to the *bereginy* on house fronts along the Volga River. The forms of household objects, such as the duck-shaped *kovsh*, used for ceremonial occasions and once embodying specific beliefs, gradually became conventional; in a sense, the natural forces grew domesticated and were incorporated into the daily life of household and village.

One example of a possible carry-over from ancient beliefs was the depiction of animals on wheatcakes and spicecakes. After the rise of Christianity, the pagan Slavs used animal-shaped cakes in rituals, perhaps to replace sacrifices mentioned by chroniclers. In eleventh-century Novgorod, cakes were made of a special white flour, in the shapes of cows and deer. Later, in the eighteenth and nineteenth centuries, spicecake animals were made for St. George's Day, when the herds were sent out to pasture after the winter.[18] The original functions of the wheatcakes are unknown, but the rituals were undoubtedly meaningful to the Slavic inhabitants of Rus' even after Christianization, and they remained important to their descendants. Eventually, the spicecake figures became like toys, and the ritual a game. But the forms provided a sense of continuity and security; it was believed that the cakes helped to protect the herd. They also preserved a tangible element of an ancient ritual.

The Slavic tribes did not live in isolation. Settling along rivers, they had contact with other tribes, and with townspeople of Kiev, Novgorod, and other cities. But they kept their distinctive forms of ornament and their belief in the powers of nature. One of the few surviving large-scale monuments from the tenth century offers a clue about the ways images changed their emphasis from protection of agrarian communities to symbols of centralized authority. Attributes of Perun are evident on the so-called Zbrucz (Zbruchskii) idol (fig. 10.2), found in 1848 in Galicia, southeastern Poland, on the Zbrucz River, a tributary of the Dniestr.[19] It is a four-sided stone pillar carved at its peak with four human faces, each with a conical hat or helmet, looking out in the four directions. Below the faces, in a series of registers in low relief, are torsos with crossed arms and, on the tunic of one, a running horse. In the register below these are smaller female figures with hands outstretched; and finally, at the base, human faces or masks much more shallowly carved than those at the top. This four-faced idol may have symbolized Perun's power to protect, or it may have signified an attempt to bring diverse aspects of divinity together under one crown. In this sense it corresponded to Kievan Prince Vladimir's policy of centralizing the Slavic pantheon by erecting the group of idols with Perun at their head.

The names of pagan gods were evoked for dramatic purpose in the *Tale of Igor's Campaign*,[20] written by a Christian poet in the twelfth century; they still had resonance because author and audience were part of a culture based in the dual-belief system, *dvoeverie*. As Kievan power and Christianity grew, large sculptures representing pagan dieties disappeared: according to legend, after Vladimir was baptized he had the idols cast into the Dniepr River. But the images persisted in amulets and jewelry. Kievan artists adapted the Slavic bird forms to their elegant work in cloisonné enamel and filigree; such pieces were found in twelfth-century sites near the St. Mikhail Monastery. The more active figurative motifs such as horses and stags may have appealed to the Varangian military clans and princely retinues that began to dominate Kievan territory; these motifs were gradually combined with designs from Scandinavia, and with motifs such as gryphons and hero warriors from Greek and Byzantine lands.[21] Elements of Slavic ornament persisted, without their original cult meanings, in the decoration of churches in Kiev, Vladimir, Novgorod, and Moscow, on the covers and in marginal ornaments of gospel books, in secular ornament of the Muscovite tsars and boyars, and in peasant art.

The process by which pagan belief was absorbed into Christian practice was complex, but one aspect important for folk art was the continued role of visual imagery and physical participation in religious celebration. When the Kievan state took on the governing and military role, the once-powerful sky gods Perun and Khors declined in importance, but the cults of Mokosh and Mother Moist Earth remained essential to the agrarian communities.[22] Secondary figures—Volos, protector of herds; Iarilo and Kupalo, associated with the sun, fire, and male youth; Rod and Rozhanitsa, deities related to ancestor worship and rituals of death and birth (*rod* means "kin" and *rozhanitsa* is "one who gives birth"); and the later additions, *rusalki* and *bereginy*, water sprites and protectors—increased in importance and were identified with rural rather than city and military life.

While some of the pagan gods retained their old identities, others took on the guises

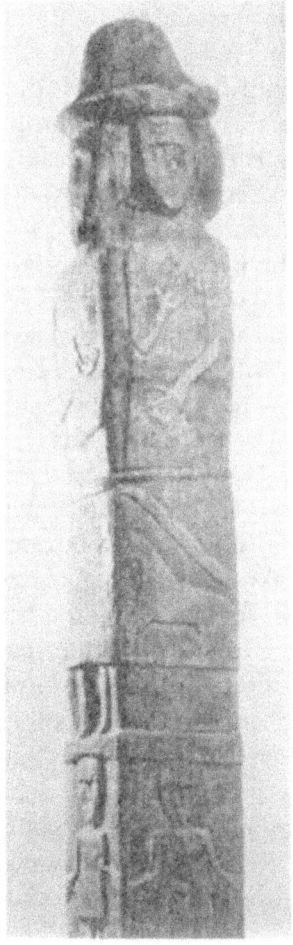

FIG. 10.2 Zbruchskii Idol. Stone pillar with low-relief carving. Dniestr River region, 10th century. National Museum, Cracow.

of Christian saints. For example, Volos was connected by a similar name and function with St. Blasius (Vlasii), who had lived among wild animals and saved a poor woman's pig from a wolf. St. George, on whose feast day (April 23) animals were led out to spring pasture, was a patron of herds and of farming, as his Greek name indicates, before becoming a warrior saint and patron of the Russian princes.[23] His slaying of the dragon connected him typologically with the Greek god Apollo, who killed Python and brought light; the Christian saint therefore absorbed some of the functions of Khors. Kupalo was celebrated at the summer solstice, St. John's Eve, with bonfires and ritual immersion in the rivers and lakes; his popular name, Ivan Kupala, suggests bathing and water (*kupat'*, "to bathe"), a literal rendering of John the Baptist's role (in contrast to his Orthodox title, Ioann Predtechi, "the Forerunner"). Iarilo, more akin to Dionysius than to any Christian figure, was celebrated in the most unrestrained midsummer festivals, often along with Kupalo. Perun and Khors were identified with the prophet Elijah ascending to heaven in his fiery chariot. Elijah (Il'ia), in turn, became a personification of sun and sky, the bringer of rain, guardian against lightning and fire, and protector of summer harvests.

In a more complex shift of identity, the mystery of Mokosh and Mother Moist Earth survived in Christian form in the person of the Byzantine Mother of God.[24] The names Theotokos in Greek and Bogoroditsa in Russian express the active role of giving birth, while the alternative terms Meter Theou and Bogomater' imply a state of being both sacred and protective. These dual emphases relate the image not only to the Byzantine sources of Kievan religious art, but also to the depiction of Mokosh as a stylized female figure with upraised hands. The early Christian *orans* pose may have been so readily understood because it was associated with the Slavic mother goddess. Another pattern of Christian adaptation was represented by Saint Paraskeva or Piatnitsa (Greek and Russian names for the fifth day, Friday), a figure whose historical origins are obscure. Paraskeva-Piatnitsa may have replaced an earlier Slavic goddess of flax and the earth, of a type represented by wooden idols found in twelfth-century sites in the north.[25] Folksongs sometimes called her Paraskeva-L'nianitsa ("linen-maker"),[26] and her image included shocks of flax, flowing water, and long hair. Women celebrated her cult on Fridays, when they abandoned spinning and weaving for orgies pagan enough to be denounced by church councils. In more decorous fashion, young women brought out towels embroidered with images of the Mother Goddess (a female figure with outstretched arms, often flanked by trees and birds, as in the examples described in chapter 12) and presented them to the icon of Paraskeva-Piatnitsa. The ceremony took place on Intercession Saturday in October, the day young women gathered to work on a veil to honor the icon of the Intercession of the Mother of God. The importance of

Paraskeva as a focal figure in the rituals of peasant women was carried over into the life of towns and cities. In Novgorod, with its practical, commercial orientation, Paraskeva-Piatnitsa became the patron saint of the weekly markets and bazaars, perhaps because the fifth day of the week was market day. The Novgorod merchants who traded in Europe dedicated a church to St. Piatnitsa "on the Market" in the twelfth century.[27]

In Russia, as in other countries, common people retained their faith in and reliance on both Christian and pagan patrons and protectors. Folk narratives about supernatural beings and experiences featured both saints and nature or household spirits.[28] Prayers addressed to saints were adaptations of pagan charms or *zagovory;* their language blended forthright directions for a task to be done and protestations of devoutness expressed with churchly formality.[29] The names of Lado and Lada, versatile deities of love and fate, appeared in songs connected with planting, harvesting, and weddings, in addition to those of St. George, St. Nicholas, and other Christian patrons.[30] Special times of year, places, trees, and crops, such as grain and flax, took on personal identities and names. Kostra, or Kostroma, was flax; twisted into a human effigy, it was used in some regions along with straw figures of Kupalo in midsummer festivals.[31] Different patterns of association connected the mythical beings *rusalka, beregina,* and *sirin* with specific aspects of nature and human life. For example, the most important spring fertility ritual, seven or eight weeks after Easter, was known in Ukraine and some other regions as "Rusalka Week," because water sprites called *rusalki* were supposed to come out of the water and live in the fields and birch groves, bringing water and fertility to the land until autumn.[32]

Rusalki, descendants of the spirits of rivers, springs, and woods mentioned by Procopius and by Russian chroniclers, had various attributes in folklore and folk art, depending on local rituals and beliefs. Encountered mainly in the north, they may have been helpful or protective nature spirits akin to the Slavic *bereginy,* known mainly in the Volga area.[33] The name *beregina* may have come from *bereg* ("shore," of a river or lake) or from *berech'* ("to protect"). Both aspects were evoked when artists carved their images on the boats and house fronts along the river. The origin of the name *rusalka* is unknown. At some point it was thought that tribes living along the rivers, close to the *rusalki,* took a similar name, *Rus',* for themselves and eventually used it for their state around Kiev; though without linguistic justification, the theory remained popular.[34] *Rusalki* were visualized as young women combing their long, swirling hair as they emerged from the water. An accretion from the Greek myth of the sirens gave rise to the idea that the *rusalki* tried to attract young men by singing and combing their hair. The influence of Christianity and, later, of Western romanticism added another dimension to the legend: *rusalki* were spirits of women who died unbaptized, or unmarried, or who drowned themselves for love, and lived forever in lakes and rivers trying to lure young men to join them. One of the first Russian operas, "Rusalka of the Dniepr" (1803), was based on this theme; later in the nineteenth century, the composers Dargomyzh-shkii and Rimskii-Korsakov and the painter Kramskoi adapted *rusalka* themes from Pushkin and Gogol.[35]

Bereginy, in the mid-Volga region, were depicted on boats and frontal boards as either female or male figures with boldly curved fish tails (fig. 10.3); their features probably derived from representations of tritons, Nereids, and other mer-figures in Western baroque art. Like *rusalki*, they were usually shown holding waterweeds or branches.[36] Hybrid creatures included the *vodianoi*, a water sprite with a human torso and fish tail; the *leshii* and *polevoi*, forest and field spirits in many different shapes and sizes; and the household spirit *domovoi*.[37] The *simargl*, part bird and part dog, lived in an oak tree at the edge of the world and spread its wings to make the wind come and distribute seeds during Rusalka Week. These mythical beings, along with lions and horses, were carved on frontal boards and tools, in strikingly appropriate ways. For instance, a battledore (*valek*) (figs. 3.10, 10.4), for beating newly woven linen against smooth stones in a river, was carved as a *rusalka* combing her long, flowing hair. Her connection with both water and flax was reinforced in songs that accompanied such work, likening the working of flax to the *rusalka* combing her hair.[38]

The *sirin* and *alkonost* (figs. 10.5, 10.6) were probably introduced by traders from Persia in the eighth or ninth century. In the port of Korsun' (Chersones) on the Black Sea and in Kiev, their images appeared on pottery dishes, gold pendants, and *kolty*, and even in borders of Christian gospel books from the tenth to the thirteenth centuries. The *sirin* or *ptitsa sirin* ("sirin bird") had a woman's head and breast, a bird's feather-covered body, wings, and a long, spreading tail, often depicted as a peacock's tail with distinctive eyes. The *sirin* usually wore a crown, but on Kievan enameled *kolty* her head was framed by a nimbus, perhaps because she was identified as the "heavenly bird" of happiness. Her counterpart, the *alkonost*, bird of sorrow, was rarely portrayed except as a balance to the *sirin*, for example on the opposite side of a door frame or cupboard panel.[39] The *sirin* took on some protective functions of the *rusalka* and those of the peacock as a paradise bird and was sometimes identified with the firebird of Russian fairytales. On *lubki*, cupboard doors, and distaffs, she was often shown perched on a flowering branch or hovering above a tree, similar to depictions of the Tree of Life in the art of many cultures.[40] Like the saints, these fantastic beings and nature spirits were, one scholar said, "close kindred of the tiller of the soil."[41] Their identities evolved in folklore and pictorial art—sometimes in response to historical circumstances, as chapters 12 and 13 show—and many remain vital and familiar figures today.

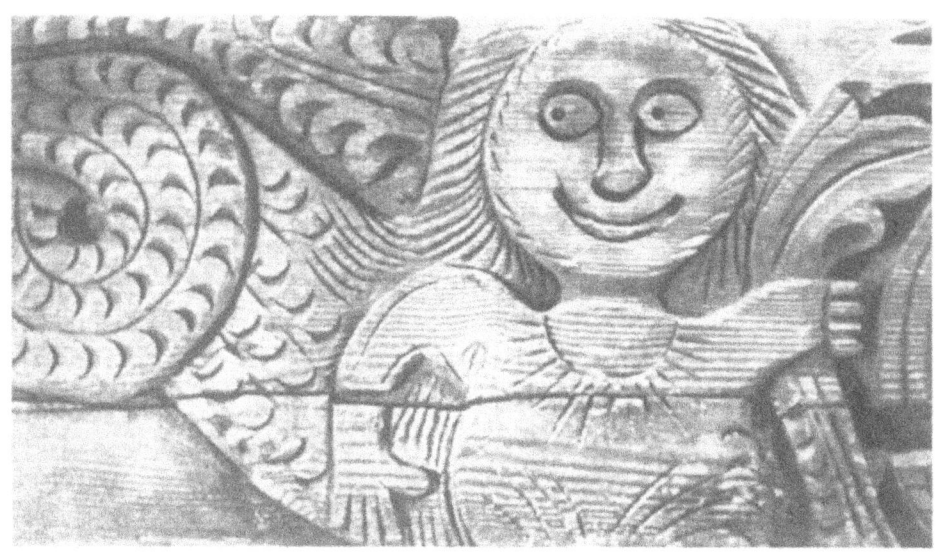

FIG. 10.3 *Beregina* on frontal board.
Carved wood. Volga region, 1855.
GIM.

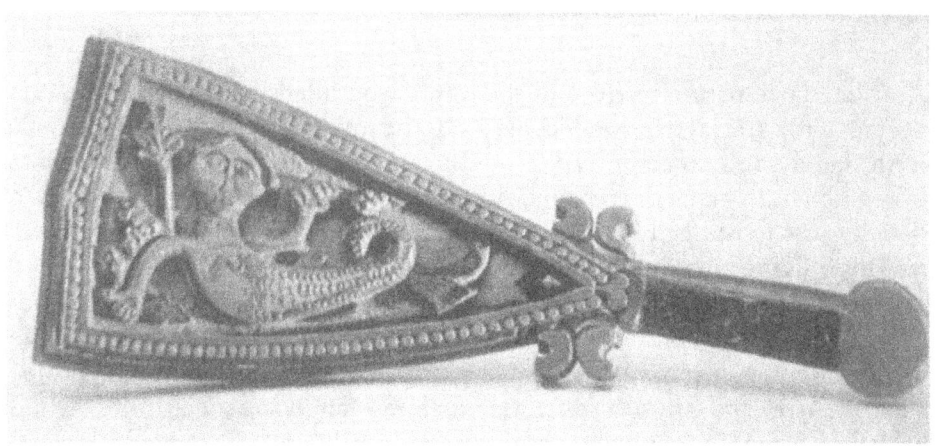

FIG. 10.4 *Beregina* or *rusalka* on *valek.*
Carved and painted wood. Nizhnii
Novgorod region, 19th century. GIM.

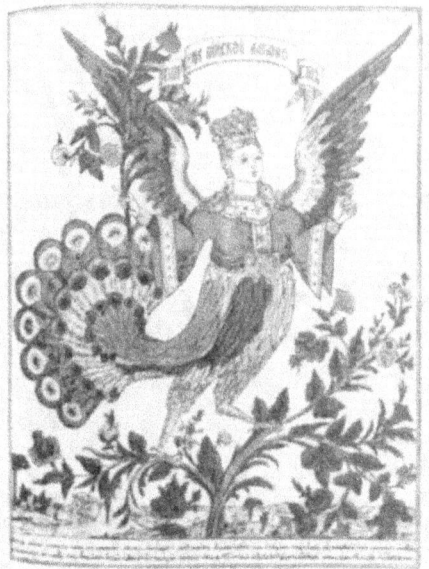

FIG. 10.5 "Alkonost." *Lubok,* colored
copper engraving. 18th century. Pushkin
Museum.

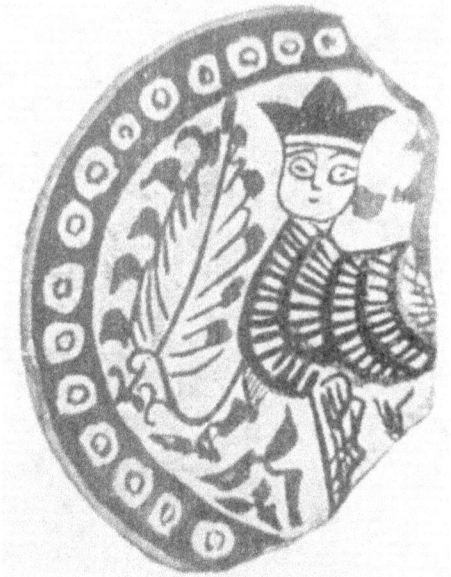

FIG. 10.6 *Sirin* on ceramic plate.
Chersones, 9th or 10th century. GIM.

The Slavic nature spirits and the saints who filled their places were connected with the agricultural cycle and the overlapping cycles of human
birth, family and community life, and death.[42] Customs varied from region
to region, and changed over time. In many villages, though, the presence of
divinity was reinforced by specific rituals and objects. These folk art objects
and their usages were tied directly to aspects of rural life in the nineteenth
and twentieth centuries, and less directly to the distant past, through traditions handed down in each locality. Ceremonies attending the crucial stages
of life often involved sympathetic magic, acts to bring luck or to protect
against harm, and physical objects indicating family or social roles. Childbirth, for example, might be eased by untying knots and opening locks or
boxes, acts common in many cultures. In some places, more specific physical symbols identified the child: an axe for a male child and a distaff for a
female.[43] Betrothal and marriage required courtship gifts, dowries, feasts,
and special costumes and headwear. Death was marked by many symbolic
tokens of pagan origin as well as Orthodox rites.

Peasant wedding ceremonies were dramatic. Specific activities, costumes,
and roles of the many participants varied from one region to another, as re-

cent research shows, but many features were widespread in the nineteenth century. Some stages of courtship took place at *posidelki* and during the seasonal festivals described below. Behind the scenes, negotiations among parents and matchmakers covered the nature of the bride's dowry (*pridanoe*) and the groom's contribution to wedding costs; the expenses of betrothal and wedding ceremonies could be heavy. In some areas, especially in the north, they were avoided by conventionalized elopement or bride theft. In winter, the courtship season, young people gathered after church to ride in sleighs until dusk; a young man would race off with his intended bride, pursued by her relatives. After escaping safely, the couple returned to beg forgiveness of the woman's parents, who refused to take her back and eventually gave their blessing.[44] Ironically, the custom reinforced the chain of authority and the duties of marriage: to show their approval, the bride's mother gave her a saucepan, while the father gave his son-in-law a whip.

Distaffs, clothing, and bed linens were important physical accessories to marriage. In parts of central Russia, a betrothed woman or her fiancé burned her distaff,[45] and she received a new one as an engagement or wedding present. Freed from chores in her parents' house, she spent the time before marriage embroidering the shirts, clothing, towels, and bed linens for her *pridanoe*.[46] The handwork was displayed to wedding guests, its quality a sign of the bride's skill; in the late nineteenth century, though, some of the traditional linens were made professionally, or purchased. Similarly, the "laments" sung by the bride and her friends while working on the dowry linen, and other songs at the wedding ceremony were sometimes performed by professionals.[47]

On the eve of the wedding, parties took place at the bride's and groom's houses. In many areas, these events featured symbolic objects and gestures, such as bathing and braiding the bride's hair and throwing hops, grain, or small coins at the couple. On the wedding morning, the bride's friends dressed her and set the wedding *kokoshnik* in place; blessed by parents and godparents, she was left to wait for the groom. Meanwhile, the groom's party set off for the bride's house (fig. 15.1); stopped by a barricade placed across the road by the bride's family, they had to buy off the guardians with jests and songs. Small gifts were paid to enter the house and to "buy" the place next to the bride, perhaps a survival of early bride-purchase customs.[48] When the party left for the church, they displayed an icon, shot off guns, cracked whips, and shouted to drive off evil spirits. Specially decorated horse yokes, often depicted on distaffs (fig. 3.3), were used for the wedding sleigh or carriage. The wedding ceremony (fig. 14.2), feasting, and post-wedding celebrations continued in some places for several days, with skits, dances, and a long series of songs composed for the occasion.[49] Throughout the betrothal and marriage ceremonials, traditional phrases, actions, and physical objects were important: embroidering the dowry linens, singing laments, touching the earth, barricading the procession, buying the seat next to the bride, flinging grain and coins at the pair. All the expected details marked the change of social roles for the newly married couple, and simultaneously celebrated the shared experience of the community.[50]

Death and funeral ceremonies combined Orthodox and pagan elements. In some areas, certain actions were thought to ease the passing of the soul and to protect the living. For instance, in Ukraine, a dying person was laid on a straw pallet on the earthen floor in the belief that the earth would lessen the pain; in the north, the *okhlupen'* was broken at the householder's death, and elsewhere an opening was cut in the wall to help release the spirit.[51] The dead body was placed so that the head was near the icons and the feet pointed toward the door of the *izba;* when the coffin was carried out the door or window, great care was taken not to let it touch any part of the house, so that the corpse would not return to harm the living.

After the funeral, the family ate a meal of *bliny* (yeast pancakes), *kisel'* (a starch-based jelly), *kut'ia* (small cakes of roasted grains with honey), and vodka. The dead person's place was set and left vacant, as if he or she were present. The funeral followed the Orthodox rite, and additional memorial services were held on the ninth, twentieth, and fortieth days after death, again six months and one year later, and on days of the church calendar designated for remembrance of the dead.[52] The dead were also remembered in local festivals of pagan origin honoring family and clan ancestors, such as Radunitsa in early spring, when eggs were placed on graves. Funerary chants and laments had dual functions of protecting the living family and maintaining meaningful ties with the dead. Many performed by famous wailers of the late nineteenth and early twentieth centuries, Irina Fedosova and Nastasiia Bogdanova, retained stylistic formulas and imagery of lamentations recorded in medieval literature, with allowance for improvisation to fit the individual.[53]

The agrarian calendar and its rituals fell into two sections, winter and summer. The old Russian calendar year, before Peter I's reforms, began in autumn: in the country, autumn and winter were times of preparation for the renewal of fertility. The autumn-winter cycle began after harvest and the Feast of the Intercession (October 1) with a social season centered on *posidelki*, culminating in winter festivals (later linked with the feast of St. Nicholas and Yuletide) at which songs were sung, gifts exchanged, fortunes told, and marriages planned.[54]

The winter festivities, often depicted in *lubki*, included processions in costumes and masks of a horse, bull, goat, and bear, recalling those of early traveling performers, *skomorokhi*. Bands of costumed singers went from house to house singing songs called *koliadki*, to wish for a good harvest and invoke Koliada, a personification of the season.[55] Without the pressures of farm work, winter offered the best opportunities for courtship, and many betrothals and weddings took place around Epiphany Sunday. Winter revelry was energetic and participatory, whether or not it resulted in marriage. Bands of mummers in masks and motley costumes ran through the streets with noisemakers and fireworks.[56] Besides wearing the traditional animal masks, horse, goat, bull, and bear, mummers took on other roles, an Old Man and Old Woman, the witch Baba Iaga, and the *kikimora*, a household spirit who took care of poultry.[57] The antics took many forms, erotic, abusive, or mock-heroic, and perhaps recalled pagan rites with animals.[58]

The most important winter festival was Maslenitsa (Shrove or "Butter" Tuesday, from *maslo*, "butter"), the week marking the end of Carnival and the beginning of Lent. Each day of the week had its specified entertainment, feasting on *bliny*, visiting, strolling through the town or village enjoying dancing, music, or street jesters. The revelry, gluttony, and sexual license of the festivities were not only a last fling before the great Lenten fast imposed by the church, but also a type of homeopathic magic, meant to bring fertility and plenty to the village. In some areas, horsemen carried the circular *bliny* around a village or group of settlements in a circular route evoking the path of the returning sun; villagers carried wheels fastened to tall poles around the village for the same purpose.[59] A high point of the week was the procession of Maslenitsa. There were several local variants, but most centered around a doll made of wood or straw and dressed in a *rubakha*, *sarafan*, and kerchief, or a male peasant dressed in women's clothes. "Maslenitsa" was carried through the town in a parade that ended in a mock battle (recalling the European battle between Shrove and Lent) and a funeral, in which the Maslenitsa costume was torn off, set aflame, and scattered, to the accompaniment of songs.[60]

A favorite Shrovetide entertainment in the north was tobogganing on specially ornamented sleds down steep hills or artificial slopes made of wood and packed with snow and ice. This was not just fun; it was a ritual of courtship. In villages on the Northern Dvina, men made special sleds (fig. 10.7), with carved and brightly painted designs of rayed suns and geometric patterns, for their daughters or intended brides.[61] In parts of Iaroslavl' Province, women slid down hills on their distaffs to encourage a good crop of flax.[62] Frequently depicted on distaffs and *lubki*, often with identifying inscriptions, the sleigh ride was a major social activity between Epiphany and the Maslenitsa week.

Several peasant customs marked the coming of spring, between Maslenitsa and Trinity Sunday, seven weeks after Easter.[63] Pastries in the shape of larks, the heralds of spring, were baked at the time of the spring equinox and tossed into the air or tied to poles in the garden. Pussy willows, among the first signs of spring, were blessed in church and used in Palm Sunday processions, as they were in Germany and other northern countries. On St. George's Day, cattle were switched with the blessed pussy willows, fed animal-shaped or circular cakes, and led to pasture, their safety ensured by both Christian and pagan protection.

The Christian festival Easter did not replace a specific seasonal ritual, but two pagan holidays that took place the following week carried similar empha-

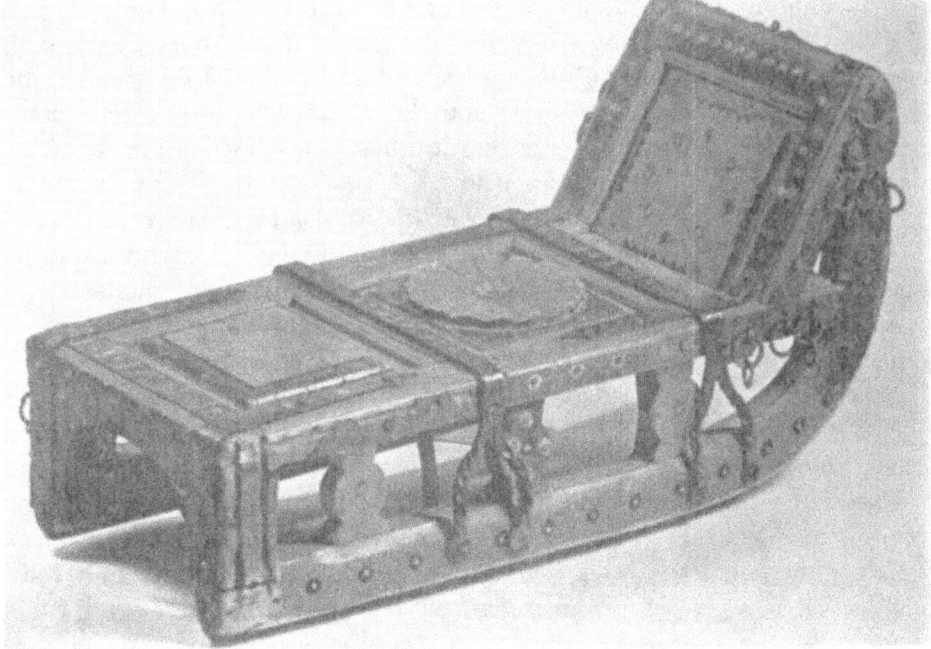

FIG. 10.7 Sled for Maslenitsa festival.
Carved and painted wood, iron. North
Russia, 19th century. Sergiev-Posad.

sis on death and rebirth. On a holiday called Krasnaia gorka ("Red Hill"),
young women, sometimes with men, gathered to dance and sing, using a loaf
of bread and an egg dyed red as symbols of fertility and the sun. On Radunitsa, an ancient holiday commemorating family ancestors, eggs painted red,
purple, and brown were placed on graves as gifts for the dead (in some places
cooked eggs were offered), and embroidered towels were fastened to the
grave markers.

The major celebration of spring and fertility was Semik. The name, derived from the root *sem'*, had two meanings: "seven," referring to the seventh
(or sometimes eighth) Thursday after Easter, and "seed" or "family" (*sem'ia*). In
the church, the Feast of the Ascension or Trinity Thursday was a time for
memorial services for the dead, and some peasants believed that ancestors
returned to life at the time when nature was being reborn, to dwell on earth
until Pentecost.[64] Even in towns, people took drives in wheeled carriages to
celebrate spring weather and decorated their houses with greenery. But the

main part of the Semik festival centered on unmarried women, *rusalki*, and birch trees.

Trinity Week was known as Green Week or Rusalka Week in Ukraine and some other regions, because the *rusalki* were supposed to leave their rivers and climb into the birch trees like the ascending sap. In many localities, young women went into the woods to select a special birch tree and clothe it with ribbons, beads, garlands, and embroidered towels. Men did not take part, and feared to enter the realm of the *rusalki* during this week. The women continued the ritual in the forest the next day, bringing food for the ancestors, singing to the *rusalka* in the tree, sometimes braiding stalks of grain into its branches or bending them to make circular wreaths. Nineteenth-century *lubki* show women garlanding the tree, with the words of songs to the *rusalka* printed beneath the pictures (fig. 10.8). The tree was cut, brought into the village, and placed in one of the houses, where everyone paid visits and treated it as an honored guest until Trinity Sunday, when the young women took the birch to the river or lakeside, ritually undressed it, and threw it and their wreaths into the water. In some places, accompanying songs told of the *rusalka* going back into the water and bringing rain to make the grain grow well.[65]

This group of events, culminating on Trinity Sunday, ended the winter cycle, with its preparations for working the soil, and symbols evoking fertility.[66] The summer cycle emphasized not potential but actual fertility. The most dramatic festival, vividly described by Nikolai Gogol in the 1830s, was that of John the Baptist and Ivan Kupala on Midsummer's Eve, celebrated with bonfires and bathing in rivers and lakes.[67] Boys and girls jumped over the bonfires or drove cattle through them. In some villages they threw old plows, sleds, or other farm tools into the fire, and at the end burned the remains of birch branches gathered during Semik, or in other places made flax dolls in the form of Kupalo (or Kupalo and Morena, a male and female pair), to burn in the fire. A closely related midsummer ritual was Kostroma, in which flax figures representing Kostroma or Iarilo were burned, buried, or drowned. Participants acted out stories about the illness and death of Kostroma, sometimes adding comic games and songs, ending on St. Peter's Day, June 29, with a funeral procession and burial of Kostroma.[68]

On St. Peter's Day, Petrovki, just before haymaking began (in some areas on St. Elijah's Day, July 20, at the beginning of harvest), women and girls sat on swings and sang about reaping the flax or wheat, lamenting as if the sheaves suffered when cut. The whole village worked together, the men with scythes, the women with sickles and rakes, to finish haymaking, and then went on to harvest cereal crops, such as rye and barley, and finally hemp and flax. Traditionally, a special *rubakha* was worn for the beginning of harvest (fig. 7.1). In some places, the first sheaf of grain or flax was left in the field until the end of harvest, when the women carried it ceremonially back to the

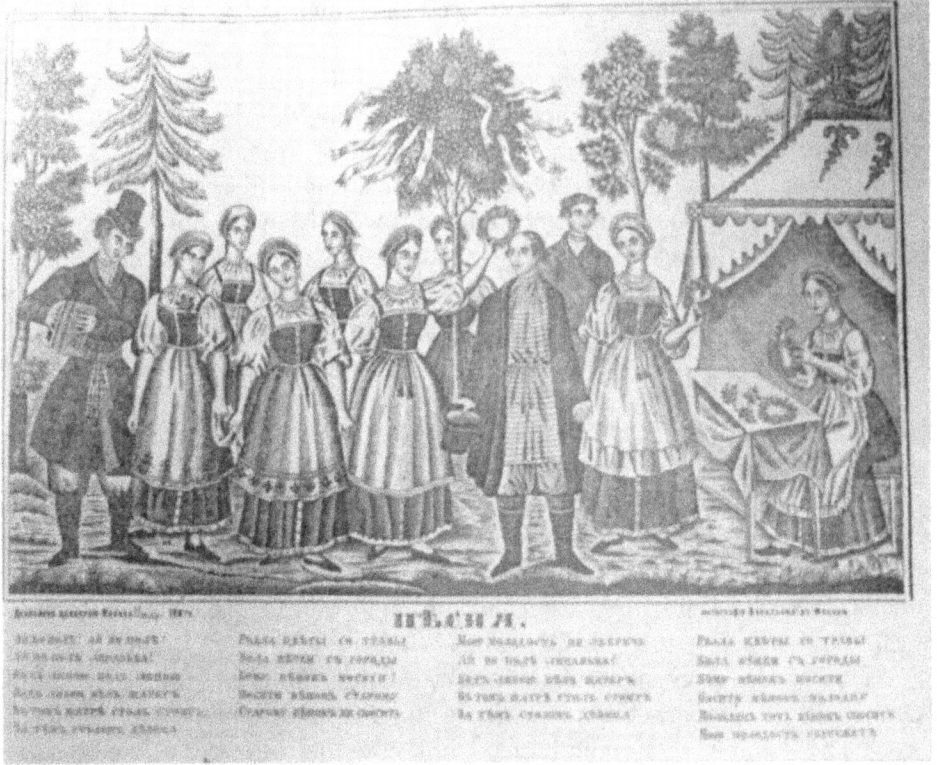

FIG. 10.8 "Song." *Lubok* with scene of
Semik festival. Moscow, 1887.

village (painter P. E. Zabolotskii depicted such a scene in the Novgorod region in 1822). The sheaf was taken to an elder's *izba* and placed in the icon corner to be kept over the winter and plowed back into the earth the following spring.[69]

After midsummer, as the days shortened, rural ceremonies not only expressed thanks for good harvests but also anticipated the hardships of winter. In the early nineteenth century, Ivan Snegirev observed that peasants prayed on July 20 to St. Elijah (Il'ia), patron of cattle and protector against fire, and dedicated a sheaf of rye to Volos, the pagan protector of herds. On August 18, the feast of Florus and Laurus, patron saints of horses, they took the animals to be blessed with holy water, and took a sheaf of oats to the icon corner, to save until October 1, Intercession Day, when it was given to the cattle that would be slaughtered for winter. Early fall, after harvest and before the cold weather, allowed a brief respite from heavy field work. In parts of Russia, a second St. George's Day in November allowed some peasants to pay their debt, *obrok*, to their landowners, and move from one village to another.[70] Beginning on St. Simon's Day, September 1, *Bab'e leto* ("Old Women's Summer"), new beer was brewed, flax was prepared for spinning, and marriages were arranged. The end of the summer cycle was marked by Intercession Saturday, a day also devoted to the celebration of Paraskeva-Piatnitsa. The mock mourning songs of betrothed women on this day denoted a change of status, a loss of freedom that was quite real, and the assumption of a new round of domestic tasks. Almost all the spinning, weaving, sewing of garments, and embroidering of shirts and ceremonial towels was done during the late fall and winter, under the auspices of Paraskeva-L'nianitsa. It was a time to care for tools or engage in handcrafts, and to prepare for the midwinter festivals.

These rituals or participatory dramas, with many variations from one region to another, were still performed in the nineteenth and early twentieth centuries. If their original functions were half-forgotten, they were still effective in particular ways for rural communities. The enactments related to agriculture and fertility were held in the places where fertility mattered, in the fields, in the forests, or on the banks of a lake or river. The people involved in the drama, at once actors and audience, were the same people who depended on the results of the rituals in real life. The masks and dolls of flax, straw, and wood were not props imitating real things, but personifications of natural forces—both functional and symbolic in the way that tokens and amulets of the Slavic cults may have been.

The pervasive animism of Russian peasants, and the tendency to personify nature in seasonal rituals, helps to explain the importance of traditional materials and forms in art. Peasants evidently believed that animals and trees understood human speech. In the spring they recited verses to their cattle before sending them out to pasture; they sang to the rivers and to the sun.[71] The objects peasants made also had voices, through their imagery and through greetings, wishes, and proverbs inscribed on them.

This was true regardless of medium or function, but in most of Russia two materials, flax and wood, were especially important and endowed with personal and ritual meaning. Flax was personified in the image of Paraskeva-L'nianitsa and, in another way, in the effigy of Kostroma. Flax was the universal material of the textile arts, the focus of all the skills and processes used to make fabric for daily wear and embroidered garments and towels used in seasonal and life-stage rituals. Wood, deeply connected with Slavic mythology and with the daily lives of Russian peasants, was used for shelter and for almost every tool; it offered durable and easily worked surfaces for decoration. During Rusalka Week, the birch tree, personified as the *rusalka*, embodied fertility and the return of spring. In weaving and embroidering ceremonial textiles and in making wooden tools for the textile arts, peasant

DESIGNS AND THEIR MEANINGS

artists sought to make the decoration worthy of its significance in the essential activities, social customs, and rituals that had marked the life of the community for generations.

Transformation of
the Slavic Legacy

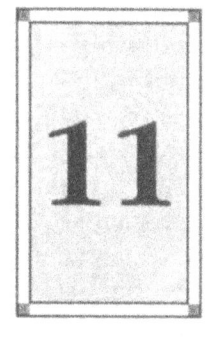

As pagan beliefs merged with Kievan state, both Slavic and gradually modified in the cre- Christian ceremony in the Byzantine visual forms were ation of Russian art. The changing purposes of art introduced distinctions between folk and court art, comparable to those between oral lore and written literature. But there were areas in which the spheres of folk styles and pagan imagery overlapped and penetrated those of the court and church.

When Prince Vladimir converted to Christianity in 988, he ordered the pagan temples destroyed and churches built in their stead. He brought teams of masons and artists from Byzantium, and they taught Russian workmen. Kievan art developed through the mingling of traditions from Byzantium, from local craftsmen, and from the Scandinavian heritage of the rulers. It was partly to keep control of the vast Scandinavian trade routes—from Staraia Rusa on Lake Il'men', down the Volkhov, Oka, Volga, and Dniepr rivers to Kiev, the Black Sea, Byzantium, and Baghdad—that Rurik and his Varangian warriors had been called "from over the Sea" around 860, the beginning of Russian history in the Kievan Primary Chronicle.[1] When his descendant Vladimir allied his city with Byzantium a century later, the decision was a matter of economics and prestige, as well as religion.

The forms of religious ritual and art were tied to the authority of the ruling elite not only in Kiev but also in the Rurik dynasty's northern bases,

Novgorod and Vladimir-Suzdal'. Each center had its distinct role. Kiev, the political, intellectual, and spiritual capital, by the eleventh century ranked as one of Europe's great cities, with 400 to 600 churches and numerous markets and manufacturing centers.[2] Novgorod, surrounded by forests and waterways, was a trading center, self-sufficient for five centuries, until it was sacked by Ivan the Terrible. Suzdal' and Vladimir, between the Oka and Volga rivers amid forest and open land with large deposits of white limestone, prospered when the south was weakened by Mongol incursions.

It was in the northern centers—with their mixture of Slavic, Finno-Ugric, and Scandinavian populations, and well-developed metalworking and wood-carving traditions—that the introduction of Kievan-Byzantine forms and techniques resulted in genuine artistic interaction. This interaction gave rise to the styles of architecture, painting, and decorative arts that dominated the Russian church and court until the eighteenth century. The same interaction affected the development of folk art, whether apart from or in contact with monastic and urban schools. Examining certain images and stylistic traits of both folk and court art reveals differing patterns of evolution. The survival of archaic forms with some accretions in folk art was inherently different from the deliberate historicizing revival of Byzantine and Slavic motifs in Musco-vite court art and in post-Petrine academic art.

Builders of the eleventh-century churches in Kiev and Novgorod em-ulated the great churches of Constantinople. Mosaic and fresco programs in the apses and domes followed the canonical imagery and hieratic com-positions of Byzantine prototypes. But active figure groupings, narrative se-quences, and a variety of decorative patterns appeared in marginal areas and borders,[3] just as relatively free compositions embellished margins of manu-scripts, small-scale church utensils, and secular objects. The twelfth-century churches of Vladimir and Suzdal', with their graceful exterior decorations of carved white limestone, showed the influence of indigenous northern styles of carving as well as Byzantine iconography. The elegant Church of the Interces-sion of the Virgin, Pokrov on the Nerl, built for Andrei Bogoliubskii in 1165, had a broad program of carving arranged within the three arched divisions on the upper part of three facades, above an arcade of engaged columns resting on sculpted corbels. The compositions of the south, west, and north facades centered around the seated figure of King David, holding a harp with his right hand raised in blessing, flanked by lions, doves, and other figures carved in high relief. The Kievan chronicles recorded that "God brought artists to Andrei from all parts of the earth," and the influx of builders and craftsmen, probably from Germany, Armenia, and Georgia, helped to transform the in-herited Byzantine styles into distinctively Russian forms of architecture and decoration.[4]

The churches built by Andrei's successors, St. Dmitrii in Vladimir, the Ca-thedral of the Nativity of the Virgin in Suzdal', and St. George at Iur'ev-Pol'skii, demonstrate how native decorative forms began to blend with those based on Kievan sources or brought to Russia by foreign craftsmen. The wealth of the relief carvings and the manner in which human and animal forms were combined with interlaced patterns of foliage may point to northern Russians who had carved such motifs in wood.[5] A striking feature of the decoration was its orderliness. The dense compositions on the facades of St. Dmitrii were arranged in neat rows; each block of stone contained a single bush, bird, lion, or mythological creature, and they were grouped so that three similar blocks were placed at each side of the narrow windows. This manner of placing figures and ornaments in horizontal bands, perhaps following practices already common in the region, certainly influenced later decoration of churches with patterned brickwork and tile. The clarity, symmetry, and small scale of the ornament in relation to the height and breadth of the walls gave an effect of harmony that later came to epitomize Russia's golden age.[6]

The sculptural themes of all the Vladimir-Suzdal' churches were echoed in the "Golden Gates" (fig. 11.1), the south and west doors of the Cathedral of the Nativity of the Virgin in Suzdal', made about 1222–25.[7] The oak doors

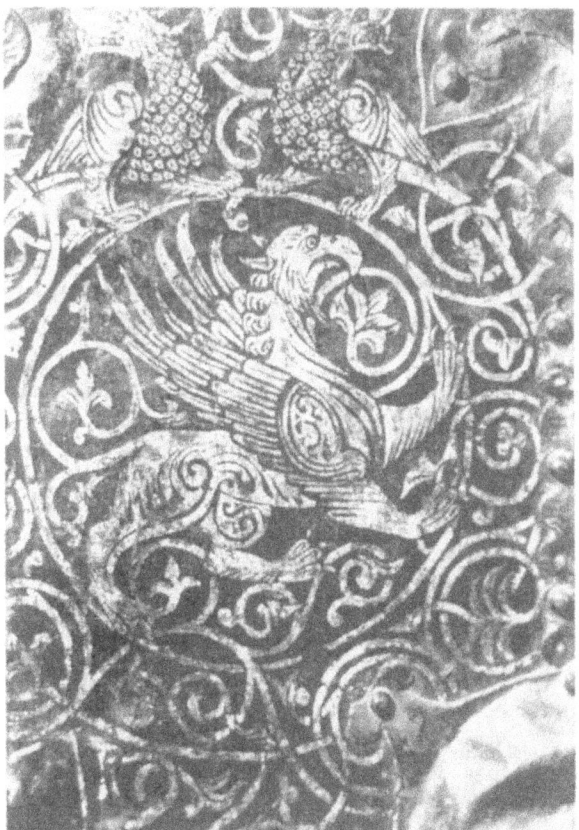

were covered with copper plates worked in a technique similar to niello, known as "fired gold," in which a plate was covered with matte black lacquer and wax, a design was engraved into its surface, and a mixture of mercury and molten gold was poured into the grooves so that, when fired, the mercury evapo-

FIG. 11.1 "Golden Gates," Cathedral of the Nativity of the Mother of God. Niello on copper, on wood. Detail of gryphon and *simargl.* Suzdal', 12th century.

DESIGNS AND THEIR MEANINGS

rated, leaving the gold fused to the copper plate. The shimmering effect was most striking in the angular highlights on garments and the repeated patterns of halos. The twenty-eight panels of each portal, with scenes from the life of the Virgin, the life of Christ, and the patron saints of the Vladimir-Suzdal' princes in canonical Byzantine style, were framed by slender columns decorated with swirling tendrils of floral ornament. Round bosses at each intersection of the frames bore plant forms and heraldic beasts: lions, gryphons, a falcon, a pair of roosters, a double-headed eagle, a dragon, a lion attacking a scaly monster, a gryphon attacking a bear. The lowest rows of panels showed lions and gryphons surrounded by rhythmic spirals of stylized vines and, above each composition, pairs of dog-faced birds, *senmurvy* or *simargli*. The "Golden Gates" elaborated the fantastic components of the carved stone ornament on the Cathedral, and at the same time united these elements with biblical scenes familiar from frescoes and manuscripts.

The interaction of cosmopolitan and local traits in the arts of Novgorod and Vladimir-Suzdal' was especially fertile in wooden architecture and carved ornament. As early as the eleventh century, a chronicle referred to Novgoroders as "carpenters."[8] No early wooden building survives, but excavations and documents suggest similarities to eighteenth-century wooden churches in the Novgorod, Suzdal', and Kizhi preserves. An important church feature influenced by the northern tradition of woodcarving was the iconostasis. Developed in the late fourteenth century, it was an extension of the rail that separated the altar from the nave in Byzantine and Kievan churches and sometimes supported local icons or images devoted to feasts. In the north, the barrier was heightened to allow the placement of icons of the twelve church feasts in a row above the local icons. Finally the iconostasis took the form of a wooden screen reaching to the ceiling and extending across the entire width of the apse, completely covered with icons arranged in rows, *chiny*, in a prescribed order.

The iconostasis allowed display of lavish carved and painted or gilt ornament, especially striking in contrast to the plain exteriors of most northern churches. There were many levels of quality and styles of carving, ranging from nearly flat interlace backgrounds surrounding cameo-like figures of saints (fig. 11.2) to deeply carved vines and leaves surrounding columns which had been carved out from inside to achieve a lacelike effect (fig. 11.3).[9] The wood could be left unpainted, but in wealthy churches the columns and carved panels of the Royal Doors were covered with gold leaf or painted dark red or black with fine gold highlights, in foliage patterns like those of the Golden Gates of Suzdal'. The style, called "herbaceous" painting, *travchataia pis'ma*, was used in the seventeenth century on lecterns and candlesticks, on borders of icons, and, later, on the painted wooden dishes of Khokhloma.

Icons and deesis rows (the Savior flanked by the Mother of God, John the Baptist, and other saints) carved in shallow relief were also common in the

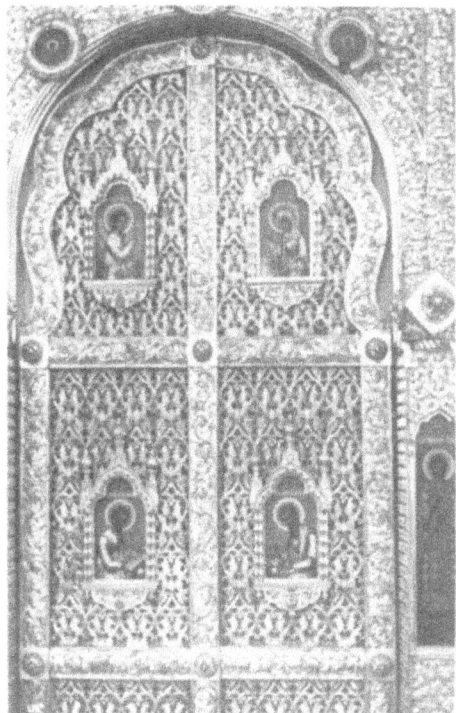

FIG. 11.2   Royal doors from iconostasis. Carved and gilded wood. North Russia, 19th century. Kolomenskoe.

FIG. 11.3   Iconostasis column. Carved and gilded wood. Detail of foliage. North Russia, 18th or 19th century. Kolomenskoe.

north.[10] The artists approached the task of modeling figures by relying more on the conventional angular drapery folds of painted icons than on actual depth of carving. If the figure was attached to a panel, part of the background and the halo might be elaborated by interlace, spirals, and other complex geometrical patterns, in a manner suggesting Scandinavian models.[11] Some works, however, are more comparable to metal gospel covers and mountings for icons produced in Moscow workshops. The question of influence and borrowing is difficult because dating is rarely secure, but it is clear that artists working in churches were exposed to many stylistic sources.

While the iconostasis was the focal point of the church, other furnishings, such as lecterns, canopies, boxes for holy books, candlesticks, crosiers, and crosses, were also decorated with dense carved designs, especially in the north. An exceptionally fine piece, the Liudogoshenskii Cross (fig. 11.4), was made for the Church of Saints Florus and Laurus in Novgorod in 1359, as a carved inscription indicates.[12] Using a single large pine board, the artist, Iakov Fedosov, fashioned the cross shape within a circular form. The outer contour of the circle was broken by angular protrusions suggesting twigs or leaves at the end of each arm and at the top of the cross. The inner part was articulated by openwork circles with four tiny crosses at their cardinal points. The artist covered the entire face of the cross with a dense, vinelike interlace. This framed and set off several roundels carved in shallow relief, resembling cameos or medals, with figures or figural groups completely fitting the circular frames. The images included a crucifixion at the top, a deesis arranged in several roundels across the cross-arm, and several saints and narrative scenes evidently popular in Novgorod: St. Jerome and the lion, Samson and the lion, St. George and the Dragon, Elijah fed by a raven; Saints Theodore Tiron and Theodore Stratilates, Kosmas and Damian, Florus and Laurus, and Simeon Stylites. The Liudogoshenskii Cross combined the formal properties of the circle, the cross of Christ's death, and the branches of the Tree of Life. The work of a highly original artist who planned and executed the entire design, it was as unusual in its iconographic scope as in its formal intricacy. The Liudogoshenskii Cross was a unique rendering of popular religious concepts in a style blending Slavic, Scandinavian, and Byzantine elements.[13]

During the fourteenth and fifteenth centuries, individual and regional styles appeared in all art forms. The Mongol inva-

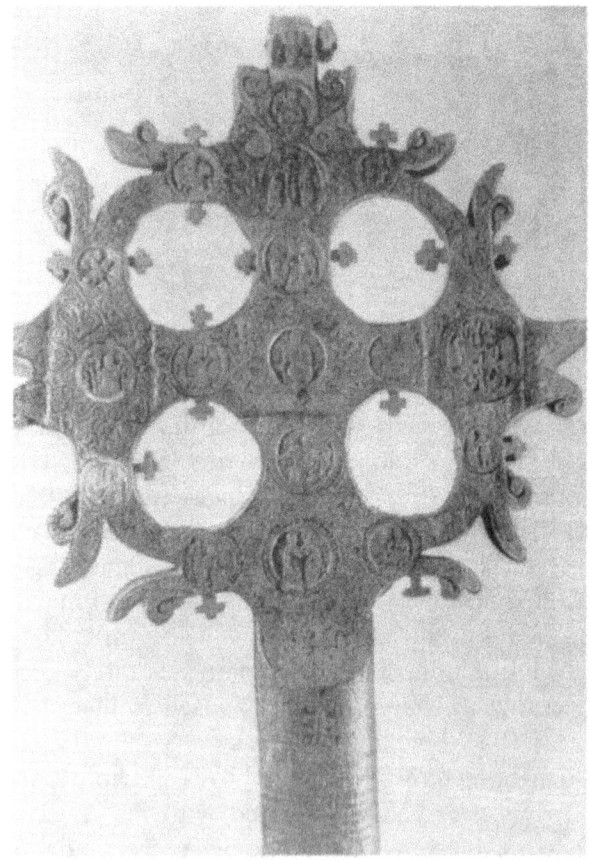

FIG. 11.4 Iakov Fedosov, Liudogoshenskii Cross. Carved wood. Novgorod, 1359. Novgorod Kremlin Museum.

sions and occupation of Russia, beginning about 1237, had not curtailed the development of Russian art, despite the initial destruction of churches, libraries, and cities, the conscription of craftsmen to work for the khan, and the economic hardships caused by tribute demands.[14] Even under the Mongol yoke, Novgorod and Moscow were large cities by European standards, with an estimated 50,000 to 100,000 inhabitants.[15] However, the long occupation left the country economically drained and culturally provincial. Builders, sculptors, and painters had access to Byzantine models, but they lacked the regular contact with current Byzantine art and the interaction among the sophisticated courts and ecclesiastical centers that had characterized Kievan Rus'. This relative isolation undoubtedly stimulated icon painting and other arts, as Russians relied increasingly on their own resources.

Local styles emerged in Novgorod, Pskov, Suzdal', Vologda, Rostov, and Moscow, in monasteries, and in the remote provinces. Even within the framework of Orthodox iconography, interpretation was tinged by local interests and beliefs. Distinctive portrayals of such saints as St. Nicholas and St. George, special protectors of common people, are particularly evident in

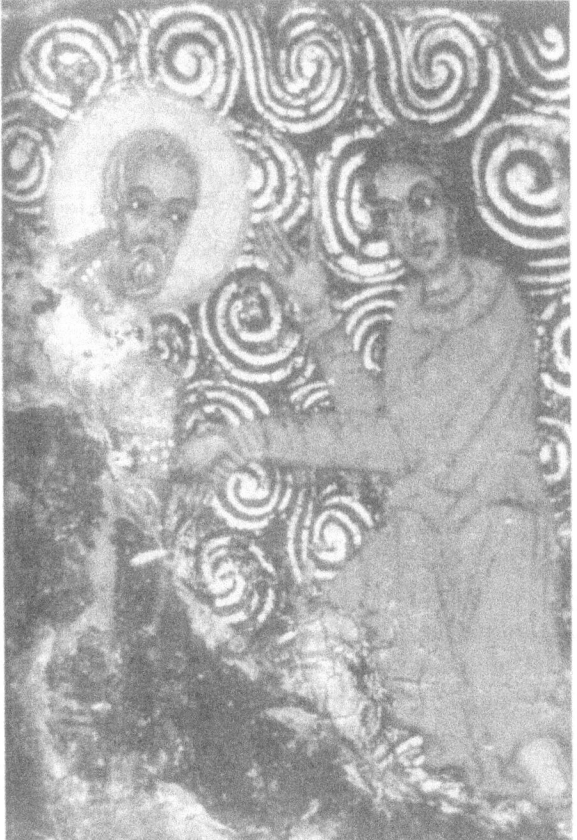

accessory details and the narrative scences, *zhit'e*, in the borders of their icons. On a fourteenth-century icon from the village of Kargach in Vologda Province (fig. 11.5), the scenes of St. Nicholas sailing and rescuing Demetrius from the bottom of the sea expressed the power of wa-

FIG. 11.5 Icon, St. Nicholas, from Church of Sts. Boris and Gleb. Tempera on wood. Detail of border. Kargach Village, Vologda Province, late 14th century. GTG.

ter almost abstractly, through vigorous spiral patterns of black and white. In contrast, the depiction of the saint driving devils out of a tree showed Nicholas pushing back his sleeve and lifting his axe to take a swing as any woodsman might.[16] The many aspects of St. George, protector of farmers, patron of warriors, and Christian martyr, gave his icons many different emphases, depending on period, region, or the worshippers for whom they were made. On some icons, details conveyed underlying connections with pagan nature gods: a round shield in the form of a stylized rosette on a twelfth-century icon; a more richly decorated shield with a central boss in the shape of a sun with a human face and petal-like rays; and a saddle cloth ornamented with a star, a rayed sun, and a tree on a late fifteenth-century icon.[17] Even centuries later, the northern environment affected the presentation of Christian imagery. The painter of a seventeenth-century icon of St. John the Baptist was probably trained in Moscow, but he used his own ideas about nature in depicting the saint not in a desert but at the edge of a dense forest inhabited by deer, horses, lions, and other wild beasts.[18]

The rise of Muscovy as the Mongol yoke slowly weakened brought enormous development of decorative and liturgical arts. Eventually the styles of Moscow spread throughout Russia and both directly and indirectly influenced peasant art. It was a complex relationship. Court schools revived forms from pre-Mongol Kiev and Vladimir-Suzdal'. Articles used in court rituals and presentations, such as silver and gilt *kovshy* shaped like swimming birds, were based on ancient wood prototypes but gained new glamour in their court setting; they, in turn, offered models for traveling artisans and folk artists in the provinces. In almost every medium of art and at every social level of patronage, designs of pre-Christian origin sometimes melded with Byzantine images, and sometimes lost their original meanings and acquired new associations related to their specific court, urban, or rural settings.

Insignificant before the Mongol period, Moscow was settled by Viatichian Slavs and by northern traders. By the twelfth century, its people practiced a variety of occupations and religions, as material from excavations revealed.[19] Reliquaries, miniature icons, and crosses from Kiev, and secular objects such as a two-part metal lock in the shape of a lion, pointed to trade ties with Kiev and the Crimea; but extensive local craft production and artistic exchange with other towns or countries developed only in the post-Mongol period.[20] Moscow's political role became manifest nearly a century after the first efforts to resist the Mongols, when Grand Duke Ivan III took the title "Tsar Ioann" (the Slavic version of Caesar), adopted the double-headed eagle of the Byzantine Empire as his insignium, and began an ambitious renovation of the Kremlin. Ivan III strengthened Russia's ties with both Byzantium and Europe in 1472, when he married the niece of the last ruling Byzantine emperor, Zoe Paleologa.[21] Known as Sophia, and famed for her intelligence throughout Europe, she had grown up in Italy as a ward of the pope. By marrying Sophia,

Ivan became heir to the Byzantine imperial mantle, and also gained access to the artistic culture of Renaissance Italy. Within months, Ivan sent agents to Italy to find the best architects, artists, and "craftsmen of every kind, suitable for our needs" and invite them to Russia to direct work on the Kremlin and to train local artists.[22] Like Andrei Bogoliubskii, he became one of Russia's great patrons of art, overshadowed only centuries later by Peter I and Catherine II.

The reconstruction of the Kremlin[23] swept away haphazard wooden structures and resulted in a new civic and national center that recalled the majestic churches and palaces of pre-Mongol Russia. Architect Aristotele Fioravanti of Bologna based the Cathedral of the Dormition on that of Vladimir, in order to affirm the spiritual authority of Moscow. He combined traditional features from Vladimir, Suzdal', and Novgorod buildings with a Renaissance spaciousness and clarity of proportion, creating a synthesis of traditional and modern styles. A comparable blend of old and new characterized the residences built for Ivan III and his successors. The oldest, the Faceted Palace (*Granovitaia palata*), with an exterior of white cut stone, looked like a north Italian palace, but the interior, especially the vaulted throne room, was almost oppressively Byzantine, according to descriptions by foreign emissaries.[24] Both the Faceted Palace and the seventeenth-century Terem Palace (fig. 11.6) featured deliberate recollections of the centuries-old Vladimir-Suzdal' style. Lions, gryphons, and unicorns were combined with the imperial double-headed eagle in elaborate stone and tile framing of doors and windows and on gilded iron gates.

As Russia's political center, the Kremlin had to fill two functions that did not always mesh smoothly: it should identify Moscow with the heritage of Rus' and at the same time express Moscow's status as a new world power. The goal of projecting an image of imperial power and religious authority required magnificent buildings and sumptuous decoration. Transforming a provincial wooden city into a "third Rome" necessitated the formation of a court style and a cohort of professional artists. After a destructive fire in 1547, Tsar Ivan IV recruited craftsmen from Novgorod and Pskov to restore the damaged icons and paint new ones. The painters were quartered in the Armory Palace in the Kremlin, under the authority of the state treasury. This was the beginning of the Kremlin workshop; it attracted the best painters, and specialists in other crafts, especially metalwork, soon became part of the system. A court workshop was not a new phenomenon. In the eleventh century there had been a royal school for embroidery and weaving in Kiev.[25] Training was equally essential for icon painting, working in metal and precious stones, and other luxury arts with which rulers could endow churches and monasteries, decorate their palaces, or reward their subjects.

The state schools and workshops provided young artists with models for emulation, and resulted in highly refined, consciously historicizing styles, especially evident in gold and silver work with niello and enamel. Seventeenth-century gospel covers, censers, bowls, and *kovshy* reflected styles from Kievan

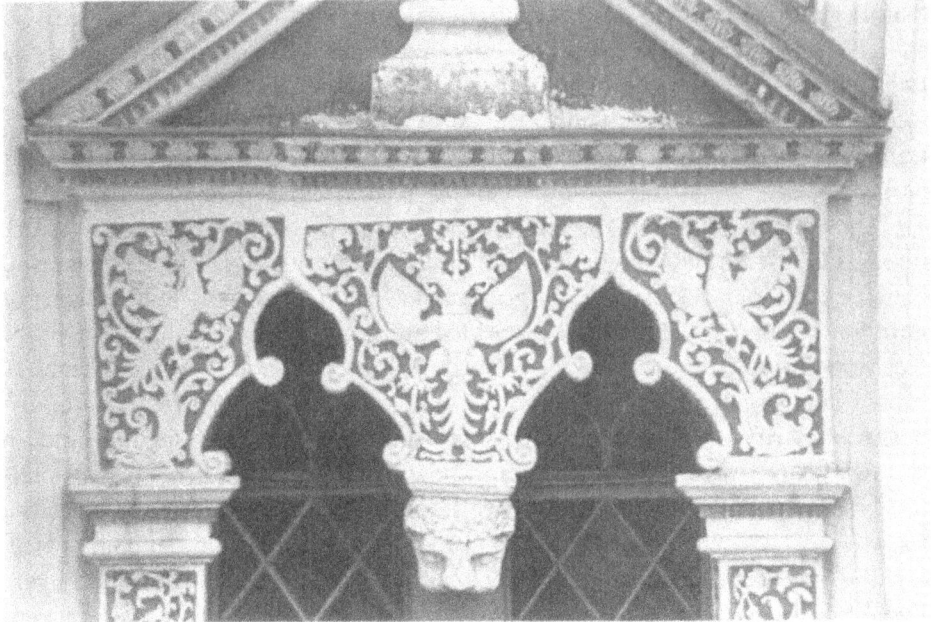

FIG. 11.6   Terem Palace. Detail of
window surround, with heraldic beasts.
Moscow Kremlin, 17th century.

Rus'. The lions, gryphons, and other heraldic beasts of Vladimir and Suzdal',
already in the repertoire of Muscovite architectural ornament, were equally
favored on *kovshy*, jewelry, and other luxury goods. A lidded box, probably
made in the "Silver Row" adjacent to the Kremlin, was ornamented with the
figures of *sirin*, gryphon, *rusalka*, and unicorn arranged in compartments
around its circumference.[26] Jewelry recalled even earlier forms: for example,
two pairs of crescent-shaped earrings of gold and silver filigree work, enamel,
and gems had hanging pearls in the shapes of Viatichian pendants.[27]

One school rivaled the Kremlin: the Stroganov workshop. The Stroganov
family of Novgorod had left the city when it fell to Ivan the Terrible, and
went east to the largely unexploited territories of Vologda Province. Their salt
mines on the Northern Dvina River produced the wealth to build residences
in Sol'vychegodsk grander than Moscow palaces. The Stroganovs commissioned icons from the best artists available, including some from the Kremlin
workshops. Two family members were painters, and others encouraged the
decorative arts, especially enamelwork on copper, for which Sol'vychegodsk
became famous. Many icons from both the Kremlin and the Stroganov

schools were signed and dated, attesting to the new status of professional artists in the seventeenth century.[28] Ironically, the emergence of individual names and documented works was not accompanied by individual inventiveness in Muscovite court and church art. The schools enforced standards of quality and determined acceptable styles. A famous edict of the 1658 Stoglav, the church council, declared: "He who shall paint an icon out of his imagination shall suffer endless torment." The overall result of these rulings was to separate the highly trained court "professionals" from untaught and unsupervised "folk" artists.

The conventional picture of a court art estranged from the genuine sources of creativity in native Russian culture is only partly true, however. The political success of Moscow and the wealth of the court, nobles, merchants, and ambitious pioneers such as the Stroganovs created unprecedented demand in all areas of decorative art. The availability of raw materials of all kinds—gold, silver, copper, and precious stones from the Urals; river pearls, mother-of-pearl, and ivory from the north; wood and flax, plentiful everywhere—in addition to new techniques of engraving, enameling, glazing, and printing, stimulated the formation of craft workshops and factories all over Russia.

Despite enormous distances, commerce expanded, especially after the English and Dutch opened the trade route through the North Sea, the Gulf of Murmansk, and the White Sea to Arkhangel'sk in 1584. A map of Russia published in Amsterdam in 1613 shows more detail in Vologda Province and more notations of towns and settlements along the Northern Dvina and Sukhona rivers than in any other part of Russia's territory.[29] Early in his reign, Peter the Great made the thousand-mile, two-week journey between Moscow and Arkhangel'sk more than once. Artists also traveled the river route between Arkhangel'sk and Velikii Ustiug, one reason for the many shared stylistic traits in northern painting.[30] With the rapid increase in trade, cities such as Sol'vychegodsk, Velikii Ustiug, Iaroslavl', and Vologda began to earn reputations for production of specialized crafts and luxury goods. As they expanded, the city workshops employed bonded serfs (who were allowed to work for fees which they paid to their owners according to an established system) and also attracted free peasant craftworkers. Prosperous monasteries remained major employers of craftworkers and sponsors of markets. In practical terms, the rise of Moscow and the success of a growing merchant class led to increased opportunities for artists at all levels.

Fundamental differences existed between rulers and people, between the city and the country, throughout the history of Russia. Prophetically, the first written record of Suzdal' concerned a popular uprising in 1024, after a crop failure led the city elders and priests to try to enserf the peasants.[31] The institution of serfdom had great consequences for Russian art, to be examined in chapter 14. In the Muscovite period, the entire population was divided into estates: the service estate, nobles and later bureaucrats; the working estate, including merchants, artisans, and peasants, who paid taxes or gave labor; and the clergy. By the seventeenth century, boyars, hereditary nobles, were required to supply revenues and troops to the tsar, and were compensated by land grants and laborers to work the land in time of peace. Peasants were bound to the land as serfs, under the authority of the landowner;[32] they provided a constant supply of cheap labor for building projects or manufacturing enterprises. Some fortunate serfs were given specialized training in crafts, and so might pay off their "debt" to their owners and become free peasant artisans or even owners of factories.

A result of the estate system was that nobles grew dependent on the court, estranged from the land and from peasant culture. An obvious symbol of the separation of the urban property owner from the peasant was Peter I's decree that all men, except priests and peasants, must shave their beards, abandon traditional Russian costume, and dress like Europeans. Nonetheless, Russian peasants and gentry did have contact with one another, especially on rural estates, and above all during childhood. Well-to-do households had peasant nurses, cooks, maids, footmen, and grooms, at least one of whom was bound to be a storyteller. As numerous memoirs and fictional writings attest, a shared folklore, along with shared religion and devotion to the tsar, was part of a common Russian identity until the twentieth century.

In terms of style and imagery, the relationship between court and folk art was complex and interactive. Superficially, the interaction meant the presence of Slavic and Scandinavian elements in the architecture and the applied arts of the Kremlin, and pagan motifs in embroidery, manuscript illuminations, or icons. It meant a formal similarity between articles used in court rituals, such as the inscribed silver *kovshy*, and humbler ceremonial utensils of wood, decorated with carving and paint—both based on ancient wooden prototypes.

Another dimension of the relationship was the quotation of court and church forms in folk art. A particular decoration on an *izba* or a distinctive shape of a wooden *kovsh* or *bratina* from an isolated area might embody a local tradition from the distant past, but could also signify an imitation of an impressive building or object seen once, or described by a traveler. The styles of courts and major monasteries were introduced to the provinces by professional artists who went to fill commissions for icons, royal doors, or church utensils, and stayed to make imitations of luxury goods in inexpensive materials for local consumption.[33] On another level, the songs and fairytales handed down orally through generations of village singers were replete with images of the magnificent palaces of tsars and boyars—images reflected on many northern distaffs. Though based on much earlier sources, including Slavic myths and Kievan hero legends or *byliny*, most of these tales were thoroughly Muscovite in their coloration.

During the long history of the growth and consolidation of the Russian nation, customs and beliefs of both pagan and Christian origin were expressed through ancient visual forms which evolved in all spheres of art. The accretions of successive generations survived and developed, or fell away, or lost their former meanings and added new ones. This evolutionary process was essential in the formation of a Russian cultural identity from the tenth through the seventeenth centuries. It was at this point, a watershed in the history of Russia, that differences between folk art and court art became more significant than circumstantial differences in backgrounds or clientele of the artists. They were conceptual, based on the meanings of objects or images for the artists who made them and for the people who used them. Both conceptual and visual differences become understandable when we examine forms such as the horse, the lion, mythical beings, and ritual scenes in folk art, and see how their evolution differed from their usages in court art.

Heraldic Beasts and
Guardian Figures:
The Evolution of
Motifs

Folk art shared with Kievan and Muscovite decoration a body of imagery and abstract design derived in part from ancient Slavic forms. In many types of folk art, and in much of pre-Petrine court art, the forms of horses, birds, mythical creatures, abstract symbols of natural forms, and ritual scenes appeared in symmetrical three-part compositions or as repeated border patterns: the design played a role in determining the meaning of a motif in its given context. Another kind of decoration showing figures engaged in action, found in *zhit'e* on icons, became common in eighteenth- and nineteenth-century folk painting, especially in the north. Many works had more than one type of decoration, and each motif reinforced or altered the meaning of the other components of a design.

A horse, a horse with a rider (fig. 12.1), and a composition in which a pair of horses with riders flank a standing figure or a tree are obviously different, but the relationships among these images and their permutations are subtle. The wide range of designs based on a single animal figure, a symbol, or a ritual scene indicates the extent to which images changed and gained new meanings by association with other forms. The horse was connected with the vital power of the sun among the Slavs and many other cultures. In folk sculpture, horse heads on the *okhlupen'* and carved horses on looms and sewing devices sometimes had exaggerated manes with spikes like sunrays.[1] In sculpture, painting, and embroidery, the shape of a horse was often accompanied by a rhomboid or a rayed circle; the figurative and abstract forms paralleled and therefore strengthened one another.[2]

In Kievan times, the horse and rider were legendary military heroes, the *bogatyri* Alesha Popovich, Usynia Gorynich, Il'ia of Muromets, Bova Korolevich, Solovei Razboinik, or their almost mythic prototype Aleksandr Makedonskii, Alexander the Great. The hero image was equally important in Vladimir-Suzdal' and Muscovy, and became familiar everywhere in the seventeenth and eighteenth centuries through *lubki*, tiles, and spicecakes. This figure gathered accretions in folk art. Among the few surviving works by seventeenth-century folk masters are painted wood trunks and chests from Velikii Ustiug and other areas in the north. Many of these depict

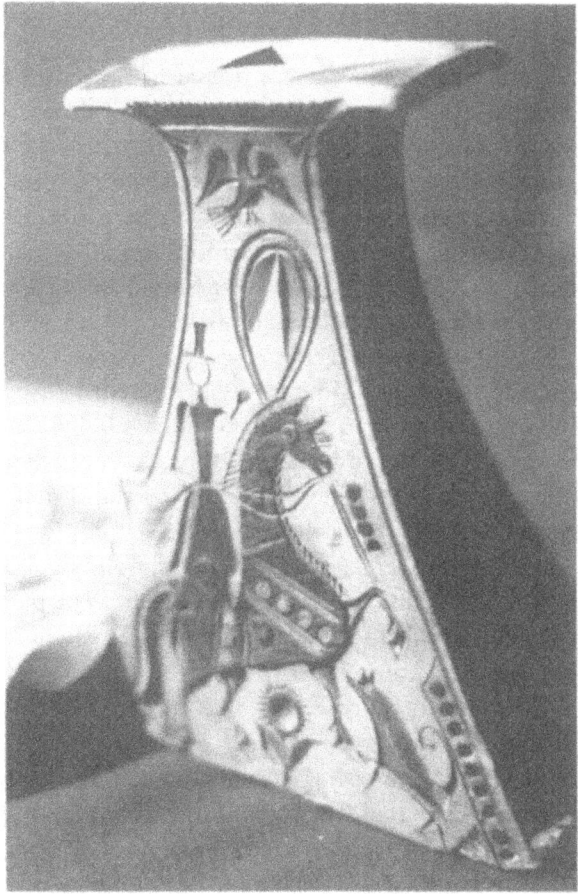

bogatyri or the kindred half-mythical character, the *kitovras* ("centaur") Polkan (fig. 8.8).[3] Polkan entered Russian legend not from Greek myth but from a story about King Solomon and his centaur brother. Polkan's adventures were later absorbed into tales of the *bogatyri*, and he appeared on painted trunks, always with bow and arrow, often shooting at a large parrot. The bril-

FIG. 12.1 Distaff socket with horse and rider. Wood, incrustation. Gorodets, mid-19th century. GIM.

liant bird first appeared in Russia in 1490, when an ambassador from Rome presented one to Tsar Ivan III; it was so well received that emissaries from other countries brought parrots, and by the seventeenth century one could find them in markets. With no iconographical reason for its presence, the parrot had a prominent place in such compositions for the sake of exoticism and color.

Polkan, the *bogatyri*, or the biblical hero Samson with his lion, accompanied by parrots and other birds, appeared on the lids of trunks and chests for valuables with no narrative connection other than shared reputations for bravery. The loose association of legends became more specific, though, when paintings on the sides of the trunks represented real battle scenes. One such subject was the storming of the Swedish fort Noteburg (Oreshek) by Peter I in 1702, a victory that opened the Neva River passage from Lake Onega to the Baltic.[4] Peter the Great was a popular figure in some parts of the north because of his involvement with shipbuilding and developing northern ports, though he was also fiercely opposed for other reasons. Images of this sort, quite different from both satire and official propaganda, not only connected Peter's triumphs with those of legendary heroes, but absorbed him into their ranks.

The motif of the horse with and without a rider continued to develop by processes of accretion, alteration, and renewal of earlier meanings. The archaic designs of running horses, running deer, or flying formations of swans on distaffs from the remote Mezen' River area preserved the ancient forms most faithfully. The graphic zigzags, hatchings, and spirals recalled the devices on early Slavic amulets. On distaffs made by Grigorii and Mikhail Novikov at the end of the nineteenth century (fig. 12.2),[5] a single horse surrounded by a border of rhomboids encasing double spirals was shown with bridle and reins but without a rider. In place of the rider was an x-shaped cross with arms crossed by short hatching strokes; a similar cross, embellished by small, hatched oval shapes, was placed directly beneath the horse's belly, and another cross, with circles at the ends of the arms, slightly to the side. The substitution of abstract forms for a figure might reflect a familiar local or family convention, or it might suggest vestiges of earlier ornamental traditions.

In Borok painting, horses pulled sleighs or carriages. Not symbolic figures in their own right, they were essential components in scenes that were part genre and part ritual: outings during the festivities of Epiphany, Maslenitsa, Semik, and wedding journeys. Distaff painters often treated the spoked carriage wheels to show their resemblance to a rayed sun, like those of Elijah's chariot, and like the wheels of the real carriages in which couples drove to welcome spring. Additional motifs on the horses' yokes and on distaffs, such as the *sirin* or birds and lush flowers, reinforced the symbolism of spring and fertility.

Gorodets distaffs decorated with contour carving, incrustation, and painting combined carriage rides with other symbolic motifs, including pairs of riders flanking a flowering tree with a bird hovering above it, or mounted soldiers paired with women. Despite the contempory costume, both motifs reflected ancient rituals. Several Gorodets distaffs had reinforcing motifs on the sides of the projecting socket into which the blade was inserted (fig. 12.1). This wedge-shaped area often contained a prancing horse on one side and a peacock (a common modification of the *sirin*) on the other. The horse and bird were clearly understood as parallel images.

This pattern of reinforcing symbolic meanings by association allowed great flexibility. For example, a horse might be paired with a duck, traditionally connected with both sun and water, or with the *rusalka*, primarily a water divinity. One fanciful mutation of the horse existed in a folk legend from the Viatka region about a winged, fire-breathing horse that lived in the river.[6] At midwinter and midsummer festivals, the songs, dances, bonfires, and river baths also connected the *rusalka* with Iarilo. On a more mundane level, the presence of horses and *rusalki* on tools for making linen—the loom, *trepalo*, *valek*, and *rubel'*—underlined the importance of both water and sun not only to grow the flax, but for a major stage in producing the fabric. In early spring, after the winter weaving was done, village women took their linen to the river, soaked it, beat it, smoothed it, and spread it over the grass and bushes to dry in the sun. They invited the help of nature divinities in this onerous task by singing songs full of vivid poetic images, likening the spinning of flax to the *rusalka* combing her hair and to fall-

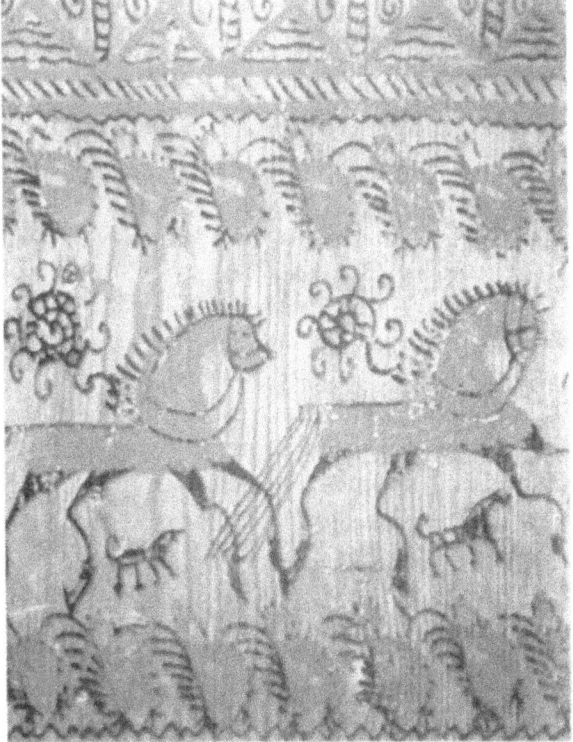

FIG. 12.2 Mikhail Novikov, distaff. Painted wood. Mezen', late 19th century. Sergiev-Posad.

ing rain, or a tuft of wool to soft clouds.[7] These songs, along with the decorated tools, linked myth and nature with domestic crafts.

Lions, gryphons, and other heraldic beasts from Vladimir and Suzdal' that were brought into the repertoire of Muscovite decorative art were also depicted on boxes, chests, and cupboard doors in the houses of merchants and well-to-do peasants, on birch-bark boxes, and in *lubki* (fig. 12.3). Lions appeared as guardian figures on carved frontal boards as often as *bereginy* and *rusalki*. They were paired at either end of a frontal board, or arranged in multifigured friezes with *vodianye* or *bereginy*. Since Russian peasants never saw real lions, they might have used cats as models, or copied images from bestiaries, emblem books, or icons. Usually the lion had a human face, with eyes facing front and an engaging grin, sometimes with bristling whiskers like those of Peter I.

The *sirin* appeared in Kievan and early Muscovite art: on *kolty*, on the "Golden Gates" and the white stone walls of Vladimir and Suzdal' churches, and in manuscript illuminations. The *sirin*, with doves, peacocks, and other birds, could be found among trailing and interlacing foliage borders, and at the heads of pages in the twelfth-century Gospel from Iur'ev and the fourteenth-century Onega Psalter. In seventeenth-century manuscripts and books, the *sirin* and peacock were used almost interchangeably. They were among the favorite motifs for decorating cupboards, trunks, and other items in the household. The *sirin* represented good fortune, while her counterpart, the *alkonost*, signified sorrow.

But one unusual rendering, on the lid of an iron-bound trunk from Olonets Province painted in 1710, shows that foreign elements had begun to change the nature of the image. This *sirin* (fig. 12.4), a large, sturdy figure with spreading tail, softly contoured feathers, long, thick braids, and a peaked crown, has a subtly modeled face turned slightly to the side and a direct, somber gaze. She stands solidly on a thick branch from which vines and heavy bunches of grapes sprout. The inscriptions label the figure "Sirin Bird of holy, blessed heaven," and the fruit "grapes," and give the date in Old Slavonic letters. A longer text in small letters explains a legend about the *sirin* who lives in the sea and sings enchantingly, so that sailors dive from their ships and are dashed against the cliffs to become her prey.[8] This text shows that the Greek myth of the siren, which might earlier have been applied to stories of the water sprites, *rusalki*, had become identified with the name *sirin*. The branch with its grapes also reflected an alteration of traditional legends. According to a north Russian tale based on the biblical story of the Garden of Eden, God provided everything for Adam and Eve, but gave them one divine command: not to eat the fruit of the great tree of grapes that grew in Eden.[9] Apparently, apples were too common to be the forbidden fruit, but few Russians had ever tasted or even seen grapes. The artist may have imitated carved grapevines on the columns of an iconostasis; such a source would have reinforced the associ-

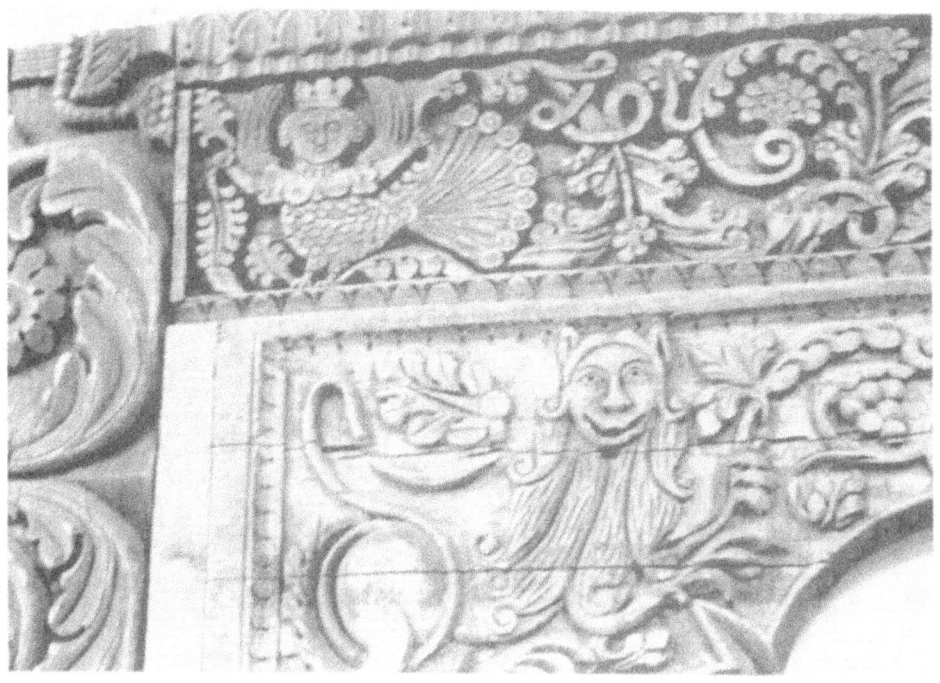

FIG. 12.3   Gate with images of lion
and *sirin*. Carved wood. Volga region,
19th century. Sergiev-Posad.

ation of grapes with the Tree of Eden and the Tree of Life. This *sirin* filled the
role of a stern archangel, warning against trespass.

On another level, the image may have expressed conservative opposition
to the westernizing practices of Peter the Great. Some Old Believers, who
had settled in the area along the White Sea, had a fanatical hatred of the
heretical Peter and his non-Russian wife Catherine.[10] The religious theme, the
presence of such a long inscription, and the sophistication of the painting
technique all point to an Old Believer community. The conflation of a Greek
myth or a biblical theme with traditional Russian folk imagery was not unusual, but here the portrait-like alteration of the *sirin* character seems to emphasize a specific issue and message.

For the most part, the *sirin* remained protective and joyful, qualities emphasized in texts accompanying her images on *lubki* (fig. 12.5). In the later
eighteenth and the nineteenth centuries, on the frontal boards of houses
along the Volga, and on painted serving utensils, lighting fixtures, and distaffs from Arkhangel'sk and Permogore, the *sirin* was often set apart at the

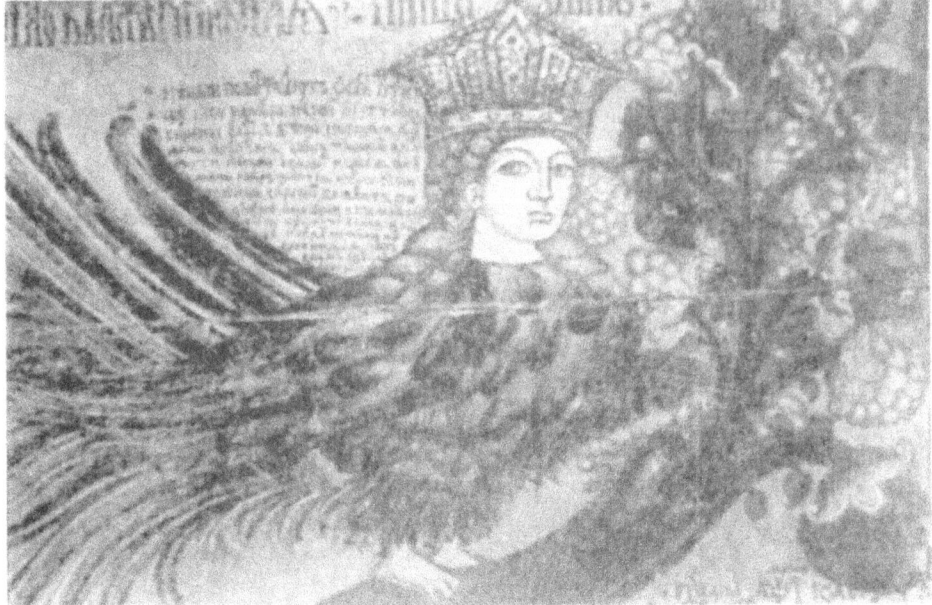

FIG. 12.4 *Sirin* perched on grapevine,
lid of trunk. Painted wood. Olonets,
1710. GIM.

center of a bowl or canister or in a roundel surrounded by foliage ornament (fig. 12.6). The Borok painter Pelageia Amosova called the central portion of a distaff the "bird" section, because that was where the *sirin* was supposed to be painted. The *sirin* was also a component of the compositional group with paired horsemen, female figures, birds, and animals surrounding the Tree of Life.

The unicorn, another creature popular in folk art from the seventeenth century and later, was not part of Slavic mythology. It probably entered Russia through European emblem books. The first Moscow printing house used the battle of the lion and the unicorn in its coat of arms in the sixteenth century. In the north, however, the image took on a more dramatic and mythic meaning as an enactment of the endless battle between the powers of the earth and those of the underground realm, and it appeared on a number of chests and trunks.[11]

One of the most sophisticated interpretations appears inside the lid of a chest for valuables made in 1688 for Nikita Potapov, a merchant living in the Borok area on the Northern Dvina (fig. 12.7).[12] The beasts seem not to fight but to embrace one another around the slender trunk of a deep-rooted, broad-

Heraldic Beasts and Guardian Figures: The Evolution of Motifs

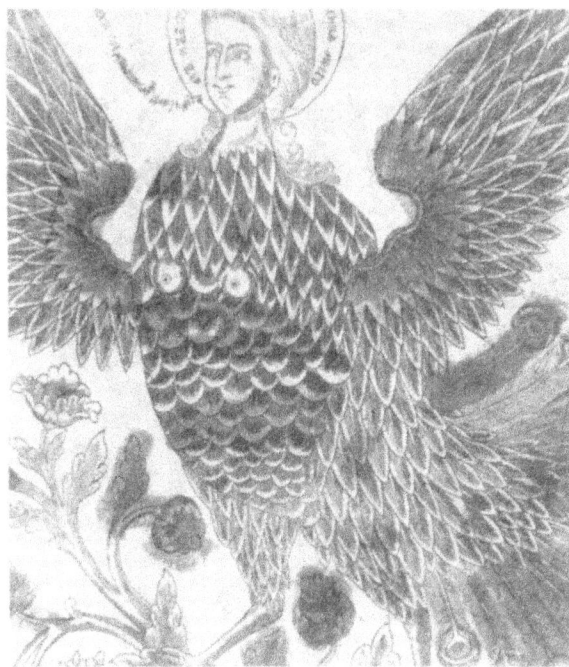

FIG. 12.5 "Sirin, the heavenly bird." *Lubok*. Late 18th or early 19th century. GRM.

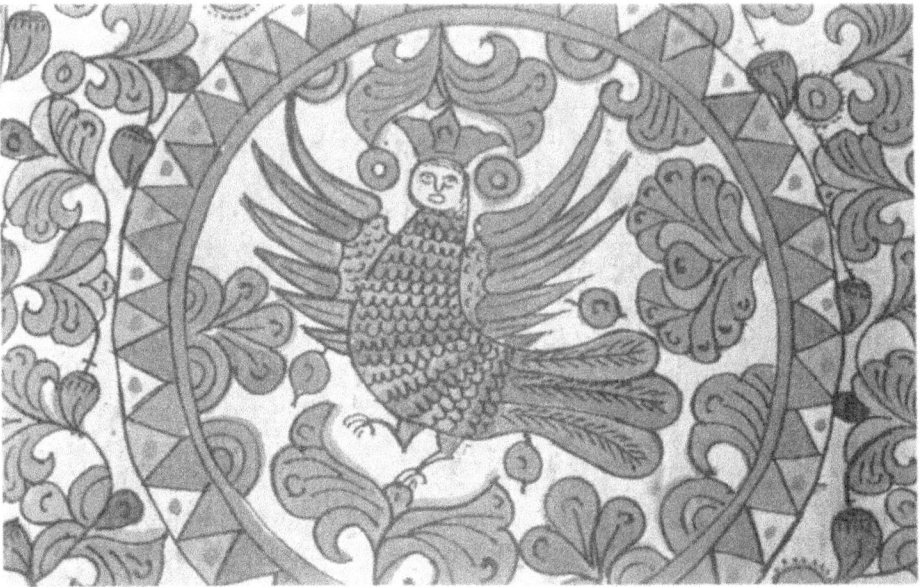

FIG. 12.6 Egor Iarygin, distaff blade with *sirin*. Painted wood. Permogore, early 20th century. Sergiev-Posad.

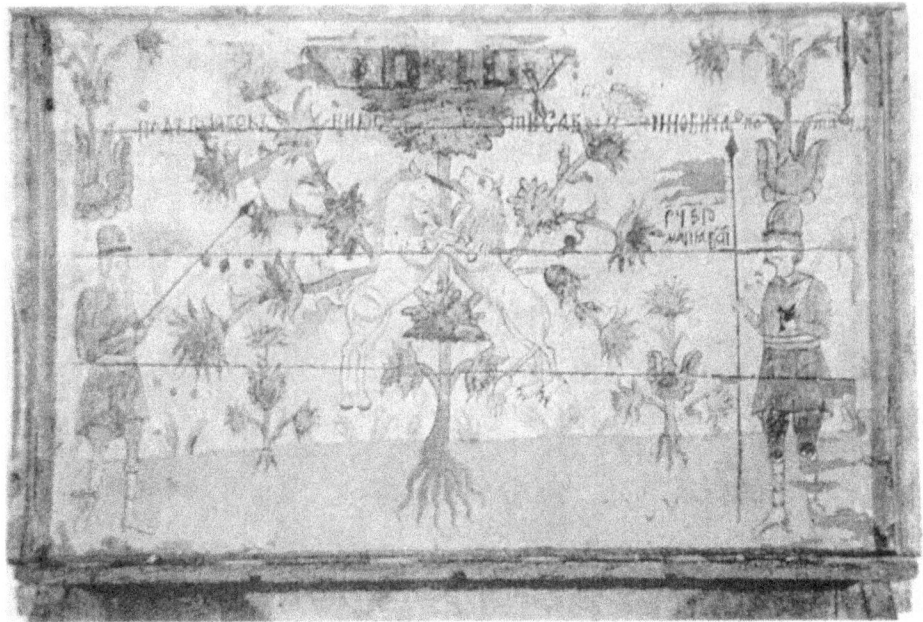

FIG. 12.7   Treasure chest made for
Nikita Potapov. Wood, metal, paint. Lid
with lion and unicorn, guards. Borok,
1688. GIM.

branched, flowering tree in which two birds are perched. At either side stand
human figures, an old man with a spear and a youth with a sword and standard, both wearing long Russian shirts, fur-lined caps, and soft boots. These
figures are guards, evidently from Potapov's household, whose role is to protect the treasure chest.

The elegant drawing, the clear blue-green and dark red against a yellow-
ish ground, and the natural poses of the figures indicate an experienced artist,
perhaps a painter of icons or manuscripts.[13] The patron was a man of wealth
and taste, probably from one of the Novgorod boyar families exiled after
Moscow annexed the city in the late fifteenth century.[14] The entire northern
territory, from Lake Ladoga to the Urals, had been part of the Novgorod
Principality before the reign of Ivan IV, and from this time to the seventeenth
century, when many of the Old Believers went into exile in the north, the area
enjoyed cultural advantages, substantial wealth, and a high level of literacy.
Local place names, such as Mokraia Edoma and Borok on the Northern
Dvina, came from Novgorod families, the Edemskiis and Boretskiis. With the

boyars came artisans and icon painters, who established the stylistic traits which Borok folk painters were later to develop.

The clear contours, light background, and harmonious balance in the composition of this trunk and others of the time were emulated by Iakov Iarygin in the late eighteenth century, and by the Amosovs and other painters in the nineteenth and early twentieth centuries. The lion and unicorn composition filled the upper portion of several early nineteenth-century distaffs from the Borok area, the heraldic creatures poised above the roofline of a house which, in the lower register, opened to reveal interior scenes of domestic activity, such as spinning (fig. 12.8).[15] Stylistically and thematically, the secular works made for well-to-do patrons in the seventeenth century were the link between Novgorodian icon painting and later northern folk art.

The central form, the tree around which the lion and unicorn pranced or in which the *sirin* or peacock perched, was the fulcrum that gave the compositions unity and symmetry. It was also the thematic link among different conceptual layers within the work. In heavily forested Russia, trees had both practical and mythic significance; birch trees and their *rusalki* had personalities, and every other species had qualities known to woodworkers. But the Tree of Life was a more complex symbol. The idea of life beyond human measure, renewing itself each year, and the tree's strength and towering height made it both a symbol of everlasting life and the central axis of the world, linking the lower world, the middle earth, and the sky.[16] These were valid meanings in both pagan and Christian contexts. In Western baroque emblems, the roots were analogous to snakes, dragons, and other primal forces; the trunk, like the rampant lion, unicorn, or horses, expressed the idea of elevation and striving; the foliage was the domain of birds and heavenly bodies. A tree bearing vines or fruit was related to the biblical Tree of Jesse, and to the Tree of Knowledge of Good and Evil. Variations on these images occurred in icons, but the most common form in folk art was the tree flanked by two animals, birds, or human figures.

The Potapov artist effectively combined the separate elements of the iconography by emphasizing formal parallels. The twisting bare roots of the tree and the smaller roots of the bushes at either side were paired with the feet of the beasts and the guards. An indication of a ground line in a dark ocher shade separated the lower world from the rest of the background. The trunk was linked with the rearing bodies of the animals and the spears held by the men; the lush foliage was united with the birds and with fantastic blossoms placed above each guard's head.

On another northern piece, a dowry chest made in the early eighteenth century (fig. 6.2), painted bright vermilion against a warm gold background, the tree motif appears in several different guises, but not as the symbolic Tree of Life. On the front, standing at either side of the lock, are human guards; on either side of them are trees with roosting birds. On the short ends of the chest, trees with birds occupy the center of the space while the flanking human figures enact specific roles. On one end a hunter aiming at a bird is balanced visually by his dog; on the other end, boys climb up the slender trunks of the flanking trees to gather the abundant fruit and nuts. Finally, on the back, two large trees, with foliage like exotic flowers found in manuscript margins, fill the center panels, and pine trees, quite realistic in contrast, stand at each end. The activities of the two men beneath the pine trees are clearly described. One with an axe and the other with a special long-handled chopper make the cuts necessary to tap the tree for pine tar, an important export since the sixteenth century.[17] This decoration recalls the style of Novgorod and contains some traditional imagery of fruitfulness and the good life, but it does so more descriptively than symbolically.

The most widespread form of the Tree of Life composition consists of a flowering tree, sometimes highly stylized, with a bird above it and horses with riders or humans standing at either side. This motif is closely linked visually and thematically to that of the Goddess attended by horsemen or birds or flanked by trees. Such scenes are most fully represented on distaffs from Iaroslavl', Vologda, and Gorodets, and in embroidery. In some cases, motifs of apparently different origins are combined in ways that reveal connections between the different genres.

The ritualistic character of a scene depicted on a box, distaff, or embroidered border may be hidden amid contemporary details and other embellishments. It may become clear only when the key symbols are identified and related to their traditional contexts. For example, a distaff base from Gorodets (fig. 12.9) contains two scenes separated by a geometrically decorated band. In the upper section are a bird hovering above a tree with two smaller birds perched on its branches, and horsemen with sabers at each side. Below the border, framed by a broad arch embellished with dots, is a woman holding a parasol, with bushes at either side; outside the arch are bushes and large birds, and below the woman are two dogs.[18] At first glance, the personages are mounted cavaliers and a fashionable lady, similar to painted wooden toys made in the Gorodets district. But the composition is also ritualistic; the key elements of bird, tree, and flanking horsemen and frontally placed female figure correspond to those in other scenes of worship before a nature goddess. The woman with the parasol, standing beneath an arch like a rainbow, suggests the rain and fertility associated on a very deep level with Mokosh or Mother Moist Earth. The tree, the Tree of Life, links her to the upper, active zone of the sky and sun, identified with the hovering bird.

Two contour-carved Iaroslavl' distaffs from the early nineteenth century show how Tree of Life motifs could be updated and made to seem part of social encounters.[19] One, depicting the meeting of a bride and bridegroom, shows the two figures in a park, posed frontally and perfectly balanced on either side of a branching tree. The other scene (fig. 5.2), a "quadrille," shows two pairs of young girls dancing at either side of a rather spikey shrub; this scene fills a section just below a scene of tea drinking, in which the large and carefully detailed samovar is exactly aligned with the tree. These are genre scenes, but in a curiously insistent way they relate the social activity to more stylized rituals, such as garlanding the birch trees during Semik or Rusalka Week.

Embroidered borders of towels and bed valances represent the most intricately interwoven forms and motifs connected with the Tree of Life and Goddess themes (fig. 7.5).[20] An example from Kargopol', in Arkhangel'sk Province,[21] combines all the elements in one horizontal band. A female figure with outstretched hands holding small trees stands at the center. On either side, horses with tails branching like peacocks' tails are ridden by male figures with upraised hands; and beyond them stand female figures with upraised hands. Variations on rhomboids and angular spirals make up the rest of the decoration. A wedding towel from Torzhek (fig. 12.10) shows the Goddess flanked by riders and birds. A valance from Olonets brings the legendary *sirin* and *alkonost* and the heraldic double-headed eagle into juxtaposition with the Tree of Life (fig. 12.11).[22] A tree covered with varicolored fruit is at the center; perched at its top are two small *alkonost* figures facing each other. At either side, a much larger *sirin* stands, grasping a flowering branch in one claw. A

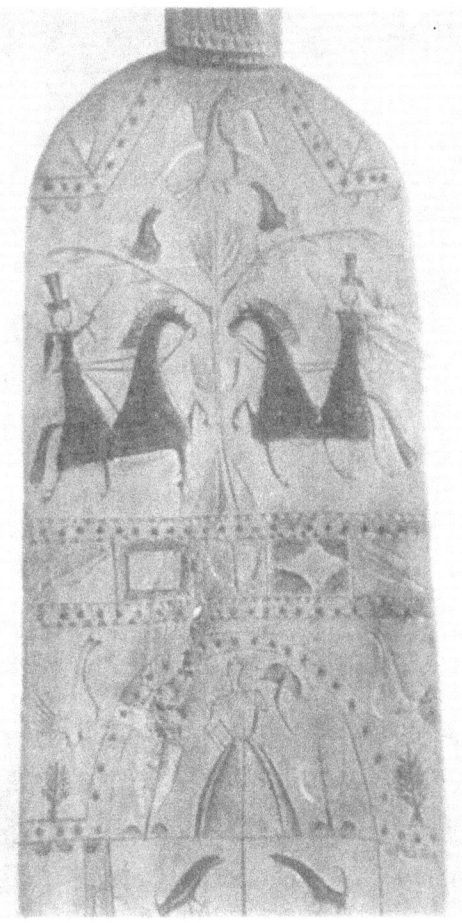

FIG. 12.9 Distaff base. Wood, incrustation. Detail of base with horsemen, Tree of Life, woman with parasol. Gorodets, 19th century. GIM.

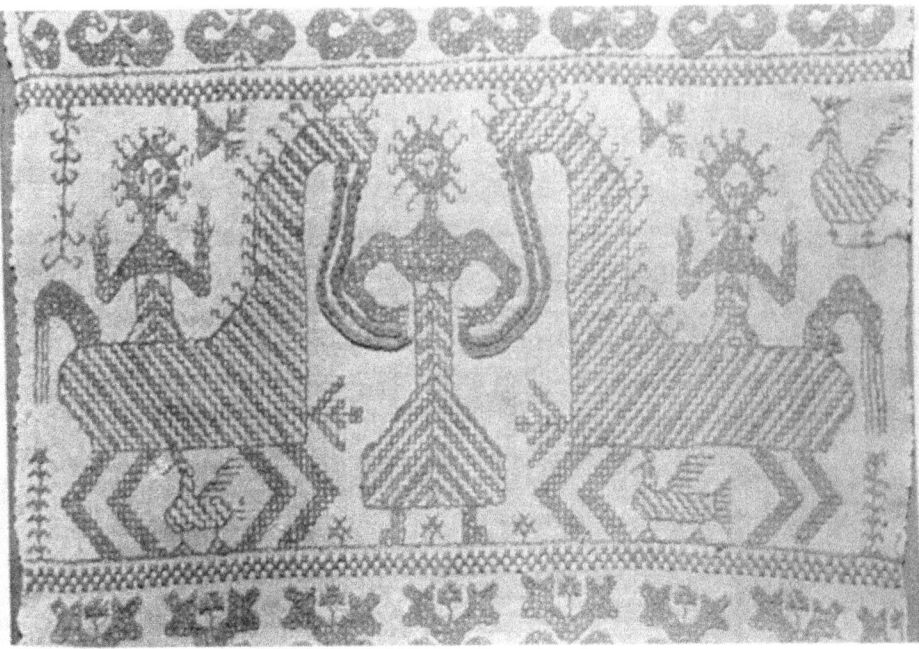

FIG. 12.10 Border of wedding towel.
Detail of female figure, riders, birds.
Torzhek, Tver' Province, 1886. Sergiev-
Posad.

small male figure with a staff at the top of each branch may signify a traveler
lured by the *sirin* or siren, according to the legend depicted on the earlier
painted chest from the same region. Finally, at the ends of the valance are
large figures, not quite identical, which seem to be variations on the double-
headed eagle form; around the three borders are small patterns of stylized
birds and flowers.

Embroidery from Tver' Province, in the northwestern part of central
Russia, preserved an especially rich range of archaic designs related to agrarian cults. Many towel borders combined highly stylized tree forms with a
female figure with upraised hands (figs. 12.12, 12.13). These represented
fertility rituals connected with Mother Moist Earth. Some may have illustrated the custom of garlanding the birch tree with flowers, ribbons, and embroidered towels during Rusalka Week, since the figures hold flowers or
branches in their hands.[23] The motifs suggest that these towels were actually
used to dress the *rusalki*. On some examples, the trees are extremely geometrical, with rhomboids, triangles, and featherlike projections arranged with

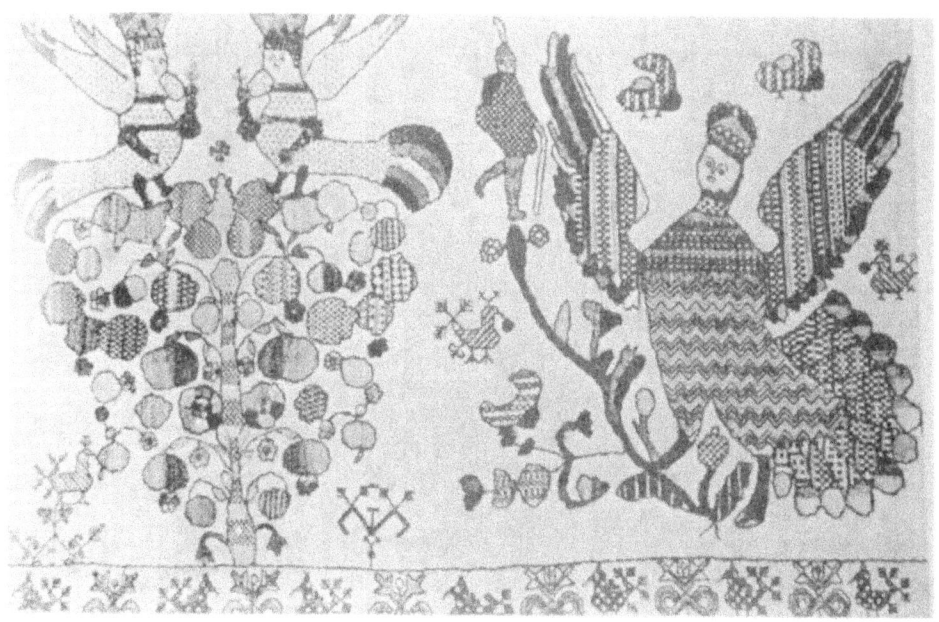

FIG. 12.11 Valance. Tambour embroidery on linen. Olonets, mid-19th century. GIM.

radial symmetry as if to suggest parts of both birds and trees. Some borders have no human or horse figures but only stylized trees, with rhomboids or birds forming extensions of the branches; others combine trees with large birds or horses, which are bilaterally symmetrical and have two heads (fig. 12.14).[24] Another kind of ritual motif, related to midsummer harvest festivals, is suggested in combinations of the double-headed eagle and the peacock or firebird with abstract symbols of the sun or fire. A swastika or rhomboid might take the place of branches or even the head of a goddess or a rider, because the presence of Kostroma, Iarilo, or Ivan Kupala would be understood.[25]

The techniques of embroidery allowed and encouraged more stylization, abstraction, and intricate connections among figures of different form and scale than did those of painting or carving. The arrangement of embroidered figures within a fairly restricted border made the forms highly concentrated and hierarchical. The fineness of the handwork was as important as the intensification of mythical or symbolic imagery, because the textiles embroidered with these motifs were worn or used during rituals, for instance to decorate the birch or *rusalka*, and in betrothal or marriage ceremonies. The meaning of

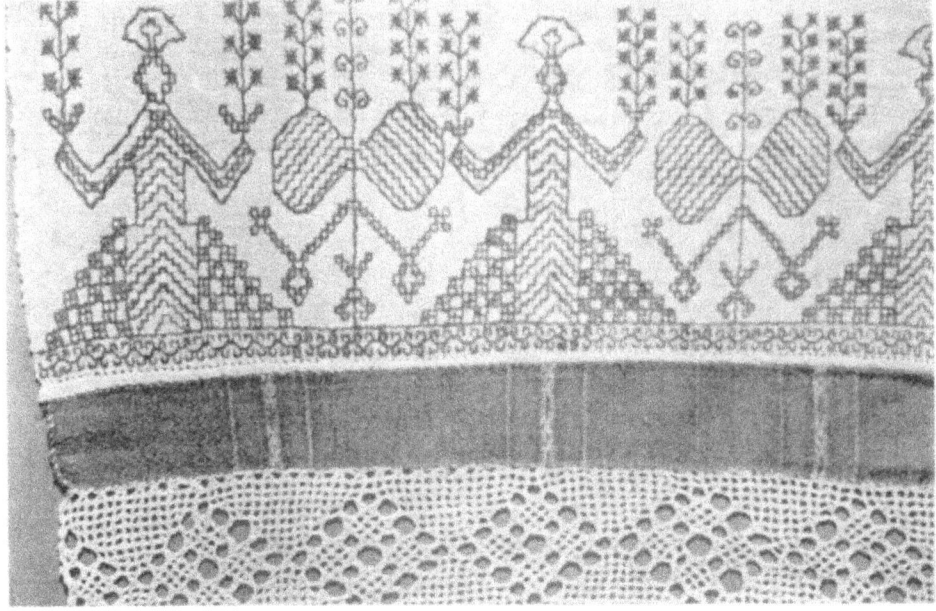

FIG. 12.12   Towel border.
Embroidery, lace. Female figures with
trees. Tver' Province, 19th century.
Sergiev-Posad.

the participatory activity and the imagery on the articles that accompanied
the ritual were mutually essential. In this respect, folk embroidery continued
to fulfill the earliest functions of visual art forms.

What of the design principles in folk art, the relationships among the
form of an object, the figurative and abstract motifs, and the background or
border elements? The main formal principles shared by most types of folk art
were bound to a reverent attitude toward physical objects and the natural
world that Russian peasants inherited from their distant ancestors.

Symmetry within each part of a composition and clear, hierarchical order-
ing of the whole composition are the rule in the art forms of Slavic and Christian Russia and in folk art. This does not mean that rigid formulas kept
designs from developing and interacting with other forms. On the contrary,
the principle of symmetry established a framework for growth based on association of parallel forms. For instance, in ancient Slavic ornaments, a solar disk
and crescent moon could combine and generate petals or axe shapes. Similarly, on a carved distaff or an embroidered border, small geometrical units

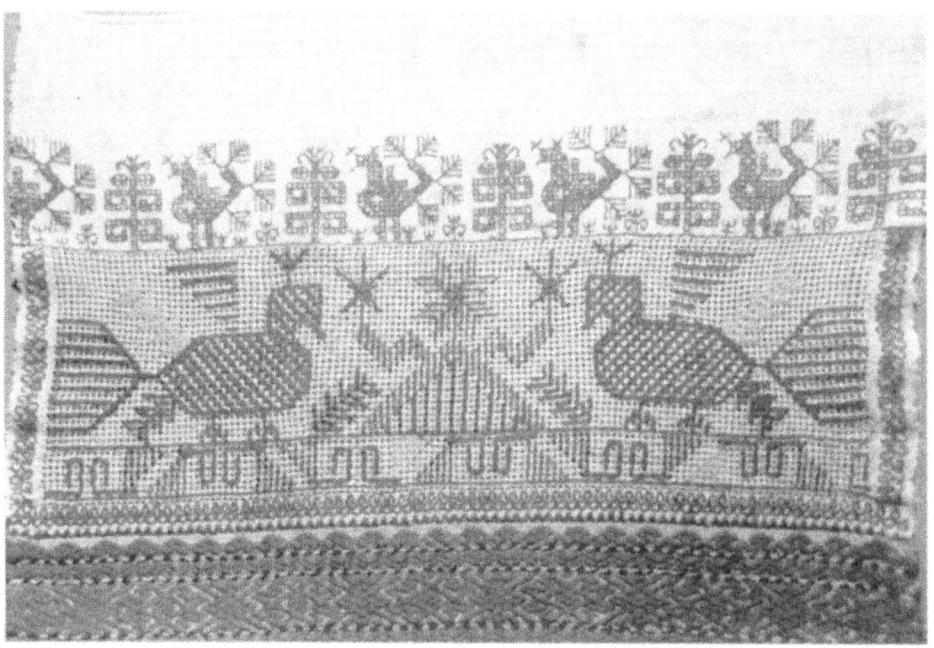

FIG. 12.13 P. I. Povareshkina, towel border. Embroidery on linen. Birds with stylized female figure and trees. Tver' Province, 1900s. Sergiev-Posad.

might form rhomboids and rosettes and, in combination with parallel group-ings, might make up an allover abstract pattern or the shape of a tree. Even on an architectural scale, from the carved pediment of an *izba* to a church facade with relief sculpture, the unit gave rise to additional parts, connected through orderly, linear articulation.

In figurative art, in frescoes, architectural carving, metalwork, icons, and folk painting, figures were normally placed frontally and centrally, in pairs or in rows. Any one figure or group would be related to other units. This could be achieved through placement: one figure above the other; paired figures at either side of a window or column; similar forms at either end of an embroi-dered towel. A different meaning was conveyed by hierarchical relationships: on an icon, a saint surrounded by smaller figures or *zhit'e* scenes; in embroi-dery, a horse, bird, goddess, or tree interspersed with small abstract forms or figures. Finally, meaning was conveyed through formal parallels, such as the wheels of a wedding carriage echoing the roundel in which a *sirin* is perched above the scene.

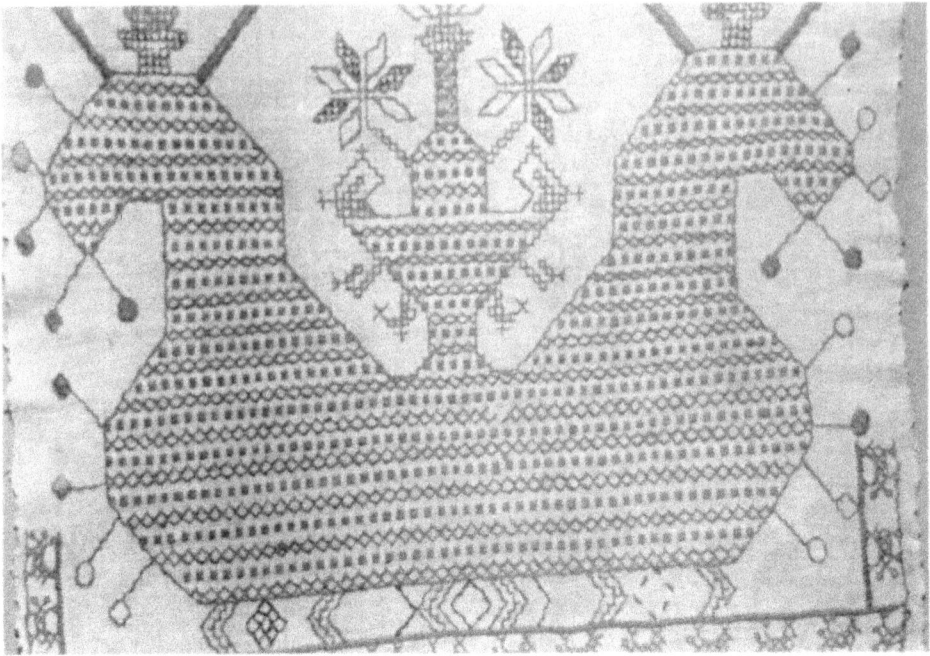

FIG. 12.14 Towel border. Embroidery
on linen. Double-headed horse with
figure. Tver' Province, second half of
the 19th century. Sergiev-Posad.

The familiar two-part symmetry in folk art has been compared to the
question-and-answer forms of songs and riddles that made up an important
part of folk rituals.[26] Two-part symmetry created a sense of participation, regular movement back and forth, and also an effect of stability; three-part compositions, with a dominant central figure and parallel appendages, created an
effect of focus and ritual power. Repetition of like forms—as on Mezen' distaffs, overall patterns in weaving, printed cloth, and chip carving, and the
herbaceous motifs in painting from the Northern Dvina and Khokhloma—
might either diffuse or concentrate a motif, creating either calm or intensity.

Another kind of symmetry or parallelism was not formal but iconographical. In ancient Slavic ornaments, an abstract pattern, such as cross-hatching or
a circle with a central dot, was often combined with a figure, a horse, or a
duck in a way that would strengthen its meaning, its symbolic connection
with the sun or other natural powers. In later art, too, the symbolic meaning
of one type of form could be augmented by a different form with a similar

meaning: for instance, on Permogore distaffs, the *sirin* was often framed by and accented by a circle patterned with zigzags or rays. Embroidered designs on a towel reinforced the symbolic imagery of garlanding the birch tree, or the verses sung while dressing a bride. The notion of symmetry and parallelism is crucial to the interaction of visual form and participatory activity in virtually every aspect of folk art and ritual.

Scenes from Life
and Forms from
the Past

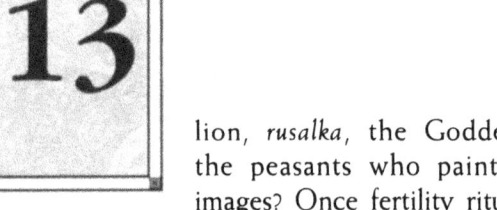

What did the horse, bird, and the Tree of Life mean to carved, or embroidered these lion, *rusalka*, the Goddess, the peasants who painted, images? Once fertility rituals were no longer essential for survival of the community, did they degenerate into popular pastimes, as some critics claimed? Did visual symbols, which once had magical powers to protect both peasant and prince, also become confused and merely decorative?

The evidence of expeditions in northern Russia—both objects and transcriptions of interviews with folk artists—shows that the original images remained valid in many ways. Whether or not a peasant believed that a lion would protect his house, that a *sirin* would bring happiness, or that Saints Nicholas and Paraskeva-Piatnitsa would protect and bring prosperity to his family, he kept these forms because they animated the home in a familiar way. Even when the ancient meanings of archaic forms were forgotten, they remained essential to the nature of an object, such as a duck-shaped dipper or a horse-shaped handle of a *rubel'*. The objects in peasant households kept alive images once vital for the individual and the community.[1] The physical objects, words, songs, and activities that accompanied daily life and seasonal rituals were also vehicles of community celebration and identification, symbols or distillations of shared experience.[2]

The continuing validity of traditional forms was fundamental to the nature of folk art, and a key factor that distinguished folk art from the decorative arts made for courts, cities, and estates. As we have seen, the ancient forms based on pagan symbols for natural forces, the interlace designs made by northern carvers, and images of legendary heroes and mythical beasts were revived in Muscovite decorative arts to evoke the cultural legacies of Kievan Rus'. In folk art, however, these forms kept their primary connection with nature, while coexisting with and evolving along with the accretions of later periods.

In the seventeenth and eighteenth centuries, when the environments of folk and court or urban art grew farther apart, the introduction of ideas and forms from Western culture made the differences even greater. Peasants had contact with Western art only in special circumstances. For instance, when the woodcarvers who worked on ships for Peter the Great's fleet used Western models for sea creatures, these forms affected the representation of *bereginy*. Northern bonecarvers, patronized by the court, were given commissions for decorative objects employing classical motifs. The demand for native artists to adapt their techniques to Western forms affected virtually all types of folk art which came into the sphere of court and gentry. There are many opinions as to whether these contacts and requirements denatured the folk impulse. Along with the closely related problem of serf art, these points will be examined later.

Meanwhile, the normal pattern of evolution, in which forms retained some of their original aspects while acquiring new associations over time, was most evident in types of folk art decorated with both symbolic motifs and images from the artists' environments. The presence of genre, while not entirely new in eighteenth-century Russian folk art,[3] was a sign of a growing individualism and a growing interest in the surrounding world. Painted wooden articles from the Northern Dvina area exhibited a wide range of genre images; distaffs from Iaroslavl' and Gorodets reflected similar interests, though with less variety.

An early representation of a scene from life is on a late eighteenth-century distaff from the Shenkursk region of Arkhangel'sk Province (figs. 13.1, 13.2).[4] The outer side of the distaff presents an architectural setting: a three-story house, like many in the north, with two upper rows of windows embellished with geometrical patterns and perching birds; a main level with a central door and two large windows or panels with rosette designs; and a ground level with a steep, ornamented staircase, supported by a central column ascending to the door. The only figures are an old man with a basket and cane climbing the stair on the left and a youth on a horse looking up from the opposite corner.

The significance of the scene is explained by its counterpart on the other side of the blade, showing a sleigh ride with two figures, a young man and woman, both in fine costumes ornamented with embroidery. In spite of the snow on the ground, there are large, tulip-like flowers or bushes in bloom, adding to the joyful nature of the scene, the traditional wedding journey. The first picture clearly relates an early stage of the courtship, when the suitor comes to the house with a gift and must wait below while the old father takes it inside. The young woman is not to be seen behind all the closed windows. An inscription beginning below the sleigh-ride scene, continuing on the ornamental knobs and the stem, serves as a dedication: "Stepanaida Dmitrovna Chiurakova, silverworker, Kurgomenskaia Volost."[5] The carefully lettered inscription and the identification of the bride by her craft were typical of the Novgorodian culture of this region.

Similar images adorn many other Northern Dvina distaffs from the early nineteenth century, including one with several figures (but not the bride) visible in windows and doorways, and one in which the young woman does appear, and smiles as the boy takes off his cap.[6] On other distaffs from the Borok area, the outer side depicts a carriage in front of an elaborate three- or four-story house, with details that evoke fairytale descriptions of the tsar's palace. Such refinements were in keeping with the elevated character and language of wedding ceremonies in some areas, in which fantasy titles were given to the chief participants: the peasant groom and bride were called "prince" and "princess,"

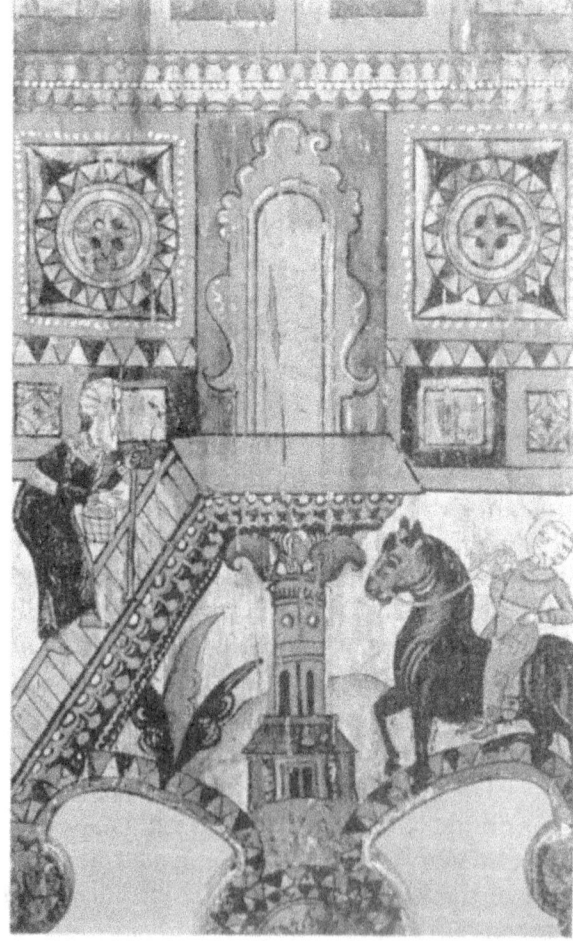

FIG. 13.1 Distaff. Painted wood. Front of blade, the suitor's visit. Borok, Arkhangel'sk Province, end of the 18th century. GIM.

and the most honored guests were designated "boyars." The order of seating, the arrangement of the table, and other details of peasant weddings were remarkably similar to those in records of weddings of the grand dukes and tsars of the fifteenth and sixteenth centuries, as if this crucial ceremony took place on a level above that of ordinary life.[7]

On the inner side of one such distaff is a much more humble genre scene with a boy blowing a horn while a girl drives cattle from a stable into the fields.[8] The subject recalls the ritual of taking the herds out to pasture on St. George's Day. But there is nothing ritualistic about the style; the animals wander all over. Another distaff of the same type shows an imposing house with two covered staircases on the front and, on the reverse, the slaughter of cattle in preparation for a feast.[9] It is specific and workmanlike: three men begin to skin and drain the blood from one carcass, while another raises an axe ready for the next victim. The style is close to that of Novgorodian icon painting, and the imagery is not appreciably different from that in marginal scenes from the lives of St. George or St. Nicholas. But the images did not need to be based on early models. The scenes with herd animals, like hunting scenes on other pieces, were typical of the region and part of the artists' experience.

The artist who best represents the increasing variety and vividness of

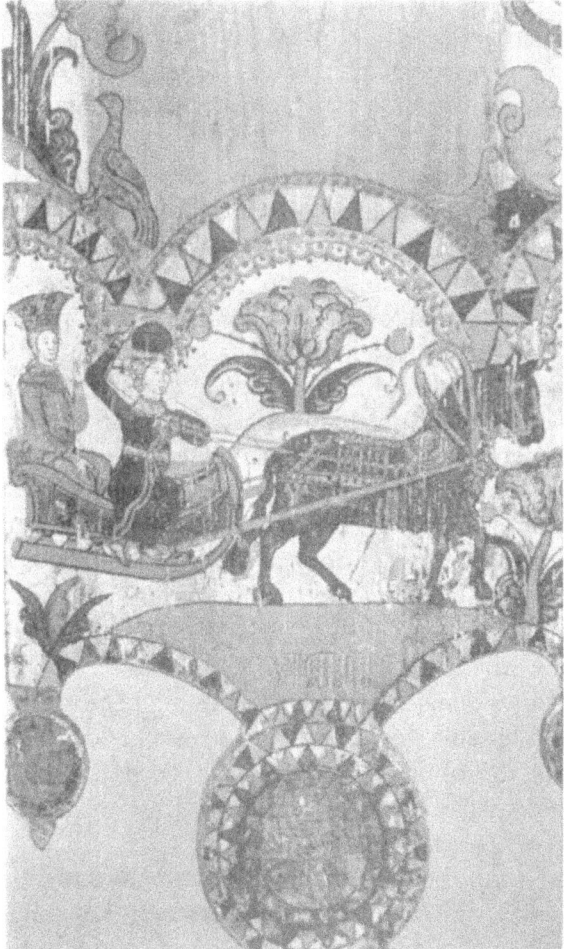

FIG. 13.2 Distaff. Painted wood. Back of blade, wedding journey and inscription. Borok, Arkhangel'sk Province, end of the 18th century. GIM.

genre, partly because a large body of his art is known, is Iakov Iarygin, who worked in the village of Bol'shoi Bereznik, near Mokraia Edoma in the Borok area, in the early nineteenth century.[10] On some of his distaffs, Iarygin juxtaposed carriage rides with interior scenes rather than exterior facades (fig. 13.3); the lion and unicorn poised above one roof (fig. 12.8) may have served as substitutes for the traditional *okhluphen'*; below the roof, the walls opened to reveal domestic activities, such as *posidelki*, reading, and tea drinking. The artist might have known similar compositions in manuscript miniatures, such as a page from an anthology of stories and parables showing two men conversing inside a house while a woman spins on the porch, and in an upper frame, the same figures at dinner.[11] Iarygin's interiors seem to combine ideas from icons and manuscripts, from the local styles of "herbaceous" ornamentation, and perhaps from designs actually used on the walls of northern houses.

Iarygin painted a great variety of genre scenes on all kinds of wooden articles, sleds, yokes, cradles, dishes, containers, and distaffs. A bread box and several bast storage containers depicted domestic tasks, including weaving, sewing, and spinning, and leisure activity such as fortunetelling and tea drinking. Iarygin even made two comic versions of the tea-drinking ceremony, pairing a man and woman seated at either side of a samovar with a couple of chickens at an identical samovar.

The artist often combined domestic and outdoor scenes in apparently informal ways, especially on birch canisters and baskets for gathering berries. One cylindrical container depicts a sequence of genre scenes: a woman with a basket and a boy leading a white dog walk into the woods to gather berries or mushrooms; behind them a boy rides a galloping horse; next, a woman sits spinning and a bearded man and boy sit reading at a table; after them, a woman sits at a cradle; and then the woman, boy, and dog reappear. Genre scenes are arranged with a different effect on the oval lid of a bread box: at one end a tea party, at the other a family dinner, with the two scenes oriented in opposite directions. Centered between them is an abstract ornament, a circle with an interior eight-petaled flower and projecting rays; and all around the domestic scenes are floral garlands, a pair of birds, and a lion and unicorn. The heraldic motifs, together with the ornamental patterning and balanced distribution of colors, help to unify the entire design and make the genre scenes part of a larger whole. On the larger surfaces of an infant's cradle, Iarygin painted on one side a sleigh ride with a small dog running behind, and at the foot a hunting scene with the same dog, and two men aiming shotguns at a wild pigeon perched at the top of a swaying tree, with other animals prancing among the flowers and leaves. These scenes recall those on trunks from the Northern Dvina painted a century earlier.

Iarygin's works probably show the activities he and his family and friends pursued: hunting, gathering berries and mushrooms in the forest, spinning, drinking tea, reading, and writing. One vignette shows a lesson, in which the

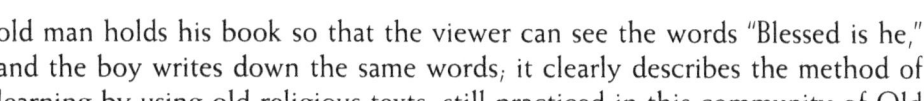
old man holds his book so that the viewer can see the words "Blessed is he," and the boy writes down the same words; it clearly describes the method of learning by using old religious texts, still practiced in this community of Old Believers.[12]

Iarygin may have been the first folk artist to paint a self-portrait. One of his early works, a cylindrical container made in 1811, shows the artist at work (fig. 4.6). The workshop is described in great detail: there is a large window, with the table placed directly under it to catch the best light; on the wall to the right is a hanging shelf for dishes and containers; on the table are small bowls for mixing pigments, and nearby on the floor is a larger bowl, perhaps used for preparing the ground on which to paint. The artist is beginning to decorate a horse yoke; he steadies it against the table with his left hand and holds a goose-quill pen in his right. There are a few other tools, but most of the space is filled, though not densely crowded, with herbaceous ornament. Iarygin's work is easily recognizable for its combinations of lush, almost self-sufficient herbaceous ornament with remarkably direct scenes of familiar activities.

Artists from Iaroslavl', Mezen', and Gorodets used different approaches to genre. Iaroslavl' contour-cut distaffs presented social rituals, such as tea drinking and dancing, aligned along a vertical axis (fig. 5.2). Mezen' distaffs, covered on the outside surface with horizontal rows of galloping horses or deer, often had simple genre scenes on the reverse; the most common were hunting scenes similar to the Tree of Life composition, but usually with some individual detail or inscription. An emphatically modern motif was the steamboat. Paddle-wheeled steamboats worked up and down the Northern Dvina and Volga rivers in the later part of the century, and were often depicted on Mezen', Borok, and Gorodets distaffs and boxes. Usually the boats, wharves, and buildings were outlined schematically, with specific written identifications: "This is Barge No. 2," or "This is the wine shop."[13] One northern distaff depicts the ship *Nevka* (fig. 13.4),[14] with steam blowing and flags flying, filling the center of the blade; a large-scale sailor signals from the deck, and just to the side, an even larger uniformed sailor stands at attention. Beneath the ship scene is a sleigh ride, with the sailor astride the sled. At the top of the blade is a tea-drinking scene. Since the sailor appears several times on the distaff, it seems likely that the artist was portraying himself, ready to go on leave, and anticipating the social activities of his village. Awkward in handling the composition and ornamental motifs, the artist was nonetheless able to use the main elements of the traditional design and rework them to express his pride in his ship and his eagerness to reach home.

Around the turn of the nineteenth to the twentieth century, Gorodets painters altered the traditional forms of two-part distaffs to allow for expanded genre scenes. The compositional type developed around 1860, using incrustation or combinations of carving, inlay work, and painting, usually contained a symmetrical, ritual motif with horsemen, tree, and bird filling the upper half of the base; an ornamental band; and smaller scenes of spinning, tea drinking, or other genre motifs. In the following decades, however, Ignatii Lebedev, Petr Sundukov, Ignatii Mazin, and other Gorodets artists abandoned the tight, symmetrical arrangement in favor of much more pliant lines and freer placement of figures. They transformed the tea-drinking ritual into a lively social occasion, with elements of narrative and contemporary urban fashion (fig. 6.6). As Mazin stated, even peasants enjoyed these scenes more than the traditional images.[15] Similar changes occurred in other forms of folk art. Wooden and ceramic toys, with their natural tendency toward the comic, were especially quick to pick up new social types and forms of entertainment.

Genre subjects chosen to decorate domestic articles often reflected events in the life of the artist or the intended recipient. On objects made for market, the scenes would be more generic, though they usually had something to do with the function of the piece: *po-sidelki* were among the favorite motifs on distaffs; festive meals were often depicted on bread boxes and other containers. Many pieces included several scenes, representing a variety of familiar occupations or suggesting a connected narrative. On distaffs from the Northern Dvina, traditionally arranged in three distinct zones, the sequence of scenes was easy to read: a *po-sidelka* or a visit by a suitor to the house of the fiancée would be followed, on the other side of the dis-

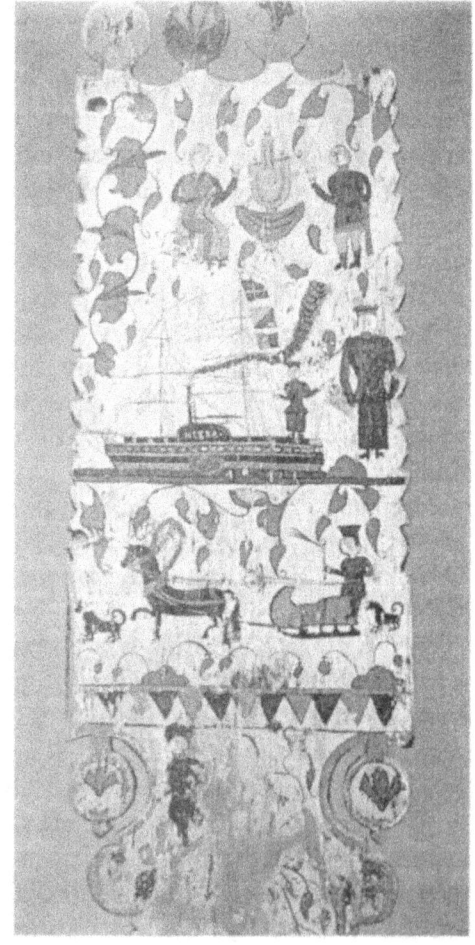

FIG. 13.4 Distaff. Painted wood. Front of blade with steamship *Nevka*, sailor, sleigh ride, and tea drinking. Permogore, late 19th century. Sergiev-Posad.

taff, by a wedding journey (fig. 13.5). This sort of narration not only provided attractive entertainment but also emphasized the ritual meanings of social traditions by embellishing the scenes with lush floral patterns and birds, symbols of plenty and good fortune, and guardian emblems such as the lion and unicorn or the *sirin*.

Decoration was meant not only to express the practical function of the object, but to recall the occasion for which it was made, such as an engagement or wedding. The genre images did not replace traditional symbolic motifs, but they added something specific and memorable to them. The few genre images in embroidery or lace — for example, a bed valance done in a tambour outline stitch showing a man and woman wearing brightly striped garments of modern cut, the woman holding a wedding kerchief[16] — served, like the initials, dates, and messages accompanying them, to add a personal note to a conventional image.

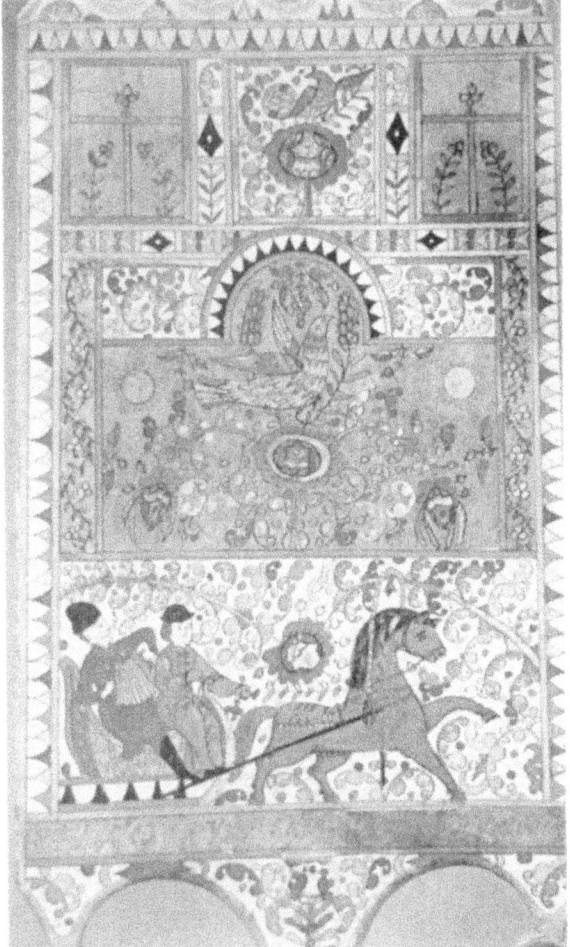

Some kinds of folk art did not incorporate genre elements at all; lacquered tableware from Khokhloma, for example, remained purely decorative, though a few new patterns based on natural forms were introduced. Most types of distaffs also retained traditional carved patterns or painted geometrical or floral forms as their only ornament.

It was mainly in regions such as Borok, where icon- and manu-

FIG. 13.5 Vasilii Amosov, distaff. Painted wood. Blade with wedding journey. Borok, early 20th century. Sergiev-Posad.

script-painting traditions had made artists adept at both ornamental and figurative motifs, and along the Volga, with the stimuli of trade and markets,
that genre became part of the folk repertoire. Even there, genre scenes filled
only a portion of the composition. They were usually set off by a framing
device from the symbolic or heraldic elements, but even an artist such as
Iarygin, who juxtaposed various types of images without obvious borders,
maintained a clear balance between genre and symbol.

The characteristic separation of the genre element from the rest of the
decoration on an object distinguished folk genre from the depiction of a
scene from peasant life within a continuous, illusionary space by academically
trained artists. In the next section we will clarify these differences, and determine whether a folk esthetic survived during the course of several revivals of
interest in folk art in the nineteenth and twentieth centuries. In traditional
folk art, scenes from life fit into forms from the past. Genre details often
helped to identify a piece with its function, owner, or maker, but they did not
interfere with the overall scheme of decoration based on meaningful, emblem-
atic forms and on principles of order, proportion, and symmetry developed
over many centuries and mastered by each artist.

PART IV

Preservation
and
Revival
of
Russian
Folk
Art

Serf Artists, Peasant Painters, and the Rise of Genre

You can let Grigorii paint some interior in your house . . . some
room where he can instinctively feel at home. Do not let him paint heads
and figures for another three or four months.

— Aleksei Venetsianov, 1842 or 1843[1]

There have been cases in which serf [artists], having been awarded
medals but not having received their freedom . . .
fell into despair and died.

— Academy of Arts Council, 1829[2]

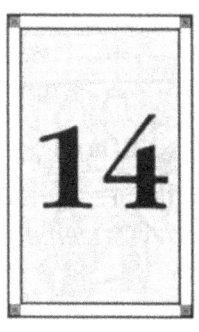

A decline in the vigor, originality, and quality of folk art in the mid-nineteenth century was attributed, ironically, to the breakdown and eventual abolition of serfdom, the migration of labor to the cities, and the unforeseen hardships experienced by the free but impoverished peasants. Some peasants had always earned varying amounts of money each year by selling surplus produce or items made during the winter, such as textiles, bast shoes, carved utensils, and toys, at regional markets. But trade in *kustar'* or domestic handcraft goods came increasingly under the control of commercial jobbers, who bought by the pound and did not pay for quality. Some traditional arts, such as bonecarving and niello work, were not easily adapted to the *kustar'* system, and were virtually extinct by the end of the nineteenth century.[3]

A more fundamental cause of decline, many observers believed, was a loss of purpose, integrity, and artistic innocence that had begun much earlier, when images and styles foreign to native traditions were introduced from the West. The expanded range of art forms coincided with an expanded patronage, that of nobles and merchants as well as church and court. The influx of Russian and foreign masters into Moscow and their concentration in the "German Suburb" encouraged a large-scale sharing of styles and techniques throughout the eighteenth century.[4] The effects of systematic training were even more far-reaching. Peter I's ambitions for his new capital gave impetus to training in architecture and allied arts, and set the stage for the founding of the Academy of Arts in the 1750s. The cosmopolitan orientation of the upper levels of society, combined with the economic dependence of the peasantry, also gave rise to the peculiar category of serf art.

Because serf art developed outside of the normal evolution of regional folk art traditions, it has scarcely been studied as an entity,[5] and has even been dismissed as non-Russian. Although contacts between peasant artists and those trained in monastic, urban, and court centers had been frequent and productive in many parts of Russia in the past, the relationship between serf artist and gentry-class master was very different in character. But regardless of their circumstances or the particular qualities of their work, the presence of serf artists was as significant as the role of markets and manufacturing centers in the overall composition of visual culture in eighteenth- and early nineteenth-century Russia.

Most serf art, required to imitate European styles of painting and decorative arts, seems remote from peasant life. Only a few works known to be by serfs reveal the hardships familiar to the artists. For example, one serf painter of the early nineteenth century gives a laconic treatment of a harsh subject: the selling of a woman serf (fig. 14.1).[6] A row of men across the middle of the composition includes an old peasant, a bailiff, the buyer in military uniform, the owner's agent, and a group of ten peasants with the woman kneeling in front of them. Some shading gives the figures volume, and facial expressions are individually characterized. But they are matter-of-fact, not emotional, and the poses are stiff. Although the subject was evidently observed from life, the representation was probably based on a *lubok*. This work shows an aspect of serf art that is difficult to interpret, because there is little context for it. The subject does not occur in traditional folk painting. But the treatment of the figures in the space is similar to that of genre scenes by Iarygin and other early nineteenth-century painters of the north, or later Gorodets painters, and to compositions of other types of peasant art and urban folk art. The work fits into a pattern already observed among folk artists: they incorporated new subjects, adapted new materials, but retained certain traits of their local traditions.

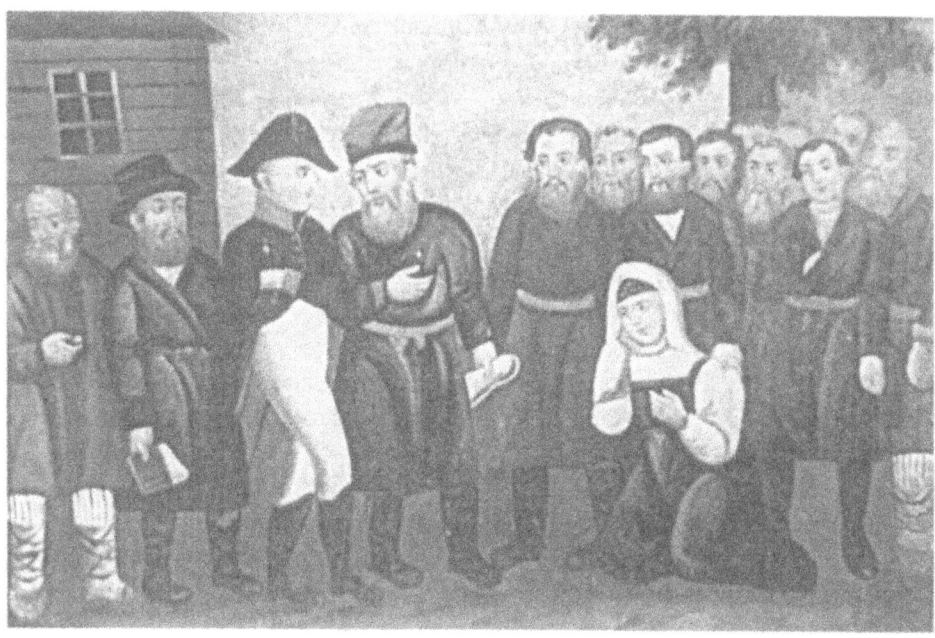

FIG. 14.1 Anonymous serf artist,
Selling a Serf. Oil on canvas. Early 19th
century. Arkhangel'skoe Estate Museum.

Peasants living in heavily agricultural central Russia had two obligations
to the owners of land and village: a specified amount of work on the land
(*barshchina*) or a portion of its produce, and payment (*obrok*) for the debt or
interest on the debt incurred for the loan of grain, tools, or other necessities.
Initially the payment was also for protection against enemies, a threat in the
open lands of the south; in the north, the system of *barshchina* was never as
entrenched, and the *obrok* was discharged by hunting, carpentry, or other
skills and crafts, by work in towns or factories away from the estate, or by
trade. In one year alone, authorities issued over one million internal passports
allowing serfs to travel away from their villages.[7] Poor soil and a short growing season meant less dependence on agricultural labor and greater importance of crafts and trade; these factors contributed to the continued vitality of
traditional folk art in the north.[8]

Serfs were bound to the land, and legally could not be sold except with
their land. But they could be mortgaged; their labor could be rented out to
other landowners or manufacturers; and they could be sent to Siberia or into
the army at the whim of their masters. In practice, serfs were bought and sold

with little restriction. Peasants could even buy men to take their places in the army, and landowners encouraged this commerce, making their most valuable serfs pay high prices for substitutes.[9] When common field serfs might be bought for 100 rubles, army substitutes cost ten or twenty times that much; when female house serfs sold for 50 rubles, men paid 500 or more for attractive young women, by private arrangement or at established markets.[10]

Serfs with special skills were worth 1,000 to 5,000 rubles. Prince Grigorii Potemkin reportedly paid 40,000 rubles for a fifty-piece serf orchestra.[11] Landowners who possessed more than the hundred or so serfs needed to run a household and till the land of a small estate sometimes invested in specialized training for serfs showing aptitude. One Moscow family kept 243 domestic serfs, of whom 72 were identified as painters, carpenters, locksmiths, icon painters, or other craftsworkers.[12] One of Russia's wealthiest families, the Sheremetevs, counted 73,500 male "souls" in their accounts for 1765. Between that year and the end of the century, the Sheremetevs undertook major building projects at their estates Kuskovo and Ostankino in the Moscow suburbs. They employed serfs trained as architects, carpenters, painters, gilders, ornamental plasterers, and masters in some twenty other crafts.[13] They established a theater composed of serf actors and musicians, with special facilities designed by serf architects.

As pioneers in a new kind of patronage, the Sheremetevs made their holdings into showplaces of art and incubators of talent. They made methodical efforts to increase the numbers of skilled artists available for their projects, hiring experienced masters to train young serfs in skills that would be needed for building or for maintaining and conserving works of art. After two to five years of training and general schooling at home, the most talented serfs were sent to study in St. Petersburg. Among the Sheremetev serfs who became recognized artists were the architects Mironov and Dikushin, the painters Krasovskii, Funtusov, and Mukhin, the cabinetmaker and mechanic Priakhin, and the remarkable Argunov family, with two architects and three painters.[14] Other serf painters were well known in this early period; among them Mikhail Shibanov, a serf of Prince Potemkin, was noted for his portraits of Catherine II and her court. His scenes of peasant life, *Celebrating the Marriage Contract* and *Peasant Dinner*, unusual subjects for the 1770s,[15] show dignified sympathy rather than the idealization of peasant life that became common later. The role of serf artists has sometimes been too positively presented as a unique Russian phenomenon that transformed foreign sources into the beginnings of a genuine Russian art. It has also been criticized as cultural tyranny. In any event, the Argunovs, Shibanov, and other talented artists would not have accomplished so much without the training provided by their masters.

The scale of the Sheremetevs' establishment, the high quality of the training, and the abilities of their serf artists were exceptional. But by the mid-eighteenth century, many serfs trained in specialized crafts worked on estates and in factories, chiefly in cabinetmaking, porcelain, and metalwork. Some owners of poor farmland came to depend on the *obrok* their serfs paid in lieu of labor. Encouraged by the government, landowners built factories on their estates or on holdings in the metal-rich Urals. One of the most successful industries, employing thousands of serfs and free laborers, was the metalworks founded by Nikita Demidov, a state peasant who had worked as a gunsmith in Tula, attracted the attention of Peter I, gained various favors, and acquired land in the Urals. Before he died in 1725, he had a 100,000-ruble income, and his heirs expanded the factories. A more common situation was for factories actually owned by peasants (who could not buy real property) to be registered in the name of a landowner; the Sheremetevs were nominal owners of many peasant-owned textile mills in Ivanovo, Vladimir Province. A peasant named Sokov was among the first to print cotton on a large scale around 1800; his method was copied by other peasant manufacturers, and within forty years there were 130 cotton-printing factories in Ivanovo.[16] A sizable share of ceramic production was controlled by peasants, especially in the villages of Gzhel', and in the larger porcelain factories free peasants and serfs often worked side by side. On estates, serfs trained in specialized techniques worked on projects along with other trained serfs and sometimes professional masters.

Did serf artists contribute distinct features to Russian art? The question has not been adequately studied, and it is complex. Certainly the decorative projects at Ostankino and Kuskovo shared the stylistic traits of eighteenth-century Russian decorative art and architecture.[17] But more specific questions can be raised. Did the styles and techniques of folk arts influence serf artists to the extent that folk traits might be seen even in work based on European models? From a different perspective, did serf art have any effect on folk art — did contact with the work of trained serf artists influence other peasant artists? A consistent pattern of influence is unlikely, since situations and practices varied with each region, estate, and factory, and changed over time. But individual cases suggest some interaction and cross-fertilization between folk styles and introduced forms, especially in manufacturing and market centers, where contact between peasant and urban artists already existed.

Serfs chosen for special training were not always those who would have been artists in peasant villages. One noble landowner wrote to his Moscow office that he was sending three boys from a country estate to the city: "see if they are apt for domestic service," he instructed the agent, "or if they should be sent out for training in a craft, as woodworkers, blacksmiths, or something of the sort."[18] Wealthy owners sent serfs to St. Petersburg or Moscow; others arranged to enroll their serfs with neighbors who kept accomplished painters or cabinetmakers on their estates. Owners made contracts stipulating the amount of time needed for the training and the schedule of payment, for instance, fifty rubles in three installments for training a serf in bootmaking.

Part of this payment usually came from the serf's *obrok*, but after completing his training, a serf artist anticipated a yearly bonus higher than those given to untrained serfs.[19]

By the late eighteenth century, many estates afforded training, facilities, and materials as good as those of major cities. Landowners imported fine hard and soft woods from Africa, the Americas, and Asia. They obtained varnishes, glues, gold leaf, and high-quality tools, and expected their serf cabinetmakers to fill orders for chairs, card tables, writing desks, and other European furnishings, as well as the parquet floors, gilt or marbled columns, and fine paneling required in noble houses. Anything beyond their capabilities had to be ordered from a city firm, such as the Moscow furniture studio of Spol', where the well-known carver Fedor Nikiforov, a serf belonging to Princess Shcherbatova, worked, along with other serf artisans.[20]

The types of furniture made in this period differed from traditional Russian forms almost as much as did the decoration. Inlay work using veneers of exotic woods to create perspectival vistas was highly prized, and some pieces were signed. One of the best serf cabinetmakers was Matvei Iakovlevich Veretennikov, who identified himself as "servant-craftsmaster" of His Excellency State Councillor Aleksandr V. Saltykov.[21] Little is known about his training. Engraving and inlay were Russian techniques, but his views of Constantinople indicated training in Western rules of perspective and scale, and even such conventions as a tree or a figure in the lower left foreground to serve as a framing device.

Much of the furniture made in the early nineteenth century by serfs and independent masters was indistinguishable from French Empire pieces. But a few works show the hands of artists who apparently tried to relate the imported forms to more familiar, Russian ones. Such an adjustment appears in a divan made by a serf from the Goncharov estate in the 1820s. The Karelian birch suited the smooth, curving lines of the piece, as did the very simple ornament: a fanlike half-circular motif at the center of the base, with long rays extending from it to the sides, other fan shapes at the ends of the arms, and circular rosettes at the junctions of the arms with the base. These patterns were simplifications of widely used designs in folk carving, rather than copies of French Empire motifs.[22] A serf who made a Karelian birch dressing table with legs shaped like reclining lions also compromised between Russian and foreign forms. The lions approximate European models, but the low relief and squarish shapes make them seem closer to the lions of Russian decorative and folk art. The carved columns, baskets, and vases framing the mirror also suggest traditional woodcarving as well as fashionable European motifs. Few works show awkwardness in the adaptation of European forms, however, since only expert carvers would be allowed to work with the fine materials.

The facility with which serf artists learned demanding techniques, and became expert in styles that had no precedent in folk art, suggests that esthetic inclinations could be altered to suit new requirements. Familiarity with wood as a basic household material, or with other materials such as metal or clay, may have given Russian serfs advantages in learning how to work with these materials, regardless of style.

More serfs were trained in the decorative arts than in painting, a circumstance due both to the desires of owners and to the systematization of artistic education in the eighteenth century. Peter I gave training for architects and builders priority. The Chancellory for Building placed twelve-year-old boys in training programs in carpentry, smithing, and other building skills. The Academy of Sciences took over education in architecture and applied arts, and sought to balance specialized and general training by requiring a drawing class for all disciplines. The concept of drawing as the foundation for an encyclopedic curriculum of specialties was realized in the Academy of Arts, begun in the reign of Elizabeth in 1755, and permanently chartered in 1764 by Catherine II. The French Academy was the authority for the high status of the classical "paragon" of architecture, painting, and sculpture. But the Russian Academy differed in bringing all branches of art together under one roof, and offering classes in ornamental sculpture, carving in wood, work in bronze, niello and casting from molds, goldsmithing, miniature painting, and cabinet-making.[23] Students who completed the course might be sent away to gain further experience: painters to Italy to copy masterpieces, and decorative artists to the Imperial Porcelain Factory, the Imperial Tapestry Works, or other official enterprises.[24]

The centralization and inclusive scope of academic training suited the requirement for steady production of fine and decorative arts in St. Petersburg. Gradually, the influence of the Academy penetrated to the provinces, much as the court style of the Kremlin workshops had in the seventeenth century. During the eighteenth century, only two kinds of painting existed in the provinces: icon painting, done in workshops attached to monasteries or by itinerant painters, and secular painting, done by serf artists to decorate the country houses of the gentry. Serf painters imitated models from the capital, sometimes at second or third hand, taking compositions and motifs from medals, niello objects, tiles, and *lubki*, in place of inaccessible original paintings by professional or foreign artists. Some serf artists may have adapted local folk styles of painting on wood. A late eighteenth-century painting of a wedding by an anonymous artist (fig. 14.2), probably a serf in an old-fashioned household, depicts the wedding party, guests in *sarafany* and *kokoshniki*, and the array of food in neat horizontal rows on the table, above a diamond pattern indicating a parquet floor.[25]

In the nineteenth century, the spread of Western and urban fashions created a demand for art of professional quality, first in the wealthy trading cities, such as Tver', Iaroslavl', Nizhnii Novgorod, and Saratov, then in other central Russian cities, including Arzamas, Penza, Voronezh, and Kaluga, and the

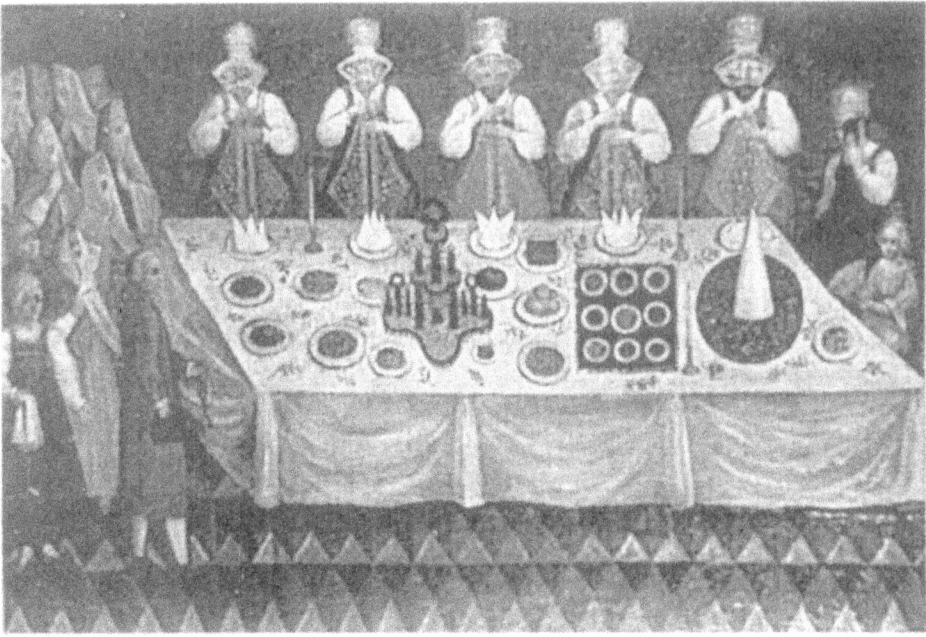

FIG. 14.2 Anonymous, *Wedding at Toropets*. Oil on canvas. End of the 18th century. GIM.

manufacturing cities of the Urals and Siberia.[26] The greatest demand was for portraits; most portraits of merchants, merchants' wives, landowners, and officials from the 1820s and 1830s were done by undocumented or little-known artists, most likely serfs. The painters placed their sitters solidly in the middle of a dark background, and gave great attention to precise depiction of facial features, clothing, and accessories such as medals, buttons, pearl necklaces, rings, lace collars, and woven shawls.[27] Dignified and stiff, these portraits showed the influence of icons and the few examples of Western-style portraiture available to provincial artists, styles already sadly outmoded in Moscow and St. Petersburg.

Many landowners commissioned views of their estates. A view of Zobnino, an estate near Tver', painted in the late eighteenth century by the serf Fedorov, shows an impossibly elevated viewpoint based on ground plans and architectural drawings rather than observation, and enlivened by figures, shrubbery, sunlight, and clouds.[28] The wealthy Demidov family commissioned paintings of their estate and copper works in Nizhnii Tagil from Vasilii Raev, a former serf with professional training, and ordered their

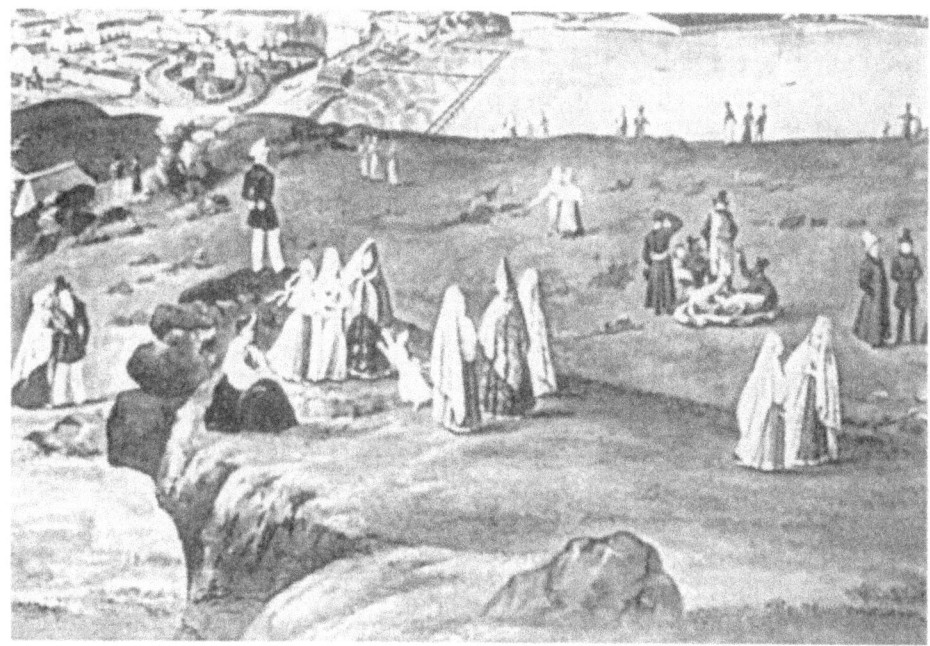

FIG. 14.3 I. Khudoiarov, *Festival on Bald Mountain.* Paint on metal lid of wedding trunk. Nizhnii Tagil, mid-19th century. GIM.

own serf artists to depict the factory in operation, some of the first such scenes in Russian art.[29] The artists, members of the Khudoiarov family, specialized in painting on iron sheets with a lacquer developed at the factory. Some of these paintings on trays and trunks were floral decorations, but the most notable were broad vistas, such as *Festival on Bald Mountain* by I. Khudoiarov (fig. 14.3). The depiction of the sheet-pressing section of the Demidov factory by P. F. Khudoiarov showed his experience in handling complex scenes using the fast-drying lacquer. This scene and others of the series were full of accurate observations of technical processes and the actions of the workers.[30]

Academy graduates set up studios in many parts of the country. The first important provincial school opened in Arzamas. Aleksandr Stupin, a local icon painter, went to the Academy of Arts in 1800 for two years. On his return he transformed his icon-painting workshop into a well-run school, approved by the Academy; Raev was among the graduates. Stupin accepted young boys, including serfs, trained them for six years, and then reported to the Academy on the most promising. The Academy authorized Stupin to award medals, but stopped the practice in 1829, after a tragic event. One of Stupin's most talented pupils, a serf named Miasinikov, committed suicide, apparently because he was not permitted to attend the Academy. The official decision read: "because there have been cases in which serfs, having been granted medals but not having received their freedom from their owners, have fallen into despair and died."[31]

Academy policy prohibited masters from enrolling serfs, though students of humble backgrounds were admitted. From a philosophical viewpoint, freedom was necessary to allow proper study of the fine arts, as opposed to mere crafts. Measures were taken to increase the selectivity and professional level of the Academy, such as raising the age of admission and letting outside schools take over preparatory instruction.[32] But by the middle of the century, new ideas about the role of art in society began to eclipse purely pedagogical concerns.

The contrasting experiences of two outstanding painters who were serfs, Vasilii Tropinin, born in 1776 and still active at midcentury, and Grigorii Soroka, who belonged to the next generation but died early, illustrate the range of attitudes and circumstances that affected serf artists. Tropinin, born a serf of one noble family, was transferred to another as part of a dowry. He showed talent early and was sent by his master to St. Petersburg to learn the arts of the confectioner. He attended free drawing classes at the Academy, and in 1799 he was admitted to advanced portrait classes as an auditor. The painting he showed at the 1804 student exhibition, *Boy Grieving over His Dead Bird*, was praised by the Academy's vice-president; encouraged by this success, his professor wrote to Count Morkov that the young artist should either be given his freedom and enrolled as a regular student or be taken out of the Academy.[33]

Count Morkov took his serf away to an estate in Ukraine and assigned him the jobs of lackey, pastry cook, supervisor of the property, painter for the local church and the house, and drawing teacher for the children. The good-natured artist painted landscapes, made copies of Italian, Dutch, and French works, and painted many portraits of his master's children and of his own wife and son, much admired for their freshness and sensitivity. Friends urged Morkov to free Tropinin, but the count replied that he did not want to lose "his talented artist," and agreed only in 1823.

Tropinin began painting professionally in Moscow. One of his most striking works, *Lacemaker* (fig. 14.4), the first of many unpretentious and lively portraits of peasants, was so highly acclaimed that the Academy offered Tropinin the chance to qualify for the rank of Academician. By the 1830s he was an established portraitist, and for two decades he continued to paint both commissioned portraits and those of anonymous peasants.[34] Tropinin's distinctive self-portrait, painted in 1846 when he was seventy, shows the artist posed with palette, brushes, and maulstick against a backdrop of the Moscow Kremlin, as a vigorous and confident professional.

Grigorii Vasil'ev, called Soroka, was a more original artist, but he never had the chance to become a professional painter and never exhibited his work. Born in 1823 in Pokrovskaia, a village of about one hundred peasants in Vyshnevolotskii Uezd (now Vyshnii Volochek), Tver' Province, halfway between Moscow and Petersburg, Soroka belonged to the estate of the wealthy Miliukov family.[35] He learned to read and write at a local peasant school, and began to draw at an early age. At about age eighteen he was sent to be a house servant at Ostrovki, an estate on Lake Moldino, less than a mile from the village. This position gave him the chance to see books and paintings, to hear conversations about literature, culture, and current events among Nikolai Miliukov's friends, and to meet the painter Aleksei Venetsianov, who ran an art school about twenty miles away on a small estate called Safonkovo.

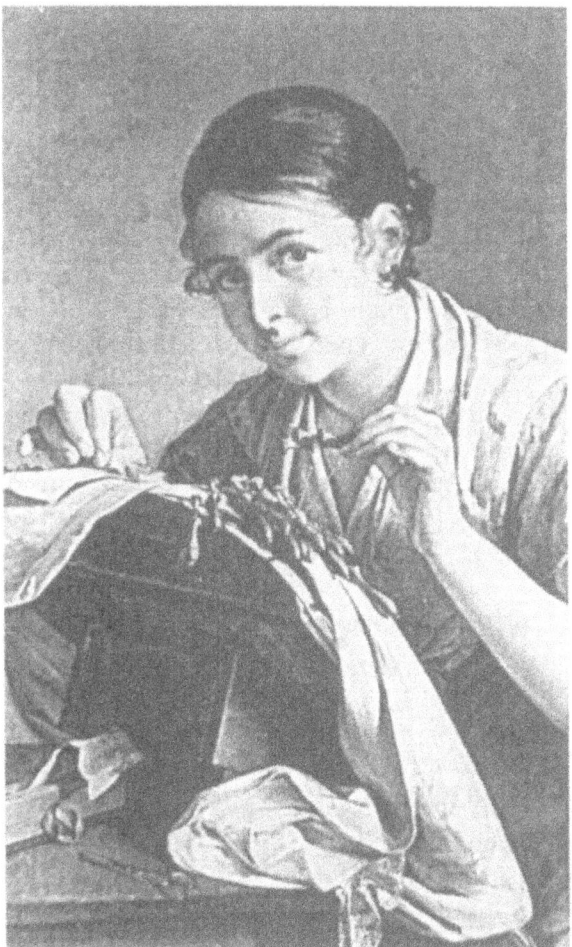

Venetsianov had earned the title of Academician and a reputation as a portraitist in the early years of the century.[36] In 1818 he retired to his estate in order to concentrate on painting nature and rural life. Venetsianov's treatment of peasant subjects was different from the quaint images of village life often used to embellish porcelain vases and other luxury goods. His close-up portraits of peasants were unprecedented in their directness

FIG. 14.4 Vasilii Tropinin, *Lacemaker.* Oil on canvas. 1823. GTG.

and absence of anecdote. Venetsianov advocated looking at nature rather than copying models from the past, and he was a forerunner of the realist tendency in Russian art. However, many of his works, such as *Spring, Plowing* and *Summer, Harvest*, were not realistic but expressed an idealized sense of the harmony and continuity of the landscape, the seasons, and the peasants' labor comparable to that felt in folklore and art.

Venetsianov intended his teaching to benefit poor students, including serfs; he helped to redeem some of them from bondage, so that they could receive academic training. He had more than seventy pupils, he recalled, some of whom were "limited, or even entirely lacking in talent." But many "filled his heart with pleasure." Though he emphasized natural light and familiar subjects and opposed routine, academic copying, he did not limit his pupils to their rural environment. He took them to Petersburg to study, he sent their work to the Academy exhibitions, and he tried to help them get professional positions. By the time Soroka met him, Venetsianov's school was at its height.

Miliukov agreed to let Venetsianov teach Soroka; he was delighted to have his serf trained to paint portraits of the family and views of the estate. But he did not let Soroka study regularly, and he wanted Venetsianov to skip time-consuming stages of instruction so that Grigorii could get on with his duties. Soroka worked as a gardener and, like other domestics, was expected to serve as an actor in evening dramatic productions. Miliukov refused to let Soroka go to St. Petersburg, despite Venetsianov's persuasion. Ultimately all Venetsianov could do for the young artist was give him extra work as his assistant in the school, and obtain a few commissions for the church and copying paintings for other landowners (for which Miliukov was paid).

Except for his self-portrait, which shows reserve and tight control, Soroka's paintings reveal no resentment about his position. His portraits of the Miliukov daughters Lidiia and Elizaveta are sympathetic and uncontrived. An interior, *The Study at Ostrovki* (fig. 14.5), shows the quiet dimness of the room and the orderliness of inkwell, pen, and papers on the desk. Most of all, the landscapes, *View of Lake Moldino* (fig. 14.6), *Fisherfolk*, and *View of the Lake at Ostrovki*,[37] with their wide skies reflected in smooth water, are so luminous in tone and delicately balanced in composition that they convey almost unimaginable peace and harmony.

When Venetsianov died in 1847, Soroka was an accomplished artist, valuable property, and totally vulnerable. He petitioned for his freedom in vain. In the 1850s he married, moved back to Pokrovskaia, and became the village icon painter. Ostrovki accounts show that he paid an annual *obrok* of twenty rubles, which he earned by local painting jobs and from pupils. Finally, in 1861, Soroka was freed in the general emancipation of serfs. He joined other peasants in buying some of Miliukov's farmland, and because

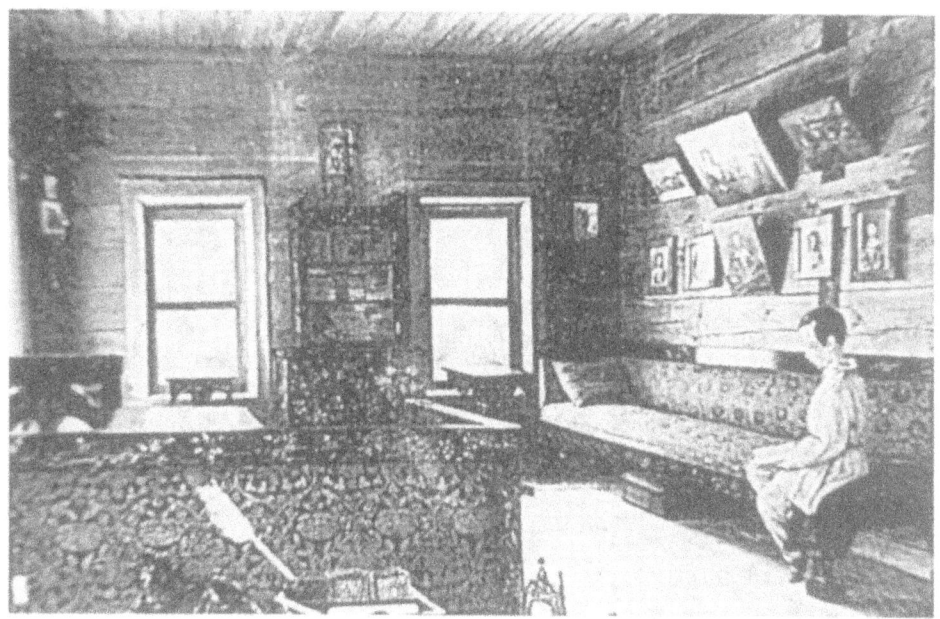

FIG. 14.5 Grigorii Soroka, *Study at Ostrovki.* Oil on canvas. Detail. 1840s. GRM.

the conditions set by the landowner were so harsh, Soroka agreed to compose a petition, addressed to Tsar Alexander II. Unfortunately, the letter fell into Miliukov's hands. He spitefully lodged a complaint, and in April 1864 Soroka was arrested, charged with "having committed crudeness and spread false rumors in the district," and sentenced to three days in prison and corporal punishment. After this experience, according to witnesses, Soroka fell ill, grew melancholic, and wandered about the village in a daze. Within days he hanged himself from a beam in the pottery barn on the Ostrovki estate.

Soroka's suicide, Miasinikov's suicide thirty-five years earlier, and the unrecorded deaths and failures of other serfs who could not withstand the tension between their abilities and their circumstances, were symptomatic of larger problems, as the Academy's 1829 statement on serf artists indicated. The situations of Soroka, Miasinikov, and even the more fortunate Tropinin were different from those of serf artists such as the Khudoiarovs in the distant provinces, and wholly unlike those of peasant artists in traditional village environments. Their frustrations, foreign to traditional folklife, were the result of new conditions and exposure to new ideas and goals.

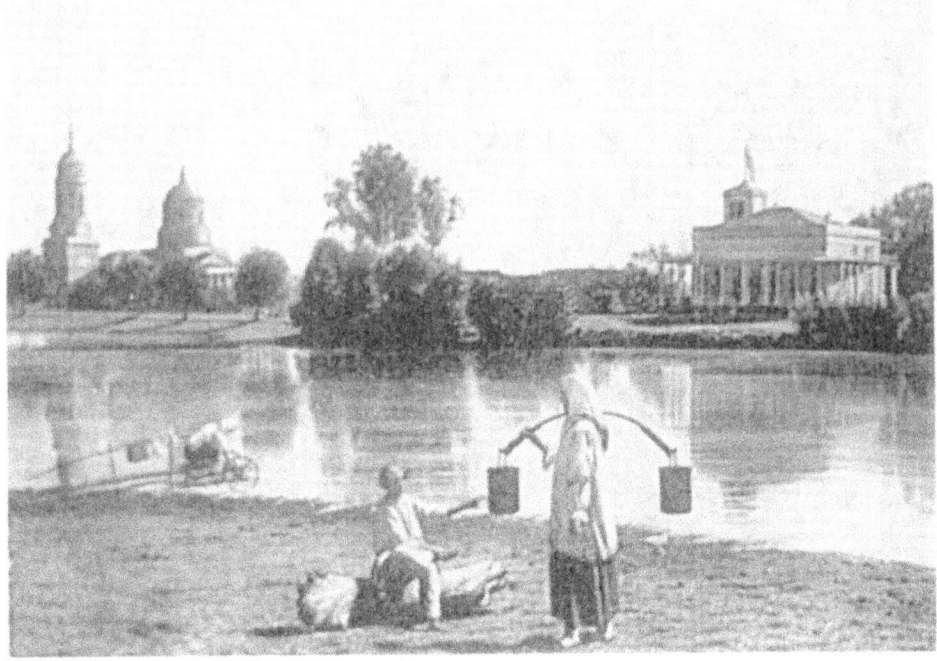

FIG. 14.6 Grigorii Soroka, *View of
Lake Moldino*. Oil on canvas. Late 1840s.
GRM.

Some serf artists adjusted to new circumstances. Venetsianov had at least
seven pupils of serf background who were given freedom and the opportunity
to study at the Academy or even abroad.[38] Sergei Zarianko, son of a household serf, was taken to Petersburg by Prince Liubomirskii, and was allowed to
attend a gymnasium and later to study with Venetsianov, who helped him to
enroll in Academy classes as an auditor. He received medals for interior
scenes, and in 1850 was granted the title of Professor for a portrait of Fedor
Tolstoi, vice-president of the Academy. He went on to teach at the Moscow
School of Painting, Sculpture, and Architecture, and counted founding members of the realist art association, the *Peredvizhniki*, among his pupils. Grigorii
Mikhailov, of rural serf background, painted small portraits of serfs under
Venetsianov's guidance; however, at the Academy he entered the studio of the
leading historical painter and portraitist, Karl Briullov, and became adept at
society portraits and the idealized scenes of humble life fashionable among
buyers. Fedor Slaviansky was a serf on an estate not far from Safonkovo; his
master let him study there, and in 1838 Venetsianov redeemed him and took

him to St. Petersburg. He audited Academy classes while working with Venetsianov, earning the title of artist within five years. He was nominated for membership in the Academy for *On the Balcony (Family Portrait)* (fig. 14.7), showing his wife, her mother, three young children playing, and the artist himself with his palette, in a scene full of light, quiet pleasure, and intimacy.

Serfs who did not belong to Venetsianov's circle also became active professional artists. Vasilii Raev, serf of Count Kushelev, was sent to Stupin's school in the 1830s, then to the Academy, and even to Rome, with the help of private supporters. He earned the title of Academician and worked as a landscapist and mosaicist. Vasilii Sadovnikov was a serf of Princess Golitsyna, who let him study with private teachers and gave him his freedom in 1858; the same year he earned the title of Free Artist without Rank from the Academy. He was known for watercolor views of Petersburg, its aristocratic suburbs, and interiors of palaces. Kanoshenkin, a serf of the notoriously severe former war minister, Count Arakcheev, managed to take art lessons while remaining a serf, and produced lithographs and drawings of architectural vistas.

Gurii Krylov, a serf from a Novgorod estate, was sent to St. Petersburg to study drawing, and was given his freedom in 1828. He studied at the Academy of Arts and the Surgical Academy. There is no evidence that he worked with Venetsianov, but his domestic interiors suggest familiarity with the school.[39] *Kitchen* (fig. 14.8), probably painted in 1826 or 1827, shows a simple but spacious room with shelves for utensils, an oven, water barrels, cleaning rags, a cooking stove, kindling, and a samovar all clearly arranged; a narrative note is introduced as a woman points to fowl pecking grain while a cat basks in the open doorway. To eyes familiar with Novgorodian icons and northern folk painting, the composition would appear balanced, harmonious, and familiar. The artist might have improved upon simple enumeration of details by adding a more naturalistic handling of space, through the perspective of oven and floorboards, and a realistic oblique light, possibly learned from Dutch paintings in the Hermitage.

Most painters involved with Venetsianov's school and with the rise of genre painting in the 1820s to 1850s were, if not serfs, from modest, provincial backgrounds, the sons of priests, soldiers, or small merchants; stylistic differences were individual, and not matters of class identity. Two of Venetsianov's early pupils, Nikifor Krylov and Aleksandr Denisov, though not serfs, were particularly sensitive to rural and small-town environments. Krylov's luminous, sharply delineated *Winter* of 1827 (fig. 14.9), one of the first winter scenes painted outdoors, received an Academy medal. Denisov excelled in interiors with oblique light softly haloing figures and objects; he also received medals and showed such promise that Venetsianov helped to send him to Berlin to study. Aleksandr Alekseev, Venetsianov's assistant from 1826 through the early 1830s, painted an informative scene showing students in Venetsianov's Petersburg studio busy with plaster casts and a model in peasant cos-

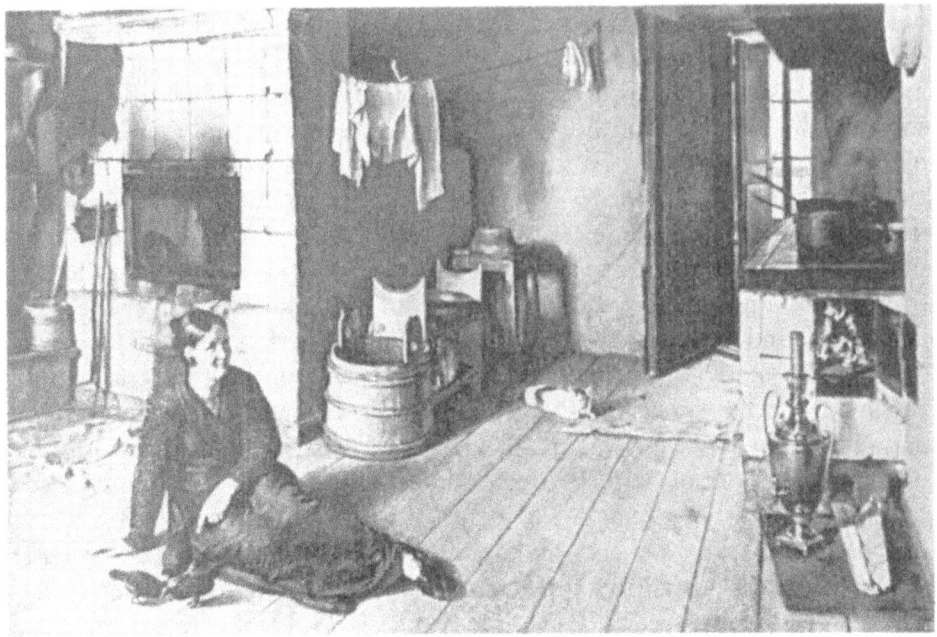

FIG. 14.8 Gurii Krylov, *Kitchen.* Oil on cardboard. 1826 or 1827. GRM.

tume; Alekseev went on to become a drawing teacher first in Pskov and later in distant Arkhangel'sk. Evgraf Krendovskii, from the Ukraine, attended Stupin's Arzamas school before studying with Venetsianov and at the Academy. He painted group scenes, such as *Preparations for the Hunt,* and precise landscapes, such as *Square in a Provincial Town.*[40] Lavr Plakhov studied with Venetsianov, went on to the Academy in the early 1830s, and later worked in Düsseldorf and Berlin. He became known for scenes of common laborers and artisans at work or at rest, such as *Stonecutters, At the Forge, Carpentry Workshop,* and *Coachmen's Room at the Academy of Arts;* he was one of the first to specialize in urban genre, and to work in photography.[41]

What these artists shared, in terms of preferred styles and subjects, were not consequences of serf origins; many serf artists did not follow Venetsianov's precepts, while some exponents of his ideas came from different backgrounds. However, contact with Venetsianov certainly strengthened individual interests in nature, qualities of light, activities of daily life, details of faces, and the physical environment. These aspects of art were not entirely neglected even in the Academy; especially after the defeat of Napoleon, the Academic Council promoted Russian themes, among them subjects from

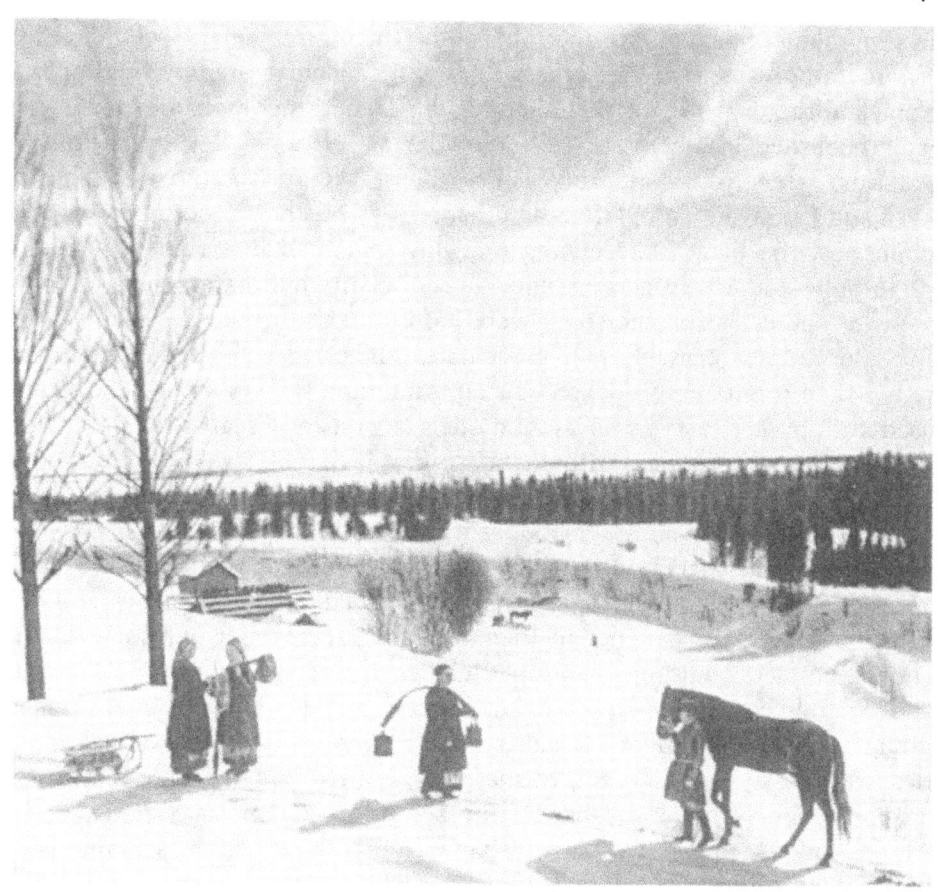

FIG. 14.9 Nikifor Krylov, *Winter.* Oil on canvas. 1827. GRM.

"popular life." One examination assignment in 1824 was to "depict a peasant family playing checkers."[42] However, study from life was overshadowed in the curriculum by copying from "originals" (casts and reproductions of classical and Renaissance art), and by the rules of composition necessary for prestigious historical painting. Significantly, none of Venetsianov's pupils, and no serf artists, even those who studied with Briullov, made careers in historical painting or large-scale, "parade" portraiture.

Available facts about the lives and careers of the artists in Venetsianov's circle do not support generalizations about their attitudes toward peasant life and folk art. Details in genre paintings and portraits show familiarity with peasants' costumes, tools, and occupations. But these images are no more or less revealing of peasant life and folk culture than were vignettes of village life painted on ornamental vases and table services manufactured by the Imperial Porcelain Factory,[43] or the colored engravings and lithographs of similar subjects published in albums under such titles as "National Representations of Artisans, Taken from Nature in St. Petersburg," "Representations of Labor in City and Country," and "The Magic Lantern."[44] Neither Venetsianov nor his pupils lost the habit of idealizing rural life ingrained in eighteenth-century philosophy and art. In genre scenes, overall clarity and harmonious arrangement of figures within the space were more important than details or narrative. Portraits of peasants, while accurate, suggested calm and permanence rather than spontaneity. Alekseev's studio interiors showed how Venetsianov used both plaster casts and peasant models, a woman in scarf and *sarafan* with her needlework, or a man with a staff, so that his pupils could look from one kind of model to the other and relate their observations of individuals to classical proportions and timeless beauty.

There is little likelihood that the artists of Venetsianov's circle had direct knowledge of the folk painting of the northern regions, Arkhangel'sk and Vologda provinces, at least not in their formative stages. But like some of the anonymous serf paintings mentioned earlier, the scenes of provincial towns and country estates by Krendovskii, Soroka, and Krylov and interiors and group scenes by Slavianskii, Denisov, and Plakhov show strong visual affinities with the styles of Iarygin, Misharin, and other contemporary folk painters.[45] The integrity of the image, the subordination of small parts to the whole, and the unifying of many shapes and textures within a harmonious framework of firm horizontal divisions and clear vertical accents—traits evident in all these works—are also traits of folk art. They are also qualities of classical art, as Venetsianov understood classicism, based on the enduring harmonies of nature rather than ephemeral effects. Whether or not Venetsianov's pupils would have mastered traditional folk art forms had they remained in their villages, it seems that their studies at Safonkovo helped to confirm and develop their innate sensitivity to form, structure, and design. Venetsianov's teaching did not alter his pupils' esthetic predispositions in the way that training in imported styles of decorative arts or academic copying of approved models sometimes obliterated native feelings for form and structure.

Ironically, it was not serf art and idealized peasant genre painting that disrupted the unity of folk art traditions and peasant life and caused the perceived decline in the originality and quality of folk art. The harsh daily experience of serfs and peasants was not expressed in folk art or serf art. It was the emergence of socially critical realism in the mid-nineteenth century that upset the harmonious relationship between rural life and its depiction in art. Neither the institution of serfdom nor the imposition of foreign styles on serf artists affected folk art as drastically as did the collapse of serfdom and the disruption of rural social structures in the mid-nineteenth century.

National Art and
Folk Art

Socially critical genre paint-ing of the mid-nineteenth century upset the harmonious relationship between classical styles and rural settings. Real-ism, as a philosophical posi-tion, did not allow the omission of jarring details for the sake of visual unity or beauty. Representations of peasants by realist painters such as Vasilii Perov, Vasilii Pukirev, Illarion Prianishnikov, Grigorii Miasoedov, and Vladimir Makovskii used "folk" motifs as indications of backwardness, in contrast to the former idealization of the peasant community. Although many artists sympa-thized with the poor, and were drawn to the populist movement of the 1870s, they did not want to share the hardships of peasant life. Their professional identification distanced them from the peasantry and from peasant or town artisans, and contributed to the process, begun in the seventeenth century, of separating the spheres of folk and professional artists. The realists' paintings about peasant life and the Russian countryside, sociologically more accurate than the romantic images of the first part of the century, were esthetically much farther removed from folk traditions.

Details of folk costume, embroidered linen towels, painted wooden dishes, and other furnishings of *izby* in genre paintings of the 1870s, such as Vasilii Maksimov's *Arrival of the Enchanter at the Peasant Wedding* (1875) and Vladimir Makovskii's *Wedding Procession* (1888) (fig. 15.1), helped to convey a sense of the reality of such rituals in peasant life. For similar reasons, historical

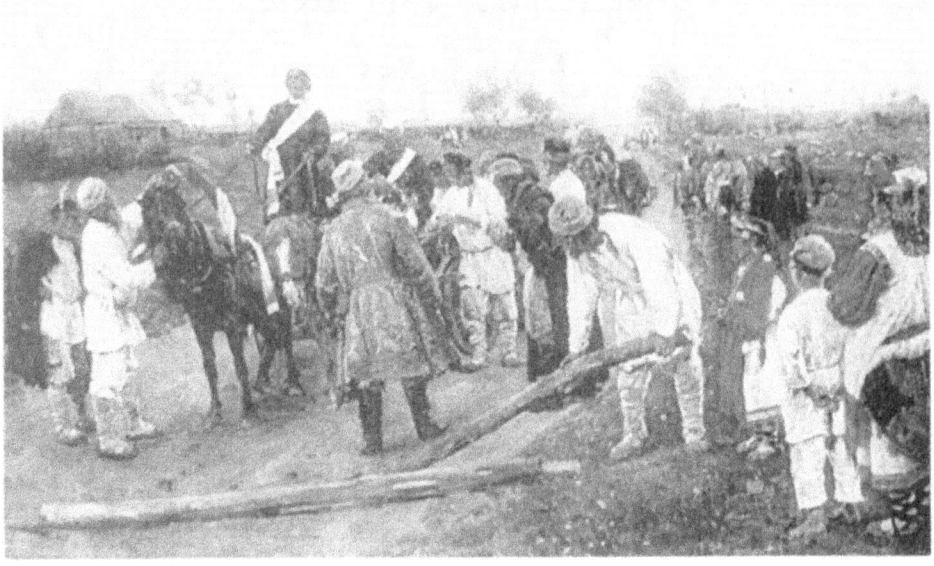

FIG. 15.1 Vladimir Makovskii,
Wedding Procession. Oil on canvas. 1888.
Private collection.

painter Vasilii Surikov included examples of Muscovite architecture, costumes, and icons in such paintings as *Boiarynia Morozova* (1887), and composers used fragments of folk melodies and the sound of the Kremlin bells to establish atmosphere in Russian historical opera.

Regardless of their class origins or early surroundings, most painters did not use folk elements spontaneously, but quoted them consciously, almost academically. The forms were valuable not in themselves but because they served to make genre and historical scenes "national." This nationalism and historicism were related to searches for national styles taking place all over Europe and in America during the same period. What distinguished the phenomenon in Russia was the tendency, especially among Slavophiles, to equate folk culture with the entire historical legacy of Russia before westernization. This attitude affected perceptions of folk art and resulted in new forms of interaction between folk art and high art in subsequent periods.

Historicism meant not only appreciation for the heritage of earlier times but also the desire to evoke ideas connected with certain periods through historical styles and images. Early examples of evocation of the Russian past were the palaces and churches of the Kremlin built under Ivan III and his successors. Catherine II knew the value of historicism: when she decided to have the decaying tsars' palace at Kolomenskoe demolished, she ordered a precisely scaled wooden model. She commissioned architect Giacomo Quarenghi to make drawings of the Moscow Kremlin, considered the most sensitive interpretations of an architectural style that seemed exotic and meaningless to many westernized aristocrats in the eighteenth century.[1] While her preference was for Palladian classicism, Catherine commissioned buildings, such as Kazakov's Petrovskii Palace, in the old Muscovite style. She wore the *sarafan* and *kokoshnik* on occasion, and had traditional *kovshy* made for ceremonies. Catherine's historical interests had much to do with projecting a legitimate Russian identity for herself. But in most of her patronage of Russian arts and industries—ivory carvings from Kholmogory, metal and lapidary work from factories in Velikii Ustiug, Tula, and the Urals, and porcelain from the Imperial Porcelain Factory—she followed her own cosmopolitan tastes.[2]

In academic painting and sculpture, elevated subjects from Russian history found a place alongside themes from the Bible and from Greek and Roman history and mythology. The first painting of this kind, Anton Losenko's *Vladimir before Rogneda*, exhibited in 1770, exemplified the balance of tension and restraint in such classical subjects as Andromache and Hector, painted by Losenko and his Russian and European contemporaries.[3] Aside from their titles, there was little here or in other works set in early Kiev, Novgorod, or Moscow, such as *The Oath of Marfa Posadnitsa* and *The Election of Mikhail Fedorovich Romanov as Tsar*, to set them apart from international neoclassicism. In sculpture, a "national" effect was achieved by clothing classical nudes with appropriate Russian garb, as in the monument to Minin and Pozharskii, the butcher and the prince who drove the Poles out of Moscow in the seventeenth century, erected in front of St. Basil's Cathedral in 1818.

Archeological exoticism was a component of historicism. The aura of remoteness and mystery, achieved in Western painting by Egyptian, archaic Greek, primitive Celtic, or American Indian settings, was equally strong in scenes of ancient and medieval Russia. With the rise of national opera, historical research became essential for theatrical decoration. For productions of Alexander Serov's *Rogneda* in 1865 and 1867, the archeologist V. A. Prokhorov and the artist N. Ellert made drawings based on early manuscripts and frescoes from St. Sophia in Kiev for the costumes of the noble characters, and used actual peasant costumes for the peasants. In Aleksandr Tolstoi's 1867 drama *The Death of Ivan the Terrible*, some of the props were authentic objects from the period. The sets for these productions, for Mikhail Glinka's *A Life for the Tsar*, and for Pushkin's tragedy *Boris Godunov* included such landmarks as Novodevichii Convent and the Palace Square in the Kremlin, a practice continued in later operas.[4] Painters eagerly took up stories of pre-Petrine Russia and used similar methods, as works by Pavel Chistiakov and Viacheslav

Shvarts show. Historical genre became popular, as it did in European salon painting, and costume pieces set in fortresses and *teremy*, based on legend as much as history, attracted attention at exhibitions throughout the century. Even the realists Vasilii Perov, Nikolai Ge, Vasilii Polenov, Il'ia Repin, and Ivan Surikov turned to historical themes; Surikov in particular made painstaking studies of historical artifacts in preparation for *Boiarynia Morozova, The Execution of the Strel'tsy*, and other major works.

A distinct type of painting focused on ordinary individuals in historical, "folk" settings. Rostislav Felitsin's *Grievous News (Reading the Letter)* of 1856 (fig. 15.2) shows two women comforting one another in a dimly lit room. They wear folk costume, one an embroidered *rubakha* and the *kokoshnik* of a married woman, the other a printed *sarafan*, with the braided hair of an unmarried woman. A Vologda distaff and spindle stand to the side, showing that normal life has been interrupted by the death of the woman's soldier husband. She clutches his last letter to her breast; the fully legible text, in a stiff, archaic folk style, tells the young wife not to worry and to take care of their little son.[5] Painting at the end of the Crimean war, Felitsin wanted to comment on the tragedy of war for ordinary people; he employed the evocative, national setting to avoid censorship and suggest universality.

Historical painting and genre had separate spheres in the Russian academic system, but the two areas grew closer as realist artists stopped using classical models and based their main characters on people from their own circles and their bystanders and crowds on peasants. The changing emphasis in scenes from Russian history was related to changing perceptions of peasant life in mid- and late nineteenth-century art. Russian folklife, preserving the customs, physical settings, and "national spirit" that had been replaced in St. Petersburg and Moscow by European forms, seemed to offer a valid contact with the Russian past, more vital than strict archeology. Late in the century, Il'ia Repin tried to capture the free, vigorous life of Ukrainian cossacks in his ambitious historical painting *The Zaporozhian Cossacks Write a Letter to the Turkish Sultan* (1891); and Viktor Vasnetsov combined archeological and folk sources, legendary characters, and peasant models in *Three Bogatyri* (1898) to express his feeling for the timeless spirit of Russia.

In music, the nostalgic idealization of peasants through romances incorporating folksongs gave way to "national" operas on subjects from history and folklore and, increasingly, from village life. Historical, legendary, and fairytale themes, such as *A Life for the Tsar, Il'ia Bogatyr'*, and the *Rusalka* series, shared the stage with folk genre operas such as *Posidelki* and *The Bride's Wedding Party*.[6] Composers Mili Balakirev, Modest Musorgskii, and Nikolai Rimskii-Korsakov incorporated folksongs into their historical operas to represent the voice of the Russian people,[7] and they also turned to subjects from village life, such as Musorgskii's *Sorochinskii Fair*, based on the midsummer Kupalo festivities, and Rimskii-Korsakov's *May Night*, set in Rusalka Week.

In contrast to the tendency in painting and music to equate peasant culture with national culture of the past, the trend in literature was toward concern for the actual lives of peasants. Nikolai Karamzin's sentimental novel *Poor Liza* of 1792 paved the way for sympathetic portrayals of peasants in the 1840s and 1850s, but few of these works employed details of real life or genuine folk idioms. A radically different approach was introduced by the populist journalist and poet Nikolai Nekrasov in the 1850s to 1870s. In "On the Volga," "Red-nose Frost," "Who Lives Well in Russia?" and "Children's Tears," he used traditional rhythms and refrains of folksong (many collected by the revolutionary populist Khudiakov) to give life and conviction to his voices of suffering peasants.[8] Nekrasov's work was carefully researched and accurate in fact and feeling, and much of it was memorized by peasants and accepted as something of their own. The poems were published in illustrated editions and collectors' albums, and also in cheap editions for peasants. With their "popular" style, Nekrasov's works invite comparison with songs and stories printed for peasant or lower-middle-class urban audiences in *lubok* books. Many had heroic, fantastic, or Western themes, but some of the writers were of serf or peasant background who wrote from experience, reflecting the tensions of the post-emancipation period.[9]

The most prolific illustrator of Nekrasov's work, Aleksandr Lebedev, employed descriptive detail to reinforce the poems' village settings. For instance, a drawing for "Who Lives Well in Russia?" showed the old peasant Savelii and the woman spinning with a distaff of a Iaroslavl' type,

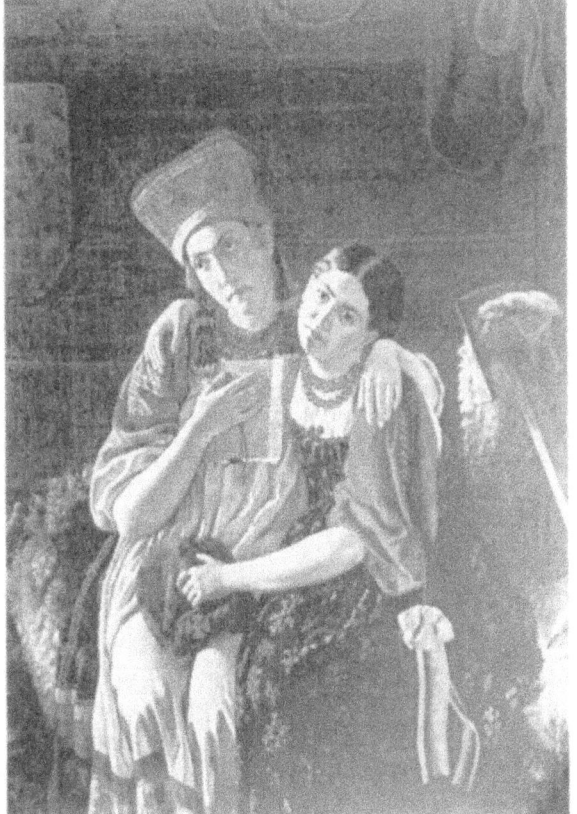

FIG. 15.2 Rostislav Felitsin, *Grievous News (Reading the Letter)*. Oil on canvas. 1856. GRM.

seated on benches next to the icon corner in the *izba*.[10] The painter closest in spirit to Nekrasov, Vasilii Perov, painted many of the same subjects. *Accompanying the Dead* (fig. 15.3), from 1865, less than a year after "Red-nose Frost," expressed the despair of the peasant woman driving with her husband's coffin out to the frozen burial ground.[11] Perov was interested in Russian folklore and popular life, and sketched scenes of Semik festivities, episodes from the life of popular hero Stenka Razin, and images from Aleksandr Ostrovskii's poem *Snegurochka*.[12] But neither Perov nor any of the other realist artists, however sincerely concerned with the conditions of the peasantry, attempted to use stylistic elements of folk art to express the character of peasant life.

Such a goal was not considered or articulated until the last decades of the nineteenth century, when folk culture seemed to be in danger of disappearing and serious folk art revival efforts began. Meanwhile, folk style was firmly connected with ideas of nationalism through the overlapping concepts of *narod* as "folk" and "nation." Nostalgia for the unity and integrity of rural life reinforced a determination to draw some lessons from its decline. Historians, social reformers, and official policymakers as well as artists believed that restoring the forms of historical and folk culture could help to restore the traditional values threatened by modern conditions. This motivation does much to explain some scholars' determination to find ancient Slavic roots for customs and art forms observed among nineteenth-century peasants. This conservative attitude was also part of the reason for Alexander III's official nationalism in the arts at the end of the nineteenth century.[13]

Historicizing in architecture meant applying Byzantine, Novgorodian, or Muscovite features, and designs derived from manuscript interlace and architectural woodcarving where they could make the greatest impact, on the exteriors of buildings. The St. Petersburg Society of Architects sponsored competitions promoting "nationalism" in architecture and design. Although one architect, Lev V. Dal', complained that "mere byzantinizing" interfered with the goal of creating a genuine Russian style, in fact both "Byzantine" and "folk" styles were recognized as components of an architectural eclecticism typical of the late nineteenth century.[14] In the applied arts the best examples of historicism were fine jewelry and silver and enamel utensils in Kievan and Muscovite forms; a "Russian folk style" was one of many period styles used in luxury goods with commercial success from the middle of the century.[15]

Peasant artists in the remote villages of Arkhangel'sk, Olonets, and Vologda provinces continued to work as they had earlier in the century, sometimes adding new motifs, particularly genre subjects, in painting or embroidery, and increasing the complexity of surface ornament in many media.[16] But economic changes greatly affected the urban arts, ceramics, metalwork, lacquerware, and textile printing. The situation actually improved for some manufactures. The Lukutin lacquer factory reached the height of its produc-

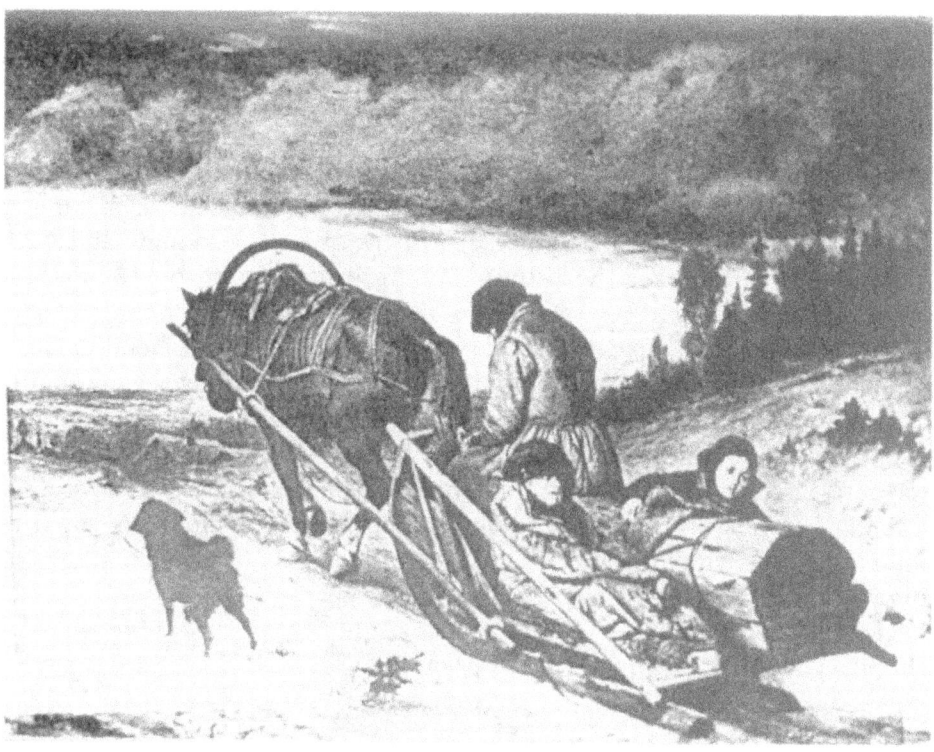

FIG. 15.3 Vasilii Perov, *Accompanying the Dead.* Oil on canvas. 1865. GTG.

tion in the 1860s and 1870s; prosperity led to higher artistic quality until pressure for continued expansion brought a decline in the level of design and execution. Large ceramic and textile firms benefited from the emancipation of serfs in 1861; they employed hundreds of peasants at low wages, added machines, and expanded the practice of division of labor. The Kuznetsov ceramic factory near Gzhel' was able to double its output every ten years, so that by 1896 it was producing half of the ceramics in all of Russia, about 4,300,000 rubles' worth.[17] Ceramics and glass factories also produced dishes for peasants and common inns, which easily undersold handmade pottery dishes or woodenware at regional fairs. Similarly, calico from factories in Moscow and Vladimir provinces, decorated with flowers or with printed imitations of traditional embroidery motifs, in the so-called "Russian border" design (fig. 15.4), also found a ready market among peasants.[18] Some peasant women used manufactured materials creatively, to add to the decoration of *ponevy* and *sarafany.*

These cheap, readily available goods threatened to replace utensils and fabrics made by peasants for the market, and gave rise to efforts by government commissions and private individuals to establish workshops for traditional crafts, the basis of the *kustar'* or handcraft revival movement. A commission to study and improve crafts began work in the 1870s, and many specialized studies of various *kustar'* industries, ranging from lacemaking to toys, were organized through the Department of Rural Economy and Agricultural Statistics, under the Ministry of Agriculture.[19] In the 1890s there were probably about 7,500,000 *kustari*, peasants engaged in home-industry crafts, many more than were employed in factories, throughout Russia.[20] Some of the intellectual circles founded in the 1860s to study the antiquities and ethnography of Russia—the Moscow Archeological Society, the Society of Lovers of Natural Sciences, Anthropology, and Ethnography, the Petersburg Society of Architects, and the Russian Historical Society—gave attention to folk art.[21] Finally, several populist-inspired groups devoted to improving the condition of workers and peasants organized *kustar'* workshops. The Society for Encouragement of Industriousness concentrated on "the general development of women's work, as a means of creating assistance to needy women of all conditions, and also with the goal of acting for the most profitable return on various forms of indigent women's labor."[22] Philanthropic motives went hand in hand with the

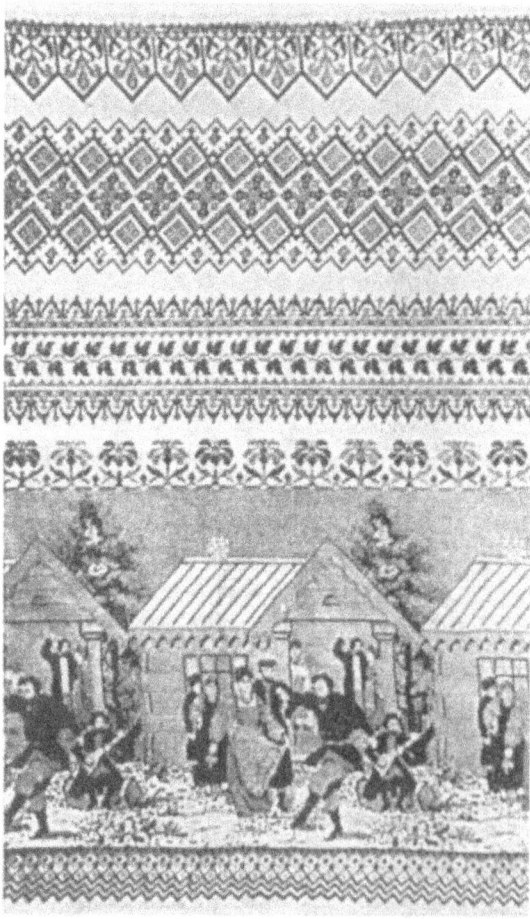

FIG. 15.4 "Russian border." Printed calico. 1870s. GIM.

belief that saving traditional folk arts could help to preserve fragile links with Russia's past.

Efforts by landowners and artists at Abramtsevo and other art colonies described in the next chapter coincided with the programs supported by the government; many of their aims and results were identical. Some artists were active in both private and government-sponsored projects. Viktor Vasnetsov introduced theater costumes and sets based on folk art sources in the Mamontov Private Opera's *Snegurochka* in 1885, and almost immediately turned to a government commission, taking charge of the ponderously historicizing decoration for the Church of St. Vladimir in Kiev, built to commemorate nine centuries of Christianity in Russia.

Nationalism and historicism in art were supported by scholarly study, collection, and exhibition of early Russian art and folk arts. The Slavophile historians of the 1820s and 1830s had already established the concept of the *narod* as the preserver of the genuine elements of Russian culture. Many scholars and research societies studied ancient linguistic and artistic forms and sought traces in folklore and art. Beginning in the 1860s, the Moscow and the St. Petersburg Archeological Societies, the Commission for the Preservation of Ancient Monuments, and other scholarly bodies and their publications established a framework for research for the rest of the century. Historians Ivan Zabelin, Ivan Golyshev, Ivan Snegirev, and Dmitrii Rovinskii, among others, wrote about daily life, church and domestic architecture, and crafts in early Russia.[23] Vladimir Stasov published a detailed, illustrated study of ornament in early Russian art and folk art in 1872 (fig. 1.5, 15.5), and he continued to write on many aspects of folk music, ornament, images of the peasantry in realist painting, and, eventually, the uses of folk styles by Elena Polenova and Viktor Vasnetsov.[24]

The great national collections of Russian antiquities and art, including the Historical Museum in Moscow and the Imperial Russian Museum in St. Petersburg, and exemplary private collections such as that of Petr Shchukin were formed in the 1880s and 1890s. In 1885, the Moscow *zemstvo* founded the Moscow Kustar' Museum to house a substantial collection of *kustar'* goods, explain techniques and materials to the public, and provide raw materials and an outlet for sales for practicing *kustar'* artists.[25] Similar museums were organized in St. Petersburg, Kostroma, Nizhnii Novgorod, and Viatka. Government policy not only advocated retrospective nationalism but encouraged development of native industries and trades by means of applied arts schools, statistical studies, and some eighty regional, national, and international exhibitions, which included folk and *kustar'* arts in the category of industrial and applied arts or rural economy, rather than fine art.[26]

The art schools of the nineteenth century, like the early Academy, combined foundation courses in drawing and the grammar of ornament with instruction in woodworking, ceramics, textile arts, and other media. The

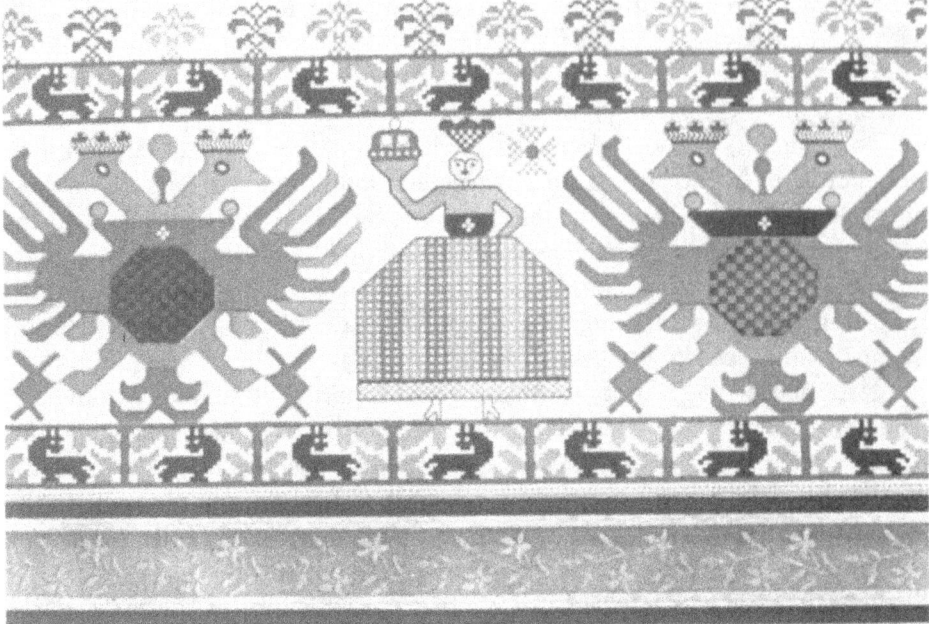

FIG. 15.5 "Towel border," plate 58
from Vladimir Stasov, *Russkii narodnyi
ornament* (1872).

courses taught skills needed for modern applied arts and manufacturing prac-
tices, rather than those of folk arts. The Stroganov School in Moscow and the
Stieglitz School and the Society for the Encouragement of Artists school in
St. Petersburg were the most influential, but there were many smaller schools
throughout Russia, especially in manufacturing and trading cities such as
Iaroslavl', Ekaterinburg, and Saratov.[27]

Count Sergei Stroganov founded the First Moscow Drawing School in
1825 to teach basic techniques of drawing to future craftsmen, so that graduates could render any type of object correctly in any style required. Soon the
school added a Women's Drawing Section, attracting mainly women who
planned to teach drawing for a living. A Second Drawing School was formed
as a branch of the Moscow Court Architectural School (later part of the
School of Painting and Sculpture). Its function was to prepare draftsmen for
applied arts manufactures, textiles, furniture, porcelain, and jewelry, and it
opened branches in villages near the major factories. In St. Petersburg, the
preparatory drawing school of the Society for the Encouragement of Artists

added applied arts instruction. In the 1870s the society founded a museum of artistic manufacture and opened a permanent exhibition "where all year long there would be displayed for sale examples of all types of fine production executed in local workshops and factories and also by the students of the School."[28] Finally, the Stieglitz (Shtiglits) School of Technical Drawing, founded in 1879 by Baron Stieglitz, represented a new stage in art training, with more demanding foundation courses than the other schools required and a wider range of specialized courses. Between 1880 and 1900 the school offered classes in majolica, carving, decorative painting, embroidery and lacemaking, xylography and aquatint, painting on porcelain, drawing patterns for machine-woven and printed fabrics, engraving, painting on glass, and theatrical design.

All the schools received commissions from the court, the church, and wealthy patrons, and assigned them to students. One teacher recorded an ambitious interior design project for Tsar Alexander II's yacht *Derzhava*, to be done in a "Russian style" with harmonizing porcelain dinner services.[29] Publications of drawings for use by craftsmen aided the dissemination of approved historical models through the schools and regional *kustar'* centers.[30] The schools operated until the Revolution in 1917 (when many were renamed and reorganized), and they were instrumental in achieving a high quality of manufactured goods and a high status for the applied arts in Russia. Teachers, artists, and cultural leaders hoped not only that the schools would improve manufactures and handcrafts but, in Stasov's words, that the "hundreds of young men and women" who graduated would go on to teach in towns and villages all over Russia, and "elevate the level of art in popular life."[31]

While valuing this goal, Stasov and others began to fear that consistent standards of training and production, growing foreign contacts, and participation in international trade and crafts exhibitions might undermine the distinctive qualities of Russian regional styles. It was a serious dilemma. The growth of the capitalist economy, the multiplication of factories, and railroads had already changed the rural economy and threatened the survival of folk arts and cottage industries. Some specialized crafts had declined to the point of extinction. Interfering with local crafts and traditional methods of passing on skills, design principles, and figurative or decorative motifs could accelerate the denaturing and falsification of folk art. Although many different viewpoints existed within the folk art revival movement, most participants and government officials agreed that ignoring the problem would lead not only to the loss of a part of Russian culture, but also to economic decline in the Russian countryside.[32] The goals of the folk art revival efforts were not simple or one-sided. The government considered the improvement of the *kustar'* industries crucial to stabilizing the national economy. Elena Polenova, Elizaveta Mamontova, and others at Abramtsevo, and Princess Mariia Tenisheva and her colleagues at Talashkino were motivated by both philanthropic and artistic concerns; they wanted to nurture the creative impulses of the peasants, and they hoped that revitalized folk arts would help to reinvigorate national art in the broadest sense.

Artistic Renewal

There is no doubt, Russian folk art is dying; it has nearly died.
The currents of modern life sweep it away, and only in a few places,
deep in the most remote areas, do its last feeble sparks still smolder.

—Ivan Bilibin, 1904[1]

Our goal is to capture the still-living art of the people, and give it
the opportunity to develop.

—Elena Polenova, 1885[2]

The most attention-getting art in popular life took place but in art colonies on private efforts to improve the level of not in applied arts schools estates. Elena Polenova and other professional artists sought to intervene in the decline of traditional crafts and to stimulate the development of contemporary folk art by providing suitable training and models for local peasants. The products of the joinery and embroidery workshops at Abramtsevo, Talashkino, and smaller establishments changed the character of Russian *kustar'* art,[3] and the folk art revival movement as a whole changed the concepts of "national" and "folk" culture.

Abramtsevo was a modest estate about forty kilometers northeast of Moscow owned by Savva and Elizaveta Mamontov; he was a progressively minded railway magnate and she was a member of the Sapozhnikov family, owners of a silk-weaving factory in the Moscow district. Beginning in the 1870s, the Mamontovs invited artists to spend summers on the estate: Vasilii Polenov, Viktor Vasnetsov, Il'ia Repin, and later Elena Polenova, Valentin Serov, Mikhail Nesterov, and Mikhail Vrubel' were some of the leading painters of their times, though not all were involved in applied arts and folk art revival. Polenov, son of an archeologist, had spent his childhood on the family estate Imochentsy in forested northern Olonets Province, and was always attracted to Russian folklore, history, and peasant life. Vasnetsov, the son of a priest from remote Viatka Province, was more closely tied to folk traditions. Both artists painted portraits and genre scenes of peasants, such as the village storyteller from Imochentsy or a group of peasants at a kiosk selling books and *lubki*.[4]

Vasnetsov was fascinated by Russian folklore; even while studying abroad he worked on ideas for *Warrior at the Crossroads, Three Bogatyri,* and other monumental paintings of legendary heroes. Throughout his career, he painted scenes from the Kievan epic "The Tale of Igor's Campaign," and from fairytales still told to children, "Alenushka and Her Brother Ivanushka," "Three Tsaritsas from the Underground Kingdoms," "Ivan Tsarevich and the Gray Wolf," and images related to several folk sources, such as *Sirin and Alkonost, Songs of Joy and Sorrow* (fig. 16.1). He employed the realistic style of historical painting; he included authentic historical and folk costumes in all his works, and he found many of his models among local peasants, such as Ivan Petrov, who posed for the Bogatyr' Il'ia Muromets.[5] Vasnetsov believed that the Russian peasant preserved the positive traits of Old Russia.

The difference between illustrating folktales and actually incorporating elements of folk style, so crucial in retrospect, was no more important for Vasnetsov than for Perov or other realist genre painters—at least in respect to easel painting. The fact that some works were commissions for Mamontov's railroad—for example, the three tsaritsas from the underground kingdoms were meant to symbolize the mineral wealth of the Donets Basin[6]—may have discouraged experimentation. But in group endeavors, the church at Abramtsevo, plays and operas for Mamontov's theater, and various applied art projects, Vasnetsov and his friends grew more adventurous in their use of early Russian and folk art sources.

The building of the Church of the Savior in 1881 was not the first historicizing project at Abramtsevo: in 1873, Mamontov had commissioned Viktor Hartman to build a workshop and a peasant hospital and Ropet (pseudonym of Ivan Petrov) to build a bathhouse in the established Russian "folk" style. But it drew upon Russian traditions important to many members of the group: early religious architecture and a community approach to work. Polenov and Vasnetsov made plans based on ancient churches in the Olonets and Novgorod regions; Vasnetsov's, modeled on the Church of the Savior at Nereditsa, was chosen, and he took charge of the exterior of the church and the windows. Polenov designed the iconostasis and painted icons and ornaments; Repin and Mamontova painted icons; Mamontova, Polenova, and Mariia Iakunchikova embroidered vest-

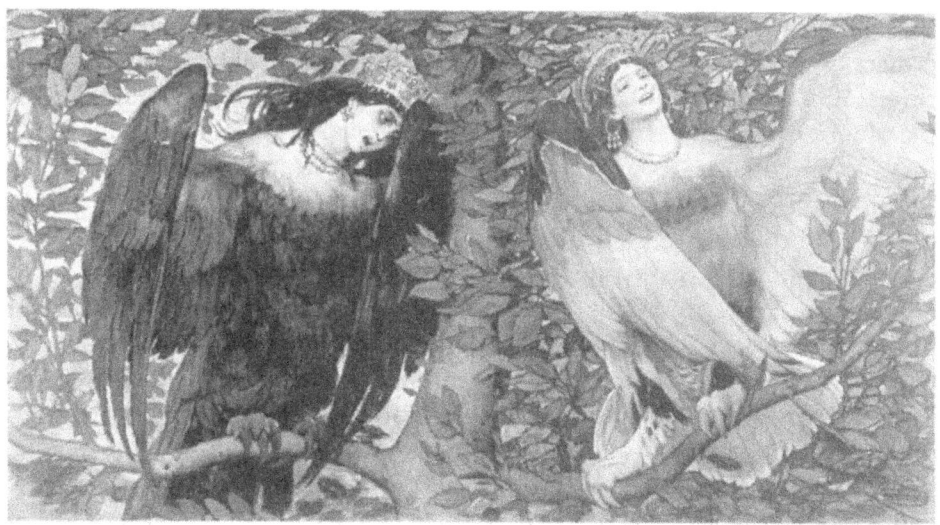

FIG. 16.1   Viktor Vasnetsov, *Sirin and Alkonost, Songs of Joy and Sorrow.* Oil on canvas. 1896. GTG.

ments; Mark Antokol'skii carved stone sculptures, assisted by Savva Mamontov and his young son Andrei.

The church project was deeply satisfying to the participants, but it revealed awkward contradictions between goals and means. Mikhail Nesterov, who joined the group later, mentioned the rumor that Elizaveta Mamontova "secretly rubbed the walls with grass, so that they would look mildewed, and thus seem older," and that the gilded cupola had been purposely blackened for an antique effect. Inside, the icons by Polenov and Repin clashed with the Novgorodian architecture and ornament.[7] This first group project suffered from the common confusion of antiquity with Russianness. Yet, for Vasnetsov it represented an embodiment of a cherished dream: "It seemed that the artistic impulse of creativity of the Renaissance and Middle Ages had spouted forth anew."[8]

While working on the church, the group took trips to Rostov, Iaroslavl', and other old towns to study church ornamentation. On one trip, passing through the nearby village of Repikhovo, Polenov and Repin saw a carved frontal board and admired it so much that they persuaded the owner to sell it.[9] This acquisition marked the beginning of a folk art museum and a conscientious study of local folk art, which distinguished the Abramtsevo group's interests from the more common pattern of mingled historicism and nostalgia.

The breakthrough, the incorporation of folk art forms into a new artistic project, was in theatrical decoration, a sphere of art combining painting, architecture, design, and a constant search for new decorative sources. The Mamontovs and their friends often held evenings of reading aloud while drawing or working in clay, and these entertainments led to pantomimes, adaptations of famous scenes, and even full-length plays and operas, with costumes and sets designed by the artists. What began as a diversion became a major commitment. Some saw the theater as a vehicle for exploring the possibilities of decoration on an unprecedented scale; others saw it as a means of reaching audiences who might be indifferent to more traditional art forms. Polenov later wrote of their hope "by means of subjects and settings taken from the world of history and folklore, to raise children up out of the commonplace tenor of daily life into the realm of heroism and beauty."[10] The Mamontov opera evoked the heroism and beauty of Russian history and legend in *Boris Godunov, Khovanshchina, Sadko, The Tsar's Bride, Prince Igor,* and *The Tale of Tsar Saltan.*

Snegurochka (The Snow Maiden), Aleksandr Ostrovskii's play in verse based on a Russian fairytale about the coming of spring, was performed in Mamontov's Moscow house in the winter of 1882/83 as a play, and in 1885/86 as an opera by Rimskii-Korsakov. Vasnetsov designed the costumes and sets. The chorus of villagers wore "genuine Russian garments" borrowed by Abramtsevo village elder Alekseich from peasants in his birthplace in Tula Province south of Moscow; other costumes had embroidered designs based on "antique" models found by Polenova.[11] Avoiding the pedantic archeologizing or superficial picturesqueness of earlier stage designs, Vasnetsov's sets were visually lively. For the village of Berendeevka in the first act (fig. 16.2), Vasnetsov modeled the simple hut of the poor old couple Bobyl and Bobylikha and the solid *izba* of the wealthy Murash, with its covered stairway and carved window frames, on north Russian types. Each *izba* had a prominent *okhlupen'*, one a schematic duck shape, the other an elaborately carved figure like a *rusalka*. The palace of Tsar Berendei in Act Two was based on the vaulted chambers of the Faceted and Terem Palaces of the Kremlin, with arched windows opening onto a view of distant domes and towers. Brilliant red, yellow, and blue flowers, fruits, and figures covered the walls and columns; on the dark blue vaults, stylized forms of animals, birds, fish, sun, moon, and stars stood out in light gold. These motifs evoked Vladimir-Suzdal' stonecarving, and perhaps owed something to the Slavic and Scythian ornaments found in excavations in southern Ukraine since the 1830s.[12]

Vasnetsov's juxtaposition of ancient forms with colors and decorative motifs from folk painting, carving, and embroidery made his set perfectly expressive of the traditional fairytale setting "in a certain kingdom," long, long ago. Ostrovskii himself added ideas to the simple tale of the Snow Maiden, adopted by the old peasant couple, who learns to feel love but melts away with the coming of spring. Setting the drama in prehistoric times, he included scenes of Mas-lenitsa frolics, songs about nature, the deity Lado, bards, and *skomorokhi*, a birch grove, deep woods, and, for the final act, the valley of Iarillo and the lake from which the Red Sun of summer rises. The choruses celebrating Maslenitsa and Iarillo, two-part songs with much repetition of phrases and sounds, were given vigorous, folksong settings by Rimskii-Korsakov. The combined effects of verse, music, movements of the figures, and the brilliant costumes and settings were truly overwhelming, Natal'ia Polenova reported. "When the poor old peasant and his wife made their exit, and . . . Berendei's people, the vast carni-val including the genuine goat-mask figure of ancient plays, and when the women began their dance . . . [painter Vasilii Surikov] burst forth in tumultu-ous applause which filled the whole theater."[13]

Vasnetsov's designs owed much to the collection of carved wood ornament, utensils, and textiles begun at Abramtsevo in 1881 (figs. 1.1, 16.3). The artist most directly concerned with the folk art collection, Elena Polenova, appreci-ated Vasnetsov's instinctive feeling for these sources. "I did not study with Vas-netsov," she said, "but somehow, in his company, I acquired an understanding of

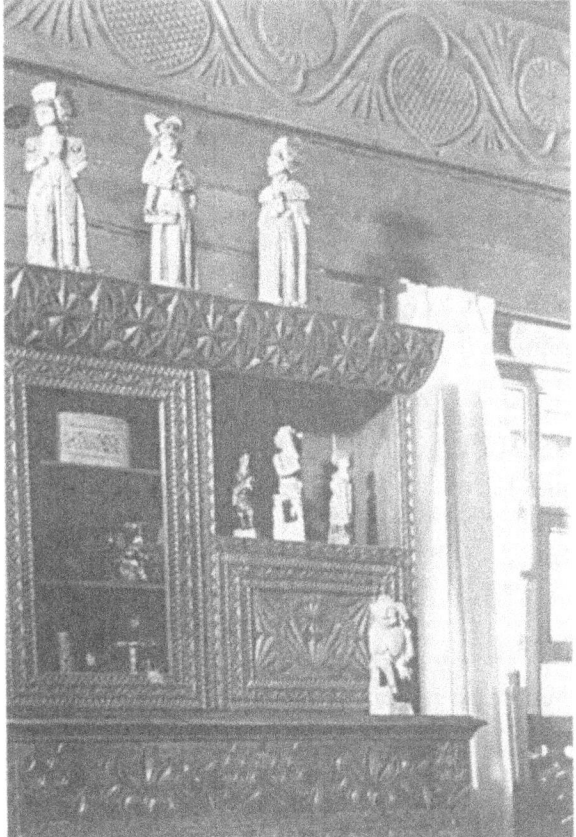

the Russian folk spirit."[14] In the performance of *Snegurochka*, she was keenly aware of the connection between the visual forms based on folk art and the choruses with "that sin-cere, Russian note in the music," and she often mentioned musical ele-ments in folk art.[15]

Polenova's approach to folk art was both prac-

FIG. 16.3 Room in Abramtsevo studio, with Bogorodskoe carving and other objects from collection; cupboard made at Abramtsevo.

tical and intuitive. Her initial goals were to study and collect folk art and to preserve its traditions, but she also hoped to assimilate the forms and the underlying feeling, the "music" of folk art, in her own creative work. What began as a search for antiquities in the ancient towns of Rostov, Iaroslavl', and Vladimir, and then became a hunt for anything "suitable for Snegurochka,"[16] grew into a search for new sources to revitalize both *kustar'* crafts and contemporary art.

Elizaveta Mamontova had started a joinery and carpentry workshop in 1876 as part of the elementary school she founded for peasants on the estate. Her main intention was to train local peasants so that they could earn money with *kustar'* crafts during the winter and not have to search for work in the city. The shop produced simple furniture far inferior, Mamontova realized, to the carved woodwork found around the countryside. Polenova, Mamontova, and Vasilii and Natal'ia Polenov discovered that they had "no need to go to Rostov in search of antiquities."[17] They visited villages in the Moscow district and farther afield, made notes, drawings, and photographs of architectural details, and collected all kinds of objects, ranging from carved frontal boards and lintels of gates to distaffs, saltcellars, and spoons. One evening, Natal'ia and Vasilii Polenov were invited into an *izba* by an old peasant woman, and Natal'ia saw "beside me on the bench, a piece of linen with a *valek* on top. I turned it over. It was carved . . . with deep contours, a fantastic image, very crude but interesting. We bought it for fifty kopeks."[18] In the course of one week, they found three distaff blades, four *val'ki*, one saltcellar, several embroidered towels, a silk scarf, and many *arshiny* of striped linen fabric. "The word has gone around, and now people bring things to us," Natal'ia Polenova reported, adding that in the villages of Men'shovo and nearby Valishchevo, "all the old things [handed down] from their grandparents are still preserved."[19]

At Abramtsevo, Elena Polenova arranged objects not by their material or type, but in ways that allowed her to examine similar forms or compare certain objects with drawings in her album.[20] By 1885, a small museum of folk arts was installed as part of the craft workshop. Its concentration on the art of adjacent districts (Moscow and Vladimir provinces) and its connection with continuing work in the crafts made the museum different from the dozen or so other private collections formed in the 1880s.[21]

Mamontova and Polenova wanted to teach crafts to children in the Abramtsevo village primary school, joinery for the boys and needlework for the girls, in order to awaken their pride in traditional skills and a feeling for their native culture. They believed that good models for instruction would improve the work of practicing *kustari* and, further, that appropriate models and control of quality would establish a valid artistic direction for the production of useful goods.[22] Polenova expressed these ideas in a letter to her friend Pelageia Antipova:

We have made it a rule not to rely on . . . published material [and] not to depend on drawings of well-known monuments or [objects] in public museums. Our goal is to capture the still-living art of the people, and give it the opportunity to develop. What turns up in publications is mostly dead and forgotten. . . . The thread is broken and it is terribly difficult to retie it artificially. If you tell a peasant to copy from a monument of the thirteenth or fourteenth century . . . it would seem just as strange to him as to copy something from Mauritania or ancient Greece. And that is why we look for inspiration and models mainly by going around the *izby* and examining things that are part of the environment, trying, of course, to exclude foreign novelties.[23]

Identifying the difference between "living" models and the "Russian" motifs adapted from manuscript interlace and Muscovite architecture used by Hartman, Ropet, and other architects and by manufacturers of porcelain and printed cotton, was a major step toward clearing up the confused notion of "national" style. However, Polenova's work in the carpentry studio was concerned with stimulating the development of *kustar'* arts rather than restoring the integrity of traditional folk art. Polenova was a pioneer in her use of genuine folk sources, but she employed those sources in ways that corresponded to her social and esthetic ideals, not to the nature of folk art.

When Mamontova and Polenova reorganized the workshop in 1885, they agreed that Polenova would devise models based on authentic folk objects and supervise the young pupils in executing the pieces. Mamontova undertook to find a commercial outlet, essential for establishing the Abramtsevo *kustar'* artists on a sound basis. The Moscow Zemstvo Kustar' Museum, established in 1885, provided an ideal but temporary venue for exhibiting and selling the workshop products. In 1886 Mamontova opened a store for the "Sale of Items Carved in Wood by Pupils in the Carpentry Studio of Abramtsevo Village," and in 1890 she established a "Shop of Russian Handwork" in a good business location.[24] Students of the Abramtsevo workshop had a three-year training course, followed by an optional year of paid work at Abramtsevo or an affiliated workshop in Sergiev-Posad, when their pieces were bought through the Kustar' Museum or the store at set prices. On completing the course, the boys were given sets of tools and sent back to their villages. As practicing *kustari*, they would make items for sale during the winter months and deal with local customers or the Moscow store directly. Equipped with a repertoire of Abramtsevo designs, some of them began to add features of their own invention. Polenova once mentioned her astonishment when she saw a beautifully carved *valek* in a neighboring village, asked to buy it, and found out that it had been made by a twelve-year-old village boy trained at Abramtsevo.[25] This experience suggests that the workshop could improve skills without unduly altering the common shapes and styles of utilitarian objects still preserved in the villages. However, it is impossible to gauge the overall effects of the program for the careers of the *kustari* back in their villages, because few of the former students are known;[26] almost all the information and material preserved at Abramtsevo concerns the work done at the Abramtsevo workshop and its branches.

The workshop was not just a matter of educating peasants and giving them a marketable skill. A crucial problem was determining what designs would be right for the peasant artists, suitable to the objects, and appealing to buyers. Polenova and Vasnetsov spent some time in 1885 experimenting with carved and painted designs on utilitarian objects (fig. 16.4), decorating a kitchen cupboard with "all kinds of designs in the old Russian taste," including "stylized birds" and "stylized foliage forms" on the door.[27] At this point, as in *Snegurochka*, the artists were more interested in exploiting the myriad possibilities of folk ornament than in discovering its underlying formal principles.

Teaching in the joinery workshop forced Polenova to pay attention to the basic components of carved design. Since the pupils were not experienced, she and her assistants had to find models of geometrical carving, and work out the steps and types of incisions needed to make the designs. Most of the models were saltcellars, distaffs, and other objects in the Abramtsevo museum, a few *nalichniki*, horse yokes, or parts of carts. Using these pieces, photographs, and watercolor sketches from her albums, Polenova selected interesting motifs from various sources and arranged them to fit the cupboards, shelves, or stools she designed for the students. One cupboard, for example, had doors taken from a shelf from the nearby village of Komiagino, a handle based on a distaff from Valishchevo, and columns from the village of Bogoslovo in Iaroslavl' Province.[28] "Our work in the [joinery] studio is going well," Polenova wrote in the summer of 1885, "especially the collection of materials. Russian folk art has turned out to be a completely untouched sphere, and it seems that there is not a single Russian village from which we cannot bring out something interesting."[29]

While Polenova collected new models and worked out designs for the workshop, she entrusted much of the training of students and execution of pieces to two peasant assistants, Ivan Antonovich Komissarov, the senior joiner (*stoliar*), and Semen (other names not recorded), a joiner and painter from Komiagino, who did most of the painting. As she and Mamontova prepared to exhibit the workshop products in September 1885, Polenova suggested having Komissarov make replicas of small and large cupboards, shelves, corner shelves, and other pieces, sometimes with variations in the form of the doors or the carved patterns.[30] Komissarov was also an excellent teacher who encouraged the boys' enthusiasm.[31] Semen was less reliable, and more individualistic. When Polenova visited his workshop she said, "The impression it made on me was simply poetic. He sits there in his sheepskin jacket, brushes and paints spread around him, and close to him at the table two pupils intently outlining little flower designs." Semen's drawback as a supervisor of students was that "he positively cannot copy; there is too much creativity in him." Some of his inventions were appealing, but others were esthetically unpleasant; Polenova hoped that she could persuade him to see things her way without "spoiling" him.[32] Reluctantly, for the sake of consistency, Polenova took over the supervision of painting.

The furniture and other items made at Abramtsevo had the value of "novelty, originality, and style," in Polenova's words, but they were not all of high quality; the success of the store encouraged a fashion for "Abramtsevo style" objects, and large orders sometimes resulted in technically poor work.[33] A more serious criticism was the lack of authenticity in Polenova's designs. With several years of study in villages around Abramtsevo and Sergiev-Posad and in other centers, including Rostov and Iaroslavl' to the northeast, Kostroma, Vladimir, and Suzdal' to the east, and Tula to the south, Polenova knew the distinctive regional decorations of architectural carving and household objects. Her records were accurate, and her earliest shelves and saltcellars were direct copies of the authentic folk pieces she had collected. But over the next few years, Polenova began to combine motifs from several sources that she felt had affinities to one another or expressed similar feelings for nature. She began to contradict her initial decision to use only works of "living" folk art as models, and subjected folk designs to her own more inclusive understanding of principles of ornamentation.

Polenova had studied ancient Scythian gold

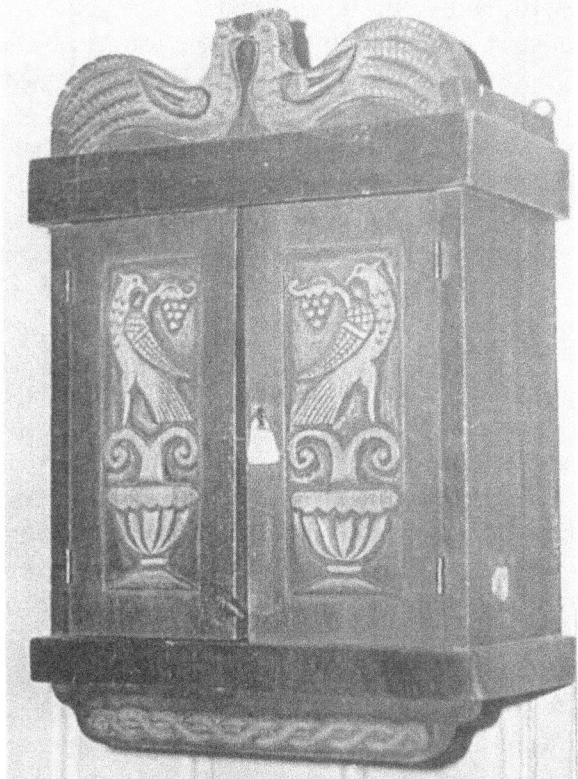

FIG. 16.4 Cupboard made at Abramtsevo Workshop, with bird motifs in low-relief carving. Abramtsevo Estate Museum.

objects in the Hermitage, and may have discussed them with historian Ivan Zabelin, a friend of her father.[34] Later she noticed affinities between Russian ornaments and "kindred forms" from Norway, which she saw on trips to Munich and Berlin, and she paid special attention to peasant art from Auvergne as well as more exotic exhibits from North Africa and the Sandwich Islands shown at the Paris Universal Exposition in 1889.[35] Unlike most viewers and even museum curators, who regarded such objects as curiosities or indicators of the degree of mechanical skill among exotic peoples,[36] Polenova examined the elements of ornamentation common to many cultures, based on animal and foliage forms and geometrical patterns. Her ideas about the application of designs from various artistic sources to new works of art took concrete shape in her designs for the Abramtsevo workshops and her illustrations to Russian fairytales.

Polenova's albums contained drawings of carved objects and details of carving from carts, cupboards, houses, and riverboats; embroidery on old Russian textiles, folk garments, and towel borders; sketches of flowers, branches, and other natural forms to be used for invented ornamental motifs; and designs for carved ornament to be executed in the Abramtsevo workshop.[37] She made notes on floral and geometrical ornamentation, the relationships between high- and low-relief carving, and the patterns of borders. In designs for the workshop, Polenova often used patterns and motifs taken from architectural ornament for chair backs or cupboard doors. Such adaptation was easy and reasonable, since cupboards, benches, looms, and other furnishings in peasant houses shared patterns with architectural ornament.

Adaptation was more complex and questionable when embroidery designs or motifs traditionally painted were used for relief carving, or when furniture shapes were based on those of Moscow boyar dwellings instead of the simpler peasant forms. Most Abramtsevo furniture was more massive than peasant models and more emphatic in its decoration. While geometrical patterns of three-faceted chip carving remained the basic type of ornament, stylized flowers and rosettes became prominent, along with animal forms known to be of ancient origin, such as horses, ducks, and stags (the latter, rare in folk carving, may have come from Scythian jewelry). Although few Abramtsevo pieces were signed or dated, there was a progression from the early, simple chip carving to a more plastic relief style based on frontal boards and carving on boats, and finally to fanciful combinations of animal and fairytale figures.

When Stasov raised the question of authenticity with Polenova, she replied that all her designs for the workshop and for her illustrations of fairytales were "taken directly from the soil," based on objects she had collected in isolated villages and monasteries.[38] Her work did not duplicate what had already been made, such as commercial reproductions of antique or provincial furnishings; rather, it was meant to continue the evolution of folk art in a natural way. Polenova had felt for some years that the workshop was successful but had reached a plateau: the peasant artists were still not "self-sufficient" or "resourceful,"[39] and contriving models for replication did not satisfy her.

Polenova's mission was to keep a feeling for ornament active and fertile in Russian art and in daily life. Her illustrations of fairytales showed her interest in recent scholarly study of folklore. While working on costumes for *Snegurochka*, she reread stories familiar from her childhood in the edition published by Aleksandr Afanas'ev in 1883; she learned local variants of the tales from master storytellers in villages near Abramtsevo.[40] Polenova studied the poetic styles and compared versions of the stories she heard, much as she studied folk ornament, with the idea of discovering how to render the character of these stories visually. She wrote of her plans to do a series of watercolors expressing "the poetic attitude toward nature of the Russian people":

> I want to clarify . . . the ways in which the Russian landscape has influenced, and has found expression in, the Russian folk epic and lyric poetry. In a word, to express the connection between the soil and the works that grow up out of the soil. . . . As subjects I shall take fairytales, songs, and poetic proverbs. I should like to identify and express those inventive, creative forms which enliven and nourish the imagination of the Russian peasant.[41]

The imaginative elements of her fairytale illustrations were as important for Polenova as literal or ethnographical accuracy. Her first set of watercolor illustrations, "The War of the Mushrooms,"[42] combined close-up depictions of mushrooms and other woodland plants with images based on icons, *lubki*, and embroidery, and purely decorative elements. In a later group of illustrations for stories adapted from Afanas'ev—"The White Duck," "Wolf and Fox," "Grandfather Frost," "Why the Bear Lost Its Tail," "The Goat Family," and "Synko-Filipko"—the alternation between accurate description and decorative treatment of the page was more evident. For "Synko-Filipko," the story of a boy carved from a block of wood by an old peasant, interior scenes were based on an *izba* in Kostroma Province,[43] and other scenes emphasized evocative colors, contrasts of scale, and the compositon of the page as a whole. Polenova knew German and English children's book illustration and the work of Walter Crane and William Morris; her later watercolors show the influence of modern graphic art in France, where she spent much time between 1895 and 1898.[44] Like her contemporaries in Russia and Europe, Polenova was eager to absorb new visual ideas from many sources, and to experiment with unconventional techniques and compositions, sometimes disregarding the essential connection between the form of an object and the ornament applied to it.

In order to concentrate on her illustrations and paintings, Polenova left the Abramtsevo joinery workshop in 1893. It continued to operate successfully, under the direction of a former pupil, Egor Zelenko.[45] Polenova stayed involved in applied arts through her interest in the embroidery workshop founded by Mariia Fedorovna Iakunchikova (née Mamontova, Savva's niece) at Solomenko in Tambov Province.[46] Iakunchikova wanted to expand the *kustar'* revival to include embroidery and other textile arts, improving on Elizaveta Mamontova's small embroidery workshop at Abramtsevo; by this time several upper-class women had organized embroidery, spinning, and weaving schools in various districts.[47] In 1891, Iakunchikova invited the young artist Natal'ia Davydova to supervise the design and production of such articles as tablecloths, wall hangings, purses, and dress trim based on patterns found on embroidered towels, *rubakhi*, and aprons. She persuaded Polenova to create designs for the Solomenko workshop. Polenova adapted a subject from a second group of fairytales, the Firebird guarding the tree of golden apples, for a large embroidered *panneau*. At the 1896 All-Russian Exhibition in Niznhii Novgorod, this stunning life-size panel,[48] measuring twelve by seven feet and worked in brilliant vermilion, yellow, gray-green, and indigo with heavy, cloisonné-like outlines, was an inspiration for Davydova, Aleksandr Golovin, and other young artists experimenting with applied art techniques. Abandoning the traditional forms and techniques, which the *kustar'* revival had initially set out to preserve, these artists expressed their own conceptions of a "Russian spirit" through stylized forms of forest and water plants, swans, and fanciful creatures.

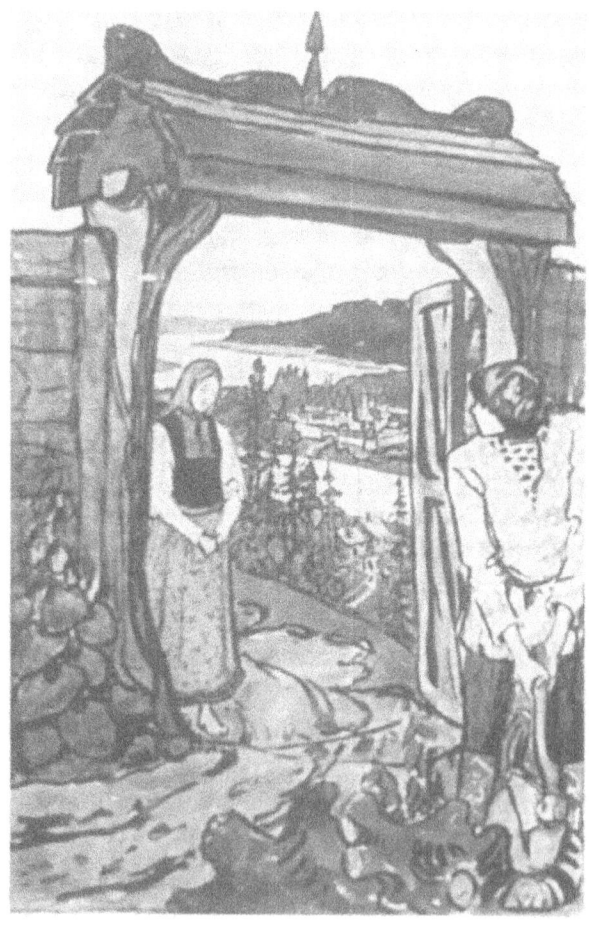

FIG. 16.5 Elena Polenova, illustration for fairytale. Watercolor. 1890s. GRM.

Polenova and her colleagues planned to demonstrate the range of *kustar'* products and their own creative works at the Paris Exposition Universelle of 1900. After Polenova died late in 1898, her friends made the exhibit a tribute to her achievements as the leader in the *kustar'* revival. The works were housed in a special Russian "village" designed by Konstantin Korovin and built by peasant carpenters from a workshop at the Trinity-Sergiev Posad, near Abramtsevo. Golovin arranged the interior to display many samples of furniture and ceramics from Abramtsevo and a large cupboard, designed by Mariia V. Iakunchikova and built by the Trinity-Sergiev joiners, containing examples of old and "improved" *kustar'* art. Hanging on the walls and draped across furnishings were examples of Solomenko embroidery and *naboika* prints made from old blocks and from Davydova's new drawings.[49]

The designs for carving and for embroidered and appliqué panels made by Polenova and her colleagues at Abramtsevo, at the Solomenko workshop, and later at Talashkino were closer in inspiration and appearance to *art nouveau*, the Russian *stil' modern*, than to folk art. The same was true of illustrations for fairytales, in editions of Pushkin's "Golden Cockerel," "The Tale of Tsar Saltan," and other tales by Nesterov in 1889, Sergei Maliutin between 1898 and 1910, and Ivan Bilibin between 1901 and 1910. The closeness of "folk" style to *art nouveau* was apparent in theatrical productions, with sets by Korovin, Vrubel', Maliutin, and others; in paintings and decorative panels inspired by fairytales by Mariia V. Iakunchikova, Davydova, and Golovin; and in inventive ceramic tile panels depicting the *sirin, bogatyri*, and other figures of Russian legend by Vrubel'. Vrubel' approached ceramics much as Polenov and Vasnetsov had approached stage design and other artists approached various applied arts: as a means of breaking away from the conventional subjects and stylistic restrictions of easel painting and work on a greatly expanded scale, with textural and coloristic effects that had not yet been achieved on canvas. Vrubel' said that these images and effects would convey a distinctive "national note," different from the "pale" conventions of the West.[50]

At the turn of the century, Princess Mariia Tenisheva tried to surpass the Abramtsevo group's work and bring about a cultural revival on a vast scale.[51] The lavish scope of her efforts was supported by her husband, Prince Viacheslav Tenishev, a wealthy industrialist, who gave her the estate Talashkino near Smolensk. Tenisheva was interested in educational reform: in 1892 she organized a factory school at the Tenishev ironworks in Smolensk, and in 1894 she turned to art education and hired Repin to direct her private studio in St. Petersburg as a preparatory school for young artists. Tenisheva was a competent painter, but her passion was enamelwork. Besides making enameled objects, and creating enamel-like effects in other media, she studied ancient Russian metal ornaments from excavations in Kiev, Smolensk, and Novgorod. She wrote a dissertation on the history of enamel, defending it at the Moscow Archeological Institute. Tenisheva's interests coincided with the fashion for

silver and enamel tea sets and other luxury items in the "Russian style" produced by the firms of Ovchinnikov, Khlebnikov, and Fabergé, some of whose
designs were inspired by jewelry found in the excavations. But her convictions
and goals were closer to those of the Abramtsevo artists.

Tenisheva established a drawing school in Smolensk intended, like applied arts schools in the capitals, to attract craftspeople and give them the
skills needed to improve the artistic level of their work. Because Smolensk was
in a linen-producing area, she opened an embroidery studio in the city, giving
training and employment to two thousand peasant women.[52] The crafts studios at Talashkino included a woodworking shop, directed by Maliutin, who
was also responsible for most of the building on the estate; a ceramics studio,
directed by Ivan Barshevskii, a noted archeologist and authority on Russian
antiquities; and an embroidery and textile section, headed by Anna Pogoss-
kaia, a Smolensk embroiderer and activist in the *kustar'* movement. Artists
from the Abramtsevo circle occasionally contributed designs for ceramics,
textiles, and novelty items such as painted balalaikas. Working at Talashkino,
Vrubel', Maliutin, Iakunchikova, Golovin, Dmitrii Stelletskii, and Nikolai Rerikh produced experimental pieces of applied art based on adaptations of folk
art or old Russian and Byzantine forms.

Maliutin, a peasant by birth, and part of the Abramtsevo circle in the
1890s, where he designed the first *matreshka* doll, became Tenisheva's closest
collaborator in major projects: planning a church; building a studio, the "Teremok," in 1901–1903; organizing a woodworking workshop; and designing
chairs, door frames, and knick-knack shelves. Already an experienced artist,
interested in Russian history and folk art, Maliutin kept detailed notes and
sketches of every kind of ornament. Some of these motifs, foliage forms, grinning lions, and *rusalki* based on folk carving, he used in the "Teremok" and in
later design projects for private houses (fig. 16.6).[53] The "Teremok," with its
fancifully decorated facade painted in jewel-like colors, was visually and thematically quite different from the "Russian style" buildings Hartman and
Ropet built for Mamontov. Here, and in many of Tenisheva's other projects,
intuition and fantasy replaced historicism. A notable aspect of the work done
at Abramtsevo and Talashkino was the close connection between experimentation in all areas of applied arts—woodworking, embroidery, ceramics, illustration, and theatrical design—and a sense of liberation through the richness
and fantasy of the Russian folk tradition.

Along with members of the Abramtsevo group and the Solomenko workshops, Tenisheva contributed to the Russian pavilion at the Paris Exposition
Universelle of 1900, for which her husband, Prince Tenishev, was one of the
commissioners. To create a market for Talashkino crafts, Tenisheva opened a
store in Moscow called *Rodnik*, "The Source," with an interior designed by
Maliutin.[54] In 1898 she founded a Museum of Russian Antiquities and Folk Art
at Talashkino, to display approximately two thousand objects acquired with

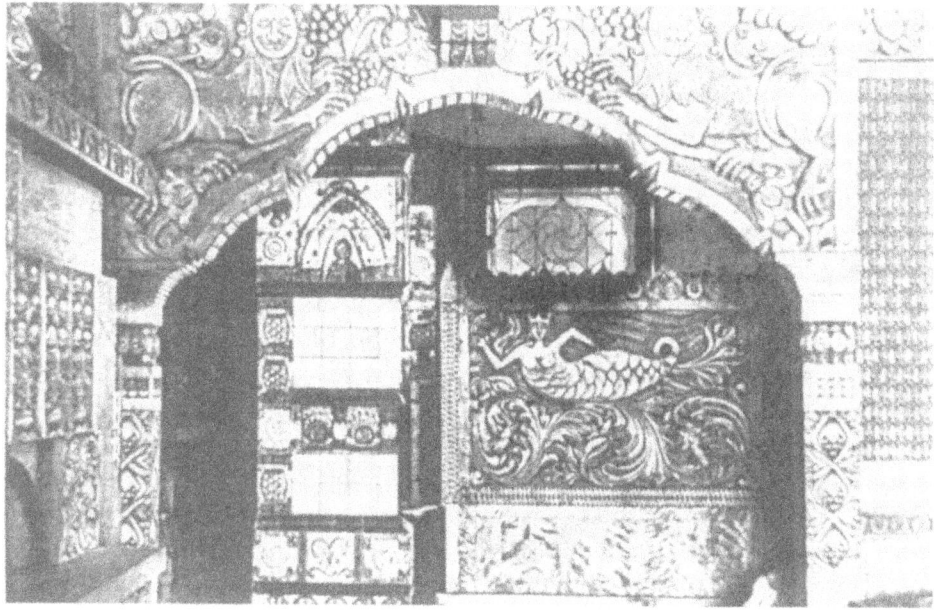

FIG. 16.6   Sergei Maliutin, interior of Pertsov house, Moscow.

the help of antiquarians Adrian Prakhaov and Ivan Barshchevskii on a trip through the Russian provinces.[55] The collection later grew to about ten thousand pieces, and in 1905 Tenisheva, with Maliutin's and Vasnetsov's help, built a museum in Smolensk to house it; most of it is still displayed there. Alarmed by political disturbances, including walkouts in her embroidery workshop, Tenisheva closed Talashkino and left for Paris in 1906, taking part of the collection. Before returning the works to Smolensk, she exhibited them at the Musée des Arts Decoratifs in 1907. This was among the early exhibitions that helped to awaken international interest in Russian antiquities and decorative arts.[56]

The art colonies' efforts to recover authentic Russian art and revive the traditional *kustar'* arts were aided for a time, and given a broader international base, by the "World of Art" (*Mir iskusstva*) group, Alexandre Benois (Benua), Sergei Diaghilev, and others.[57] Their goals overlapped most significantly in the theater, where they aimed to produce spectacles that would arouse in any audience a feeling for the beauty and expansiveness of the Russian cultural heritage. Diaghilev's early operas and ballets, including *Boris Godunov* in 1907, *Prince Igor* in 1910, *Petrushka* in 1911, and *The Rite of Spring* in 1913, rapidly showed audiences the enormous range of expression inherent in the history of Muscovy, the remote conflicts of Kievans and the tribes of the steppes, the poignancy of urban Maslenitsa customs, and the shocking severity of pagan rituals. From the outset, the color and theatricality of Russian national art appealed to Diaghilev.

Mamontov and Tenisheva gave financial support to the journal *Mir iskusstva*. Selections from the Abramtsevo folk art collection and *kustar'* items from the workshop were illustrated in the first issue. Vasnetsov's and Polenova's works were also featured; one of Polenova's illustrations for "Synko-Filipko" was on the cover of the second issue in 1899.[58] Two members of the group, Benua and Bilibin, wrote eloquently but very differently about Russian folk arts. Benua identified with the urban, cosmopolitan character of St. Petersburg, but he felt the nostalgic charm of folk art when he visited the Russian Pavilion at the Paris Exposition of 1900. In his review for *Mir iskusstva*, he commented on peasant crafts: "painted boxes of birch bark, charming little toys, curious and so childlike, *naboika* which is having such success among Parisians, ceramics, embroidery, lace, and so forth—everything glorious, lush, unpretentious in form and beautiful in color." But, he added, "one feels sad that all this splendor is now in decline."[59]

Bilibin's article on the art of northern Russia, illustrated with his photographs and drawings, occupied most of a later issue of the journal (fig. 16.7).[60] Bilibin had studied with Repin in Tenisheva's St. Petersburg school before meeting the *Mir iskusstva* artists, Vasnetsov, and some of the Moscow group in 1899. While a student he completed several illustrations for the Russian fairytales "Marfa Morevna" and "The White Duck," as well as vignettes with old Russian motifs for *Mir iskusstva*. In 1902 he went on an expedition to Vologda Province to collect samples of folk art and photograph wooden architecture for the ethnographic department of the Russian Museum. He went to Vologda and Arkhangel'sk provinces the next summer, and in 1904 to Tver' and Olonets provinces, and published articles on "Folk Art of the Russian North" and "Remnants of Art in the Russian Village."[61] Best known for fairytale illustrations that echoed the heroic and epic character of Vasnetsov's work with more inventive compositions and decorative devices, Bilibin had the ability to include pieces of folk art in his scenes without denaturing the works. His conservation of authentic folk elements was largely due to the profound impressions the northern Russian countryside made on him.

Bilibin wrote in *Mir iskusstva* that folk art was dying, and that only in the most remote places did "its last feeble sparks still smolder." He understood the historical changes and knew that the "enchanting, fairytale time" when pure folk art had flourished could never be retrieved. His message was that remnants of folk art should be preserved and allowed to develop naturally, in their own environment. Bilibin was against isolating folk art in museums, or reviving only media and styles that were fashionable or commercially viable. He urged that authentic folk ornament be taught in all the art schools and among the wider public, so that new artists could learn the nearly forgotten forms. His views echoed those initially held at Abramtsevo, but he disagreed with the group's adaptations and alterations of folk art, and opposed the emphasis on *kustar'* revival. His main interest was in preserving and strengthening the traces of folk culture rather than using them to invent something new.

By this time, attitudes toward nationalism, historicism, and folk culture had changed from the Slavophile positions of the early nineteenth century, from the official *narodnost'* of Alexander III, and even from the original goals of the Abramtsevo group. The hopes that theater and art could counterbalance the "commonplace tenor of life" by drawing on "the realm of heroism and beauty" enunciated by Polenov, and Polenova's goal "to capture the still-living art of the people and give it the opportunity to develop,"[62] were not abandoned, but the emphasis changed. At the turn of the century, Russian folk art was no longer a source of models for improving the *kustar'* industries, but an inspiration for experimentation and renewal by professional artists. In his *History of Russian Painting in the Nineteenth Century*, published in 1902, Benua identified

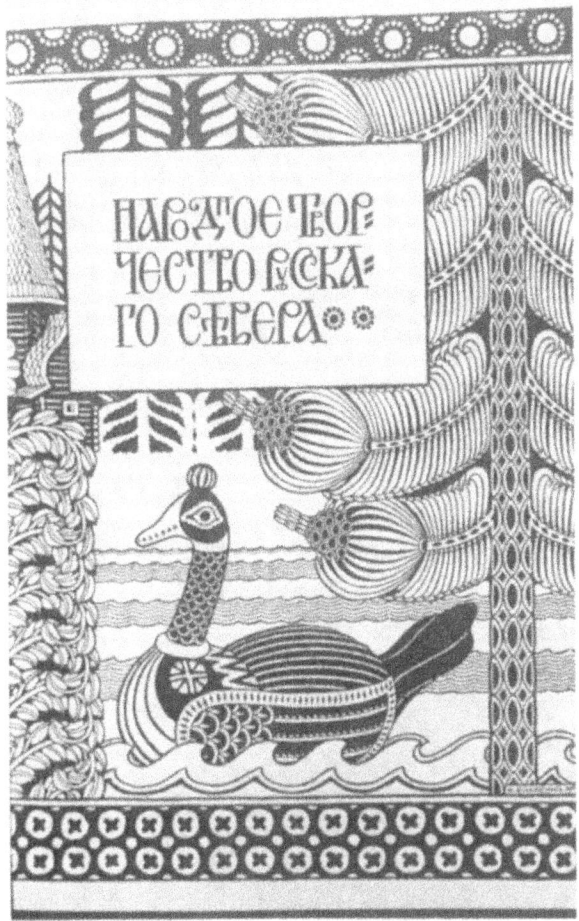

FIG. 16.7 Ivan Bilibin, "Folk Art of the Russian North," title page for *Mir iskusstva* (1904).

the Abramtsevo group's achievements not only with a "renaissance of decorative art" but also with a significant new direction which many European artists were taking, a search for "the very *language* of art."[63] Benua's statement was prophetic of radically new approaches to folk art and old Russian culture in the early twentieth century.

Folk Art and New
Languages of Art

For the point of departure in our art we take the *lubok*, the primitive art
form, the icon, since we find in them the most acute, most direct
perception of life.

—Aleksandr Shevchenko, 1913[1]

Through icons I came to understand the emotional art of the peasants.

—Kazimir Malevich, 1933[2]

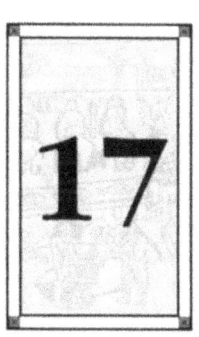

For artists as deeply con-scious of their Russian and
Eastern heritage as were the pioneers of Russian avant-
garde art in the early twenti-eth century, folk art had value
both as a token of identity in a rapidly shifting world and as a symbol of the
untapped powers of a non-European culture. Vasilii Kandinskii and Natal'ia
Goncharova, in particular, took great pains with their research into folk art,
but preservation and revival of folk art were not the main goals for either
artist. During the first decade of the century, the energetic neoprimitivist
movement replaced nostalgia toward folk art with a new emphasis on the
vitality and essential modernity of its forms and design principles.

Kandinskii visited the north of Russia and felt the intense visual effects
of painted houses and brightly costumed villagers in the summer of 1889.
Then a law student at Moscow University, Kandinskii was conducting field
research on deities, religious beliefs, and judicial procedures among a non-
Russian people, the Zyrians (today, Komi), living near the Susola and

Vychegda rivers in the remote northeastern part of Vologda Province. His work resulted in two scholarly articles still cited in ethnographic literature, and the experience later had a profound influence on his art.[3] Unlike Bilibin, Kandinskii did not write about the folk art or record his observations visually at the time. But the sensory impressions of the trip developed in his mind over the next two decades, coming to the surface in forms, colors, and various details in drawings, woodcuts, and paintings. Passages in his memoirs, written in 1913, emphasize these visual effects and suggest that Kandinskii's awareness of the connection between sensory and spiritual perception may have begun with this trip.

Describing the journey by train to Vologda, by steamboat up the Sukhona River to Velikii Ustiug and Kotlas, and by coach into Zyrian territory, he emphasized the "unending forests, between brightly hued hills," and the feeling of "immersing" himself in the environment. When he reached his goal, he felt that he had entered a completely new world, crossed a threshold into a painting, with the people in their colorful costumes and painted faces seeming "like brightly colored living pictures," and their houses like painted folksongs.[4] These first impressions, remembered so many years later, show that Kandinskii was affected by the feeling of magic and fantasy in the village. His awareness of specific motifs and artifacts was subsumed by an overwhelming internal experience of form and color.

> In these extraordinary huts I first encountered the miracle that became subsequently one of the elements of my work. It was here that I learnt not to look at the picture from the side, but to *revolve in the picture* myself, to live in it. I can remember vividly stopping on the threshold of this amazing spectacle. The table, the benches, the stove so imperious and so huge, the closets, the sideboards — everything had been painted with multi-colored and bold ornaments.[5]

Kandinskii may not have worked out the implications of these perceptions before he began to study painting in 1896. His article on Zyrian religion, with its references to *domovye* and nature gods, to icons, and to rituals and taboos of both pagan and Christian origins, shows that he appreciated the complex relations between visual forms and magic properties within an animistic folk culture. On a more mundane level, he evidently knew some of the village crafts, since his friend N. A. Ivanitskii was active in reviving and reorganizing the cottage industry of carving from bone and horn.[6] Although Kandinskii was not interested in the projects of the Abramtsevo group at this early stage, a comparable approach to combining the fields of folk art, religious imagery, and theater would become important in the Blaue Reiter period. His attraction to Zyrian beliefs and customs showed an appreciation for the values of diverse cultures and the possibility of divergent ways of perceiving the physical world. This attitude was later expressed in *Concerning the Spiri-*

tual in Art, and was essential to the creation of new relationships between form and meaning.

Works reflecting Kandinskii's Vologda experiences include paintings, woodcuts, and glass paintings done between about 1902 and 1913, with folk, fairytale, or religious motifs, and later works, done mainly in Paris in the 1940s, containing magical signs to embody principles of shamanistic creation. Among the earlier works, *Golden Sail,* a color woodcut of 1903, and the tempera painting *Russian Beauty in a Landscape* of 1904 resemble Bilibin's fairytale illustrations of the same period.[7] But many were far more complex. *Motley Life* of 1907 included both "old Russian" images and symbols from Zyrian religious lore. The prominent figure of a shaman might be interpreted as both a healer and an artist.[8] This kind of personal identification with folkloristic imagery was quite different from the retrospective attitude of late nineteenth-century symbolism. Soon Kandinskii began assimilating ethnographic and religious images of Asia and Africa as well as Russia into his philosophy of artistic creation. Speaking for the Blaue Reiter group, he said:

> When there is a similarity of inner tendency in the whole moral and spiritual atmosphere, a similarity of ideals, . . . a similarity in the inner feeling [between one period and another], the logical result will be a revival of the external forms which served to express those inner feelings in an earlier age. An example of this today is our sympathy, our spiritual relationship, with the Primitives. Like ourselves, these artists sought to express in their work only internal truths, renouncing in consequence all consideration of external form.[9]

This statement clarifies the differences between Kandinskii's attitudes to folk art and those of the Abramtsevo group and Bilibin. Far from advocating preservation or revival of folk art forms, Kandinskii implied that such forms would appear when needed to express internal truths. Certainly they appeared in his own works to express his innermost conception of the artist's dual roles: as a shamanistic magician-healer and as the legendary Christian warrior St. George, helped by his powerful horse, the artistic gift, to conquer the dragon.[10]

Kandinskii's identification of "primitivism" in art with the striving to express "internal truth" without relying on external forms was part of an increasingly animated debate about the nature of artistic creation, central to modern art movements in Europe and Russia. The *Blaue Reiter Almanac,* published in 1912, offered an unusually thorough and concentrated exploration of "primitive" art, illustrated with *lubki,* Bogorodskoe wooden toys, votive images, masks, and other folk art from many cultures; some of these items were in the second Blaue Reiter exhibition.[11] Reference to examples in his own collection helped to anchor Kandinskii's theoretical discussions in the realm of the tangible.

Kandinskii presented his paper "On the Spiritual in Art" at the Second All-Russian Congress of Artists in St. Petersburg in 1911. Most of the congress was practically oriented, with sessions on art education, painting techniques, architecture and cities, Russian antiquity and its preservation, industrial art and *kustar'* art, and art in the theater. Kandinskii spoke in the theoretical session on "Problems of Esthetics and Art History," in which a few other papers, on harmony, rhythm, and music in art and history, had some relation to his theme. The paper was well received by a large, diverse audience, and regarded as a thoughtful attempt to explain modern art, though not particularly innovative.[12]

By this time, the personal and spiritual elements so important to Kandinskii's art were being questioned by members of the Moscow avant-garde. Paradoxically, several artists, including Natal'ia Goncharova, Mikhail Larionov, David Burliuk, and later Kazimir Malevich, based their new styles on characteristics of folk and "primitive" art. Goncharova, Larionov, and Burliuk exhibited with Kandinskii and the Blaue Reiter group; an article by Burliuk and a drawing by Goncharova were published in the *Almanac*. It is small wonder that interpretations of primitivism current at the time sometimes overlapped and sometimes contradicted one another.

Stimulated by simultaneous discoveries of Russian icons, folk art, and popular art, the indigenous arts of other cultures, and the creative uses of "primitive" art forms by Gauguin and Matisse,[13] the younger artists shared Kandinskii's multicultural interests. But while Kandinskii continued to search for the "internal truths" of "primitive" arts, Goncharova, Larionov, and Malevich wanted to use them as starting points in a search for new formal systems. Identifying the significance of primitivism, Sergei Makovskii wrote that the symbolist painters exploring "the music of color and line" were on the verge of something new and important: "They have heralded that *primitivism* to which modern painting has come in its search for a rebirth at its very sources—in spontaneous creation unweakened by the weight of historical experience."[14]

Makovskii anticipated a major shift in Russian art, a turning away from the symbolism and estheticism indebted to Western modernist movements. He saw Russia and the East as the birthplaces of a "new primitivism," which could revitalize art. The rhetoric of the neoprimitivist movement, delivered in numerous statements and manifestos between 1910 and 1913, finally erased the vestiges of historicism and nostalgia associated with folk art. This new attitude also justified combining elements of folk art with formal ideas picked up from European modernists. Strikingly, in a booklet entitled "Neoprimitivism: Its Theory, Its Potentials, Its Achievements," Aleksandr Shevchenko connected the primitive with forms of modern technology: "the simple, unsophisticated beauty of the *lubok*, the severity of the primitive, the mechanical precision of construction . . . that is our password and our slogan."[15]

Shevchenko went on to extol specific "primitive art forms—icons, *lubki*, trays, signboards, fabrics of the East, etc." as "specimens of genuine value and painterly beauty." The types of art admired and collected by these artists belonged to provincial towns, markets, and fairgrounds rather than to villages on rural estates or in northern forests. In other words, the neoprimitivists sought out examples of living folk art, not the remnants of the disintegrating village cultures mourned by Bilibin. Some artists expressed disinterest in and even scorn for the popularized and commercialized *kustar'* production aimed at middle-class and foreign buyers.[16] Larionov showed works imitating *lubki* and shop signs in the "Knave of Diamonds" exhibition of 1910, and in 1913, at the "Target" exhibition, he gave wall space to "easel painters, house painters, and sign painters," *lubki*, children's paintings, and so-called "naive" art, including several shop signs and portraits painted on tin and black oilcloth by Niko Pirosmanashvili, a self-taught Georgian painter "discovered" by friends of Larionov on a visit to Tbilisi.

Native Russian arts were attracting attention at national and international exhibitions, including the Second All-Russian Folk Art Exhibition held in 1913 in St. Petersburg and the exhibition of newly cleaned and restored icons organized that year by the Institute of Archeology in Moscow. An exhibition of Russian folk art and crafts, part of the Russian section of the Paris Salon d'Automne in the same year, may have been equally important in changing attitudes about the value of folk art. In the nineteenth century, folk and *kustar'* art had been exhibited with industrial and applied arts, rather than fine arts, but now folk art was seen to have much in common with contemporary art. The exhibit included examples of toys, *lubki*, spicecake molds, *matreshki*, and icons, some from the collections of Bilibin, Larionov, and other artists. One of the organizers, Iakov Tugendhol'd, a respected critic of modern European and Russian art, stated in the introduction to the catalogue that the goal was "to show original folk art, and to contrast it with the pseudo-Russian style" that had dominated handicraft exhibitions abroad. "In selecting materials, the organizers were guided solely by the artistic level of each object, independent of its historical or ethnographical meaning."[17] This principle confirmed the young artists' rejection of the nineteenth-century retrospective approach to folk art.

Larionov used *lubki*, signboards, and graffiti as models for his visually and thematically crude paintings of soldiers and prostitutes. One critic commented on the "deliberate simplification and vulgarization of form" at the "Knave of Diamonds" exhibition,[18] and some observers compared the lack of refinement in these works to the poor artistic quality of *kustar'* art. Larionov was more interested in the stylistic characteristics of *lubki*: the placement of major figures in a shallow foreground plane, the distribution of subsidiary forms without regard for illusionary space, and the interaction of texts and images. The well-known satirical *lubok Barber Cutting Off the Beard of an Old*

Believer was a source for several barbershop scenes by Larionov and Burliuk. The flattening of space, distortion of figures, and enlargement of key objects such as scissors and razors not only pointed to *lubok* style but rejected the traditional criteria of academic art. Larionov quoted another popular *lubok* image, the "Cat of Kazan" as if sketched on a wall behind a reclining nude, in *Venus* of 1912. *Lubki* depicting *bogatyri* or "cavaliers" were sources for figures in some soldier paintings, such as *Galloping Soldier* of 1908.[19] The colors and the manner of applying paint flatly within emphatic outlines may have been based partly on painted toys, furniture, and decorative panels from Gorodets, such as those by Mazin and Lebedev described in chapter 6. Larionov was not pious about his sources, and was not concerned with the problems of authenticity and integrity that vexed artists of the older generation.

Despite his reputation for crudeness, Larionov also showed sensitivity toward folk culture. In *Autumn*, from his 1912 cycle *Seasons of the Year*, he divided the canvas into four compartments and drew the figures in white against a blue background, creating a stiff symmetry much like that of contour-carved *terem* distaffs from Iaroslavl'. The courting couple, branching tree, and female with upraised hands flanked by birds were elements of archaic folk ritual appearing on distaffs and embroidery, not on objects of urban folk art.[20] During the following decade, after the neoprimitivist phase had ended, Larionov returned to images reflecting rural folk culture in stage and costume designs for Diaghilev's ballet.

Goncharova and Malevich both used *lubki* as stylistic models, especially for graphic works, including illustrations for futurist poems by Aleksei Kruchenykh and Velimir Khlebnikov, and Malevich's anti-German posters during World War I.[21] They responded to the directness and formal order of provincial icons and rural folk art most strongly in paintings of peasant subjects, such as Goncharova's *Grain Harvest* (fig. 17.1) and *Washing Linen* of 1910 and Malevich's many drawings of village scenes (fig. 17.2) and such paintings as *Peasant Woman with Buckets and Child*, *Harvesting Rye*, and *The Woodcutter* of 1912.[22] Il'ia Mashkov, Petr Konchalovskii, Pavel Filonov, Vladimir Tatlin, and many other contributors to the neoprimitivist exhibitions explored the possibilities of folk arts and icons with widely varied results. Mashkov painted several large still lifes of brightly colored fruit, vegetables, and loaves of bread arranged in neat rows or pyramidal piles against black backgrounds, just as they were on signboards for bakers' and grocers' shops. Konchalovskii also imitated signboards and paintings on tin trays, and in some still life paintings included embroidered towels and bowls and spoons from Khokhloma. Filonov, in his 1912 drawings *Musicians* (fig. 17.3) and *Orientation on the Russian Lubok (Three Horsemen)* and the painting *Maslenitsa* of 1913–1914, referred to *lubok* compositions and carved wooden carriages, as well as themes from folk life.[23] Tatlin's paintings *The Fishmonger* and *The Sailor*, exhibited in 1912, emphasized the structural elements of icons, curved contours, and "reversed" perspective. His costume and stage designs

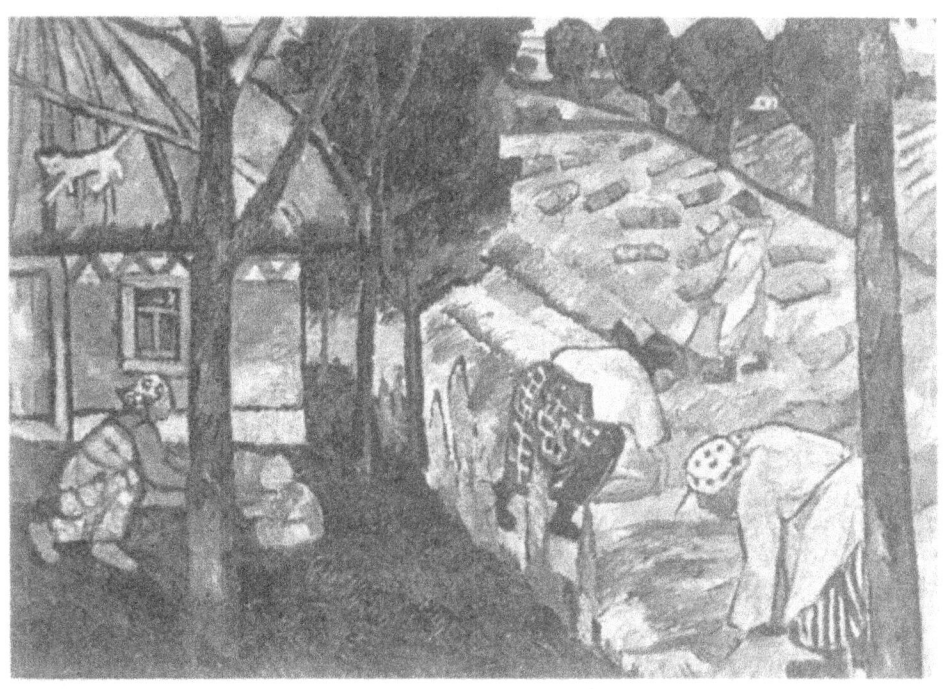

FIG. 17.1 Natal'ia Goncharova, *Grain Harvest*. Oil on canvas. 1908. GRM.

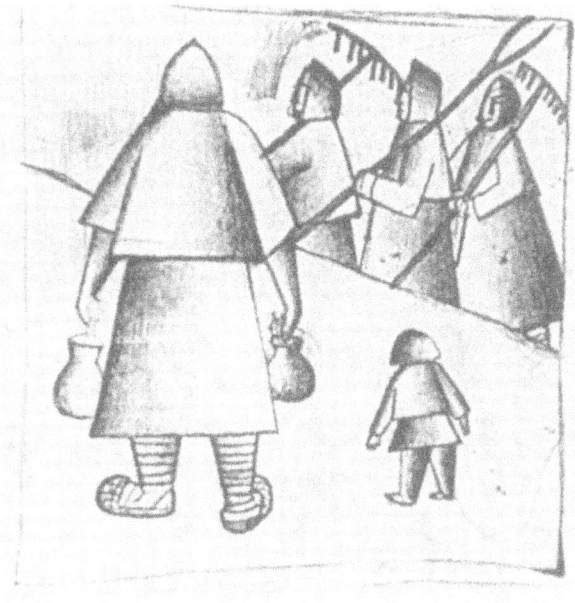

FIG. 17.2 Kazimir Malevich, *In the Field*. Pencil on paper. 1911–12. GRM.

for a "folk drama," *The Emperor Maximilian and His Disobedient Son Adolf,* suggested characters in *lubki.* In 1913, Tatlin made lithographs to illustrate the poem "To Signboards," Vladimir Maiakovskii's verbal expression of the neoprimitivists' delight in this vigorous folk art form: "these books of iron" replete with "fish, smoked and cured, and golden-headed turnips."[24]

Goncharova and Malevich worked with folk and icon sources in a somewhat different spirit. According to Malevich, both had a strong "social concern," and were interested in the peasants as people, not only in visual qualities of folk art.[25] In *The Woodcutter,* Malevich treated the figure and cut logs with a conscientious regularity and smoothness like that of brightly painted toys turned on a lathe and worked by rods or strings. The intense, luminous white, yellow, red, green, and black and the emphatic geometry recall northern Russian icons as well as folk painting on wood; the subjective association of the visual fullness and intensity with religious feeling is reinforced by the painting on the back of the canvas, *Peasant Women at Church.* These paintings stand apart from other neoprimitivist works with their monumentality and dignity. Much later, Malevich explained this stage of his work in an autobiographical note: "Through icon painting, I came to understand the emotional art of the peasants, which I had loved earlier, but whose meaning I had not fully understood."[26]

Malevich recalled that as a child he had watched in amazement while an ordinary housepainter transformed the roof of a building by painting it green; he cited this story as prophetic of his later understanding of the elemental, or primitive, power of color.[27] The story also explains two crucial aspects linking the development of abstract art in Russia to neoprimitivism and the rediscovery of folk art. The recognition of the functions of applied art went hand in hand with the understanding that color and form have expressive value without depending on representation.

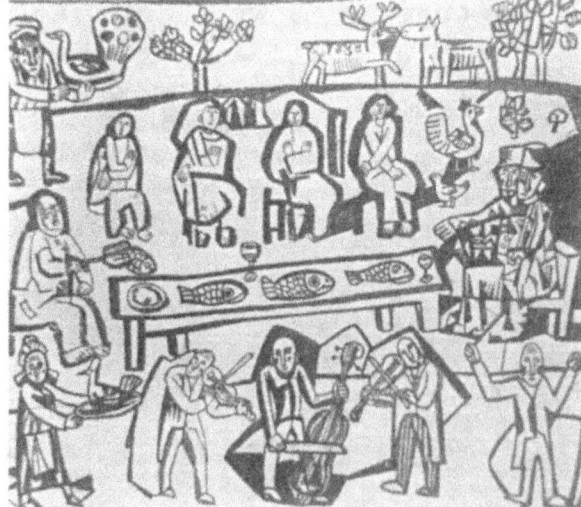

FIG. 17.3   Pavel Filonov, *Musicians.* Pencil and ink on paper. 1912. GRM.

Through icons and folk art, Goncharova discovered the keys to a national culture, distinct from that of the West. "The art of my country is incomparably more profound and important than anything that I know in the West," she wrote in 1913.[28] Like many contemporaries she believed that the art of "the East" would generate the art of the future. Goncharova had grown up on an estate near Tula in central Russia, where an ancestor had founded a linen factory. She knew the familiar rhythms of the repeated tasks of farming, preparing flax, and spinning, weaving, and washing the linen. She did not have to search far for stylistic sources, though she learned their value after studying at the Moscow School of Painting, Sculpture, and Architecture, meeting Larionov, and becoming involved with modernist experimentation. Access to modern Western art in Sergei Shchukin's and Ivan Morozov's collections, and to icons collected by Il'ia Ostrouknov and Sergei Riabushinskii among others, was of great importance, as was Larionov's growing collection of shop signs, folk ornaments, and toys. Goncharova's training in sculpture undoubtedly helped her to visualize the chunky forms of the carved wooden toys in terms of their rhythmic possibilities for paintings of peasants dancing, harvesting grain, fishing, or washing linen.

By the time the main tendencies within the avant-garde were defined in the "Knave of Diamonds," "Donkey's Tail," and "Target" exhibitions, Goncharova was ready to declare her rejection of the theorizing of European-oriented members of the avant-garde in favor of a more down-to-earth attention to the real elements and structures of art. In an impromptu speech in 1912, she declared: "Cubism is a positive phenomenon, but it is not altogether a new one. The Scythian stone images, the painted wooden dolls sold at fairs are those same cubist works . . . . For a long time I have been working in the manner of cubism."[29]

Early works, including *In Church*, *Evangelists*, and *Elder with Seven Stars*, were based on icons of provincial rather than court schools; though some of them shocked viewers,[30] the artist was not trying to debase religious forms but rather attempting to convey a feeling of popular or folk spirituality. Soon she adopted an almost missionary attitude toward Russian art. In her preface to the catalogue of her first solo exhibition in 1913, she made the most sweeping statement about the importance of Eastern and Russian sources for modern art:

> Hitherto I have studied all that the West could give me. . . . Now I shake the dust from my feet and leave the West. . . . My path is toward the source of all arts, the East. The art of my country is incomparably more profound and important than anything that I know in the West.[31]

Goncharova continued working with images from icons, manuscripts, and church art after many contemporaries had abandoned these forms and turned to abstraction. Early Russian applied arts and folk art inspired much of her work for the theater. When Diaghilev asked her to design sets and costumes for Rimskii-Korsakov's *Coq d'or (The Golden Cockerel)* in 1913, Goncharova was enchanted by the fairytale subject and the visual material. "I visited archaeological museums, where I was inspired by peasant costumes," she told an interviewer. "I discovered such treasures as the magnificent rings of our Tsars and boyars. I had discussions with artisans. The Russian people have an innate taste for art."[32] Echoing the enthusiasm for Russian sources expressed by participants in Mamontov's theatrical spectacles, Goncharova underlined the resiliency of Russian themes for Diaghilev's ballet. Later performances of *Coq d'or* and other ballets including *Liturgie* in 1914, *Les noces* in 1918 designed by Goncharova, and *The Midnight Sun* of 1915 and *Les contes russes* of 1917 designed by Larionov, contained direct references to peasant customs and folklore, and obvious quotations from *lubki*, peasant toys, and architectural carving.

Goncharova's neoprimitivist interpretations of traditional forms developed in two new directions between 1912 and 1914, toward expressionism on the one hand and toward abstraction on the other. *Mystical Images of War*, a suite of lithographs based on icons, *lubki*, and passages in the Book of Revelation, begun when war was declared in 1914, were among her strongest expressionistic works.[33] Interest in primitive forms and in the material substances and tools belonging to folk art also led Goncharova to explore elementary principles of form, color, graphic line, contrast, and other elements of structure and decoration. Having worked in primitive and cubist styles, and on virtually abstract "rayist" paintings and drawings, Goncharova began a series of decorative paintings based on patterns and textures of women's clothing and accessories. This series, explained as "an investigation of an abstract artistic problem," was not based only on folk costume, but it reflected a shared interest in applied arts and design among many avant-garde artists, including Ol'ga Rozanova, Aleksandra Ekster, Vladimir Tatlin, and Liubov' Popova.[34] One contemporary writer, Ivan Aksenov, recognized the underlying connection between this kind of investigation of form and a "distinct folk character" still to be perceived in Russian culture. This was "not the kind of folk character that requires a whole arsenal of ethnographic material to become manifest, but that direct sensation of folk character that penetrates the works . . . certain of their motifs become the bases of new forms, of domestic, handicraft art."[35]

Emphasizing the essential "folk character," beyond specific references to *lubki*, painted trays, and shop signs, in the work of Il'ia Mashkov, Aristarkh Lentulov, Petr Konchalovskii, and Aleksandra Ekster, Aksenov went on to discuss the importance of returning to "ancient tradition" in order to work out the essential synthesis of traditional and new for a regeneration of the "fundamental meaning of form" in contemporary art.[36] Writing at about the same time that Goncharova declared that Russian sources gave her independence from the West, Aksenov clearly considered "folk character" as something not particularly national. Rather, he concluded, through the work of contemporary artists, it would lead to a "high level of pure painting unprecedented in our country."[37] This interpretation of "folk" as universal rather than Russian was echoed by Naum Gabo, an early associate of Malevich, who played a major role in the international constructivist movement in the 1920s. Commenting briefly on Russian folk art in a lecture at the National Gallery of Art in Washington in 1959, he said:

> The history of Russian folk art does not go very deep; there are very few relics of antiquity left in Russia. . . . The imagery in that art contains very little of those symbolic aspects which we find in the ancient cultures. Russian mythology is limited to a very few subjects, all concerned with the domestic life of the people, and this imagery played a secondary part in the visual consciousness of the Russian artists.
>
> The fundamental elements of visual expression—lines, shapes, colors, and forms—are revealed as the focal theme and the main point of interest to the artist in his pictorial language, and in that respect it can be characterized as what is now called abstract.[38]

The attempt to consider an indefinite "folk" art or "folk" character as a basis for abstraction required considerable oversimplification of its underlying formal principles, denial of the role of symbols, and reduction of the specific physical traits of its various media to "lines, shapes, colors, and forms." A different process of deriving modern artistic forms from the principles of folk art also existed within the avant-garde. Emphasizing motifs from urban rather than folk culture, artists working in a new style known as cubo-futurism created collages and collage-like paintings utilizing words and commonplace objects related to familiar trades and occupations: barbershops, laundries, seamstresses' work tables, a knife-grinder's stand. Many paintings by Rozanova, Malevich, Goncharova, and Udal'tsova, among others, retained traces of the shop signs and *lubki* of earlier works;[39] despite their shifting forms and fragmented planes, they emphasized what later became known as a "culture of materials."

Malevich identified color and form as the primary elements of all arts, and the self-sufficient bases of pure abstraction, in his Suprematist work between 1915 and 1919. During the same years, he and Ivan Puni, Rozanova, Udal'tsova, and Liubov' Popova, in collaboration with Natal'ia M. Davydova and Evgeniia Pribylskaia (organizers of an embroidery and weaving workshop at Verbovka near Kiev), created abstract designs to be embroidered by the peasant craftswomen. The resulting items, at least four hundred handbags, scarves, and blotters, were exhibited and sold not only at craft outlets but at a special exhibition in the Museum of Figurative Arts in Moscow in 1919.[40] Their success was largely due to the professional artists' genuine interest in folk and applied arts, and to a spirit of collaboration very much in the tradition of Abramtsevo, Solomenko, and Talashkino. Similar projects would continue under the auspices of new art institutions after the Revolution. Eventually, formal discoveries based partly on folk and applied arts were used in the creation of new art forms for the new society. The revolutionary idea of bringing art into daily life called upon all the connotations of the term *narodnoe iskusstvo*, as national, folk, and popular art.

Expressing themselves in verbal declarations and in representational, abstract, and applied art, many artists developed new theories, forms, and materials to correspond to a new era. For the neoprimitivists and futurists, the "new" signified factories, airplanes, streetlights, and "primitive art forms— icons, *lubki*, trays, signboards."[41] After the Revolution, the "New Way of Life" attracted many artists to work in applied art forms, especially textiles and graphic design. Some new designs for garments and fabrics were based on the functional and festive components of traditional peasant costume. Many other articles preserved the organic unity of form and function inherent in folk art and essential to products made for use.

Artists of the twentieth-century avant-garde, in search of new formal languages, rejected the historicism and estheticism of nineteenth-century approaches to folk art. First, they emphasized individual vision; later, many stressed social and communal values. Neither attitude was entirely in keeping with the character of folk art. The nature of the folk community had been changing since the mid-nineteenth century; by the turn of the century, the definition of "folk art" was blurred by the growth of professionally guided *kustar'* industries, and by the vitality of an expanding urban popular culture. Perhaps the concept of a genuine folk art was no longer valid, as Bilibin had concluded. After the Revolution, the "folk" changed more completely than Bilibin could have anticipated. The roles of fine and applied art in society also changed radically, and these very changes opened up new possibilities for the development of folk arts from within the communities of peasant and town artisans, and for traditional images and decorative forms to take on new significance.[42]

Reshaping Folk Art
in the Soviet Era

Peasant art is the healthy blood of the *kustar'* industry.
—Vasilii Voronov, 1925[1]

Decorative and applied folk art, an inalienable part of Soviet Socialist
culture, exerts an active influence on the shaping of the people's
artistic tastes, enriches professional art and the possibilities of
industrial design.
—Central Committee of the Communist Party of the Soviet Union, 1975[2]

Architecture and the applied arts were essential tools for
restructuring society in the early Soviet period, as they
had been for Peter the Great's efforts to transform Russian
culture. Familiar and practical forms, textiles, tableware, furniture, and *lubok*-
like posters were ideal vehicles for disseminating new political concepts and
positive images of workers and peasants. In contrast to previous revivals and
adaptations of folk art, with their concentration on personal perceptions and
styles, the Soviet applications of folk art stressed social and community
values.

Celebrations expressing the popular euphoria of the February and October revolutions of 1917 were remarkably close to folk ritual in form and
essence.[3] The May Day festivities of 1918 in Petrograd seemed to have the
carnival atmosphere of Maslenitsa revels, with dancing, street performances,
torchlight parades, fireworks, and bright ribbons and garlands decorating

ships in the Neva River. Speeches, concerts, and public pageantry recalled the Russian Orthodox liturgy. Although belief in the Communist International was supposed to replace religion and parochial superstition, in effect the early May Day celebrations called upon both pagan and Christian traditions of participatory ritual. Many forms of celebration, commemoration, and propaganda—mass pageants and reenactments of revolutionary events, films, songs, banners, posters, temporary and permanent decorations for city squares, books, clothing, and even "fine" arts—repeated forms and imagery of nineteenth-century peasant art, seasonal rituals, and urban popular entertainment.

In addition to reenactments of the events, the Bolsheviks planned permanent monuments to record and symbolize the Revolution. Lenin's scheme of monumental propaganda included inscribed plaques and sculptures depicting revolutionary heroes or symbolizing Communist ideals. Under the supervision of Anatolii Lunacharskii, People's Commissar of Enlightenment, fifty or sixty monuments were erected, many in the temporary medium of plaster.[4] More successful in communicating the ideas of the Revolution were the more immediate and experiental forms such as parades, floats, pageants, posters, films, and stories. By the time the anniversary of the October Revolution was celebrated, November 7, 1918, a vocabulary of ritual was in place.[5] It included such concrete symbols as the worker's hammer and peasant's sickle, and the more abstract forms of spotlights, red bunting, and futuristic designs evoking the striving and utopian ambitions of the new state. But new "proletarian" art forms were not enough to substantiate the legitimacy of the new government. This required the reconstruction of an identifiable Russian heritage.

Art programs instituted during the early years of Communism were based on the theory that art should be given to the masses as a "legacy" and as a powerful tool to be used in the creation of a new social order.[6] The association of folk art with communal values was underlined by Aleksandr Bogdanov's promotion of a "conscious realization of collectivism," through "the direct collaboration of many people, even of the masses."[7] This approach had the virtue of rejecting the elitism, intellectualism, and imperialism of the nineteenth-century art establishment—a major consideration when iconoclasm was an agent of the political revolution.

The despoiling of tsarist monuments was a needed catharsis for the proletariat, just as vandalizing and burning manor houses was an outlet and symbol of revenge for the aroused peasantry.[8] However, the culture of the past, of the court, the bourgeoisie, and the church, included meaningful national symbols that had to be saved or replaced. A Commission for the Preservation of Monuments and Antiquities was organized immediately after the revolution; the Military Revolutionary Committee made Malevich commissar in charge of the Kremlin monuments; others were responsible for turning former imperial palaces into museums for the people, preserving buildings of historical interest in the cities and provinces, and registering private collections of art. The artists and scholars involved in this commission and in various art education programs had the difficult task of preserving the genuine monuments of the people's cultural heritage, while ridding them of hated tsarist and capitalist references.

Igor Grabar', an artist and art historian from the "World of Art" group and new director of the Tretiakov Gallery, headed the Commission for the Preservation of Artistic Treasures in 1919. In his pamphlet *Why We Must Preserve and Collect the Treasures of Art and Antiquity*, Grabar' explained that what made a nation unique and distinct from others was its cultural legacy.[9] Even the "trifles of everyday life" inherited from the past gave a picture of the habits, tastes, and opinions of our ancestors and, like works of fine art, they should be preserved. Grabar' attempted not only to convince local leaders of the need for emergency measures in the face of widespread vandalism, but also to instruct them on how to collect, store, and register the objects; the pamphlet provided sample inventory forms to be sent to the central commission.[10]

Lunacharskii planned to develop mass culture by supporting "the existing and emergent workers' and peasants' studios, which are seeking new paths within the visual arts, music, the theater, and literature," by opening workers' departments in institutions of art education, and "by introducing art into everyday life and into industrial production at large."[11] Although Lunacharskii purposely linked peasants' and workers' cultures in order to emphasize one of the goals of Communism, these were still different spheres. Aiding their development often required different measures, just as propaganda directed at the peasantry and the urban proletariat utilized distinct idioms. The nature of professional artists' involvement also varied, ranging from designing clothing, clubs, entertainment, and propaganda for "the people," to teaching and supervising in schools and artels for traditional peasant crafts, to conducting research and theoretical work in the field of "folk" and "popular" art.

Lunacharskii understood better than most politicians the connections between the neoprimitivists' and futurists' rejection of elitist "fine" art and the constructivists' work with new materials and forms to bring art into the framework of daily life. He saw the potential of these energetic forces for Narkompros (the People's Commissariat of Enlightenment) and wrote that their "dynamism and methods of collective creative work . . . certainly stand in some sort of relationship to what the proletariat may create in the artistic field."[12] Lunacharskii's enthusiasm waned as he realized that the radical styles of the "leftist" artists were unacceptable to the "proletariat and peasantry."[13]

Folk art motifs and design principles sometimes proved more useful than abstract forms for propaganda purposes. Window posters for the Russian Telegraph Agency (ROSTA) were intended to be viewed by large groups, because a paper shortage made large editions of posters or notices impossible to produce. Designed by Vladimir Maiakovskii, Mikhail Cheremnykh, and Vladimir

Lebedev among others, the posters employed toylike figures, compositions based on *lubki,* and simplified stereotypes of bloated capitalists and *bogatyri* in Red Army uniforms to make their exhortations clear and vivid. Lebedev adapted the typical composition of a Gorodets distaff for a poster with two main scenes separated by a band of letters in place of geometric designs (fig. 18.1). The upper part, showing a stout bourgeois in a carriage above a row of bowing peasants, corresponded to the printed message "Peasants, if you don't want to feed the landlords . . ." while below, a peasant leading a horse with a cart full of food showed the conclusion: "feed the men at the front, who are defending your land and freedom."[14] Aleksei Radakov's poster *The Illiterate Is like a Blind Man,* Elizaveta Kruglikova's *Women! Learn Your Letters!* and Aleksandr Apsit's *Organize Reading Rooms* (fig. 18.2) all focused on peasants and included familiar details of costume and setting. Radakov's quoted folk art style, with the *lubok*-like peasant stepping off the edge of a cliff, and a border of red and black zigzags like those separating sections of a painted distaff.[15]

Even "agitation" trains and steamboats, the most modern vehicles for propaganda and often futuristic in their decor, were sometimes toned down to appeal to peasant taste by means of floral motifs borrowed from distaffs and embroidery.[16] Peasants were harder to reach than urban workers, not only because of physical distances separating villages, but because many Communist practices were alien to rural social and familial customs.[17] Familiar styles were intended to make the pro-

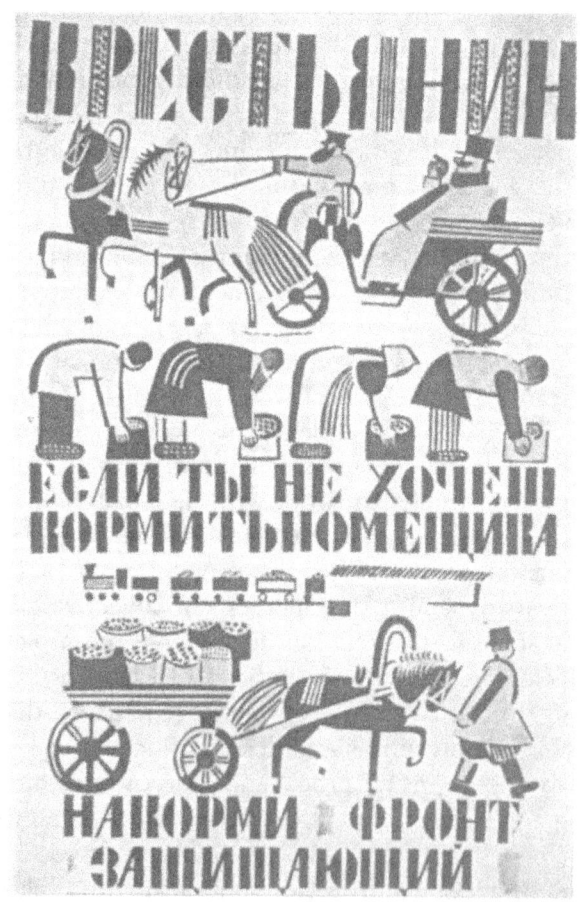

FIG. 18.1 Vladimir Lebedev, ROSTA poster. 1920.

paganda accessible and acceptable. An additional reason for the frequency of "folk" motifs was the quest for legitimacy and "Russianness" or *narodnost,*' the quality of belonging to "the people."

When the peasantry and proletariat proved less responsive to new art forms than planners had hoped, the alternative was to create a proletarian culture as if from the grassroots through artistic education. Modern agencies and acronyms, IZO (Department of Fine Arts), SVOMAS (Free Art Studios), VKhUTEMAS (Higher State Artistic Technical Studios), and INKhUK (Institute of Artistic Culture), replaced such reminders of tsarist, aristocratic, or mercantile patronage as Imperial Academy of Fine Arts or Stroganov School. The Stieglitz School of Technical Drawing became the State Labor Training Workshops for the Decorative Arts in 1918. Most Soviet educational programs were adaptations of practices already employed in the late nineteenth and early twentieth centuries to improve training in the industrial and applied arts.

According to Lunacharskii, art education had two goals: "One is to introduce people to art as widely as possible, the other is to bring to the fore men and women and whole communities capable of conveying popular sentiment through an artistic medium."[18] The amateur art movement was part of the effort to develop proletarian art. As early as 1918, free schools and art studios were opened to peasants and workers who wished to develop their skills with the help of professional artists. Cadres of amateurs took part in decorating clubs, factories, and propaganda trains. The Petrograd Palace of Arts (the former Winter Palace) held a joint exhibit of amateur and professional

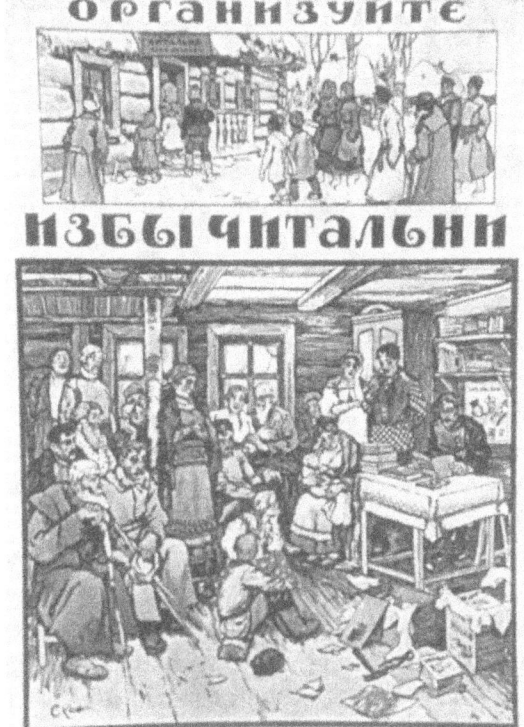

FIG. 18.2 Aleksandr Apsit, "Organize Reading Rooms." 1919.

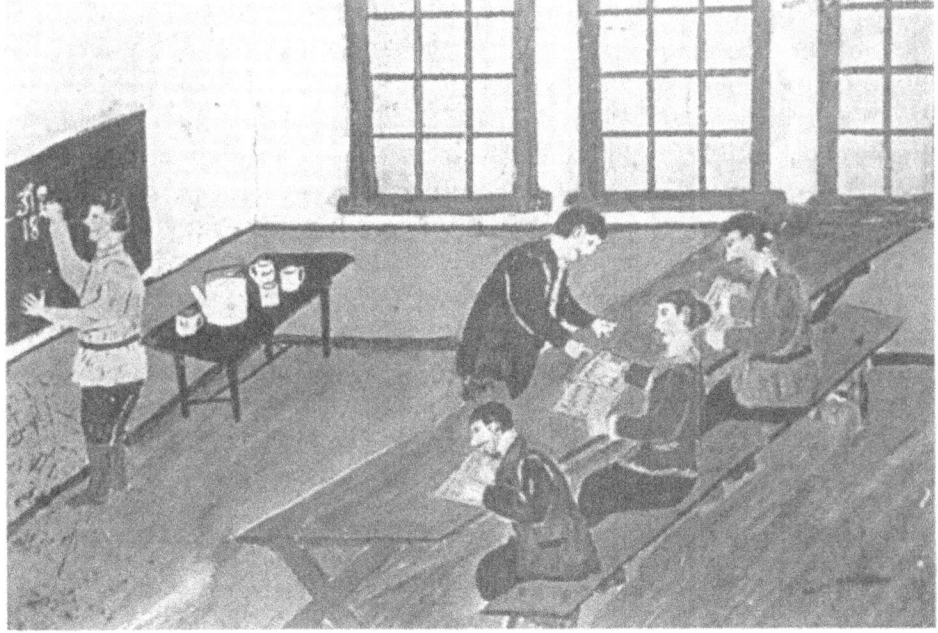

FIG. 18.3   A. Eremin, *Adult Literacy
School*. Oil on canvas. 1931. Extramural
People's University of Art, Moscow.

artists in 1919, and during the next two decades, trade unions and clubs
sponsored numerous amateur art societies, traveling picture galleries,
classes, and exhibitions.

Working with odd scraps of canvas and cardboard, beginning artists often
depicted scenes in factories, in adult literacy classes, and on collective farms;
some imitated reproductions of well-known realist genre scenes, or emulated
the romantic landscapes and flower pictures of upper-class decor.[19] In contrast
to serf artists or folk artists trained in academic conventions of representation
and ornamentation, amateur painters worked empirically, devoting attention
to placement of figures and objects and to details of costumes, furnishings,
and landscape. For example, A. Eremin's *Adult Literacy School* of 1931 (fig. 18.3)
shows a large classroom with three windows and a table with a teapot and
four cups in one corner, a man in a peasant shirt and boots doing an arithme-
tic problem at the blackboard, and a man in suit and tie instructing three
peasants, two men and a woman, seated at a long table with their reading
exercise books. M. Utkin's *Dubrovskii Collective Farm* of the same year (fig. 18.4)
shows a large field of wheat filling most of the picture; in the foreground, a

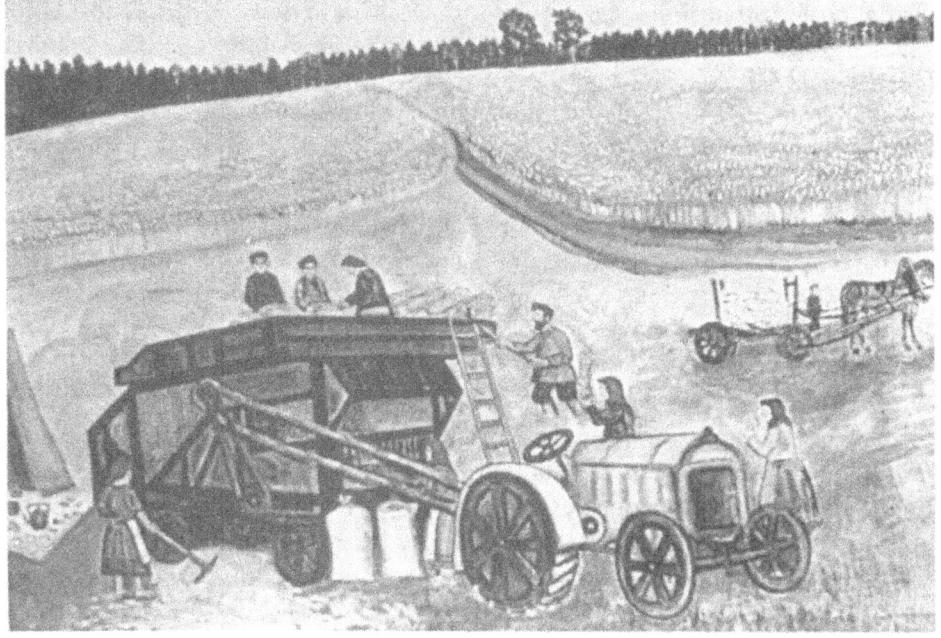

FIG. 18.4   M. Utkin, *Dubrovskii Collective Farm.* Oil on canvas. 1931. Extramural People's University of Art, Moscow.

harvesting scene around a tractor and thresher, with five women and three men raking and pitching the grain; a smaller man and a horse in the distance; and a tent with tea things at the left edge of the scene. Both pictures describe particular activities; they do not establish mood or emphasize the harmonious balance between peasant life and the natural world so important for Venetsianov and his followers a century earlier. These paintings, and undoubtedly many lost works, show genre motifs that appeared in nineteenth-century painting on distaffs and boxes from the Northern Dvina and Gorodets areas, scenes of daily life familiar to the artists. Though without the symbolic and decorative elements of traditional folk art, they display a recognizable folk esthetic.

Preserving the "naiveté" of amateur artists was not an established policy everywhere, but it was a goal in some of the best free studios. At the Krupskaia Central House of Popular Creative Art, founded in Moscow in 1934 and later called the Extramural People's University of Art, instructors encouraged students to try new techniques but did not teach rules of composition or representation. Many professionals understood the value of retaining and developing local art traditions; they wanted to avoid earlier mistakes in "improving" folk and *kustar'* art with standardized "Russian" designs. Some debated whether amateurs should be taught at all, but by the 1930s there was general agreement that amateur work in all media could absorb and utilize technical instruction along with influences from contemporary culture, posters, films, illustrated magazines, and fine art.[20] The first All-Russian Exhibition of Collective Farmer Amateur Art opened in Moscow in 1935, with 657 works in all media by 214 amateur artists from all over the Russian federation, including areas of the far north previously unexposed to easel painting. In 1937, amateur paintings were sent to the Paris World's Fair, where a self-taught painter from the Urals won a Grand Prize.[21]

In the area of folk art, continuation and adaptation of earlier approaches to reviving and supporting the folk and *kustar'* arts prevailed, without any major change of policy. Between about 1902 and 1910, approximately one hundred schools staffed by professional artists offered training in specialized crafts and applied arts to peasants and workers throughout Russia. The revival of local craft production—lacquered tableware in Khokhloma, woven carpets in Kursk, carved bone and tusk in Kholmogory, jewelry in Rostov and Krasnoe Selo, and carved wooden toys in Gorodets, Bogorodskoe, and Sergiev-Posad—begun in the prerevolutionary period, continued under Soviet sponsorship. As many as 40,000 people were involved in folk and applied arts projects in a given year between 1917 and 1930.[22] In the early 1920s, probably over 400,000 *kustari* were enrolled in government-sponsored unions and artels.[23]

The late-nineteenth-century trend toward centralizing regional craft production continued after the Revolution. Lenin signed a decree, "On Measures to Assist the *Kustar'* Industries," in April 1919, calling for the centralization of regional *kustar'* industries under the authority of Narkompros, and the mobilization of professional artists to support *kustar'* development.[24] By the end of that year, there were seven major state workshops for fabric weaving and printing, woodworking, lacemaking, stonecutting, and other arts; eight regional schools and workshops, in Viatka, Pskov, Smolensk, Ivanovo-Voznesensk, Mstera, Petrozavodsk, and other towns, each with a regional specialization; and several district workshops, some still being established. Competitions, exhibitions, and courses were organized "to aid in propagandizing" the crafts and to establish them on a sound economic footing.[25] Later documents recorded information on artists whose works were exhibited and sold at international exhibitions in Venice, Paris, Milan, Leipzig, Frankfurt, Prague, and Stockholm.[26] In the early 1930s, a firm called Eksportnabivtkan', specializing in hand-printed *naboika* fabric, was so well run and produced fabric of such high quality that it earned some eighteen million rubles in foreign sales.[27] These international contacts were important for the Soviet economy during the difficult years of the Civil War and the New Economic Policy.

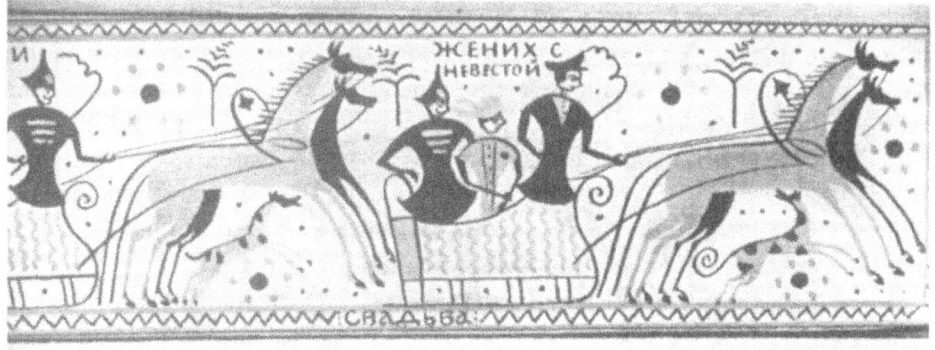

FIG. 18.5 V. I. Golitsyn, *Wedding Ride.* Panel, wood painted in Mezen' style. 1920s. MNI.

In remote areas of Arkhangel'sk and Vologda provinces, the political revolution scarcely affected local traditions, but economic changes were more disruptive. Widespread access to manufactured goods, especially textiles, meant less work for weavers, dyers, and makers of printing blocks and distaffs. Scholars and planning commissions sought alternative directions for displaced specializations; artists also found solutions for themselves. Some artists were able to adapt traditional techniques and favorite decorative motifs to other kinds of objects: for instance, Gorodets distaff painters Lebedev and Mazin became known for panels depicting scenes of village life; painter V. I. Golitsyn used a variety of regional styles, including that of Mezen' River distaffs, for ornamental panels to be sold at markets (fig. 18.5).[28] Abramtsevo was "reorganized" and designated a "central workshop" under Narkompros in 1919; according to a government survey, forty carvers and joiners from neighboring villages worked there, and furniture production showed "strong development."[29]

The woodcarving and toymaking enterprises of Sergiev-Posad (renamed Zagorsk after the Revolution), Semenovo, and Bogorodskoe flourished, with cadres of experienced peasant masters, professional artists, and talented pupils. A large portion of their production followed traditional forms, probably because these styles were already successful with buyers abroad, and one of the main concerns was to keep the *kustar'* industries on a sound economic footing. The museum of folk art established in 1920 in the Trinity Monastery, the Zagorsk (Sergiev-Posad) State History and Art Museum-Preserve, was to serve as a repository of models for woodcarving workshops in the area. This region was subject to exhaustive statistical surveys of *kustar'* activity and other "light industries" both before and after the Revolution. In 1927, D. I. Vveden-

skii was able to identify changes in the *kustar'* population (such as the proportions of men and women or the numbers of peasants and townspeople
working in each craft), changes in the expenses and selling prices of various
articles, and even trends in preferences for specific materials and styles. In the
toymaking field, the range of materials and forms increased significantly between 1912 and 1927: carved and lathe-turned wooden toys and molded clay
figures were still numerically dominant, but there were also more toy musical
instruments, "soft" toys, and playthings of mixed media.[30]

The most impressive story of artists adapting local traditions to create a
new craft industry was that of the lacquer-painting collectives in the villages
of Palekh, Mstera, and Kholui in Vladimir Province. Icon painting, the specialty of the area, had developed under the influence of the Vladimir and
Suzdal' schools in the thirteenth century and of the Kremlin workshops in the
seventeenth century; by the mid-eighteenth century the three towns produced large quantities of cheap icons painted on basswood or printed on paper and expensive commissioned icons drawn in a miniaturist technique and
accented with gold.[31] Although the trade had slackened by the early twentieth century, 3,465 people in Mstera, the majority of the population, and comparable numbers in the other villages were engaged in icon making.[32]

After the Revolution, icon painters tried other crafts but without much
success until 1921, when an artist from Palekh, Ivan Golikov, visited the Kustar' Museum and saw lacquered papier-mâché boxes from Fedoskino. He told
his fellow artists about the boxes, and they tried applying icon-painting techniques, using egg-based tempera instead of oils, to lacquered surfaces. The
results were brilliant. Golikov had the inspiration of using the icon-painting
style to depict Russian fairytales, legends of the *bogatyri*, and other national
images in addition to motifs from rural life such as harvesting and dancing,
already familiar in decorative art.

The Palekh products were immediately successful. Golikov and his colleagues I. M. Bakanov, I. V. Markichev, N. M. Zinov'ev, and others formed a
craft collective, the Artel of Early Painting, in 1924. Former icon painters in
Kholui and Mstera also founded cooperatives, including the extremely productive Proletarian Art artel. The initiative was supported by Narkompros,
and Lunacharskii wrote in the introduction to the first scholarly book on lacquer painting that "the art of the Palekh craftsmen, far from being ruined, has
expanded, consolidated and [been] saved for the future."[33]

Stylistically close to seventeenth-century icons and manuscript miniatures, the lacquer paintings of the 1920s and 1930s and later also reflected
current events. An artist might paint a scene from the epic "Tale of Igor's
Campaign," a folktale recounted by Afanas'ev or Pushkin, a celebration of
rural electrification, or an image of Lenin exhorting a crowd in front of a
factory. The latter subjects particularly pleased such luminaries of Soviet culture as Lunacharskii and Maksim Gor'kii, who received a painting of Lenin by

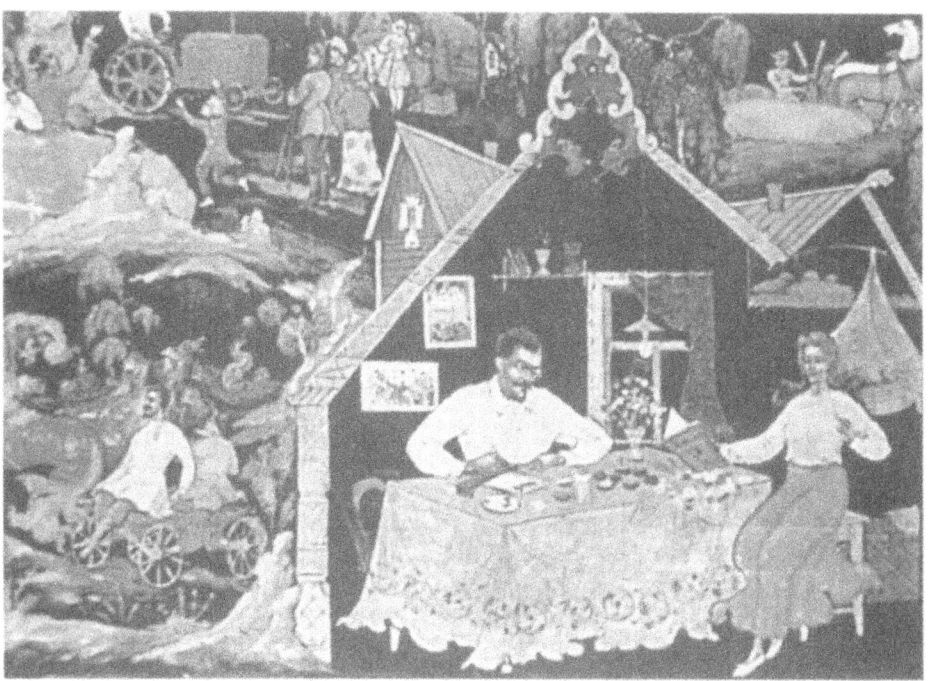

FIG. 18.7 M. Shemarov, *The Story of Ivan Golikov*. Tempera and lacquer on papier-mâché. Palekh, 1969. State Museum of Palekh Art.

Golikov as a gift from the inhabitants of Palekh.[34] One Palekh box made by a younger master depicted Ivan Golikov's inspired career (fig. 18.7). Genre scenes on lacquer boxes and plaques often included quotations from *lubki*. Fedoskino painter A. E. Kulikov's *Radio in the Village* (fig. 18.8), an interior scene with a *lubok* on the back wall, is strikingly akin to Larionov's work. The same artist's rendering of a popular subject, *Izba Reading Room*, shows men, women, and children in peasant dress reading newspapers and paperback books, and discussing them with eager expressions and vigorous gestures;[35] Kulikov may have based this scene on a poster similar to Apsit's *Organize Reading Rooms*, published in 1919.

Throughout the years of war and industrial growth, the delicate art of lacquer miniature painting remained remarkably resilient in its ability to convey contemporary propaganda and at the same time retain its traditional elegance. The high quality of the work, supported by four-year training programs, and the international recognition it received were part of its continuing success. This art form, based on religious and courtly styles but actually a Soviet phenomenon, testifies to the flexibility and resourcefulness of the artists and to the value of traditional formal idioms for the communication of new themes.

For the most part, newly revived crafts adhered to traditions of the media; professional artists served as staff of the Kustar' Museum, and as teachers and directors of collectives, but they rarely introduced their own interpretations, as had their predecessors at Abramtsevo and Talashkino. Occasionally, professional designers made timely changes in otherwise traditional images. For instance, *Chastushki (Rhymes)*, a three-piece appliqued and embroidered panel designed by B. I. Lange in 1925 (fig. 18.9), incorporated words from a popular song, and gave the suitor a peaked Red Army cap.[36] Traditional forms of textiles, woodcarving, painting on wood, lacquerware, tin trays, ceramic figures, and toys in all media readily absorbed new figures and themes of the Red Army, collective farms, dam building, and rural electrification.

The development of "revolutionary" imagery in porcelain, a luxury art, was a dialectic contradiction of the idealized images of peasants found in eighteenth- and early nineteenth-century pieces. Figurines of workers, women sewing red banners and distributing leaflets, chess pieces representing red and white armies, platters and plates depicting parades, commissars, workers, and the new Soviet heraldry conveyed remarkably clear messages. Although porcelain was definitely not a

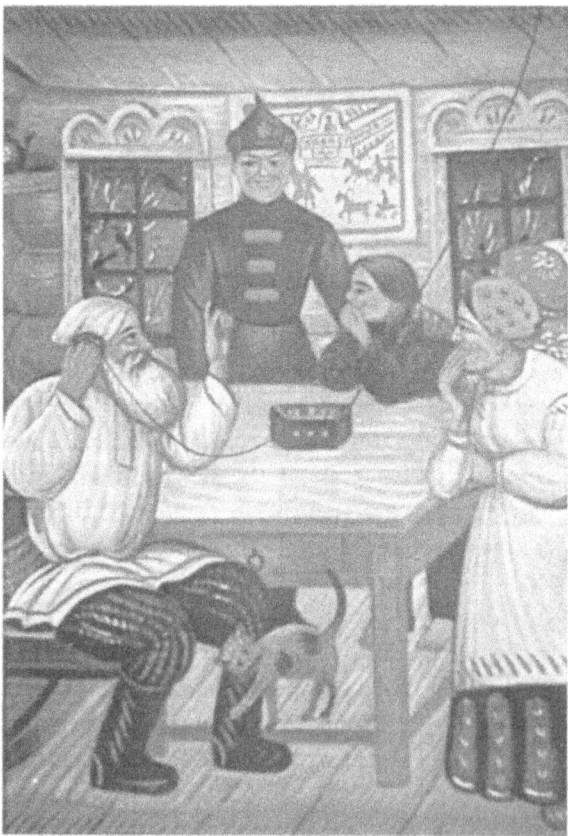

FIG. 18.8 A. Kulikov, *Radio in the Village*. Oil and lacquer on papier-mâché. Fedoskino, 1925. MNI.

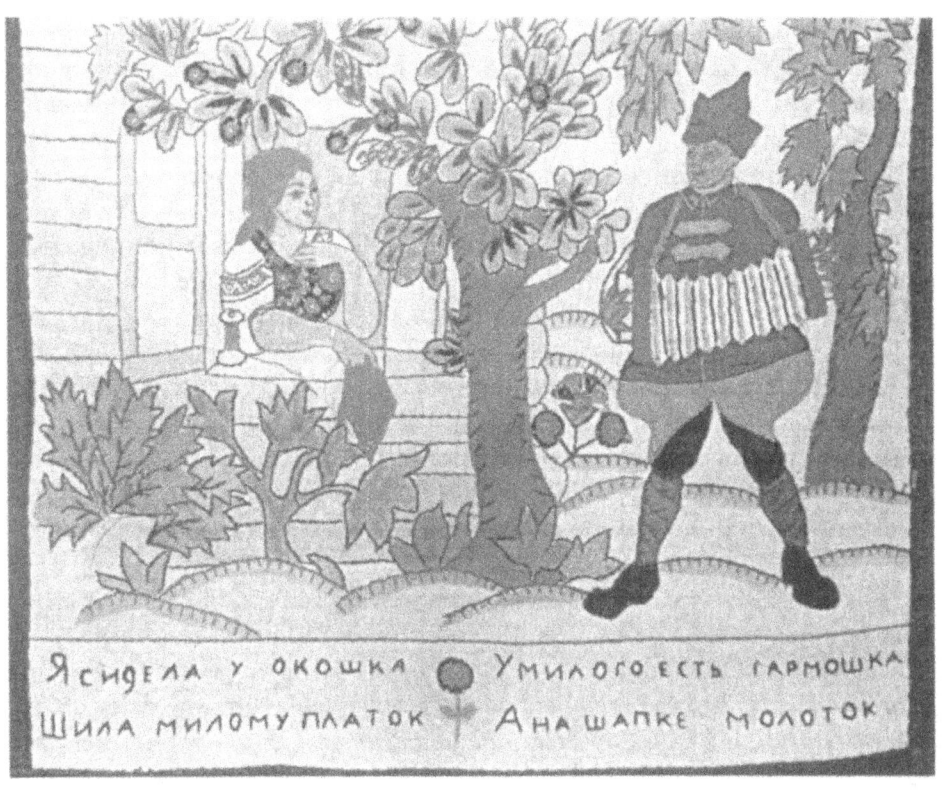

Я СИДЕЛА У ОКОШКА ● УМИЛОГО ЕСТЬ ГАРМОШКА
ШИЛА МИЛОМУ ПЛАТОК А НА ШАПКЕ МОЛОТОК

FIG. 18.9 E. I. Lange and B. N. Lange, *Chastushki.* Linen, calico, appliqué, and embroidery; one of three panels. Moscow, 1925. MNI.

folk or mass art form, artists readily adapted it to the requirements of the new state. Faced with a severe shortage of paper for posters, they were delighted to discover hundreds of unpainted blanks for plates in the storerooms of the former Imperial Porcelain Factory. Sergei Chekhonin, a painter and graphic artist, thought that these smooth, uniform surfaces would be ideal vehicles for propaganda, and he cleverly adapted the traditional designs to new imagery, replacing the imperial double-headed eagle with the hammer and sickle or a red star and decorating the borders with garlands of fruit and sheaves, farm tools, or industrial motifs instead of military trophies.[37] The project involved many leading artists of the avant-garde, including Vasilii Kandinskii, Kazimir Malevich, Liubov' Popova, Natan Al'tman, and Vladimir Lebedev, who introduced new styles resembling those of posters with *lubok*-like figures of soldiers, workers, and peasants, dynamic geometrical shapes framing slogans and commemorative dates, and even decorative forms based on folk painting and embroidery. One artist especially interested in folk motifs was Aleksandra Shchekotikhina-Pototskaia, who came from an Old Believer family and traveled widely in the north of Russia. Direct observations of village life and customs such as *posidelki* were reflected in "Wool Winders," produced in several versions, showing a young man and woman in festive garments smiling coyly as they wind yarn (fig. 18.10). Such a nostalgic image reassured viewers that traditional patterns of life would continue under the new regime.[38] Other artists adapted painting techniques of cheaper ceramic ware, using broad brushes to paint flowers and foliage like those on Gzhel' pottery, in order to make their works seem less elite, more appropriate to mass culture. However, propaganda porcelain was not intended for a mass market, and design and production were chiefly in the hands of professional artists; these examples represent purposeful quotation of traditional forms rather than genuine interaction between folk and professional artists.

Among artists who worked more directly with peasant and amateur artists were not only those who had been involved with the prerevolutionary *kustar'* revival, Nikolai Bartram, Natal'ia Davydova, Mariia F. Iakunchikova, and Sergei Maliutin, but also members of the avant-garde. Kazimir Malevich, for example, was the first to propose opening free art schools for workers and peasants, in October 1917; Ol'ga Rozanova headed the applied art section of IZO until her death in 1918. Textile and clothing design, directly tied to the requirements of daily life, attracted leading constructivist artists, including Aleksandra Ekster, Vladimir Tatlin, Aleksandr Rodchenko, and particularly Liubov' Popova and Varvara Stepanova, who worked in design and production at the First Textile Print Factory.[39] Sculptor Vera Mukhina and dress designer Nadezhda Lamanova were interested in combining traditional textile techniques such as embroidery and *naboika* with new designs appropriate to contemporary life. Some dresses featured "authentic" details embroidered by peasant women or specified using *kustar'*-made linen towels with embroidered borders (fig. 18.11). The designers published patterns which anyone could sew, in magazines such as *Iskusstvo v bytu* (*Art in Daily Life*).[40]

Lamanova worked out an organizational plan for a workshop of contemporary costume in 1919. To integrate theory and practice in the curriculum, she specifically considered the relationship of traditions, including folk art, to contemporary needs. "Folk art, its history and techniques, the importance of the Russian peasantry . . . as a primary source of decorative art in its various manifestations" was one of the "auxiliary disciplines" of the program.[41] She wrote about "how to adapt the style and character of folk costume to our everyday clothing," emphasizing the "versatility of folk costume," the "sensible" design for hard work and ease of embellishment for special occasions.[42] Throughout the 1920s, textile specialists and historians of art were conscious of the artisan traditions of textile weaving and printing, the appeal of *"lubok* motifs,"* and the need to preserve the best of these stylistic elements while introducing compatible modern designs.

Some of the most effective fabric designs employed repeated geometrical motifs like those of pattern weaving and embroidery, or the floral patterns of multicolor or indigo *naboika* (fig. 18.12). An enormous range existed even within the category of peasant motifs: from designs based on Bilibin's folktale illustrations to "realistic" harvest scenes, to modernistic renderings of tractors and railways. The goal of the professional artists was to develop patterns that were practical and "dynamic, variable and able to accommodate individuality."[43] Garments for the new Soviet body had to be modern, not nostalgic. However, as in any propaganda, the use of familiar forms in textiles and garments promoted a positive attitude toward change.

The ability to combine national traditions with modern functions was fundamental to early Soviet art policy. The period was one of extreme contrasts and surprising compromises; some of the very artists who urged the rejection of outworn traditions and their replacement with a wholly new visual and physical culture actually worked in formal "languages" that combined folk or popular idioms with modern functions.[44]

Considerations of national identity and relevance to contemporary life affected not only the applications of folk art styles to new purposes but also the policies regarding the study and collecting of folk art. Immediately after the Revo-

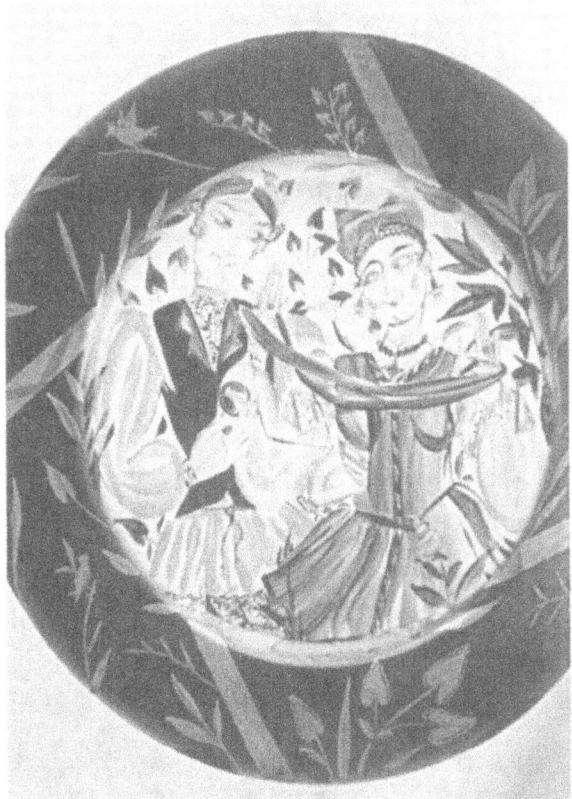

FIG. 18.10 Aleksandra Shchekotikhina-Pototskaia, *Wool Winders.* Porcelain plate. Petrograd, 1921. Private collection.

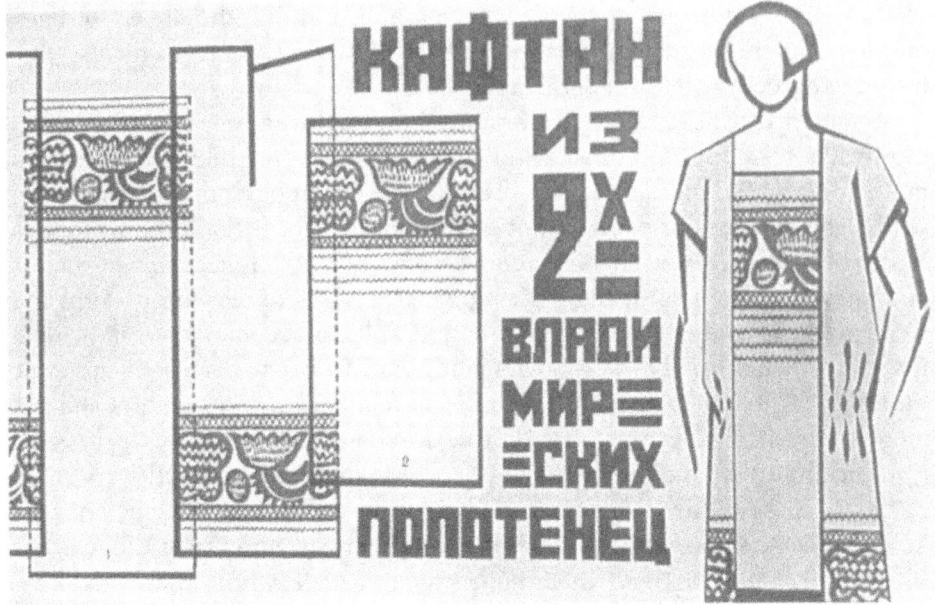

FIG. 18.11 Nadezhda Lamanova,
kaftan made from two Vladimir towels.
Design printed in *Iskusstvo v bytu* (1925).

lution, Grabar's Commission for the Preservation of Artistic Treasures
included folk art objects along with decorative arts within its purview. The
1920s and 1930s saw major expeditions and publications, some connected
with exhibitions of Russian folk art at the Historical Museum in Moscow in
1921, at the All-Union Exhibition of Arts and Handcrafts in 1923, and at
Soviet exhibits at the World's Fairs between 1925 and 1939.

The opening of the renovated Kustar' Museum in 1925 marked an important change in the treatment of folk art and in defining its role in contemporary life. In his introduction to the Museum guidebook, Vasilii Voronov
stated:

> The *kustar'* industry was and remains at the root of peasant art. Its further develop-
> ment under the new conditions of political and economic life must preserve these
> organic bonds and centuries of interwoven connections. Peasant art is the healthy
> blood of the *kustar'* industry.[45]

Voronov held that the characteristics of genuine *kustar'* art, originally
drawn from the "old way of life of the Russian peasantry," had become dis-

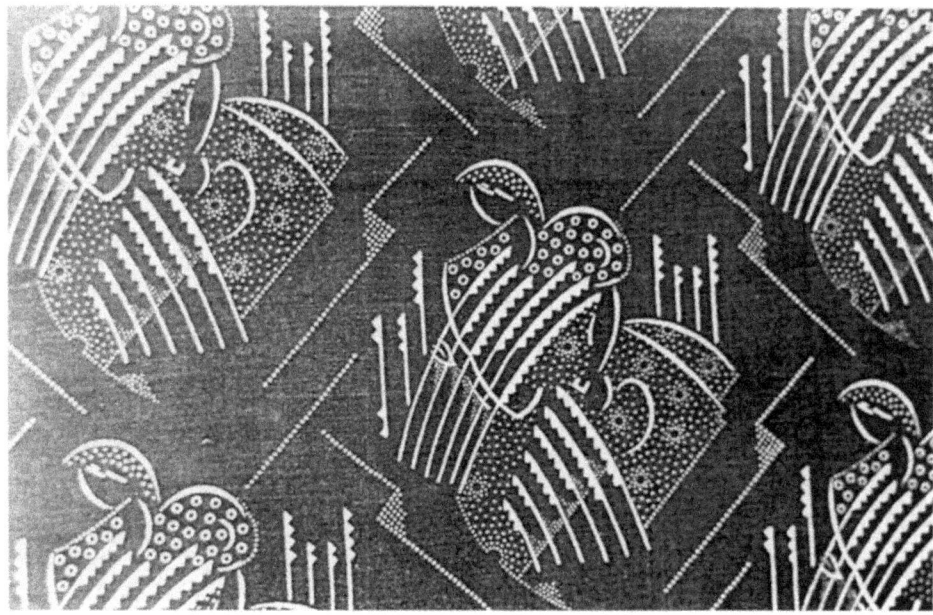

FIG. 18.12 Liubov' Silich,
"Harvesters" fabric. Indigo printed
indienne. Ivanovo, late 1920s or early
1930s. GIM.

torted by the demands of urban markets and, more seriously, by the involvement of professional artists in folk art "revival" schemes. He blamed the artists
at Abramtsevo and Talashkino for subjective, often incorrect interpretations
of folk art forms. He complained of the tendency to use *kustar'* and folk as
interchangeable categories, and denounced the exploitation of folk and *kustar'*
art for commercial motives.[46] Voronov's vehemence on these points arose
from his own background. His grandfather had been a serf, and Voronov grew
up in Moscow in a modest, servant-class family. Fond of drawing, he entered
the Stroganov School and graduated at age nineteen in 1906. To pursue new
interests in history and archeology, he attended Moscow University while
working as a drawing teacher; he began studying children's art and folk art
and was going on expeditions, collecting materials, and publishing on both
subjects between 1910 and 1915.[47] Having begun work in folk and applied art
at a time when the stylized forms of Russian *modern* were fashionable, Voronov
was both attracted and repelled by the invented forms. When he studied authentic materials systematically, he became convinced of the need to "recon-

struct the fabric of peasant life" by preserving genuine folk art and assisting living peasant masters.[48]

The permanent collections of the Kustar' Museum and the exhibitions Voronov organized there and at the Historical Museum provided examples and models to help *kustar'* artists combat the "deformation" of traditional forms.[49] Voronov and other specialists tried to clarify the meanings of *kustar'*, folk, and peasant art, after a long period in which the distinctions had been ignored by artists and scholars alike. Voronov introduced the term "peasant art" into the scholarly discourse, because it was flexible enough to include regional variations, historical changes, and the continuing contacts among villages, markets, and towns characteristic of the peasant milieu. He explained his position in the 1921 exhibition "Russian Peasant Art" at the Historical Museum, and in his major book, *Peasant Art*, published in 1924. He believed that the meanings of "folk" and "peasant" were very close in Russian culture and that true folk art, both in its historical evolution from pagan times and in the present, was tied to the collective life of the people.[50] But he insisted that peasant artists always drew upon their perceptions of life around them. When the cultural environment changed, the "old peasant art" lost part of its vital connection to daily life. Rather than trying to turn back time and restore old forms and techniques, contemporary *kustari* should absorb "nourishment" from folk traditions and use them to develop further, always striving for integrity rather than imitation. For Voronov, the purpose of museum collections and scholarly studies was to support the "living connection between old peasant art and contemporary *kustar'* art industry."[51]

Much research before and just after the Revolution was devoted to finding examples of folk art and classifying them according to techniques and regional variations. Aleksandr Bobrinskii's finely illustrated book on peasant woodcarving, completed in 1911 and meant to serve as a guide in reviving traditional art forms, was one of the most important early studies of the subject.[52] Bilibin continued his researches in the north, and reported on local distaff carvers and their markets.[53] In the 1920s, several scholars investigated the entire complex of folk arts in certain regions: P. G. Istomin led expeditions to the Northern Dvina, S. Tomilov studied the folk art of the Mezen' and Pinega areas, and D. V. Prokop'ev worked in the Gorodets and Nizhnii Novgorod area of the Volga.[54] Studies of the arts of the non-Russian peoples of the Soviet Union also expanded in this period. The same decade saw the first methodical studies by V. Gorodtsov and others, examining ancient pagan beliefs and visual art forms as sources for forms and symbols in folk art.[55]

Following research of the 1920s that defined the major qualities of Russian folk art, emphasis shifted in the 1930s to potential values of folk art for pedagogy and social development. For example, Lunacharskii's preface to N. M. Tseretelli's important book on folk toys published in 1933 urged readers to use "a correct Marxist analysis" to obtain insights into social psychology, "into the class structure of the peasantry . . . the creators of these toys." Both he and the author stressed the need for more research into the "sociology of toys," the roles of the factory and cottage production, the interaction of peasants and bourgeois townspeople, and the importance of toys as models of behavior for children.[56] Equally important were practical measures to encourage the development of folk arts and to emphasize the contributions of national art forms to Soviet applied art and design. The title of a later theoretical study by Soviet folk art scholar Aleksandr Saltykov, *The Utilization of Folk Traditions in the Development of Soviet Applied Art*, summarized this approach.[57] In addition to gathering materials for the Kustar' Museum, the Historical Museum, and other repositories of folk arts, Voronov, Bakushinskii, and other scholars worked with folk masters to invigorate local arts, such as Khokhloma tableware, Palekh and Fedoskino lacquerware (fig. 18.13), Kholmogory bone-carving, Zhostovo tray painting (fig. 18.14), and Velikii Ustiug niello. At the same time, stimulus for folk art research came from professional artists' searches for "national" decorative principles to use in designing textiles, dishes, and furnishings, or in other technical and industrial applications. The

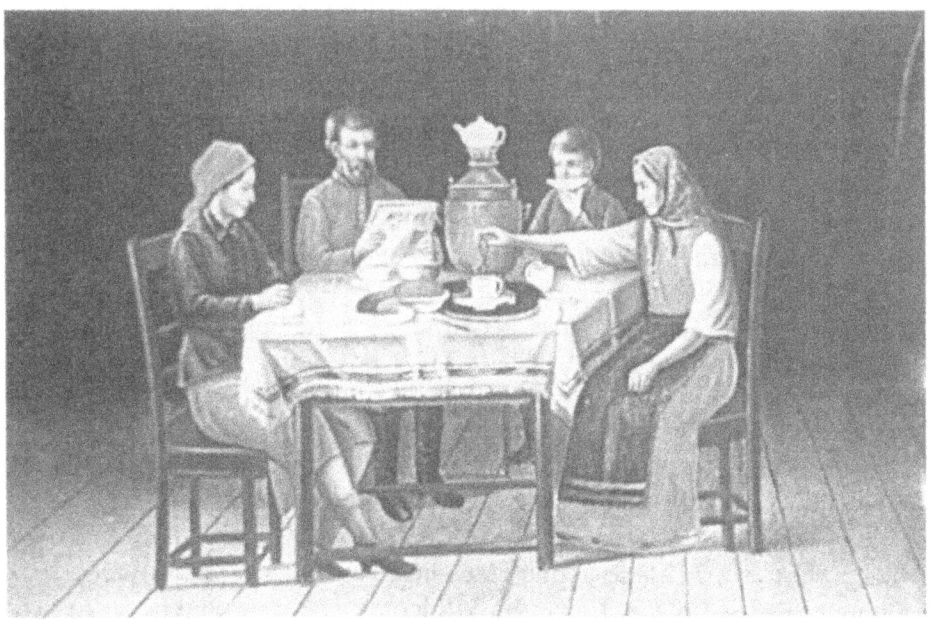

FIG. 18.13   I. Semenov, *Tea Drinking*. Oil and lacquer on papier-mâché. Fedoskino, 1934. MNI.

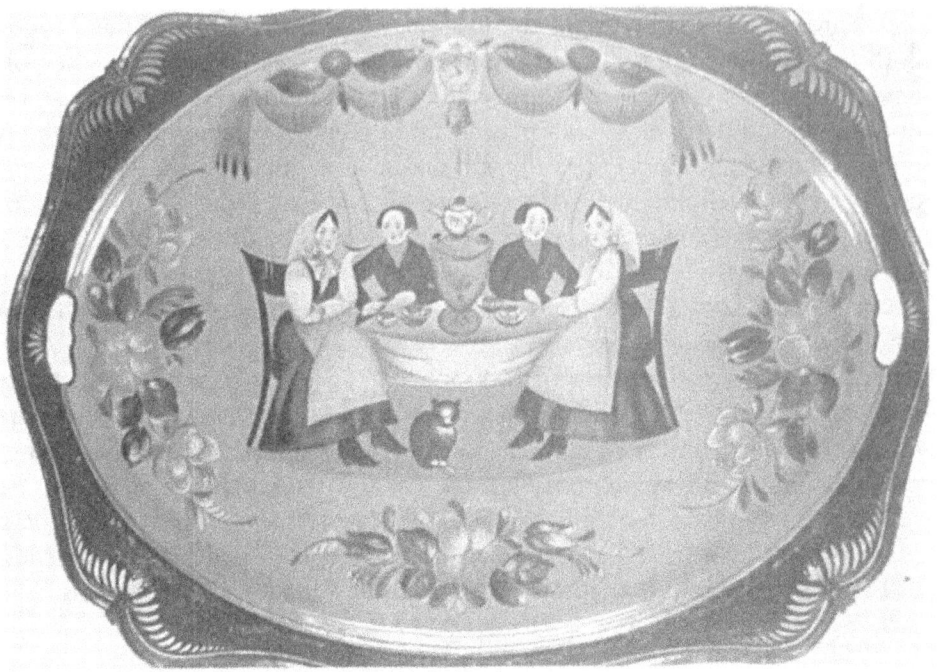

FIG. 18.14   A. Leznov, after K. Osipov, *Tea Drinking*. Painted tin tray. Zhostovo, 1931. MNI.

reorganization of the Museum of Folk Art and the establishment of the Research Institute for Decorative Arts in 1932 were part of this trend.[58]

Official documents of the 1930s not only defined goals such as achieving nationality in Soviet art, but also revealed serious problems with materials, physical facilities, and transport. For instance, an inquiry at the Stalin Industrial Collective concerning production of Khokhloma ware in the Semenov district pointed out that both the railroad and the Volga River were over forty-five kilometers distant, and there were no highways; even in 1932, horse carts were used to carry products to Gorodets or Nizhnii Novgorod. The population was almost ninety percent employed in Khokhloma painting, without any other industry and dependent on food brought in from outside the area; there were mature linden and pine trees needed for the industry, but within two years those within a thirty-kilometer radius would be exhausted.[59] Practical measures, including tighter organization of the artels and schools, helped in many cases, most notably in Khokhloma, in the Kholmogory and Tobol'sk ivory-carving artels, in Palekh, Mstera, and Kholui lacquer artels, in the production of enamel and painted metalwork in Zhostovo and Rostov, and in various woodworking enterprises at Abramtsevo-Kudrino, Sergiev-Posad, and Bogorodskoe.

During the 1930s and 1940s, while "intensive ideological and artistic restructuring" took place, the presence of artists from the older generation, those who had helped in the revitalization of the crafts under the *zemstvo* organizations, ensured, according to one authority, that "the best traditions of folk art never died."[60] Certain types of applied art, such as porcelain plates and vases made at the State Porcelain Factory to be displayed in Party offices and embassies abroad, were used to commemorate Stalin's military victories and vast building projects, just as movies, concerts, fiction, and other forms of popular culture were exploited. On a deeper level, Stalin's advisers tapped the Russian oral tradition of *bylini*, tales of legendary heroes recited by village storytellers; they commissioned genuine folksingers, who traditionally performed at weddings, funerals, and other village ceremonies, to make up new songs, dubbed *novini*, in honor of Stalin's feats.[61]

Visual forms of folk art were less subject to this kind of manipulation. The ideological requirements of Soviet Socialist Realism impinged tangentially on the types of folk art with figurative elements. For example, bone and ivory carvers began to carve human and animal figures in the round, and entire scenes from daily life, such as seal hunting or gathering outside a trading post with sleigh and reindeer.[62] Bogorodskoe carvers also represented contemporary genre scenes, such as the multifigured composition *Kolkhoz of Woodcarvers* of 1938. An imposing piece carved in 1948 by three Bogorodskoe masters, entitled *Friendship of the Peoples of the USSR*, came closest to exemplifying Stalinist esthetics with its tiered composition: three figures (a male worker, a soldier, and a woman farmer) on a pedestal embellished with the seals of the Soviet republics, and beneath them, around the base of the platform, smaller figures in national costumes with grain, fish, sheep, and other symbols of their republics' resources.[63]

Textiles reflected changing values in different ways. Soviet textile and fashion design still existed on two levels, for home consumption and for export. Some of the leading high-fashion designers of the late 1930s, including Elena Savkova, worked closely with the Scientific Research Institute of Art Industry to revive a "Russian style" dress with details in traditional embroidery and lace patterns.[64] For the mass market, the abstract or semi-abstract forms of stylized gears, tractors, airplane propellers, and factory chimneys, briefly popular in the 1920s, were largely replaced by floral motifs in the 1930s. Some textile patterns imitated traditional *naboika*, while others, such as the "Blackberry" printed linen from the artel Eksportnabivtkan', produced from 1934 to 1938,[65] resembled Khokhloma painting. These fabrics and dress patterns of fuller cut and softer lines than the austere constructivist designs suggested an appeal to more traditional, perhaps feminine, taste.

Images of peasant women (or collective farmworkers) in photographs, movies, posters, monumental mosaics and murals in public places, and easel paintings often included brightly printed calico dresses and scarves. Healthy bodies, plentiful food, colorful garments, bright sunlight, and happy faces also supported the optimistic propaganda of Socialist Realist depictions of holidays on the *kolkhoz*, for example by Arkadii Plastov and Sergei Gerasimov in 1937; Plastov's work highlighted a portrait of Stalin with red banners bearing the slogan "Life has become better, life has become happier!"[66] The principle of reassuring the public through familiar images, employed in the early Communist years, still seemed useful for supporting, and disguising the harsh consequences of, Stalin's agricultural policies. Similarly, paintings of the World War II and immediate postwar period, such as Sergei Gerasimov's *Mother of a Partisan* (1943) and Tat'iana Iablonskaia's *Bread* (1949), included authentic details of peasant dress to reinforce the theme of the steadfast strength of Russian peasant women.[67]

War imagery appeared in a different guise in folk and applied art. The repertoires of lacquered boxes and carved bone plaques expanded to include partisan brigades galloping across battlefields. More typical reflections of the wartime spirit were scenes of Aleksandr Nevskii fighting the Germans on a lacquered writing set and ivory statuettes of the seventeenth-century hero Ivan Susanin,[68] images also revived in opera and film in this period. Printed fabric and lace tablecloths and hangings were decorated with images of *bogatyri* or with modern soldiers, tanks, and airplanes. Bogorodskoe toys with moving parts often depicted mounted soldiers, tanks, and other military subjects. Materials were scarce during the war, and many craftsmen were sent to the front. Although a government decree of 1942 released many masters from service in order to maintain at least a minimal level of production in the crafts artels, few could achieve a normal standard until the end of the war.[69]

During the postwar years, from the late 1940s through the 1960s, cultural authorities tried to bring folk artists fully into the framework of industrial production, urging overfulfillment of production goals in keeping with the Stakhanovite mentality of the period.[70] *Kustar'* work in craft collectives was equated with mere execution rather than creation of forms. Aleksandr Saltykov spoke against this system, asserting that the "most valuable" components of the art industry were not the products but the "people, masters and artists, the conservators of wonderful traditions."[71] A new generation of scholars, Viktor Vasilenko, Mikhail Zvantsev, Ol'ga Kruglova, and Serafima Zhegalova, among others, continued regional studies, through ethnographic and collecting expeditions, and also pursued research based on archeological material and folklore and linguistic studies. Less concerned than their predecessors with finding "national" styles suitable for contemporary application, most scholars concentrated on specific media or types of folk art, such as architectural woodcarving, carved and painted distaffs and utensils, or textiles.

Broadly based studies of the semantic structures and symbolic languages of folk art, incorporating comparative material from other cultures, rare before the war, became increasingly important. At the same time theoretical and practical discussions of the problems of developing folk arts in the modern world were aired at regional and national conferences.[72] Study of folk art as a branch of art history and development of practical programs to train artists and promote regional folk arts were closely coordinated in the former Soviet Union.

In 1975, the Central Committee of the Communist Party issued a decree, recalling those of the early Soviet period, declaring that folk art was an "inalienable part" of Soviet culture. The decree required the state to "protect folk masters and create the best possible working conditions for them" and called for all-union exhibitions and conferences every five years to survey the current work of "masters of folk art industries" and examine problems of theory, production, and training in folk art.[73] The first exhibition and conference, held in Moscow in 1979/80, covered the entire geographical extent of the Soviet Union, and included both forms traditional to various regions and new specializations. Speakers discussed such issues as creating "traditions" in contemporary folk art; evaluated recent expeditions to collect work and interview artists; described progress in regional folk art industries; surveyed work in various media; and listed problems, such as the organization of workshops, economic conditions in the villages, and quality of production, that should be addressed by regional or national authorities.[74]

The next all-union exhibition and conference, in 1990, entitled "Folk Art and Contemporary Culture: Problems of Preservation and Development of Tradition," was coordinated with an exhibition (fig. 18.15) and introduced a definite theme and agenda: the urgent need to conserve the natural and social "ecologies" within which folk arts evolved and should continue to develop.[75] Several presenters abandoned the time-honored manner of enumerating achievements and directed attention to issues. For example, a report on folk art production in Arkhangel'sk emphasized the "confrontational interaction" of village and urban cultures; the discussion of daily life and contemporary folk art in Belarus' dealt with the effects of radiation from the Chernobyl disaster.[76] Although the conference was mandated by government decree and sponsored by the Ministry of Culture and other high-level agencies, it did not present an overly optimistic picture of progress. More than one participant bemoaned the poor quality of production in his or her craft and the rapid growth of touristic kitsch.

Some of the problems raised at the conferences, now occupying folk art scholars, administrators of regional folk arts industries, and practitioners of various forms of folk art, were inherited from the folk and *kustar'* revival movements of the late nineteenth century, and from the reorganization of crafts industries in the early Soviet period. Extracting folk art forms, images, and patterns from their natural settings, even with laudable intentions, caused distortion and denaturing of the art, as Voronov and other scholars had realized in the 1920s. The expansion of the souvenir industry (fig. 18.16) in the past thirty years exacerbated the problem. "Russian Souvenir" sections of department stores, foreign currency shops, and even temporary kiosks and tables of street vendors feature types of work thought to appeal to tourists; they rely heavily on predictable, imitative, and cute designs. The worst examples of Gzhel' figurines, *matreshka* dolls, Rostov enamel, and pseudo-Palekh containers are comparable to variety-show production numbers based loosely on folksongs. Some are well executed, but with no taste, the fault of poor designs by commercial artists; some pieces sold as "Palekh" or "Rostov" are Moscow products.[77] These abuses are serious, but they do not negate the quality of many crafts produced in workshops and homes under regular supervision in accordance with decrees on "folk art industries." The rampant commercialism and the presence of fakes and kitsch are external problems, but there are also real difficulties with the very process of organizing and protecting folk arts: the problem of "collectivization," identified by Aleksandr Kantsedikas and other scholars.[78]

In most of European Russia, folk arts have been organized or promoted by professionals for nearly a century, but in a few areas, such as the northern Caucasus, parts of Siberia, the Baltic, and the northern parts of Arkhangel'sk and Vologda provinces, some folk arts are still practiced as do-

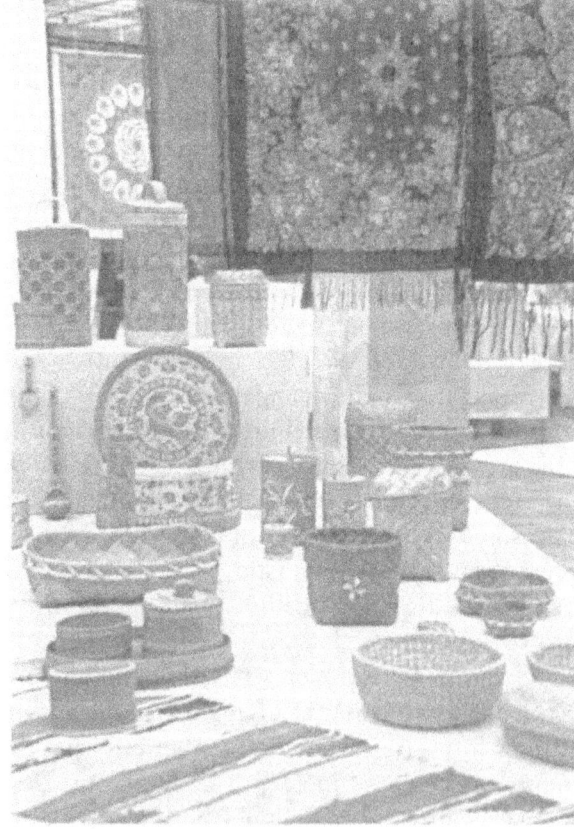

FIG. 18.15 Central and north Russian crafts at "Folk Art and Contemporary Culture" exhibition, Academy of Arts, Moscow, 1990.

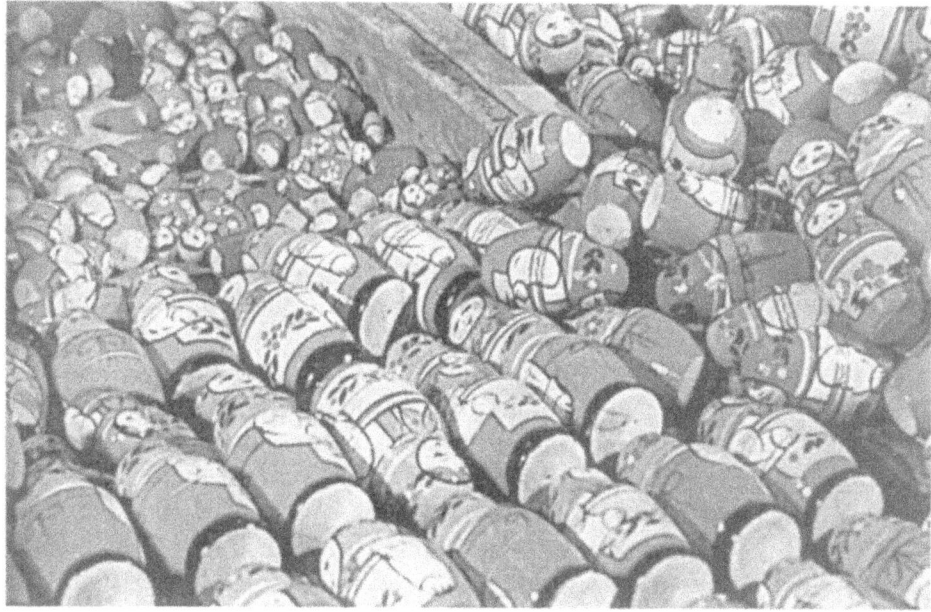

FIG. 18.16 *Matreshka* dolls ready for assembly at Sergiev-Posad Toy Factory, 1980s.

mestic work, for household use or for local markets. Increased attention to the individuality of folk art masters in recent years, and the use of a new vocabulary in conferences and publications, replacing *kustar'* with *master* or *khudozhnik* ("artist"), has already had some effect.[79]

Within each branch of folk art, contemporary practitioners are highly conscious of the legacy of the artists who founded or rejuvenated local craft industries: Mikhail Chirkov, founder of the Northern Niello artel in Velikii Ustiug in the 1920s; Andrei Chushkin, who worked with Nikolai Bartram at Bogorodskoe and carved peasant figures engaged in common occupations; and Ivan Golikov, the founder of the Palekh painting artel. In many places, folk masters brought new energy to traditions still preserved in remote areas, such as pattern weaving in villages on the Pinega River in northern Arkhangel'sk Province. Anastasiia Beliaeva, born after the Revolution, learned weaving techniques and the accompanying songs from her mother; she urged other local weavers and several novices to join an informal collective. The women weave geometrical borders for towels used in weddings and funerals and draped around family photographs; they regularly perform as a folk chorus, wearing local costumes.[80]

PRESERVATION AND REVIVAL OF RUSSIAN FOLK ART

Some exceptional artists created new local traditions. Birch-bark carver Martyn Fatianov, with his own family and the large Petukhov family, introduced the Shemogodsk crafts of plaited birch-bark baskets and "birch-bark lace" containers to the Arkhangel'sk and Mezen' River area, so that now two or three masters of birch-bark carving work in each of several villages.[81] Ul'iana Babkina of Kargopol', born in 1888 in Grinevo, a small village where many peasant families worked as potters or practiced traditional forms of embroidery, pattern weaving, and woodworking, modeled clay toys as a child. She later invented new figures, painted them with tempera and gouache, and made up stories to go with them, sometimes elaborating on tales of the *bogatyri* and Polkan the centaur.[82] Babkina's figures intrigued local children, and some of them learned how to model clay and became masters themselves. The craft spread from Grinevo to other villages around Kargopol'. Babkina was awarded the title "Hereditary Master of Kargopol' Toys" before her death in 1977. Though most of her original students had died by the 1980s, the "Kargopol' Toys" enterprise is still flourishing with their former pupils, Valentin Shevelev and other young masters. Countless other folk masters working in established local art forms or developing new specialties could be mentioned. Many are more widely known than their predecessors, and have more direct contacts with other artists, with folk art scholars, and with the public. One especially fertile type of contact is quite recent: art students from institutes in Moscow, St. Petersburg, and other cities who want to learn folk art styles and techniques have been sent for periods of apprenticeship or internship to villages in Arkhangel'sk and Vologda provinces, where local folk artists serve as their mentors.[83] Some folk artists were members of the Union of Artists and received recognition as "Honored People's Artists" from the Soviet government. Many take part in conferences and send works to national and international exhibitions. The majority live in small towns and villages. Though many work in artels, some have small home workshops: the weavers of Pinega use large looms in their *izby*; potters and makers of clay figures in Kargopol' and Viatka have ovens in their yards and display finished works on fenceposts in front of their houses.

Articles made by folk masters are no longer routinely used in the household, since they are too valuable to use for the tasks now done with the help of manufactured goods. But embroidered hangings and painted wooden dishes, like those described earlier in this book, appear for special occasions. Moreover, folk artists are free to use their creativity and skill for their own pleasure. Stepan Veselov, a master of Khokhloma painting, known for introducing stylized roosters and other birds into the traditional foliage ornament of the lacquered wooden dishes, was interviewed and photographed with some of his pieces in 1980. Posing for one picture, taken outdoors in a hayfield, he held a large wooden *kovsh* shaped like a waterbird, while his wife carried an ordinary galvanized bucket painted with large roosters in vigorous strokes of red, gold, and black, clearly the work of Veselov.[84] In a simple, un-self-conscious way, this artist found outlets for esthetic expression in his home.

Validity and integrity are still key themes in discussions of folk art by Russian scholars. Veselov's decorated bucket does not raise the issue, because it is not presented as "art." However, the artist's wish to embellish a household utensil, and his use of a familiar and natural skill to do so, seems entirely within the framework of folk art as a part of peasant life. Even some commercially motivated adaptations of traditional folk motifs or techniques — for example, embroidered borders on napkins or aprons, or breadboards painted in the styles of Borok or Gorodets — are reasonably consistent with the patterns of adjustment of regional art forms to economic changes experienced in the late nineteenth and early twentieth centuries. Recent changes in laws concerning personal and real property have encouraged many city dwellers to buy or build houses in rural villages, while many villagers are improving their dwellings. A substantial number of new houses are made of logs, cut and numbered for easy assembly; even those with concrete block foundations, plywood walls, and manufactured windows are embellished with bright paint and elaborate sawn *nalichniki* and other traditional features of peasant *izby* (fig. 18.17). The distinctive style of this small building boom clearly reflects rediscovered values.

Returning to some of the questions raised at the beginning of this book, we can consider what the preservation of traditional forms of folk art means in Russia. Do the images of the *sirin*, the *bogatyr'*, Mother Moist Earth, the Tree of Life, or the geometrical abstractions of natural forces, such as the rhomboid, circle, and zigzag, still have significance when artists no longer believe in these powers? The question raised by Voronov, Vasilenko, and other scholars has not yet been fully answered, and perhaps cannot be. For folk artists today, belief in pagan gods or in Christian saints may be less important than artistic conviction. In other words, the validity of a given form of folk art depends on the artists' confidence in the traditions of that form, understanding of the geographical and social setting in which it developed, and ability to work within the technical and stylistic requirements in a way that gives personal satisfaction. While the emphasis on a dialectic relationship between the "individual" and the "collective" in Soviet folk art theory is beginning to disappear,[85] the broader concept of cumulative originality within a local or regional art tradition is still a valid basis for contemporary development of folk art in Russia.

The study of folk art and the encouragement of local crafts industries from the late nineteenth century to the present were not discrete projects isolated from the rest of life. The deliberate revival of folk art forms and the use of folk and popular art as the basis for cultural revival were inevitable and natural, part of a pattern established centuries earlier by the Muscovite princes. The inherent conservatism of folk culture included the capacity to absorb a variety of influences—forms introduced by traders, portable art objects, or visiting artists; patterns and motifs taken from one source and adapted to fit another medium; events and personalities causing changes in the country's way of life—and flexibility to grow without losing its essential character.

At the beginning of the twentieth century, Bilibin expressed the concern that efforts to protect and revive Russian folk arts were doomed because folk culture had changed too much. "Folk art has ended. That means that the folk has stopped being the author of its own further development in design and handwork."[86] His concern was shared by Voronov and contemporaries in the 1920s, aware of social and economic changes brought by industrialization and Communism. It is shared by scholars today, facing changes in artistic perception and taste brought about by mass communication, by decades of state support for souvenir and crafts industries, by the abrupt loss of government patronage, and by recent attempts at Western-style capitalism. However, local folk traditions survive in many places, and folk masters and their pupils still occupy positions in their villages and cooperatives similar to those of their grandparents. Handmade articles are still used and displayed in ordinary households. Decoration offers esthetic nourishment, and periodic celebrations, whether religious, secular, or official in character, provide necessary spiritual release. Whether or not specific images communicate their original meanings, the continued presence of these forms in homes and, for artists, the processes of making utensils, textiles, toys, or other crafted items for personal use or for sale help to preserve a sense of identification with national culture.

The role of folk art studies and practices today is not the link to the distant past cherished by nationalist sentiment; nor is it the artistic and philanthropic mission envisioned by the Abramtsevo group, the liberating source enjoyed by the avant-garde neoprimitivists, or the building tool of mass culture advocated by the framers of early Soviet arts policies. The contemporary folk art industry embodies aspects of all these approaches, but it is based on the work and experiences of practicing folk artists. Russian folk art is still evolving.

Glossary

alkonost.	Mythical bird-woman, counterpart of *sirin*.
arshin.	Old Russian measurement, approximately 71.12 cm.
beregina.	Mythic creature, part fish, part woman, often winged; carved on house fronts to offer protection.
bloki.	Pulleys on loom.
boyar (*boyarina, boyarshchina*).	Old Russian nobility.
bratina.	Early form of bowl used for festivals.
burak.	Birch container with handled lid, for liquids (*tuesok*).
bylina.	Heroic tale of ancient Russia.
chelnoki.	Shuttles, for weaving.
dontse.	Base of distaff (cf. *prialka*).
endova.	Festive vessel with a spout.
fronton.	Pediment.
greben'.	Comb of distaff (cf. *prialka*).
guberniia.	Province.
izba.	Peasant house.
izrazets.	Clay tile, stamped or painted and glazed, used to decorate tile stoves and facades of buildings.
inkrustatsiia.	Incrustation, wood inlay work characteristic of Gorodets.
kaftan.	Most common garment for men in pre-Petrine Russia.
klet'.	Simple, rectangular log frame of an *izba*.
kovsh.	Ancient Russian dish for beverages.
kokoshnik.	Headdress for women, often embroidered, with river pearls; worn by boyarinas before Peter I, later used only among peasants and the merchant class.
korob.	Trunk made of wood and bast.
kumgan.	Tall ceramic pitcher with spout.
kustar'.	Practitioner of a handicraft; often itinerant, but in late nineteenth century connected with home industry.
kvass.	Traditional beverage made from black bread and malt.
lapti (*sg. lapot*).	Bast sandals.
larets.	Casket, small chest.
lobnaia doska.	Frontal board of *izba* at base of pediment.

Glossary

lopaska.	Blade of a distaff, often carved or painted (cf. *prialka*).
lubok (pl. *lubki*).	Woodcut or metal engraving of religious, moral, satirical, or entertaining subjects.
matreshka.	Nested wooden dolls.
mochesnik.	Small bast box for spindles, knitting needles, and yarns.
nabilki.	Parts of loom to which threads are fixed.
nabirukhi.	Small bast boxes for gathering berries.
naboika.	Fabric with designs printed from a carved wooden board (*nabivnaia doska*).
nagrudnik.	Short jacketlike garment for women.
nalichnik.	Carved window or door frame.
oblast'.	Region.
ochele.	Panel decorating top of window or gate, carved in deep relief or openwork; sometimes brightly painted.
ofenia.	Itinerant salesman of small items, notions, icons.
okhlupen'.	Roof ridge, often decorated with carved horse or duck.
panka.	Primitive wooden doll.
paneva.	Tunic-like garment for women.
pelena.	Ecclesiastical embroidery, icon covers; altar frontals.
perednik.	Woman's apron.
podklet'.	Lower part of an *izba*, usually for storage.
poneva.	Ornamented skirt worn by peasant women.
posad.	Commercial or industrial part of a city.
postavets.	Cupboard in an *izba*, usually placed on a bench.
prialka.	Tool for hand spinning, consisting of a vertical blade with a "comb" at the top edge to hold the flax, and a horizontal base on which the spinner sits.
prianik.	Flat honeycake, like gingerbread, stamped with designs.
prituzhalnik.	Part of loom for stressing warp.
raskol'niki.	Old Believers, schismatic sect that refused to accept reforms of Patriarch Nikon; many were exiled to Vologda region and farther northeast.
rubakha.	Long embroidered shirt.
rubel'.	Hand-held tool with ridged base for rocking over linen fabric to smooth it.
rukomoi.	Hanging pitcher with spout for washing hands.
salonitsa.	Saltcellar.
sarafan.	Tunic-like garment for women.
shveika.	Sewing implement, an upright stem topped by a pincushion and a base on which the sewer sits.
sirin.	Mythical bird of good fortune, depicted with a woman's face.
skomorokh.	Itinerant jester.
skvorechnik.	Starling box.
skobkar'.	Wooden vessel for beverages, often shaped like a waterbird.

sloboda.	Large settlement on outskirts of a city.
sunduk.	Clothes chest.
svetets.	Wrought-iron holder for wooden tapers.
teremok.	Chest or trunk based on early Russian building type (tower chamber); the base is a deep container, and the lid opens for shallow storage space.
trepalo.	Scutcher, for crushing flax to make linen.
tuesok.	Birch-bark vessel for liquids.
uezd.	District.
valek.	Battledore, for beating cloth while washing.
vereteno.	Spindle.
verst.	Measurement of distance, 3,500 feet.
volost'.	Smallest administrative division in Russia.
zemstvo.	District assembly.
zhban.	Barrel-like cask with lid.

Notes

Preface

1. Alois Riegl, *Stilfragen* (Berlin, 1893), echoed in Helmut T. Bossert, *Volkskunst in Europa* (Berlin, 1926), Preface. See Robert Goldwater, *Primitivism in Modern Art* (New York, 1938, 1966), for broader discussion of theories and issues, though without reference to Russian folk art.

2. Quotations from Holger Cahill (1932), Alfred H. Barr, Jr. (1942), Sidney Janis (1942), John A. Kouwenhoven (1950), in Jean Lipman, "Foreword," in *American Folk Painters of Three Centuries* (New York, 1980), p. 10.

3. "Art belongs to the people. It should stretch its deepest roots into the very thick of the broad mass of workers. It should be understood, and loved, by the masses." Quoted in S. K. Zhegalova, *Russkaia narodnaia zhivopis'* (Moscow, 1975), p. 5.

4. See Tat'iana M. Razina, *Russkoe narodnoe tvorchestvo* (Moscow, 1970); Tat'iana S. Semenova, *Narodnoe iskusstvo i ego problemy: Ocherki* (Moscow, 1977); Aleksandr S. Kantsedikas, *Iskusstvo i remeslo: K voprosu o prirode narodnogo iskusstva* (Moscow, 1977), for this approach.

5. Viktor M. Vasilenko, along with Vasilii Voronov, Aleksandr Bakushinskii, and other researchers, worked with folk artists in newly established craft workshops in the 1930s. Today, many scholars connected with the Institute of Art History, the Academy of Arts, the Institute of Applied and Industrial Art, and regional schools are concerned with standards of quality in the various craft workshops and guilds. See M. A. Nekrasova and K. A. Makarova, eds., *Problemy narodnogo iskusstva* (Moscow, 1982).

1. Tradition and Discovery

1. A. E. Ershov, reply to interview question, in A. B. Saltykov, *Samoe blizkoe iskusstvo* (Moscow, 1968), pp. 52–53, also quoted in Zhegalova, *Russkaia narodnaia zhivopis'*, p. 6.

2. V. Kandinskii, *Tekst khudozhnika* (Moscow, 1918), p. 28, quoted in John E. Bowlt and Rose-Carol Washton Long, eds., *The Life of Vasilii Kandinsky in Russian Art: A Study of "On the Spiritual in Art"* (Newtonville, Mass., 1980), p. 2.

3. Ershov's technique, known as "incrustation," is described in chapter 5. His comments are from transcripts of Saltykov's 1958 interviews, reprinted in A. B. Saltykov, "O spetsifike i narodnosti dekorativnogo iskusstva (besedy s masterami)," in Saltykov, *Samoe blizkoe iskusstvo*, pp. 41–56.

4. Saltykov, *Samoe blizkoe iskusstvo*, pp. 52–53.

5. Saltykov, *Samoe blizkoe iskusstvo*, p. 53.

6. The term is used in the article "Folk Art" in the *Encyclopedia of World Art* (New York, Toronto, and London, 1961), vol. 5, p. 454. I developed this idea in a paper, "Folk Tradition and Individuality in Northern Russian Art," in Sharon K. Tune, ed., *Proceedings of the American Historical Association, 1988* (Ann Arbor, Mich., 1989).

7. See M. Zvantsev, "Narodnaia rez'ba: Imena russkikh masterov," *Dekorativnoe iskusstvo SSSR*, 1960, no. 1, pp. 29–32; O. V. Kruglova, "Nadpisi na proizvedeniiakh russkogo narodnogo iskusstva," in *Soobshcheniia Zagorskogo istoriko-khudozhestvennogo muzeia-zapovednika*, 1958, no. 2, pp. 65–66. Relatively few objects with written names or initials have survived.

8. The relationships between structure and decoration and between form and function are essential to any study of folk art. The literature is vast, but a summary of the concepts of function, utility, and form is in George Mills, "Art: An Introduction to Qualitative Anthropology," reprinted from the *Journal of Aesthetics and Art Criticism*, 1957, vol. 16, no. 1, pp. 1–17, in Charlotte M. Otten, ed., *Anthropology and Art* (Garden City, N.Y., 1971), pp. 722–75.

9. M. A. Nekrasova, *Narodnoe iskusstvo kak chast' kul'tury* (Moscow, 1983), p. 17; L. M. Baktin, "Tip kul'tury kak istoricheskaia tselostnost'," *Voprosy filosofii*, 1969, no. 9.

10. V. M. Vasilenko, *Narodnoe iskusstvo: Izbrannye trudy* (Moscow, 1974), pp. 16–17.

11. P. I. Mel'nikov (Andrei Pecherskii), in *V lesakh* (2nd ed., St. Petersburg, 1881; reprint, Moscow, 1956), wrote of the remote settlements of Old Believers in the 1850s.

12. Novgorod excavation material was published in A. V. Artsikhovskii and B. A. Kolchin, *Trudy novgorodskoi arkheologicheskoi ekspeditsii* (Moscow, 1956). Major studies include V. M. Vasilenko, *Russkaia rez'ba i rospis'* (Moscow, 1947); L. A. Dintses, "Drevnie cherty v russkom narodnom iskusstve," in N. N. Voronin and M. K. Karger, eds., *Istoriia kul'tury drevnei Rusi* (Moscow and Leningrad, 1948–51), vol. II, pp. 465–91; B. A. Rybakov, "Prikladnoe iskusstvo i skul'ptura," in *Istoriia kul'tury drevnei Rusi*; S. K. Prosvirkina, *Russkaia dereviannaia posuda* (Moscow, 1957); G. K. Vagner, *Mastera drevnerusskoi skul'ptury: Rel'efy Iur'eva-Pol'skogo* (Moscow, 1966); O. V. Kruglova, *Russkaia narodnaia rez'ba i rospis' po derevu* (Moscow, 1974).

13. V. S. Voronov, "Krest'ianskoe iskusstvo" (Moscow, 1924), reprinted in V. S. Voronov, *O krest'ianskom iskusstve* (Moscow, 1972), p. 36.

14. See the work of L. Dintses, I. Boguslavskaia, A. Kantsedikas, T. Razina, B. Rybakov, T. Semenova, and V. Vasilenko in the bibliography, and further discussion in chapters 10 and 12.

15. See Victor Turner, ed., *Celebration: Studies in Festivity and Ritual* (Washington, D.C., 1982), p. 16, for a general discussion.

16. Voronov, Vasilenko, and other Soviet scholars mention these contacts only briefly; Voronov notes "the important problem of the similarity of Russian peasant art to folk arts of other countries" but invites "other scholars to take on the subject," in "Problemy izucheniia narodnogo iskusstva" (1939), in *O krest'ianskom iskusstve*, p. 292. On

the archeology of Northern Slavic sites in Germany and Poland from the Weser River to the Western Dvina, see Joachim Herrmann, "The Northern Slavs," in David M. Wilson, *The Northern World: The History and Heritage of Northern Europe,* A.D. 400–1100 (New York, 1980), pp. 183–206.

17. Bossert, *Volkskunst in Europa;* Helmut T. Bossert, *Ornamente der Volkskunst: Gewebe, Teppiche, Stickereien* (Tübingen, 1958) and *Ornamente der Volkskunst: Neue Folge. Keramik, Holz, Metall* (Tübingen, 1962); Bernward Deneke, *Europaische Volkskunst* (Propylaen Kunstgeschichte, Supplementband V) (Frankfurt a.M., Berlin, and Vienna, 1980); Reinhard Peesch, *Ornamentik der Volkskunst in Europa* (Leipzig, 1981). A comparative study focusing on one medium, wood, is G. N. Bocharov et al., *Derevo v arkhitekture i skul'pture slavian* (Moscow, 1987); for a broader approach to world folk art see Henry Glassie, *The Spirit of Folk Art: The Girard Collection at the Museum of International Folk Art* (Santa Fe and New York, 1989).

18. The Museum für Deutsche Volkskunde (Staatliche Museen Preussischer Kulturbesitz), Berlin, is a rich source for folk arts of Eastern Europe. See bibliography and "Folk Art" in *The Encyclopedia of World Art,* vol. 5, pp. 451–506. A recent illustrated survey covering many nationalities of the former Soviet Union is T. Razina, N. Cherkasova, and A. Kantsedikas, *Folk Art in the Soviet Union* (New York and Leningrad, 1990).

19. Ivan Stoliarov, *Zapiski russkogo krest'ianina* (Paris, 1986), describes his family's trips to sell clay dishes at the local bazaar and at larger peasant markets in Voronezh.

20. Much of the essential field research, recording of interviews, and developing of censuses of artists and their works was done in expeditions sponsored by the State Historical Museum, the State Russian Museum, and other institutions from the late 1950s through the 1970s. Ol'ga Kruglova and Serafima Zhegalova collected objects and interviewed artists in the Northern Dvina villages; Aleksandr Saltykov and M. P. Zvantsev worked in the Volga region, Viktor Vasilenko in the Volga area, Ukraine, and the north; and in the 1960s and 1970s Mariia Nekrasova and others interviewed and photographed artists at work in many areas.

21. Nekrasova, *Narodnoe iskusstvo kak chast' kul'tury,* pp. 63–68, discusses these distinctions with different conclusions. The conclusion that folk art is based on a "core" of tradition rather than a rigid canon is from G. K. Vagner, Introduction to Vasilenko, *Narodnoe iskusstvo,* pp. 11–12.

22. Johann Gottlieb Georgi, *Opisanie vsekh v rossiiskom gosudarstve obitaiushchikh narodov . . .* (St. Petersburg, 1776–77), and reports of explorations by Simon Pallas (1773) and Gavriil Sarychev (1802) in the State Hermitage Museum.

23. P. I. Chelishchev, *Puteshestvie po severu Rossii v 1791 godu: Dnevnik P. I. Chelishcheva* (St. Petersburg, 1886), pp. 79–98.

24. Evdokii Ziablovskii, *Zemleopisanie Rossiiskoi imperii dlia vsekh sostoianii* (St. Petersburg, 1810), vol. 4, pp. 8–9.

25. See Donald Fanger, "The Peasant in Literature," in Wayne Vucinich, ed., *The Peasant in Nineteenth-Century Russia* (Stanford, 1968), pp. 235–36.

26. Fanger, "The Peasant in Literature," pp. 244–46 on Grigorovich's "The Village" and Turgenev's *Sportsman's Sketches.*

27. See Margarita Mazo, "Folk Song in Russian Culture" (unpublished paper, Colloquium of the Kennan Institute for Advanced Russian Studies, Washington, D.C., 1988), p. 14. See Y. M. Sokolov, *Russian Folklore,* trans. Catherine Smith (New York, 1950), pp. 62–85, for a survey of early folklore studies in Russia.

28. V. P. Bezobrazov, *Narodnoe khoziaistvo Rossii, Moskovskaia (tsentral'naia) promyshlennaia oblast'* (St. Petersburg, 1882–89), vol. 1, p. 82.

29. Sergei Kravchinskii (pseud. Stepniak), *The Russian Peasantry: Their Agrarian Condition, Social Life and Religion* (New York, 1888), p. 158. This book, written in English for foreign readers, was largely concerned with the contradictions of peasant religion.

30. See P. Krachkovskii, ed. and trans., *Puteshestvie Ibn-Fadlana na Volgu* (Moscow and Leningrad, 1939), p. 79. N. Pomerantsev, *Russkaia dereviannaia skul'ptura* (Moscow, 1967), illustrates tenth-to-twelfth-century sculptures excavated in Novgorod and Vologda, which may resemble these idols.

31. Laurence Oliphant (1852) on trade pavilions, quoted in Robert Sears, *An Illustrated Description of the Russian Empire* (New York, 1855), pp. 104–107. For other comments, see Suzanne Massie, *Land of the Firebird: The Beauty of Old Russia* (New York, 1980), p. 186.

32. Jacob Reitenfels (1671, published as "Chteniia v obshchestve istorii i drevnostei rossiiskikh," Moscow, 1905), p. 93, quoted in Vasilenko, *Narodnoe iskusstvo*, p. 38. For Chancellor, Giles Fletcher, Sigismund von Herberstein, and other travelers, see F. Wilson, *Muscovy: Russia through Foreign Eyes* (London, 1970).

33. Theophile Gauthier, *Voyage en Russie* (1856), translated as *Russia: Descriptive and Illustrative* (Paris, 1905), vol. I, pp. 430–34.

34. George Kennan, *The Marquise de Custine and His "Russia in 1839"* (London, 1972), pp. 74–86, citing Le Marquis de Custine, *La Russie en 1839* (Paris, 1843).

35. *The Englishwoman in Russia: Impressions of the Society and Manners*, by a Lady ten years resident in that country (1855; reprint, New York, 1970), p. 32.

36. C. L. Dodgson, "Journal of a Tour in Russia in 1867," in Dodgson, *The Russian Journal and Other Selections from the Work of Lewis Carroll* (New York, 1935), pp. 95–107.

37. F. L. M. August von Haxthausen-Abbenburg, *Russia Observed: The Russian Empire, Its People, Institutions and Resources*, trans. Robert Farie (London, 1856), vol. 1, Preface, pp. xiv–xvi. Haxthausen was in Russia in 1843. See Richard Pipes, *Russia under the Old Regime* (New York, 1974), pp. 10–12, for comment on Haxthausen's evaluation of the rural economy.

38. Haxthausen, *The Russian Empire*, vol. 1, pp. 101–102.

39. Haxthausen, *The Russian Empire*, vol. 1, p. 144.

40. Haxthausen, *The Russian Empire*, vol. 1, pp. 106–107, 113–16.

41. Sears, *An Illustrated Description of the Russian Empire*, p. 98.

42. Sears, *An Illustrated Description of the Russian Empire*, pp. 528–30, 557.

43. *The Englishwoman in Russia*, p. 39.

44. *The Englishwoman in Russia*, p. 39.

45. See Galina N. Komelova, *Stseny russkoi narodnoi zhizni kontsa XVIII–nachala XIX vekov* (Leningrad, 1961), for engravings in the Hermitage. Among the photographs are a series of street types taken in St. Petersburg by William Carrick in the 1860s, reproduced in Chloe Obolensky, *The Russian Empire: A Portrait in Photographs* (New York, 1979), pp. 86–89.

46. Sir Donald Mackenzie Wallace, *Russia: Its History and Condition to 1877* (Boston, 1910), vol. I, pp. 128–38; his chapter on the peasants of the north describes festivals, crafts, and trade artels also covered by other books of this period, including Francis H. E. Palmer, *Russian Life in Town and Country* (New York, 1901), and Howard P. Kennard, *The Russian Peasant* (Philadelphia, 1908).

47. Isabel Florence Hapgood, *Russian Rambles* (Boston and New York, 1895; reprint, 1970), pp. 266–70.

48. E. E. Viollet-le-Duc, *L'art russe, ses origines, ses éléments constitutifs, son apogée, son avenir* (Paris, 1877), pp. 136–71.

49. V. V. Stasov, *Russkii narodnyi ornament* (St. Petersburg, 1872), 2 vols. See chapter 15.

50. Nikolai Leskov, *The Sealed Angel and Other Stories*, ed. and trans. K. A. Lantz (Knoxville, 1984).

51. Il'ia Repin, *Dalekoe blizkoe*, ed. K. Chukovskii, 4th ed. (Moscow, 1953), pp. 55–56.

52. Repin, *Dalekoe blizkoe*, p. 74. Repin's contemporaries Aleksei Bogoliubov and Fedor Vasil'ev wrote about folk carving on barges on the Volga.

53. Kandinskii, *Tekst khudozhnika*, in Bowlt and Long, *Kandinsky*, p. 2. Kazimir Malevich, "Autobiographical Notes, 1923–1925," trans. Xenia Glowacki-Prus and Arnold McMillin, in Troels Andersen, *K. S. Malevich: Essays on Art* (Copenhagen, 1968), vol. 2, pp. 147–55.

2. Village and *Izba*

1. Viollet-le-Duc, *L'art russe*, p. 251.

2. I. V. Makovetskii, *Arkhitektura russkogo narodnogo zhilishcha: Sever i verkhnee Povolzh'e* (Moscow, 1962), pp. 14–46, 47–66, on types of villages and their main structures.

3. See Pipes, *Russia under the Old Regime*, pp. 16–19.

4. *The Englishwoman in Russia*, p. 39.

5. Stoliarov, *Zapiski russkogo krest'ianina*, p. 14.

6. Makovetskii, *Arkhitektura*, p. 14, citing the chronicle of Nestor, "Povesti vremennykh let."

7. Among others, a sixteenth-century Solovetskii icon (State Historical Museum) shows construction methods; a Novgorod icon (Tretiakov Gallery) of St. Anthony includes a detailed representation of his monastery.

8. On early dwellings, see Makovetskii, *Arkhitektura*, pp. 7–46; I. M. Bibikova and N. A. Koval'chuk, *Dereviannaia rez'ba krest'ianskikh zhilishch verkhnego Povolzh'ia* (Moscow, 1954); M. P. Zvantsev, *Domovaia rez'ba* (Moscow, 1935). On wood architecture in Russia and eastern Europe, see Heinrich Nickel, *Osteuropaische Baukunst des Mittelalters* (Leipzig, 1981).

9. Makovetskii, *Arkhitektura*, p. 16, refers to the Kievan chronicles' sensational story of Grand Duchess Ol'ga, who took revenge on the killers of her husband, Igor', by inviting them to wash in her bathhouse (*istopka*), then locking them in and setting the building ablaze.

10. Basic sources are Makovetskii, *Arkhitektura*, and Basile Kerblay, *L'isba russe d'hier et d'aujourd'hui* (Lausanne, 1983), especially pp. 49–59.

11. V. T. Shmakova, "Printsipy dekora krest'ianskikh domov i izb," in *Russkoe narodnoe iskusstvo severa* (papers from a conference at the State Russian Museum) (Leningrad, 1968), pp. 60–68.

12. M. P. Zvantsev, *Nizhegorodskaia rez'ba* (Moscow, 1969), pp. 6–9, diagrams pp. 25ff.

13. T. V. Staniukovich, "Vnutrenniaia planirovka, otdelka i meblirovka russkogo krest'ianskogo zhilishcha," in V. A. Aleksandrov et al., eds., *Russkie: Istoriko-etnograficheskii atlas* (Moscow, 1970), pp. 61–88.

14. Stoliarov, *Zapiski russkogo krest'ianina*, p. 15.

15. Mary Matossian, "The Peasant Way of Life," in Vucinich, *The Peasant in Nineteenth-Century Russia*, p. 29.

16. Makovetskii, *Arkhitektura*, pp. 74–78.

17. Ol'ga Sevan, "Rospis' krest'ianskogo doma," *Dekorativnoe iskusstvo SSSR*, 1979, no. 10, p. 16.

18. Vasilii Baradulin, "Rospis' krest'ianskogo doma," *Dekorativnoe iskusstvo SSSR*, 1979, no. 3, pp. 20–21, identifies major centers and masters, based on expeditions of the 1960s and records of painters in *Permskie gubernskie vedomosti* for 1869.

19. Shmakova, "Printsipy dekora krest'ianskikh domov i izb," p. 67, finds evidence of such designs as early as the eighteenth century in a miniature from the manuscript *Zhitiia Aleksandra Svirskogo*, in the State Historical Museum. This interior includes icons and a geometric meander pattern on the wall. Other illustrations of painted interiors of the 1880s to 1900s are in S. Zhegalova, S. Zhizhina, Z. Popova, and Iu. Cherniakhovskaia, *Prianik, prialka i ptitsa sirin*, 2nd ed. (Moscow, 1983), p. 30; and *Painted Handcrafts of the Urals* (Moscow, n.d.), pp. 24–25, 41–42.

20. Kandinskii, "Reminiscences" (1901–13), in *Complete Writings on Art*, ed. Kenneth Lindsay and Peter Vergo (Boston, 1982). On the importance of Kandinskii's ethnographic expedition in 1889, see Peg Weiss, "Kandinsky and 'Old Russia': An Ethnographic Exploration," in G. Weisberg, L. Dixon, and A. Lemke, eds., *The Documented Image: Visions in Art History* (Syracuse, 1988), pp. 187–222.

3. Domestic Tasks and Tools

1. D. A. Rovinskii, *Russkie narodnye kartinki* (St. Petersburg, 1881), p. 113, no. 128. (Muzh lapti pletet / a zhena nitki priadet. Obogatet' khotiat / ognia ne gasiat.)

2. Nikolai N. Sobolev, *Russkaia narodnaia rez'ba po derevu* (Moscow and Leningrad, 1931–34), pp. 335–44; *Russkaia dereviannaia posuda XVII–XX vekov*, exhibition catalogue, State History Museum (Moscow, 1982), passim.

3. The word *skobkar'* is of unknown origin: it may have described the technique of scraping (*skobit'*) with an adze or drawknife (*skobel'*) or referred to the dug-up tree root (*kopan*) from which the vessel was made. An inscription on one vessel from Arkhangel'sk, "Adriona Kuznetsova skop'kar'," suggests that the word meant "carver." See *Russkaia dereviannaia posuda*, cat. no. 1.

4. Seventeenth-century records from the Ustiug and Moscow markets mention *stavtsi* from Tver', Kaluga, Kostroma, Vologda, Viatka, Sol'vychegodsk, and other centers.

5. Cf. Sobolev, *Russkaia narodnaia rez'ba*, pp. 340–43.

6. Several inscribed spoons are from the Solovetskii Monastery and may have been souvenirs. Descriptions are in *Russkaia dereviannaia posuda*, cat. nos. 101–123.

7. I. Rabotnova, "Mnogoznachnost' soderzhaniia: Voprosy izucheniia narodnogo iskusstva," *Dekorativnoe iskusstvo SSSR*, 1973, no. 11, pp. 28–29.

8. Sobolev, *Russkaia narodnaia rez'ba*, pp. 352–56.

9. O. V. Kruglova, *Russkaia narodnaia rez'ba i rospis' po derevu* (Moscow, 1974), p. 19.

10. See summary of material in chapters 1 and 10.

11. Kruglova, *Russkaia narodnaia rez'ba*, p. 20.

12. S. K. Zhegalova, "Istoriia odnoi ekspeditsii," in *Prianik, prialka i ptitsa sirin*, p. 40.

13. V. S. Voronov, "Russkie prialki" (1916–1920), first published in full in Voronov, *O krest'ianskom iskusstve*, pp. 200–49; O. V. Kruglova, I. A. Piatnitskaia, and N. A. Vorob'eva, *Severnye prialki* (Vologda, 1969), catalogue of an exhibition at the Vologda Regional Research Museum and the Sergiev-Posad State History and Art Museum-Preserve; Kruglova, *Russkie prialki* (Zagorsk, 1971); N. V. Taranovskaia and N. V. Mal'tsev, *Russkie prialki* (Leningrad, 1970).

14. Trinity-Sergiev Monastery, No. 2772. The icon, from about 1420, is attributed to Rublev's workshop. Reproduced in Kruglova, *Russkaia narodnaia rez'ba*, fig. 92.

15. Seasonal activities were noted by many of the travelers cited in chapter 1. Sir Donald Mackenzie Wallace, *Russia: Its History and Condition*, pp. 128–41, relates the rural calendar to specific crafts. Also see Matossian, "The Peasant Way of Life," pp. 20–39.

16. Stoliarov, *Zapiski russkogo krest'ianina*, p. 65, describing winter tasks and the lack of books or other amusements for children.

17. V. I. Averina, "Gorodetskaia rez'ba i rospis' na predmetakh krest'ianskogo remesla i domashnei utvary" (dissertation, Research Institute of Artistic Industries, Moscow, 1955), pp. 57–63.

4. Specialization and Originality

1. Shmakova, "Printsipy dekora," pp. 63–65; Baradulin, "Rospis' krest'ianskogo doma," pp. 20–23; S. K. Zhegalova, "Narodnyi master rospisi Iakov Iarygin," in *Muzei narodnogo iskusstva i khudozhestvennoi promyshlennosti: Sbornik* (Moscow, n.d.), pp. 192–208; Zvantsev, "Narodnaia rez'ba."

2. A. V. Bakushinskii, "Nizhegorodskaia rospis'," in *Issledovaniia i stat'i* (Moscow, 1981), pp. 286–97 (this article, from an unfinished book, was the first scholarly study of Khokhloma work). D. V. Vvedenskii, *Gorod Sergiev, Moskovskoi gubernii: Melkie promysly* (Moscow, 1927), pp. 9–11 on toys.

3. Ziablovskii, *Zemleopisanie Rossiiskoi imperii*, vol. 4, pp. 8–9.

4. Ziablovskii, *Zemleopisanie Rossiiskoi imperii*, vol. 3, pp. 236–37.

5. Ziablovskii, *Zemleopisanie Rossiiskoi imperii*, vol. 3, pp. 210–11, 147–85, 136.

6. Chelishchev, *Puteshestvie po severu Rossii v 1791 godu*, pp. 79–98 on Arkhangel'sk, with an appendix listing 261 craftsmasters. On Kholmogory, pp. 119–21; on Velikii Ustiug, pp. 164–72; on Vologda, pp. 211–48.

7. Chelishchev, *Puteshestvie po severu Rossii*, pp. 164–72.

8. Chelishchev, *Puteshestvie po severu Rossii*, pp. 167–68.

9. Chelishchev, *Puteshestvie po severu Rossii*, p. 170. I wish to thank Svetlana Zhizhina for additional information on Velikii Ustiug.

10. See S. K. Prosvirkina, *Russkaia dereviannaia posuda* (Moscow, 1957).

11. Ziablovskii, *Zemleopisanie Rossiiskoi imperii*, pp. 61, 236–37; Chelishchev, *Puteshestvie po severu Rossii*, p. 237; major fairs were held at Sergiev-Posad on the tenth Friday after Easter and on the Feast of the Assumption (August 15); at Makarevskii Monastery on July 20 and January 19 and 25; at the Kirillo-Belozerskii market on St. Kirill's Day (June 9) and on the feasts of the Ascension and the Presentation of the Virgin.

12. Bezobrazov, *Narodnoe khoziaistvo Rossii*, vol. 1, p. 231.

13. Bezobrazov, *Narodnoe khoziaistvo Rossii*, vol. 1, pp. 177–231, includes tables of sales figures. See Jerome Blum, *Lord and Peasant in Russia* (Princeton, 1961), pp. 124, 286, on markets and annual fairs in general.

14. S. K. Zhegalova, "Novye materialy po istorii severodvinskoi rospisi," in *Russkoe narodnoe iskusstvo severa*, pp. 34–44. A Novgorodian manuscript dated 1627 in the St. Petersburg Public Library shows characteristic treatment of costumes, horses and carriages, and buildings found later on distaffs from the Northern Dvina region.

15. State Historical Museum, *Russkaia dereviannaia posuda*, p. 3.

16. Averina, "Gorodetskaia rez'ba," pp. 15–30, citing A. Bobrinskii, *Narodnye russkie dereviannye izdeliia* (Moscow, 1911), and material from excavations in the Gorodets area, now in the Nizhnii Novgorod Art and History Museum.

17. Averina, "Gorodetskaia rez'ba," pp. 41–47.

18. Hapgood, *Russian Rambles*, pp. 350–52, narrates an episode centering on a Gorodets spicecake.

19. Averina, "Gorodetskaia rez'ba," pp. 40, 44; V. S. Boikova, *Russkii narodnyi prianik*, exhibition catalogue, State Museum of Ethnography of the Peoples of the USSR (Leningrad, 1976).

20. See Zhegalova, "Istoriia odnoi ekspeditsii," in Zhegalova et al., *Prianik, prialka i ptitsa sirin*, pp. 32–43; Averina, "Gorodetskaia rez'ba," pp. 136–42.

21. Sobolev, *Russkaia narodnaia rez'ba*, pp. 14–15.

22. Kruglova, "Nadpisi," pp. 66–70.

23. Kruglova, "Nadpisi," pp. 68–69. Other spicecake inscriptions are noted by Iu. Cherniakhovskaia, "Gorod-prianik," in Zhegalova et al., *Prianik, prialka i ptitsa sirin*, pp. 83–97.

24. Kruglova, *Russkaia narodnaia rez'ba*, p. 194; Kruglova, "Nadpisi," pp. 65–66; Zvantsev, "Narodnaia rez'ba," p. 29. A facade from the village of Malye Vishenki carved by Malishev with the initials MMM and the date 1882 on the frontal board is in the Sergiev-Posad Museum.

25. Zvantsev, "Narodnaia rez'ba," pp. 29–32, includes Semen Udalov, Master Goriachev, Ivan Kalugin, E. Zirinov, G. Kokurkin, Molov, Skoblikov, Gunin, Merlushkin, I. Semenov, V. Petukhov, I. Zolin, V. Vasil'ev, Fedor Konkin, Aleksandr Rodionov (1875), A. Molodtsov (1889), and Grigorii Krylov. See Bibikova and Koval'chuk, *Dereviannaia rez'ba krest'ianskikh zhilishch verkhnego Povolzh'ia*.

26. Shmakova, "Printsipy dekora," pp. 64–66.

27. Sevan, "Rospis' krest'ianskogo doma," pp. 25–26.

28. Shmakova, "Printsipy dekora," p. 66.

29. Shmakova, "Printsipy dekora," p. 66, especially the houses of A. Likhachev, P. Tiuliubaeva, M. Iarygin, M. Parfenov, M. Misharin, K. Koriaeva, M. Anisimova, and A. Opiakin.

30. *Painted Handcrafts of the Urals*, pp. 23–25, illustrating work by Riabkhov, the Mal'tsev brothers, Mashkovtsev, and others.

31. Distaffs from villages near Mokraia Edoma, Arkhangel'sk region, in the Sergiev-Posad Museum, Kruglova, *Russkaia narodnaia rez'ba*, figs. 70, 73; in the State Historical Museum, Vasilenko, *Narodnoe iskusstvo*, figs. 63, 67. Shmakova, "Printsipy dekora," p. 67, discusses early evidence of such patterns.

32. See O. Kruglova, *Narodnaia rospis' severnoi Dviny* (Moscow, 1987), for a full, finely illustrated discussion of these styles.

33. Zhegalova, *Russkaia narodnaia zhivopis'*, pp. 106–15; S. K. Zhegalova, "Khudozhestvennye prialki," in S. K. Zhegalova et al., *Sokrovishcha russkogo narodnogo iskusstva: Rez'ba i rospis' po derevu* (Moscow, 1967), pp. 128–30. Works by Iarygin, Misharin, and other Borok painters are in the State Historical Museum and the Sergiev-Posad Museum-Preserve. See Kruglova, *Russkaia narodnaia rez'ba*, no. 75.

34. Zhegalova was the rediscoverer of Iarygin; her publications on the artist include "Ekspeditsiia Gosudarstvennogo istoricheskogo muzeia na severnuiu Dvinu," *Sovetskaia etnografiia*, 1960, no. 4; "Severodvinskaia rospis' po derevu," in S. K. Zhegalova et al., *Russkoe khudozhestvennoe derevo: Trudy Gos. ordena Lenina istoricheskogo muzeia*, no. 56 (Moscow, 1983), pp. 117–49, with a catalogue, pp. 149–71. See Vasilenko, *Narodnoe iskusstvo*, pp. 110–11.

35. Zhegalova, "Istoriia odnoi ekspeditsii," pp. 27–28.

36. Zhegalova, "Istoriia odnoi ekspeditsii," pp. 37–39, includes Pelageia Amosova's description of her working methods; additional information is in Zhegalova, "Khudozhestvennye prialki," pp. 130–32.

37. Svetlana G. Zhizhina, "Severnaia reznaia beresta XVIII–XX vekov" (dissertation, Institute of Art History, Moscow, 1976); S. G. Zhizhina, "Severnaia reznaia beresta," in Zhegalova, *Russkoe khudozhestvennoe derevo*, pp. 83–116; pp. 84–86 on monastic origins; pp. 94–96 on artistic connections with metalwork and other arts of Novgorod and Velikii Ustiug.

38. Chelishchev, *Puteshestvie po severu Rossii*, p. 170.

39. Zhizhina, "Severnaia reznaia beresta," pp. 85–86; *Otchet o Vserossiiskoi khudozhestvenno-promyshlennoi vystavke* (Moscow, 1882), vol. 5, p. 67.

40. Zhizhina, "Severnaia reznaia beresta," p. 88.

41. Zhizhina, "Severnaia reznaia beresta," pp. 87–88. Besides Ivan Afanas'evich and Foma Anisimovich Veprev, local archives contained the names of other Veprevs: Afanasii Ivanovich, Prokopii Timofeevich, Iakov Fedorovich, Ivan Mikhailovich, Andrei Mikhailovich, Grigorii Mikhailovich, Savvatei Osipovich, and Nikolai Fomich.

42. Zhizhina, "Severnaia reznaia beresta," p. 87, quoting a letter from Nikolai V. Veprev (the artist's grandson) to V. Vasilenko (1961).

43. Zhizhina, "Severnaia reznaia beresta," p. 88.

44. The Russian *kustar'* exhibit is discussed by Wendy Salmond in "The Solomenko Embroidery Workshops," *Journal of Decorative and Propaganda Arts*, Summer 1987, pp. 138–40, and in her dissertation, "The Modernization of Folk Art in Russia: The Revival of the Kustar Art Industries, 1885–1917" (University of Texas at Austin, 1989, forthcoming as a book).

45. See S. G. Zhizhina, "Khudozhestvennye izdeliia iz beresty," in Zhegalova et al., *Sokrovishcha russkogo narodnogo iskusstva*, pp. 221–32.

46. Zhizhina, "Severnaia reznaia beresta," p. 88.

47. V. S. Voronov, "Mastera narodnogo iskusstva" (1937), in *O krest'ianskom iskusstve*, pp. 280–81.

48. S. Zhegalova and S. Zhizhina, "O chem rasskazali dereviannye reznye figury i figurki liudei," in Zhegalova et al., *Prianik, prialka i ptitsa sirin*, pp. 63–82, describe Savinov's work and summarize his biography.

49. Zhegalova and Zhizhina, "O chem rasskazali," pp. 66–70.

50. Zhegalova and Zhizhina, "O chem rasskazali," pp. 70–71.

51. The date inscribed here should be 1890, according to Zhizhina, but at some time the figure 9 was altered so that it appeared as 1820 and the piece could be sold as an earlier antique.

52. The collection is now in the Egor'evskoe Regional Museum; most of Savinov's work is now in the State Historical Museum in Moscow and in the Sergiev-Posad Museum-Preserve.

53. See Nekrasova, *Narodnoe iskusstvo kak chast' kul'tury*, and Mariia A. Nekrasova, ed., *Narodnye mastera: Traditsii, shkoly* (Moscow, 1985).

54. Ershov, in Saltykov, *Samoe blizkoe iskusstvo*, p. 53.

5. Wood and Carved Ornament

1. Ziablovskii, *Zemleopisanie Rossiiskoi imperii*, vol. 3, p. 128.

2. General works covering materials and techniques are M. Kamenskaia, "Narodnoe iskusstvo," and V. M. Vasilenko, "Narodnoe iskusstvo pervoi poloviny XIX veka," in I. E. Grabar', V. Kemenov, V. Lazarev, et al., eds., *Istoriia russkogo iskusstva* (Moscow, 1954–64), vol. 7, pp. 415–48; vol. 8, book 2, pp. 567–616.

3. Cf. Ziablovskii, *Zemleopisanie Rossiiskoi imperii*, vol. 4, pp. 325–77. As a rule, a workshop (*masterskaia*) was small, with two or three workers engaged in the same craft; a factory (*fabrik*) employed four or more workers, though most were much larger.

4. B. A. Rybakov, "Makrokosm v mikrokosme narodnogo iskusstva," *Dekorativnoe iskusstvo SSSR*, 1975, no. 1, pp. 30–33, 51; no. 3, pp. 38–43. On the structure and design of the *izba*, see Bibikova and Koval'chuk, *Dereviannaia rez'ba krest'ianskikh zhilishch verkhnego Povolzh'ia*; Makovetskii, *Arkhitektura*; M. P. Zvantsev, *Nizhegorodskaia rez'ba* (Moscow, 1969); Staniukovich, "Vnutrenniaia planirovka," pp. 61–88; Shmakova, "Printsipy dekora," pp. 60–68.

5. V. Voronov, "Problemy izucheniia narodnogo iskusstva" (1939), in *O krest'ianskom iskusstve*, pp. 294–96.

6. Pomerantsev, *Russkaia dereviannaia skul'ptura*, figs. 1, 5, includes figures from B. A. Kolchin's Novgorod excavations and Charonda village, Vologda Province.

7. Arkhangel'sk, Museum of Fine Arts, in Pomerantsev, *Russkaia dereviannaia skul'ptura*, figs. 14–17.

8. An unusual secular sculpture depicting Peter the Great on horseback was made by a Smolensk artist, Mark Borodavkin. Russian wood sculptures from the seventeenth and eighteenth centuries are in the Priliutskii Monastery Museum-Preserve, near Vologda, in the Smolensk State Museum Reserve of History, Architecture, and Art, and in the Russian Museum, St. Petersburg.

9. N. Mal'tsev, "Dereviannaia skul'ptura," in I. Boguslavskaia, ed., *Dobrykh ruk masterstvo* (Leningrad, 1976), pp. 43–44.

10. Voronov, "Problemy izucheniia narodnogo iskusstva" (1939), in *O krest'ianskom iskusstve*, p. 296.

11. Averina, "Gorodetskaia rez'ba i rospis'," pp. 61–82 and Appendix II, describes the techniques and applications of carving. The eight techniques are (1) *vyemchato-trekhgran-*

naia rez'ba (three-faceted grooved), (2) *vyemchato-nogtevidnaia* (fingernail-shaped groove), (3) *melko-uzornaia vyemchataia* (fine outline groove), (4) *konturnaia* (contour), (5) *skobchataia s inkrustatsii* (scraped-out with incrustation), (6) *plastichno-rel'efnaia* (plastic, or high-relief), (7) *plosko-rel'efnaia* (low-relief), and (8) *prorez'* (cut through or openwork).

12. This outline of basic cuts and patterns is based on A. A. Abrosimova, N. I. Kaplan, and T. V. Matlianskaia, *Khudozhestvennaia rez'ba po derevu, kosti i rogu* (Moscow, 1978), and Averina, "Gorodetskaia rez'ba i rospis'," Appendix. The same terms to describe cuts are still used today, as a recent handbook on woodcarving shows: N. S. Stepanov, *Rez'by ocharovanie* (Leningrad, 1991), pp. 78–104.

13. The distaff, dated December 19, 1890, signed by Master Stepan Ogloblin, is in the Sergiev-Posad Museum (no. 5444), illustrated in Kruglova, *Russkaia narodnaia rez'ba*, no. 53/54.

14. Zhegalova, *Russkaia narodnaia zhivopis'*, p. 139.

15. Averina, "Gorodetskaia rez'ba i rospis'," pp. 101–12; Iu. Cherniakhovskaia, "Koni iz gorodtsa," in Zhegalova et al., *Prianik, prialka i ptitsa sirin*, pp. 108–109.

16. Examples of the types and usages are given in N. Mal'tsev, "Prianichnye doski," in Boguslavskaia, *Dobrykh ruk masterstvo*, pp. 56–57, and Boikova, *Russkii narodnyi prianik*.

17. Cherniakhovskaia, "Gorod-prianik," pp. 89–91.

18. State Historical Museum, Moscow; see Cherniakhovskaia, "Gorod-prianik," p. 92.

19. Cf. Mal'tsev, "Prianichnye doski," p. 65, and V. Voronov, "Prianichnye doski" (1926), in *O krest'ianskom iskusstve*, p. 253.

20. Hapgood, *Russian Rambles*, pp. 266–70.

21. State Historical Museum, Moscow, in Cherniakhovskaia, "Gorod-prianik," p. 97.

22. Kruglova, *Russkaia narodnaia rez'ba*, pp. 21–22. I would like to thank Ol'ga Kruglova for demonstrating these to me in the Sergiev-Posad Museum.

23. A place-setting board and tablecloth are in the State Russian Museum, St. Petersburg.

6. Painting on Wood

1. Averina, "Gorodetskaia rez'ba i rospis'," p. 146.

2. These villages were the center of an artistic renewal in the 1920s, with the founding of the lacquer box-painting industry by Palekh icon painter Ivan Golikov and others; see chapter 18.

3. See Mel'nikov (Pecherskii), *V lesakh*, and Leskov, "The Sealed Angel."

4. S. K. Zhegalova, "Severodvinskaia rospis' po derevu," in Zhegalova et al., *Russkoe khudozhestvennoe derevo*, pp. 117–49.

5. Khokhloma was one of several villages in which the art was practiced. The others were Novopokrovskoe, Semino, Khriashchi, and Kuligino, all near the town of Semenovo in Nizhnii Novgorod Province. See Vasilenko, "Khokhlomskaia rospis' i podmoskovnaia rez'ba," in *Narodnoe iskusstvo*, pp. 130–38.

6. According to Vasilenko, aluminum powder was used in the past few decades for the same process. Information on methods comes from interviews with Khokhloma masters by Vasilenko and Bakushinskii, scholars who were instrumental in reviving the art in

the twentieth century. See A. V. Bakushinskii, "Nizhegorodskaia rospis'," in *Issledovaniia i stat'i* (Moscow, 1981), pp. 286–97; Vasilenko, "Khokhlomskaia rospis'," pp. 130, 133.

7. Vasilenko, "Khokhlomskaia rospis'," pp. 137–38, citing N. Mneva, "Drevnerusskaia zhivopis' Nizhnego Novgoroda," in *Materialy i issledovaniia* (Moscow, 1958), p. 36. In the late nineteenth century there were instances of professional artists introducing motifs from historical sources (e.g., medieval manuscripts) to peasant artists; see chapter 16.

8. Zhegalova, *Russkaia narodnaia zhivopis'*, pp. 65–69.

9. The distaff blade, from the end of the eighteenth century (State Museum of Ethnography, no. 5502–39), is one of the oldest examples of Permogore painting. Kruglova interprets the inscriptions and style in *Narodnaia rospis' severnoi Dviny*, plates 1, 2, 3, and commentary (unpaged).

10. Novgorodian miniatures dated 1627 in the St. Petersburg Public Library, reproduced in the portfolio "Miniatures from Old Russian Illuminated Manuscripts" (Leningrad, 1980), offer close parallels. See Shmakova, "Printsipy dekora," p. 67, for a comparison of wall painting with an eighteenth-century miniature.

11. Several villages located within a radius of about 15 to 20 km, including Skobeli, Puchuga, and Pervaia Zherlyginskaia, represent the "Borok" style; see Zhegalova, "Ekspeditsiia . . . na severnuiu Dvinu," and Kruglova, "Severodvinskie rospisi," p. 20.

12. Zhegalova, "Istoriia odnoi ekspeditsii," pp. 37–39; Zhegalova, "Khudozhestvennye prialki," p. 131. Kruglova, *Narodnaia rospis' severnoi Dviny*, makes this distinction between Permogore and Borok styles.

13. Kruglova, *Narodnaia rospis' severnoi Dviny*, nos. 112–126.

14. V. M. Vishnevskaia, "Svobodnye kistevye rospisi," in *Russkoe narodnoe iskusstvo severa*, pp. 7, 8. This article summarizes the results of expeditions in the 1950s and 1960s.

15. See Vishnevskaia, "Svobodnye kistevye rospisi," pp. 9–12, on the dissemination of fresco painting from ancient Kiev to the north of Russia, and the importance of teams of artists invited from Moscow to paint the stone churches of Vologda, Kirillovo, Kargopol', and other northern cities in the seventeenth century.

16. Kruglova, *Russkaia narodnaia rez'ba*, p. 14, figs. 65, 66.

17. I. Boguslavskaia, "Rospisi na korobakh Gorodetskogo raiona Gor'kovskoi oblasti," in *Soobshcheniia Gosudarstvennogo russkogo muzeia* (Moscow, 1974), no. 10, pp. 84–90.

18. V. M. Vasilenko, "Russkaia narodnaia rez'ba i rospis' po derevu XVIII–XX vv.," in *Russkoe narodnoe iskusstvo*, pp. 124–25, citing his own conversation with the artist in 1936; this distaff is in the State Historical Museum. Mazin, whose father was a minor Gorodets painter, studied with Varvara Konovalova, a traditional folk painter. He was a successful artist by the 1890s and after the Revolution helped to establish a Gorodets painting school. He painted panels illustrating folklife and crafts for the Nizhnii Novgorod Museum in 1927–28. See Voronov, "Mastera narodnogo iskusstva," pp. 283–84.

7. Textile Arts and Costume

1. See Ivan Bilibin, "Narodnoe tvorchestvo russkogo severa," in *Mir iskusstva* (St. Petersburg, 1904), vol. 12, no. 6, pp. 267–302 (album of photographs) and 303–18 (text).

2. See M. N. Shmeleva and L. V. Tazikhana, "Ukrasheniia russkoi krest'ianskoi odezhdy," in *Russkie*, pp. 89–123, for a systematic summary of peasant costume; L. N.

Molotova and N. N. Sosnina, *Russkii narodnyi kostium* (Moscow, 1984); I. Ia. Boguslavskaia, *Russkoe narodnoe iskusstvo* (Moscow, 1984); and the State Historical Museum handbook, *Russkii narodnyi kostium* (Moscow, [1982]).

3. Hapgood, *Russian Rambles*, p. 256.

4. On designs related to weddings: L. N. Molotova, "Shenkurskie svadebnye golovnye ubory," in K. Chistova and T. Bernshtam, eds., *Russkii narodnyi svadebnyi obriad* (Leningrad, 1978), pp. 220–31; L. N. Molotova, "K voprosu o funktsiiakh devich'ikh golovnykh uborov v severorusskom svadebnom obriade XVIII–XIX vv.," *Sovetskaia etnografiia* (Moscow, 1979), no. 1, pp. 116–21. On motifs related to Rozhanitsa, the Slavic goddess of birth: S. V. Zharnikova, "Some Archaic Motifs in the Embroidery of Sol'vychegodsk *Kokoshniks* [Headdresses] of the Northern Dvina Type (Based on Materials from the Vologda Oblast Museum of Local Lore, History and Economy)," *Soviet Anthropology and Archaeology* (Armonk, N.Y., 1987), Winter 1986/87, vol. 25, no. 3, pp. 3–16 (reprinted from *Sovetskaia etnografiia*, 1985, no. 1).

5. L. V. Efimova and R. M. Belogorskaia, *Russkaia vyshivka i kruzhevo: Sobranie Gosudarstvennogo istoricheskogo muzeia* (Moscow, 1982), includes examples of all major types of *kokoshniki* and portraits of peasant and merchant-class women wearing them; works by the serf artists Ivan Argunov and Grigorii Shibanov also show many types. The State Historical Museum, the Museum of Ethnography, the Russian Museum, and the Sergiev-Posad Museum-Preserve have important collections.

6. This summary is based on several sources, including a special exhibit on flax and linen at the Smolensk Regional Museum.

7. Ol'ga Gordeeva, senior researcher, State Historical Museum, Moscow, in a discussion of costume in the Volga area during a conference at the museum, December 23, 1982.

8. Semenova, *Narodnoe iskusstvo i ego problemy*, pp. 171–87.

9. See Efimova and Belogorskaia, *Russkaia vyshivka i kruzhevo*, pp. 11–19, plates 1–28. Stasov, *Russkii narodnyi ornament*, Part I ("Shit'e tkani, kruzhevo"), one of the first studies of embroidered ornament, covered historical development, regional styles, and four basic types of motifs: geometrical, forms from the plant world, animals and birds, and human figures.

10. Shmeleva and Tazikhana, "Ukrasheniia russkoi krest'ianskoi odezhdy," p. 94.

11. M. Lukin and N. Davydova, *Umel'tsy Velikogo Ustiuga* (Arkhangel'sk, 1977), pp. 63–70.

12. Shmeleva and Tazikhana, "Ukrasheniia russkoi krest'ianskoi odezhdy," p. 93. The "white-eye" style meant the following arrangement of threads: one red, three white, two green, three white, one red; the "red-eye" pattern was three red, two white, four red, three green, two red, three white.

13. A similar factory was started by Vera Eliseeva in Voronezh Province, and others were founded later. The work was extremely taxing; Merlina employed only women aged 17 to 27, since they often became blind and crippled after that time. She awarded retired workers with freedom from serfdom. See E. V. Arseneva, *Russkie platki i shali* (Moscow, 1982), pp. 3–4.

14. See L. E. Kalmykova, *Narodnaia vyshivka tverskoi zemli* (Leningrad, 1981), for illustrations, technical descriptions, and analysis of specialized forms and motifs.

15. Shmeleva and Tazikhana, "Ukrasheniia russkoi krest'ianskoi odezhdy," p. 106.

16. Zharnikova, "Some Archaic Motifs," pp. 3, 5. See G. S. Maslova, *Ornament russkoi narodnoi vyshivki, kak istoriko-etnograficheskii istochnik* (Moscow, 1978).

17. Kalmykova, *Narodnaia vyshivka tverskoi zemli*, pp. 31–32. On earlier embroidery, see T. Manushina, *Khudozhestvennoe shit'e drevnei Rusi v sobranii Zagorskogo muzeia* (Moscow, 1983).

18. P. M. Belogorskaia, in Efimova and Belogorskaia, *Russkaia vyshivka i kruzhevo*, pp. 151–52, 154–59.

19. I. A. Alpatova, "Khudozhestvennye osobennosti russkoi naboiki" (dissertation, Institute of the History of Art, Moscow, 1972), esp. pp. 91–186, for a description of the main types and techniques of *naboika*.

20. Efimova and Belogorskaia, *Russkaia vyshivka i kruzhevo*, pp. 22–23 and nos. 112–115, 121.

21. Sofiia Davydova, *Russkoe kruzhevo: Russkie kruzhevnitsy. Issledovanie istoricheskoe, tekhnicheskoe i statisticheskoe* (St. Petersburg, 1892), esp. pp. 139–49. See Salmond, "The Modernization of Folk Art in Russia," chap. 2.

22. Hapgood, *Russian Rambles*, p. 284.

23. Zhegalova, "Istoriia odnoi ekspeditsii," p. 40.

8. Beyond the Village

1. Bilibin, "Narodnoe tvorchestvo russkogo severa," pp. 267–381.

2. S. G. Zhizhina, "Severnaia reznaia beresta," pp. 83–116; Lukin and Davydova, *Umel'tsy Velikogo Ustiuga*, pp. 20–27.

3. I. A. Piatnitskaia, "Istoricheskie korni i evoliutsiia shemogodskoi rez'by," in *Russkoe narodnoe iskusstvo severa*, pp. 145–51.

4. Andrei Bolotov, quoted by S. G. Zhizhina, "Dereviannoe kruzhevo," in Zhegalova et al., *Prianik, prialka i ptitsa sirin*, pp. 124–25.

5. Chelishchev, *Puteshestvie po severu Rossii*, p. 170.

6. Lukin and Davydova, *Umel'tsy Velikogo Ustiuga*, p. 22.

7. Zhizhina, "Severnaia reznaia beresta XVIII–XX vekov," p. 18. The box is in the Sergiev-Posad Museum.

8. I wish to thank Svetlana Zhizhina for showing me this box and others in the State Historical Museum.

9. The ivory throne in the Kremlin, believed to have been made in Constantinople for the marriage of Ivan III and Sophia Paleologa, but probably made by Italian or German craftsmen, had a great influence on Moscow artists. In the north, monastic scribes and artists may have used bone plaques for the purpose of working out interlace designs before transferring them to parchment.

10. V. M. Vasilenko, "Severnaia reznaia kost'," in *Narodnoe iskusstvo*, pp. 178–79.

11. Peter I made a walrus ivory chandelier, now in the Hermitage Museum. The scientist Lomonosov came from Kholmogory, practiced bonecarving and mosaic work, and probably helped to raise the status of these arts. Some ivory carvers also worked in mother-of-pearl. Irina Ukhanova, "Iz istorii rez'by po perlamutrovym rakovinam v Rossii," in *Soobshcheniia Gosudarstvennogo Ermitazha* (Leningrad, 1982), no. 47, pp. 25–27.

12. The *teremok* may not have originated from this architectural model. The same shape is characteristic of twelfth-century Byzantine pieces from Ravenna (Museo Nazion-

ale). The intrinsic value of ivory made it likely that such works were presented as diplomatic gifts, later to become models for native artists.

13. Vasilenko, "Severnaia reznaia kost'," pp. 193–96, on motifs and sources.

14. S. Rozhdestvenskaia, "Prosechnoe zhelezo v arkhitekture Vorsmy i ego mastera," in Nekrasova, *Narodnye mastera: Traditsii, shkoly,* pp. 158–67.

15. Lukin and Davydova, *Umel'tsy Velikogo Ustiuga,* pp. 42–50.

16. A. A. Gilodo, S. V. Gnutova, and G. S. Kirillova, *Russkii samovar* (Moscow, 1991), pp. 5–22, on samovar types; pp. 202–205 list major firms and masters in Tula.

17. State Historical Museum, *Mednye izdeliia ural'skikh zavodov* (Moscow, n.d. [1982]), p. 3. Law required that metal products be stamped with the factory trademark, date, and maker's initials, so these works are easily identified.

18. G. Vilinbakhov, "Russkie znamena XVII veka s izobrazheniem edinoroga," in *Soobshcheniia Gosudarstvennogo Ermitazha* (Leningrad, 1982), vol. 47, pp. 22–24. See chapter 12.

19. See Chelishchev, *Puteshestvie po severu Rossii,* p. 170. Earrings of metal wire and river pearls were worn with *kokoshniki* on festive occasions; many examples are in the Hermitage Museum, the Russian Museum, the Museum of Ethnography, and the Sergiev-Posad Museum-Preserve.

20. A form of niello was used in ancient Rome and in Saxon Britain; the technique developed in mid-fifteenth-century Italy also gave rise to the art of metal engraving for prints. See Arthur M. Hind, *A History of Engraving and Etching* (Boston, 1923), pp. 42–43.

21. Mikhail Chirkov, the master who established the *Severnaia chern'* ("Northern Niello") workshop in Velikii Ustiug, was a popular hero because he did not sell the secret to foreigners. V. Voronov, "Mastera narodnogo iskusstva," in *O krest'ianskom iskusstve,* pp. 281–82, and S. Maslenitsyn, "Master ustiuzhskoi cherni M. P. Chirkov," in *Narodnye mastera: Traditsii, shkoly,* pp. 89–97. Technical information is in Lukin and Davydova, *Umel'tsy Velikogo Ustiuga,* pp. 53–54.

22. Dmitrii A. Rovinskii, *Russkie narodnye kartinki* (St. Petersburg, 1881), first identified the sources and traced the development of the prints, chaps. 1, 2, fig. 2. Rovinskii's later compendium of Russian copper engravings, *Podrobnyi slovar' russkikh graverov* (St. Petersburg, 1895), includes some of this material.

23. S. K. Zhegalova, "O stilisticheskom edinstve lubochnykh kartinok i severnykh rospisei po derevu XII–XIII veka," in *Narodnaia graviura i fol'klor v Rossii XVII–XIX vv.* (Proceedings of a conference at the Pushkin Museum of Fine Arts) (Moscow, 1976), pp. 131–39.

24. Zhegalova, "O stilisticheskom edinstve lubochnykh kartinok," p. 136.

25. Rovinskii, *Russkie narodnye kartinki,* pp. 18, 38, for examples of Ushakov's printed icons and *lubki* based on church frescoes.

26. Rovinskii, *Russkie narodnye kartinki,* pp. 66, 78.

27. Rovinskii, *Russkie narodnye kartinki.* This summary follows the order of Rovinskii's treatment.

28. Rovinskii, *Russkie narodnye kartinki,* p. 356.

29. I wish to thank Irina Ukhanova for showing me examples of this technique in the State Hermitage.

30. In the 1840s a colored woodcut of a single sheet size cost 1 or 1½ kopeks. Rovinskii, *Russkie narodnye kartinki,* p. 65.

31. See S. Nikitin, "Ob obshchikh siuzhetakh v fol'klore i narodnom izobrazitel'nom iskusstve," in *Narodnaia graviura i fol'klor*, pp. 320–50.

32. Iu. Lotman, "Khudozhestvennaia priroda russkikh narodnykh kartinok," in *Narodnaia graviura i fol'klor*, p. 60, on the connection between theater and "stories in pictures." S. Zhizhina related *lubok* images to fireworks in a discussion during a conference at the State Historical Museum, December 23, 1982. For panoramas and other urban popular entertainment, see A. F. Nekrylova, *Russkie narodnye gorodskie prazdniki, uveseleniia i zrelishcha konets XVIII–nachalo XX veka* (Leningrad, 1988). On the development of *lubki* and *lubok* books in the nineteenth century, see Jeffrey Brooks, *When Russia Learned to Read* (Princeton, 1985), pp. 62–72, 73–79, 80–96.

33. The early development of lacquers is summarized in S. Zhizhina and I. Remizova, *Russkie khudozhestvennye laki XVIII–XX vekov* (Moscow, 1982) (unpaged), and in N. Golybina, "Russkie laki," in Boguslavskaia, *Dobrykh ruk masterstvo*, pp. 164–73.

34. The techniques are described in Zhizhina and Remizova, *Russkie khudozhestvennye laki*. I wish to thank Irina Ukhanova for showing me unfinished cardboard forms in the Hermitage collection.

35. Repin's painting (1879, Russian Museum) was copied on a tea caddy by the Vishniakov factory; most peasant genre scenes, like those adapted to other luxury arts, were idealized.

36. A. V. Bakushinskii, *Iskusstvo Palekha* (Moscow, 1934), reprinted in *Issledovaniia i stat'i*; V. M. Vasilenko, "Mstera i Kholui" and "Palekhskaia zhivopis'," in *Narodnoe iksusstvo*, pp. 233–37, 238–42; V. Porudominskii, *Otkrovenie Ivana Golikova* (Moscow, 1977).

37. V. Kotov, "Iskusstvo Palekha i narodnaia kartinka," in *Narodnaia graviura i fol'klor*, pp. 234–46. Kotov discusses twofold connections: between local icon painting and printed paper icons from Suzdal' in the nineteenth century, and early twentieth-century Palekh designs based on *lubki*, pp. 241–44.

38. The palace in the Kremlin in Uglich exemplifies this treatment. See I. I. Sergeenko, *Russkii izrazets* (Moscow, 1982), pp. 1–5, for historical background and examples of main types. The State Historical Museum has a collection of about 7,500 tiles.

39. Examples of *izrazets* friezes are in the Kolomenskoe Museum: friezes from the Church of Koz'ma and Damian in Sadovniki, the porch of the cathedral of the Danilov Monastery, and the drum of the Church of the Assumption in Gonchary decorated with nearly life-size figures of the Apostles, modeled in high relief and colored with blue-green, yellow, brown, and white enamels.

40. Sergeenko, *Russkii izrazets*, p. 3.

41. Sergeenko, *Russkii izrazets*, p. 4.

42. T. I. Dul'kina and N. S. Grigor'eva, *Gzhel'* (Moscow, 1982), and T. I. Dul'kina and N. S. Grigor'eva, *Keramika Gzheli XVIII–XX vekov* (Leningrad, 1988).

43. Dul'kina and Grigor'eva, *Gzhel'*, pp. 38–39.

44. N. Grigor'eva, "Goncharnoe iskusstvo," in Boguslavskaia, *Dobrykh ruk masterstvo*, pp. 108–12.

45. Stoliarov, *Zapiski russkogo krest'ianina*, pp. 17–21, describing the pottery making of Karachun, about 30 miles from Voronezh.

46. Stoliarov, *Zapiski russkogo krest'ianina*, pp. 18–19.

47. Stoliarov, *Zapiski russkogo krest'ianina*, pp. 18–20.

9. Toys in All Media

1. Sears, *Illustrated Description of the Russian Empire*, p. 557.

2. In Russian museums, folk art is distributed among many curatorial departments according to medium—wood, ceramics, textile, metal—and toys are sometimes classified this way. The exception is the Sergiev-Posad Museum of Toys (an affiliate of the Academy of Pedagogical Sciences).

3. D. I. Vvedenskii, *Gorod Sergiev, Moskovskoi gubernii: Melkie promysly* (Moscow, 1927), pp. 9, 15, 32, 42.

4. G. L. Dain, *Russkaia narodnaia igrushka* (Moscow, 1981), p. 44. This ceremony is also described in I. Ia. Boguslavskaia, "Figurki iz gliny," in *Dobrykh ruk masterstvo*, p. 198, and N. Tseretelli, *Russkaia krest'ianskaia igrushka* (Moscow, 1933), p. 99, citing A. Den'shin, *Viatskie starinnye glinianye igrushki* (Viatka, 1926).

5. Ivan Zabelin, *Domashnii byt russkikh tsarei (i tsarits) v XVI–XVII v.*, 2nd ed. (Moscow, 1872; reprint, Ann Arbor, Mich., 1972), Part II, pp. 80–137.

6. Tseretelli, *Russkaia narodnaia igrushka*, p. 30, citing "Sbornik vypisok iz arkhivnykh bumag o Petre Velikom" (Moscow, 1872), Part II, pp. 127–73.

7. The Bogorodskoe carving industry was supported by N. D. Bartram and V. I. Borutskii, pioneer scholars of toymaking, at the turn of the century; a *kustar'* carving artel and schools were organized in 1913 and greatly expanded under the Soviets in the 1920s. After setbacks during the war years, a new Bogorodskoe Factory of Artistic Carving was established in 1961. Aleksandr Grekov, *Bogorodskaia igrushka* (Moscow, 1987), unpaged album.

8. Orlovskii's print (1820, Hermitage) is an early example of social satire; these subjects appealed to the toymakers. Tseretelli, *Russkaia narodnaia igrushka*, pp. 135–36, illustrates both works.

9. Tseretelli, *Russkaia narodnaia igrushka*, pp. 79–80.

10. See V. P. Vil'chinskii, ed., *Russkoe narodno-poeticheskoe tvorchestvo protiv tserkvi i religii* (Moscow, 1961); I thank Marjorie Balzer for this source.

11. Descriptions of these and other toys are based on examples in the Sergiev-Posad Museum of Toys; I thank curator Galina I. Dain for showing me the collection and discussing the pieces with me.

12. G. I. Dain, *Russkaia igrushka* (Moscow, 1987), p. 46.

13. D. Vvedenskii, *U Sergievskogo igrushechnika* (Moscow, 1926), p. 49, cites records of transport kept by the railway.

14. G. P. Durasov, "Ul'iana Babkina—narodnyi master Kargopolia," in Nekrasova, *Narodnye mastera: Traditsii, shkoly*, p. 101.

10. Amulet, Ornament, and Ritual

1. Stasov, *Russkii narodnyi ornament*, vol. 2, p. 372.

2. V. S. Voronov, *Krest'ianskoe iskusstvo* (Moscow, 1924), p. 114.

3. Roman Jakobson, "On Russian Fairy Tales," commentary on Aleksandr Afanas'ev, *Russian Fairy Tales*, trans. Norbert Guterman (New York, 1945), pp. 632–33.

4. See Marija Gimbutas, *The Slavs* (New York and Washington, 1971), pp. 36–49, 67–71, 80–97; P. N. Tret'iakov, "Slavs," in *The Modern Encyclopedia of Russian and Soviet History* (Gulf Breeze, Fla., 1978), vol. 35, pp. 232–36; Joachim Herrmann, "The Northern Slavs," in David M. Wilson, ed., *The Northern World* (New York and London, 1980), pp. 184–206. Tamara Talbot Rice, *The Scythians* (New York, 1957), pp. 178–96.

5. Objects from the Kherson region are in A. Leskov, *Novye sokrovishcha kurganov Ukrainy* (Leningrad, 1972). Two of the largest collections are in the Hermitage and in the Museum of Historical Treasures of Ukraine in Kiev.

6. Tret'iakov, "Slavs," p. 235; S. A. Tokarev, "Slavic Religion and Mythology," in *The Modern Encyclopedia of Russian and Soviet History* (Gulf Breeze, Fla., 1978), vol. 35, pp. 212–13.

7. Linda J. Ivanits, *Russian Folk Belief* (Armonk, N.Y., and London, 1989), p. 13, quoting the Primary Chronicle.

8. See Ivanits, *Russian Folk Belief*, pp. 12–17, for a summary of the pagan deities and of the scholarship on the subject.

9. E. A. Riabinin, *Zoomorfnye ukrasheniia drevnei Rusi X–XIV vv.*, a special issue of *Arkheologiia SSSR*, ed. V. A. Rybakov (Leningrad, 1981), illustrates, analyzes, and classifies the grave objects.

10. G. K. Vagner, *Problema zhanrov v drevnerusskom iskusstve* (Moscow, 1974), p. 47; A. Ambroz, "O simvolike russkoi krest'ianskoi vyshivki arkhaicheskogo tipa," *Sovetskaia arkheologiia*, 1966, no. 1, pp. 72–73; V. Vasilenko, "Slavianskoe iazychestvo," *Dekorativnoe iskusstvo SSSR*, 1968, no. 2, pp. 19–20.

11. P. I. Utkin, *Russkie iuvelirnye ukrasheniia* (Moscow, 1970), pp. 13–14.

12. V. M. Vasilenko, "Slavianskoe iazychestvo XI–XIII vv." (1968) and "Razmyshleniia o viaticheskikh kol'tsakh" (1972), first published in *Narodnoe iskusstvo*, pp. 243–49, 250–59; Utkin, *Russkie iuvelirnye ukrasheniia*, p. 14; Gimbutas, *The Slavs*, pp. 160–69.

13. See Turner, *Celebration*, p. 16.

14. Vasilenko identified the petaled crescent with a dual symbol for the moon and sun. The flower with even, rounded petals might be a wild relative of the chamomile (known today in Bulgaria and elsewhere as "Perun's flower" because of its color and form). The ornaments always had seven petals or rays, suggesting a symbolic association with the seven days of the week or the seven phases of the moon. Vasilenko, "Razmyshleniia," pp. 254–55. Talbot Rice, *The Scythians*, pp. 181–82, notes that the Slavs, unlike the Scythians, had both a solar cult and one centered on a goddess whose powers were connected with the earth and forests.

15. Vasilenko, "Razmyshleniia," pp. 257–58. The cult of Perun was widespread even after the rise of Kiev. Manifestations include Peryn' in Novgorod, Perkunas in Lithuania, and Perunika in Bulgaria; these might ultimately be related to the ancient Indian Pariania, who takes the form of a storm cloud.

16. Riabinin, "Zoomorfnye ukrasheniia," pp. 101, 110, illustrates several combinations; Vasilenko, "Razmyshleniia," pp. 257–58, describes household items from Novgorod, such as spoons decorated with bird shapes, rhomboids, and solar disks. On the concept of increasing effectiveness by increasing the number of symbols, see V. P. Darkevich, "Simvoly nebesnykh svetil v ornamente drevnei Rusi," *Sovetskaia arkheologiia*, 1960, no. 4.

17. Dintses, "Drevnie cherty v russkom narodnom iskusstve," in N. N. Voronin and M. K. Karger, eds., *Istoriia kul'tury drevnei Rusi* (Moscow and Leningrad, 1948–51), pp. 465–67, on textile fragments from Severian and Krivichian *kurgany,* bone fragments from many sites, with rhomboid and cross designs.

18. Vasilenko, "Slavianskoe iazychestvo," p. 246, also discusses another type of ritual cake, the round *kalachi* (from *kolo* or *koleso,* "wheel"), baked on St. Peter's Day, in connection with the ancient sun-disk ornament. See Ivanits, *Russian Folk Belief,* pp. 12–13.

19. Vagner, *Problema zhanrov,* pp. 69–75 and fig. 6. The idol resembles descriptions of the idols of Perun and the other gods set up by Vladimir in Kiev, and after the conversion cast into the river, where they were covered with layers of sediment. The Zbrucz idol is in the Krakow Museum in Poland. See Gimbutas, *The Slavs,* pp. 153, 155.

20. *Slovo o polku Igoreve,* discovered and edited in 1795, was composed by an unnamed poet, possibly a member of Igor's retinue, a Christian believer who had strong ties to Slavic traditions: he calls himself a descendant of Veles, god of cattle and plenty, and perhaps also a patron of artistic talent, like Hermes. See George P. Fedotov, *The Russian Religious Mind* (New York: Harper, 1960), pp. 315–43, on the mingling of Slavic, Hellenic, and Christian elements in the epic.

21. Vagner, *Problema zhanrov,* p. 61; A. Rybakov, "Prikladnoe iskusstvo kievskoi Rusi IX–XI vekov," in Grabar', Kemenov, Lazarev, et al., *Istoriia russkogo iskusstva,* vol. 1 (Moscow, 1954), p. 262. For Scandinavian comparisons, see James Graham-Campbell and Dafydd Kidd, *The Vikings* (New York, 1980), and Wilson, *The Northern World,* esp. pp. 171–73.

22. See George Vernadsky, *The Origins of Russia* (Oxford, 1959), pp. 137–39; Fedotov, *The Russian Religious Mind,* pp. 14–20; V. N. Lazarev, "Zhivopis' i skul'ptura Novgoroda," in Grabar', Kemenov, Lazarev, et al., *Istoriia russkogo iskusstva,* vol. 2 (Moscow, 1954), p. 236, on the *dvoeverie* and popular piety.

23. See M. V. Alpatov, "Obraz Georgiia Voina v iskusstve Vizantii i drevnei Rusi," in Alpatov, *Etiudy po istorii russkogo iskusstva* (Moscow, 1967), vol. 1, pp. 154–69.

24. See Joanna Hubbs, *Mother Russia: The Feminine Myth in Russian Culture* (Bloomington, Ind., 1988), pp. 87–123.

25. Cf. N. Pomerantsev, *Russkaia dereviannaia skul'ptura* (Moscow, 1966). Fig. 5 represents "Aunt Anna," progenitress of the clan and goddess of weaving, Charonda village, Vologda region. On comparable metamorphoses and conflations of gods and saints in western Europe, see Pamela Berger, *The Goddess Obscured: Transformations of the Grain Protectress from Goddess to Saint* (Boston, 1985), pp. 49–54.

26. V. I. Chicherov, *Russkoe narodnoe tvorchestvo* (Moscow, 1959), p. 363.

27. M. K. Karger, "Novgorodskoe zodchestvo," in Grabar', Kemenov, Lazarev, et al., *Istoriia russkogo iskusstva,* vol. 2, pp. 38–39. The church was begun around 1158 and completed in 1207; it has recently been restored.

28. See Linda J. Ivanits, ed., "Russian Folk Narratives about the Supernatural," in *Soviet Anthropology and Archaeology* (Armonk, N.Y., 1987), vol. 26, no. 2, pp. 15–17, 59–68, 69–83.

29. Vasilenko, "Russkaia narodnaia rez'ba," in *Narodnoe iskusstvo,* pp. 47–59; Sokolov, *Russian Folklore,* pp. 246–55. Divination, frowned upon by the church but popular to the present day, was aided by special *lubok* almanacs and divination booklets.

30. Ivan Snegirev, *Russkie prostonarodnye prazdniki i suevernye obriady* (Moscow, 1838), pp. 23–30, 75–80.

31. V. Propp, *Russkie agrarnye prazdniki: Opyt istoriko-etnograficheskogo issledovaniia* (Leningrad, 1963); N. I. Kravtsov, ed., *Russkoe narodnoe poeticheskoe tvorchestvo* (Moscow, 1971), pp. 36–37, 49–50; Ivanits, *Russian Folk Belief*, pp. 10–12. See Sir James Frazer, *The Golden Bough* (1890; rev. ed., Great Meadows, N.J., 1959), pp. 262–69, on festivals and ritual names connected with crops, trees, water, and fire; though inaccurate in some details, Frazer's study relates Slavic and Russian practices to those of other cultures.

32. Propp, *Russkie agrarnye prazdniki*, p. 78, includes a description of the *rusalki* dancing and swinging from the branches. See Propp's introduction and Roberta Reeder's notes in Roberta Reeder, ed., *Down along the Mother Volga* (Philadelphia, 1975), pp. 7, 82–84, for variations.

33. Vasilenko, "Russkaia narodnaia rez'ba i rospis' po derevu," pp. 46–47, quoting sources from the sixth to the twelfth centuries; pp. 46–51 on relationships between *rusalki* and *bereginy*.

34. V. M. Vasilenko mentioned this interpretation to me in 1982. Omelian Pritsak, *The Origin of Rus'* (Cambridge, Mass., 1981), pp. 3–7, summarizes explanations of the word *rus'* in relation to Slavic or Scandinavian sources of *Rus'*; he does not include this idea.

35. Nikolai Krasnopol'skii's *Dneprovskaia rusalka* was an adaptation of a Viennese opera, *Das Donauweibchen*, with Russian songs by Stepan Davydov. The romantic *rusalka* pieces were prototypes for Russian fairytale operas by Glinka and later Slavophile composers. See Malcolm H. Brown, "Native Song and National Consciousness," in Theofanis G. Stavrou, ed., *Art and Culture in Nineteenth-Century Russia* (Bloomington, Ind., 1983), p. 64. The later operas and Kramskoi's *Rusalki* (1871, Tretiakov Gallery) were based on Pushkin's "Rusalka" and Gogol's "May Night."

36. Vasilenko, "Russkaia narodnaia rez'ba," p. 57, citing A. Afanas'ev, *Poeticheskie vozzreniia slavian na prirodu* (Moscow, 1869), vol. 3, p. 132.

37. See Ivanits, "Russian Folk Narratives," pp. 59–68, 68–83.

38. Vasilenko, "Russkaia narodnaia rez'ba," p. 56, gives several examples of songs and images.

39. An early eighteenth-century painted cupboard in the State Historical Museum, Moscow, shows the *sirin* and *alkonost* with a long text recounting their legend. I wish to thank curator Zoia Popova for showing this piece to me.

40. See J. E. Cirlot, *A Dictionary of Symbols* (New York, 1962), pp. 328–32.

41. Lazarev, "Zhivopis' i skul'ptura Novgoroda," p. 236.

42. This discussion emphasizes the visual or physical aspects of life-stage ceremonies and seasonal rituals. General summaries of birth, betrothal, marriage, and death customs, based on studies of Tver', Tambov, and other central Russian provinces in the 1850s and 1860s, are in Matossian, "The Peasant Way of Life," pp. 20–30; Stephen P. Dunn and Ethel Dunn, *The Peasants of Central Russia* (New York, 1967), pp. 94–104; Y. M. Sokolov, *Russian Folklore* (New York, 1950), pp. 203–34, includes wedding chants and funeral laments.

43. Matossian, "The Peasant Way of Life," p. 22.

44. John Bushnell, "Russian Peasant Bride Theft, and Russia's Bride Theft Zone: Preliminary Observations" (American Association for the Advancement of Slavic Studies an-

nual meeting, Boston, 1987). I wish to thank the author for sending me this paper. A similar custom in Old Believer villages beyond the Volga is described in Mel'nikov (Pecherskii), *V lesakh*, pp. 78–80. Sokolov, *Russian Folklore*, pp. 209–10, describes abductions on horseback and other variants.

45. Dunn and Dunn, *The Peasants of Central Russia*, pp. 96–97.

46. Dunn and Dunn, *The Peasants of Central Russia*, pp. 99–100, note that in the mid-twentieth century, a *pridanoe* was still obligatory in Viriatino, Tambov region. It included a down puff with three slipcases, four valances for the marriage bed, one sheet, four bedspreads, two down pillows with four cases each, one calico bed curtain, several curtains for closets and kitchen shelves and windows, four towels for the icons and photographs on the wall, a lace cover for the icon table, two tablecloths, and an oilcloth for the kitchen table. In addition, the bride prepared a set of clothes for the groom.

47. Sokolov, *Russian Folklore*, pp. 206–207.

48. Dunn and Dunn, *The Peasants of Central Russia*, pp. 98–99; Sokolov, *Russian Folklore*, p. 210.

49. Sokolov, *Russian Folklore*, pp. 213–22, on songs and chants, and information on paid composers and chanters.

50. See Turner, *Celebration*, p. 16, for a more general statement of the multiple functions of such community rituals.

51. Matossian, "The Peasant Way of Life," p. 29.

52. Dunn and Dunn, *The Peasants of Central Russia*, pp. 103–104; Sokolov, *Russian Folklore*, pp. 224–34. Many Russian cemeteries still have tables for visitors at each gravesite.

53. Sokolov, *Russian Folklore*, pp. 230–34.

54. V. I. Chicherov, *Zimnii period russkogo zemledel'cheskogo kalendaria XVI–XIX vekov* (Moscow, 1957), pp. 156–85.

55. Elizabeth A. Warner, *The Russian Folk Theater* (The Hague, 1977), pp. 3–17, on the *koliadki*, processions, and masks; Chicherov, *Russkoe narodnoe tvorchestvo*, pp. 367–70, on *koliadki*. The word *koliadki* derived from the name of the Greco-Roman new year holiday, *kalanda* (*calendae*). See Sokolov, *Russian Folklore*, pp. 179–87.

56. Recorded as early as the eleventh century, the custom may have originated as a way of tricking evil spirits, and later it may have taken on additional elements from popular, half-understood church plays. Warner, *The Russian Folk Theater*, pp. 5–8, cites a description of the mummers by Adam Olearius in 1636.

57. Warner, *The Russian Folk Theater*, p. 7.

58. Performances with real animals also took place; dancing bears and bear baiting were condemned by the Russian church. Warner, *The Russian Folk Theater*, pp. 15–16.

59. See Sokolov, *Russian Folklore*, p. 188.

60. Warner, *Russian Folk Theater*, pp. 18–22; Kravtsov, *Russkoe narodnoe poeticheskoe tvorchestvo*, pp. 44–45; Ivanits, *Russian Folk Belief*, pp. 7–8; Sokolov, *Russian Folklore*, p. 190.

61. Examples from the early twentieth century are in the Sergiev-Posad Museum and the State Historical Museum, Moscow. I wish to thank S. Zhegalova and S. Zhizhina for describing the custom to me.

62. O. Kruglova, "Drevniaia simvolika v proisvedeniiakh narodnogo iskusstva Iaroslavskoi oblasti," *Sovetskaia arkheologiia*, 1971, no. 1, p. 265.

63. Kravtsov, *Russkoe narodnoe poeticheskoe tvorchestvo*, pp. 46–48; Reeder, *Down along the Mother Volga*, pp. 6–7, 78–83; Ivanits, *Russian Folk Belief*, pp. 7–9; Matossian, "The Peasant Way of Life," pp. 34–36.

64. Ivanits, *Russian Folk Belief*, p. 9.

65. Kravtsov, *Russkoe narodnoe poeticheskoe tvorchestvo*, pp. 47–48; Reeder, *Down along the Mother Volga*, pp. 7, 81–84; Frazer, *The Golden Bough*, p. 81; Warner, *The Russian Folk Theater*, p. 22. The sequence had varied forms, including garlanding young girls with branches to replace the birch trees, and games in which peasants exchanged stock questions and answers in riddle form.

66. See Chicherov, *Russkoe narodnoe tvorchestvo*, pp. 359–80; the rituals and labors are also described by the foreign observers cited in chapter 1, including Robert Sears (1855), "the Englishwoman in Russia" (1855), and Sir Donald Mackenzie Wallace (1877).

67. Nikolai Gogol's "Saint John's Eve," in *Evenings on a Farm near Demianka* (1831–32), describes Kupalo rituals. The magic of fire and water and secret herbal drinks acquired overtones of satanism in some versions, including Modest Musorgskii's *A Night on Bald Mountain* (1867) and Andrei Tarkovskii's film *Andrei Rublev* (1965).

68. See Frazer, *The Golden Bough*, pp. 269–70. Warner, *Russian Folk Theater*, pp. 24–26, for several regional variants; Kravtsov, *Russkoe narodnoe poeticheskoe tvorchestvo*, pp. 49–50, includes a ritual practiced in Soviet times.

69. P. E. Zabolotskii, *After the Harvest* (1822, Russian Museum), depicts "Uspenskii," the estate of A. Tomilov near Staraia Ladoga.

70. Snegirev, *Russkie prostonarodnye prazdniki*, pp. 79–80. See below, chapters 13 and 14, on serfs' obligations.

71. Vasilenko, "Russkaia narodnaia rez'ba," p. 55, citing A. Afanas'ev, *Poeticheskaia vozzreniia slavian na prirodu* (Moscow, 1869), vol. 3, p. 141.

11. Transformation of the Slavic Legacy

1. There is little archeological material for this period; most modern writing either emphasizes or denies the importance of the Varangians in the formation of Rus'. See Pritzak, *The Origin of Rus'*. On physical material see N. N. Voronin and V. N. Lazarev, "Zakliuchenie k pervym dvum tomam," in Grabar', Kemenov, Lazarev, et al., *Istoriia russkogo iskusstva*, vol. 2, pp. 379–85.

2. Jerome Blum, *Lord and Peasant in Russia* (Princeton, 1961), pp. 15, 16, cites Rybakov's identification of some sixty specialized crafts in Kiev and other cities in B. A. Rybakov, *Remeslo drevnei Rusi* (Moscow, 1948), pp. 501–22.

3. G. H. Hamilton, *The Art and Architecture of Russia*, 2nd ed. (Harmondsworth, 1972), pp. 62–64. A similar separation between formal, liturgical images and more active figure scenes existed in much of medieval pictorial art. Borders in St. Sophia in Kiev included geometrical patterns, gryphons, and other exotic beasts along with seraphim frescoes of the southwest tower. Similar geometric forms and mythic creatures decorated the borders along the vaults at St. Sophia in Novgorod, St. George in Staraia Ladoga, and The Savior in Nereditsa. The frescoes at Nereditsa were destroyed in World War II, but photographs show the presence of several artists, and the use of different styles for different iconogra-

phy. See V. N. Lazarev, "Zhivopis' i skul'ptura Novgoroda," in Grabar', Kemenov, Lazarev, et al., *Istoriia russkogo iskusstva,* vol. 2, pp. 96–99.

4. See Hamilton, *Art and Architecture of Russia,* pp. 39–40; a now lost chronicle stated that Frederick Barbarossa sent artists to Andrei in Suzdal', according to V. N. Tatishchev's *Istoriia rossiiskaia* (1774). The Kievan princes had trade and dynastic ties with the Caucasian kingdoms, and the exterior relief sculpture of Armenian and Georgian churches may have been known to Russian and Western artists.

5. Carvers combined Scandinavian and Slavic (or Scythian) styles on a wooden column carved with shallow interlace and gryphon and lion motifs, probably made for a shrine in Novgorod in the eleventh century (in the Institute of the History of Material Culture, Academy of Sciences), illustrated in N. N. Voronin, "Itogi razvitiia drevnerusskogo iskusstva," in Grabar', Kemenov, Lazarev, et al., *Istoriia russkogo iskusstva,* vol. 4, p. 617.

6. On the program of St. George at Iur'ev-Pol'skii, partly restored under Ivan III, and on the facades of the Cathedral of the Nativity of the Virgin in Suzdal', see G. K. Vagner, *Mastera drevnerusskoi skul'ptury: Rel'efy Iur'eva-Pol'skogo* (Moscow, 1966), and G. K. Vagner, *Belokamennaia rez'ba drevnego Suzdalia* (Moscow, 1975).

7. Vagner, *Belokamennaia rez'ba,* pp. 97–142. The doors were unique in their time, but two other sets of "fired gold" doors were made in 1336 for the cathedrals of Novgorod and Tver'.

8. M. K. Karger, "Novgorodskoe zodchestvo," in Grabar', Kemenov, Lazarev, et al., *Istoriia russkogo iskusstva,* vol. 2, pp. 16–17, citing the term *plotniki* in the Ipat'ev Chronicle for 1016.

9. Parts of iconostases, including royal doors, are displayed in many Russian museums, notably the Kolomenskoe Museum-Preserve.

10. Examples from Novgorod, Rostov, and Moscow are illustrated in Pomerantsev, *Russkaia dereviannaia skul'ptura,* pp. 45–57. Later, artists from Vologda made more refined carved and painted icons of St. George and St. Paraskeva.

11. For example, a doorway from the twelfth-century Hylestad church in Setesdal, Norway, is carved in a similar style.

12. The date appears in a long inscription carved around the staff stating that the cross was placed in the Church of Saints Florus and Laurus by the inhabitants of Legoshaia Street in Novgorod.

13. I. I. Pleshanova, "Dva pamiatniki drevnerusskoi rez'by po derevu v sobranii Russkogo muzeia," in *Soobshcheniia Gosudarstvennogo russkogo muzeia* (Moscow, 1974), vol. 10, pp. 107–14, discusses the ornamentation of the cross in relation to royal doors and other church carving.

14. Charles Halperin, *Russia and the Golden Horde* (Bloomington, Ind., 1985), pp. 120–25; Blum, *Lord and Peasant in Russia,* p. 63.

15. Blum, *Lord and Peasant in Russia,* pp. 62–63, cites estimates based on tribute to the Mongols at the rate of 2 rubles per hundred inhabitants; in 1446 Moscow paid 2,000 rubles. In the fourteenth century, Milan and Venice had populations of about 100,000, Paris about 80,000, Florence about 55,000 (after the Black Death).

16. Icon from the Church of Saints Boris and Gleb, Kargach, now in the Tretiakov Gallery, Moscow; a comparable image is an icon from Novgorod in the Russian Museum, Leningrad.

17. The icons, both from Novgorod, are in the State Hermitage and the Tretiakov Gallery. The fifteenth-century icon is discussed in a different context in Alpatov, "Obraz Georgiia Voina v iskusstve Vizantii i drevnei Rusi," pp. 154–59.

18. The icon, painted ca. 1620–30, is in the Tretiakov Gallery. See Iu. Dmitriev, "Stroganovskaia shkola zhivopisi," in Grabar', Kemenov, Lazarev, et al., *Istoriia russkogo iskusstva,* vol. 3 (Moscow, 1955), pp. 661–63.

19. Dates of excavation layers in Moscow are difficult to interpret because building during Moscow's ascendancy disturbed the ground levels. Excavations of the Kremlin and surrounding areas by the Institute of Archeology in the 1960s yielded ivory, bronze, and crystal ornaments, and many gravestones decorated with solar disks, from two to six on each stone, instead of crosses. M. G. Rabinovich, "Kul'turnyi sloi tsentral'nykh raionov Moskvy"; N. S. Sheliapina, "Arkheologicheskie nabliudeniia v moskovskom kremle v 1963–65 gg."; and G. P. Latysheva, "Torgovye sviazi Moskvy v XII–XIV vv.," in N. N. Voronin et al., *Drevnosti moskovskogo kremlia* (Moscow, 1971), pp. 17, 30, 80, 138, 146, 215–23.

20. Latysheva, "Torgovye sviazy Moskvy," ill. p. 217; A. Iakobson, "Khudozhestvennye sviazy moskovskoi Rusi s Zakavkazem i Blizhnim Vostokom v XVI v.," in Voronin et al., *Drevnosti moskovskogo kremlia,* pp. 230–33.

21. V. O. Kluchevsky, *A History of Russia,* trans. C. Hogarth (London and New York, 1917), vol. 2, pp. 16–17, on the marriage of Ivan and Sophia and the "self-realization" of the Muscovite Empire. Richard Pipes, *Russia under the Old Regime* (New York, 1974), pp. 72–73.

22. Aida Nasilova, *The Faceted Chamber in the Moscow Kremlin* (Leningrad, 1978), p. 5, citing *Pamiatniki diplomaticheskikh snoshenii Rossii s derzhavami inostrannymy* (St. Petersburg, 1853), p. 93.

23. See V. Ia. Libson, *Pamiatniki arkhitektury Moskvy. Kreml', Kitai-gorod, Tsentral'nye ploshchadi* (Moscow, 1982).

24. Hamilton, *The Art and Architecture of Russia,* pp. 156–57, citing Augustin von Meyerberg in 1661. The palace was restored in the nineteenth century. See Nasilova, *The Faceted Chamber,* for reproductions of the complete decorative program.

25. V. Lazarev, "Zhivopis' i skul'ptura Novgoroda," in Grabar', Kemenov, Lazarev, et al., *Istoriia russkogo iskusstva,* vol. 2, pp. 270–77.

26. State Historical Museum; illustrated in M. M. Postnikova-Loseva, "Prikladnoe iskusstvo XVI–XVII vekov," in Grabar', Kemenov, Lazarev, et al., *Istoriia russkogo iskusstva,* vol. 4 (Moscow, 1959), pp. 561, 606.

27. Armory Palace and the State Historical Museum; the earrings are illustrated in Postnikova-Loseva, "Prikladnoe iskusstvo XVI–XVII vekov," pp. 564–65.

28. Another sign of the status of court artists was their housing: Simon Ushakov, master of the Kremlin school, was given a spacious, three-story stone house for himself and his assistants adjacent to the Church of the Trinity "in Nikitinki," not far from the Kremlin. Libson, *Pamiatniki arkhitektury Moskvy,* pp. 454–56.

29. "Tabula Russiae," published in H. Gerrits, *Atlas major sive Cosmographia* (Amsterdam, 1613); facsimile published as an insert in Libson, *Pamiatniki arkhitektury Moskvy.*

30. S. K. Zhegalova, "Novye materialy po istorii severodvinskoi rospisi," in Boguslavskaia and Suslova, *Russkoe narodnoe iskusstvo severa,* p. 41.

31. See A. Milovskii, *Suzdal'* (Moscow, 1981), p. 7.

32. See Blum, *Lord and Peasant in Russia*, and Pipes, *Russia under the Old Regime*, pp. 86–97, for details on the system and distinctions among categories of peasants and serfs. The "service" class made up less than 1% of the population. The workers paid their obligation in money or labor, called *tiaglo*. The process of turning peasants into land-bound serfs did not seriously affect the northernmost regions, as it was not economical. According to Chicherov, *Russkoe narodnoe tvorchestvo*, p. 203, the absence of serfdom was a key aspect of northern culture.

33. See Iakobson, "Khudozhestvennye sviazi moskovskoi Rusi," in Voronin et al., *Drevnosti moskovskogo kremlia*, pp. 230–33.

12. Heraldic Beasts and Guardian Figures

1. Vasilenko, "Russkaia narodnaia rez'ba i rospis' po derevu," p. 55.

2. For example, the association of the wheel of St. Elijah's chariot with the sun is suggested by visual parallels of spokes or rays combined with a circle. For the concept that the effectiveness of symbols increased with repetition, see V. Darkevich, "Simvoly nebesnykh svetil v ornamente drevnei Rusi," *Sovetskaia arkheologiia*, 1960, no. 4. Relating both figurative and abstract symbols (horse and circle) to natural powers (the sun) is suggested by the concept of the "multi-vocal" symbol in Victor Turner, *The Ritual Process* (Ithaca, N.Y., 1977).

3. Zhegalova, *Russkaia narodnaia zhivopis'*, pp. 26–49. A. N. Veselovskii connected legends of Solomon and *Kitovras* with Indian and Western analogs in his 1872 dissertation, cited in Sokolov, *Russian Folklore*, pp. 85, 101.

4. There are two similar trunks from Velikii Ustiug, one in the State Historical Museum, the other in the Hermitage. Zhegalova, *Russkaia narodnaia zhivopis'*, pp. 47–50.

5. Grigorii Novikov's distaff (1880, State Historical Museum) is illustrated in Zhegalova, *Russkaia narodnaia zhivopis'*, p. 132. Two distaffs with abstract sun symbols placed around horses, painted by Mikhail Novikov around 1898, are in the Sergiev-Posad Museum; see Kruglova, *Russkaia narodnaia rez'ba i rospis' po derevu*, figs. 81, 82.

6. See Vasilenko, "Russkaia narodnaia rez'ba," p. 55, and pp. 54–56 on water deities' manifestations. Some ancient mythologies associated the horse with both sky and sea, including the Greek myths of Poseidon and Apollo.

7. Vasilenko, "Russkaia narodnaia rez'ba," p. 56.

8. Painted trunk (State Historical Museum). Zhegalova, *Russkaia narodnaia zhivopis'*, pp. 75–76.

9. Zhegalova, *Russkaia narodnaia zhivopis'*, p. 77.

10. Zhegalova, *Russkaia narodnaia zhivopis'*, p. 79, suggests that the face was a portrait of Peter's wife, Catherine I.

11. Zhegalova, *Russkaia narodnaia zhivopis'*, pp 59–60, 64–65; examples from Velikii Ustiug and the Northern Dvina. See Vilinbakhov, "Russkie znamena XVII veka s izobrazheniem edinoroga," for examples on military banners.

12. Zhegalova, *Russkaia narodnaia zhivopis'*, pp. 64–69.

13. See I. N. Ukhanova, "Knizhnaia illiustratsiia XVIII v. i pamiatniki narodnogo dekorativno-prikladnogo iskusstva russkogo severa (Severnaia Dvina)," in T. V. Alekseeva, ed., *Russkoe iskusstvo pervoi chetverti XVIII veka* (Moscow, 1974), pp. 210–26.

14. Zhegalova, "Novye materialy po istorii severodvinskoi rospisi," pp. 39–40.

15. Distaffs from Mokraia Edoma (Sergiev-Posad Museum), in Kruglova, *Russkaia narodnaia rez'ba,* fig. 70.

16. The Scandinavian Tree of Life, Yggdrasil, as described in the Eddas, was very close to the northern Russian image, and may have been an early source, though there is no supporting evidence. See Roger Cook, *The Tree of Life: Image for the Cosmos* (New York, 1974), for illustration and discussion of the image in many cultures.

17. Zhegalova, "Novye materialy po istorii severodvinskoi rospisi," p. 44.

18. Gorodets distaff from the V. E. Arkharov-Fredynskii collection, illustrated in V. S. Voronov, "Russkie prialki" (1916–20), in *O krest'ianskom iskusstve,* opposite p. 232.

19. Distaffs from Iaroslavl' Province (1817 and 1835, Sergiev-Posad Museum), illustrated in Kruglova, *Russkaia narodnaia rez'ba,* figs. 47, 48.

20. Dintses, "Drevnie cherty v russkom narodnom iskusstve," pp. 469–77, discusses weaving and embroidery with images of Mokosh, horses and riders, and other elements of the "pre-Christian" *chin* (icon row).

21. Towel border (Museum of Folk Art, Moscow), illustrated in Voronov, *O krest'ianskom iskusstve,* fig. 75.

22. Embroidered valance from Olonets Province (mid-nineteenth century, State Historical Museum), in Efimova and Belogorskaia, *Russkaia vyshivka i kruzhevo,* no. 90.

23. Three towel borders from the Ves'egonsk region of Tver' Province (1848 and second half of nineteenth century, Sergiev-Posad Museum), in Kalmykova, *Narodnaia vyshivka tverskoi zemli,* nos. 68, 69, 70.

24. Examples from Ves'egonsk (second half of nineteenth century, Sergiev-Posad Museum), illustrated in Kalmykova, *Narodnaia vyshivka tverskoi zemli,* nos. 59, 64, 65, 66, 80, 81.

25. Kalmykova, *Narodnaia vyshivka tverskoi zemli,* p. 14.

26. T. M. Razina, "Poetizatsii drevnikh siuzhetov," *Dekorativnoe iskusstvo SSSR,* nos. 7, 11 (1973) and no. 6 (1974), on the semantics of folk art, compares the rhythmic structure of embroidery to that of oral folk poetry. Vagner, *Problema zhanrov v drevnerusskom iskusstve,* pp. 52–56, discusses two-part songs. V. M. Vasilenko pointed out the composition of riddles to me. Margarita Mazo relates wedding songs, songs to saints, and other folk music to peasant embroidery in her work on "Folk Music and Beliefs of the Contemporary Russian Village" (forthcoming article).

13. Scenes from Life and Forms from the Past

1. V. M. Vasilenko, "Narodnoe iskusstvo pervoi poloviny XIX veka," in Grabar', Kemenov, Lazarev, et al., *Istoriia russkogo iskusstva,* vol. 8, book 2 (Moscow, 1964), p. 575.

2. Turner, *Celebration,* p. 16, defines celebration as expression of shared purposes and values, the "essential life" of a community, and the "distillation and typification of its corporate experience."

3. Early genre scenes include frescoes of musicians playing in St. Sophia in Kiev; domestic details in icons, such as a maidservant spinning in an Annunciation scene

(Sergiev-Posad Museum); and manuscript miniatures showing workers building churches, such as a late sixteenth-century "Life of St. Sergei of Radonezh" (Russian State Library). Later books, influenced by Western models, included many genre scenes. See A. A. Sidorov, "Graviura XVI veka," in Grabar', Kemenov, Lazarev, et al., *Istoriia russkogo iskusstva,* vol. 3, pp. 615, 617.

Genre as a category of the fine arts was recognized in the Academy of Arts in the 1750s and '60s, but it did not influence folk art. See chapter 14 and T. Alekseeva, "Bytovoi zhanr," in Grabar', Kemenov, Lazarev, et al., *Istoriia russkogo iskusstva,* vol. 7 (Moscow, 1961), pp. 231–82.

4. State Historical Museum, Moscow. Zhegalova, "Novye materialy," pp. 36–37, and *Russkaia narodnaia zhivopis',* pp. 116–18, dates it shortly before 1797 on the basis of the inscription giving the place name Kurgomenskaia Volost', which was changed in that year.

5. Zhegalova, "Istoriia odnoi ekspeditsii," in Zhegalova et al., *Prianik, prialka i ptitsa sirin,* pp. 18, 45.

6. Both distaffs in the State Historical Museum, illustrated in Vasilenko, *Narodnoe iskusstvo,* nos. 78, 82.

7. See Sokolov, *Russian Folklore,* pp. 211–12, citing descriptions published by Nikolai Novikov, *Drevniaia Rossiiskaia Bibliofika* (St. Petersburg, 1775), Part 8.

8. State Historical Museum, in Zhegalova, *Russkaia narodnaia zhivopis',* pp. 120–21.

9. Zhegalova, *Russkaia narodnaia zhivopis',* pp. 122, 123. A similar scene on a distaff in the Museum of Folk Art is illustrated in Vasilenko, *Narodnoe iskusstvo,* nos. 85, 86.

10. On Iarygin see S. K. Zhegalova, "Ekspeditsiia Gosudarstvennogo istoricheskogo muzeia na severnuiu Dvinu," *Sovetskaia etnografiia,* 1960, no. 4, pp. 177–82; Zhegalova, "Narodnyi master rospisi Iakov Iarygin," in *Sbornik: Muzei narodnogo iskusstva i khudozhestvennoi promyshlennosti* (Moscow, [n.d.]), pp. 192–208; Zhegalova, *Russkaia narodnaia zhivopis',* pp. 89–100, 114–15; and Zhegalova, "Severodvinskaia rospis' po derevu," in Zhegalova et al., *Russkoe khudozhestvennoe derevo,* pp. 117–48, and catalogue of 60 known works, pp. 149–71. See also Vasilenko, "Russkaia narodnaia rez'ba," pp. 101–11.

11. Early eighteenth-century manuscript "Anthology" with 135 illustrations, Library of the Academy of Sciences, in Ukhanova, "Knizhnaia illiustratsiia i pamiatniki narodnogo iskusstva," pp. 216–17, ill. 146.

12. Canister (ca. 1810, State Historical Museum), in Zhegalova, "Severodvinskaia rospis'," p. 126, catalogue, no. 2. Old Believers preserved the forms of writing used before Patriarch Nikon's reforms; see Brooks, *When Russia Learned to Read,* pp. 25–26.

13. Painted boxes from Gorodets, late nineteenth century, in Vasilenko, *Narodnoe iskusstvo,* nos. 113, 114, 115.

14. Distaff from Arkhangel'sk region (Sergiev-Posad Museum), in Kruglova, *Russkaia narodnaia rez'ba,* no. 76.

15. Vasilenko, "Russkaia narodnaia rez'ba i rospis' po derevu XVIII–XX vv.," pp. 124–25.

16. Valance from Nizhnii Novgorod (State Historical Museum), illustrated in Efimova and Belogorskaia, *Russkaia vyshivka i kruzhevo,* nos. 81, 82.

14. Serf Artists, Peasant Painters, and the Rise of Genre

1. A. G. Venetsianov, letter to N. O. Miliukov, owner of serf artist Grigorii Soroka, Tretiakov Gallery Archive (*fond* 38), reprinted in K. V. Mikhailova, *Grigorii Soroka 1823–1864* (Leningrad, 1975), p. 100.

2. Session of the Council of the Academy of Arts (1829), cited in G. G. Pospelov, "Provintsial'naia zhivopis' pervoi poloviny XIX veka," in Grabar', Kemenov, Lazarev, et al., *Istoriia russkogo iskusstva*, vol. 8, book 2, p. 358.

3. By 1900, only two master bonecarvers were working in Kholmogory, and only one niello master, M. P. Chirkov, in Velikii Ustiug; the icon-painting workshops in Palekh were nearly abandoned. See T. M. Razina, "Narodnoe iskusstvo," in Grabar', Kemenov, Lazarev, et al., *Istoriia russkogo iskusstva*, vol. 10, book 2 (Moscow, 1969), p. 460.

4. V. A. Kovrigina, "Zolotye i serebrianye mastera moskovskoi nemetskoi slobody (konets XVII–pervaia chetvert' XVIII v.)," *Vestnik Moskovskogo universiteta* (Istoriia), ser. 8, no. 4, 1981, pp. 60–71, notes that Russians outnumbered foreign masters, and that Russians and foreigners often worked in the same artels.

5. There are studies of individual serf artists, including the Argunov family and Soroka; of estate architecture and serf architects; of serf theaters and orchestras; and of the most influential masters of serf artists, the Sheremetevs. Works on decorative arts sometimes identify serf artists. Biographical information is fragmentary and works are scattered.

6. The painting is illustrated in N. Shkarovskaia, *Narodnoe samodeiatel'noe iskusstvo* (Leningrad, 1975), fig. 17.

7. Blum, *Lord and Peasant in Russia*, p. 426, citing data for 1857; the documents were needed for travel over 30 versts.

8. Chicherov gave this reason for the preservation of folk rituals in the north, *Russkoe narodnoe tvorchestvo*, p. 203.

9. See Blum, *Lord and Peasant in Russia*, pp. 422–33, on sales and other abuses.

10. Blum, *Lord and Peasant in Russia*, pp. 426–27.

11. Blum, *Lord and Peasant in Russia*, p. 426.

12. V. S. Dediukhina, "K voprosu o roli krepostnykh masterov v istorii stroitel'stva dvorianskoi usad'by XVIII v. (Na primere Kuskovo i Ostankino)," *Vestnik Moskovskogo universiteta* (Istoriia), ser. 8, no. 4, 1981, p. 85, on the household of Prince Cherkasskii in Moscow, later transferred to the Sheremetevs.

13. Dediukhina, "K voprosu o roli krepostnykh masterov," pp. 85–86, citing material from the Sheremetev archives and accounts.

14. Dediukhina, "K voprosu o roli krepostnykh masterov," pp. 86–91. These artists also supervised many projects. Mukhin worked on set design for the Sheremetev theater; the architects Mironov, Dikushin, and P. Argunov supervised building and decorating projects at Ostankino and Kuskovo, including the theater, Egyptian Pavilion, and Italian Pavilion, and had authority over the free outside artisans who were sometimes brought in. Two of the Argunovs served as advisors in acquiring works of art from abroad.

15. Shibanov was active from about 1772 through the 1780s. *Peasant Dinner* (1774) and *Celebrating the Marriage Contract* (1777) are in the Tretiakov Gallery. T. V. Alekseeva,

"Bytovoi zhanr," in Grabar', Kemenov, Lazarev, et al., *Istoriia russkogo iskusstva*, vol. 7 (Moscow, 1961), pp. 244–52.

16. Blum, *Lord and Peasant in Russia*, pp. 299–301.

17. Dediukhina, "K voprosu o roli krepostnykh masterov," pp. 83–84, 93. For a study of Russian estates see Priscilla Roosevelt, *The Russian Country Estate: A Social and Cultural History* (New Haven, 1994).

18. Zoia Popova, "Krepostnoi master Matvei Iakovlev, syn Veretennikov," in Zhegalova et al., *Prianik, prialka i ptitsa sirin*, p. 157, citing a letter from Prince Kurakin, 1777.

19. Popova, "Krepostnoi master," pp. 158–60. House serfs received a monthly payment in food or other necessities, in lieu of the share of crops for a farming peasant; they got clothing and boots every two or three years. Skilled workers normally had an annual bonus ranging from about six rubles for an apprentice, to ten to twenty for a craftsman, to perhaps fifty or more for especially valuable artists like the Argunovs. Dediukhina, "O roli krepostnykh masterov," pp. 89–92.

20. Popova, "Krepostnoi master," p. 146.

21. Popova, "Krepostnoi master," p. 156. Card table with views of the colonnade in the garden of the Turkish sultan and Justinian's obelisk in Constantinople, with signed inscriptions in Russian and French dated 1797 (State Historical Museum).

22. V. A. Shelkovnikov and T. N. Iakovleva, "Dekorativnoe i prikladnoe iskusstvo pervoi poloviny XIX veka," in Grabar', Kemenov, Lazarev, et al., *Istoriia russkogo iskusstva*, vol. 8, book 2 (Moscow, 1964), pp. 524–25, illustrates the Goncharov divan (State Historical Museum), the birch dressing table (private collection), and other pieces of serf-made furniture.

23. I. A. Pronina, "O prepodavanii dekorativno-prikladnogo iskusstva v XVIII v.," in Alekseeva, *Russkoe iskusstvo pervoi chetverti XVIII veka*, pp. 82–83.

24. Pronina, "O prepodavanii," p. 86.

25. Anonymous, *Wedding in Toropets* (Historical Museum, Moscow), in Shkarovskaia, *Narodnoe samodeiatel'noe iskusstvo*, fig. 12.

26. G. G. Pospelov, "Provintsial'naia zhivopis' pervoi poloviny XIX veka," in Grabar', Kemenov, Lazarev, et al., *Istoriia russkogo iskusstva*, vol. 8, book 2, pp. 345–73.

27. N. Fedorova and S. Iamshchikov, *Iaroslavskie portrety XVIII–XIX vekov* (Moscow, 1984), illustrates 134 portraits from Iaroslavl', including works by Nikolai Myl'nikov and Ivan Tarkhanov; they are strikingly similar to those of American portraitists of the same period.

28. Shkarovskaia, *Narodnoe samodeiatel'noe iskusstvo*, pp. 8–9, fig. 18.

29. Vasilii Raev, a serf freed by his master in the 1830s to study at the Arzamas Art School, traveled widely and became well known for his landscapes. Invited by the Demidovs to paint landscapes and interiors of the Nizhnii Tagil factories, he undoubtedly influenced local painters. Pospelov, "Provintsial'naia zhivopis'," p. 356, n. 1.

30. I. Khudoiarov's painting, on a wedding trunk made in Nizhnii Tagil, is in the Historical Museum, Moscow; P. F. Khudoiarov's works are in the Nizhnii Tagil Regional Museum. Pospelov, "Provintsial'naia zhivopis'," pp. 355–56, suggests a similarity between the factory scenes and *lubki*.

31. Pospelov, "Provintsial'naia zhivopis'," p. 358, n. 1, mentions this case, quoting the Academic Council statement (Central State Archives of Literature and Art, *fond* 789).

32. The drawing school run by the Society for the Encouragement of Artists in St. Petersburg was the most important. See S. Frederick Starr, "Russian Art and Society, 1800–1850," in Stavrou, *Art and Culture in Nineteenth-Century Russia*, pp. 101–105, for other implications of these points.

33. N. N. Kovalenskaia and A. A. Savinov, "V. A. Tropinin i portretisti nachala XIX veka," in Grabar', Kemenov, Lazarev, et al., *Istoriia russkogo iskusstva*, vol. 8, book 1 (Moscow, 1963), pp. 514–40.

34. Most of Tropinin's works are in the State Tretiakov Gallery and the Museum of V. A. Tropinin and Moscow Artists of His Time, catalogue by G. Kropivnitskaia, *Muzei V. A. Tropinina i moskovskikh khudozhnikov ego vremeni* (Moscow, 1975); see A. Amshinskaia, *Tropinin* (Moscow, 1976).

35. Biographical material is from Mikhailova, *Grigorii Soroka*, pp. 3–32, and the exhibition catalogue, Mikhailova, *Grigorii Soroka*. Other sources are T. V. Alekseeva, *Grigorii Vasil'evich Soroka* (Moscow, 1955), T. V. Alekseeva, *Khudozhniki shkoly Venetsianova* (Moscow, 1958), and T. V. Alekseeva, "Razvitie bytovogo zhanra," in Grabar', Kemenov, Lazarev, et al., *Istoriia russkogo iskusstva*, vol. 8, book 2, pp. 248–55.

36. See A. Savinov, *Venetsianov* (Moscow, 1955); T. V. Alekseeva, "A. G. Venetsianov i razvitie bytovogo zhanra," in Grabar', Kemenov, Lazarev, et al., *Istoriia russkogo iskusstva*, vol. 8, book 1 (Moscow, 1963), pp. 546–98; G. V. Smirnov, *Venetsianov i ego shkola* (Leningrad, 1973).

37. Soroka's album of drawings (1820s–1840s) is in the State Russian Museum. The self-portrait (1840s) is in a private collection in Moscow, the portrait of Lidiia Miliukova (1840s) is in the Hermitage, and *View of Lake Moldino* (1847) is in the Tver' Provincial Picture Gallery. The other works mentioned here, the portrait of Elizaveta (1840s), *Study at Ostrovki* (1844), *Fisherfolk* (1840s), and *View of the Lake at Ostrovki* (late 1840s–early 1850s), are in the State Russian Museum.

38. The information on Venetsianov's pupils and associates is based on Alekseeva, "A. G. Venetsianov i razvitie bytovogo zhanra" and "Razvitie bytovogo zhanra"; catalogue entries by John E. Bowlt and Alison Hilton for *The Art of Russia, 1800–1850* (Minneapolis, 1978), pp. 56–58, 60, 65, 72, 74.

39. *The Art of Russia, 1800–1850*, no. 31, p. 56.

40. Krylov's *Winter* (1827), Denisov's *Sailors in a Cobbler's Workshop* (1832), and Alekseev's *In the Studio of A. G. Venetsianov* (1827) are in the Russian Museum. Krendovskii's paintings, from the 1830s, are in the Tretiakov Gallery.

41. Lavr Plakhov's works are at the Russian Museum: *Stonecutters* (1830s), *At the Forge* (1845), *Preparing for Work* (1830s), and *Coachmen's Room at the Academy of Arts* (1834); and the Tretiakov Gallery: *Carpentry Workshop* (1845). At the end of the 1840s he stopped painting and turned to photography. See Alekseeva, "Razvitie bytovogo zhanra," p. 232.

42. K. V. Mikhailova and G. V. Smirnov, *Zhivopis' XVIII–nachala XX veka: Iz fondov Gosudarstvennogo russkogo muzeia* (Leningrad, 1982), p. 86 and nos. 68, 69.

43. Besides dinner services, vases and porcelain figurines of idealized peasants were made by the Imperial, the Gardner, the Gur'ev, and other porcelain factories; B. Shelkovnikov and T. Iakovleva, "Dekorativnoe i prikladnoe iskusstvo," in Grabar', Kemenov, Lazarev, et al., *Istoriia russkogo iskusstva*, vol. 8, book 2, pp. 534–39; I. Ivanova, *Russian Applied Art* (Leningrad, 1976), pp. 57–58, 114–19.

44. See Komelova, *Stseny russkoi narodnoi zhizni*, pp. 12, 18–19.

45. See Alison Hilton, "Russian Folk Art and 'High' Art," in Stavrou, *Art and Culture in Nineteenth-Century Russia*, pp. 250–52.

15. National Art and Folk Art

1. Hamilton, *The Art and Architecture of Russia*, p. 235.
2. See G. N. Komelova et al., *Catherine the Great: Treasures of Imperial Russia from the State Hermitage Museum, Leningrad* (Leningrad, 1990).
3. *Vladimir before Rogneda* (1770) is in the State Russian Museum. See Alla Vereshchagina, *Khudozhnik. Vremia. Istoriia: Ocherki russkoi istoricheskoi zhivopisi XVIII–nachala XX veka* (Moscow, 1973), pp. 11–19 and illustrations. See Robert Rosenblum, *Transformations in Late Eighteenth Century Art* (Princeton, 1967), pp. 10–15, 27–39, for parallels.
4. See F. Ia. Syrkina, "Teatral'no-dekoratsionnoe iskusstvo," in Grabar', Kemenov, Lazarev, et al., *Istoriia russkogo iskusstva*, vol. 9, book 1, pp. 149–52, on historical stage design 1830s–1870s.
5. Felitsin, from the Moscow bourgeoisie, made long visits to peasant friends in central Russia. Mikhailova and Smirnov, *Zhivopis' XVIII–nachala XX veka: Iz fondov Gosudarstvennogo russkogo muzeia*, pp. 91–92, no. 78.
6. Malcolm H. Brown, "Native Song and National Consciousness," in Stavrou, *Art and Culture in Nineteenth-Century Russia*, pp. 63–65.
7. See Richard Taruskin, "Realism as Preached and Practiced: The Russian Opera Dialogue," *Musical Quarterly*, July 1970, vol. 56, no. 53, pp. 431–55. Vladimir Stasov wrote about the use of popular motifs in Russian national music in "Twenty-five Years of Russian Art" (1882–83), in *Selected Essays on Music*, trans. Florence Jonas (London, 1968), pp. 102–10.
8. Murry Peppard, *Nikolai Nekrasov* (New York, 1967), pp. 65–66, 118–19, 138–39; N. Nekrasov, *Poems*, trans. J. M. Soskice (London, 1929); N. A. Nekrasov, *Poslednie pesni*, ed. G. Krasnov (Moscow, 1974). Khudiakov was a student of ethnography committed to populism; he studied with the eminent F. I. Buslaev, an authority on the history of Russian art and literature, and devoted much of his life to collecting peasant songs, stories, and proverbs. His *Collection of Historic Popular Songs of the Great Russians*, published in 1860, revealed that peasant songs contained seeds of protest, and had enormous influence on intellectuals, including Nekrasov. He also published *Russian Booklet*, a collection that brought together traditional peasant songs and stories with works by Nekrasov and other populists. See Franco Venturi, *Roots of Revolution*, trans. Francis Haskell (New York, 1960), pp. 338–41.
9. Brooks, *When Russia Learned to Read*, pp. 82–89, on the peasant writers Ivan Ivin and Matvei Ozhegov; some former peasants, including I. Morozov, E. Gobanov, and I. Sytin, became major publishers of *lubok* books, see pp. 96–100.
10. Lebedev's undated drawing is reproduced in E. I. Smirnova, "Aleksandr Ignat'evich Lebedev," in A. I. Leonov, ed., *Russkoe iskusstvo seredina deviatnadtsatogo veka* (Moscow, 1958), opposite p. 224.
11. Other Nekrasovian works by Perov are *Rural Death*, *Drowned Woman*, and *Parents at the Grave of Their Son*, and many portraits of peasants and poor city children, in the Tretiakov Gallery.

12. See V. I. Plotnikov, "V. G. Perov i russkii fol'klor. (K probleme narodno-poeticheskoi temy v russkom iskusstve vtoroi poloviny XIX veka)," in *Problemy razvitiia russkogo iskusstva* (Leningrad, 1971), no. 1, pp. 45–65.

13. The different "russification" policies of Nicholas I and Alexander III and similarities between official Slavophilism and bourgeois taste are discussed by L. Suprun, "Professional'nye khudozhniki i narodnoe iskusstvo v Rossii kontsa XIX–nachala XX veka" (dissertation, Research Institute of Artistic Industry, Moscow, 1971), pp. 24–31, 41–44.

14. L. V. Dal', "Istoricheskoe issledovanie pamiatnikov russkogo zodchestva," *Zodchi*, 1872, no. 2, cited in M. A. Il'in and E. A. Borisova, "Arkhitektura," in Grabar', Kemenov, Lazarev, et al., *Istoriia russkogo iskusstva*, vol. 9, book 2 (Moscow, 1965), p. 262. Examples of historicizing architecture include Grimm's Georgian and Byzantine Church at Khersones, Ropet and Hartman's Teremok at Abramtsevo, Parland's Savior on the Blood in Petersburg, the Church of St. Vladimir in Kiev decorated by V. Vasnetsov and others, Shervud and Semenov's Historical Museum in Moscow, Chichagov's Moscow City Duma, and Pomerantsev's Mercantile Rows (now GUM) in Moscow. See William C. Brumfield, *The Origins of Modernism in Russian Architecture* (Los Angeles, 1991).

15. A recent, broad, well-illustrated treatment of this topic is Evgenia Kirichenko, *Russian Design and the Fine Arts, 1750–1917* (New York, 1991).

16. Vasilenko, "Narodnoe iskusstvo," in Grabar', Kemenov, Lazarev, et al., *Istoriia russkogo iskusstva*, vol. 9, book 2, pp. 325–30, 354, on differences between the first and second halves of the nineteenth century.

17. N. P. Levinson, "Khudozhestvennaia promyshlennost'," in Grabar', Kemenov, Lazarev, et al., *Istoriia russkogo iskusstva*, vol. 9, book 2, pp. 214–15.

18. Levinson, "Khudozhestvennaia promyshlennost'," pp. 325–27, for examples of cotton prints.

19. See Suprun, "Professional'nye khudozhniki," pp. 69–74, 83.

20. Suprun, "Professional'nye khudozhniki," p. 74. Figures from *zemstva*, probably low, are 1,800,000 *kustari* in 40 provinces; cited in Brooks, *When Russia Learned to Read*, pp. 10–11. *Kustari* lived better and had higher rates of literacy than factory workers or landbound peasants. See Blum, *Lord and Peasant in Russia*, pp. 301–303.

21. Suprun, "Professional'nye khudozhniki," pp. 80–83.

22. Suprun, "Professional'nye khudozhniki," p. 80, quoting Central State Archives of the City of Moscow, 1866 (*fond* 16).

23. I. E. Zabelin, *Domashnii byt russkogo naroda v XVI i XVII st.* (1872) and *Domashnii byt russkikh tsarei (i tsarits) v XVI–XVII v.* (1915); I. Golyshev, *Pamiatniki starinnoi russkoi rez'by po derevu po Vladimirskoi gubernii* (1876); I. Snegirev, *Russkie prostonarodnye prazdniki i suevernye obriady* (1838), *Russkaia starina v pamiatnikakh tserkovnogo i grazhdanskogo zodchestva* (1851), and *Lubochnye kartinki russkogo naroda v Moskovskom mire* (1861); D. A. Rovinskii, *Istoriia russkikh shkol ikonopisaniia do kontsa XVII veka* (1856) and *Russkie narodnye kartinki* (1881). Besides the major commissions, small provincial circles, such as the "Northern Circle of Amateurs" in Vologda, also held congresses and published reports, such as *Vremennik iziashchnykh iskusstv*, Vologda.

24. V. Stasov, *Russkii narodnyi ornament* (St. Petersburg, 1872), 2 vols.; *Slavianskii i vostochnyi ornament* (St. Petersburg, 1884–87); articles on Vasnetsov (1896) and Polenova (1899), originally in *Iskusstvo i khudozhestvennaia promyshlennost'*, reprinted in V. Stasov, *Stat'i i zametki, ne voshedshie v sobraniia sochinenii* (Moscow, 1954), vol. 2, pp. 154–220, 221–68.

25. Suprun, "Professional'nye khudozhniki," pp. 84–85; see Salmond, "The Modernization of Folk Art in Russia," pp. 100–102.

26. Suprun, "Professional'nye khudozhniki," Appendix, pp. 320–23, "List of Regional, All-Russian, and International Exhibitions in Russia from 1883 to 1904."

27. See N. Moleva and E. Beliutin, *Russkaia khudozhestvennaia shkola vtoroi poloviny XIX–nachala XX veka* (Moscow, 1967), pp. 171–77, and Levinson, "Khudozhestvennaia promyshlennost'," pp. 329–30.

28. Levinson, "Khudozhestvennaia promyshlennost'," p. 330, quoting P. Stolpianskii, *Staryi Peterburg i Obshchestvo pooshchreniia khudozhestv* (Leningrad, 1928), p. 50.

29. The porcelain service, in the Russian Museum, is illustrated in Kirichenko, *Russian Design*, p. 122. Suprun, "Professional'nye khudozhniki," pp. 32–34, citing M. E. Makarenko, *Shkola Imperatorskogo obshchestva pooshchreniia khudozhestv, 1839–1914* (Petrograd, 1914), p. 61.

30. Suprun, "Professional'nye khudozhniki," pp. 73–74; the Commission to Publish Drawings for Craftsmen was organized in 1897 under the Kustar' Museum in St. Petersburg; the first edition of drawings was published in 1900, in 1,000 copies.

31. V. V. Stasov, "Vystavki dvukh khudozhestvenno-promyshlennykh shkol," in *Khudozhestvennye novosti* (St. Petersburg, 1889), vol. 7, no. 2, columns 25–35, reprinted in Stasov, *Stat'i i zametki, ne voshedshie v sobraniia sochinenii*, vol. 2, pp. 42–51.

32. See Salmond, "The Modernization of Folk Art in Russia," p. 8, on commissions on *kustar'* industries under the Ministry of State Domains and the *zemstva* (local governing units).

16. Artistic Renewal

1. Bilibin, "Narodnoe tvorchestvo russkogo severa," p. 303.

2. Elena Polenova, letter to P. Antipova, April 16, 1885, in E. Sakharova, ed., *V. D. Polenov—E. D. Polenova: Khronika sem'i khudozhnikov* (Moscow, 1964), p. 362.

3. Sources on the art colonies include N. Pakhomov, *Abramtsevo, muzei-usad'ba* (Moscow, 1953); Dora Kogan, *Mamontovskii kruzhok* (Moscow, 1972); Mark Kopshitser, *Savva Mamontov* (Moscow, 1972); Stuart Grover, "Savva Mamontov and the Mamontov Circle, 1870–1905: Art Patronage and the Rise of Nationalism in Russian Art" (Ph.D. dissertation, University of Wisconsin, 1971); M. K. Tenisheva, *Vpechatleniia moei zhizni* (Paris, 1933; reprint, Leningrad, 1991); L. Zhuravleva, *Teremok* (Moscow, 1972); John Bowlt, "Two Russian Maecenases: Savva Mamontov and Princess Tenisheva," *Apollo*, December 1973, vol. 98, no. 142, pp. 444–53; Boris Lossky, "The Popular Arts in Russia and Their Revival," *Apollo*, December 1973, vol. 98, no. 142, pp. 454–59. The most thorough study of the *kustar'* art revival is Salmond, "The Modernization of Folk Art in Russia."

4. Polenov's *Nikita Bogdanov, Teller of Bylini* (1876, Russian Museum), Vasnetsov's *Book Kiosk* (1875–76, Tretiakov Gallery). On Polenov, see O. A. Liaskovskaia, "V. D. Polenov," in Grabar', Kemenov, Lazarev, et al., *Istoriia russkogo iskusstva*, vol. 9, book, 2, pp. 119–35, and Sakharova, *Polenov—Polenova*, Introduction, pp. 6–45. On Vasnetsov, N. N. Kovalenskaia, "V. M. Vasnetsov," in Grabar', Kemenov, Lazarev, et al., *Istoriia russkogo iskusstva*, vol. 9, book 2, pp. 93–118.

5. Among his works on legendary and folk themes are *Warrior at the Crossroads* (1878–79, Russian Museum), *Three Tsaritsas of the Underground Kingdoms* (1879–84, Kiev State Museum of Russian Art), *Three Bogatyri* (completed 1898), *After the Battle of Igor Sviatoslavovich against the Polovtsians* (1880), *Alenushka* (1881), *Ivan Tsarevich and the Gray Wolf* (1889), *Sirin and Alkonost* (1896), and *Bard* (*Vayan*) (1899), all in the Tretiakov Gallery; the portrait study of Petrov (1883) is in the Tretiakov Gallery.

6. Grover, "Savva Mamontov," pp. 250, 365, points out the commercial objectives behind Mamontov's commissions.

7. M. Nesterov, letter to A. V. Nesterova, July 18, 1888, in A. Rusakova, ed., *M. V. Nesterov: Iz pisem* (Leningrad, 1968), p. 18.

8. N. Morgunov and N. Morgunova-Rudnitskaia, *Viktor Mikhailovich Vasnetsov: Zhizn' i tvorchestvo* (Moscow, 1962), p. 214; also quoted in M. Davydova, *Ocherki istorii russkogo teatral'no-dekoratsionnogo iskusstva* (Moscow, 1974), p. 79.

9. Elizaveta Mamontova's notes on the church project, in "Letopisi sel'tsa Abramtseva," Summer 1881; see Kogan, *Mamontovskii kruzhok*, p. 164.

10. V. Polenov, "O narodnom teatre," handwritten notes, State Tretiakov Gallery, Manuscript Division, no. 54/16, sheet 2. Quoted in Syrkina, "Teatral'no-dekoratsionnoe iskusstvo," in Grabar', Kemenov, Lazarev, et al., *Istoriia russkogo iskusstva*, vol. 9, no. 2, pp. 174–75. See Davydova, *Ocherki istorii russkogo teatral'no-dekoratsionnogo iskusstva*, pp. 72–90.

11. Natal'ia Polenova, notes dated 1885, in N. Polenova, *Abramtsevo* (Moscow, 1922), quoted in E. Sakharova, *Elena Polenova* (Moscow, 1952), p. 14.

12. Vasnetsov does not comment on the ornaments from Kul Oba and Chertomlyk, in the Hermitage, but Polenova studied the exhibits and made drawings of some of them, labeled "Scythians—Hermitage," in a sketchbook of 1881–82, Polenov Estate Museum, Polenovo, nos. 445/5–20. Vasnetsov's watercolor set designs (1885) are in the Tretiakov Gallery.

13. N. Polenova, notes from 1885, in Sakharova, *Polenova*, p. 14.

14. Polenova's statement was made to Stasov, quoted by him in his article "Elena Dmitrievna Polenova," in *Stat'i i zametki*, p. 243.

15. Polenova, letter to Vasnetsov, October 21, 1885, quoted in Kopshitser, *Mamontov*, p. 108. I wish to thank Tat'iana Makarova, formerly at the Abramtsevo Estate Museum, for discussing this point with me and for lending me her unpublished manuscript, "Samoe zavetnoe (Tvorchestvo E. D. Polenovoi 80–90x godov)."

16. Polenova, letter to E. Mamontova, August 6, 1885, from the village of Men'shovo, on the Lopukhin estate, where Polenova spent the summer painting and collecting examples of folk art, Sakharova, *Polenov—Polenova*, p. 359; see Suprun, "Professional'nye khudozhniki," p. 105.

17. N. Polenova to E. Polenova, July 11, 1885, Sakharova, *Polenov—Polenova*, p. 358.

18. N. V. Polenova to E. Polenova, June 7, 1885, from Men'shovo, Sakharova, *Polenov—Polenova*, p. 360.

19. N. Polenova, letter to E. Polenova, July 11, 1885, Sakharova, *Polenov—Polenova*, p. 358; other letters report similar acquisitions; most of these pieces are now in the Polenov Estate Museum in Polenovo, Tula Province.

20. Polenova's studies of folk objects are preserved in several albums in the Abramtsevo Estate Museum.

21. Major collectors were M. K. Tenisheva, V. P. Sidamon-Eristova, N. L. Shchabel'skaia, the Khanenko family in Kiev, V. A. Gartmann (embroidery); S. M. Bem (clay toys); A. A. Bobrinskii, P. I. Shchukin, I. A. Golyshev (wood); D. V. Grigorovich (glass); and K. A. Dalmatov (lace, embroidery). Some collectors were scholars and teachers, and some donated important collections to the Historical Museum. See Suprun, "Professional'nye khudozhniki," pp. 111–12, and Vasilenko, "Narodnoe iskusstvo," in Grabar', Kemenov, Lazarev, et al., *Istoriia russkogo iskusstva*, vol. 9, book 2, pp. 354–58.

22. Statement by Mariia F. Iakunchikova and Aleksandra S. Mamontova, dated January 6, 1910, in the Central State Archives of Literature and Art (TsGALI), *fond* 395, no. 1, unit 1873, pages 6–8, quoted by Suprun, "Professional'nye khudozhniki," p. 114. Letters by Polenova to Stasov, 1894, in Sakharova, *Polenova*, pp. 17–18, and *Polenov—Polenova*, p. 513, corroborate these goals. See Alison Hilton, "Domestic Crafts and Creative Freedom: Russian Women's Art," in H. Goscilo and B. Holmgren, eds., *Russia • Women • Culture* (forthcoming).

23. Elena Polenova, letter to P. Antipova, April 16, 1885, in Sakharova, *Polenov—Polenova*, pp. 362–63.

24. I wish to thank Tat'iana Makarova of the Abramtsevo Estate Museum for information on the organization of the workshop and the commercial enterprise. Additional material is in Kogan, *Mamontovskii kruzhok*, pp. 164, 168, Suprun, "Professional'nye khudozhniki," pp. 125–32, 136–44, and Salmond, "The Modernization of Folk Art in Russia," pp. 24–30. Vasilenko, "Narodnoe iskusstvo," in Grabar', Kemenov, Lazarev, et al., *Istoriia russkogo iskusstva*, vol. 9, book 2, pp. 355–56, comments on the effect of adapting folk art forms to urban tastes.

25. See Suprun, "Professional'nye khudozhniki," p. 124.

26. Salmond, "The Modernization of Folk Art in Russia," p. 45, n. 41, notes that Polenova told Stasov in 1894 that there were 19 students and 28 graduates, but an 1898 census listed only 12 joiners in the district still connected with the workshop or working from their homes for Mamontova. The best-known pupils of Polenova were Egor Zelenkov, who ran the workshop after 1893, and V. P. Voronskov, who founded a workshop in nearby Kudrino in 1906. I have found no information on Abramtsevo *kustari* working independently in villages.

27. Polenova, letter to Antipova, April 16, 1885, Sakharova, *Polenov—Polenova*, p. 352.

28. Polenova's notations on a page from an album of sketches, reproduced in N. V. Polenova, *Abramtsevo*, pp. 57–58.

29. Polenova, letter to P. Antipova, August 9, 1885, Sakharova, *Polenov—Polenova*, p. 360.

30. E. Polenova, letter to E. Mamontova, August 21, 1885, Sakharova, *Polenov—Polenova*, pp. 360–61.

31. E. Polenova, letter to N. Polenova, September 21, 1885, Sakharova, *Polenov—Polenova*, p. 362.

32. E. Polenova, letter to N. Polenova, September 21, 1885, Sakharova, *Polenov—Polenova*, pp. 361–62.

33. E. Polenova, letter to P. Antipova, March 3, 1886, Sakharova, *Polenov—Polenova*, p. 366. In a letter to Mamontova, December 15, 1885, she describes a commission from Natal'ia Naryshkina, lady-in-waiting to the empress, for 30 mirror frames modeled on

Vologda distaffs in the Abramtsevo museum to be given to the empress and grand duchesses at the annual Winter Palace ball. Sakharova, *Polenov—Polenova*, p. 403.

34. Polenova's sketchbook of 1881–82 contains drawings from the exhibits of Kul Oba and several other excavations, Polenov Estate Museum, nos. 445/5–20, in D. V. Polenov, ed., *Gos. muzei-usad'ba V. D. Polenova: Katalog* (Leningrad, 1964), pp. 151–52.

35. Polenova, letter to Stasov, October 1894, in Sakharova, *Polenov—Polenova*, p. 506.

36. See Robert Goldwater, *Primitivism in Modern Art* (1938), rev. ed. (New York, 1967), pp. 3–9, on the founding of ethnological museums in Europe and America and the development of an ethnological approach to "primitive" art; this approach was affirmed in the work of Franz Boas and his colleagues on Eskimo and North Pacific Coast art in the 1890s through the 1920s. See M. Mead and R. Bunzel, *The Golden Age of American Anthropology* (New York, 1960), pp. 306–17, 331–39, for comparisons of anthropological approaches to art.

37. See Polenov, *Gos. muzei-usad'ba V. D. Polenova*, pp. 156–60. Polenova also made sketches from reference books and archeological journals, including *Russkie drevnosti*, *Pamiatniki drevnerusskogo zodchestva*, and Stasov's *Slavianskii i vostochnyi ornament*.

38. Polenova, letter to Stasov, October 1894, Sakharova, *Polenov—Polenova*, pp. 505–508; Stasov was vehement because he thought Polenova's free interpretation of forms a sign of "decadence." Their correspondence on these points continued intensively for several months, and intermittently until Polenova's death in 1898.

39. E. Polenova, letter to Mamontova, March 13, 1889, Sakharova, *Polenov—Polenova*, p. 419.

40. Polenova, letters to Stasov, April 2, September 30, 1894, Sakharova, *Polenov—Polenova*, pp. 497, 504. A. N. Afanas'ev, *Russkie detskie skazki* (Moscow, 1883), English translation by Norbert Guterman, *Russian Fairy Tales* (New York, 1945). Polenova knew the village singers of *byliny*, N. Bogdanov and V. Shegolenkov, painted by Polenov and Repin at Abramtsevo in the 1870s. On a trip to another village, she met a literate peasant boy who wrote down the words of an old storyteller for her.

41. Polenova, letter to P. Antipova, October 25, 1886, Sakharova, *Polenov—Polenova*, p. 373.

42. Polenova credited the story to her grandmother, V. N. Voeikova. A manuscript copy with the original watercolors (1886) is in the Museum of Books, Russian State Library, Moscow. This was the only story published in Polenova's lifetime: *Voina Gribov: Narodnaia skazka* (Moscow, 1889). Natal'ia Polenova edited a posthumous edition of all of Polenova's fairytales, in three volumes with illustrations in color, *Russkie narodnye skazki i pribautki, pereskazannye dlia detei i illiustrirovannye E. D. Polenovoi* (Moscow, 1906).

43. Sakharova, *Polenov—Polenova*, p. 759; the drawing was made during a visit to her friend Antipova.

44. Polenova, letters to Stasov, 1894, in Sakharova, *Polenova*, p. 20, and May 19, 1897, Sakharova, *Polenov—Polenova*, p. 568; she says that though Walter Crane's books were English stories and of completely different character from hers, they pleased her very much. Crane's children's books first appeared in 1865. Morris's Kelmscott Press was founded in 1891, and during the mid-1890s there were many discussions of the Pre-Raphaelites and of Morris among the Abramtsevo artists. The English magazine *Studio* planned an issue with Polenova, but illness kept her from participating. See Sakharova,

Polenov—Polenova, pp. 780–82. On contacts in France, letters from summer 1895, Sakharova, *Polenov—Polenova*, pp. 532–35.

45. Salmond, "The Modernization of Folk Art in Russia," p. 49, n. 54, citing Galina Dain, "Istoriia problemy promysla i Abramtsevo-Kudrinskaia rez'ba," *Dekorativnoe iskusstvo SSSR*, 1987, vol. 6, no. 355, p. 42.

46. Mariia Fedorovna Mamontova had married Vasilii Iakunchikov, the brother of Natal'ia Vasil'evna Polenova, Vasilii Polenov's wife; her husband was also the half-brother of the painter Mariia Vasil'evna Iakunchikova, Polenova's close friend. See Wendy Salmond, "The Solomenko Embroidery Workshops," *Journal of Decorative and Propaganda Arts*, Summer 1987, pp. 128–43 on M. F. and M. V. Iakunchikova, Polenova, and the role of textile arts in *kustar'* revival.

47. Salmond, "The Modernization of Folk Art in Russia," pp. 50–55, describes the women's *kustar'* workshops, pointing out the leading role of upper-class women, landowners' wives, in efforts to improve traditional women's arts.

48. E. Polenova, letter to V. Stasov, January 29, 1896, Sakharova, *Polenov—Polenova*, pp. 543–44.

49. See Salmond, "The Solomenko Workshops," p. 139, for discussion and photographs.

50. Polenova, Mark Antokol'skii, and Iakunchikova were also experienced ceramicists. But Vrubel' was most interested in the technical aspects of the art; he became head of the Abramtsevo ceramic studio in 1890 and worked closely with the young chemist Petr Vaulin on developing metallic bases for glazes, producing a variety of textures and colors ranging from opaque to clear. I am grateful to William Nevskii, conservator of ceramics at the Abramtsevo Museum, for showing me results of the technical experiments in the museum archive.

Vrubel' connected the "national note" to his experiments in ceramics in a letter to his sister, Anna Vrubel', summer 1891, in E. P. Gomberg-Verzhbinskaia et al., *Vrubel': Perepiska, vospominaniia o khudozhnike*, 2nd ed. (Leningrad, 1976), pp. 56–57.

51. See Bowlt, "Two Russian Maecenases," pp. 450ff.; Zhuravleva, *Teremok*; Salmond, "The Modernization of Folk Art in Russia," pp. 151–83; Tenisheva, *Vpechatleniia moei zhizni* (reprint, 1991), pp. 125–32, 140–42, 203–205.

52. See Suprun, "Professional'nye khudozhniki," pp. 176–78, citing E. N. Kletonova, *Simvolika narodnykh ukras Smolenskogo kraia* (Smolensk, 1927), on the significance of the textile arts revival.

53. TsGALI (Central State Archives of Literature and Art), Moscow, *fond* 2023, no. 1, item 36 (1894–1913), has about 30 sketches and studies, including a large gouache of a *sirin*, painted in blue and white with gold highlights; items 38, 39, and 40 contain over 20 designs of ornaments and architectural plans.

54. A descriptive catalogue was printed: "Rodnik: Khudozhestvennye krest'ianskie izdeliia pod rukovodstvom Kn. M. K. Tenishevoi i A. B. Pogosskoi" (Moscow, 1903); see Bowlt, "Two Russian Maecenases," p. 453.

55. Suprun, "Professional'nye khudozhniki," p. 175.

56. Suprun, "Professional'nye khudozhniki," pp. 150–53. See Bowlt, "Two Russian Maecenases," pp. 452–53. Between 1880 and 1904 there were about 80 regional exhibitions of *kustar'* and applied arts in Russia, the Baltic capitals, and Warsaw; after the Paris Exposition Universelle in 1900, there were no major representations in the West until the

Russian Section at the Paris Salon d'Automne of 1913 included a large folk art exhibition. See Suprun, "Professional'nye khudozhniki," pp. 77 and 320–23 (Appendix: "List of Exhibitions").

57. See Janet Kennedy, *The "Mir iskusstva" Group and Russian Art* (New York, 1976).

58. Diaghilev admired Vasnetsov's work, although most members of the group thought it outdated. Diaghilev made extraordinary efforts to produce the Polenova issue, and to organize a memorial exhibition of her work as a special section of the First International Exhibition of the World of Art at the end of 1898. Polenova's later graphic work, more than her *kustar'* activity, was admired by the group.

59. A. Benua, "Pis'ma so Vsemirnoi vystavki," *Mir iskusstva*, 1900, no. 17–18, pp. 108–109, quoted in Razina, "Narodnoe iskusstvo," in Grabar', Kemenov, Lazarev, et al., *Istoriia russkogo iskusstva*, vol. 10, no. 2, p. 456.

60. Bilibin, "Narodnoe tvorchestvo russkogo severa," *Mir iskusstva*, 1904, no. 11, pp. 267–318.

61. Bilibin, "Narodnoe tvorchestvo" and "Ostatki iskusstva v russkoi derevne," *Zhurnal dlia vsekh*, 1904, no. 10, pp. 609–18. The *Mir iskusstva* article and a short article on Russian costume (1909) are reprinted in S. V. Golynets, ed., *Ivan Iakovlevich Bilibin: Stat'i, pis'ma, vospominaniia o khudozhnike* (Leningrad, 1970), pp. 31–46, 47–48.

62. Polenov, "O narodnom teatre," in Syrkina, "Teatral'no-dekoratsionnoe iskusstvo," pp. 174–75. Polenova, letter to P. Antipova, April 16, 1885, in Sakharova, *Polenov—Polenova*, p. 26.

63. Aleksandr Benua, *Istoriia russkoi zhivopisi v XIX veke* (St. Petersburg, 1902), pp. 223–26, 252, 262–64.

17. Folk Art and New Languages of Art

1. Aleksandr Shevchenko, *Neo-primitivizm: Ego teoriia, ego vozmozhnosti, ego dostizheniia* (Moscow, 1913), trans. in John E. Bowlt, ed. and trans., *Russian Art of the Avant-Garde: Theory and Criticism* (New York, 1976), p. 46.

2. Kazimir Malevich, "Fragments from 'Chapter from an Artist's Autobiography,' 1933," trans. Allan Upchurch, reprinted in *Kazimir Malevich, 1878–1935*, exhibition catalogue (Los Angeles, 1990), pp. 144–45.

3. V. Kandinskii, "Iz materialov po etnografii Sysol'skikh i Vychegodskikh Zyrian: Natsional'nye bozhestva (po sovremennym verovaniiam)," *Etnograficheskoe obozrenie*, 1889, no. 3, pp. 102–10; and "O nakazaniiakh po resheniiam volostnykh sudov Moskovskoi gubernii," in *Trudy Etnograficheskogo otdela Imperatorskogo obshchestva liubitelei estestvoznaniia, antropologii i etnografii* (Moscow, 1889), vol. 9, pp. 13–19. The sponsoring organizations had been active in organizing expeditions and conferences since the 1860s; Suprun, "Professional'nye khudozhniki," pp. 79–80. See Weiss, "Kandinsky and 'Old Russia,'" in Weisberg, Dixon, and Lemke, *The Documented Image*, pp. 187–222; and Peg Weiss, *Kandinsky and "Old Russia"* (New Haven, 1995). I wish to thank the author for sharing her article and insights with me.

4. Weiss, "Kandinsky and 'Old Russia,'" p. 188, citing Kandinsky, *Complete Writings on Art*, ed. Kenneth C. Lindsay and Peter Vergo (Boston, 1982), p. 891, nn. 47, 48.

5. Kandinskii, *Tekst khudozhnika* (Moscow, 1918), p. 28, quoted in Bowlt and Long, *The Life of Vasilii Kandinsky in Russian Art*, p. 2.

6. Weiss, "Kandinsky and 'Old Russia,'" p. 188, citing Lindsay and Vergo, *Kandinsky*, p. 891, n. 45.

7. *Golden Sail* and *Russian Beauty in a Landscape* are in the Stadtische Galerie im Lenbachhaus, Munich. Kandinskii and Bilibin may have met in Munich, as Kandinskii attended Anton Azbé's studio between 1897 and 1899, and Bilibin studied there for a few months in the spring and summer of 1898. They could also have had contact through Igor' Grabar' and *Mir iskusstva:* Kandinskii reviewed Munich exhibitions for the journal in 1902, and Bilibin, a member of the group since 1900, wrote his major article on folk art of the Russian north in 1904. Coincidentally, both studied law before turning to art. Surprisingly, there is no record of correspondence between the two.

8. *Motley Life* is in the Stadtische Galerie im Lenbachhaus, Munich. See Weiss, "Kandinsky and 'Old Russia,'" pp. 189–90, 196–205.

9. Wassily Kandinsky, *Concerning the Spiritual in Art*, trans. M. T. H. Sadler as *The Art of Spiritual Harmony* (London, 1914; rev. ed., New York, 1977), p. 1. This point is discussed at length in Goldwater, *Primitivism in Modern Art*, pp. 127–29, and in a different sense by Weiss, "Kandinsky and 'Old Russia,'" pp. 194–95, 202–206. On Kandinskii and the Russian symbolists, see Bowlt and Long, *The Life of Vasilii Kandinsky in Russian Art*, pp. 12–15.

10. See Weiss, "Kandinskii and 'Old Russia,'" pp. 197–203, 206–14, on Kandinskii's personal symbolism.

11. See Wassily Kandinsky and Franz Marc, *The Blaue Reiter Almanac*, ed. Klaus Lankheit (New York, 1974). Eight *lubki* were shown in the Blaue Reiter exhibition; one was illustrated in the catalogue. The *Blaue Reiter Almanac* included seven folk prints, pp. 76, 77, 118, 216, 220, 221, 225; a wood sculpture, p. 73, evidently from Bogorodskoe, depicts a *bogatyr'*, probably Erusian Lazarevich, killing a many-headed dragon.

12. Bowlt and Long, *The Life of Vasilii Kandinsky in Russian Art*, pp. 23–24.

13. Larionov, in Paris in the fall of 1906, saw the Gauguin retrospective and probably the fauvist works at the Salon des Indépendants. The "Golden Fleece" exhibition in Moscow in 1908 featured Cezanne, Gauguin, and Matisse along with French and Russian symbolists. The Moscow collectors Sergei Shchukin and Ivan Morozov, with important works by these artists and later by Picasso, invited Russian artists to see the paintings.

14. S. Makovskii, "'Golubaia roza,'" *Zolotoe runo*, Moscow, 1907, no. 5, p. 25, quoted in Bowlt and Long, *The Life of Vasilii Kandinsky in Russian Art*, p. 15. Although Makovskii was reviewing a symbolist exhibition, his comments also applied to other experimental art.

15. Shevchenko, *Neo-primitivizm*, in Bowlt, *Russian Art of the Avant-Garde*, p. 45. Slightly later, American artists and writers drew parallels between folk art and machine esthetics; see Alison Hilton, "Narodnoe iskusstvo i sovremennost' v epokhu kul'turnogo obnovleniia v SShA i v SSSR," in M. A. Nekrasova and K. A. Makarov, eds., *Narodnoe iskusstvo i sovremennaia kul'tura* (Moscow, 1991), pp. 160–74.

16. See Salmond, "The Modernization of Folk Art in Russia," pp. 220–22.

17. Ia. A. Tugendkhol'd, *Russkoe narodnoe iskusstvo na vystavke "Salon d'Automne,"* 1913, quoted in Suprun, "Professional'nye khudozhniki," p. 77. A different version of the article is given as the preface to the French catalogue of the exhibition in Ia. A. Tugendkhol'd, *Iz istorii zapadnoevropeiskogo, russkogo i sovetskogo iskusstva*, ed. T. Kazhdan (Moscow, 1987), p. 296. The other organizers were N. Bartram, G. Lukomskii, N. Rerikh, and N. Vrangel'.

18. V. Lobanov, *Khudozhestvennye gruppirovki za 25 let* (Moscow, 1930), p. 62, quoted in John E. Bowlt, "Neo-primitivism and Russian Painting," *The Burlington Magazine*, March 1974, p. 138.

19. Larionov's many barbershop scenes, painted between 1907 and 1911, and the series of soldiers relaxing, 1908–1911, are in the Tretiakov Gallery, the Russian Museum, the Centre Pompidou, and private collections; *Galloping Soldier* (1908) is in the Tate Gallery.

20. Larionov's *Seasons of the Year* (1912) and related paintings are in the Tretiakov Gallery and the Centre Pompidou, Paris. All contain similar figures arranged in compartments, with short texts; some include more modern or graffiti-like forms in addition to archaic symbols.

21. See Mary Chamot, "Russian Avant-garde Graphics," *Apollo*, December 1973, pp. 494–501 on Goncharova. Malevich's posters satirized German soldiers much as *lubki* had ridiculed French invaders in the early nineteenth century.

22. These works by Goncharova are in the State Russian Museum and the Tretiakov Gallery; those by Malevich are in the Stedelijk Museum.

23. Filonov's works are in the Russian Museum; see E. Kovtun et al., *Pavel Nikolaevich Filonov, 1883–1941*, exhibition catalogue (Leningrad, 1988), nos. 12, 15, 189.

24. Tatlin's *Fishmonger* (1911, Tretiakov Gallery), *Sailor* (1911, Russian Museum); designs for "Emperor Maximilian" (1911) are in the Tretiakov Gallery, the Bakhrushin Museum, Moscow, and the Lobanov-Rostovsky collection, London. Makovskii's poem "To Signboards" ("Vyveskam," 1913) is quoted in Shkarovskaia, *Samodeiatel'noe iskusstvo*, p. 23.

25. Camilla Gray, *The Russian Experiment in Art, 1863–1922* (London, 1962; rev. ed., New York, 1986), p. 134.

26. Malevich, "An Artist's Autobiography," pp. 144–45.

27. Kazimir Malevich, "From 1/42: Autobiographical Notes, 1923–25," trans. Xenia Glowacki-Prus and Arnold McMillin, in Troels Andersen, *K. S. Malevich: Essays on Art* (Copenhagen, 1966–78), vol. 2, pp. 147–55.

28. Natal'ia Goncharova, "Predislovie k katalogu vystavki," in A. Guber, ed., *Mastera iskusstva ob iskusstve* (Moscow, 1970), vol. 7, pp. 487–90; translated in Bowlt, *Russian Art of the Avant-Garde*, pp. 55–56.

29. Goncharova transcribed the remarks in a letter (manuscript section, Russian State Library, Moscow) trans. Bowlt, *Russian Art of the Avant-Garde*, p. 78.

30. *In Church* (1909) and *Elder with Seven Stars* (1910) are in a private collection; *Evangelists* (1910) is in the Tretiakov Gallery. Three paintings exhibited in 1909 were confiscated by the police, and religious works shown at the "Donkey's Tail" exhibition in 1912 were ordered removed; see Mary Chamot, *Goncharova Stage Designs and Paintings* (London, 1979), pp. 9–10.

31. Goncharova, "Predislovie," in Bowlt, *Russian Art of the Avant-Garde*, pp. 55–56.

32. Franck Jotterant, *L'Illustré*, September 24, 1959, p. 65, quoted by Chamot, *Goncharova*, p. 15.

33. Chamot, *Goncharova*, pp. 10, 55. The apocalyptic passages in Revelation (chaps. 8–10 and 18:21) are evoked through iconic and modern images (e.g., angels combined with airplanes). See Alison Hilton, "Natalia Goncharova and the Iconography of Revelation," *Studies in Iconography*, Fall 1991, pp. 232–57.

34. See Alison Hilton, "'Bases of the New Creation': Women Artists and Constructivism," *Arts Magazine*, October 1980, pp. 142–45. Goncharova also sold dress designs based on folk costumes.

35. Ivan Aksenov, "Concerning the Problem of the Present State of Russian Painting" (on the "Knave of Diamonds," Moscow, 1913), quoted in Larissa Zhadova, *Malevich, Suprematism and Revolution in Russian Art, 1910–1930* (London, 1982), p. 15; also translated in Bowlt, *Russian Art of the Avant-Garde*, p. 63.

36. Aksenov, "Concerning the . . . Present State of Russian Painting," referring chiefly to Ekster's work.

37. Aksenov, "Concerning the . . . Present State of Russian Painting," in Bowlt, *Russian Art of the Avant-Garde*, p. 69.

38. Naum Gabo, *Of Divers Arts* (The A. W. Mellon Lectures in the Fine Arts, National Gallery of Art, Washington, D.C., 1959) (London, 1962), p. 123.

39. E.g., Rozanova's *Workbox* and *Hairdresser's* (both 1915, Tretiakov Gallery); Malevich's *Knife Grinder* (ca. 1913, Yale University Art Gallery); Goncharova's *Laundry* (1912, Tate Gallery); and Udal'tsova's *Barbershop* (ca. 1914, location unknown).

40. Zhadova, *Malevich*, pp. 33–34.

41. See M. Larionov and N. Goncharova, "Rayonists and Futurists: A Manifesto" (Moscow, 1913), and Shevchenko, *Neo-primitivizm*, in Bowlt, *Russian Art of the Avant-garde*, pp. 89, 45.

42. "Folk art has ended. That means that the folk has stopped being the author of its own further development in design and hand-work." Bilibin, "Narodnoe tvorchestvo russkogo severa," p. 304.

18. Reshaping Folk Art in the Soviet Era

1. V. S. Voronov, introduction to the guidebook of the Kustar' Museum, "Putevoditel' po Kustarnomu muzeiu" (Moscow, 1925), reprinted in *O krest'ianskom iskusstve*, p. 191.

2. Decree of the Central Committee of the Communist Party of the Soviet Union, "On Folk Art Industries," *Pravda*, February 27, 1975.

3. See Richard Stites, "The Origins of Soviet Ritual Style: Symbol and Festival in the Russian Revolution," in Claes Arvidsson et al., *Symbols of Power* (Stockholm, 1987), pp. 23–42.

4. Stites, "Origins of Soviet Ritual Style," pp. 34–36; John Bowlt, "Russian Sculpture and Lenin's Plan of Monumental Propaganda," in H. Millon and L. Nochlin, eds., *Art and Architecture in the Service of Politics* (Cambridge, Mass., 1978), pp. 182–93; examples illustrated in Mikhail Guerman, *Art of the October Revolution* (Leningrad and New York, 1979), nos. 277–291.

5. See Stites, "Origins of Soviet Ritual Style," pp. 33–36, on the "standardization of symbols."

6. Aleksandr Bodganov, "The Proletarian and Art" (1918) and "The Paths of Proletarian Creation" (1920), in Bowlt, *Russian Art of the Avant-Garde*, pp. 176–82, exemplify the ideals and rhetoric of the period.

7. Bodganov, "The Paths of Proletarian Creation" (1920), in Bowlt, *Russian Art of the Avant-Garde*, pp. 181–82.

8. Richard Stites, "Iconoclastic Currents in the Russian Revolution: Destroying and Preserving the Past," in Abbott Gleason, Peter Kenez, and Richard Stites, eds., *Bolshevik Culture* (Bloomington, 1985), pp. 1–24.

9. I. E. Grabar', *Dlia chego nado okhraniat' i sobirat' sokrovishcha iskusstva i stariny*, Committee for the Preservation of Artistic Treasures, under the Council of the All-Russian Cooperative Congresses (Moscow, 1919), pp. 3–4.

10. Grabar', *Dlia chego nado*, pp. 16–22, 23–30.

11. Anatolii Lunacharskii and Iuvenal Slavinskii, "Theses of the Art Section of Narkompros and the Central Committee of the Union of Art Workers concerning Basic Policy in the Field of Art" (1920), in Bowlt, *Russian Art of the Avant-Garde*, pp. 184–85.

12. A. Lunacharskii, *Ob izobrazitel'nom iskusstve* (Moscow, 1967), vol. 2, pp. 301–302, quoted in Sheila Fitzpatrick, *The Commissariat of Enlightenment* (Cambridge, 1970), p. 127.

13. Lunacharskii, *Ob izobrazitel'nom iskusstve*, pp. 115–16, quoted in Fitzpatrick, *Commissariat*, p. 127.

14. Vladimir Lebedev, ROSTA window (1920), in Guerman, *Art of the October Revolution*, no. 44.

15. Posters by Radakov (1920), Kruglikova (1923), and Apsit (1919), illustrated in Guerman, *Art of the October Revolution*, nos. 81, 82, 84.

16. Camilla Gray, *The Russian Experiment in Art, 1863–1922*, rev. ed. (New York, 1986), pp. 224–25, illustrates the "Red Cossack" train; also in Guerman, *Art of the October Revolution*, no. 339.

17. See Beatrice Farnsworth, "Village Women Experience the Revolution," in *Bolshevik Culture*, pp. 243–46, 247–53, on peasant women's resistance to collectivization and the success of some gradual changes "along familiar lines."

18. Lunacharskii, *Ob izobrazitel'nom iskusstve*, vol. 2, p. 73, quoted in Shkarovskaia, *Narodnoe samodeiatel'noe iskusstvo*, pp. 26–27.

19. Shkarovskaia, *Narodnoe samodeiatel'noe iskusstvo*, pp. 31–32, nos. 49–53; very little work survives from the 1920s and 1930s.

20. See Shkarovskaia, *Narodnoe samodeiatel'noe iskusstvo*, pp. 36, 48–49; related problems of training contemporary folk artists are discussed in Iu. F. Lashchuk, "O vospitanii spetsialistov dlia narodnykh khudozhestvennykh promyslov," in Irina Boguslavskaia, ed., *Tvorcheskie problemy sovremennykh narodnykh khudozhestvennykh promyslov* (Leningrad, 1981), pp. 325–35.

21. See Shkarovskaia, *Narodnoe samodeiatel'noe iskusstvo*, pp. 27–37.

22. See T. M. Razina, "Narodnoe iskusstvo," in Grabar', Kemenov, Lazarev, et al., *Istoriia russkogo iskusstva*, vol. 10, book 2 (Moscow, 1969), pp. 455–74, on the support and development of folk arts in this period. On Kholmogory bonecarving, Khokhloma ware, and Palekh, Mstera, and Kholui lacquers, see Vasilenko, *Narodnoe iskusstvo*, pp. 177–232, 130–49, and 233–40. Salmond, "The Modernization of Folk Art in Russia," pp. 211–12, cites *zemstvo* statistics on the increase in budgets for *kustar'* workshops and exhibitions.

23. Salmond, "The Modernization of Folk Art in Russia," p. 230, citing E. Pribylskaia, "Khudozhestvenno-kustarnaia promyshlennost' SSSR," *Zhenskii zhurnal*, 1923, no. 4, p. 16.

24. "Dekret VTsIK i SNK o merakh sodeistviia kustarnoi promyshlennosti," April 25, 1919, in M. A. Nekrasova and S. M. Temerin, eds., *Narodnye khudozhestvennye promysly 1917–1932* (Moscow, 1986), vol. 1, pp. 19–20.

25. "Iz obzora deiatel'nosti podotdela khudozhestvennoi promyshlennosti otdela izobrazitel'nykh iskusstv Narkomprosa o razvitii khudozhestvennykh promyslov," November 27, 1919 (Central State Archive, RSFSR), published in Nekrasova and Temerin, *Narodnye khudozhestvennye promysly*, vol. 1, pp. 35–39.

26. "Iz otnosheniia Vsekompromsoiuza vsesoiuznoi zapadnoi torgovoi palate o zakliuchenii torgovykh sdelok na khudozhestvennye izdeliia eksponiruiushchiesia na mezhdunarodnykh vystavkakh" (1928) and "Svedeniia Vsekompromsoiuza o chisle kustarei izgotovliaiushchikh dlia eksporta khudozhestvennye izdeliia na 1 sentiabria 1928 g." (1928), in Nekrasova and Temerin, *Narodnye khudozhestvennye promysly*, vol. 1, pp. 111–13, 114–15; on international exhibitions and sales, pp. 206–207.

27. S. M. Temerin, "Khudozhestvennaia promyshlennost'," in Grabar', Kemenov, Lazarev, et al., *Istoriia russkogo iskusstva*, vol. 11 (Moscow, 1957), p. 579. See this article and the same author's "Khudozhestvennye promysly" in Grabar', Kemenov, Lazarev, et al., *Istoriia russkogo iskusstva*, vol. 11, pp. 558–73 and pp. 574–95, for developments in a variety of "artistic industries."

28. See Nekrasova and Temerin, *Narodnye khudozhestvennye promysly*, nos. 117–125.

29. "Iz obzora deiatel'nosti podotdela khudozhestvennoi promyshlennosti otdela izobrazitel'nykh iskusstv Narkomprosa o razvitii khudozhestvennykh promyslov," November 27, 1919, in Nekrasova and Temerin, *Narodnye khudozhestvennye promysly*, p. 36. The Abramtsevo workshop still used Polenova's models; see Salmond, "The Modernization of Folk Art in Russia," p. 232.

30. D. I. Vvedenskii, *Gorod Sergiev, Moskovskoi gubernii: Melkie promysly* (Moscow, 1927), p. 10 and passim. (141 pp. with tables.)

31. Robert L. Nichols, "The Icon and the Machine in Russia's Religious Renaissance, 1900–1909," a paper read at the American Association for the Advancement of Slavic Studies meeting, October 21, 1990, discussed the range of icon-painting enterprises, from the *kustar'* level (*bogomazy*) to machine-printed and tintype icons; in 1901 an imperial commission to preserve the ancient standards of icon painting was founded.

32. A. Bakushinskii, "Palekhskaia ikonopis'," in A. V. Bakushinskii, *Issledovaniia i stat'i* (Moscow, 1981), pp. 235–49; O. Voronova, *Lacquer Miniatures from Mstiora* (Leningrad, 1980), summarizes the history.

33. A. Lunacharskii, introduction to A. Bakushinskii, *Iskusstvo Palekha* (Moscow and Leningrad, 1938), p. 3. A novel about Golikov and his work is V. I. Porudominskii, *Otkrovenie Ivana Golikova* (Moscow, 1977).

34. Lenin's speech is depicted on a writing set, "Ten Years of October," painted in 1927 by Golikov and presented by the inhabitants of Palekh to Maksim Gor'kii; now in the A. M. Gor'kii Museum, Moscow.

35. Kulikov's *Radio in the Village* (1926) and *Izba Reading Room* (1925) are in the Museum of Folk Art, Moscow.

36. Museum of Folk Art, Moscow; in Nekrasova and Temerin, *Narodnye khudozhestvennye promysly*, vol. 2, no. 216.

37. See Nina Lobanov-Rostovsky, *Revolutionary Ceramics: Soviet Porcelain, 1917–1927* (New York, 1990), for detailed treatment of the topic, and Ian Wardropper, Karen Ketter-

ing, John E. Bowlt, and Alison Hilton, *News from a Radiant Future: Soviet Porcelain from the Collection of Craig H. and Kay A. Tuber* (Chicago, 1992), for selected themes.

38. Alison Hilton, "Soviet Propaganda Porcelain and the Russian Folk Heritage," in Wardropper et al., *News from a Radiant Future,* pp. 50–65.

39. The late Tatiana Strizhenova was among the first to study Soviet clothing design; an English-language publication of her work is Tatiana Strizhenova, *Soviet Costume and Textiles 1917–1945* (Moscow, Paris, and Verona, 1991). See Natalia Adaskina, "Constructivist Fabrics and Dress Designs," *Journal of Decorative and Propaganda Arts,* Summer 1987, pp. 144–51; Alison Hilton, "Bases of the New Creation," pp. 142–45; John Bowlt, "From Pictures to Textile Prints," p. 19; and Tatiana Strizhenova, "The Soviet Garment Industry in the 1930s," *Journal of Decorative and Propaganda Arts,* Summer 1987, pp. 162–75, on adaptations of folk designs in clothing.

40. Adaskina, "Constructivist Fabrics and Dress Designs," p. 146; this publication was a supplement to the journal *Krasnaia niva* in 1925.

41. N. Lamanova, "Organizational Plan for a Workshop of Contemporary Costume" (1919), in Lidiya Zaletova et al., *Revolutionary Costume: Soviet Clothing and Textiles of the 1920s* (New York, 1989), p. 170.

42. N. Lamanova, "Russian Fashion," in Zaletova, *Revolutionary Costume,* p. 172.

43. Strizhenova, "The Soviet Garment Industry," pp. 167, 175.

44. See Strizhenova, "The Soviet Garment Industry," p. 167, on the issue of "textile language" in the 1930s.

45. Voronov, "Putevoditel' po Kustarnomu muzeiu," p. 191.

46. Voronov, "Putevoditel'," and "Kustar'-master i rukovoditel'-khudozhnik" (1925), in *O krest'ianskom iskusstve,* pp. 178–88.

47. V. Vasilenko, "Poet narodnogo izobrazitel'nogo iskusstva," and M. Kamenskaia, "V. S. Voronov," in *Dekorativnoe iskusstvo SSSR,* 1960, no. 10 (special issue on Voronov).

48. Vasilenko, "Poet narodnogo izobrazitel'nogo iskusstva." Voronov (1887–1940) began working at the State Museum of Russian History in 1919, systematizing existing collections, organizing expeditions, and writing articles and books. He finished a dissertation on Russian distaffs, and published his first book, *Krest'ianskoe iskusstvo,* in 1920. On three major expeditions, in 1928, 1929, and 1930, to Arkhangel'sk, northern Vologda Province, the Pinega River area, and the southern Urals, he visited over 800 households in 72 locations, acquiring more than 600 objects for the museum. In 1930 he began teaching at the Architectural, Technical, and Art School and later at the Institute of Artistic Industry, and concerned himself chiefly with peasant masters working in traditional art forms.

49. Voronov, "Kustar'-master," p. 178.

50. Voronov, *Krest'ianskoe iskusstvo* (Moscow, 1924), in *O krest'ianskom iskusstve,* pp. 28–128; also pp. 13–14.

51. Voronov, "Krest'ianskoe iskusstvo i kustarnaia khudozhestvennaia promyshlennost'" (1924), in *O krest'ianskom iskusstve,* p. 170.

52. A. A. Bobrinskii, *Narodnye russkie derevlannye izdeliia* (Moscow, 1911).

53. I. Bilibin, "Prialochnye promysel," in *Mestnaia promyshlennost' i torgovlia,* 1927, nos. 5–6, cited in Vasilenko, *Narodnoe iskusstvo,* p. 22.

54. See Vasilenko, *Narodnoe iskusstvo,* pp. 21–32, for the history of Soviet folk art studies.

55. V. A. Gorodtsov, "Dako-sarmatskie religioznye elementy v russkom narodnom tvorchestve," in *Trudy Gosudarstvennogo istoricheskogo muzeia* (Moscow, 1926), no. 1, was one of the first studies of the sources of folk iconography. See Vasilenko, *Narodnoe iskusstvo*, pp. 24–25, on other archeological studies.

56. Tseretelli, *Russkaia krest'ianskaia igrushka*, pp. 10, 216.

57. A. B. Saltykov, *Ispol'zovanie narodnykh traditsii v razvitii sovetskogo prikladnogo iskusstva* (Moscow, 1956); the book deals primarily, and sometimes quite critically, with trends in the 1940s and 1950s.

58. N. I. Ivanova et al., *Muzei narodnogo iskusstva* (Moscow, 1972), pp. 6–7.

59. "Spravka eksportnogo sektora kul'tpromob"edineniia Vsekopromsoveta o razvitii khudozhestvennogo khokhlomskogo promysla . . ." (1932), in Nekrasova and Temerin, *Narodnye khudozhestvennye promysly*, vol. 1, pp. 181–82.

60. S. Temerin, "Khudozhestvennye promysly," in Grabar', Kemenov, Lazarev, et al., *Istoriia russkogo iskusstva*, vol. 11, pp. 594–95.

61. See Frank J. Miller, *Folklore for Stalin: Russian Folklore and Pseudofolklore of the Stalin Era* (New York, 1991).

62. E.g., V. Denisov, *Northern Trading-Post* (1936, Museum of Folk Art), in Vasilenko, "Severnaia reznaia kost'," *Narodnoe iskusstvo*, fig. 202. Professional artists from Moscow influenced this change. See discussion in Temerin, "Khudozhestvennye promysly," pp. 588–92.

63. Mikhail Stulov, *Kolkhoz of Woodcarvers* (1938); Vasilii Zinin, Nikolai Maksimov, and Nikolai Savin, *Friendship of the Peoples of the USSR* (1948, Sergiev-Posad Museum), illustrated in Grekov, *Bogorodskaia igrushka*; a photograph of the masters posing with the latter sculpture, from Grekov's collection, is reproduced in Nekrasova and Temerin, *Narodnye khudozhestvennye promysly*, vol. 2, no. 130.

64. See Strizhenova, *Soviet Costume and Textiles*, pp. 282–90.

65. S. Temerin, "Khudozhestvennye promysly" (1934–1941), in Grabar', Kemenov, Lazarev, et al., *Istoriia russkogo iskusstva*, vol. 12 (Moscow, 1961), p. 537.

66. Sergei Gerasimov, *Kolkhoz Holiday* (1937, Tretiakov Gallery); Arkadii Plastov, *Kolkhoz Holiday* (1937, Russian Museum). Murals by Vladimir Favorskii in a kindergarten and in the House of Models in Moscow (1933 and 1935) show the influence of old Russian frescoes as well as folk motifs (dancing figures, boys with accordions, horses); illustrated in V. P. Tolstoi, "Monumental'naia zhivopis'," in Grabar', Kemenov, Lazarev, et al., *Istoriia russkogo iskusstva*, vol. 12, pp. 309–10.

67. Gerasimov's and Iablonskaia's works, in the Tretiakov Gallery, exemplify a very large category of Socialist Realist art. These themes and related images of peasant women in Soviet posters are discussed in Alison Hilton, "Feminism and Gender Values in Soviet Art," in M. Liljeström, E. Mäntysaari, and A. Rosenholm, eds., *Gender Restructuring in Russian Studies*, Slavica Tamperensia (Tampere, Finland, 1993), pp. 99–116.

68. E.g., I. Morozov, *Partisans* (Mstera, 1944); M. Rakov, *Pursuing the Retreating Enemy* (Tobol'sk, 1942) and *Defending the Northern Border* (1944); I. Zinov'ev, *Aleksandr Nevskii Battling the German Knights* (Palekh, 1943); S. Evangulov, *Ivan Susanin* (1944); and others discussed or illustrated in V. Vasilenko, "Khudozhestvennye promysly i khudozhestvennaia promyshlennost'" (1941–1945), in R. S. Kaufman, M. L. Neiman, G. Iu. Sternin, and O. A. Shvidkovskii, eds., *Istoriia russkogo iskusstva*, vol. 13 (Moscow, 1964), pp. 348–58.

69. Vasilenko, "Khudozhestvennye promysly . . . ," pp. 347, 357, 365.

70. See M. A. Nekrasova, "K voprosu o poniatii 'narodnyi master,' " in Nekrasova, ed., *Narodnye mastera: Traditsii, shkoly,* pp. 9–10.

71. A. B. Saltykov, *Izbrannye trudy* (Moscow, 1962), p. 27, quoted by Nekrasova, "K voprosu o poniatii 'narodnyi master,' " p. 10.

72. V. Vasilenko, T. Razina, T. Semenova, B. Rybakov, G. Maslova, and A. Kantsedikas worked on imagery, ornament, and the formal syntax of folk art. Exemplifying the practical approach are I. Boguslavskaia, ed., *Tvorcheskie problemy sovremennykh narodnykh khudozhestvennykh promyslov* (Leningrad, 1981), a volume of papers for a conference at the State Russian Museum, and M. A. Nekrasova and K. A. Makarov, eds., *Problemy narodnogo iskusstva* (Moscow, 1982), a volume of essays published jointly by the Research institute of the Theory and History of Fine Arts and the Academy of Arts.

73. Decree of the Central Committee of the Communist Party of the Soviet Union, "On Folk Art Industries," *Pravda,* February 27, 1975.

74. Transcript of the conference "Obsuzhdeniia pervoi vsesoiuznoi vystavki proizvedenii masterov narodnykh khudozhestvennykh promyslov, organizovannoi soglasno postanovleniiu TsK KPSS 'O narodnykh khudozhestvennykh promyslakh' v 1979–1980 gg." (Moscow, 1983). Major theoretical papers were by I. Boguslavskaia, M. Nekrasova, and A. Kantsedikas. Specific questions addressed included the situations of folk artists working at home instead of in artels, the connections between folk art and amateur art, "rare" genres of folk art, and surveys of republics and regions, including Moldavia, Georgia, Belarus', and Kirghizia.

75. "Programma vsesoiuznoi s mezhdunarodnym uchastiem nauchno-prakticheskoi konferentsii 'Narodnoe iskusstvo i sovremennaia kul'tura: Problema sokhraneniia i razvitiia traditsii'" (Moscow, 1990).

76. N. Fileva on Arkhangel'sk, E. Sakhuta on Belarus', papers given March 21, 1990, published in M. A. Nekrasova and K. A. Makarov, eds., *Narodnoe iskusstvo i sovremennaia kul'tura: Problemy sokhraneniia i razvitiia traditsii* (Moscow, 1991), pp. 55–64, 253–61.

77. A. Kantsedikas, "Razrabotka teoreticheskikh problem i ikh znachenie dlia sovremennoi praktiki narodnykh khudozhestvennykh promyslov," in transcript of the 1979/80 conference "O narodnykh khudozhestvennykh promyslakh," pp. 73–77.

78. Kantsedikas, "Razrabotka teoreticheskikh problem," pp. 70–72.

79. See Nekrasova, "K voprusu o poniatii 'narodnyi master,'" in Nekrasova, ed., *Narodnye mastera: Traditsii, shkoly,* pp. 9–10.

80. N. A. Fileva, "Uzornoe tkachestvo na Pinege," in Nekrasova, ed., *Narodnye mastera: Traditsii, shkoly,* pp. 122–29.

81. N. A. Fileva, "Martyn Fat'ianov i dinastiia Petukhovykh: Mastera uzornoi prorreznoi beresty," in Nekrasova, ed., *Narodnye mastera: Traditsii, shkoly,* pp. 108–21, 282.

82. G. Durasov, "Ul'iana Babkina: Narodnyi master Kargopolia," in Nekrasova, ed., *Narodnye mastera: Traditsii, shkoly,* pp. 98–107. Babkina's work was noted and photographed by the ethnographer G. S. Maslova in 1947, and became widely known in the 1960s.

83. This information comes from answers to my questions about a decorative board modeled on Permogore distaffs, made in 1992 by a young artist, Ol'ga Nikolaeva, who had studied in Permogore.

84. S. P. Veselov, photographed by M. Nekrasova, 1980, in Nekrasova, *Narodnoe iskusstvo kak chast' kul'tury,* p. 326.

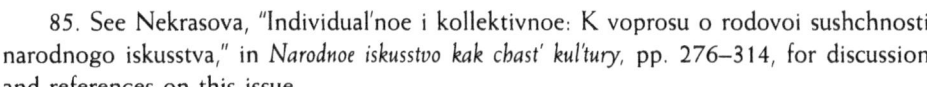

85. See Nekrasova, "Individual'noe i kollektivnoe: K voprosu o rodovoi sushchnosti narodnogo iskusstva," in *Narodnoe iskusstvo kak chast' kul'tury*, pp. 276–314, for discussion and references on this issue.

86. Bilibin, "Narodnoe tvorchestvo russkogo severa," p. 304.

Selected Bibliography

Abrosimova, A. A.; N. I. Kaplan; and T. V. Matlianskaia. *Khudozhestvennaia rez'ba po derevu, kosti i rogu.* Moscow, 1978.

Afanas'ev, Aleksandr. *Russian Fairy Tales.* Edited and translated by Norbert Guterman. New York, 1945.

Aleksandrov, V. A.; P. I. Kushner; and M. G. Rabinovich, eds. *Russkie: Istoriko-etnograficheskii atlas. Iz istorii russkogo narodnogo zhilishcha i kostiuma . . . seredina XIX–nachala XX veka.* Moscow, 1970.

Alekseeva, T. V., ed. *Russkoe iskusstvo pervoi chetverti XVIII veka.* Moscow, 1974.

Aleshina, T. S., ed. *History of Russian Costume from the Eleventh to the Twentieth Century.* Exhibition catalogue, Metropolitan Museum of Art. New York, 1977.

Alpatov, M. P. *Etiudy po istorii russkogo iskusstva.* Moscow, 1967.

Alpatov, M. P., ed. *La grande tradition du bois sculpte russe: Ancien et moderne.* Exhibition catalogue, Grand Palais. Paris, 1973.

Alpatova, I. A., "Khudozhestvennye osobennosti russkoi naboiki." Dissertation, Institute of the History of Art, Moscow, 1972.

Ambroz, A. K. "O simvolike russkoi krest'ianskoi vyshivki arkhaicheskogo tipa." *Sovetskaia arkheologiia,* 1966, no. 1, pp. 61–76.

Arbat', Iurii A. *Russkaia narodnaia rospis' po derevu: Novye nakhodki. Sistemizatsiia.* Moscow, 1970.

Arseneva, E. V. *Russkie platki i shali.* Moscow, 1982.

Averina, V. I. "Gorodetskaia rez'ba i rospis' na predmetakh krest'ianskogo remesla i domashnei utvary." Dissertation, Research Institute of Artistic Industries, Moscow, 1955.

————. *Gorodetskaia rez'ba i rospis' na predmetakh krest'ianskogo remesla i domashnei utvari.* Gor'kii, 1957.

Baedeker, Karl. *Russia.* Leipzig, 1914.

Bakushinskii, A. V. *Iskusstvo Palekha.* Moscow, 1934.

————. *Iskusstvo Palekha.* 2nd ed. Moscow and Leningrad, 1938.

————. *Issledovaniia i stat'i.* Moscow, 1981.

Baldina, O. D. "Russkie narodnye kartinki i ikh sviazy s prikladnym iskusstvom (XVIII v.)." Dissertation, Moscow State University, 1971.

Baradulin, Vasilii. "Rospis' krest'ianskogo doma." *Dekorativnoe iskusstvo SSSR,* 1979, no. 3, pp. 20–24.

Selected Bibliography

Bartenev, I., and B. Fedorov, *North Russian Architecture*. Translated by Kathleen Cook. Moscow, 1972.

Bartram, N. D. *Izbrannye stat'i: Vospominaniia o khudozhnike*. Moscow, 1979.

Beliaev, A. T.; B. A. Gushchin; and V. A. Gushchina. *Gosudarstvennyi istoriko-arkhitekturnyi i etnograficheskii muzei-zapovednik "Kizhi": Katalog*. Petrozavodsk, 1973.

Benua, A. "Kustarnaia vystavka." *Mir iskusstva*, 1902, no. 3.

_____. *Russkie igrushki*. St. Petersburg, 1905.

Bezobrazov, Vladimir P. *Narodnoe khoziaistvo Rossii, Moskovskaia (tsentral'naia) promyshlennaia oblast'*. St. Petersburg, 1882–89.

_____. *Otchet o Vserossiiskoi khudozhestvenno-promyshlennoi vystavke 1882 goda v Moskve*. 6 vols. St. Petersburg, 1883–84.

Bezsonov, S. V. *Krepostnye arkhitektory*. Moscow, 1938.

Bibikova, I. M. "Russkaia dereviannaia rez'ba: Monumental'no-dekorativnye rel'efy XI–XIV v." Dissertation, Academy of Arts, Moscow, 1963.

Bibikova, Irina M., and N. A. Koval'chuk. *Dereviannaia rez'ba krest'ianskikh zhilishch verkhnego Povolzh'ia*. Moscow, 1954.

Bilibin, Ivan. "Narodnoe tvorchestvo russkogo severa." *Mir iskusstva*, St. Petersburg, 1904, vol. 12, no. 6, pp. 265–318.

Blasius, I. H. *Reise in Europäischen Russland in den Jahren 1840 und 1841*. Braunschweig, 1844.

Blum, Jerome. *Lord and Peasant in Russia*. Princeton, 1961.

Bobrinskii, A. A. *Narodnye russkie dereviannye izdeliia*. Moscow, 1911.

Bocharov, G., and V. Vygolov. *Vologda. Kirillov. Ferapontov. Belozersk*. Moscow, 1966.

Bocharov, G. N., et al. *Derevo v arkhitekture i skul'pture slavian*. Moscow, 1987.

Boguslavskaia, I., and V. A. Suslova. *Russkoe narodnoe iskusstvo severa*. Leningrad, 1968.

Boguslavskaia, I. Ia. *Russkaia narodnaia vyshivka*. Moscow, 1972.

_____. "Drevnie motivy russkoi narodnoi vyshivki: K probleme obrazovaniia i razvitiia ornamental'nykh form v narodnom iskusstve." Dissertation, Leningrad State University, 1973.

_____. "Rospisi na korobakh Gorodetskogo raiona Gor'kovskoi oblasti." *Soobshcheniia Gosudarstvennogo russkogo muzeia*, Moscow, 1974, no. 10, pp. 84–90.

_____. *Severnye sokrovishcha*. Arkhangel'sk, 1980.

_____. *Russkii narodnyi kostium*. Moscow, [1982].

_____. *Russkoe narodnoe iskusstvo*. Moscow, 1984.

Boguslavskaia, I. Ia., ed. *Dobrykh ruk masterstvo*. Leningrad, 1976.

_____. *Tvorcheskie problemy sovremennykh narodnykh khudozhestvennykh promyslov*. Leningrad, 1981.

Boikov, V. S. *Russkii narodnyi prianik*. Leningrad, 1976.

Boikova, L. N. "Tul'skaia narodnaia vyshivka v sobranii Zagorskogo muzeia." *Soobshcheniia Zagorskogo gos. istoriko-khudozhestvennogo muzeia-zapovednika*. Zagorsk, 1960.

Bossert, Helmut T. *Volkskunst in Europa*. Berlin, 1926.

Bowlt, John E. "Two Russian Maecenases: Savva Mamontov and Princess Tenisheva." *Apollo*, 1973, vol. 98, no. 142, pp. 444–53.

Bowlt, John E., ed. *Russian Art of the Avant-Garde: Theory and Criticism*. New York, 1976.

Burtsev, A. E. *Zhizn' russkogo naroda: Ego nravy i obychai v kartinakh khudozhnikov i v snimkakh s natury*. St. Petersburg, 1914.

Chalif, Louis H. *Russian Festivals and Costumes for Pageant and Dance*. New York, 1921.

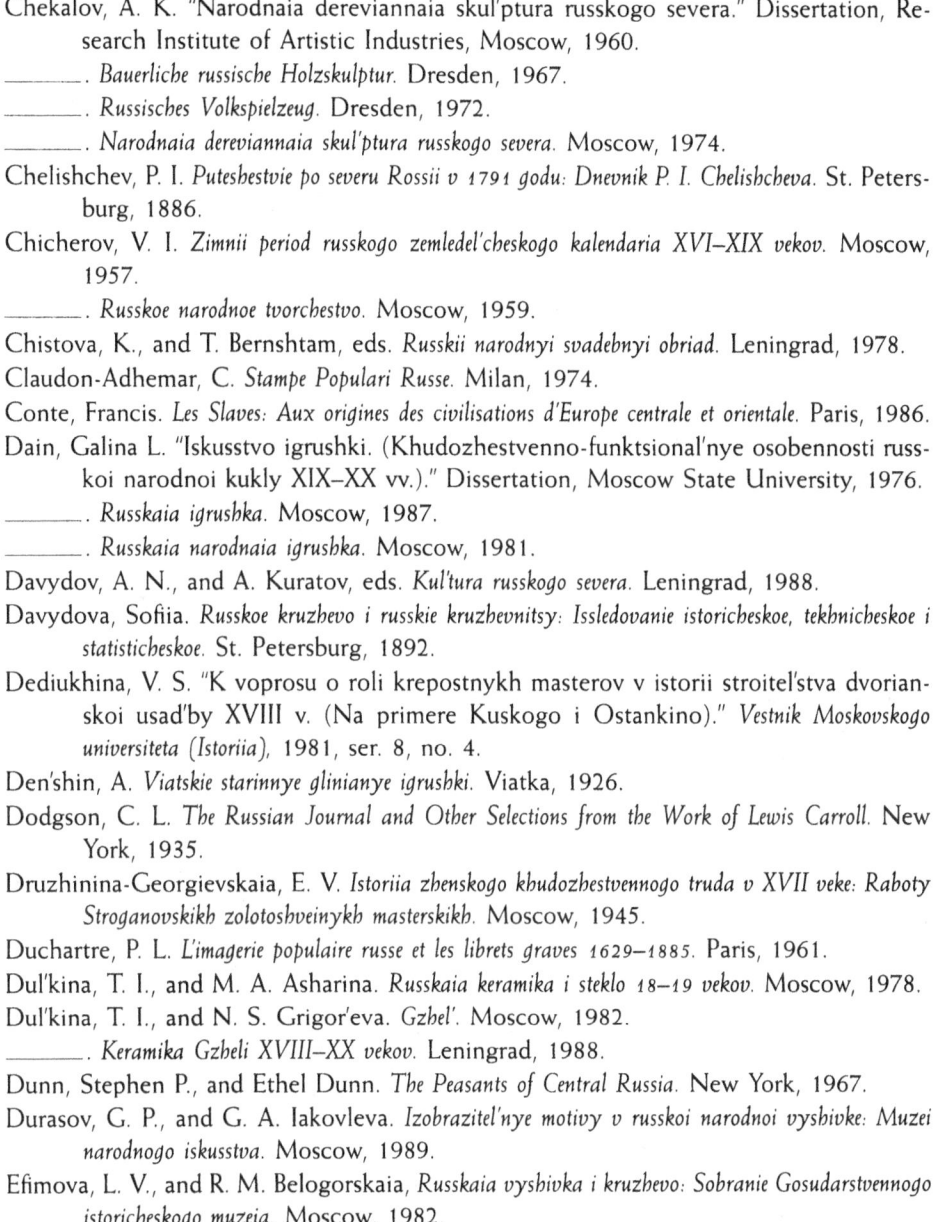

Chekalov, A. K. "Narodnaia dereviannaia skul'ptura russkogo severa." Dissertation, Research Institute of Artistic Industries, Moscow, 1960.

―――. *Bauerliche russische Holzskulptur.* Dresden, 1967.

―――. *Russisches Volkspielzeug.* Dresden, 1972.

―――. *Narodnaia dereviannaia skul'ptura russkogo severa.* Moscow, 1974.

Chelishchev, P. I. *Puteshestvie po severu Rossii v 1791 godu: Dnevnik P. I. Chelishcheva.* St. Petersburg, 1886.

Chicherov, V. I. *Zimnii period russkogo zemledel'cheskogo kalendaria XVI–XIX vekov.* Moscow, 1957.

―――. *Russkoe narodnoe tvorchestvo.* Moscow, 1959.

Chistova, K., and T. Bernshtam, eds. *Russkii narodnyi svadebnyi obriad.* Leningrad, 1978.

Claudon-Adhemar, C. *Stampe Populari Russe.* Milan, 1974.

Conte, Francis. *Les Slaves: Aux origines des civilisations d'Europe centrale et orientale.* Paris, 1986.

Dain, Galina L. "Iskusstvo igrushki. (Khudozhestvenno-funktsional'nye osobennosti russkoi narodnoi kukly XIX–XX vv.)." Dissertation, Moscow State University, 1976.

―――. *Russkaia igrushka.* Moscow, 1987.

―――. *Russkaia narodnaia igrushka.* Moscow, 1981.

Davydov, A. N., and A. Kuratov, eds. *Kul'tura russkogo severa.* Leningrad, 1988.

Davydova, Sofiia. *Russkoe kruzhevo i russkie kruzhevnitsy: Issledovanie istoricheskoe, tekhnicheskoe i statisticheskoe.* St. Petersburg, 1892.

Dediukhina, V. S. "K voprosu o roli krepostnykh masterov v istorii stroitel'stva dvorianskoi usad'by XVIII v. (Na primere Kuskogo i Ostankino)." *Vestnik Moskovskogo universiteta (Istoriia),* 1981, ser. 8, no. 4.

Den'shin, A. *Viatskie starinnye glinianye igrushki.* Viatka, 1926.

Dodgson, C. L. *The Russian Journal and Other Selections from the Work of Lewis Carroll.* New York, 1935.

Druzhinina-Georgievskaia, E. V. *Istoriia zhenskogo khudozhestvennogo truda v XVII veke: Raboty Stroganovskikh zolotoshveinykh masterskikh.* Moscow, 1945.

Duchartre, P. L. *L'imagerie populaire russe et les librets graves 1629–1885.* Paris, 1961.

Dul'kina, T. I., and M. A. Asharina. *Russkaia keramika i steklo 18–19 vekov.* Moscow, 1978.

Dul'kina, T. I., and N. S. Grigor'eva. *Gzhel'.* Moscow, 1982.

―――. *Keramika Gzheli XVIII–XX vekov.* Leningrad, 1988.

Dunn, Stephen P., and Ethel Dunn. *The Peasants of Central Russia.* New York, 1967.

Durasov, G. P., and G. A. Iakovleva. *Izobrazitel'nye motivy v russkoi narodnoi vyshivke: Muzei narodnogo iskusstva.* Moscow, 1989.

Efimova, L. V., and R. M. Belogorskaia, *Russkaia vyshivka i kruzhevo: Sobranie Gosudarstvennogo istoricheskogo muzeia.* Moscow, 1982.

The Englishwoman in Russia: Impressions of the Society and Manners. By a Lady ten years resident in that country. London, 1855. Reprint, New York, 1970.

Fedorova, N., and S. Iamshchikov. *Iaroslavskie portrety XVIII–XIX vekov.* Moscow, 1984.

Fedotov, G. P. *The Russian Religious Mind.* New York, 1960.

Frazer, Sir James. *The Golden Bough.* 1890. Rev. ed., Great Meadows, N.J., 1959.

Gauthier, Theophile. *Voyage en Russie.* Paris, 1905.

Gimbutas, Marija. *The Slavs.* New York and Washington, 1971.

Glassie, Henry. *The Spirit of Folk Art.* New York, 1989.

Selected Bibliography

Glavnoe upravlenie zemleustroistva i zemledeliia. *Russkoe narodnoe iskusstvo: Al'bom.* Petrograd, 1913.

Goldwater, Robert. *Primitivism in Modern Art.* New York, 1938.

Golitsyn, Prince F. S. *Kustarnoe delo v Rossii: V sviazi s umstvenno-dukhovnym razvitiem russkogo naroda.* St. Petersburg, 1904–1913.

Golyshev, Ivan. "Rez'ba po derevu." In *Sobranie sochinenii.* St. Petersburg, 1899.

Gorodtsov, V. A. "Dako-sarmatskie religioznye elementy v russkom narodnom tvorchestve." In *Trudy Gos. istoricheskogo muzeia,* pp. 7–36. Moscow, 1926.

Gostelow, Mary. *Embroidery of All Russia.* New York, 1977.

Grabar', I. E. *Dlia chego nado okhraniat' i sobirat' sokrovishcha iskusstva i stariny.* Moscow, 1919.

Grabar', I. E.; V. Kemenov; V. Lazarev; et al., eds. *Istoriia russkogo iskusstva.* 13 vols. Moscow, 1954–64. (Vol. 13 edited by R. S. Kaufman, M. L. Neiman, G. Iu. Sternin, and O. A. Shvidkovskii.)

Gray, Camilla. *The Russian Experiment in Art, 1863–1922.* London, 1962. Revised by Marian Burleigh-Motley, ed., New York, 1986.

Groshov, G. "Al'bom Meierberga kak istochnik po istorii russkogo krest'ianskogo zhilishcha." *Sovetskaia etnografiia,* Moscow, 1955, no. 1, pp. 164–71.

Guerman, Mikhail. *Art of the October Revolution.* Leningrad and New York, 1979.

Guliaev, V. A. *Russkie khudozhestvennye promysly 1920-kh godov.* Leningrad, 1985.

Gushchin, A. *Pamiatniki khudozhestvennogo remesla drevnei Rusi X–XIII vv.* Moscow and Leningrad, 1939.

Hamilton, George H. *The Art and Architecture of Russia.* 2nd ed. Harmondsworth, 1972.

Hapgood, Isabel Florence. *Russian Rambles.* Boston and New York, 1895. Reprint, New York, 1970.

Hasalova, Vera, and Jaroslav Vajdis. *Folk Art of Czechoslovakia.* New York, 1974.

Haxthausen-Abbenburg, August F. L. M. von. *Russia Observed: The Russian Empire, Its People, Institutions and Resources.* Translated by Robert Farie. London, 1856. Reprint, New York, 1970.

Hilton, Alison. "Russian Folk Art and 'High' Art in the Early Nineteenth Century." In Theofanis G. Stavrou, ed., *Art and Culture in Nineteenth-Century Russia,* pp. 237–54. Bloomington, Ind., 1983.

————. "The Peasant House and Its Furnishings: Decorative Principles in Russian Folk Art." *Journal of Decorative and Propaganda Arts,* Winter 1989, no. 11, pp. 10–29.

————. "Piety and Pragmatism: Orthodox Saints and Slavic Nature Gods in Russian Folk Art." In William C. Brumfield and Milos M. Velimirovic, eds., *Christianity and the Arts in Russia,* pp. 55–74. Cambridge, 1991.

————. "Narodnoe iskusstvo i sovremennost' v epokhu kul'turnogo obnovleniia v SShA i v SSSR." In M. A. Nekrasova and K. A. Makarov, eds., *Narodnoe iskusstvo i sovremennaia kul'tura,* pp. 160–74. Moscow, 1991.

————. "Remaking Folk Art: From Russian Revival to Proletcult." In John O. Norman, ed., *New Perspectives on Russian and Soviet Artistic Culture,* pp. 80–94. New York, 1994.

Hofer, Tamás, and Edit Fél. *Hungarian Folk Art.* Oxford, London, and New York, 1979.

Holme, Charles, ed. *Peasant Art in Russia.* London, 1912.

Hubbs, Joanna. *Mother Russia: The Feminine Myth in Russian Culture.* Bloomington, Ind., 1988.

Iakovleva, V. *Arkhangel'skaia narodnaia vyshivka.* Moscow, 1954.

————. *Riazanskaia narodnaia vyshivka.* Leningrad, 1959.

Il'in, M. *Russkoe narodnoe iskusstvo*. Moscow, 1959.

Itkina, Elena. *Russkii risovannyi lubok kontsa XVIII–nachala XX veka*. Moscow, 1992.

Ivanits, Linda J. *Russian Folk Belief*. Armonk, N.Y., and London, 1989.

Ivanits, Linda J., ed. "Russian Folk Narratives about the Supernatural." In *Soviet Anthropology and Archaeology*, vol. 26, no. 2. Armonk, N.Y., 1987.

Ivanova, N. N., et al. *Muzei narodnogo iskusstva*. Moscow, 1972.

Kalmykova, L. E. "Novye dannye po istorii Eletskogo kruzhevnogo promysla." In *Soobshcheniia Zagorskogo istoriko-khudozhestvennogo muzeia-zapovednika*, pp. 71–76. Zagorsk, 1958.

———. *Narodnaia vyshivka tverskoi zemli*. Leningrad, 1981.

Kalmykova, L. E., ed. *Zagorskii istoriko-khudozhestvennyi muzei-zapovednik: Sovetskoe dekorativno-prikladnoe iskusstvo*. Moscow, 1973.

Kamenskaia, M. N. *Russkaia narodnaia dereviannaia skul'ptura*. Leningrad, 1948.

Kandinsky, Wassily, and Franz Marc. *The Blaue Reiter Almanac*. Edited by Klaus Lankheit. New York, 1974.

Kantsedikas, Aleksandr S. *Iskusstvo i remeslo: K voprosu o prirode narodnogo iskusstva*. Moscow, 1977.

Kaufman, R. S.; M. L. Neiman; G. Iu. Sternin; and O. A. Shvidkovskii, eds. *Istoriia russkogo iskusstva*. Vol. 13. Moscow, 1964.

Kennard, Howard P. *The Russian Peasant*. Philadelphia, 1908. Reprint, New York, 1980.

Kerblay, Basile. *L'isba russe d'hier et d'aujourd'hui*. Lausanne, 1983.

Kharuzin', Aleksei N. *Slavianskoe zhilishche v severo-zapadnom krae*. Vilnius, 1907.

Khvorostov, A. "Konturnaia rez'ba." *Nauka i zhizn'*, 1980, no. 9, pp. 132–35.

Kirichenko, Evgenia. *Russian Design and the Fine Arts, 1750–1917*. New York, 1991.

Kluchevsky, V. O. *A History of Russia*. Translated by C. Hogarth. London and New York, 1917.

Komelova, G. N. *Stseny russkoi narodnoi zhizni kontsa XVIII–nachala XIX vekov*. Leningrad, 1961.

Koval'chuk, N. A. "Rez'ba po derevu v narodnom zodchestve Povolzh'ia." Dissertation, Moscow Architectural Institute, 1951.

Kovrigina, V. A. "Zolotye i serebrianye mastera moskovskoi nemetskoi slobody (konets XVII–pervaia chetvert' XVIII v.)." *Vestnik Moskovskogo universiteta (Istoriia)*, 1981, ser. 8, no. 4.

Kravchinskii, Sergei. *The Russian Peasantry: Their Agrarian Condition, Social Life and Religion*. New York, 1888. Reprint, Westport, Conn., 1977.

Kravtsov, N. I., ed. *Russkoe narodnoe poeticheskoe tvorchestvo*. Moscow, 1971.

Krest'ianskaia odezhda naseleniia evropeiskoi Rossii XIX–nachala XX v.: Opredelitel'. Moscow, 1971.

Kruglova, O. V. "Nadpisi na proizvedeniiakh russkogo narodnogo iskusstva." *Soobshcheniia Zagorskogo istoriko-khudozhestvennogo muzeia-zapovednika*, 1958, no. 2, pp. 65–70.

———. "Zhanrovye rospisi russkogo severa." *Soobshcheniia Zagorskogo istoriko-khudozhestvennogo muzeia-zapovednika*, 1960, no. 3, pp. 196–204.

———. "Novye dannye o rasprostranenii volzhskoi domovoi rez'by." *Soobshcheniia Zagorskogo istoriko-khudozhestvennogo muzeia-zapovednika*, 1960, no. 3, pp. 212–17.

———. "Severodvinskie nakhodki." *Dekorativnoe iskusstvo SSSR*, 1960, no. 3, pp. 33–35.

———. *Russkie prialki*. Zagorsk, 1971.

———. *Russkaia narodnaia rez'ba i rospis' po derevu*. Moscow, 1974.

Selected Bibliography

———. *Narodnaia rospis' severnoi Dviny*. Moscow, 1987.

Kruglova, O. V.; I. A. Piatnitskaia; and N. A. Vorob'eva. *Severnye prialki*. Exhibition catalogue, Vologda, 1969.

Libson, V. Ia. *Pamiatniki arkhitektury Moskvy: Kreml', Kitai-gorod, Tsentral'nye ploshchadi*. Moscow, 1982.

Likhacheva, L. D. *Drevnerusskoe shit'e XV–nachala XVIII veka*. Exhibition catalogue, Russian Museum. Leningrad, 1980.

Loukomski, G. K. *La vie et les moeurs en Russie de Pierre le Grand à Lenine*. Paris, 1928.

Lukin, M., and N. Davydova, *Umel'tsy Velikogo Ustiuga*. Arkhangel'sk, 1977.

Maiasova, N. A., and O. V. Kruglova. *Narodnoe iskusstvo: Katalog*. Zagorsk, 1957.

Makovetskii, I. V. *Pamiatniki narodnogo zodchestva russkogo severa*. Moscow, 1955.

———. *Arkhitektura russkogo narodnogo zhilishcha: Sever i verkhnee Povolzh'e*. Moscow, 1962.

Mal'tseva, N. "Russkaia tokarnaia posuda." *Dekorativnoe iskusstvo SSSR*, 1979, no. 1, pp. 21–23.

Maslikh, S. A. *Russkoe izraztsovoe iskusstvo XV–XIX vekov*. Moscow, 1976.

Maslova, Galina S. *Ornament russkoi narodnoi vyshivki: Kak istoriko-etnograficheskii istochnik*. Moscow, 1978.

Massie, Suzanne. *Land of the Firebird: The Beauty of Old Russia*. New York, 1980.

Mavrina, Tat'iana. *Gorodetskaia zhivopis'*. Leningrad, 1970.

Mel'nikov, P. I. (Andrei Pecherskii). *V lesakh*. St. Petersburg, 1881.

Mikhailova, K. V. *Grigorii Soroka 1823–1864*. Leningrad, 1975.

Millar, James R., ed. *The Soviet Rural Community*. Urbana, Chicago, and London, 1971.

Moiseenko, Elena. *Russkaia vyshivka v sobranii Ermitazha*. Leningrad, 1978.

Moleva, N., and E. Beliutin. *Russkaia khudozhestvennaia shkola vtoroi poloviny XIX–nachala XX veka*. Moscow, 1967.

Molotova, L. N., ed. *Narodnoe iskusstvo Rossiiskoi federatsii iz sobraniia Gosudarstvennogo muzeia etnografii narodov SSSR*. Leningrad, 1981.

Molotova, L. N., and N. N. Sosnina. *Russkii narodnyi kostium*. Moscow, 1984.

Moskovskoe gubernskoe zemstvo. *Igrushechnyi promysel v Sergievom posade*. Moscow, 1916.

Narodnaia graviura i fol'klor v Rossii XVII–XIX vv. Proceedings of a conference, Pushkin Museum of Fine Arts. Moscow, 1976.

Narodnoe dekorativno-prikladnoe iskusstvo russkogo severa. Proceedings of a conference, State Russian Museum. Leningrad, 1965.

Nekrasov, A. I. *Russkoe narodnoe iskusstvo*. Moscow, 1924.

Nekrasova, M. A. *Narodnoe iskusstvo kak chast' kul'tury*. Moscow, 1983.

———. *Narodnye mastera: Traditsii, shkoly*. Moscow, 1985.

Nekrasova, M. A., and K. A. Makarov, eds. *Problemy narodnogo iskusstva*. Moscow, 1982.

———. *Narodnoe iskusstvo i sovremennaia kul'tura*. Moscow, 1991.

Nekrasova, M. A., and S. Temerin, eds. *Narodnye khudozhestvennye promysly 1917–1932*. Moscow, 1986.

Nekrasova, Mariia A. "Iskusstvo Palekha." Dissertation, Institute of Art History, Moscow, 1963.

Nekrylova, A. F. *Russkie narodnye gorodskie prazdniki, uveseleniia i zrelishcha konets XVIII–nachalo XX veka*. Leningrad, 1988.

Netting, A. "Images and Ideas in Russian Peasant Art." *Slavic Review*, 1976, vol. 35, no. 1, pp. 48–68.

Nikitina, Iu. I.; A. S. Pavliuchenkov; and E. K. Pagel'skaia. *Novgorodskii istoriko-arkhitekturnyi muzei-zapovednik: Katalog.* Leningrad, 1963.

Opolovnikov, A. V. *Russkii sever.* Moscow, 1977.

Ovsiannikov, Iu. *Lubok.* Moscow, 1968.

Palmer, Francis. *Russian Life in Town and Country.* New York, 1901. Reprint, 1970.

Pantelić, Nikola, and Miodrag Djordjević. *Traditional Arts and Crafts in Yugoslavia.* Belgrade, 1984.

Peacock, Netta. "The New Movement in Russian Decorative Art." *The Studio,* 1901, vol. 22, no. 98, pp. 268–76.

Pipes, Richard. *Russia under the Old Regime.* New York, 1974.

Pleshanova, Izilla, and Liudmila Likhacheva. *Drevnerusskoe dekorativno-prikladnoe iskusstvo v sobranii Gosudarstvennogo russkogo muzeia.* Leningrad, 1985.

Polenova, N., ed. *Russkie narodnye skazki i pribautki, pereskazannye dlia detei i illiustrirovannye E. D. Polenovoi.* Moscow, 1906.

Pomerantsev, N. *Russkaia dereviannaia skul'ptura.* Moscow, 1967.

Pomerantsev, V., ed. *Russkie khudozhestvennye promysly vtoroi poloviny XIX–XX v.* Moscow, 1965.

Popova, O. S., and N. I. Kaplan. *Russkie khudozhestvennye promysly.* Moscow, 1984.

Popova, Zoia P. *Russkaia mebel'.* Moscow, 1957.

Pritsak, Omelian. *The Origin of Rus'.* Cambridge, Mass., 1981.

Prokudin-Gorskii, Sergei. *Photographs for the Tsar.* New York, 1980.

Pronin, Alexander, and Barbara Pronin. *Russian Folk Arts.* New York, 1975.

Pronina, I. "Russkaia akademicheskaia shkola dekorativno-prikladnogo iskusstva v kontse XVIII–pervoi poloviny XIX veka." Dissertation, Moscow State University, 1968.

Propp, V. *Russkie agrarnye prazdniki: Opyt istoriko-etnograficheskogo issledovaniia.* Leningrad, 1963.

Prosvirkina, S. K. *Russkaia dereviannaia posuda.* Moscow, 1957.

Rabotnova, I. "Dekorativnoe reshenie russkoi zhenskoi odezhdy XIX–nachalo XX vv." Dissertation, Academy of Arts, Moscow, 1956.

————. *Russkaia narodnaia vyshivka.* Leningrad, 1957.

————. *Russkaia narodnaia odezhda.* Moscow, 1964.

————. "Mnogoznachnost' soderzhaniia: Voprosy izucheniia narodnogo iskusstva." *Dekorativnoe iskusstvo SSSR,* 1973, no. 11, pp. 28–29.

Ralston, William. *Russian Folk-Tales.* New York, 1873. Reprint, New York, 1977.

Razina, T. M. "Russkoe narodnoe dekorativnoe iskusstvo i problemy narodnogo tvorchestva." Dissertation, Academy of Arts, Moscow, 1969.

————. *Russkoe narodnoe tvorchestvo.* Moscow, 1970.

————. "Poetizatsii drevnikh siuzhetov." *Dekorativnoe iskusstvo SSSR,* 1973, nos. 7, 11; 1974, no. 6.

Razina, T. M.; N. Cherkasova; and A. Kantsedikas. *Folk Art in the Soviet Union.* New York and Leningrad, 1990.

Reeder, Roberta, ed. *Down along the Mother Volga.* Philadelphia, 1975.

Riabinin, E. A. *Zoomorfnye ukrasheniia drevnei rusi X–XIV vv.* Special issue of *Arkheologiia SSSR.* Leningrad, 1981.

Roskoschny, Hermann. *Russland: Land und Leute.* Leipzig, [1882].

Rovinskii, D. A. *Russkie narodnye kartinki.* St. Petersburg, 1881.

Selected Bibliography

344 🍀

Russkaia dereviannaia posuda XVII–XX vekov. Exhibition catalogue, State Historical Museum. Moscow, 1982.

Russkoe narodnoe iskusstvo severa: Sbornik statei. Leningrad, 1968.

Rybakov, B. A. "Drevnie elementy v russkom narodnom tvorchestve: Zhenskoe bozhestvo i vsadniki." *Sovetskaia etnografiia,* 1948, no. 1, pp. 90–106.

————. *Russkoe prikladnoe iskusstvo X–XIII vekov.* Leningrad, 1971.

————. "Makrokosm v mikrokosme narodnogo iskusstva." *Dekorativnoe iskusstvo SSSR,* 1975, no. 1, pp. 30–33, 51; no. 2, pp. 38–43.

Rybchenkov, Boris, and Aleksandr Chaplin, eds. *Talashkino.* Moscow, 1971.

Sakharova, E., ed. *V. D. Polenov–E. D. Polenova: Khronika sem'i khudozhnikov.* Moscow, 1964.

Salmond, Wendy. "The Solomenko Embroidery Workshops." *Journal of Decorative and Propaganda Arts,* Summer 1987, no. 5, pp. 126–143.

————. "The Modernization of Folk Art in Russia: The Revival of the Kustar Art Industries, 1885–1917." Dissertation, University of Texas at Austin, 1989.

Saltykov, A. B. *Ispol'zovanie narodnykh traditsii v razvitii sovetskogo prikladnogo iskusstva.* Moscow, 1956.

————. *Russkaia narodnaia keramika.* Moscow, 1960.

————. *Samoe blizkoe iskusstvo.* Moscow, 1968.

Sears, Robert. *An Illustrated Description of the Russian Empire.* New York, 1855.

Semenova, T. S. *Narodnoe iskusstvo i ego problemy: Ocherki.* Moscow, 1977.

Sergeenko, I. I. *Russkii izrazets.* Moscow, 1982.

Sevan, O. "Rospis' krest'ianskogo doma." *Dekorativnoe iskusstvo SSSR,* 1979, no. 10, pp. 17–20.

Shevelev, Vladimir. "Zolotoe shit'e Kargopolia." *Dekorativnoe iskusstvo SSSR,* 1973, no. 5, pp. 46–47.

Shkarovskaia, N. *Narodnoe samodeiatel'noe iskusstvo.* Leningrad, 1975.

Shmakova, V. T. "Printsipy dekora krest'ianskikh domov i izb." In *Russkoe narodnoe iskusstvo severa,* pp. 60–68. Leningrad, 1968.

Shmeleva, M. N., and L. V. Tazikhana. "Ukrasheniia russkoi krest'ianskoi odezhdy." In *Russkie: Istoriko-etnograficheskii atlas,* pp. 89–123. Moscow, 1970.

Sirelius, U. T. *Die Vogel und Pferdmotive der karelischen und ingermanlandischen Brodegien.* Helsingfors, 1925.

Smirnov, G. V. *Venetsianov i ego shkola.* Leningrad, 1973.

Snegirev, Ivan. *Russkie prostonarodnye prazdniki i suevernye obriady.* Moscow, 1838.

————. *Krestnye khody v Moskve.* Moscow, 1861.

————. *Lubochnye kartinki russkogo naroda v Moskovskom mire.* Moscow, 1861.

Sobolev, N. N. *Naboika v Rossii: Istoriia i sposob raboty.* Moscow, 1912.

————. *Russkaia narodnaia rez'ba po derevu.* Moscow and Leningrad, 1931–34.

Sobolevskii, N. *Khudozhestvennye promyshlennosti podmoskov'ia.* Moscow, 1948.

Sokolov, Y. M. *Russian Folklore.* Translated by Catherine Smith. New York, 1950.

Staniukovich, T. V. "Vnutrenniaia planirovka, otdelka i meblirovka russkogo krest'ianskogo zhilishcha." In V. A. Aleksandrov et al., eds., *Russkie: Istoriko-etnograficheskii atlas.* Moscow, 1970.

Stasov, V. V. *Russkii narodnyi ornament.* St. Petersburg, 1872.

————. *Stat'i i zametki, ne voshedshie v sobrannye sochineniia.* Moscow, 1954.

Stavrou, Theofanis G., ed. *Art and Culture in Nineteenth-Century Russia*. Bloomington, Ind., 1983.

Stites, Richard. "The Origins of Soviet Ritual Style: Symbol and Festival in the Russian Revolution." In C. Arvidsson et al., *Symbols of Power*, pp. 23–42. Stockholm, 1987.

Stoliarov, Ivan. *Zapiski russkogo krest'ianina*. Paris, 1986.

Suprun, L. "Professional'nye khudozhniki i narodnoe iskusstvo v Rossii kontsa XIX–nachala XX veka." Dissertation, Research Institute of Artistic Industries, Moscow, 1971.

————. "Traditsionnoe i samodeiatel'noe: O narodnom iskusstve." *Dekorativnoe iskusstvo SSSR*, 1976, no. 4, pp. 38–40.

Svinin, Pavel P. *Sketches of Russia*. London, 1814.

Sytova, Alla. *The Lubok: Russian Folk Pictures 17th–19th Century*. Leningrad, 1984.

Taranovskaia, N. V. *Russkaia dereviannaia igrushka*. Leningrad, 1968.

Taranovskaia, N. V., and N. V. Mal'tsev, *Russkie prialki*. Leningrad, 1970.

Tenisheva, M. K. *Vpechatleniia moei zhizni*. Paris, 1933. Reprint, Leningrad, 1991.

Tian-Shanskaia, Olga S. *Village Life in Late Tsarist Russia*. Edited and translated by David L. Ransel. Bloomington, Ind., 1993.

Tokarev, S. A. "Slavic Religion and Mythology." In *The Modern Encyclopedia of Russian and Soviet History*. Gulf Breeze, Fla., 1978.

Tseretelli, N. *Russkaia krest'ianskaia igrushka*. Moscow, 1933.

Turner, Victor, ed., *Celebration: Studies in Festivity and Ritual*. Washington, D.C., 1982.

Ukhanova, Irina N. "Dereviannye val'ki russkoi rez'by XVIII–pervoi poloviny XIX veka." *Soobshcheniia Gos. Ermitazha*. Leningrad, 1961.

————. *Rez'ba po kosti v Rossii XVIII–XIX vekov*. Leningrad, 1981.

Ukhanova, Irina N., ed. *Dekorativno-prikladnoe iskusstvo Rossii i zapadnoi Evropy: Sbornik nauchnykh trudov Gos. Ermitazha*. Leningrad, 1986.

Utkin, P. I. *Russkie iuvelirnye ukrasheniia*. Moscow, 1970.

Vagner, G. K. "Drevnie motivy v domovoi rez'be Rostova-Iaroslavskogo." *Sovetskaia etnografiia*, 1962, no. 4.

————. *Mastera drevnerusskoi skul'ptury: Rel'efy Iur'eva-Pol'skogo*. Moscow, 1966.

————. *Problema zhanrov v drevnerusskom iskusstve*. Moscow, 1974.

————. *Belokamennaia rez'ba drevnego Suzdalia*. Moscow, 1975.

Vallance, Aymer. "Russian Peasant Industries." In *Studio*, p. 243. London, 1906.

Vasilenko, Viktor. *Russkaia rez'ba i rospis'*. Moscow, 1947.

————. "Russkoe narodnoe iskusstvo XVIII–XX vekov. (Khudozhestvennaia kul'tura russkoi derevni)." Dissertation, Moscow State University, 1970.

————. *Narodnoe iskusstvo: Izbrannye trudy*. Moscow, 1974.

————. "Zakliuchenie diskussii o semantike." *Dekorativnoe iskusstvo SSSR*, 1975, no. 3. p. 44.

————. *Russkoe prikladnoe iskusstvo: Istoki i stanovlenie*. Moscow, 1977.

Velimirovic, Milos. "Peasant Culture and National Culture: Examples from the Arts." *Balkanistica III*, 1976, pp. 145–49.

Verkhne-volzhskaia etnologicheskaia ekspeditsiia. *Krest'ianskie postroiki Iaroslavsko-Tverskogo kraia*. Leningrad, 1926.

Vernadsky, G. *The Origins of Russia*. Oxford, 1959.

Selected Bibliography

Viollet-le-Duc, E. E. *L'Art russe, ses origines, ses éléments constitutifs, son apogée, son avenir.* Paris, 1877.

Volkov, F. K., ed. *Materialy po etnografii Rossii.* 4 vols. St. Petersburg, 1910.

Voronin, N. N., and M. K. Karger, eds. *Istoriia kul'tury drevnei Rusi.* Moscow and Leningrad, 1948–51.

Voronin, N. N.; M. K. Karger; et al., eds. *Drevnosti moskovskogo kremlia.* Moscow, 1971.

Voronov, V. S. *Krest'ianskoe iskusstvo.* Moscow, 1924.

———. *O krest'ianskom iskusstve.* Moscow, 1972.

Voronov, V. S., and A. Topornin. *Severnaia istoriko-bytovaia ekspeditsiia. (Krest'ianskii byt XVIII–XIX vv).* Moscow, 1929.

Vremennik iziashchnykh iskusstv. Vologda, 1916.

Vucinich, Wayne, ed. *The Peasant in Nineteenth-Century Russia.* Stanford, 1968.

Vvedenskii, D. V. *Gorod Sergiev, Moskovskoi gubernii: Melkie promysly.* Moscow, 1927.

Wallace, Sir Donald Mackenzie. *Russia: Its History and Condition to 1877.* Boston and Tokyo, 1910.

Warner, Elizabeth A. *The Russian Folk Theater.* The Hague, 1977.

Wilson, Francesca M. *Muscovy: Russia through Foreign Eyes, 1553–1900.* London, 1970.

Zabelin, Ivan. *Domashnii byt russkikh tsarei (i tsarits) v XVI–XVII v.* Rev. ed. Moscow, 1915.

Zhegalova, S. K. *Russkaia dereviannaia rez'ba XIX veka: Ukrashenie krest'ianskikh izb verkhnego Povolzh'ia.* Moscow, 1957.

———. "Ekspeditsiia Gosudarstvennogo istoricheskogo muzeia na severnuiu Dvinu." *Sovetskaia etnografiia,* 1960, no. 4.

———. *Russkaia narodnaia zhivopis'.* Moscow, 1975.

Zhegalova, S. K., et al., eds. *Russkoe khudozhestvennoe derevo: Trudy Gos. ordena Lenina istoricheskogo muzeia,* no. 56. Moscow, 1983.

Zhegalova, S. K.; S. Zhizhina; Z. Popova; S. Prosvirkina; and Iu. Cherniakhovskaia. *Sokrovishcha russkogo narodnogo iskusstva: Rez'ba i rospis' po derevu.* Moscow, 1967.

———. *Prianik, prialka, i ptitsa sirin.* Moscow, 1967. Rev. ed., 1983.

Zhiguleva, V. M. *Narodnoe iskusstvo Penzenskoi oblasti kontsa XIX–XX vekov. (Vyshivka, tkachestvo, keramika v sobranii Zagorskogo muzeia).* Moscow, 1989.

Zhizhina, S. G., and I. Remizova. *Russkie khudozhestvennye laki XVIII–XX vekov.* Moscow, 1982.

Zhizhina, Svetlana G. "Severnaia reznaia beresta XVIII–XX vekov." Dissertation, Institute of Art History, Moscow, 1976.

Zhuravleva, Larisa S. *Teremok.* Moscow, 1974.

Zhuravleva, Larisa S., ed. *Russkoe narodnoe reznoe i raspisnoe derevo v sobranii Smolenskogo gos. ob"edinennogo istoricheskogo i arkhitekturno-khudozhestvennogo muzeia-zapovednika.* Moscow, 1985.

Ziablovskii, Evdokii. *Zemleopisanie Rossiiskoi imperii dlia vsekh sostoianii.* St. Petersburg, 1810.

Zvantsev, M. P. *Domovaia rez'ba.* Moscow, 1935. Rev. ed., 1970.

———. "Narodnaia rez'ba: Imena russkikh masterov." *Dekorativnoe iskusstvo SSSR,* 1960, no. 1, pp. 29–32.

———. *Nizhegorodskaia rez'ba.* Moscow, 1969.

Index

Abramtsevo, estate and workshops, 227–39, 325n50, 331n29

Academy of Arts, 203–206, 223

Afanas'ev, Aleksandr, 237

Agriculture. *See* Farming

Aksenov, Ivan, 254–55

Alekseev, Aleksandr, 211–12, 214

Aleksei Mikhailovich (Tsar), 102, 116

Alexander III (Tsar), 220, 243

Alkonost (nature spirit), 144, 146, 179, 308n39

Al'tman, Natan, 269–70

Amateur art movement, 261–64

Amosov, Vasilii, 193

Amosova, Pelageia, 52–54, 79–80, 97, 174

Amulets: as heirlooms and toys, 124; motifs of early Slavic, 139

Antokol'skii, Mark, 229, 325n50

Apsit, Aleksandr, 260, 261

Archeology: excavations in Novgorod and early folk art, 6, 20, 102, 292n30; physical remains of early Slavic tribes, 137–39; historicism and, 217; excavations in Moscow, 312n19

Architecture: travelers' accounts of, 11; ceramic tiles, 115, 116–18; of Kremlin, 163–64, 217; historicism and, 220, 320n14. *See also* Houses; *Izba*

Argunov, Ivan, 301n5

Arkhangel'sk: distaffs from, 40–41, 187–88; interaction of peasant and town economy, 43; icon painting, 76; craft production in Soviet period, 265; contemporary practitioners of folk art, 282; inscription on vessel from, 294n3

Art, Russian: inclusion of folk art in nineteenth-century works on, 14–15; influence of folk art on, 15–16; serfs and history of, 198–214; folk art and development of national style, 215–26;

neoprimitivism in early twentieth century, 245–56. *See also* Decorative arts

Austen Factory (Moscow), 114

Avant-garde, 244, 248, 255, 256

Babkina, Ul'iana, 129–30, 282

Bakanov, I. M., 266

Bakushinskii, Aleksandr, 289n5, 299–300n6

Balakirev, Mili, 218

Balts, 138

Baradulin, Vasilii, 294n18

Barshevskii, Ivan, 240, 241

Bartram, Nikolai, 127, 270, 305n7

Bast paper, 109

Battledores, 36, 37

Beliaeva, Anastasiia, 281

Benois (Benua), Alexandre, 241, 242, 243–44

Bereginy (water spirits), 24, 26, 143–45, 172, 187

Beseda (community activity), 14, 38. *See also* *Posidelka*

Bezobrazov, V. P., 10, 44–45

Bibles, early printing of, 109

Bilibin, Ivan, 99, 242–43, 256, 274, 284, 327n7, 329n42

Birch bark: storage containers of, 33; painting on, 46; boxes made by Veprev family, 54–56; carving of as specialized art form, 99–101; niello engraving, 107; contemporary production of, 282

Birch tree: in Russian folklore and folklife, 99, 153, 177, 310n65

Bird boxes, 56–57

Birds, as motif, 170. *See also* *Alkonost; Sirin*

Blacksmiths, 104–105

Blasius, St., 142

Boas, Franz, 324n36

Boatbuilding, influence of on woodcarving, 21, 45, 66, 187

Bobrinskii, Aleksandr, 274

Bochkarev, Stepan, 100, 101

Index

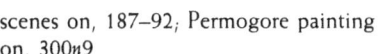

Index

Index

Index

ALISON HILTON is Wright Family Professor of Art History and Director of the M.A. Program in Art and Museum Studies at Georgetown University. She is author of *Kazimir Malevich, 1878–1935* and (with Norton T. Dodge) of *New Art from the Soviet Union: The Known and the Unknown.*

www.ingramcontent.com/pod-product-compliance
Lightning Source LLC
Chambersburg PA
CBHW080007210526
45170CB00015B/1855